THE IMPLICATIONS OF LITERACY

*Written Language and Models of Interpretation
in the Eleventh and Twelfth Centuries*

THE IMPLICATIONS OF LITERACY

*Written Language and Models
of Interpretation in the Eleventh
and Twelfth Centuries*

BRIAN STOCK

PRINCETON UNIVERSITY PRESS

PRINCETON, NEW JERSEY

FOR MY MOTHER

PREFACE

The problems raised by a study which attempts to cross the boundaries of several disciplines are never easy to solve. The strategy employed in the present volume is relatively straightforward. Throughout, an effort has been made to provide accurate working summaries of important historical, philosophical, or theological texts before an analysis is undertaken in relation to the book's central theme. This procedure has been adopted for a number of reasons. It could not be assumed that even among medievalists those who were knowledgeable in one field under investigation were widely read in others. The inaccessibility of certain works under discussion was another factor: the chronicles of the early Pataria are not available in translation, and the treatises on the eucharist present unusual problems of interpretation. As an alternative, quotations could have been made in the originals, and, wherever warranted, this has been done. However, a mass of evidence cited only in Latin would have rendered the book incomprehensible to critical theorists, to social scientists, and to non-medievalists in cultural history, on whose behalf in part it has been written.

As far as I am aware, the central argument of the book is my own, and I alone am responsible for the study's theoretical or practical limitations. Yet I owe a large debt to a number of generous colleagues. Among those who read earlier drafts of various chapters, I especially thank J. N. Hillgarth, B. W. Merrilees, Walter H. Principe, A. G. Rigg, and Professor Raoul Manselli. Caroline W. Bynum and John T. Gilchrist read the entire manuscript in an earlier version and made many helpful suggestions. Franz H. Bäuml, Edward Peters, and Heather Phillips kindly read the completed draft, while Maruja Jackman brought to the discussion the sorts of questions which a medievalist might not normally have asked.

To others I owe more general debts: to Gerhart Ladner, for his pioneering studies of the idea of reform; to Georges Duby, for his contributions to eleventh-century *mentalité*; and to Cinzio Violante, whose analysis of the early Patarene movement laid the foundation for all subsequent inquiry. Two good friends, John O'Neill and Natalie

vii

Davis, have for many years offered me the benefits of their insights into critical theory and anthropological history respectively. Giles Constable and Robert L. Benson made it possible for me to attend and to comment on the important reassessments submitted to the colloquium on "the renaissance of the twelfth century," while Milton Yinger made a place for my views on church, sect, and group organization within the interdisciplinary panel of the meeting of the American Sociological Association in 1977. An invitation from Jacques Le Goff provided me with the occasion of lecturing on the book's subject at the Ecole des Hautes Etudes en Sciences Sociales, Paris, during the spring of 1981. There is no adequate way I can thank my colleague and friend for the interest he has expressed in problems of mutual concern since my own student sojourn in the former VIe Section.

I should never have embarked on a study of such complexity had I not been sustained by the unusual research environment of the Pontifical Institute of Mediaeval Studies. I have received much encouragement over the years from J. Ambrose Raftis and Michael M. Sheehan; and I owe a special debt to Leonard Boyle, who graciously read the entire manuscript and gave me the benefit of his learned advice on paleography, diplomatics, and wider historical concerns. I should also like to thank the librarian, Rev. D. A. Finlay, C.S.B., for granting many special requests.

Finally, I should like to express my appreciation to R. Miriam Brokaw and the editors of the Princeton University Press for the care they have taken in the production of this book.

I am grateful to the former Canada Council for a Senior Killam Fellowship during 1973-1974 and to the Social Sciences and Humanities Research Council of Canada for subsequent grants, without which the study could not have been completed.

Toronto   B.S.
1982

CONTENTS

CONTENTS

THE IMPLICATIONS OF LITERACY

*Written Language and Models of Interpretation
in the Eleventh and Twelfth Centuries*

INTRODUCTION

This book is a study of the rebirth of literacy and of its effects upon the cultural life of the eleventh and twelfth centuries.

Literacy itself is the subject of Chapter One. The other four chapters treat heresy and reform, the eucharistic controversy, language and theological reality, and ideas and society. No attempt is made to oversimplify the internal development of these historical problems for the sake of setting up a unitary perspective. Yet the choice of topics as well as the manner of presentation are intended to lay the foundation for a broader thesis linking literacy's rise to the emergence of similar modes of thought in different branches of the period's cultural life. These, I argue, may be described as literacy's implications.

The book's principal theoretical tenets may be stated briefly as follows. Before the year 1000—an admittedly arbitrary point in time—there existed both oral and written traditions in medieval culture. But throughout the eleventh and twelfth centuries an important transformation began to take place. The written did not simply supersede the oral, although that happened in large measure: a new type of interdependence also arose between the two. In other words, oral discourse effectively began to function within a universe of communications governed by texts. On many occasions actual texts were not present, but people often thought or behaved as if they were. Texts thereby emerged as a reference system both for everyday activities and for giving shape to many larger vehicles of explanation. The effects on higher culture were particularly noticeable. As methods of interpretation were increasingly subjected to systematic scrutiny, the models employed to give meaning to otherwise unrelated disciplines more and more clustered around the concept of written language. Standing, therefore, behind much of the renaissance of intellectual life is a set of assumptions about language, texts, and reality.

basic thesis

The rapprochement between the oral and the written consequently began to play a decisive role in the organization of experience. The results can be seen in sets of dichotomies based upon linguistic considerations which lie beneath the surface of a number of the period's

3

key cultural issues. One of these was the relation of human action to the formal written models by which, it was thought, random events could be set in order. A distinction likewise arose between the content of what was perceived and the status in reality assigned to it by the process of sifting, classifying, and encoding. At a more abstract level, philosophers revived the opposition between what was really taking place when events were described in words and what was merely thought or said to be taking place. A barrier was also introduced between traditional accounts of how the universe worked and scientific constructs, which were normally the byproduct of a logically articulated cosmic design. Sets of rules, that is, codes generated from written discourse, were employed not only to produce new behavioural patterns but to restructure existing ones. Literacy thereby intersected the progress of reform. At an individual level, a change was brought about in the means by which one established personal identity, both with respect to the inner self and to external forces. And the writing down of events, the editing so to speak of experience, gave rise to unprecedented parallels between literature and life: for, as texts informed experience, so men and women began to live texts.

In sum, what eventually came about was the simultaneous existence of different provinces of meaning based upon logical and linguistic considerations, each having its own assumptions about how knowledge was communicated. Moreover, it was in the fundamental process of categorization, rather than in the content of knowledge alone, that the Middle Ages broke irrevocably with the interpretive patterns of later antiquity and moved towards those of early modern Europe. There had of course been widespread literacy in the classical world and occasional revivals of latinity in the period before the millennium, the most impressive being associated with the Carolingian reforms of speaking and writing the ancient tongue. Although styles of script and methods of book production were in constant evolution, the eleventh century's major innovations did not take place in the techniques of reading and writing. The novelty arose from the range, depth, and permanence of literacy's influence, which, over the course of time, was gradually brought to bear on a broader field of activity than ever before, and from the altered status of oral discourse in relation to real or putative texts. In fact, one of the demonstrable signs of a changed environment was the ambivalence with which many textual models were greeted by the medievals themselves.

The study of the cultural context of the spoken word is of course not new. In fact, it is widely recognized by historians, students of literature, and social scientists that the appearance of literacy in a society formerly dependent on oral communication can contribute to the way in which individuals perceive issues, frame them in language, and evolve systems of interpretation. But the process by which this takes place is as yet poorly understood, both within earlier phases of western civilization and in contemporary communities which until recently had only a slight acquaintance with the written word. At first, historians focused on proving the existence of literacy during the Middle Ages, on establishing its alleged connections with economic development, and on tabulating as best they could the numbers of readers and writers. However, it has become clear that, in a society, whether past or present, in which the researcher's assumptions about the centrality of the written word in culture are not shared, mere statistics can be misleading, especially if taken out of their social context. During the medieval period the implanting of a society that acknowledged literate criteria in a wide variety of circumstances required more than a simple increase in the use˜of scribal techniques. A different style of reflection also had to question long-established habits of thought, which, if not actually produced by oral tradition, were nonetheless maintained in the system of human interchange by means of the spoken word.

The attempt to impose such a broad, if flexible, framework of analysis on a number of separate medieval cultural activities has some obvious limitations. Since the early nineteenth century, when the study of the Middle Ages first entered the secular university curriculum, the field has been confounded from time to time by large hypotheses, which only accounted for one aspect of development by neglecting others. One has only to recall the various stage theories, the reduction of culture to an epiphenomenon of material change, or the still popular notion of periodic renascences. The present volume offers no palliatives for those in search of oversimplified pictures of historical growth, still less for those seeking to illustrate contemporary theories in the social sciences through the anecdotal use of medieval data. However, it does propose three perspectives on a seminal century and a half, which, in the author's view at least, has too long suffered from the complementary deficiencies of overspecialization and undergeneralization. The first is the replacement of much linear, evolutionary thinking with a contextualist approach, which describes phases of an integrated cultural transformation happening at the same time. For "humanity," C. S. Lewis observed, "does not pass through phases as a train passes through stations: being alive, it has the privilege of always moving yet never leaving anything behind."[1] The second is the reaffirmation of a theory of the middle range,[2] which is better suited to the present, imperfect state of thinking in the cultural sciences than universal tenets. Finally, the book attempts to place the problem of language and culture at the centre of the discussion. For, without such a shift in emphasis away from purely factual and historical description, little progress in understanding beyond the comparison of content is possible.

The adoption of these perspectives, it goes without saying, requires the employment of literary and historical styles of analysis at once. Also involved are the use and reuse of three concepts, namely literacy, textuality, and orality, which merit clarification at the outset.

Of the three, literacy is the most difficult to define and the most troublesome to use. The term's connotative field in English has no precise equivalent in other languages. Worse, no matter how literacy is characterized, there is, even within English, no universally agreed, value-free definition. The conceptual vocabulary evolved for debating the issues everywhere betrays an ineradicable bias towards written tradition.

Little light is shed on the question by referring back to medieval precedents, since, throughout the period, *litteratus*, the word most closely corresponding to "literate," indicated a familiarity, if not always a deep understanding, of Latin grammar and syntax.[3] There was also vernacular literacy, or rather literacies, although their early record is fragmentary when compared to Latin. The literate, in short, was defined as someone who could read and write a language for which in theory at least there was a set of articulated rules, applicable to a written, and, by implication, to a spoken language. Even today, such terms as "preliterate" and "illiterate," which are commonly used to describe earlier phases of culture, imply a semantic norm linked to the use of texts. The study of past or present communities less dependent on writing than our own has provided correctives to one-sided views. Yet, inescapably, we are better equipped intellectually to outline the role of literacy among people like ourselves, or among those presumably desirous of becoming so, than in societies functioning all or partly by word of mouth. Of course, tracing the roots of

---

[1] *The Allegory of Love* (Oxford, 1936), 1.

[2] R. K. Merton, "On Sociological Theories of the Middle Range," in *On Theoretical Sociology. Five Essays, Old and New* (New York, 1967), 39-40.

[3] H. Grundmann, "Litteratus-illitteratus. Der Wandel einer Bildungsnorm vom Altertum zum Mittelalter," *Archiv für Kulturgeschichte* 40 (1958), 1-15; discussed below, Ch. 1, pp. 14ff.

modern literacy is a valid dimension of the subject. But it is no substitute for reconstituting another society's system of communication on its own terms.

The imprecision of the idea of literacy, as well as the uneven state of the documentation, make it preferable in a medieval context to speak of the occasioned uses of texts. Distinguishing between literacy and textuality can also help to isolate what was original in the medieval achievement.

Literacy is not textuality. One can be literate without the overt use of texts, and one can use texts extensively without evidencing genuine literacy. In fact, the assumptions shared by those who can read and write often render the actual presence of a text superfluous. And, if common agreement obviates the need for texts, disagreement or misunderstanding can make them indispensable. Texts, so utilized, may be symptomatic of the need for explanation and interpretation, even at times of functional illiteracy.

If ancient, medieval, and early modern society shared a similar bias towards a literate official culture, the high Middle Ages differed from periods before and after it in the complexity of its attitudes towards texts. In the classical world, as nowadays, one assumes a widespread recognition of literate norms in education and society, even if in practice genuine literacy is not universal. But, down to the thirteenth century, written traditions were largely islands of higher culture in an environment that was not so much illiterate as nonliterate. As a consequence, texts served a broader range of purposes than they do in a society in which literacy is the axis of educational theory and practice. On many occasions, texts merely recorded oral transactions, telling us little of the cultural level of the participants other than that they employed the services of a scribe. On others, they functioned as evidential documents, that is, as a sort of insurance policy in case the oral record was forgotten or obliterated. On still others, they served what diplomatics calls a dispositive role, which effectively superseded oral arrangements, even though the signatories to a document may have pledged their faith by verbal, formal, and gestural means. To investigate medieval literacy is accordingly to inquire into the uses of texts, not only into the allegedly oral or written elements in the works themselves, but, more importantly, to inquire into the audiences for which they were intended and the mentality in which they were received.

The status of texts, then, is one side of the problem of medieval literacy. The other is the status of oral discourse, or, more precisely,

7

the manner in which its functions changed under the influence of the written word.

Medieval orality has given rise to much scholarly controversy. As the term is employed in what follows, it refers to one of two states of affairs. Very occasionally, mention is made of what may be called pure orality, that is, verbal discourse uninfluenced by the written mode. Medieval documentation provides little direct evidence for such orality, although one catches glimpses of it in accounts of gestures, rituals, and feudal ceremonial. These activities are presumed to take place in a world that is preliterate: in theory at least, they arise not from an ignorance but from an absence of texts.

The type of orality for which the Middle Ages furnishes the most abundant evidence is verbal discourse which exists in interdependence with texts, as, for instance, do the normal spoken and recorded forms of a language, which impinge upon each other in complex ways but remain mutually exclusive. The medievals did not understand, as indeed we do not, how spoken and written styles of interchange influence each other. However, from about the millennium, the written word, if directly affecting only a minority, had once again begun to be widely adopted as a basis for discussions of cultural activity and even as a standard of cultural progress. Inevitably, there was a certain amount of tension: for, in this "traditional" society, in which the new was almost always framed in terms of the old, the rules of the game were radically altered when the sole means of establishing a position's legitimacy was assumed to be the discovery of a written precedent.

There were of course both negative and positive consequences. On the negative side, a different set of value judgments emerged. The preliterate, who managed without texts, was redefined as an illiterate, that is, as a person who did not understand the grammar and syntax of a written language.[4] Literacy thereby became a factor in social mobility: the lower orders could neither read nor write, but their lives were increasingly influenced by those who could. On the positive side, the revival of writing added a new dimension to cultural life, very often, as noted, incorporating the oral into a real or implied textual framework. An example is the role of spoken testimony within codified statutes, which transcended the oral legal formalism of the early Middle Ages and gradually evolved within literate jurisprudence.

This second type of orality, it should be stressed, is an essential

---

[4] Cf. F. H. Bäuml, "Varieties and Consequences of Medieval Literacy and Illiteracy," *Speculum* 55 (1980), 237-43, 246-49, discussed below, Ch. 1, pp. 19ff.

ingredient of modern communications systems, in which words and texts are normally interdependent. However, it is important to note that the medieval version of this state of affairs came about by two different routes. One took place within written tradition itself and involved its gradual extension into formerly oral sectors of life and thought. The other took place within oral tradition and involved an equally slow acculturation[5] of the written mode. As an example, we may consider the influence of canonical penitential theory on unwritten Irish and Anglo-Saxon legal codes between the sixth and eighth centuries. From the canon lawyer's point of view, oral adapted to written law. But, from the viewpoint of the practitioner of oral law, writing first appeared as a foreign element. In the second case, as long as law functioned orally, the presence of writing alone was not indicative of literacy. Instead, there was a complex process of assimilation by a different mentality, in which states of textuality, rather than the oral or the written alone, comprised the operative element. Only when the underlying social psychology had changed can we speak of a genuine shift to scribal culture.

The stages were complicated and often imperceptible, as histories of education oriented around the survival of the classical tradition do not sufficiently emphasize. There is in fact no clear point of transition from a nonliterate to a literate society. For, even at the high point of oral usage, let us say, in the medieval context, continental Europe during the tenth century, writing was not by any means absent from everyday transactions; and, when literate norms were firmly re-established in law and government, that is, by the mid-twelfth, the spoken word did not cease to play a large cultural role. _The change_, as suggested, was not so much from oral _to_ written as from an earlier state, predominantly oral, to various combinations of oral _and_ written. In some areas of human activity like property law, orality was very largely superseded; in others, oral and written forms found their equilibrium with respect to each other, dividing responsibility so to speak for important institutions of culture, as was the case for instance of oral confession within structured penitential theology. The balance between oral and written modes of communication brought about during the Middle Ages persisted in many areas long afterwards. Medieval linguistic evolution thereby provides an example, rare in cultural

---

[5] On the notion of acculturation in historical research, a review of methods is presented by A. Dupront, "De l'Acculturation," _XIIe Congrès International des Sciences Historiques_ (Vienna, 1965), 7-36.

9

history, of *la longue durée*,[6] that is, of a relatively stable model adapted afterwards to different times, places, and circumstances.

A study of medieval literacy's implications, then, cannot be carried out as if society had already adopted the norms and values which are in fact literacy's byproducts. Further, merely surveying the field, or limiting oneself to statistics, begs a large question: why "literacy" at all, and, more particularly, why the style of discourse in administration, the professional life, and the quest for higher knowledge, which, Weber noted long ago,[7] is the hallmark of socially useful rationality? A successful treatment of the second theme requires that one take, so far as possible, a neutral position with respect to cultural change. In other words, one must dissociate oneself from the modernist perspective, along with the bias towards one type of culture which it implies, and try to reach the understanding of the issues in the minds of the original participants. For the "first feudal age," as Marc Bloch called it, was above all a period of reawakening to modes of communication and to a sense of cultural discontinuity.[8] When texts were introduced into communities hitherto unfamiliar with writing, they often gave rise to unprecedented perceptual and cognitive possibilities: they promised, if they did not always deliver, a new technology of the mind.[9] How favorably did persons at different levels of society respond to the widening of horizons? What cracks appeared in the bedrock of long-unquestioned attitudes? How did traditional values weather the storms of innovation? If a plausible connection is to be made between literacy and other mutations of culture, such questions must first be asked.

As noted, this book moves from specific to more general historical issues. Chapter One attempts to establish the central premise, namely that, after the year 1000, oral discourse increasingly functioned within a framework of legal and institutional textuality. Chapters Two to Five present a series of case histories, each of which is designed to

[6] F. Braudel, "Histoire et sciences sociales: la longue durée," *Annales, E.S.C.*, 13 (1958), 725-53; J. Le Goff, *Pour un autre Moyen Age. Temps, travail et culture en Occident: 18 essais* (Paris, 1977), 9-11, *et passim*.

[7] Max Weber, *Wirtschaft und Gesellschaft*, 5th ed., ed. J. Winckelmann (Tübingen, 1972), 1.I.3, pp.2-3; 1.II.2, pp.12-13.

[8] *La société féodale*, vol. 1: *La formation des liens de dépendance* (Paris, 1939), book 2, chs. 2-3.

[9] Cf. F. de Saussure, *Cours de linguistique générale*, ed. T. de Mauro (Paris; 1981), 45-47, and, on the connection between logic and writing, the explorations of J. Derrida, *De la grammatologie* (Paris, 1967), ch. 2 (pp. 42-108). For a broader review of oral performance within hermeneutic principles, see in general, R. E. Palmer, *Hermeneutics* (Evanston, 1969), 12-32,48-54, and 201-17, with a bibliography, 254-74.

open out onto a broader problem. These larger issues are four in number: literacy and social organization (Chapter Two), the criticism of ritual and the related emergence of empirical attitudes (Chapter Three), the philosophical question of language, texts, and reality (Chapter Four), and the broader interconnections between texts, ideas, and society (Chapter Five). The questions treated in the book, I argue, were not only linked at a purely historical level, the heretics, for instance, described in Chapter Two, facing some of the same dilemmas as the theoreticians of Chapters Three and Four. They also illustrate the manner in which the growth of literate culture found expression in different aspects of medieval life and learning at once. In other words, there is both an external history, visible in events, debates, and legislation, and an internal history, by which similar problems and orientations turn up in otherwise unrelated areas of endeavour about the same time. For literacy, as it actually penetrated medieval life and thought, brought about a transformation of the basic skills of reading and writing into instruments of analysis and interpretation. It was, so to speak, the ontological cement binding the apparently isolated activities. Accordingly, the book's proper subject is not only a set of interrelated themes in eleventh- and twelfth-century history, but, viewed from the inside, the exploration of potential links between content and communicative form.

I.

ORAL AND WRITTEN

The study of medieval literacy's implications presupposes an understanding of the broader transition to a type of society in which oral discourse exists largely within a framework of conventions determined by texts.

What follows is an introductory account of that development. A deliberate attempt is made to place the growth of literacy in a wide context and to illustrate its connections with linguistic, legal, and institutional changes. But three themes mentioned in the Introduction, which are of special relevance to the subsequent chapters, are also stressed. One is a de-emphasizing of the problem of origins and along with it a purely evolutionary perspective in favour of a functional approach. What we wish to know about oral and written culture in the Middle Ages is not where each component came from, although that would be useful too, but how the two actually worked together. To understand these often complex relations, however, we must maintain a loose distinction between habits of thought and modes of communication. The one is not a synonym for the other. As noted, ways of thinking associated with orality often survived in a textual environment; writing them down did not always eliminate their links with oral exchange. The persistence of orality, or rather its transformation, raises in turn the questions of anachronism and of values. The rise of literacy helped to re-introduce the notion of archaism, and, more generally, the separation of culture into learned and popular sectors. Oral tradition became identified with illiteracy. Such labels, of course, were not established by texts themselves but by their human commentators, and, by implication, through attitudes towards earlier models of interpretation. When major issues regarding the cultural heritage arose, it was men's conception of the past, not the past in an objective sense, which largely shaped the nature of the responses. In the medieval mind, as in ours, whether the record was preserved orally or in writing was of critical importance.

12

1. TWO TRADITIONS

Let us begin with a fundamental question: how useful is the distinction between "oral" and "written" and how do the categories illuminate the medieval evidence?

There is, as noted, no hard and fast line between them. A text does not cease to be structured discourse, obedient to the laws of grammar and syntax, simply because it is spoken aloud. And oral exchange, if recorded, may still preserve many of its original features, for instance, formulae, repetition, and encyclopedism. Written texts are continually being re-performed, offering continuities to human behaviour over time. Oral interpolation may derive from improvisation or from texts.

Despite the untidiness of the terms, there are practical reasons for retaining them. Some are historical: men and women were conscious of the difference, especially after the millennium, when writing and its diverse functions began to undergo a sustained revival. Moreover, the evidence, such as it is, suggests that at no point in the subsequent three centuries was a significant percentage of laymen able to read and to write.[1] Medieval and early modern society hovered between the extremes: there was a tiny minority who were truly literate and a much larger majority for whom communication could take place only by word of mouth. Down to the age of print and in many regions long afterwards, literacy remained the exception rather than the rule. Despite primary schools, cheap paper, spectacles, and the growing body of legal and administrative material, the masses of both town and countryside as late as the Reformation remained relatively indifferent to writing.[2] For this vast group, marginal to literacy, the graphic world represented only a complex set of signs, frequently tied to re-

[1] An excellent recent assessment of evidence from English sources is M. T. Clanchy, *From Memory to Written Record: England, 1066-1307* (London, 1979), 182-201. Earlier surveys include V. H. Galbraith, "The Literacy of the Medieval English Kings," *Proceedings of the British Academy*, 5th Series, 21 (1935), 201-38; J. W. Thompson, *The Literacy of the Laity in the Middle Ages* (Berkeley, 1939); and M. B. Parkes, "The Literacy of the Laity," in D. Daiches and A. Thorlby, eds., *The Mediaeval World* (London, 1973), 555-77. A more general account is C. M. Cipolla, *Literacy and Development in the West* (Harmondsworth, 1969), 41-54.

[2] See in general N. Z. Davis, "Printing and the People," *Society and Culture in Early Modern France* (Stanford, 1975), 189-226; and, on the psychological impact of printing, E. L. Eisenstein, *The Printing Press as an Agent of Change. Communications and Cultural Transformations in Early Modern Europe* (Cambridge, 1979), vol. 1, pp. 225-72.

lations of authority.[3] There was no universal language. The majority
of people spoke a vernacular dialect which varied from place to place
and which could clearly be distinguished even within regions from
the more refined speech habits of the upper strata of society. Ignorance
of Latin was widespread, despite its association with grammatical correctness.[4] Although scribal pressures rose from many directions and
gathered momentum as the age of print neared, many peasants,
burghers, and even aristocrats remained essentially within oral-aural
culture.

The first reason, then, for maintaining a working dichotomy between oral and written communication is descriptive. The second is
explanatory.

To the contemporary mind the rise of textuality is self-evident,
while the persistence of orality is difficult to account for. But to the
medievals just the opposite was true. Oral discourse, as a means of
communicating and storing facts, was well suited to a society that
was regionalized, highly particularized, and more conscious of inherited status than of achievement through pragmatic social roles. Oral
culture possessed its own characteristics, some of which have been rediscovered through the study of contemporary communities that lack
writing.[5] In all such societies without texts language exists only in a
verbal form. The fundamental categories of classification, through which,
Durkheim argued, the world is interpreted, are handed down by word
of mouth. The continuity of culture depends on individuals who verbally transmit the heritage from one generation to the next. The form
and content of knowledge, whose logical properties are not differen-
tiated as in textual tradition,[6] are passed on in a series of face-to-face

[3] Cf. J. Le Goff, "Culture cléricale et traditions folkloriques dans la civilisation mérovin-
gienne," *Annales, E.S.C.*, 22 (1967), 780-91; repr., *Pour un autre Moyen Age*, 223-35.

[4] H. Grundmann, "Litteratus-illitteratus," 1-15.

[5] See above all J. Vansina, *Oral Tradition. A Study in Historical Methodology*, trans. H. M.
Wright (London, 1965), where there is a review of earlier approaches, pp. 2-8. The work of
British anthropologists is discussed by M. T. Clanchy, "Remembering the Past and the Good
Old Law," *History* 55 (1970), 166-72. Broader in scope is M. de Certeau's illuminating study,
L'écriture de l'histoire (Paris, 1975), esp. pp. 213-88.

For an anthropological perspective on the impact of literacy, see J. Goody and I. Watt, "The
Consequences of Literacy," *Comparative Studies in Society and History* 5 (1962-63), 304-45, together
with the studies edited by J. Goody in *Literacy in Traditional Societies* (Cambridge, 1968), and
J. Vansina, "The Power of Systematic Doubt in Historical Enquiry," *History in Africa* 1 (1974),
109-27. For a brief *aperçu* of recent issues, see J. Goody, *The Domestication of the Savage Mind*
(Cambridge, 1977), chs. 2-4. For a positive assessment of oral sources in social history, see P.
Thompson, *The Voice of the Past. Oral History* (New York, 1978), 19-64.

[6] J. A. Notopoulos, "Mnemosyne in Oral Literature," *Transactions and Proceedings of the Amer-*

encounters. Such meetings are rich in gesture, ritual, and ceremony: men communicate not only by what they say but by how they behave. The human sensorium is oriented around the ear.[7] The meaning of words is not generalized into a series of standard definitions which can then act as points of reference: consequently, "in an oral-aural culture one can ask about something but one cannot look up anything."[8] Speech and action form a cohesive whole: "the meaning of each word is ratified in a succession of concrete situations, accompanied by vocal inflexions and physical gestures, all of which combine to particularize both its specific denotation and its accepted connotative usage."[9] Meaning arises as a compromise between a standard set of rhetorical figures and an individual interchange to which they are adapted.[10]

The single great storehouse of meaning is memory. The mnemonic devices through which epic, legal, and religious information is recalled help to structure the way in which the individual thinks about the facts transmitted.[11] Of course, memory is selective. In any society, Freud noted, what people forget is as important as what they recall. In oral as in written culture, memory functions within the social group, which, with its particular conventions, traditions, and institutions, acts as a conceptual filter for image formation and recollection.[12] But, in oral tradition, one cannot check what is recalled against a presumably "correct" version of events. Hence, the constitution of the social group, together with its "folk-memory," determines the relationship of the new elements to the old.[13] The past, whether conceived abstractly or concretely, can be present, if relevant to ongoing cultural needs. Oral culture is therefore conservative, if only in the

---

ican Philological Association 69 (1938), 465-93; the important study of E. A. Havelock, Preface to Plato (Cambridge, Mass., 1963), 215-33; and, on the linguistic mechanisms, the older but still useful account of M. Jousse, Etudes de psychologie linguistique. Le style oral rythmique et mnémotechnique chez les Verbo-moteurs (Paris, 1924), 133-232.

[7] M. McLuhan, The Gutenberg Galaxy (Toronto, 1962), 22-29; 40-45; W. J. Ong, The Presence of the Word (New Haven, 1967), 1-9, 17-35.

[8] Ong, op.cit., 23.

[9] Goody and Watt, art.cit., 306.

[10] Cf. E. R. Curtius, European Literature and the Latin Middle Ages, trans. W. R. Trask (New York, 1953), 61-68.

[11] See, in general, F. A. Yates, The Art of Memory (London, 1966).

[12] F. C. Bartlett, Remembering (Cambridge, 1932), 253-55. Bartlett's approach is briefly criticized by A. D. Baddeley, The Psychology of Memory (New York, 1976), 9-15, who reviews other issues in the field relevant to this volume, chs. 12, 13, and 14 (pp. 300-69). For a literary approach, see in general G. Dumézil, Mythe et épopée, 3 vols. (Paris, 1968-73).

[13] M. Halbwachs, Les cadres sociaux de la mémoire (Paris, 1925).

15

literal sense of the term.[14] It suits small, isolated communities with a strong network of kinship and group solidarity. The reaction to the outside world is frequently one of fear and hostility. To put the matter another way: if, as some argue, communications media are among the chief building-blocks of civilization,[15] then oral culture is limited to particularist societies in which "the structure of . . . linguistic material is inexorably mixed up with, and dependent upon, the course of the activity in which the utterances are imbedded."[16] In such societies, "the controls of action are informal; they rest on the traditional obligations of largely inherited status, and are expressed in talk and gesture and in the patterns of reciprocal action."[17]

Medieval society after the eleventh century was increasingly oriented towards the scribe, the written word, the literary text, and the document. In Italy and southern France, the tradition of Roman legal and rhetorical studies never really disappeared.[18] In the north, the spoken word played a predominant role in both administration and literary culture down to about 1050. The Carolingian period was a midpoint. The clear, beautiful minuscule reformed the "national" Insular, Visigothic, and Beneventan hands, just as Charlemagne's coronation on Christmas Day, 800, created a new empire out of formerly warring principalities. But the written did not supersede the oral. The concise enumeration of ecclesiastical holdings in Irminon's polyptique of the abbey of St. Germain creates one impression. The capitularies issued by the emperors in the eighth and ninth centuries create another. These bodies of ordinances treat a wide variety of legislative matters in legal, ecclesiastical, military, administrative, and commercial areas. But their format varies little. They were "not usually drafted in official full texts by the royal chancery, but were notes or title lists set down to recall the contents of royal commandments made orally."[19] In their written form they often exist as verbal orders

[14] Goody and Watt, art.cit., 307-08.

[15] H. A. Innis, *The Bias of Communication*, repr. (Toronto, 1964), 3-60; *idem, Empire and Communications*, 2nd ed. (Toronto, 1972).

[16] B. Malinowski, "The Problem of Meaning in Primitive Languages," in C. K. Ogden and I. A. Richards, *The Meaning of Meaning* (Cambridge, 1923), 311.

[17] R. Redfield, *The Primitive World and its Transformations* (Ithaca, N.Y., 1953), 14.

[18] Curtius, *European Literature*, 61-68.

[19] R. C. van Caenegem, "Capitularies, Imperial and Ecclesiastical," *New Catholic Encyclopedia* vol. 3, p. 89. On this question see A. Dumas "La parole et l'écriture dans les capitulaires carolingiens," *Mélanges Louis Halphen* (Paris, 1951), 208-16, who presents in my view a more balanced view than F. L. Ganshof, "Charlemagne et l'usage de l'écrit en matière administrative," *Le Moyen Age* 57 (1951), 1-25.

or prohibitions. There was no authoritative text because the text was not the authority: that came from the *bannum*, the spoken word of the emperor. The extant specimens of Ottonian diplomas create a similar impression. They are magnificent reminders of the imperial presence, not substitutes for it.

The change to administrative activity involving scribes took place between the eleventh and thirteenth centuries with the Norman kingdom, as Haskins emphasized, acting as a bridge. The contrast can be seen by comparing the diplomas of Robert the Pious or Henry I with those of Louis VI. The twelfth century emerges as "the period in which diplomatic script attained its apogee."[20] Of course, one cannot judge the literary output of a whole nation by the activity of the royal chancery. But in the countryside the picture is not so different. After the brief Carolingian renaissance, written records declined sharply in quantity and quality. From the tenth to the early twelfth century "social relations were once again founded on spoken words, acts and ceremonies rather than on written documents. . . . The rights and duties of each individual were laid down and maintained with some flexibility by custom and ancient usage."[21] From about 1150, records of all sorts become more plentiful. The information they provide is more precise. "A group of specialists in administration emerges, whose particular technical expertise is based on the written word and on reckoning, and who are occupied in registering, counting, valuing and surveying."[22] The transformation does not take place in all regions at the same time. Ecclesiastical estates and properties with cash crops near marketing centres precede the more outlying areas. The larger villages and nascent towns adopt literacy more rapidly than the countryside, where commercial instincts are held in check by long-established custom. The cursive reappears: one wrote more quickly, Pirenne noted, because commercial occasions for writing were more numerous.[23] Even allowing for regional and occupational variations, by the mid-twelfth century the presence of scribal culture is one of

---

[20] M. Prou, *Manuel de paléographie* (Paris, 1892), 110.

[21] G. Duby, *Rural Economy and Country Life in the Medieval West*, trans. C. Postan (Columbia, S.C., 1968), 61.

[22] *Ibid.*, 62.

[23] "L'instruction des marchands au Moyen Age," *Annales d'histoire économique et sociale* 1 (1929), 18. On the contribution of monastic schools, see the revisions of P. Riché, "L'instruction des laïcs au XIIe siècle," *Mélanges Saint Bernard* (Dijon, 1953), 214-17. For a recent review of the question, see R. S. Lopez, "The Culture of the Medieval Merchant," in D.B.J. Randall, ed., *Medieval and Renaissance Studies*, No. 8 (Durham, N.C., 1979), 54-62.

the few universalizing forces that the western Middle Ages knows as a whole.

"Administration," wrote Hilary Jenkinson, "is founded on precedent, that is on memory; and it grows with the adoption for its own uses of artificial memory, that is of writing."[24] But not only the style of government is changed. Other areas of society and culture are also affected. Memory is oral-aural and visual at the same time; records are only visual. The change is not irreversible, but once it has taken place it entails other consequences. What begins as a practical necessity can easily finish as an altered social psychology.

For the new use of texts is not merely "the graphic counterpart of speech."[25] It has a structure and logical properties of its own. In societies functioning orally the advent of the written word can disrupt previous patterns of thought and action, often permanently. Above all it transforms man's conception of himself in society. When written models for conducting human affairs make their appearance, a new sort of relationship is set up between the guidelines and realities of behaviour: the presentation of self is less of a subjectively determined performance and more of an objectified pattern within articulated norms. One no longer responds through inherited principles handed down by word of mouth. The model is now exteriorized. Individual experience still counts, but its role is delimited; instead, loyalty and obedience are given to a more or less standardized set of rules which lie outside the sphere of influence of the person, the family, or the community. Moreover, one need not be literate oneself in order to be affected by such rules. A written code can be set up and interpreted on behalf of unlettered members of society, the text acting as a medium for social integration or alienation, depending on its use. Of course, the areas of life subject to textual constraints in the Middle Ages were modest by modern standards. They covered birth and death, baptism and marriage, initiations, terms of service, transfers of property, and a small number of issues in public and private law. And in most cases written documents were suffused with oral tradition. Often the record merely preserved what had always been said and done. But the important point is not the degree to which writing penetrated oral culture: it was its irrevocability. Up to the eleventh century, western Europe could have returned to an essentially oral civilization. But by 1100 the die was cast.

[24] *Palaeography and the Practical Study of Court Hand* (Cambridge, 1915), 2.
[25] D. Diringer, *Writing* (London, 1962), 13.

18

2. LATIN AND ROMANCE

The rise of literacy not only created a hiatus between oral and written tradition. It also brought to the surface and gave shape to the inherent duality of the western European languages. For, long before oral and written became tangible issues, most spoken and recorded languages had bifurcated into popular and learned forms. It is tempting to think of the one as a virtual synonym for the other. But in many ways they were different. In the early Middle Ages "oral" was not the equivalent of "popular." *Beowulf*, although perhaps composed and certainly delivered orally, was from the beginning a product of higher culture and has come down to us as a complex text.

Oral culture acquired popular associations only at the time when cultural values were beginning to be associated with literacy. Bäuml speaks of the average man after the millennium passing from "preliteracy" to "illiteracy." In the first phase writing played no very great role in legal or institutional communication. In the second, it was a question of not being able to read and write in a society in which legal and institutional communication increasingly took place in writing; in short, it was the cultural state of the culturally disfavoured.[26] No such precise distinctions can be made between popular and literary elements in language. Certainly, writing helps to standardize language.[27] But linguistic change is affected by much more than the means of preservation. Although the paucity of evidence obscures the actual mechanisms, it is clear that Latin, early Romance languages, and their written forms evolved by a process of continuous interchange. Not only were there "direct channels," Sabatini notes, between both writers and readers as well as speakers and listeners. There were also "indirect channels," that is, either "the registering of an oral discourse in a vulgarizing written language" or "the recitation of a vulgarizing text in spoken forms."[28]

[26] For a recent statement, see F. H. Bäuml, "Varieties and Consequences . . . ," 237-49.

[27] For a discussion of the problems, see E. Pulgram, "Phoneme and Grapheme: a Parallel," *Word* 7 (1951), 15-20 and *idem*, "Graphic and Phonic Systems: Figurae and Signs," *ibid.*, 21 (1965), 208-24. For a bibliography on the subject, see J. Vachek, *Written Language* (The Hague, 1973), 71-77. The evolution of different approaches is discussed by J. H. Greenberg, "Historical Linguistics and Unwritten Languages," in A. S. Dil, ed., *Language, Culture and Communication. Essays by Joseph H. Greenberg* (Stanford, 1971), 11-29.

[28] F. Sabatini, "Dalla 'scripta latina rustica' alle 'scriptae' romanze," *Studi medievali*, 3rd series, 9 (1968), 326 and H. Lüdke, "Die Entstehung romanischer Schriftsprachen," *Vox Romanica* 23 (1964), 12. Cf. P. Wunderli, "Die ältesten Texte unter dem Gesichtswinkel von Protokoll und Vorlesen," *ibid.*, 24 (1965), 44-63; C. A. Mastrelli, "Romania-Germania: Mündliche und

The duality of the Romance languages, their rough division into popular and literary forms, was a legacy of the history of Latin. The starting point was the importation into Rome of the speech and educational habits of a foreign people, the Greeks, through which an alien grammar, syntax, and rhetoric were imposed onto the paratactic, verbally unsophisticated structure of early Latin. From Rome's earliest foreign conquests to the end of the Antonine period in A.D. 192, the linguistic expansion of Latin followed the political. Latin first vanquished the other dialects of the Italian peninsula. It then became the language of administration throughout the republic and later the empire, except in the Greek-speaking east.

As Horace wryly noted, the conquest of Greece had backfired: the physical submission only speeded up Rome's assimilation into the wider framework of Hellenistic culture, which became bilingual. In the process, Latin underwent a rapid development, of which the most important feature was the appearance of a literary vehicle. Romans had little or no native literature of their own; so they imported and adapted what they did not have. Linguists roughly date the earliest dissimilarities between spoken and literary Latin from the second half of the third century.[29] Not by accident, Livius Andronicus, a freed Greek slave, began composing his plays and Latin *Odusia* about the same time. Livius was an archaiser, a conscious creator of poetic diction.[30] Later authors, while imitating Greek models less crudely, followed his example. But the emulation went far beyond language-training and literature: it "prepared the way for modern forms of humanism that are based on a second language, a cultural lingua franca which is used to transmit a tradition generally recognized as having an essential superiority over all others, and therefore to be imitated."[31] An identification was made between the correct attitude towards the classical heritage and the style of life considered appro-

schriftliche Überlieferung," in H. Bekker-Nielsen *et al.*, eds., *Oral Tradition, Literary Tradition* (Odense, 1977), 83-92.

[29] F. Altheim, "Die Anfänge des Vulgärlateins," *Glotta* 20 (1932), 153; R. A. Hall, Jr., "The Reconstruction of Proto-Romance," *Language* 26 (1950), 19; C. Mohrmann, "Les formes du latin dit 'vulgaire,' " *Latin vulgaire, latin des chrétiens, latin médiéval* (Paris, 1955), 5. For earlier bibliography on the subject, see K. Strecker, *Introduction to Medieval Latin* trans. and rev. R. B. Palmer (Berlin, 1965), 28-34.

[30] E. Fränkel, "Livius," *Paulys Realencyclopädie der classischen Altertumswissenschaft*, Suppbd. V, 605.

[31] H. I. Marrou, *A History of Education in Antiquity*, trans. G. Lamb (London, 1956), 342. On the medieval development of this notion, see B. Bischoff, "The Study of Foreign Languages in the Middle Ages," *Speculum* 36 (1961), 209-24.

priate for the educationally privileged sectors of society. This pattern,
once established, was adapted to different linguistic situations. In the
Middle Ages it drove a wedge not between Latin and Greek but between the official culture, which was in Latin, and the unofficial cultures which existed in vulgar Latin or early vernaculars. During the
Renaissance a similar theory of high culture helped to legitimize literary Italian, French, and German.

The early medieval phases of these complicated transformations cannot be observed directly. Latin is grammatically inert; there is no
substantial body of records delineating the spoken languages; and the
manuscript tradition for both cursive and formal scripts is at times
fragmentary. Paleography, diplomatics, philology, and comparative
linguistics have traditionally approached the lacunae from two directions. One looks forward from the ancient world and is based on the
alleged evolution of popular versus learned Latin. Through an analysis
of deviations from known classical norms, attempts have been made
to describe how new words appeared, were assimilated and passed
through stages of technical, colloquial, savant, or literary usage. The
other method works back from the known Romance or Germanic
languages. Through philological, etymological, and syntactical reconstruction, together with the study of comparative phonology, hypotheses are offered about missing links. Both approaches have been
aided by the scientific dating of extant records and the historical analysis of handwriting.

In attempting to place chronological limits around the changes,
attention has naturally shifted to the Late Latin period, that is, roughly
between A.D. 200 and 600. The first boundary corresponds to the
age of Tertullian and the early martyrologies, which, Löfstedt persua-
sively argues, are as useful an indicator of linguistic shifts as the death
of Tacitus around A.D. 117, the event normally taken to signal the
end of the classical age.[32] More importantly, the third century also
saw the introduction of a new cursive which by 367 had become the
"common script" everywhere except the imperial chancery.[33] This *scripta
latina rustica* took its vocabulary from popular usage; it absorbed morphology and syntax, as well as traces of phonology; and it adopted
new graphic signs to express the sounds actually spoken.[34] Many factors influenced the linguistic and scribal changes: the interplay of
social classes and levels of education; migration from the countryside

[32] E. Löfstedt, *Late Latin* (Oslo, 1959), 1.
[33] J. Mallon, *Paléographie romaine* (Madrid, 1952), 123.
[34] F. Sabatini, "Dalla 'scripta latina rustica,' " 334.

21

to the towns and from the peripheries of the contracting empire to the metropolis; the conflict of different generations, ethnic groups, and religions, through which the vulgarisms of one period became the fashionable styles of the next; and above all political considerations like the *Constitutio Antoniniana* of 212, which bestowed Roman citizenship on all inhabitants of the empire regardless of origin.[35]

Among the forces contributing to the growth of popular Latin in the later empire a special place is reserved for Christianity. Members of the new faith constituted virtually a "third race" after Romans and Jews, no less marked than the latter by their refusal to participate in official cults and by their sense of exclusiveness.[36] One of the clearest ways to delineate boundaries was through the spoken or written word. What was created was "not quite a new language, but certainly new forms of expression."[37] Whether in everyday, literary, or liturgical Latin, Christians introduced words and phrases drawn from ordinary speech and occasionally from Greek.[38] The novelty arose both in language and style. The Old Latin versions of the Bible, which drew heavily on colloquial usage, influenced speech patterns among Christian communities, and this linguistic phenomenon, reflecting in turn the often low social origins of the converts, allowed a measure of freedom within the restrictions of the literary language. Notions of genre were similarly affected. Christian "literature," Auerbach observed, that is, stories from the Bible, dealt by and large with topics that did not fit into the classical oratorical divisions.[39] Their forms of expression were "humble" but their matter "sublime." New canons of taste were obviously at work. The Bible, or its translations, attempted to make God's word accessible to all, no matter what the level of education. It intermingled high and low in both audience and inner message: the complexity depended not on rhetorical figures—

---

[35] For general reviews of the issues, see W. von Wartburg, *Die Entstehung der romanischen Völker*, 2nd ed. (Tübingen, 1951), chs. 3-5, and F. Wieacker, *Vulgarismus und Klassicizmus im Recht der Spätantike* (Sitzungsberichte der Heidelberger Akademie der Wissenschaften, Phil.-hist. Kl., Abh. 3, 1955), 7-44.

[36] A. Harnack, *The Mission and Expansion of Christianity in the First Three Centuries*, trans. and ed. J. Moffatt, re-ed. J. Pelikan (New York, 1961), vol. 1, 273-75.

[37] Löfstedt, *Late Latin*, 68.

[38] C. Mohrmann, "L'étude de la latinité chrétienne," *op. cit.*, 19-34; *idem*, "Latin (in the Church)," *New Catholic Encyclopedia*, 8, 413. For a balanced historical and critical assessment of the question, see Löfstedt, *op.cit.*, ch. 5, or J. de Ghellinck, "Latin chrétien ou langue latine des chrétiens?" *Les études classiques* 8 (1939), 449-78.

[39] E. Auerbach, *Literary Language and its Public in Late Latin Antiquity and in the Middle Ages*, trans. R. Manheim (London, 1965), 46.

although these, Augustine showed, were found in abundance—but in the desire of the faithful for spiritual enlightenment.[40] The blending of classical stylistics and biblical themes greatly influenced the development of medieval Latin and the Romance languages. The gradual abandonment of the classical curriculum in the schools after Justinian could not but promote the acceptance of spoken Latin, whose rhythms were now not far from those of the translated Bible itself.

Religious forces contributed to widening the gap between popular and literary Latin from within the empire. Political forces often came from outside. Chiefly they consisted of intrusions into the Latin-speaking world by linguistic foreigners, which began as early as the Roman defeat by Armenius in A.D. 9, and continued until Otto the Great routed the Magyars at the River Lech in 995 and the Arabs were expelled from their last Italian stronghold by Roger of Sicily after 1061. By and large, the outsiders did not disturb the morphology or syntax of Latin as spoken or written, except in Rumania, where the penetration of the Avars in the century or so after the death of Justinian brought about a fusion of Romance and Slav elements. In some cases, like the Visigoths in Spain and the Langobards in Italy, the survivals are difficult to distinguish from the general influx of Germanic words. In others the lexicographical legacy is greater, as for instance in France, where Germanic words influenced the vocabulary of agrarian life, feudal relations, and military hardware,[41] or Arabic Spain, where the innovations affected gardening, building, commerce, administration, literature, music, and above all science.[42] The denouement of the invasions was the reshaping of the empire in the image of the invaders, in which, from the ninth century at least, a new Romania emerged as a palpable linguistic reality. But the fate of government and language were not the same. The growing strength of the centralized monarchy after Pippin's coronation in 751 merely camouflaged the increasing decentralization of spoken languages. When Charlemagne died in 814 he had largely realized his ambition of reconstituting the empire to include what is now France, the Low Countries, greater Germany, and sectors of Italy and Spain. But ordinary people in different regions could scarcely any longer understand each other.

The hiatus, in other words, had opened not only between spoken

[40] *Ibid.*, 50-51.
[41] W. D. Elcock, *The Romance Languages* (London, 1960), 236; in greater detail, see G. Paris, "Les mots d'emprunt dans le plus ancien français," *Mélanges linguistiques* (Paris, 1909), 315-52.
[42] Elcock, *The Romance Languages*, 279.

and written languages but between spoken languages themselves, which in turn had begun to evolve distinctive written forms. But did speech influence writing, as is usually assumed, or vice versa? The actual evolution of the spoken and the written within Latin and Romance forms is subject to diverse interpretations. The traditional view— namely, that Latin and Romance coexisted as spoken languages from about the second century B.C., but had become mutually unintelligible by the ninth—is certainly oversimplified. The implicit explanation of how people spoke is based in fact on how they wrote; the connection remains hypothetical until we understand how the medievals themselves viewed the relationship between speech and writing. A growing body of evidence suggests that the evolution was not only verbal. There was also a set of incompatibilities, as yet not fully understood, between official written and unofficial spoken forms.[43] When communication between the two became too difficult for ordinary speakers, the written language, that is, Latin, probably became reduced to "an additional collection of rules."[44] Moreover, what has normally been looked upon as the "emergence" of the Romance vernaculars may in part have been only a new way of writing.[45] One may even ask whether the *Strasbourg Oaths* of 842 were the "birth certificate"[46] of the Romance languages, or whether they were indirect byproducts of Alcuin's reforms, in which "the reading aloud of written texts for the first time sounded different from the pronunciation of the same words in the vernacular."[47]

Even before this famous meeting a number of works written roughly within a century of each other in different regions of Europe underlined the passage to genuine bilingualism from "diglossia,"[48] that is, from the simultaneous use of phonologically interdependent forms of Latin and Romance in which each had specific functions. These texts

---

[43] For recent reviews of the issues, see the lecture notes of D'A. Avalle, *Alle origini della letteratura francese. I giuramento di Strasburgo e la sequenza di santa Eulalia*, ed. L. Borghi (Turin, 1966), 41-144; C. Th. Gossen, *Französische Skriptastudien. Untersuchungen zu den nordfranzösischen Urkundensprachen des Mittelalters* (Österreichische Akademie der Wissenschaften, phil.-hist. Kl., Sitzungsberichte, 253 Bd., Vienna, 1967); *idem*, "Graphème et phonème: le problème central de l'étude des langues écrites du moyen âge," *Revue de linguistique romane* 32 (1968), 1-16; R. Wright, "Speaking, Reading and Writing Late Latin and Early Romance," *Neophilologus* 60 (1976), 178-89.

[44] Wright, *art.cit.*, 178.

[45] *Loc.cit.*

[46] W. von Wartburg, *Einführung in Problematik und Methodik der Sprachwissenschaft* (Halle, 1943), 191.

[47] Wright, *art.cit.*, 185.

[48] H. Lüdke, *Geschichte des romanischen Wortschatzes* (Freiburg, 1968), ch. 5.

include the *Indovinello Veronese*, the *"Laudes Regiae"* of Soissons, the *Parody of the Lex Salica*, the *Glosses of Reichenau*, the *Glossary of Kassel*, the *Graffito romano*, and the *Glossary of Monza*.[49] The tension between written and spoken languages is also evident from a number of contemporary statements, the well-known provision for vernacular preaching in the council of Tours of 813,[50] for instance, or the mention in a Montecassino penitential of confession in *rustica verba*.[51] Again, a tenth- or early eleventh-century text from the kingdom of Leon ironically disparages those who speak *latinum circa romançum* before laymen, while nonetheless praising the use of correct but obscurantist Latin, even if understood only by clerics.[52] The statement's ambivalence suggests that the Romance languages would not have attained recognition had classical, written Latin not been reasserted. Paradoxically, Romania may in part have been a byproduct of the Carolingian "renaissance," whose real educational aim was to reform the standards for teaching, speaking, and writing Latin.[53] Wherever Latin improved, the spoken and grammatically written languages grew farther apart.

The period between the eleventh and the thirteenth centuries marks

[49] For a general review, see C. A. Mastrelli, "Vicende linguistiche del secolo VIII," *I problemi dell'occidente nel secolo VIII* (Spoleto, 1973), 805-31. Specifically, the *Indovinello* is datable from the late eighth or early ninth century; L. Schiaparelli, "Sulla data e provenienza del cod. LXXXIX della Biblioteca Capitolare di Verona (l'Orazionale Mozarabico)," ASI, series 7, 1 (1924), 106; for a philological and linguistic discussion, see C. A. Mastrelli, "L'indovinello veronese," *Archivio glottologico italiano* 38 (1953), 190-209. The *Laudes Regiae* originates between 783 and 787; P. Zumthor, "Une formule galloromane du VIIIe siècle," *Zeitschrift für romanische Philologie* 75 (1959), 214. The parody of the *Lex Salica* comes from the last quarter of the eighth century; G. A. Beckmann, "Aus den letzten Jahrzehnten des Vulgärlateins in Frankreich. Ein parodistischer Zusatz zur Lex Salica und eine Schreiberklage," *ibid.*, 79 (1963), 305-06. The *Glosses of Reichenau* are before 800; Mastrelli, "Vicende linguistiche . . . ," 827; the *Glossary of Kassel* from Fulda between the eighth and ninth centuries; *loc. cit.*; the *Graffito romano* from the first decade of the ninth; Sabatini, *art.cit.*, 322-23; the *Glossary of Monza* from the north of Italy in the first decade of the tenth; B. Bischoff and H. G. Beck, "Das italienisch-griechische Glossar der Handschrift e 14 (127) der Biblioteca Capitolare in Monza," in *Medium Aevum Romanicum. Festschrift für Hans Rheinfelder*, ed. H. Bihler and A. Noyer-Weidner (Munich, 1963), 51.

[50] *Concilium Turonense*, anno 813, MGH Concilia Aevi Karolini 1, p. 288: "in rusticam Romanam linguam aut Thiotiscam, quo facilius cuncti possint intelligere quae dicuntur." For a list of other admonitions on vernacular preaching, see M. Zink, *La prédication en langue romane avant 1300* (Paris, 1966), 87-88.

[51] Quoted in B. Migliorini, *The Italian Language*, ed. and trans. T. G. Griffith (London, 1966), 42.

[52] Quoted in R. Menéndez Pidal, *Orígenes des español*, 3rd, ed. (Madrid, 1950), 459n1: "Ille est vituperandus qui loquitur latinum circa romançum, maxime coram laicis, ita quod ipsi met intelligunt totum; et ille est laudandus qui semper loquitur latinum obscure, ita quod nullus intelligat eum nisi clerici . . . ."

[53] Cf. H. Lüdke, "Die Entstehung romanischer Schriftsprachen," 5-8. On Alcuin's influence, see in particular L. Wallach, *Alcuin and Charlemagne* (Ithaca, 1959).

the final stages of this long process. The vernacular languages of continental Europe made their first substantial appearance in textual form. Owing to economic and demographic expansion, great numbers of hitherto "voiceless" individuals were also making their first acquaintance with culture in the formal sense of an ongoing tradition dependent on the written word. The result was a profound interaction between language, texts, and society. Glimpses of the change can be caught in literature. But, unlike the age of print, when secular letters rivalled theology as a vehicle for the discussion of values, the period before 1200 was inadequately provided with a lay reading public and literary genres flexible enough for expressing the full range and depth of its emotional life. Even French, which of all the Romance languages most accurately reproduced "the relative position of written and spoken Latin in the later days of the empire,"[54] gave little evidence of a reading as opposed to a listening public. Genuine literacy remained largely a monopoly of ecclesiastical culture, which not only served as a repository for issues of dogma but acted as a laboratory for experimenting with new relations between oral and written, vernaculars and Latin. Of course, the Romance and Germanic languages existed in substance if not in grammatical form, and each was self-consciously developing a literary versus a colloquial dimension. But compared to Latin their norms were still relatively flexible. Latin owed its prestige and strength to two sources. It was the only language in which grammar could be taught; therefore, anyone wishing to learn to read and to write had to master the ancient tongue. Also, it was the only written language widely known and understood. This twofold advantage, focusing on *grammatica* and *scripta*, was a powerful asset and, from the eleventh century at least, a source of profound conflict.[55] For the comprehension of Latin not only made possible an education in formal disciplines like Roman and canon law, theology, and from about the time of Abelard, in philosophy. It also opened the door to controlling fiscal, property, and more general economic relations, which from the later twelfth century were increasingly written down.

   It is not surprising that *litteratus*, the normal term for describing

[54] M. K. Pope, *From Latin to Modern French with Especial Consideration of Anglo-Norman*, 2nd ed. (London, 1952), 3-4. On written versus spoken languages, the *status questionis* is reviewed by C. A. Robson, "Literary Language, Spoken Dialect and the Phonological Problem in Old French," *Transactions of the Philological Society, 1955* (Oxford, 1956), 117-31.

[55] For an overview of the issues, see M. Richter, "Kommunikationsprobleme im lateinischen Mittelalter," *Historische Zeitschrift* 222 (1976), 43-80.

someone who knew how to read and to write, referred almost invariably to literacy in Latin. As the norms of scribal culture were gradually adopted, the mention of literacy, first by clerics and later although less frequently by laymen, became more common. Yet, Grundmann noted, the basic meaning changed little. Between the eleventh and fourteenth centuries a literate was one who could read, write, and perhaps also speak Latin.[56]

The illiterate were known by a variety of terms: *illitterati*, *indocti*, or often simply as *laici*, but perhaps the most instructive were *rustici* and *idiotae*, words which in their philological setting convey the cultural barriers which after 1100 progressively separated the lettered from the unlettered.

Both terms contain a double set of values, at once recognizing the cultural norms associated with literacy but justifying the sacred simplicity of the illiterate. To take rusticity first: in classical antiquity *rusticitas* meant one of two things, either the way of life of the countryside or the speech habits of the people who lived there. In the eleventh century, the contrast more often lay between the vernaculars or dialects of those who knew no Latin and the written discourse, for the most part in Latin, of ecclesiastics and later of townsmen educated by them. The *rusticus* was not only a serf, a villein, or simply a peasant; to speak *rustico more* was to communicate in an unlearned tongue for which there was no written counterpart based on grammatical rules.

The ancient distinction between *urbanitas* and *rusticitas*, although occasionally involving orthography and syntax, was essentially one of pronunciation.[57] It came about after Rome had made a number of successful conquests and educated Romans were beginning to be embarrassed at their rural origins. The agrarian past was deeply imprinted on early Latin: primitive law was that of the farmer; the religion was rich in rural cults; and in contrast to Greek, with its

---

[56] H. Grundmann, "Litteratus-illitteratus . . . ," 3-15. Cf. M. T. Clanchy, *From Memory to Written Record*, 175-85. The insistence on the spoken element was underlined in the definition of *litteratus* in the late twelfth-century *Magnae Deriuationes* of Huguccio of Pisa, which was copied without alteration into the influential *Catholicon* of Giovanni Balbi of Genoa, completed ca. 1286: "Litteratus: . . . Literator uel literatus non dicitur ille qui habet multos libros et inspicit et reuoluit ut monachus qui proprie potest dici antiquarius, quia antiquas historias habet ad manum. Sed ille dicitur literator uel literatus qui ex arte de rude uoce scit formare literas in dicionibus et diciones in orationibus et orationes scit congrue proferre et accentuare." (Joannes Balbus, *Catholicon* [Mainz, 1460; repr. Farnborough, U.K., 1971], s.v.).

[57] J. Marouzeau, "Latinitas—Vrbanitas—Rusticitas," in *Quelques aspects de la formation du latin littéraire* (Paris, 1949), 11.

flexible verbal constructions so suitable for abstract thought, the conceptual vocabulary stressed the concrete thing rather than the idea, the form, or inner reality.[58] Roman authors were ambivalent towards the nation's agrarian heritage. Cicero, Vergil, and Horace all made their careers in the metropolis, but they never tired of singing the praises of the country life. Oratory and later rhetoric turned out to be the greatest enemies of Rome's former linguistic diversity. Cicero advised young orators "to avoid rustic abrasiveness and provincial novelty"[59] as well as archaism,[60] while Quintilian suggested repeatedly that *urbanitas* was preferable on most occasions *in verbis et sono et usu*.[61] Macrobius, writing as late as the fifth century, could think of no more appropriate metaphor for the barbarism of mankind's origins than a linguistic "roughness" that was simply an erudite version of the same theme.[62] But, by the time he wrote, the standard was not spoken but written Latin. It was grammar in textual form, not speech habits, which henceforth isolated the literate and by implication denoted the rustic. And the irony underlying the earlier distinctions had re-emerged in a new context. The simplicity of the countryside was largely replaced as a literary topos by that of the Bible.[63] Although Christian authors from Augustine on studied and mastered rhetoric, they were constantly reminded that Jesus and the apostles spoke in the plain language of uncultivated men.

They were, as the New Testament bore witness, *idiotae*. This term, which occurs in Acts and Paul, had a wide range of meaning in Greek; during the hellenistic period the senses were gradually adapted to the needs of Latin. In classical and patristic Greek, the ἰδιώτης was the private person or the layman: the unskilled, unprofessional, or uninitiated, as opposed let us say to the trained officer, physician, philosopher, or priest.[64] In Latin, *idiota* came to mean someone who was ignorant of a science, a doctrine, or an area of study, and as a corollary one unperfected in a practical discipline.[65] Vitruvius, for instance, distinguished "between laymen and architects."[66] Among Christian-

[58] *Ibid.*, 7-8.

[59] *De Oratore* 3.12.44, ed. J. G. Baiter and C. L. Kayser (Leipzig, 1860), 152.

[60] *Ibid.*, 3.11.42, *loc.cit.*

[61] *Institutio Oratoriae* 6.3.7, ed. M. Winterbottom (Oxford, 1970), vol. 1, p. 339.

[62] *Commentariorum in Somnium Scipionis* 2.10.6, ed. J. Willis (Leipzig, 1963), 125.

[63] There are of course references to *rusticitas* in the Vulgate: Jerem 23:3 (*rus*); Eccli 7:16 (*rusticatio*); 1 Par 27:26 and Sap 17:16 (*rusticus*).

[64] Liddell and Scott, *Greek-English Lexicon*, s.v.

[65] *Thesaurus Linguae Latinae*, s.v.

[66] *De Architectura* 6.8.10; for this and other examples, see the *Thesaurus* 7.1, p. 221.

Latin authors, who frequently had in mind a Greek antecedent, it acquired the sense of one unskilled, poorly educated, or ignorant of religious teachings. It could also refer to a person recently converted but not yet fully acceptable to the community. In medieval Latin the sense was refined further. The primary meaning of *idiota* became an illiterate. The secondary range included various types of *conversi* (who were of course often unlettered).[67]

But *idiota* too was an ambivalent notion: it harboured within its range of meaning the idea of blessed simplicity which was clearly exposed in two biblical texts.[68] In the one, at Acts 4, Peter and John, who had just brought about the cure of a lame man, were arrested by the religious authorities while addressing a large crowd. After spending the night in jail, they were summoned before the elders and asked by what power and in whose name the miracle had been performed. Peter replied excitedly, and the interrogators realized that the pair were *sine literis et idiotae*.[69] They expressed admiration that such eloquence could come from the mouths of the uncultivated.

The other passage is found in Paul's well-known praise of charity in 1 Corinthians. Paul asked which was the better of two gifts, the ability to speak mysteriously or to make prophecies. The man who speaks in mysteries, he reasoned, talks to God, not to other men. But the prophet speaks to men in order "to build, to exhort and to console." By speaking mysteries a man may strengthen his own faith, but by prophesying he strengthens the entire church. Of course, he continued, it would be otherwise if mysteries could be translated into ordinary language; but they can no more be rendered into everyday speech than the notes of a flute or a harp. The message may be profound, but it will not find an audience. So the man who has such a gift should pray for the power to interpret it for others. And this prayer, he adds, should be with both mind and spirit. For "if you pray with the spirit, how can one who takes his place among the uninstructed (*locus idiotae*) say Amen. . . ."[70] Paul does not tell us precisely who the *idiotae* are. In all probability they are not yet full

[67] J. F. Niermeyer, *Mediae Latinitatis Lexicon Minus* (Leiden, 1976), s.v.

[68] For a full review, see C. Spicq, "La vertu de la simplicité dans l'Ancien et le Nouveau Testament," RSPT 22 (1933), 5-26. Peter Damian is particularly rich in examples of sacred simplicity; see *De Sancta Simplicitate* . . . , c. 3, PL 145.697B; c. 5, 699A-C, *et passim; De Vita Eremitica* . . . , c. 5, *ibid.*, 753D-54D; c. 7, 756D-57C; *De Vera Felicitate ac Sapientia*, c. 1, *ibid.*, 831B; *De Gallica Profectione, prol., ibid.*, 865A.

[69] Actus 4:13.

[70] 1 Cor 14:16. Cf. Jerome, *Comm. ad Gal.* 3.6.18; PL 26.468B.

Christians; that is, although they take part in the gatherings, they do not yet belong.[71] During the Middle Ages, the sense of *idiota* as someone partially excluded from participation in worship was extended to monastic lay brethren[72] and even occasionally to heretics.[73] Not only were the uninstructed given membership; apostolic poverty was extolled for its own sake. As late as 1440 Capgrave wrote in his *Life of St. Katherine*: "Ryght as be twelue ydiotes, sent Austyn seyth, hee meneth the apostelis, for thei not lerned were."[74]

From the basic problem of oral and written styles of communication, then, it is a short step to the wider issue of spoken and written language, not only to the separation of Latin and Romance but to the oral and written forms of the vernaculars themselves. In the end, the arbiter of a new system of values was not language but literacy, that is, the complex interplay of orality with textual models for understanding and transmitting the cultural heritage.

3. THE EMERGENCE OF WRITTEN CULTURE

In every revolution there are winners and losers. The emergence of written culture in the Middle Ages is no different. There is only one official version of the story and it is told by the written records themselves: the rest is very largely silence.

The bias of preserved records, to which we have previously alluded, has entailed two consequences. One is the overlooking of areas of human experience for which there is little or no "literature," such as the history of technology and the family. "Until recent centuries," Lynn White notes, "technology was chiefly the concern of groups which wrote little." As a result, "the role which technological devel-

---

[71] G. Kittel ed., *Theological Dictionary of the New Testament* (Grand Rapids, Mich., 1965), III, 217.

[72] E.g., Odo of Cluny, *Vita S. Odonis*, c. 20, PL 133.71D; Ulric of Cluny, *Consuetudines Cluniacensis* 2.10, PL 149.706C; Peter Damian, *Epistolae* 2.12, PL 144.281B.

[73] Grundmann, "Litteratus-illitteratus," 55-57. E.g., Gregory VII, *Reg.* 2, *Ep.* 76, PL 148.427B. For the use of the metaphor of *rusticitas* in a similar context, see Humbert of Silva Candida, *Adversus Simoniacos* 2.25, MGH Libelli de Lite I, p. 171, 6-7; c. 2.30, *ibid.*, 179, 1-2. Cf. Manegold of Lautenbach, *Ad Gebhardum liber, prol.*, MGH Libelli de Lite I, 310-13.

[74] 1.288; quoted in OED, s.v. Cf., in Old French, *Vie Edward Conf.*, 5716, quoted in Tobler-Lommatsch, *Altfranzösisches Wörterbuch* (Wiesbaden, 1960), 1275: "Si unt a lui mult encusé Saint Ulstan de simplicité, Qu'idiote esteit e sanz letrure E qu'en croce aveir n'out dreiture." On the religious preference for the spoken, cf. M. T. Clanchy, *op.cit.*, 208-14.

opment plays in human affairs has been neglected."[75] A similar statement can be made about the internal history of the family. The relationships between the members are subject to the dicta of kinship, which, as a rule, have no articulated history.[76]

But perhaps the most injurious consequence of medieval literacy was not the subjects it simply omitted. It was the notion that literacy is identical with rationality. By and large, literate culture in the Middle Ages assumed that it was the standard by which all cultural achievement should be measured, not only in literature itself, but also in law, philosophy, theology, and science. Of course, this theory was just a reworking of the idea of high culture which originated in the West with the Latin assimilation of the Greek heritage. But there was an important difference. In the ancient world the literary language suitable for superior discourse remained in touch with orality, even when it was written down. During the Middle Ages, when Latin was increasingly a foreign tongue employed by a minority of *clerici*, it became largely identified with written tradition. The criterion was not literacy but textuality.

The study of medieval culture has no wholly adequate model for interpreting these changes, either from within the continuity of written traditions and institutions alone or as an evolutionary transition from oral to written.

The best-known approach through written tradition is the renaissance theory, which connects the rise of "rational" attitudes to the revival of ancient forms of high culture. Culture is thereby assumed to have developed, if not progressed, in a linear fashion through periodic rejuvenations of the literate disciplines themselves.

The renaissance idea expresses a partial truth. After all, the medievals recorded only what they felt deserved to survive, and this inevitably included bits and pieces of the ancient heritage. Moreover, whenever they looked back on an earlier period, the degree to which they saw order and coherence involved reconstruction through textual precedents. And the more chaotic were the times, the more they tended to see reasonableness in the past. Modern interpreters, for their part, have perpetuated a different but equally damaging sort of bias. For better or worse, periodization did not come to medieval studies until the boundaries of classical antiquity and the Renaissance were laid down. The implicit equation of literacy, higher culture, and ration-

[75] *Medieval Technology and Social Change* (Oxford, 1962), vii.
[76] P. Laslett and R. Wall, *Household and Family in Past Time* (Cambridge, 1972), 1.

31

ality gave rise to the defensive posture which justified the study of the Middle Ages mainly as an incomplete revival of classical antiquity. The understanding of the later eleventh and twelfth centuries has both benefited and suffered from this type of analysis. As a result of roughly a century of research, few historians still look upon "the Middle Ages" and "the Renaissance" as radically opposed notions. The "twelfth-century renaissance" is an acknowledged category of discussion, whose usefulness is admitted even by the advocates of a decisive break between medieval and early modern culture.[77] Yet a price has been paid for the rehabilitation. In so eloquently defending the century as an earlier version of something else, medievalists have not adequately faced the responsibility of asking how the culture shaped itself.

As a response, the thesis of a simple transition from oral to written modes of communication is superficially attractive, especially if once again the reassuring example of antiquity is invoked. The growth of written culture and, as a result, of rational attitudes would seem to have repeated with minor variations a process that unfolded in the eastern Mediterranean centuries before. Marrou speaks of "the dark age" before Hesiod and of "the Homeric Middle Ages," in which the metaphor of darkness is largely justified by the lack of a written tradition.

Other parallels between the ancient world and the Middle Ages come to mind. Writing first developed in the Near East for the purpose of government; that is, it arose "not to fix theological or metaphysical dogma . . . but for the practical needs of accountancy and administration."[78] Similarly, the utilitarian functions of writing, which included preserving and transmitting the cultural heritage, preceded the rise of individual medieval disciplines. Again, in Homeric times, the use of the alphabet went hand in hand with a widespread technical and commercial revolution.[79] In the West, from the eleventh century, innovations in agriculture, warfare, and devices for the efficient use of water and air power helped to create the conditions of economic progress;[80] and the rebirth of medieval literacy coincided with the remonetization of markets and exchange. Comparisons can also be made in literature. In Homer, as in *Beowulf*, the *Chanson de Roland*, or the

[77] For a review of the older literature, see W. K. Ferguson, *The Renaissance in Historical Thought. Five Centuries of Interpretation* (Cambridge, Mass., 1948), chs. 10-11.

[78] *A History of Education in Antiquity*, xvi.

[79] G. Childe, *What Happened in History*, repr. (Harmondsworth, 1964), 31.

[80] See in general L. White Jr., *Medieval Technology and Social Change*, and, more briefly, B. Stock, "Science, Technology, and Economic Progress in the Early Middle Ages," in D. Lindberg, ed., *Science in the Middle Ages* (Chicago, 1978), 23-32.

Nibelungenlied, poetry is a major means of transmitting ideas, values, and information. "Metrical textbooks" are memorized and publicly recited in conjunction with other gestures, rituals, and symbolic statements. Finally, in both ancient and medieval accounts of creation, pure narratives yielded in comparable educational circumstances to stories containing analytical and even scientific elements.[81]

The idea of a linear transition from oral to written tradition contains a large degree of accuracy. Within the period under study, it is paralleled by such well-known developments as, in religion, the decline of liturgical worship and the rise of theological scholarship or, in politics, the shift from the priest-king, whose connections are with an oral, pictorial, gestural, and liturgical culture, to the desacralized law-king, whose links are with the literate, the administrative, the instrumentally rational, and the constitutional. But, beyond such broad comparisons, the problem of communications in medieval culture is more complex than either the renaissance or the evolutionary theory allows. On the one hand, the spokesmen on behalf of a progressive modernity within the Middle Ages are not entirely to be trusted. The medievals believed that they were the heirs to the Greeks, seeing farther, as Bernard of Chartres claimed, only because of the eminence to which earlier achievement had permitted them to rise.[82] His point of view, like that of fifteenth-century renaissance theorists, was weighted in favour of learned tradition and in favour of cultural diffusion, the latter being more helpful in accounting for the internal development of disciplines than why new attitudes or ways of thinking came into being. On the other hand, the thesis "from oral to written" merely puts into new terminology the older stage-theory of culture, in which complex communicative processes are inevitably reduced to adjuncts of material change. With respect to epic poetry, for instance, we may ask what evidence there is for a wholly "oral" state of mind. True, the *Iliad* and the *Odyssey*, like medieval epics, are in part repositories of morals, customs, and other legal-religious material lodged in the collective memory. But epic poetry, it has long been known, also contains conceptualized texts, which resemble written forms of record in the same way that the layouts of manuscript pages anticipated the first printed books. They do not recall a living "oral" society but rather the conventions through which its literary stylists sought to render it for posterity.

[81] On the Greeks, see J. P. Vernant, "Du mythe à la raison: la formation de la pensée positive dans la Grèce archaïque," *Annales, E.S.C.,* 12 (1957), 183-206; on selected twelfth-century thinkers, see B. Stock, *Myth and Science in the Twelfth Century* (Princeton, 1972).

[82] *Metalogicon* 3.4, ed. C.C.J. Webb (Oxford, 1929), 136; discussed below, Ch. 5, pp. 517ff.

A more sophisticated approach to the problem of communications and cultural transformations must begin with the recognition that, beyond the perspectives supplied by the period's witnesses, there are clearly both diachronic and synchronic relationships to be investigated. Moreover, there is not one but rather many models, all moving at different velocities and in different orbits. Above all, medieval uses of writing must not be conceived only as revivals of earlier educational and behavioural patterns. Of course, nowhere in the West was writing actually reinvented; and, even when absent, it was so to speak present in its absentness, since ancient models were often recalled by memory and imitated orally. Also, there can be no denying that later ancient education provided the overall cultural background. Yet, the differences between the two experiences are as notable as the similarities. In Greece, the link between literacy and rationality is chiefly associated with the teaching of Socrates and Plato. In the West, inquiries into the relations between factuality, textuality, and rationality were undertaken from about the year 1050, but there was no single figure who focused attention on key issues and who acted as a spokesman for cultural evolution as a whole. Instead, the change in mentality was diffused through a number of disciplines—law, philosophy, theology, historical writing, music, and science—which did not always communicate with each other. Like the ancient world, the Middle Ages had its *Geisteswissenschaften*, but, unlike it, no integrated theory of how they functioned with respect to each other, still less of their implications for social change.

In sum, the activities of medieval scribes gradually increased their range and influence partly because Europe recreated the conditions which made written culture relevant in the first place. Had that climate of opinion not existed, the legacy of Greek and Roman learning might have remained untouched for a much longer time. But, to tell the story of oral and written evolution, one cannot simply review the forces by which writing perpetuated itself and in which literate culture grew by a series of renewals. Nor is the development of orality within textual tradition a linear process. Once again we must speak of two perspectives, one from within written culture, the other from within oral culture. Let us look briefly at each.

The Perspective of Written Tradition

The clearest instances of literacy's continuous employment are furnished by the papal chancery, royal chanceries, and the lay notariate.

Long before the *Edict of Milan* guaranteed corporate freedom for the church, the popes had employed notaries of the city of Rome for collecting the acts of the martyrs, keeping the minutes of synods, and preparing transcripts of documents. From at least the time of Damasus I these records were kept in an archive over which presided the chief scribe (*primicerius notariorum*), who was an influential member of the papal court.[83] Successive pontiffs had to find the man with the right combination of "business training and experience"[84] to act at once as curator, administrator, and supervisor of the copying of letters. Until the pontificate of Innocent III (1198-1216), "there appears not to have been a consistent archival policy."[85] The lack of original registers makes the early history of the chancery difficult to reconstruct. Yet, a virtually unbroken series of scribes has been brought to light[86] and the practices of the various popes become clearer after papyrus was replaced by parchment under Benedict VIII around 1020.[87]

The eleventh century witnessed a great rise in the volume of transactions.[88] In an increasingly litigious age, Ullmann notes, "the unparalleled advantage which the papacy had over any other institution was its own storehouse of ideological memory, the papal archives."[89] Between Benedict VIII and Innocent III, four particularly important changes took place in the manner in which the chancery handled the written word. The form of papal bulls was clarified; the offices of writing and dating were combined; the curial script was abandoned and along with it reliance on the Roman *scriniarii*; and the rules for the *cursus* were standardized.

These changes did not take place at the same time but they all moved in the same direction. First, the style of the privilege was modified. Formerly a cumbersome document best suited to ceremonial occasions, it was put into a format closer to the ordinary papal letter and thus made more suitable for everyday business. The letter in turn

[83] H. Bresslau, *Handbuch der Urkundenlehre für Deutschland und Italien*, 2nd ed. (Leipzig, 1912), vol. 1, p. 152.

[84] R. L. Poole, *Lectures on the History of the Papal Chancery* (Cambridge, 1915), 15.

[85] L. E. Boyle, *A Survey of the Vatican Archives and its Medieval Holdings* (Toronto, 1972), 7.

[86] L. Santifaller, "Saggio di un elenco dei funzionari, impiegati e scrittori della Cancelleria Pontificia dall'inizio all'anno 1099," BIS 56, 1-2 (1940).

[87] *Idem*, "Beiträge zur Geschichte der Beschreibstoffe im Mittelalter . . . I," MIöG, XVI. Ergänzungsbd, Heft 1 (1953), 87-89.

[88] See P. Kehr, "Scrinium und Palatium. Zur Geschichte des päpstlichen Kanzleiwesens im XI. Jahrhundert," MIöG, VI. Ergänzungsbd (1901), 70-112.

[89] W. Ullmann, *The Growth of Papal Government in the Middle Ages* 2nd ed. (London, 1962), 262.

had its scope expanded so that it covered matters hitherto dealt with by privileges.[90] The second change, the uniting of the offices of *scriptum* and *data*, was completed by 1144. The third was the question of a standard hand. The battle between the Roman curial script and the Caroline minuscule was decided in favour of the latter during the eleventh century.[91] By the twelfth, the exemplar of all future papal correspondence had emerged. Finally, the *cursus* was standardized. The task was begun under Urban II and completed during the pontificate of Gelasius II (1118-19). This transition, although often overlooked by the modern reader, was particularly indicative of a new mentality. The system known as the *cursus curiae romanae* had long been in use as a set of rules governing the balance and cadence of epistolary periods. *Cursus* now became identified with one of three invariable styles of endings for such sentences, *planus*, *tardus*, and *velox*. The adoption of *cursus* by the papal chancery was symptomatic of the final metamorphosis of ancient oratory into medieval rhetoric. As it was employed from the twelfth century, the *cursus* was not made up of words but of syllables in words in an accentual pattern. Ancient metre was not misunderstood; it was deliberately abandoned.[92] What originated as an oral-aural phenomenon was eventually pressed into the service of writing.

The expansion of the chancery was of course inseparable from the rise of a reformist papacy in the later eleventh century, especially during the pontificates of Nicolas II, Alexander II, and Gregory VII.[93] Gregory's career spanned the major period of change. As Hildebrand he first came to Rome in 1049 with Bruno of Toul, later Leo IX, and by him was made deacon of St. Paul outside the Walls. His influence on the curia grew steadily over the years.[94] In 1054 he presided over the synod of Tours which considered the case of Berengar. He was instrumental in electing Nicolas II in 1058 and Alexander II in 1061. The latter's "reform group" of canonists and theologians remained active throughout his papacy from 1073 to 1085.[95] His program gave

[90] Poole, *Lectures*, 115.

[91] See P. Rabikauskas, *Die römische Kuriale in der päpstlichen Kanzlei* (Rome, 1958).

[92] See Poole, *Lectures*, 76-97; for a vernacular example, J. Benedicktsson, "Cursus in Old Norse Literature," *Medieval Scandinavia* 7 (1974), 15-21.

[93] For recent reviews of the period's issues and literature, see H. Hoffmann, "Von Cluny zum Investiturstreit," *Archiv für Kulturgeschichte* 45 (1963), 165-203 and H. Fuhrmann, "Das Reformpapsttum und die Rechtswissenschaft," in J. Fleckenstein, ed., *Investiturstreit und Reichsverfassung* (Sigmaringen, 1973), 185-91.

[94] See G. B. Borino, "L'arcidiaconato di Ildebrando," *Studi gregoriani* 3 (1948), 463-516.

[95] See T. Schmidt, *Alexander II (1061-1073) und die römische Reformgruppe seiner Zeit* (Stuttgart, 1977), 134-216.

birth to a set of letters and decrees which comprise the earliest surviving papal register that is complete in its original form.

Gregory saw reform in both moral and legal terms. He believed that written law should constitute the basis of ecclesiastical administration and, more particularly, of "the translation of abstract principles into concrete governmental actions."[96] Yet his achievement cannot be viewed in isolation from the work of other eleventh-century canonists, who edited compilations and penitentials, organized them under specific titles, applied tests of authenticity to earlier legislation, and established a common doctrine for the church's increasingly widespread activities.[97] Gregory, it turns out, was less influential himself on canon law than collections like the *Seventy-Four Titles* of 1076, which was utilized among others by Anselm of Lucca, Ivo of Chartres, and Gratian.[98] But Gregory remained the chief symbol of a *societas christiana* in which legal principles bound the spiritual to the temporal:[99] he insisted that law as opposed to custom was the equivalent of truth, the search for which would lead to the restoration or renewing of the authentic practices of the apostles and the primitive church.[100]

Royal chanceries were slower than the papacy in developing scribal techniques for administration. An office specifically reserved for drafting documents was not commonly called a *cancelleria* until well into the twelfth century.[101] But the function had existed earlier, underlining, Peter Classen notes, a clear line of continuity between later Roman and Germanic practices.[102] Rudimentary archives were con-

[96] Ullmann, *Growth of Papal Government*, 262. Cf. G. Ladner, *Theologie und Politik vor dem Investiturstreit* (Baden near Vienna, 1936), 45-51.

[97] See R. Knox, "Finding the Law. Developments in Canon Law during the Gregorian Reform," *Studi gregoriani* 9 (1972), 421-66.

[98] J. T. Gilchrist, *Diuersorum patrum sententie siue Collectio in LXXIV titulos digesta* (Vatican City, 1973), xvii. On Gregory's own role, see the same author's "Gregory VII and the Juristic Sources of his Ideology," *Studia Gratiana* 12 (1967), 1-38 and "The Reception of Pope Gregory VII into the Canon Law (1073-1141)," ZRG KA 59 (1973), 35-77 and tables.

[99] J. van Laarhoven, " 'Christianitas' et réforme grégorienne," *Studi gregoriani* 6 (1959-61), 11-12, 33-98, and, for a review of major lines of interpretation, O. Capitani, "Esiste un' 'età gregoriana'? Considerazioni sulle tendenze di una storiografia medievistica," *Rivista di storia e letteratura religiosa* 1 (1965), 454-81.

[100] G. Ladner, "Two Gregorian Letters on the Sources and Nature of Gregory VII's Reform Ideology," *Studi gregoriani* 5 (1956), 236-42. For other texts, see the summary of H.E.J. Cowdrey, *The Epistolae Vagantes of Pope Gregory VII* (Oxford, 1972), Appendix A, no. 67.

[101] H. W. Klewitz, "Cancellaria. Ein Beitrag zur Geschichte des geistlichen Hofdienstes," *Deutsches Archiv für Geschichte des Mittelalters* 1 (1937), 69-77.

[102] "Kaiserreskript und Königsurkunde. Diplomatische Studien zum römisch-germanischen Kontinuitätsproblem II," *Archiv für Diplomatik* 2 (1956), 52-57, 71-73.

structed by the Visigoths, by the Langobards, and, it is thought,[103] by the Anglo-Saxons. But the model later imitated developed out of the transition from the Merovingian to the Carolingian kings. Pippin, crowned at Soissons in 751, abandoned the chaotic record-keeping of Childeric III and adopted instead the somewhat more methodological system of the palace mayors.[104] The Carolingian chancery grew in size with successive emperors, only to become fragmented with different parts of the empire after 840.

In the late ninth and tenth centuries, the royal chanceries of Provence, Burgundy, and Italy utilized the Carolingian style of diploma. Similar traditions dominated the diplomatic services of the early Ottos. They even served as a point of departure for the modest writing service of Hugh Capet.[105] The chanceries of Hugh, Robert I, Henry I, and Philip I were no more extensive than was necessary for ruling a kingdom encompassing little more than the Ile-de-France. But, from the time of Robert the Pious, a process of simplification was discernible. The new charter was smaller in dimensions and lacked many of the traditional formulae. Eventually it was simply called *scriptum, pagina*, or *carta*,[106] indicating that the text rather than its symbolic trappings constituted the message. The position of the archchancellor correspondingly rose in prestige. A case in point was Etienne de Garlande. Archdeacon of Paris, he became chancellor under Philip I in 1105-1106. He kept his office under Louis VI, and, even after his dismissal in 1127, remained an influential seneschal.[107] But genuinely "administrative kingship" does not appear in Europe until the accession of Henry I onto the English throne in 1100. Henry centralized accounting and treasury procedures, improved the quality and quantity of records, and greatly increased the royal control of justice.[108] He created a *magister scriptorii* whose office carried on its activities whether the king was present or not.[109] In order to find such a radical reform of government in France one must look forward to the reign

---

[103] See M. T. Clanchy, *From Memory to Written Record*, 14-15.

[104] G. Tessier, *Diplomatique royale française* (Paris, 1962), 40.

[105] *Ibid.*, 129.

[106] A. Giry, *Manuel de diplomatique*, 2nd ed. (Paris, 1925), 732.

[107] Tessier, *Diplomatique royale française*, 133.

[108] C. W. Hollister and J. W. Baldwin, "The Rise of Administrative Kingship: Henry I and Philip Augustus," *American Historical Review* 83 (1978), 868. For the chronology of charter writing in England, see Clanchy, *From Memory to Written Record*, 36-59, and the useful comparative chart, p. 44.

[109] *Dialogus de Scaccario*, ed. C. Johnson (London, 1950), 129. On Henry's scribes, see T.A.M. Bishop, *Scriptores Regis* (Oxford, 1961), 4-15.

of Philip Augustus after 1179.[110] Throughout the twelfth century regional chanceries also sprang into existence in the north: in Flanders from 1136, Hainault from 1180, Namur from 1180-1190, and Brabant from 1199.[111] Episcopal registers became more abundant in the thirteenth.[112]

Between the later Roman empire and the eleventh century the continuity of administrative literacy was maintained by private and public scribes to whom nowadays we give the generic title of notaries. However, Roman *notarii*, either as *scriniarii* or *cancellarii*, were civil servants who did not normally draw up or authenticate private acts. This task was left to the *tabelliones*, simple secretaries who were organized as a guild. As they had no public capacity, they were compelled to deposit acts in an appropriate branch of the imperial bureaucracy, the census, the judiciary, the municipal magistracy, or the provincial prefecture. Justinian, who was emphatic on *insinuatio*, specifically excluded *tabelliones* from the *publica fides*. There were at least two reasons. The transfer of the empire's headquarters to the Greek-speaking world meant that legislation regarding private acts inevitably had to take account of bilingualism. Also, increasing numbers of litigants were illiterate.

The case which provided the instance for the legislation *De tabellionibus*[113] clearly indicates the manner in which later imperial scribes acted as intermediaries between oral and written culture. In 536 an illiterate woman (*persona mulieris . . . scribendi ignara*) had a document drawn up by a *tabellio*. Instead of witnessing it himself, he routinely assigned it to one of his assistants. The woman later claimed that the document did not state what she had said. As the *tabellio* was not the *scriptor documenti*, he could hardly attest its veracity. (For, in Roman law, unless there was a witness, a judge could not pronounce upon the case.) Justinian's legislation provided that henceforth a *tabellio* had to be present to witness a document, especially when those contracting an agreement were illiterate (*maxime quando litteras sunt ignorantes qui haec iniungunt . . .*).[114] The link between testimony and

[110] Hollister and Baldwin, *art.cit.*, 891-905.

[111] W. Prevenier, "La chancellerie des comtes de Flandre dans le cadre européen à la fin du XII siècle," *Bibliothèque de l'Ecole des Chartes* 125 (1967), 45-48.

[112] See in general C. R. Cheney, *English Bishops' Chanceries 1100-1250* (Manchester, 1950), 1-2n and chs. 2 and 4.

[113] *Novella* 41, *Corpus Iuris Civilis*, ed. R. Schoell and W. Kroll, 4th ed. (Berlin, 1912), vol. 3, pp. 273-77.

[114] *Novella* 44, pr. 1, pp. 273-74.

writing was reinforced in *Novella* 73, which dealt with the authentication of documents. Scribes, it read, were particularly important among those having no formal education. Witnesses acquainted with the parties were essential: some could write on behalf of those with little or no knowledge of letters, while others could attest to the veracity of the act.[115] After the installation of Langobard rule, guilds of professional scribes survived in regions under Roman law, although often in a degenerate form. Local traditions proliferated. In Ravenna, the noble *notarii* were set apart from the simple drafters of private instruments.[116] In Naples, where notarial traditions were strong, secular and ecclesiastical scribes formed a single body, the *curiales*, from the tenth century, and authenticated acts written by their apprentices, the *discipuli scriptores*.[117] Scribes were also active in Gaeta, Sorrento, Amalfi, and of course in Rome.

However, decisive changes were introduced into the notariate by the Langobards. Although their precise origin remains obscure,[118] Langobard *notarii* had by the end of the ninth century acquired varying degrees of the *publica fides*. They provided the essential link not only to Frankish notarial practices, but more importantly between the rudimentary private act of the early Middle Ages and the authenticated public document which appeared with increasing frequency in Italy from the eleventh century.[119] Early Langobard legislation did not speak of the *notarius* but simply of the *scriba*, the writer. A change of function can be discerned in the legislation of Liutprand, who demanded of all who wrote documents (*qui cartolas scribent*) that they be familiar with both Langobard and Roman law, i.e., both unwritten and written tradition.[120] Schiaparelli distinguished the *notarii regis*, who were chancery officials, from the *notarii civitatis* and *ecclesiarum*,

[115] C. 8, *ibid.*, 363-64. For a review of the Justinian legislation, see M. Amelotti and G. Costamagna, *Alle origini del notariato italiano* (Rome, 1975), 19-26, 33-36, 41-43. There were of course historical reasons for the shift towards written edicts; see in general, W. Kunkel, *An Introduction to Roman Legal and Constitutional History* (Oxford, 1966), 135-48.

[116] See M. W. Steinhoff, *Origins and Development of the Notariate at Ravenna (Sixth through Thirteenth Centuries)*, diss. (New York University, 1976), chs. 5-6.

[117] See L. Schiaparelli, "Note diplomatiche sulle Carte longobarde: 1. I notai nell'età longobarda," ASI, 7th series, 17 (1932), 32-33; A. Petrucci, *Notarii. Documenti per la storia del notariato italiano* (Milan, 1958), 17-18; and G. Cencetti, "Il notaio medievale italiano," *Atti della Società ligure di storia patria*, n.s. 4 (1964), vii-xxiii.

[118] For a discussion, see Petrucci, *Notarii*, 4-11.

[119] See in general H. Bresslau, *Handbuch*, I, 583-635 and A. de Boüard, *Manuel de diplomatique française et pontificale II: l'acte privé* (Paris, 1948), 153-220.

[120] *Liutprandi Leges* de anno XV, 91, VIII, MGH Leges 4, 144-45.

the latter of whom, Petrucci maintains, were instrumental in providing scribal services for the newly established landed aristocracy.[121] Charlemagne, far from innovating, attempted to generalize the system throughout the empire, demanding in a well-known edict that every bishop, abbot, and count retain a notary.[122] He forbad priests from drafting private acts and had a list of notaries compiled for the imperial period. When the empire fragmented, notaries, particularly in Italy, became more and more identified with higher lay culture, often holding up the prestige of written law over "feudal" incursions. In 881, the count of Asti, quoting a charter, declared that laws which were neither written down nor attested publicly by a notary were inadmissible as evidence.[123]

The lay notariate was reborn in Italy during the tenth and eleventh centuries. An unbroken tradition of grammatical training, a precocious commercial development, and an early revival of Roman law combined to insure Italian preeminence. A large role was also played by the Gregorian Reform, which reiterated the Carolingian injunction against priests transacting secular business. The transformation, Alain de Boüard noted, was both diplomatic and legal.[124] Above all, it required the progressive scribalization of hitherto oral judiciary procedures. In a word, the *notarius* became *iudex*: the *confessio in jure*, when authenticated by a notary public, took the form of an autonomous legal institution. All that was really necessary was the agreement of both parties in a single written transcription, which, if sworn before a notarial tribunal, became an *instrumentum publicum*. The notary's register, which simply recorded the various items of business which passed over his desk in no apparent order, acquired a value equal to the original documents and testimonies. In principle there were two registers, a summary of the *procès-verbal* and a more extensive official record. The earliest extant register is that of the Genoese notary Giovanni Scriba, whose *notularium* begins in 1154.[125] During the later twelfth and thirteenth centuries notarial cartularies became normal features of the administration of Italian and southern French towns.

[121] Petrucci, *op.cit.*, 5. The question is fully reviewed by Amelotti and Costamagna, *op.cit.*, 153-88. On the subjective quality of Langobard contracts, see F. Calasso, *La "convenientia." Contributo alla storia del contratto in Italia durante l'alto medioevo* (Bologna, 1932), 92.

[122] *Karoli Magni Capitularia*, Dec. 805, c. 4, MGH Leges 1, 131: "Ut unusquisque episcopus et abbas et singuli comites suum notarium habeant."

[123] Quoted by de Boüard, *Manuel*, 161n1.

[124] *Ibid.*, 163-64.

[125] H. Voltelini, "Die Imbreviatur des Johannes Scriba im Staatsarchiv zu Genua," MIöG 41 (1926), 71.

From about the middle of the thirteenth century notaries also began to appear in lands of customary law.[126]

Orality within Written Tradition

The history of the papacy, of chanceries, and of the notariate, together with the chief literary genre of institutional communication, the *epistula*,[127] tells the story of literacy's rebirth largely from the viewpoint of written tradition. But the typical medieval and early modern state of affairs, as noted, is for orality to retain its functions within a system of graphic representation for language, as for instance it does in the notarial tribunal, which, in superseding oral record, nonetheless demands personal attendance and verbal testimony. What distinguished medieval from ancient literacy, it is arguable, was not the presence of such roles, but their variety and abundance.

The most instructive examples are found in diplomatics, medieval law, and feudalism, to which we now turn. Since Brunner, it has been customary for historians to differentiate roughly between the "dispositive" and "evidential" functions of writing in later Roman and early medieval private law.[128] In Roman law the juridic act was separate from its proof. Throughout the republic no particular importance was attached to the written texts of private contracts. By Justinian's time, as the legislation *De tabellionibus* suggests, just the opposite was true: in general, the proof of a contractual agreement arose in large part from its authenticated transcript.[129] The emphasis on writ-

[126] For a bibliographical review, see A. Wolff, "Das öffentliche Notariat," in H. Coing, ed., *Handbuch der Quellen und Literatur der neueren europäischen Privatrechtsgeschichte*, vol. 1 (Munich, 1973), 510-14.

[127] For a full review, see G. Constable, *The Letters of Peter the Venerable*, vol. 2 (Cambridge, Mass., 1967), 1-44 (on orality, pp. 27-28), *idem, Letters and Letter-Collections* (Turnhout, 1976), and, on the distinction between oral and written forms, J. Leclercq, "Lettres de S. Bernard: histoire ou littérature," *Studi medievali* 3rd series, 12 (1971), 5-11 (antiquity) and 11-17 (Middle Ages).

[128] The older literature on the Brunner thesis is reviewed by Bresslau, *Handbuch*, II, 81n4. Recent surveys of the question include A. de Boüard, *Manuel*, II, 43-50; H. Steinacker, " 'Traditio cartae' und 'traditio per cartam,' ein Kontinuitätsproblem," *Archiv für Diplomatik* 5-6 (1959-60), 5-15, 46-64; and P. Classen, "Fortleben und Wandel spätrömischen Urkundenwesens im frühen Mittelalter," in P. Classen, ed., *Recht und Schrift im Mittelalter* (Sigmaringen, 1977), 36-41. Other contributions include H. Fichtenau, " 'Carta' et 'Notitia' en Bavière du VIIIe au Xe siècle," *Le Moyen Age* 69 (1963), 105-09; D. P. Blok, "Les formules de droit romain dans les actes privés du haut Moyen Age," *Miscellanea Mediaevalia . . . J. F. Niermeyer* (Groningen, 1967), 17-21; and P. Toubert, *Les structures du Latium médiéval* (Rome, 1973), I, 95-113.

[129] L. Stouff, "Etude sur la formation des contrats par l'écriture dans le droit des formules du Ve au XIIe siècle," NRHD 11 (1887), 249-68.

ten records was not of course the byproduct of more widespread education but of "legal illiteracy." Like language and culture, Roman legal traditions during the empire bifurcated into "popular" and "learned" components. Between the third and the sixth centuries there arose a large number of "vulgar" practices in private law which cannot be traced to enactments in the classical system.[130] The interpolations were publicly recognized from at least the time of Constantine, who, in reaction against them, insisted that acts be drawn up not *privatim* or *occulto* but "with the knowledge of others . . . and the witness of those nearby."[131] The unearthing of an indigenous if unofficial tradition of unwritten law has rendered inoperable the simplistic contrast between supposedly oral Germanic and written Roman codes. "This presentation," Ernst Levy concluded, "rests upon a fallacy. The law books of Justinian were not yet in existence when the earliest Germanic codes were framed."[132] It was not classical but vulgar Roman law which by and large the new kingdoms adapted to their own need: "Where Germanic ideas found entrance into these codifications, as they particularly did in the law of persons, domestic relations and succession, there was the deliberate creation of something new. . . ."[133]

The novelty of course need not be regarded negatively as "vulgarity": it was less a degenerate form of correct legal precepts than a facet of a more widespread oral tradition, which, uneclipsed by Hellenism and sophistic rhetoric, reappeared and was strengthened after the third century, when dormant impulses were stirred by the customs of peoples unfamiliar with writing.[134] What was implicitly challenged was the equation of official and written culture. In both Ravenna papyri and Langobard charters, for instance, *traditio cartae* is a symbolic act, religious in origin, sworn verbally on the Bible, and, unlike *traditio*

[130] *West Roman Vulgar Law. The Law of Property* (Philadelphia, 1951), p. 6. The following paragraphs draw extensively on this study. Cf. Levy, *Weströmisches Vulgarrecht: Das Obligationenrecht* (Weimar, 1956), 1-13; idem, *Gesammelte Schriften*, ed. W. Kunkel and M. Kaser (Cologne and Graz, 1963), 163-320.

[131] *Fragmenta Vaticana* 249, 4ff. and 35, 5f., *Fontes Iuris Romani anteiustiniani*, ed. S. Riccobono, et al. (1941-43), vol. 2, resp., 513ff., and 469ff.; quoted by Classen, "Fortleben und Wandel . . . ," 34.

[132] *West Roman Vulgar Law*, 15.

[133] *Loc.cit.*

[134] On "vulgarization," see, in addition to the cited works of E. Levy, F. Wieacker, *Vulgarismus und Klassicizmus* . . . ; idem, *Allgemeine Zustände und Rechtszustände gegen Ende des Weströmischen Reiches* (Ius Romanum Medii Aevi 1, 2a, Milan, 1963), 5-16, with earlier bibliography summarized on p.13n21; and M. Kaser, *Das römische Privatrecht, zweiter Abschnitt: Die nachklassischen Entwicklungen*, 2nd ed. (Munich, 1975), 5-8, 17-31.

per cartam, not necessarily legally binding.[135] One oral tradition appears to have melted into another. The Justinian compromise between the old and the new was an interim codification of accumulated verbal practices. Germanic jurists, imitating, although not always faithfully, their Roman predecessors, attempted to set down for posterity their own hitherto unwritten customs. The link was not only between peoples but between two forms of oral culture at different stages of textualization: the *Kontinuitätsproblem*, by implication, is also a problem of communication.[136]

The innovations affected the law of property in particular. By the fourth century the classical distinction between the right to control (*dominium, proprietas*) and the fact of controlling (*possessio, servitus, ususfructus*) had broken down. *Possessio* came to mean ownership; *dominium* and *proprietas* were reduced to mere possession. In some areas of family law, such as divorce and inheritance, *dominium* was further degraded to mere *ususfructus*. Form of ownership was bound to function: in the case of state-controlled trade guilds the public tax burden was transferred along with property rights. Types of property holding were confused. The difference between *emphyteusis* and *ius privatum* evaporated; anyone who controlled land was able to keep it and to dispose of it at will, provided that he satisfied the demands of the fisc. The acts of obligation and disposal coalesced: "as the distance shrank between ownership and possession . . . , so the transfer of ownership was no longer accurately kept apart from the causal transaction aimed at it."[137] Sale became merely an exchange of goods for money, the equivalent, Isidore pointed out, of trade or barter (*commutatio rerum*).[138]

The decline of such juridic niceties placed new burdens on documentation. For, where the law was no longer understood, it had to be spelled out, illustrated, and explained. The fourth and fifth centuries saw the rise of legal instruments which classical law had con-

[135] See H. Steinacker, *Die antiken Grundlagen der frühmittelalterlichen Privaturkunde* (Leipzig and Berlin, 1927), 92-101; L. Wenger, *Die Quellen des römischen Rechts* (Vienna, 1953), 747-48; and J.-O. Tjäder, *Die nichtliterarischen lateinischen Papyri Italiens aus der Zeit 445-700: I. Papyri 1-28* (Lund, 1955), 274-75.

[136] Cf. H. Mitteis, *Die Rechtsgeschichte und das Problem der historischen Kontinuität* (Abhandlungen der Deutschen Akademie der Wissenschaften zu Berlin, Jahrgang 1947, phil.-hist. Kl., Berlin, 1947), 20. On the educational aspects of the question, see the interesting study of D. Illmer, *Formen der Erziehung und Wissensvermittlung im frühen Mittelalter* (Munich, 1971), and, on the broader changes in the schools, P. Riché, *Education and Culture in the Barbarian West*, trans. J. J. Contreni (Columbia, S.C., 1976).

[137] Levy, *West Roman Vulgar Law*, 127.

[138] *Etymologiae* 5.24.23.

sidered at best superfluous. These practices were taken over by Germanic codifiers, who freely adapted them to their own needs.

The new buyer, for instance, was not content with an informal promise to deliver goods. He insisted on physical transfer, accompanied by witnesses and a written contract. The general tendency was "to obviate the shortcomings through the use of documents."[139] It was supported by the inadequate legal education of the new citizens as well as the eastern habit of reducing legal transactions to writing. The trend became so popular that after Constantine jurists took pains to point out that *traditio* did not require the drawing up of an instrument. The transfer of the burden of taxation also increased documentation: "there can be no doubt . . . that as in the East so in the West all major sales, not only of land but also of *coloni*, slaves, and other valuable objects were usually put into writing."[140] As a consequence, only exceptionally did *traditio* alone remain a basic element in the transfer of title. By the fifth century sale normally included a public performance of the act, either before witnesses or through registration, after which the proceedings were set down in writing. Similarly, Constantine insisted that all gifts not among members of a family be recorded and the property formally handed over. As in the case of sale, it was performance, not promise or intention, that created the legal act. In other words, in all types of property transfer, more and more stress was laid on factual or physical *traditio* and attestation *per legitimas scripturas*. There was no *traditio per cartam* alone: the delivery of the *scriptura* did not take the place of the thing being transferred (*traditio rei*). In most instances the document merely served as a transcript.

Oral tradition, as a consequence, played a dual role, equally evident in the new functions for texts and in the growing emphasis on performed transfer. Justinian's compromise was that contracts could exist *sive in scriptis sive sine scriptis*:[141] but this was a halfway-house between classical practice, which was already in decline, and medieval usage, which existed in substance if not in legal form.

In contrast to Justinian's "renaissance," the Germanic codes did not attempt to restore classical norms in private law.[142] Oral tradition was rather more sure of itself, even when it was transmitted in written

[139] Levy, 128.
[140] *Ibid.*, 131.
[141] *Ibid.*, 150n159. Cf. P. Classen, "Fortleben und Wandel . . . ," 13-14.
[142] Levy, 156.

form. *Traditio per cartam* appeared only in the seventh century.[143] During the following four hundred years oral practices dominated private law in regions of Europe influenced by Germanic institutions. The *carta* was primarily a symbol of physical *traditio*, the *notitia*, as a Langobard charter put it, a text "to be retained by memory for future times."[144] From about 1050 abstract juridic principles began slowly to reappear. But the "accidental" rediscovery of the *Digest* around 1070 was both a source and a symptom of a more general reawakening of interest in the written word. Moreover, it is arguable that, throughout the period of customary law, the operative distinction was not between types of legal instrument and their supposed Roman or Germanic origins, an issue that has much preoccupied legal history: it was simply whether the written text was acknowledged to be an objective criterion in contractual agreements.

The Germanic codes presented no uniform view of writing's uses.[145] The Alamans showed an interest in dating.[146] The *Lex Ribuaria* noted the value of *scripturarum series* in such areas as dowries, freeing slaves and inheritance.[147] In Bavarian law the buying or selling of a man could be proved either through witnesses or *per cartam*.[148] Similar provisions were made by the Goths and the Burgundians. The clearest influence of Rome appeared in Visigothic law, in which provision was made for verifying subscriptions by a comparison of hands.[149] Even such reminiscences of Roman law were often "vulgar" in origin. The fifth-century *Codex Euricianus* was a case in point. It asserted that *venditio* or *emptio* (meaning either sale or barter) could be completed

---

[143] *Ibid.*, 165-66; on the reception, see the same author's essays in his *Gesammelte Schriften*, I, 201-63, and, for a thorough review of the connection between orality and proof in Frankish culture, see F. L. Ganshof, "La preuve dans le droit franc," *La preuve, deuxième partie: Moyen âge et temps modernes* (Brussels, 1965), 71-98. On the attitude toward the "good old law" up to about 800, see R. Sprandel, "Über das Problem neuen Rechts im früheren Mittelalter," ZRG KA 48 (1962), 117-37.

[144] anno 847, quoted by Stouff, "Etude," 275n1.

[145] For a recent review, see P. Classen, "Fortleben und Wandel . . . ," 20-36.

[146] *Lex Alamannorum* 42.2, MGH Leges Nat. Germ. 5.1, p. 103: "Scriptura non valet, nisi in quam annis et dies evidenter ostenditur."

[147] *Lex Ribuaria* 27, 50, 58, MGH Leges 5, 232, 240, 242.

[148] *Lex Baiuwarorum* 16, 15, MGH Leges Nat. Germ. 1.5.2, p. 441.

[149] *Lex Visigothorum* 1.5.15, MGH Leges Nat. Germ. 1.1, pp. 116-17. On the basic contrasts between Visigothic and Roman law, see E. Levy, "Reflections on the first 'Reception' of Roman Law in the Germanic States," *Gesammelte Schriften* I, 201-09. For a review of the varieties of uses for subscription, see K. Zeumer, "Zum westgothischen Urkundenwesen, 1. Subscriptio und Signum," *Neues Archiv* 24 (1899), 15-29.

per scripturam, or, "if a text were unavailable, ratified by witnesses."[150] The text "was merely a matter of evidence and not relevant for the validity of the sale,"[151] which was legalized by payment. A similar approach was taken in the Burgundian and Bavarian laws, and in the sixth-century *Formulae Marculfi*.[152] Such clear intrusions by orality rendered unworkable the normal terms of reference for contract law. In the *Codex Euricianus*, for example, "considering that there might be no *scriptura*, a *traditio cartae* or *per cartam* was out of the question."[153] In many cases, such as *hereditas* and *possessio*,[154] there was no precise vernacular equivalent for Roman legal vocabulary.

From "vulgarity," therefore, as a debased image of literate law, it is a short step to oral law, which, although assimilating writing, has not as yet been changed by it. In Salic law the land to be sold was frequently represented by a physical object, a rod or piece of sod, which, when ritually exchanged, legitimized the transfer.[155] This law was not "irrational"; its principles of operation were merely different from written law.[156]

Scribal practices almost invariably entered oral legal systems by imitating already functioning verbal institutions. Of course, neither Roman nor Germanic law admitted obligations *solo consensu*. But, whereas classical law recognized only real contracts, Germanic codes emphasized formalism. In oral law, the equivalent of the Roman contract was "only the image of the transaction for cash, an imitation of exchange."[157] Such unwritten law was made up of words, rituals, and symbols. In place of the author's signature one had a sign, a cross, or simply *manumissio*, the ceremonial placing of hands on the parchment. Witnesses did not "record" an act: on the contrary, "Germanic custom demanded that transactions be not only capable of being heard and seen, but that they be actually heard and seen."[158] Oral practices were

---

[150] c. 286, ed. K. Zeumer, MGH Leges Nat. Germ. 1.1, p. 11.

[151] *Ibid.*, 159.

[152] *Ibid.*, 158-59, 161-62.

[153] *Ibid.*, 161.

[154] A. Gurevič, "Représentations et attitudes à l'égard de la propriété pendant le haut moyen âge," *Annales, E.S.C.*, 27 (1972), 525-28.

[155] P. Ourliac and J. de Malafosse, *Histoire du droit privé 1: Les Obligations* (Paris, 1957), 64.

[156] Cf. R. V. Colman, "Reason and Unreason in Early Medieval Law," *Journal of Interdisciplinary History* 4 (1974), 571-91.

[157] J. Brissaud, *A History of French Private Law*, trans. R. Howell (Boston, 1912), 472.

[158] H. D. Hazeltine, "Comments on the Writings Known as Anglo-Saxon Wills," in D. Whitelock, ed., *Anglo-Saxon Wills* (Cambridge, 1930), ix. Cf. J. Brissaud, *French Private Law*, 486; A. Heusler, *Institutionen des Deutschen Privatrechts* (Leipzig, 1885), I, 65-75.

not limited to the north; they spread southwards into romanized Burgundy and the Midi, producing, for instance, the odd hybrid of a "dispositive" twig sown to a "probative" text.[159] The persistence of oral tradition is nowhere better illustrated than in the ceremony of *levatio cartae*. Before the charter was written, the parchment, pen, and ink were placed on the land to be sold. In the participants' minds the instruments thereby became impregnated with earthly forces. When the act was "signed," it was turned into a symbolic replica of the ritual by which the exchange was solemnized. It was both a legal record and a quasi-magical object.[160] Even a *carta sine litteris* carried weight.[161]

Anglo-Saxon uses of writing offer a number of parallels. The earliest English charters date from the seventh century; their form and style betray the attempts of clerics to impress a few Roman legal ideas onto a society hitherto ignorant of them.[162] As in Merovingian Gaul, the charters had no authenticity; the witnesses, instead of signing, were represented by a scribe who normally made a mark or cross. The text was not without value. It demonstrated the "need to communicate in writing . . . or to preserve in writing the memory of a transaction or an event, formally or informally," as a donation of Offa put it in 785, "on account of the uncertain passage of future time, since, out of ignorance or even deceit, it often happens that a denial of what truly took place arises."[163] The acculturation of writing within oral tradition is well recapitulated *in nuce* in the history of the Anglo-Saxon will, of which some fifty originals survive. In Hazeltine's view, "the dispositive act of giving *mortis causa* is an oral and formal act." When completed before witnesses, it "needs no documentation to make it valid and binding in the law." In other words, "the juristic act is complete without the writing."[164] Although the Anglo-Saxons used writing for other purposes, the recording of wills was chiefly the result of canonical influences.[165] Even after writing was introduced, the dis-

---

[159] A. de Boüard, *Manuel*, II, 104-06, gives examples.

[160] See E. Goldmann, "Cartam levare," MIöG 35 (1914), 1-59, and briefly Gurevič, "Représentations," 532-33. Two types were known at St. Gall; K. Zeumer, " 'Cartam levare' in Sanct Galler Urkunden," ZKG GA 4 (1883), 117.

[161] See M. Kos, "Carta sine litteris," MIöG 62 (1954), 97-100.

[162] Galbraith, "The Literacy of the Medieval English Kings," 217.

[163] Quoted in L. E. Boyle, "Diplomatics," in J. M. Powell, ed., *Medieval Studies. An Introduction* (Syracuse, 1976), 76; for the original, see *Chartae Latinae Antiquiores*, pt. 3, ed. A. Bruckner and R. Marichal (Olten and Lausanne, 1963), no. 222, pp. 136-37.

[164] "Comments . . . ," in D. Whitelock, ed., *Anglo-Saxon Wills*, viii.

[165] M. M. Sheehan, *The Will in Medieval England* ... (Toronto, 1963), 54-59.

positive act remained an essentially oral contract. It was merely underpinned by a written transcript. "To the proof of oral acts furnished by transaction-witnesses, . . . there was now added the evidence of writings."[166] *Cwide* did not originally mean *gewrit* but "simply speech, discourse, *dictum*."[167] The *chirographa* or copies "were not dispositive *cartae*, but merely memoranda, documents *memoriae causa, notitiae*."[168]

These functions for texts within oral culture became an intimate part of "feudalism." The notion of feudalism, both as a stage of history and as a state of mind, is lacking in precision,[169] but its relationship to the oral and written aspects of cultural development is reasonably straightforward. The feudal bond originated as a spoken contractual arrangement between two individuals, most frequently a lord and a vassal, to which certain property rights were appended. This state of affairs persisted throughout the early Middle Ages; between the eleventh and the thirteenth centuries, a somewhat different "feudal system" came into being. The personal dependencies and military obligations were retained. But, what had arisen in principle as a bond between men slowly but surely became enmeshed in the economic structures of a competitive agrarian society. Property relations became more important, especially at the local level. The oral features were either translated into written terms—*festucare*, for instance, which earlier denoted symbolic *traditio*, coming to mean "to ratify"[170]—or, like ceremonies of investiture, were framed as verbal ritual within an ever-widening network of written law. Thus, a complex set of human relations was eventually reduced to a body of normative legislation: feudalism, in Ganshof's phrase, was "realized."[171] By 1100 the conceptual framework was in place; by 1300 customaries for both secular and ecclesiastical estates were being systematized and written down.

[166] Hazeltine, "Comments," xii.

[167] *Ibid.*, xiii; and in greater detail, Sheehan, *The Will*, 39-47, 54-55.

[168] Hazeltine, "Comments," xxiv, echoing H. Brunner, *Zur Rechtsgeschichte der römischen und germanischen Urkunde* (Berlin, 1880), 44-47, and H. Bresslau, *Handbuch . . .* , I, 502-11.

[169] See in general Bloch, *Feudal Society*, trans. L. A. Manyon (London, 1961), I, xvii-xxi; G. Duby, "La féodalité? Une mentalité médiévale," *Annales, E.S.C.* 13 (1958), 765-71; E.E.R. Brown, "The Tyranny of a Concept: Feudalism and Historians of Medieval Europe," *American Historical Review* 79 (1974), 1063-88; W. Ebel, "Über den Leihegedanken in der deutschen Rechtsgeschichte," *Studien zum mittelalterlichen Lehenswesen*, ed. T. Mayer (Constance, 1960), 11-36; and, on the relationship of concepts to reality, R. Brenner, "Agrarian Class Structure and Economic Development in Pre-Industrial Europe," *Past and Present* 70 (1976), 30-75, with the various replies, *ibid.*, 78 (1978), 24-55.

[170] R. E. Latham, *Revised Medieval Latin Word-List*, s.v.

[171] *Feudalism*, trans. P. Grierson (London, 1952), 139.

The metamorphosis was so complete that the feudist lawyers of the seventeenth century had no trouble in reconstructing the entire organism from its surviving legal remains.

Feudal rites were united by a number of common features: respect for the individual and his word, the belief in the concrete over the abstract, the formalization of obligations through ritual and, just beneath the surface of many ceremonies, a somewhat nostalgic resort to the gestures of tribal warfare.[172]

The whole operated as a symbolic system, whose efficacy, Jacques Le Goff observes, was seriously impaired if any single element was omitted.[173] Like all oral ceremonial, feudal ritual was conservative. There is little difference between the rite of commendation in the Merovingian formularies and the investitures recorded by Galbert of Bruges before William, the new count of Flanders, in 1127.[174] The texts almost invariably lack contemporary glosses or commentaries, an indication that the ritual itself rather than an interpretation based upon it comprised the contractual bond. Once enacted, the relationship was in principle lifelong, in contrast to other agrarian contracts, which were in theory at least renewable. Ratification sometimes took place by an exchange of letters, but such simple forms of registration were merely accessories after the fact.[175]

The ritual was the bond. Each of the central ceremonies blended the spoken, the symbolic, and the performance of rites. In homage, for instance, the lord and the vassal stood facing each other. The vassal repeated a number of set phrases in response to statements by the lord. He then joined his hands and placed them in the lord's. The lord closed his own hands over those of the vassal. The physical gestures, which were sometimes concluded with a kiss on the mouth,

[172] On symbolism and oral culture in Germanic law, see in particular A. Heusler *Institutionen, loc.cit.* Earlier legal literature is summarized by R. Heubner, *A History of Germanic Private Law,* trans. F. S. Philbrick (Boston, 1918), 5-16. (Omitted is the important collection of M. Thévenin, *Textes relatifs aux institutions privées et publiques aux époques mérovingiennes et carolingiennes* [Paris, 1887].) A lucid English summary of the main principles is H. D. Hazeitine, "Comments . . . ," vii-xl; a useful collection of texts in translation, R. Boutruche, *Seigneurie et féodalité,* vol. I (Paris, 1968), 331-72; a recent review of anthropological perspectives, J. Le Goff, "Le rituel symbolique de la vassalité," *Pour un autre Moyen Age,* 348-420.
[173] Le Goff, "Le rituel symbolique," 365.
[174] For the Merovingian text, see Ganshof, *Feudalism,* 6-7; for Galbert, H. Pirenne, ed., *Histoire du meurtre de Charles le Bon, comte du Bruges* (Paris, 1891), 89. For a lengthier discussion of the latter, see F. L. Ganshof, "Les relations féodo-vassaliques aux temps post-Carolingiens," *I problemi comuni dell'Europa post-carolingia* (Spoleto, 1955), 69-77.
[175] Ganshof, *Feudalism,* 7.

served as a symbolic statement of the relation.[176] Homage was usually followed by the quasi-religious ceremony of fealty, in which the vassal, placing his hands over the Bible or some relics, pledged (or repledged) his allegiance. The same union of the oral and the concrete occurred in other important rites, such as marriage, which in Germanic custom consisted of *desponsatio, dotatio*, and *traditio puellae*.[177] A good example is furnished by the ceremonies surrounding the *festuca*, which was both a physical object, a rod, a wand, or, later, merely a bit of thatch, and, as subsequent lexicographers summed it up, a *signum et symbolum traditionis*.[178] In Salic law the *festuca* was either ceremonially taken up or thrown down on the ground as bonds were reaffirmed or broken. A vassal appearing before his count's tribunal might hold the staff in his left hand while he held out his right to swear an oath. He thereby symbolically re-expressed both his devotion and freedom since, in Germanic society, juridic liberty was inseparable from the right to take up arms, which seizing the *festuca* recalled. Alternately, the *festuca* was thrown down when legal conditions were not fulfilled, as for instance when, following a homicide, an appropriate *wergeld* was withheld.[179] Eventually the term *exfestucare* came to mean rupturing the bond of homage.[180] All such rituals had a common base, the early medieval belief that exchange should take place orally, between men face to face and within the framework of the gift.[181]

The decline of symbolic rites is one side of feudalism's later evolution. The other is the transformation of personal into territorial law, which subsequently developed written forms.[182]

Under the Carolingians private law had an ambivalent status. In

---

[176] See Le Goff, "Le rituel symbolique," 356-59.

[177] E. Chénon, "Recherches historiques sur quelques rites nuptiaux," NRHD 36 (1912), 624.

[178] Du Cange, *Glossarium Manuale* . . . (Halae, 1774), s.v.

[179] M. Thévenin, "Contributions à l'histoire du droit germanique," NRHD 4 (1880), 74-89.

[180] M. Bloch, "Les formes de la rupture de l'hommage dans l'ancien droit féodal," in *Mélanges historiques*, vol. 1 (Paris, 1963), 189-206. Earlier literature is reviewed on p. 190n2, including the important study of K. von Amira, *Der Stab in der germanischen Rechtssymbolik* (Abhandlungen der Kg. Bayerischen Akademie der Wissenschaften, philos., philolog., u. hist. Kl., 35, Abh. 1, Munich, 1911), pp. 1-180; on Bloch's own views, see Le Goff, "Le rituel symbolique," 378-80.

[181] On the last, see M. Mauss, "Essai sur le don. Forme et raison de l'échange dans les sociétés archaïques," in *Sociologie et anthropologie*, 4th ed. (Paris, 1968), 145-171 (originally published 1923-24), and the important revisions of M. Sahlins, "The Spirit of the Gift," in *Stone Age Economics* (Chicago, 1972), 149-83. For a recent review of the early medieval evidence, see G. Duby, *Guerriers et paysans VII-XIIe siècle* (Paris, 1973), 60-69.

[182] Following A. Esmein, *Cours élémentaire du droit français*, 13th ed. (Paris, 1920), 779-871.

general it was personal and varied with the racial origin of the subject. Yet, in principle at least, it fell within the domain of written law. Whether the laws originally descended from oral or written tradition, the judge, in rendering a verdict, was obliged to make reference to an official or authorized text.[183] Custom had no official status; a point of law could be derived only from a written precedent.

With the decline of the Frankish monarchy, this situation greatly changed. The personal laws and capitularies were used less and less; in their place arose a large number of territorial customs. Many forces were at work: economic, social, and political. Frankish personal law implied two prior conditions. The race of the defendant had to be known and the judge had to understand the law. With the intermingling of peoples, strict racial boundaries evaporated; and, as Latin literacy declined, so did the capacity to interpret the *leges*.[184] As a consequence, the use of legal texts and with it the law of personality gradually fell into neglect. In every region of the empire possessing geographical boundaries and a local character there arose a set of customs that governed everyone lay and religious within its borders without distinction of race.[185] Naturally, the inherited *leges* of the dominant group in each region furnished the model. But the codes themselves were consulted less and less. And, as personal ceded to territorial law, the oral in general replaced the written. The last vestiges of the Carolingian censuses disappeared in the eleventh century.[186] But, long before, lay and ecclesiastical *consuetudines* had sprung into being. While retaining traces of the Justinian and Theodosian codes, they represented a new legal form. The capitularies, which were also based on the law of persons, suffered a similar fate. Unlike the *leges* of each national group, they had from the outset been marred by obscurity, incompleteness, and lack of contact with popular mores.[187] Outside the church they became largely obsolete during the tenth and eleventh centuries. The disappearance of these two forms of written law meant that, for a relatively brief period, custom reigned supreme in northwestern Europe, extending its jurisdiction equally into lands of Germanic and Roman legal traditions.

Although practices varied from place to place, the custumals were

[183] *Ibid.*, 779.
[184] *Ibid.*, 782-83.
[185] R. Boutruche, *Seigneurie et féodalité*, vol. 2 (Paris, 1970), 127.
[186] Esmein, *op.cit.*, 783.
[187] *Ibid.*, 784.

united by three general principles.[188] They were local in jurisdiction. They were predominantly oral in form and function. And they were both "old and young." According to Ulpian, custom was "the silent consensus of the people, rooted in long habit."[189] Writing centuries later, Beaumanoir was in essential agreement.[190] But what constituted long habit? On occasion customs were truly immemorial. But, as they affected local property relations, often they were no older than a generation or two.[191] What gave them their timeless character was the verbal milieu in which they operated.

One branch of written law actually broadened its range during the customary period: canon law. The Carolingian *pagus* yielded to the jurisdiction not only of the manorial estate but also of the bishopric. As centralized administration weakened, the gap was filled both by local feudal and ecclesiastical courts. This was a reversal of earlier trends. In the later Roman empire, wherever civil law remained in force, the church limited itself to internal juridic questions.[192] The Carolingians marked the turning point. From Pippin's reign every attempt was made to bring church and state closer together.[193] Charlemagne, as noted, employed Latin culture as a common denominator among his various dominions.[194] The church gradually acquired a wide legal role, dealing with both civil and criminal cases affecting laymen, the clergy, or both.[195] Canon law was ideally suited to the task. It was made up of unusual elements: quotations from the Bible and the fathers, decrees of synods and councils, papal letters and decretals, borrowings from indigenous traditions, and generalizations based on the developing institutions of the church itself. Roman law was the cement binding together the parts. When Roman civil procedures all but disappeared from the ordinary law of northern Europe in the tenth

[188] Cf. E. Chénon, *Histoire générale du droit français public et privé des origines à 1815*, vol. 1 (Paris, 1926), 489-92.

[189] *Regulae* 1.4; cf. Justinian, *Inst.* 1.2.9; Gratian, *Decretum* D.12, c.6.

[190] Philippe de Beaumanoir, *Coutumes de Beauvaisis*, no. 683, ed. Am. Salmon (Paris, 1899), vol. 1, p. 346.

[191] Chénon, *Histoire*, vol. 1, 490-91. For other legal and anthropological parallels, see M. T. Clanchy, "Remembering the Past . . . ," 172.

[192] Esmein, *Cours*, 168-69.

[193] P. Fournier and G. Le Bras, *Histoire des collections canoniques en Occident depuis les fausses décrétales jusqu'au Décret de Gratien*, vol. 1 (Paris, 1931), 7-8, 78-107.

[194] M.L.W. Laistner, *Thought and Letters in Western Europe A.D. 500 to 900* (London, 1957), 189-206; C. Vogel, "La réforme culturelle sous Pépin le Bref et sous Charlemagne," in E. Patzelt, ed., *Die karolingische Renaissance*, vol. 2 (Graz, 1965), 171-242.

[195] Esmein, *Cours*, 181-86.

and eleventh centuries,[196] canon law emerged not only as the standard-bearer of the law of persons but of written legal traditions in general.[197]

From the tenth century its increased use at the local level may be attributed in large part to the weakness of seigneurial justice. The feudal magnates never really replaced the administrative authority of the central government. There was little commitment to universal jurisprudence.[198] Often, only a rough-and-ready system was maintained to keep order and to derive profits from fines and confiscations. The tone of the courts was caught by Bernard of Angers, who, speaking of a plea in 1007, remarked that "each person argues his own case, resulting in a confused outcry of intermingled voices in which it is difficult to judge the true from the false."[199] Ecclesiastical courts, whether they utilized collections of canons, or, as was often the case, less formalized directives, invariably followed procedures that were more erudite, reasonable, and objective. Germanic modes of proof of course found their way into the corpus.[200] But, from the Carolingian period, the duel was forbidden, and other *judicia Dei* were condemned progressively at the synods of Seligenstadt (1022), Geisleben (1028), Burgos (1077), and Toledo (1091).[201] And their influence was slight

[196] On this complex subject see M. Conrat, *Geschichte der Quellen und Literatur des römischen Rechts in früheren Mittelalter* (Leipzig, 1891); H. Kantorowicz, *Studies in the Glossators of the Roman Law*, ed. P. Weimar (Aalen, 1969); P. Weimar, "Die legistische Literatur der Glossatorenzeit," in Coing, *Handbuch*, 129-260; and, in detail, the various volumes of *Ius Romanum Medii Aevi*.

[197] Briefly reviewed by K. Nörr, "Die kanonistische Literatur," in Coing, *Handbuch*, 370-78, and S. Kuttner, "The Revival of Jurisprudence," in R. L. Benson and G. Constable, eds., *Renaissance and Renewal in the Twelfth Century* (Cambridge, Mass., 1982), 299-323. For a remarkable study of the medieval tradition of an influential collection, see H. Mordek, *Kirchenrecht und Reform im Frankenreich. Die Collectio Vetus Gallica, die älteste systematische Kanonessammlung des fränkischen Gallien* (Berlin and New York, 1975), 97-207. A witness to early eleventh-century attitudes is Abbo of Fleury, *Collectio Canonum*, c. 9, PL 139.482B-C, who derives *lex* from "reading" and equates legal and written tradition: "Sicut rex a regendo dicitur, ita et lex a legendo. . . . Jura vero legitima ex legibus cognosci oportebit, et a vulgari intelligentia remotiora sunt. . . . Nam lex et principium constitutio scripta; mos vero consuetudo vetustate probata, nec tamen scripta." Cf. *Ep.* 10, *ibid.*, 433A-38B.

[198] On the use of the written in decision-making, see the admittedly later evidence of Y. Bongert, *Recherches sur les cours laïques du Xe au XIIIe siècle* (Paris, 1949), 277-89.

[199] *Liber Miraculorum S. Fidis* 1.12, ed. A. Bouillet (Paris, 1897), 43.

[200] For a brief review, see F. L. Ganshof, *Frankish Institutions under Charlemagne*, trans. B. and M. Lyon (New York, 1970), 87-97.

[201] Cf. E. Vacandard, "L'Eglise et les ordalies," *Etudes de critique et d'histoire religieuse*, 2nd ed. (Paris, 1906), 197, Esmein, *Cours*, 321, and for a thorough recent review, see J. Gaudemet, "Les ordalies au moyen âge: doctrine, législation et pratiques canoniques," *La preuve, deuxième partie*, 99-135.

compared to canon law's benefits. Emanating from a single body of doctrine, canon law offered an alternative to the often overlapping jurisdictions of customs.[202] It also provided a stepping-stone to higher justice. From the local bishop a claimant could appeal to the archbishop, the metropolitan, or even the pope. Claims could be lodged directly with the papacy, a privilege whose abuse by the mid-twelfth century incurred the wrath of St. Bernard.[203] But above all canon law was attractive because it was literate. The canons were a set of organized texts, a model of early scholastic rigour later imitated in philosophy and theology; the bishop or his *officialis*[204] normally acted as judge; and canonists culminating in Gratian insisted on the importance of written evidence.[205] If there was any flaw in the system, it was its overextension into secular affairs. Despite Gregorian legislation to the contrary, ecclesiastical courts after 1100 were asked to pass judgment on an ever-increasing number of matters in private law. The court's competence came to depend less on the status of the defendants than on the *ratio materiae*.[206] In other areas, canon law effectively led the way to lay participation in justice. A good example is the *pax* or *treuga Dei*.[207] At first the peace of God attempted to limit feuding and warfare only to those entitled to bear arms, protecting as it were those who "laboured or prayed."[208] But, by 1041, the council of Narbonne spoke of the *praeceptum Dei* and the *institutiones nostrae, quae . . . scribenda sunt*,[209] that is, the texts to be recorded. Lay contact was also brought about by the episcopal investigation of heresy, the forerunner of the Inquisition.[210]

The legal renaissance undertaken from the later eleventh century eventually left continental Europe with three fields of literate juris-

[202] On the "Rechtskreise," see R. Heubner, *History of Germanic Private Law*, 3-4.

[203] *De Consideratione* 3.2.10-12, ed. J. Leclercq and H. M. Rochais, *S. Bernardi Opera*, vol. 3 (Rome, 1963), 437-39.

[204] P. Fournier, *Les officialités au moyen âge* (Paris, 1880), 2.

[205] See E. Jacobi, "Der Prozess im Decretum Gratiani und bei den ältesten Dekretisten," ZRG KA 3 (1913), 266-70.

[206] Esmein, *Cours*, 325.

[207] On early eleventh-century attempts, see H. Hoffmann, *Gottesfriede und Treuga Dei* (Stuttgart, 1964), 18-23. On the relation between Henry III's peace movement and the legal legitimacy of the empire, see G. Ladner, *Theologie und Politik vor dem Investiturstreit*, 75. On English analogies in the council of London of 1142, see F. M. Powicke, *The Loss of Normandy (1189-1204)* (Manchester, 1913), 94-95.

[208] G. Duby, "Les laïcs et la paix de Dieu," *Hommes et structures du moyen âge* (Paris and The Hague, 1973), 232-34.

[209] *Concilium Narbonense*, c. 1; Mansi 19, 827D.

[210] C. Douais, *L'inquisition. Ses origines, sa procédure* (Paris, 1906), 4-14.

prudence, Roman law, canon law, and the statutes of feudal law, which were codified from the twelfth century. Traces of Roman law had never disappeared from agrarian contracts[211] and from the time of Irnerius it increasingly permeated the customaries, just as, at the other end of the social scale, it affected Salian and Staufer conceptions of sovereignty.[212] The codification of feudal law is perhaps less a direct consequence of Roman influences than an aspect of the more wide-spread transition to literate legal institutions.[213] (Later, general principles also emerged from collections of sentences from arrests and judgments, as well as from popular collections of juridic maxims and proverbs.) For, in the *pays de coutume*, common law was custom. Municipal statutes apart, written tradition was resisted. Instead, the jurisdiction of customaries was expanded under the aegis of tribunals of appeal until they embraced large regions. Local variations, originally the backbone of the system, were eventually reduced to insignificance. The *Coutumiers* or *Livres de pratique* all embodied the same principles.[214] First, the custom became immobilized in the text; once written down, it could be modified only by a new redaction. Secondly, the custom, if recorded, was assumed to have existed in that form for all time; the natural evolution of customary law was thereby arrested. Thirdly, the influence of Roman law was curbed; once a custom entered a code, it could be influenced only by interpretation.

A still more significant mutation lay in the ensuing philosophy of law itself. Editing customs effectively made them into written laws which from that point did not derive their authority from popular consent but from the power to decree. Again, the influence of Roman traditions was ambivalent. Esmein notes: "Roman law often appeared

[211] On this much debated question, see P. Grossi, "Problematica strutturale dei contratti agrari nella esperienza giuridica dell'alto medioevo italiano," *Agricoltura e mondo rurale in occidente nell'alto medioevo* (Spoleto, 1966), 487-529.

[212] W. Ullmann, "Von Canossa nach Pavia. Zum Strukturwandel der Herrschaftsgrundlagen im salischen und staufischen Zeitalter," *Historisches Jahrbuch* 93 (1973), 265-300.

[213] An assertion which, in view of the scarcity of the evidence, must be made with caution for Normandy before the accession of William in 1035; see J. Yver, "Les premières institutions du duché de Normandie," *I Normanni e la loro espansione in Europa nell'alto medioevo* (Spoleto, 1969), 299-366; and, for the Scandinavian sources, G. Hafström, "Die politischen Institutionen des skandinavischen Wikinger und deren Probleme," *ibid.*, 57-69. On the association of Roman law with written tradition, see J. Flach, "Le droit romain dans les chartes du IXe au XIe siècle," *Mélanges Fitting* (Montpellier, 1907), vol. 1, 406-12; and, on resistance to the intrusion of Roman law, see E. Meynial, "Remarques sur la réaction populaire contre l'invasion du droit romain en France aux XIIe et XIIIe siècles," *Mélanges Chabaneau* (Erlangen, 1907), 557-84.

[214] Esmein, *Cours*, 824-25.

as *ratio scripta* but not always as *jus scriptum*."[215] On the one hand, Roman instruments for contractual obligations were almost universally adopted by the fourteenth century. Yet, in many customaries, elements of oral law were retained. A good example is provided by the regional legislation of Normandy. The Latin version of the *Très Ancien Coutumier*, the earliest compilation to have survived, is datable between 1199 and 1204 for its first part and between 1218 and 1223 for its second.[216] Yet, even at such late dates, it bears witness less to a positive reinstatement of written law than to the written record necessitated by the setting up of the Norman state.[217] In the later thirteenth-century *Grand Coutumier*, which successive generations of historians have praised for its precise jurisprudence,[218] the idea of proof nonetheless involves both *vadiatio legis* and *lex*: it moves from a solemn, ritual engagement, utilizing physical symbols, to the administration of "the institutes or laws through which disputes are terminated," in which, Besnier observes, one finds not an opposition between customary and written law but rather throughout "a formalism dominated by a principle which makes the rights of the parties dependent on the performance of external actions in which the judge does not take part."[219]

In England, by comparison, oral and written elements combined in law in a different way.[220] On the one hand, the development of the sealed writ, and, more importantly, of the royal courts, from which sprang other deputations such as the exchequer, the bench of common pleas, and the itinerant justices, offered a precocious example of literate law for which before the thirteenth century there was little

[215] *Ibid.*, 792.

[216] R. Besnier, *La coutume de Normandie* (Paris, 1935), 53.

[217] M. de Bouard, "Le duché de Normandie," in F. Lot and R. Fawtier, eds., *Histoire des Institutions françaises au moyen âge*, (Paris, 1957), I, 11-14.

[218] Esmein, *Cours*, 802; C. H. Haskins, *Norman Institutions* (Cambridge, Mass., 1925), 38; 182-89.

[219] R. Besnier, " 'Vadiatio legis et leges.' Les preuves de droit commun à l'époque des coutumiers normands," NRHD, 4th Series 19-20 (1940-1941), 93.

[220] On the matter of the following paragraphs, see in general the still useful surveys of Sir Frederick Pollock and F. W. Maitland, *The History of English Law before the Time of Edward I*, 2nd ed. intro. S.F.C. Milsom (Cambridge, 1968), chs. 2, 3 and 4 and W. S. Holdsworth, *A History of English Law*, 7th ed., ed. A. L. Goodhart and H. G. Hanbury, vol. 2, book 2, chs. 1-2; and, more briefly, R. C. van Caenegem, *The Birth of the English Common Law* (Cambridge, 1973). On the techniques of scribal culture in the same period, see the fine survey of M. T. Clanchy, *From Memory to Written Record*, pt. I: "The Making of Records," pp. 11-147.

equivalent on the Continent outside Italy.[221] A more instructive basis
for comparison arises from the methods of pleading.[222] Up to the mid-
twelfth century complaints were delivered orally. They were not dif-
ferentiated by the nature of the claim; all consisted of the same narrative
formula, which recited the breach of law and demanded compensa-
tion. The defendant replied, after which the local doomsman indicated the appropriate type of validation. Hence, as in other feudal
courts, there was, as van Caenegem notes, "no intrinsic link between
the nature of the plaint and the method of proof."[223] Judges did not
evaluate evidence; documents were introduced only to corroborate verbal statements. The Roman style of proof through witnesses, which
was reintroduced by canonists, was largely unknown. The trial consisted of oral pleading, the reading aloud of written evidence, and the
selection of an arbitrary means of determining innocence or guilt. The
latter was based on the analogy between formal and material truth;
that is, a physical sign on the defendant's part was interpreted as an
indication of inner guilt or of innocence. Truth was not abstract but
concrete; in justice, as in everyday life, it consisted of appropriate
conduct—gestures, daily rituals, speech habits, and behavioural reactions. The verdict was less an indication of who was right and wrong
than a compromise between plaintiff and defendant. The real function
of the court, the jurors, and the public was mediation.[224]

During the twelfth century, written documents replaced oral testimony and an objective method of evaluating evidence challenged
formal procedures such as duels, ordeals, and compurgations. The
innovations consisted mainly of taking evidence from witnesses, ana-
lyzing the various factors in a case, and carefully scrutinizing written
documents and records; methods, in fact, in which there were clear
parallels between Roman and common law despite the different origins
of the two systems.[225] In England, the chief vehicle for establishing
impartiality was the jury, which depended for its judgment on rec-

[221] R. C. van Caenegem, *Royal Writs in England from the Conquest to Glanvill* (London, 1959),
18.

[222] *Ibid.*, 35-37, on which this paragraph is based. On the persistence of spoken legal traditions, see M. T. Clanchy, *From Memory to Written Record*, 22-26.

[223] van Caenegem, 36.

[224] Cf. R. V. Colman, "Reason and Unreason in Early Medieval Law," 574-81.

[225] R. C. van Caenegem, "The Law of Evidence in the Twelfth Century: European Perspectives and Intellectual Background," *Proceedings of the Second International Congress of Medieval Canon
Law* (Vatican City, 1965), 298-99. For a broad review of European developments, see J.-P.
Lévy, "L'évolution de la preuve des origines à nos jours," *La preuve, deuxième partie*, esp. pp. 14-
26 and 37-54.

ognitions, that is, on formal replies to factual inquiries[226] which could simply supply the court with information, or, as was more often the case, act both as a "mode of proof in litigation" and "an adjudication as well as a verdict,"[227] the latter incorporating the court's decision. As a subspecies of the *inquisitio*, the *recognitio* was a privilege of Frankish justice. Imported to England after the Conquest, it may have amalgamated with Old English recognitions, which were a legacy of Scandinavian law.[228] The critical period of change was the reign of Henry II from 1154 to 1189, during which the widespread use of the jury system resulted in "a rationalization and laicization of the judicial process"[229] as part of the growth of the royal courts and the use of the sealed writ. *Inquisitiones* and *recognitiones* once again combined the oral and the written. Early English recognitions were wholly oral. After the Conquest, *inquisitiones* began to appear more and more frequently in writing, the most famous example being the *Domesday Book*, which is designated a *descriptio*,[230] that is, the "transcript of an official verbal investigation" concerning land holding. Other such requests for information occurred during the twelfth century, helping to establish objective methods of collecting and evaluating evidence. They paralleled the Roman and canonical practice of having evidence weighed by a legally competent judge, who also pronounced on the guilt or innocence of the accused.

Cultural Implications

Just as in law and diplomatics, the cultural implications of literacy may be viewed from two vantage points. From the one, writing represents literacy; oral transactions in themselves have no legitimate status. From the other, writing is used chiefly to record; it is ancillary to a reality conceived in physical, personal, and verbal terms.

The clearest consequence of the rebirth of literacy itself was the

[226] On their prehistory, see R. Besnier, " 'Inquisitiones' et 'Recognitiones.' Le nouveau système des preuves à l'époque des Coutumiers normands," NRHD 4th series 28 (1950), 183-212.

[227] van Caenegem, *Royal Writs*, 51.

[228] On this question, see H. Brunner, *Die Entstehung der Schwurgerichte* (Berlin, 1872), 293-308, the criticisms of C. H. Haskins, *Norman Institutions*, ch. 6, pp. 196-238, and the more recent survey of van Caenegem, *Royal Writs*, ch. 4, pp. 51-103.

[229] van Caenegem, 53.

[230] V. H. Galbraith, *The Making of Domesday Book* (Oxford, 1961), 183-84.

reawakening of a wide range of critical methods for utilizing texts as evidence.[231]

Among the various *discrimina veri ac falsi*, diplomatic examination gradually became more frequent. The earliest example dates from 1074, when a group of experts assembled at Liège to give an opinion on the authenticity of a papal privilege placing the abbey of St. Hubert under the control of the Holy See. On confirmation, the document was retranscribed "in everyday hand" for the benefit of the chief litigant, the archdeacon Boso, who claimed he could not decipher the cursive of the Roman scribes.[232]

The problem was not only legibility. By this date forgery had been raised to the level of a high art.[233] In oral culture a forger was not a person who altered legal texts; he was a traitor. He betrayed the relationship not between words and things but between men.

Only through the wedding of property claims to a written record of title did the opposite point of view come to prevail. In fact, the rise of forgery rather than its detection is about as good a witness as we have to the growth of general legal expertise. The two most famous cases were the *Donation of Constantine* of the 750s and the *False Decretals* of pseudo-Isidore, written, it is thought, in the diocese of Le Mans between 845 and 847. Both were based on genuine originals. The *Donation* utilized the *Legenda sancti Silvestri*, a fanciful account of Constantine's conversion in which the emperor allegedly "conferred a privilege" of jurisdiction over all Roman priests to the pope, and, just eight days after becoming a Christian, prostrated himself tearfully before the pontiff with crown and imperial mantle in hand.[234] The *False Decretals* were put together in a more complex manner. Isidore did not invent papal documents on his own. Mostly he supplied let-

[231] For a review, see K. Schreiner, " 'Discrimen veri ac falsi.' Ansätze und Formen der Kritik in der Heiligen- und Reliquien-verehrung des Mittelalters," *Archiv für Kulturgeschichte* 48 (1966), 1-33.

[232] *Cantatorium S. Huberti*, c. 26, ed. K. Hanquet (Brussels, 1906), 76-83, discussed by J. Stiennon, *Paléographie du Moyen Age* (Paris, 1973), 24.

[233] See H. Fuhrmann, "Die Fälschungen im Mittelalter," *Historische Zeitschrift* 197 (1963), 529-54 and his *Einfluss und Verbreitung der pseudoisidorischen Fälschungen*, vol. 1 (Stuttgart, 1972), 76-80.

[234] *Legenda, prol.*, ed. B. Mombritius, *Sanctuarium seu Vitae Sanctorum*, vol. 2 (Paris, 1910), 513, 17-19 and 25-28. On the textual transmission, see S. Williams, "The Oldest Text of the 'Constitutum Constantini,' " *Traditio* 20 (1964), 448-61; on contemporary relations with the papacy, H. Fuhrmann, "Das frühmittelalterliche Papsttum und die konstantinische Schenkung . . . ," *I problemi dell'occidente nel secolo VIII*, 257-92, with a full bibliography; and, on more general background and interpretation, see W. Ullmann, *The Growth of Papal Government*, 74-86.

ters or decrees which the sixth-century *Liber Pontificalis* stated were mislaid or lost. His major sources were the Bible, Roman law, recorded custom, capitularies, penitentials, *regulae*, patristic writings, and earlier canonical collections like the spurious *Hispana Gallica Augustodunensis*.[235] Plagiarizing hundreds of authentic documents, he constructed a virtually new legal tissue. The chief political aim of the *Decretals* was "to protect the suffragan bishops from the clutches of the metropolitans, provincial synods and the secular power"[236] in the wake of setbacks to reform after the reign of Louis the Pious and the definitive breakup of the empire in 843. They entered canon law via the *Collectio Anselmo dedicata* of the late ninth century, whence they influenced Burchard of Worms, Ivo of Chartres, and Gratian.

Although critically questioned by modern scholarship, major forgeries like the *Decretals*, the *Capitula Angilramni*, and the *capitula* of Benedict the Levite may also be viewed positively in a medieval context as assertions of written over customary law.[237] A good example on a smaller scale of how they worked is provided by a set of falsifications over property rights in the diocese of Le Mans between 832 and 837.[238] Like many Carolingian bishoprics, Le Mans lost most of its estates in the eighth century. Nor was there any surviving written evidence to document the claims. In response to the predicament, a local monk invented precedents to title for the original lands and many others besides, not only altering donation charters but reworking the oral history of the see and the lives of local saints,[239] as,

---

[235] H. Fuhrmann reviews the sources briefly in "False Decretals," *New Catholic Encyclopedia*, vol. 5, 820-24, with a concise bibliography, 823-24. Pseudo-Isidore, it is worth noting, forbad ordination to those who were *inscii litterarum*, an injunction reiterated in the influential *Seventy-Four Titles*; for Isidore, see PL 130.923C; for the later collection, the edition of J. Gilchrist, tit. 16, c. 153, p. 100.

[236] Fuhrmann, "False Decretals," 821.

[237] For a concise review, see P. Fournier, "Etude sur les fausses décrétales," RHE 7 (1906), 33-51 or L. Saltet, "False Decretals," *The Catholic Encyclopedia*, vol. 5, 773-80; in greater detail, Fuhrmann, *Einfluss und Verbreitung*, vols. 2-3 (Stuttgart, 1973, 1974). On the mentality of the medieval forger see T. F. Tout, "Mediaeval Forgers and Forgeries," *Bulletin of the John Rylands Library* 5 (1918-20), 214-15; H. Silvestre, "Le problème des faux au Moyen Age," *Le Moyen Age* 66 (1960), 351-70; and the various papers reunited in "Die Fälschungen im Mittelalter: Überlegungen zum mittelalterlichen Wahrheitsbegriff," *Historische Zeitschrift* 197 (1963), 529-601. The field is briefly reviewed by B. de Gaiffier, "Mentalité de l'hagiographe médiéval d'après quelques travaux récents," *Analecta Bollandiana* 86 (1968), 392-96, and C. Brühl, "Der ehrbare Fälscher. Zu den Fälschungen des Klosters S. Pietro in Ciel d'Oro zu Pavia," *Deutsches Archiv für Erforschung des Mittelalters* 35 (1979), 209-13.

[238] W. Goffart, *The Le Mans Forgeries* (Cambridge, Mass., 1966), 23.

[239] *Ibid.*, 29-58.

sometime later, did Eadmer in defending Canterbury's claims over York.[240] The resulting forgery displayed considerable ingenuity, maintaining, Walter Goffart notes, that "a possessory right established by originality or antiquity of title was distinct from, and prevailed over, the mere possession of land."[241] The attempt failed, but debates over *jus* and *possessio* became more frequent from the eleventh century. The whole matter entered a new phase with the rise of official chanceries and sealed charters. In developing methods for detecting diplomatic fraud the papacy took the lead. At first formularies were employed in an effort to insure correctness of style, for, as Mabillon later observed, "diplomatic has its own mode of expression, which depends less on grammatical rules than on usage."[242] But formularies only served as guides for the offenders. A more successful attempt was made in Innocent III's well-known decretal on the verification of bulls, which called for, among other things, prevention of theft, inspection of seals, and strict control of authentication.[243]

The growth of expertise in diplomatics went hand in hand with other critical instincts. Men began to think of facts not as recorded by texts but as embodied in texts, a transition of major importance in the rise of systems of information retrieval and classification. As fact and text moved closer together, "searchability" shifted "from memory to page layout."[244] The earliest alphabetically arranged reference work was the *Elementarium Doctrinae Erudimentum* of Papias, which was completed by 1053.[245] Between 1083 and 1087 Deusdedit compiled a topical subject-index to his collection of eleven hundred seventy-three canons. Around the middle of the twelfth century Gilbert of Poitiers improved upon Cassiodorus's thematic classification of

[240] See R. W. Southern, "The Canterbury Forgeries," *English Historical Review* 73 (1958), 193-226; M. Gibson, *Lanfranc of Bec* (Oxford, 1978), Appendix C.

[241] Goffart, 24.

[242] *De Re Diplomatica* 2.1.

[243] *Regesta* 1, 349 (4 Sept. 1198), ed. O. Hageneder and A. Haidacher, *Die Register Innocenz'III. 1. Pontificatsjahr 1198/99, Texte* (Graz and Cologne, 1964), 520-22, discussed by Poole, *Lectures on the History of the Papal Chancery*, 153-60.

[244] R. and M. Rouse, "*Statim invenire*: Schools, Preachers, and New Attitudes to the Page," in R. L. Benson and G. Constable, eds., *Renaissance and Renewal in the Twelfth Century*, pp. 201-25. On the thirteenth-century development of such alphabetically arranged tools for locating biblical and patristic quotations for sermons, see the same authors' "Biblical *Distinctiones* in the Thirteenth Century," AHDLMA 41 (1974), 27-37 and *Preachers, Florilegia and Sermons: Studies in the "Manipulus florum" of Thomas of Ireland* (Toronto, 1979), 3-42.

[245] On the dating, see G. Goetz, *Corpus Glossarium Latinorum*, vol. 1 (Leipzig, 1923), 175; on the lexicography, L. W. and B. A. Daly, "Some Techniques in Mediaeval Latin Lexicography," *Speculum* 39 (1964), 231-33.

the psalms by means of written symbols.[246] Also, Gilbert and Stephen of Langton both critically examined the *textus receptus* of Paul's epistles.[247] The great codifications of the period—Peter Lombard's *Sentences*, Abelard's *Sic et Non*, Gratian's *Decretum*, and, towards the century's end, Huguccio's *Magnae Derivationes*—went hand in hand with new methods for organizing knowledge. And these were reflected in codices, not only in clarity of form, expression, and genre, as well as the separation of text and commentary, but also in the design and functionality of manuscripts themselves.[248] Richard and Mary Rouse note: "Innovations in layout of the manuscript page are surely the most highly visible of all the twelfth-century aids to study—such techniques as running headlines, chapter titles in red, alternating red and blue initials and the gradation in size of initials, cross-references, and citation of authors quoted."[249] To these one may add the beginnings of alphabetized indexing.[250] Such aids moreover were not limited to law, philosophy, and theology. They also affected practical areas such as the liturgy, where efforts at standardization from the later eleventh century brought about clearer texts in the twelfth. In his *Libellus de Correctione*, for instance, Hervé de Bourgdieu proved that certain texts in the lectionary were interpolations, and sought to establish a method for separating *antiqua veritas* and *nova falsitas* in the Christian rite. His approach consisted like that of the diplomatists of finding an earlier "evangelical" or "synodal" authority for the texts.[251] Passages for which no previous documentation could be found were classified as "vulgar" custom (*usus uulgate consuetudinis, uulgi consuetudo*),[252] which, he observed, "*veritas* and *ratio* inevitably reject."[253]

If by contrast we turn from this critical renaissance to areas of

[246] Rouse and Rouse, "*Statim invenire*," 204-05.

[247] A. Landgraf, "Zur Methode der biblischen Textkritik im 12. Jahrhundert," *Biblica* 10 (1929), 456-74.

[248] Cf. M. Parkes, "The Influence of Concepts of *Ordinatio* and *Compilatio* on the Development of the Book," in J.J.G. Alexander and M. T. Gibson, eds., *Medieval Learning and Literature. Essays presented to R. W. Hunt* (Oxford, 1976), 116-19.

[249] Rouse and Rouse, "*Statim invenire*," 207.

[250] L. W. Daly, *Contributions to a History of Alphabetization in Antiquity and the Middle Ages* (Brussels, 1967), 69-84.

[251] G. Morin, "Un critique en liturgie au XII siècle. Le traité inédit d'Hervé de Bourgdieu *De correctione quarundam lectionum*," Rben 24 (1907), 37. On his antecedents, see the manuscript sources reviewed by R. E. Reynolds, "Liturgical Scholarship at the Time of the Investiture Controversy: Past Research and Future Opportunities," *Harvard Theological Review* 71 (1978), 112-18.

[252] Morin, "Un critique . . . ," 39, 40, 41.

[253] *Ibid.*, 43: ". . . quia consuetudinem racio et ueritas semper excludit."

culture more directly supported by the spoken, the symbolic and by ritual, the picture changes. Good examples are provided by relics, miracles, and the cult of local saints.[254] Rodulf Glaber drew the attention of his generation to the plethora of holy objects found throughout Europe on the eve of the millennium.[255] But the saints' pledges (*sanctorum pignora*), in his view, had to be underpinned by written proofs (*diversorum argumentorum indicia*). As in formalist *traditio*, the physical itself was not questioned; documentary support was merely subjoined. The status of the written word was largely evidential.

As it turns out, a study in depth of these issues was made just after the turn of the century in a collection of the miracles of St. Foy, who was martyred at age twelve in 303 and whose remains, taken to Agen by St. Dulcidius early in the fifth century, were seized by the monks of Conques and forcibly translated sometime before 883.[256] Books one and two of the *Miracula* were written by Bernard of Angers,[257] a sometime student at Chartres,[258] who came to Conques after 1010 to bear witness himself to the prodigies of the child saint, of whom Fulbert had given so eloquent an account.[259] On his first of three visits Bernard remained only twenty-five days,[260] sufficient time, however, to collect the most notable stories, which he later sifted, redrafted, and dedicated to his former master. Bernard's insights were unusual for his time and deserve more than a brief summary.

The *Miracula* were an immediate and lasting success.[261] Where they differ from other eleventh-century collections, like the Fleury continuation of the *Miracula Sancti Benedicti*, is not in content, which records the usual intercessions, but in the point of view of the narrator, who, as both faithful Christian and *scolasticus*, felt obliged to accept the marvels at their face value and, at the same time, to authenticate them

[254] On the belief in relics, see the thoughtful remarks of H. Fichtenau, "Zum Reliquienwesen im früheren Mittelalter," MIöG 60 (1952), 60-89. The use of miracle collections as historical evidence is discussed by R. C. Finucane, "The Use and Abuse of Medieval Miracles," *History* 60 (1975), 1-10. Cf. *idem, Miracles and Pilgrims* (London, 1977).

[255] *Historiae* 3.6.19, ed. M. Prou (Paris, 1886), 68.

[256] For the secondary literature, see P. Geary, *Furta Sacra* (Princeton, 1978), 169-74.

[257] A. Bouillet, *Liber Miraculorum Sancte Fidis* (Paris, 1897), xiii.

[258] Cf. A. Clerval, *Les écoles de Chartres au moyen âge, du Ve au XVIe siècle* (Chartres, 1895), 62.

[259] *Epistola ad domnum Fulbertum, Liber Miraculorum*, 1-2.

[260] *Liber* 1.7, p. 30.

[261] Bouillet, *Liber*, preface, xiv; on the cult, see A. Bouillet and L. Servières, *Sainte Foy, vièrge et martyr* (Rodez, 1900), 245-387.

through the examination of witnesses, the comparison of accounts, and the organization of a coherent narrative.

In his dedicatory letter to Fulbert,[262] Bernard tells us how he came to collect and to write down the *Miracula*. While a student at the cathedral school in Chartres, he was in the habit of visiting the church of St. Foy located just outside the town walls, "either for praying or for writing." The miraculous stories often came to mind, as they had been a frequent topic of conversation between Fulbert and himself. But, he adds, since the events were highly unusual (*inaudita*) and diffused popularly (*vulgarium fama*), they had at that point to be treated largely as fictional inventions (*inanis fabule commenta*). Bernard was determined to visit the place of their origin. He noted the intention *in manuali codicello*, a detail which reveals that his literary habits preceded his interest in the saint. But only three years later, after a stint of teaching grammar in Angers, was he able to journey to Conques. At first he was overwhelmed by the bulk of the material and the diversity of the accounts (*tanta a diversis relatoribus*). So he concentrated on the "redaction" of a single miracle, the story of Guibert, a priest whose eyes were unjustly torn out by his master and restored by St. Foy. On the marvel's veracity all witnesses were agreed. Guibert himself appeared, recounted the details, and displayed his scars.

Bernard related the first miracle as fully as possible, as he put it, *non solum sensum e sensu, sed etiam verbum e verbo* (not only the meaning from the sense but even word for word). The others were based on notes which he took down hastily and revised after reflection. Throughout, he focused on events from his own generation, which, he felt, were easiest to verify. In most cases there were two texts, as called for by canonical procedure, the verbal transcript of the actual testimonies and a later version (*lectio*), which he composed at leisure in Angers. He thought of himself as a recorder, not an embellisher, of events, admonishing Fulbert on receiving his collection to emend perhaps the manner of presentation but not the facts presented. For, although he was himself, or so he claimed, unskilled in rhetoric, he did not believe everything he heard or for that matter find many things related easy to believe. It was preferable, he argued, for the miracles to be published while his memory was fresh (*nunc dum sunt nova et indubia . . . tradi litteris*) rather than to wait indefinitely for the right spokesman. To facilitate matters, he organized the material not chronologically but by the nature of the miracle (*miraculorum . . .*

---

[262] *Epistola*, pp. 1-4.

similitudo). If the incredulous did not believe him, they were invited to come to Conques and to make their own inquiries.

Bernard can be described as a systematic hagiographer and an anthropological fieldworker[263] at once. An early critic of oral history, he investigated popular belief not to discredit it through a foreign rationality, although skepticism surfaces from time to time, but to verify it, utilizing the most convincing modes of proof at his disposal. From time to time he also made revealing comments about his own frame of mind. The ancients, he noted in miracle one,[264] were his predecessors. But he did not on that account underrate his own achievement. Earlier authors told of marvels through a single witness who was not always present at the event. What harm then could there be if a "modern" of admittedly lesser talent merely preserved for his own record what he saw taking place in the Auvergne, the Rouergue, or the Toulousain? Moreover, the essential issue as he saw it was not the old versus the new but simply the absence of literacy: what was lacking was not recordable activities but authors willing to put them in writing, to inscribe them, as he elsewhere put it, on the tablets of their hearts.[265] If there was a *grammaticus* in the region, he speculated, he undoubtedly felt that the mysteries of St. Foy were beyond his powers of expression or simply unworthy of notice. Rather than be guilty of such neglect or audacity, Bernard felt obliged to put the notable events of the diocese "into letters," lest someone coming afterwards cast doubt on their veracity. Moreover, he defended his methods. They were logical and systematic, endeavouring always to get at the *rei veritas* through *argumenta*. And they combined the oral and the written. Only one miracle was heard at a time, and a second marvel of a similar type was taken to confirm the divine intention of the first.[266] In addition to oaths taken in his presence or sworn on the martyr's remains, he had the evidence of trial by fire and of physical signs, like the scars around Guibert's eyes.[267] Finally, after his brief sojourn at Conques, Bernard left his manuscript with the local monks, forbidding them to transcribe it before miracles as yet unedited were

[263] Cf. J. Vansina, *Oral Tradition*, ch. 5, pp. 114-40.

[264] *Miracula* 1.1, p. 15.

[265] *Ibid.*, 1.2, p. 20.

[266] *Ibid.*, 16.

[267] *Loc.cit.*: "Hujus rei veritatem quot argumentis sollicitus indagaverim, tediosum nimis est revolvere; nam preter testimonium illorum qui michi parati vel super sanctę Martyris pignera jurare, vel judicium ignitum gerere assistunt, videas adhuc antiquas stigmatum cicatrices, sciseque cutis circa oculos deformitatem horrere."

added or before the whole collection was read and corrected by a competent authority. Only then could the *Miracula* join the ranks of *authenticae scripturae*. Even the process of editing was arduous. The notes hastily scribbled before eyewitnesses were taken to Angers, not, he reiterated, to add superfluous information, but to prune repetitions and to rework the whole into a more concise, organized literary product. As a consequence, the reader had before him not "the immense undigested library" of oral record but only the polished transcript of what was most memorable.[268]

By adding the weight of literary authority to the miracles, Bernard effectively raised a local hagiographic tradition to a higher and more universal level of culture. By implication, he treated those who refused to accept his version of events as uneducated. He clearly recognized himself to be a man of culture and learning in contrast to the lay society of Conques, as was revealed in an anecdote involving a chance meeting with an erudite abbot named Peter, en route from Rome in 1020, who immediately noted his correct and cultivated accent.[269] His individuality as an author also spoke forth in the *epistola* with which he concluded book one. Unlike Sulpicius Severus, he asserted, he did not seek anonymity, lest his *novella editio* of the miracles be thought apocryphal. To his own signature, as a sign of authenticity, he added the approbation of his monastic *confrères*, Reynold of Tours, who improved his style, Wantelme and Leowulf of Noyons, who erected a new church to the saint, and a certain "John Scot," a relative of Reynold's, who judged his work to be not inferior to the *prisci doctores*.[270]

Bernard's mentality—at once critical of oral tradition yet seeking to verify it—is perhaps best revealed in his fictive debate with a heretic in Angers, who remained incredulous at such unnatural acts as the restoration of a blind man's sight or the resurrection of a mule. There was, he asserted, no Platonic *ratio* or *necessitas*; no one of sound judgment therefore ought to waste his time in such investigations.[271] Bernard's reply was characteristically ambivalent.[272] Like the Jews, he argued, the skeptic would refuse to trust even the resurrection of Lazarus. He was the *filius diaboli*, the *minister antichristi*. He was at once thereby illiterate and dangerously learned: a rustic, devoid of all

[268] *Ibid.*, 1.7, p. 30.
[269] *Ibid.*, 2.8, p. 114: "Hic cum aliquam sermonum vim in ore meo sensisset. . . ."
[270] *Ibid.*, 1.34, p. 86.
[271] *Ibid.*, 1.7, p. 31.
[272] *Ibid.*, 31-33.

true knowledge, totally unskilled in God's ways (*rusticus, ab omni scientia alienus, prorsus totius divine virtutis inexpertus*), and, what was worse, a traitorous soul, depraved in mind, who had fallen into the same error as the Pharisees, vaunting themselves the prophets' successors but refusing to acknowledge the *signa* and *prodigia* of Christ. Having tried unsuccessfully to impede his journey to Conques by other tasks, the devil in his view resorted to heresy, not only to mislead the uninstructed (*inexperti*) but also to prevent Bernard from relating the miracles to a larger audience, that is, from acting as the *veritatis assertor*. Thus, paradoxically, the heretic, although *illiteratus et omnium bonorum inscius*, stood accused of preventing the translation of God's intentions into written form. Bernard added that the maker's ways were far from lacking "reason" and "necessity." Beasts rather than men were brought back to life on occasion because they were needed to insure the latter's livelihood.[273] Moreover, during the patristic age morals were so lax that the body did not deserve to be saved; nowadays, a resurrected mule could reaffirm the faith and show the way back to ancient probity. Bernard even demanded that the unbeliever, although in one sense illiterate (*rusticus, idiota, ignarus*), avail himself of the *antiquaria pagina*. The diatribe ended with a reminder that only canonical methods had been used to establish the facts. The stories, as recorded, were not byproducts of *fabulosa fama* or *apocripha scriptura*, but came directly from the mouths of faithful witnesses, whose words were merely set down in writing.

Bernard's rehabilitation of symbolism was similar to that of orality. The gilded statue of St. Foy was for him both a physical reminder of the saint's powers and a viaticum between popular and learned culture. Symbols abound in the *Miracula* and on occasion speak for themselves. Guibert's eyes were torn from their sockets in reparation for an alleged crime;[274] they were then borne to St. Foy by a dove as white as snow.[275] Symbols are also placed in an allegorical context. In the first miracle Bernard presents the vision of St. Foy before Guibert, then interprets the meaning of her *mirabilis habitus* for the reader. By analogy with Boethius's *Philosophia*, her ample garments represent faith's limitless protection, the infinite folds of her gown the tortuous search

[273] *Ibid.*, 32. So far as I am aware, this is the earliest statement of a link between the technical usefulness of beasts and the attainment of salvation.

[274] *Ibid.*, I.1, p. 7.

[275] *Ibid.*, 9.

for wisdom, and the four precious stones adorning her crown the cardinal virtues.[276] So evocative was the statue that it frequently stood for the child saint in apparitions.[277] St. Foy herself contributed to the interest in the physical, often demanding expensive gifts to be added to the reliquary.[278] The common people responded: freed prisoners offered their chains, which were reforged into decorations for the church gates.[279]

Bernard himself revelled in the tangible and its associations. When the saint restored the patrimony of a deceased monk to the monastery, he rejoiced that he had witnessed Pride not in an image (*non . . . imaginaliter*) as in Prudentius' *Psychomachia*, but genuinely present in substance (*sed presentialiter corporaliterque proprie*).[280] Such physical signs of divine power were linked to the public performance of miracles during pilgrimages,[281] processions,[282] or other ritual observances,[283] thereby allowing men and women of different age, social background, and educational level to participate in a common religious experience.[284] The intermingling of low and high culture was not lost on Bernard. For instance, he was struck by the peasants' venerable tradition (*mos ab antiquis*) of celebrating vigils in church with candles and torches on the eve of their arrival at the shrine. While *clerici . . . litterarum periti* sang psalms, the *ignari* sang *cantilene rustice*, or other frivolities, which he personally felt were inappropriate. But the abbot of Conques told of a miracle which clearly indicated St. Foy's approval of the custom. The monks once locked the rowdy peasants outside the church until morning, but they discovered that someone had mysteriously opened the gates during the night.[285] It is arguable that St. Foy had not only tolerated the "innocent, although rustic songs," as

[276] *Ibid.*, 10.   [277] *Ibid.*, 1.25, p. 65.   [278] E.g., 1.13, 17, 25; 2.5.

[279] *Ibid.*, 1.31, p. 77.   [280] *Ibid.*, 1.5, p. 26.

[281] E.g., 1.1, p. 7, 1.2, p. 17, 1.3, p. 21, 1.4, pp. 22-23, 1.9, p. 36, 1.10, p. 37, 1.12, p. 42, etc.

[282] E.g., 1.14, p. 49: ". . . Venerabilis illa imago . . . foras cum ingenti processione efferretur. . . ." On opposition to the practice, see Bouillet, 49-50n1.

[283] E.g., vigils, 2.12, p. 120: "Est mos ab antiquis, ut peregrini semper vigilias agant in ecclesia sancte Fidis. . . ." Cf. E. R. Labande, " 'Ad limina': le pèlerin médiéval au terme de sa démarche," *Mélanges René Crozet*, ed. P. Gallais and Y.-J. Riou (Poitiers, 1966), 287.

[284] Cf. V. Turner, "Pilgrimages as Social Processes," *Dramas, Fields, and Metaphors* (Ithaca, 1974), 166-230, who does not know E. R. Labande, "Recherches sur les pèlerins dans l'Europe des XIe et XIIe siècles," *CCM* 1 (1958), 159-69, 339-47.

[285] *Miracula* 2.12, pp. 120-22.

the abbot maintained, but also offered herself as a mediator between different levels of society.

Statuary for Bernard was a special case of symbolism, which he discussed at length in book one, chapter thirteen.[286] It was, he stated, a *vetus mos* and *antiqua consuetudo* that throughout the southwest statues of local saints were fabricated out of gold or silver. Onto the statue was often placed the saint's skull, a part of the body, or a relic. How was an educated person to look upon this practice?

Bernard's reaction was essentially skeptical, but he also interpreted the popular attitude towards statuary by analogy with the role of evidence documents in authenticating oral tradition. While on a visit to the church of St. Gerard at Aurillac, he stopped and conversed with his companion Bernier before the gem-studded statue of the saint in whose presence "several rustics" were displaying their uncultivated devotion. "What do you think of the idol?" he asked. "Would it not be worthy of Jupiter or Mars?" Bernier laughed and agreed. To both it seemed obvious that God had no need of images in stone, wood, or metal, except, as was universally acknowledged, for the crucifix. If one wished to recall a saint, one should be content with authoritative accounts (*verifica libri scriptura*), or, if visual aids were required, with wall paintings (*imagines umbrose coloratis parietibus depicte*).[287] Although perhaps an immemorial practice, the portrayal of saints by means of statues was in his view a custom born of ignorance (*idiotarum consuetudo*), inadmissible to reason. Yet the habit was so widespread, he added, that he dared not speak out against it for fear of reprisals. A similar conversation took place some three days later when the pair found themselves before the statue of St. Foy. Behind the backs of the kneeling peasants Bernard murmured derisively to himself: "St. Foy, whose relics are housed in this statue, succor me on the day of judgment!" The pair chuckled: to them, the devout crowd seemed "mute, insensate and remote from reason." But Bernard, perhaps as an afterthought, then tried to put himself in the peasants' place. Just as education naturally led to a discrediting of symbolic statuary, he maintained, so popular tradition could be justified by arguments from higher culture. St. Foy's statue, however it appeared to the literate, was not merely an oracle which one consulted blindly or an idol to which one made sacrifices. It was a likeness whose purpose was to keep alive the remembered record of a martyr (*ob memoriam reverende*

[286] *Ibid.*, 1.13, 46-49.
[287] Cf. L. Gougaud, "Muta Praedicatio," Rben 42 (1930), 168-71.

martyris . . . simulacrum). It was in that sense "evidence," even though uninterpreted by popular culture. Adalgerius, deacon and later abbot, related a miracle to support the point. A cleric called Odalric had also reviled St. Foy's physical image. But the saint appeared by night and struck him so hard that he hardly survived long enough to tell the tale. In Bernard's view, the statue was thereby affirmed to be not a *spurcissimum idolum* but rather a *sancte virginis pia memoria*.

Bernard of Anger's position on oral and written culture touches upon a number of themes central to the studies in this volume: the placing of spoken testimony within a legalistic framework determined by texts; the questioning of the formal validity of ritual and symbol, together with a literate conception of inner as genuine reality; the separation of subject and object, through which the dispassionate observer of events is isolated from a mixture of events and interpretations; and a linking of literacy with reform, by which the local, the particular, and the unwritten become elements in a programme of higher religious culture, a project which, Bernard reminds us, partly motivated him to verify Fulbert's account of the miracles in the first place. Above all, it bears witness to what, in a contemporary example, has been called the "clustered" and "discontinuous" nature of "human communication" in a region in which the little and great religious traditions are beginning to overlap.[288]

How characteristic is Bernard's obviously precocious mentality of broader aspects of eleventh- and twelfth-century religious change? In two areas at least he anticipated later developments. One, which we have noted, was the persistence of the oral, the ritualistic, and the symbolic within an increasingly literate society. For literacy's rise did not automatically spell the demise of traditional attitudes and tastes, although, as in the *Miracula*, altered values reclassified them as "popular," meaning unlettered. The other area affected was communication itself. Older forms of life and thought, whether oral or written or a combination of the two, were given new life, either through simple preservation or through the creation of a genuinely literate context involving readers, writers, and an implied audience. The latter phenomenon deserves some attention, if only because it affected many departments of medieval cultural life at once.

St. Foy herself provides a convenient focal point. Hers was one of a large number of local cults which underwent a vogue during the

---

[288] W. A. Christian, Jr., *Person and God in a Spanish Valley* (New York and London, 1972), 11.

eleventh century, the *vitae* and *passiones* alternating between the spoken and the written as lessons for the office, in public or private *lectiones*, in sermons for saints' days, or, as was the case in Normandy, as moral diversion for noble families.[289] Monastic communities generally commemorated saints throughout the liturgical year; the recollection of the abbey's patron or protector formed an integral part of the *opus divinum*. Each night before matins the monks circulated around the altar; such daily pilgrimages not only fostered interior devotion but also legitimized the symbolic veneration of relics. Accordingly, a powerful force in the rise of local cults was the search for the "material souvenirs of celestial patrons."[290] Through the office other links were forged between the textual and the physical. On saints' days, the customaries prescribed that nocturns during matins, which were normally given to the Psalms, should consist of the *vitae sanctorum*. In cults of purely literary origin, the liturgical office might be influenced by the written legend; a saint's feast might be celebrated simply because the monastery possessed an excellent *vita* assuring him local fame.[291] Conversely, instituting a feast might require the written redaction of a life, especially if the house received an important relic.[292] Thus, a monk of Stenay, which acquired the remains of St. Dagobert, was obliged to render a formerly oral account in writing.[293] When matins were finished, the legendary was not shut; public reading was repeated in the cloister, the chapter, the refectory, and even during manual labour. This *lectio* was "not merely a sort of music required by ceremonial" but also served for instruction, exhortation, and meditation. The presence of relics and the regular observance of saints' days also led to more serious hagiographic education. The subject of weekly devotion from the lectionary was chosen by the librarian, who named the appropriate readers in the choir, the chapter, and the refectory.[294] Finally, saints' lives were adapted to different audiences and occasions. Homiletic versions furnished the material for haranguing pilgrims. They were simple in form, and normally preached in the

---

[289] B. de Gaiffier, "L'hagiographe et son public," 158. On the twelfth-century *sermones subalpini*, see M. Zink, *La prédication en langue romane*, 140-49; on audience relations, the same author's "Les destinaires des recueils de sermons en langue vulgaire au XIIe et au XIIIe siècle. Prédication effective et prédication dans un fauteuil," *La piété populaire au moyen âge* (Paris, 1977), 59-74.

[290] de Gaiffier, 138.

[291] *Ibid.*, 139.

[292] *Loc.cit.*

[293] *Vita Dagoberti III, regis Francorum*, MGH SS Merov., II, 512.

[294] B. de Gaiffier, "L'hagiographe et son public," 144-46.

vernacular.[295] In an effort to accommodate themselves to an unsophisticated audience, de Gaiffier remarks, they often "counted on the ignorance they proposed to remedy."[296] Yet such rough-and-ready texts perhaps created the first lay listening audiences. From them it was a short step to vernacular translations of Latin lives (or vice versa) and the reconstitution of the reading public through hagiography, *chanson de geste*, romance, and lyric.[297]

From the authors of saints' lives it is a short step to the eclectic reception of written tradition by eleventh- and twelfth-century historians. A new mentality emerged: for, whereas, for the oral historian, all events had to be stored in the human memory, the researcher with texts could, like Adso, omit ordinary information because, as he put it, "it is found to this very day in our monastic archive."[298] One also saw the beginnings of transcripts, editing, and secretarial services. For instance, Gerard of Cambrai, in writing the life of St. Autbert, first had Fulbert, his notary, draw the relevant facts from the *sacrae ecclesiae cartulae*; then the bishop himself made his selection and drafted the final version.[299] The evanescence of oral record was still evoked: Adam of Bremen undertook his history of the Hamburg diocese because, as he put it, the recollection of events was dim and *hystoria non est tradita litteris*.[300] But more sophisticated approaches were frequent. Landulf Senior distinguished among his sources for the history of Milan, referring on one occasion to the *libri varii* and *cartulae* from which he took notes[301] and on another to his own "bits of parchment," drawn, he boasted, both from the ancients and "from digging out . . . all the books in Italian towns."[302] One of the fullest brief statements of method is found in the preface to Arnulf of Milan's own history of the city. Among God's gifts, Arnulf declared, literary ability was rare: the present age furnished much that was worth writing about but too few historians capable of seizing the opportunity. This, he added, was

[295] *Ibid.*, 155-57.

[296] *Ibid.*, 154.

[297] Cf. M. D. Legge, *Anglo-Norman Literature and its Background* (Oxford, 1963), 3-4, and the literature cited. Héloïse, it is worth recalling, in her second letter to Abelard, speaks of his love-songs, which carried his fame even to the non-lettered; PL 178.185D-86A: ". . . ut etiam illitteratos medodiae dulcedo tui non sineret immemores esse."

[298] *Vita S. Frodoberti*, c. 11, PL 137.606B.

[299] "De miraculis S. Autberti Cameracensis episcopi," c. 1, anon., *Analecta Bollandiana* 19 (1900), 200.

[300] *Gesta Hamburgensis Ecclesiae*, preface, PL 146.485C-D.

[301] *Historia Mediolanensis*, preface, MGH SS 8, p. 37.

[302] *Ibid.*, 3.2, p. 74.

a pity, since an accurate record benefitted both the more and the less learned. For this reason, he avoided the snares of philosophy and rhetoric, preferring instead to set down in plain language what he had seen himself or had learned from eyewitnesses. Such a history was in his view a sort of artificial memory, an archival storehouse on which future generations could draw.[303]

Readers of Arnulf's *Liber Gestorum Recentium* may not agree with his claim to stylistic simplicity. In fact, beneath such statements lay what Haskins thought one of the period's best examples of a renaissance of literate postures within classical genres.[304] Yet, as in law, historical writing also offered a vehicle for the transmission of a literary form whose mode of composition and inner logic retained strong links with the spoken word. The line between historical and epic narrative was not sharply drawn; and, within histories, personal accounts, dreams, visions, prophecies, and poetic insights were all taken to be reliable witnesses to events.[305] One may therefore legitimately ask with Lacroix whether "any interpretation" of medieval historical writing "is valid without understanding the mechanisms of transmission"[306] of oral tradition. Reflecting on the problem of communication, for instance, Orderic Vitalis noted that a great deal depended on one's level of education. Events that seemed incredible to the ears of the ignorant (*rudium aures*), and even strange to one's contemporaries, were those which were most in need of interpretation. Naturally, those unfamiliar with critical methods (*inexperti*) found them obscure, for the exploration of the dark places of the past was the proper work of the studious and trained (*studiosi*).[307] As an example of the sort of inquiry he had in mind, Orderic described the activities of Ansold, the son of Peter of Maule: "He studied history as it was written in the ancient records, thoughtfully investigated what he could discover from learned narrators, and, once he had heard the lives of the fathers, committed

[303] *Liber Gestorum Recentium* 1.1, MGH SS 8, pp. 6-7.

[304] *The Renaissance of the Twelfth Century* (Cambridge, Mass., 1927), 224.

[305] E.g., Wipo, *Gesta Chuonradi imperatoris*, prol., 5-8; discussed below, ch. 5 p. 518. For other examples, see N. F. Partner, *Serious Entertainments. The Writing of History in Twelfth-Century England* (Chicago, 1977), 183-93.

[306] B. Lacroix, *L'historien au moyen âge* (Paris, 1971), 50. For a useful discussion of these methods in non-western oral history, see J. Vansina, *Oral Tradition*, chs. 2-4, pp. 19-113. On western sources, see M. T. Clanchy, "Remembering the Past . . . ," 165-70. On the question of historical genres, see in general B. Guenée, "Histoires, annales, chroniques. Essai sur les genres historiques au Moyen Age," *Annales, E.S.C.*, 28 (1973), 997-1016; and, more recently, the same author's *Histoire et culture historique dans l'Occident médiéval* (Paris, 1981).

[307] *Historia Ecclesiastica* bk. 6, preface, ed. M. Chibnall, vol. 3 (Oxford, 1972), 213.

them to his tenacious memory. He detested those who told inaccurate narratives or falsified the word of God or thirsted for dishonest gains; and when he detected any dangerous sophistries, he refuted them publicly, so that they should not mislead simple people."[308]

Orderic's *History*, which was begun in the late eleventh century, provides an inventory of new directions within an increasingly literate society. A Norman by persuasion if not by birth, Orderic was himself conscious of literacy's value, not only as an antidote to monastic *otium*,[309] but also in contemporaries like Thierry of St. Evroul, who personally copied many ancient texts and helped to build up the monastic library.[310] Like William of Malmesbury he was offended by what he took to be an indifference to letters in his English countrymen.[311] Norman nobles capable of drafting their own charters and wills elicited his admiration;[312] and we know from a smattering of surviving documents, such as the will of Foucher of Chartres, that he checked his own facts with meticulous care.[313] He recorded for posterity individuals who, like his own teacher, John of Reims, rose from humble station by scribal labours.[314] He also saw the tendentious side of written archives and correspondence in the endless litigation of his own day, from which his less educated forbears had happily been spared.[315]

On two occasions in particular he spoke with insight on the problems of oral record in his own time. One occurred in connection with St. William (d. 812), whose *vita* he wished to summarize for the abbey. No copy was to be found in the region, but, by chance, An-

---

[308] *Ibid.*, bk. 5, vol. 3, p. 180: "Res gestas prout antiquis codicibus insertae sunt ediscebat, a doctis relatoribus dagaciter inuestigabat, auditasque patrum uitas tenaci memoriae commendabat. Falsidicos relatores et uerbum Dei adulterantes et turpibus lucris inhiantes exosos habebat, et detectis sophismatibus malignis ne insontes deciperent palam confutebat." (Trans. M. Chibnall, *ibid.*, 181.) Elsewhere Orderic speaks of Ansold as arguing from reasoned proofs (argutae allegationes); *ibid.*, pp. 180, 182.

[309] *Ibid.*, 5.1, vol. 2 (1969), 4.

[310] *Ibid.*, bk. 3, vol. 1, pp. 48, 50.

[311] *Ibid.*, 246: "Anglos agrestes et pene illiteratos . . ."; cf. William of Malmesbury, *De Gestis Regum Anglorum*, ed. W. Stubbs, vol. 2 (London, 1889), 304. The periodization of stages of education was of course familiar in England from Alfred's reflections. See in general J. W. Adamson, " 'The Illiterate Anglo-Saxon,' " in *'The Illiterate Anglo-Saxon' and Other Essays* (Cambridge, 1946), 1-14.

[312] *Hist. Eccles.*, 5.19, vol. 3, p. 177.

[313] *Ibid.*, 5.15, pp. 151ff. The original is Archives de l'Orne H 717 (Chibnall, 151n2).

[314] *Ibid.*, 5.18, pp. 167-68. Orderic also recorded the anecdote of a sinful monk who was saved on judgment day because the weight of his written work was one letter heavier than his sins; bk. 3, p. 50.

[315] E.g., 5.1, p. 4.

thony, a monk from Winchester, was passing through and had a text
in his possession. Anthony did not wish to remain long at St. Evroul,
and, in any case, the weather was too cold for extensive copying.
Orderic was compelled to make a summary on wax tablets which was
later transferred to parchment.[316] Commenting on the oral and written versions, he made the often-quoted remark that, while a popular
song (*cantilena*) is transmitted by jongleurs, it would be preferable to
have a reliable account (*relatio autentica*), that is, one written by scholars which could be read aloud to all the monks.[317] He spoke of oral
sources in a broader context with reference to the life of St. Evroul,
who died in 706. In a dramatic statement, he recalled that the *vita*
had passed from written records under the Carolingians to unwritten
ones afterwards. His famous declaration may well have exaggerated
the loss of contact with the past, but it summed up his age's value
judgments against oral tradition. The Carolingian sources, he said:
   "I have sought out and taken from chronicles, briefly noting them
for the information of my readers. . . . Now (he added) I will turn
back and try to relate some things I have learned not from written
sources but from the oral traditions of old men. For during the terrible disturbances that accompanied the ravages of the Danes the records of former times perished in the flames, along with churches and
other buildings; and all the ardent labour and desire of later men has
been unavailing to restore them. Some things indeed, which were
saved from the hands of the barbarians by the care of our forefathers,
have since perished (shameful to relate) by the abominable neglect of
their descendants, who took no pains to preserve the profound spiritual wisdom recorded in the writings of the fathers. With the loss of
books the deeds of old men pass into oblivion, and can in no wise be
recovered by those of our generation, for the admonitions of the ancients pass away from the memory of modern men with the changing
world, as hail or snow melt in the waters of a swift river, swept away
by the current never to return."[318]
   Orderic was born in 1075. He was just old enough to recall the

---

[316] *Ibid.*, 6.3, vol. 3, p. 218; on which see Chibnall, bk. 6, pp. 218-19n3.

[317] *Ibid.*, 219. On the oral aspects of Orderic's endeavour, see Chibnall, vol. 2, xl-xli and
R. D. Ray, "Orderic Vitalis and his Readers," *Studia Monastica* 14 (1972), 18-33.

[318] *Hist. Eccles.* 6.9, pp. 283, 285. Cf., *ibid.*, p. 306, where once again Orderic supersedes
a faulty written account through contemporary verbal testimony. After stating that he follows
Dudo of St. Quentin in singing the praises of great men and deeds, he adds: "I have already
composed (*dictaui*) an account of the monastery worthily restored in the forest of Ouche in the
time of duke William, later king. But I have been unable to find any written records of the
early days after the death of St. Evroul, and therefore I will make a special effort to record in
writing (*litteris*) the tradition I have received from my seniors (*seniores audiui*). . . ."

time when even literate clerics "shrank from bending their minds to the task of composing or writing down their traditions."[319] The sentiment was typical: similar views were voiced in 1088 by Paul of St.-Père de Chartres when speaking of the neglect of record-keeping by the monastery's *antiqui monachi*.[320]

A more specific example of the manner in which orality worked within a textual framework is furnished by oral confession within structured penitential theology, which increasingly became the norm after the millennium.[321] Moreover, it was not only the sacrament which was affected, but also a group of penitential rites interrelating lay and ecclesiastical society, such as the pilgrimage, the religious withdrawal, and the crusade. In general, literate theology crystallized the distinction between the internal and external aspects of penitential activity, thereby providing a model for interrelating theory and practice in such influential areas of life as work, contemplation, and the search for salvation.[322]

The most authoritative witness to the altered mentality is doubtless the *Corrector sive Medicus* of Burchard of Worms from the years 1008 to 1012, whose nineteenth book effectively codifies previous Irish, English, and Carolingian doctrine on the theology of penance and the tariffs for various sins.[323] But the impact of literate sensibilities is perhaps more sharply thrown into relief in a minor document, namely a letter written by an anonymous "A," who speaks of himself as an "inhabitant" of Speier, to Heribert, who became archbishop of Cologne in 999.[324] Although presenting himself as a layman (*civis*), the author reveals an insider's understanding of penitential practices, re-

[319] *Ibid.*, 5.1, p. 7.

[320] *Cartulaire de l'abbaye de St.-Père de Chartres*, c. 7, ed. B. Guérard (Paris, 1840), vol. 1, p. 48: "Utrum autem vetustate abolitae sunt (cartae), aut hostium igne crematae, aut nunquam scriptae, scribarum penuria, minime scio." On the disappearance of archaeological record, cf. Rodulf Glaber, *Historiae* 5.1.8, p. 119.

[321] For a full account of the growth of private penance, see E. Amman, "Pénitence, II. La pénitence privée . . . ," DTC 12.1, 845-948, with bibliography, 948; B. Poschmann, *Die abendländische Kirchenbusse im frühen Mittelalter* (Breslau, 1930); and P. Anciaux, *La Théologie du Sacrement de Pénitence au XIIe siècle* (Louvain, 1949), esp. pp. 8-55, with a full bibliography, x-xxvi. A useful account in English is B. Poschmann, *Penance and the Anointing of the Sick* (Freiburg, 1964).

[322] For parallels in the development of internality in other fields, see M.-D. Chenu, *L'éveil de la conscience dans la civilisation médiévale* (Montréal and Paris, 1969), 17-77.

[323] G. Le Bras, "Pénitentiels," DTC 12.1, 1176. For a full recent account, see C. Vogel, *Les 'libri paenitentiales'* (Turnhout, 1978), with a full bibliography, 17-27.

[324] *Epistola A. Civis Spirensis ad Heribertum Coloniensem archiepiscopum*, in Martène and Durand, *Veterum Scriptorum Monumentorum Amplissima Collectio* (Paris, 1724), vol. 1, 357-59; repr. PL 151.693-98.

ferring on one occasion to the views of *nonulli fratrum* which in large part he shares.[325] At first reading, he would seem only to be echoing the objections to imported penitentials expressed as early as Charlemagne's synods at Tours, Châlons, and Reims in 813.[326] But the questions he raises eventually throw light on the entire issue of literacy, interiority, and private confession.

The letter's contents may be summarized briefly. "A" accuses some of Heribert's parish priests of laxness in administering penance. Others, he adds, know better, but remain silent nonetheless. From the priest's side, the error arises from appropriating the power to forgive, which belongs only to God; from the people's, it arises from the belief that no further confession is necessary and that all sins since baptism are forgiven at once.

But the real purpose of penance, "A" underlines, is to provide an earthly tribunal for divine judgment. Like a physician, the priest first leads the leper out of town; only when he is cleansed is he allowed back into the temple. That, he adds, is the meaning of Christ's raising Lazarus from the dead.[327] Moreover, Gregory the Great stated that any priest who exercises his office for his own inclinations (*pro suis voluntatibus*) rather than the subject's merits (*pro subjectorum meritis*) is automatically deprived of the power to bind and to loose.[328] "A" does not content himself with pointing out errors of doctrine. He also maintains that the administration of the sacrament has gone astray. Penitential procedure, he insists, should be judicially correct. Only after determining guilt and punishment should phrases like *"Ego tibi dimitto"* be pronounced. Some infractions—those, for instance, involving one's family or the priest himself—may be handled with personal formulae such as *"Indulgeat tibi Dominus et ego."* But no mortal should ever declare publicly "I pardon you." Only God has such capacities, as the fathers teach. By rereading their statements, "A" concludes, and, in particular, their interpretations of Scripture for ordinary individuals, one can avoid such misrepresentations as the "new absolutions."

The letter effectively raises the question of literacy at different levels. There is a generally assumed difference between the learned and

[325] *Ibid.*, 357B.

[326] On which see E. Amman, "Pénitence," DTC 12.1, 865-66, 872.

[327] Jn 11.44. Cf. Alcuin, *Epistola* 112, PL 100.337C, 340B. Gregory, *In Evangelia L.II, Hom.* 26.5-6, PL 76.1200-01.

[328] On the other sources of this section of the letter, see P. Anciaux, *La Théologie du Sacrement . . .* , 41-42n4.

the popular, that is, between the *eruditi*, the "few . . . who have some understanding of Scripture," and the *imperita multitudo*, the *popularis intelligentia*. More subtle distinctions are made on the basis of internality and externality. Heribert's priests are accused of formalism and heresy: their "absolution and remission" is both a "public deception" and an error of doctrine, founded on "no authority." They are at once illiterate as regards the true sacrament and falsely erudite in speaking of their own ability to forgive sins. But what then is penance? Oddly, in "A's" view, it involves the same distinctions in reverse. The priest, in fact, does deal with the *visibilis species*, while truth is left for God. The priest is a mediator: purification consists of exercises *per modum legitimae satisfactionis*, that is, essentially of fasting and prayer. God remains custodian of the Word; man, of the letter. The priest's function is to administer, that is, to adhere to the *regula sanctorum patrum*. But he is also an interpreter and communicator of Scripture. This is the point of "A's" reconstruction of patristic methodology. In his opinion, the entire process led to intellectualization. The fathers treated (*tractare*), then spoke (*allocutio*), adding interpretation (*explanatio*). Only afterwards came confession and penance.

In sum, we see in the anonymous letter from Speier a number of typically eleventh-century topics in penitential theology: the rejection of general absolutions, the limitation of the power of priests as indicated by Jerome and Gregory, and the return to patristic authority accompanied by a desire for increased rigour, *more antiquitus*. But, above all, by considering oral confession within a highly textual theological framework, the letter takes us to the heart of the discussion of internality and externality, that is, to the distinction between "the attitude of repenting" and "the expiation, which, among other things, included confession and satisfaction."[329]

Still another branch of culture in which oral discourse began to operate within a textual environment during the eleventh century was literature. However, in contrast to penitential theology, there are a far greater number of models, and, as a consequence, far less scope for generalization. Indeed, the term "literature," when employed outside the field of Latin, begs as many questions as it answers.

Of course, no one doubts the presence of the spoken element as such. The Norse skalds, Roberta Frank notes, "were essentially recorders of events, advertisers, men whose profession it was to fix or stabilize memory in a brief statement that would outlast time. . . .

[329] *Ibid.*, 28n3.

The skaldic stanza used repeated patterns of sound and of images to impress discrete scenes from the past on the mind—a kind of mnemotechnics. The poem itself served as a reference library."[330] There are numerous examples of the recording function: the maxims of *Beowulf* and *Genesis B* served an encyclopedic purpose;[331] the Icelandic laws passed in the codification of 1117 "from oral preservation to written preservation."[332]

Yet, wherever texts appeared, they changed relations between authors, listeners, readers, and the real or imagined public.[333] Narrative material often shifted from oral to written form and back again without leaving a trace. In the case of the *Nibelungenlied*, the version recorded in Austria around 1200 is "the written record of an oral performance" in which a considerable distance has nonetheless arisen between the two.[334] Also, while oral composition and delivery appear to be widespread, so are the different ways in which poets and audiences interact, as the investigation of contemporary oral literatures illustrates.[335] Caution, therefore, must be observed in suggesting par-

[330] *Old Norse Court Poetry. The Dróttkvaett Stanza* (Ithaca, 1978), 25.

[331] T. A. Shippey, "Maxims in Old English Narrative: Literary Art or Traditional Wisdom?" in H. Bekker-Nielsen, et al., eds., *Oral Tradition, Literary Tradition*, 35-36.

[332] P. Foote, "Oral and Literary Tradition in Early Scandinavian Law: Aspects of a Problem," *ibid.*, 54.

[333] There seems to be agreement on this point among students of different branches of medieval literature, the wide range of whose studies cannot be adequately reflected here. On early Irish, the differing positions are summarized by H.P.A. Oskamp, *The Voyage of Máel Dúin*, (Groningen, 1970), 11-15; on Anglo-Saxon, see A. C. Watts, *The Lyre and the Harp* (New Haven, 1969); on the *Nibelungenlied*, F. H. Bäuml, "The Unmaking of the Hero: Some Critical Implications of the Transition from Oral to Written Epic," in H. Scholler, ed., *The Epic in Medieval Society* (Tübingen, 1977), 86-89. Earlier work by the same author is summarized on p. 86n6; a wider perspective is adopted in the earlier paper of M. Curschmann, "Oral Poetry in Mediaeval English, French and German Literature: Some Notes on Recent Research," *Speculum* 42 (1967), 36-52. On Old French, see J. Rychner, *La Chanson de geste. Essai sur l'art épique des jongleurs* (Geneva and Lille, 1955); S. G. Nicols, Jr., *Formulaic Diction and Thematic Composition in the Chanson de Roland* (Chapel Hill, 1961); J. J. Duggan, *The Song of Roland: Formulaic Style and Poetic Craft* (Berkeley and Los Angeles, 1973); and, more generally, H. E. Keller, "Changes in Old French Epic Poetry and Changes in the Taste of its Audience," in Scholler, *op.cit.*, 150-77. For a linguistic perspective on the entire field, see P. Zumthor, *Essai de poétique médiévale* (Paris, 1972). Recent bibliographic reviews include A. B. Lord, "Perspectives on Recent Work on Oral Literature," in J. J. Duggan, ed., *Oral Literature* (Edinburgh and London, 1975), 1-24 and F. H. Bäuml, "Varieties and Consequences . . . ," 237-65.

[334] F. H. Bäuml, "The Unmaking of the Hero . . . ," 89.

[335] See J. Goody, "Literacy and the Non-Literate," *Times Literary Supplement* (12 May 1972), 539-40, and more generally, R. Finnegan, *Oral Literature in Africa* (Oxford, 1970). For earlier bibliography, see H. Jason, "A Multidimensional Approach to Oral Literature," *Current Anthropology* 10 (1969), 413-26.

allels between the evolution of literature and that of law, theology, or historical writing. Of course, literature did not develop in complete isolation. But its conventions were different, and authors were often inclined to obey their own instincts rather than general prescriptions. In one sense, scribes had as much as style or genre to do with the creation of modern letters. But literature was not so much determined as it was simply encircled by other textually oriented types of discourse, mainly legal and administrative.

No less far-reaching than in literature were the effects of literacy on medieval art and architecture, to which in a more general fashion we may briefly turn. For, as noted, oral and written traditions made different demands on the human senses. The one emphasized the ear, the other, the eye. The new complexity of the sensorium eventually altered the form and function of the visual and plastic arts.

As in literature, the Middle Ages knew two interdependent traditions. Classical representational art was closely linked to the written text. Northerly art was more primitive and abstract. Were these the artistic equivalents of oral lays and epics? The stylistic connections are difficult to prove: yet, it is suggested that the rich, "interlaced" ornamentation of the brooches, pins, belt-clasps, drinking horns, and sword-hilts are artifacts of a "heroic" society;[336] it was the craftsmanship of migratory peoples, excelling not in sculpture or buildings but in portable objects such as jewellery, implements, and weapons. Magical properties were emphasized, the elaborately decorated swords of Anglo-Saxon and Old Norse poetry effectively recapturing the sense of awe accompanying the discovery of metal-working. Books, too, when introduced by missionaries, were seen as embodiments of divine power, in which the interwoven text and decoration achieved symbolic status. When Charlemagne embarked on his ambitious scheme of imperial revival, he also inaugurated a classical "renaissance" which consisted of imposing Mediterranean canons of taste on indigenous traditions. For, despite its intrinsic beauty, northern book art did not convey a specific religious message; it did not tell a story or illustrate a moral. By contrast, classical design afforded a convenient vehicle for integrating text and picture. It also permitted Charlemagne's scribes and artists to recreate classical civilization through their own eyes. Classical art served as another reminder that the old and the new Latin

---

[336] J. Leyerle, "The Interlace Structure of Beowulf," *University of Toronto Quarterly* 37 (1967), 1. Cf. E. Vinaver, *The Rise of Romance* (Oxford, 1971), ch. 5.

empires were indissolubly linked—or so the imperial propagandists liked to believe.

From the later eleventh century the dominant mode of artistic representation became the Romanesque church, which provided an effective signpost of religious education and learning as well as of the preservation in monumental form of traditional values. For the essential feature of the new style, Ernst Kitzinger remarks, was not only the attempt "to subordinate all parts of a building to a uniform system," but also to make of architecture "a framework for the sculpture and an integral part of the message it carries. . . . The cathedral proclaims . . . the Gospel in stone."[337] The image is apt, uniting the respect for physical *traditio* with the beginnings of an interpretive tradition based on literate institutions. Moreover, the transition to Gothic in the 1130s was similar to what took place in law and literature: the written no longer merely recorded but now dictated the principles of coherence and inner meaning. "Two aspects of Gothic architecture . . . are without precedent or parallel: the use of light and the unique relationship between structure and appearance."[338] In both cases we see a movement away from concrete symbolism, to which textual evidence may be appended, and towards an order perceptible only to the mind. As Abbot Suger pointed out, the theory derived from previous authorities like Augustine and the pseudo-Denis. But the integration of the visual with the idea of logical order could not have been achieved without the underpinning of texts. Written culture effectively imposed divisions of space and time onto experience, dividing land into precise boundaries and books into chapters. Gothic architecture merely applied the same notions of didacticism and reckoning to another area and on a grander scale. "Small wonder," Panofsky observed, "that a mentality which deemed it necessary to make faith 'clearer' by an appeal to reason and to make 'reason' clearer by an appeal to the imagination, also felt bound to make imagination 'clearer' by an appeal to the senses."[339]

But not all the senses: mostly, Gothic appealed to the visual, either to appreciate the geometrical patterns of the vaulting or the play of light through the stained glass. The interest in visual phenomena coincided with the rediscovery of the science of optics. Early in the eleventh century Ibn al-Haitham proposed an alternative to the Ptolemaic theory that rays emanate from the human eye to the object

337 E. Kitzinger, *Early Medieval Art* (London, 1940), 81-82.
338 O. von Simson, *The Gothic Cathedral* (New York, 1962), 3.
339 *Gothic Architecture and Scholasticism* (Cleveland and New York, 1957), 38.

seen, stating instead that "light issues in all directions opposite a body that is illuminated. . . ."[340] Communicated by a transparent medium, the light makes an impression on the eye, whence a message is relayed to the brain. Alhazen's theory was introduced into the West by Grosseteste, Roger Bacon, John Pecham, and Witelo. By the 1270s several versions of his doctrine were available along with scholastic commentaries.[341] Of course, the new optics was neither a direct cause nor a consequence of Gothic architecture. The two merely flourished in the same mental climate. Together with the growth of literacy, the optics acted as a scientific foundation for a type of representational art which, although medieval in its roots, came to transcend all that medieval art stood for. This was achieved through the use of perspective: it effectively combined classical representation, which was the illustration of a text, with three-dimensionality, a logical development of the emphasis on the visual.[342] If medieval art began with the importation of the written into a world in which there was no implicit connection between ornamentation and narrative, it finished by expurgating the last traces of physical symbolism, even in their refined Gothic transformation, from miniatures, sculpture, and architecture.

The growth in interest in the visual, the literal, and the mentally perceptible was paralleled by new senses of time. The great divide was the invention of the mechanical clock with a verge escapement and foliot around 1270.[343] But, previous to this revolutionary device, a number of advances in time-keeping and related disciplines can be traced to the eleventh century, if not to the tenth. Once again, both oral and written traditions were at work. Alexander Murray notes: "Roman numerals manifested and partly occasioned the paralysis of early medieval arithmetic. . . . If the dead hand . . . was to lose its grip, . . . all that was needed was a displacement of writing as a whole from its monopoly in this branch of science." Gerbert, Richer, and others bear witness to a "tendency away from writing and towards material and symbolic means of expression,"[344] which naturally fa-

---

[340] D. Lindberg, "Alhazen's Theory of Vision and its Reception in the West," *Isis* 58 (1967), 323.

[341] *Ibid.*, 330. On the cultural implications, see H. Phillips, *John Wyclif's 'De Eucharistia' in its Medieval Setting*, diss. (Toronto, 1980), ch. 2, pp. 121-231: "The Feel of Perception: From Touch to Sight."

[342] For a review of the issues, see E. Panofsky, *Renaissance and Renascences in Western Art* (Stockholm, 1960), 42-113.

[343] L. Thorndike, "Invention of the Mechanical Clock about 1271 A.D.," *Speculum* 16 (1941), 242-43.

[344] *Reason and Society in the Middle Ages* (Oxford, 1978), 163.

voured the use of the abacus, a device probably imported to medieval Europe from China.

But interest in computation also went hand in hand with the rise of grammar, logic, and textual research.[345] Bede had simplified the procedure for fixing feast-days, and the Carolingian inventories imitated Roman fiscal methods. After the millennium a number of new instruments and calculating techniques began to filter into the West. The practical applications of the abacus were studied in Lotharingia and in Reims. Another novelty was the computus, a technique for fixing feast-days using Roman numerals, which was only later antiquated by the refined calculations of Ptolemaic astronomy.[346] The astrolabe, which allowed one to estimate the altitude and position of heavenly bodies, appeared about the same time via Arabic Spain.[347] The eleventh century saw the arrival of Hindu-Arabic numerals (minus the zero)[348] and the reintroduction of the *Corpus Agrimensorum*,[349] which greatly aided land measurement. Practical needs lay behind the so-called *"Second Geometry,"* which was attributed to Boethius but was actually the work of an eleventh-century student somewhere in Lorraine.[350] To these instruments must be added the psychological change in internal time-keeping brought about by the revival of monasticism. The convent walls not only provided a haven from doubt and insecurity; they imposed upon the changes of seasons and climates a man-made system of discipline and self-control.[351] However different in origin and makeup, these forces all served a similar purpose. The importance did not lie in accuracy of measurement, although mathematization was increasingly an issue, but in interposing between men and events a system of temporal reckoning independent of both. Time was externalized, offering a parallel to the abstract, depersonalized, and apparently objective world of the text.

[345] L. M. de Rijk, *Garlandus compotista, Dialectica* (Assen, 1959), xxii-xxiii. On the lack of a link between time-consciousness and structured repetition in primitive society, see E. R. Leach, "Two Essays concerning the Symbolic Representation of Time," in *Rethinking Anthropology* (London, 1966), 124-28, 132-36.

[346] On the early development, see above all C. W. Jones, *Bedae Opera de Temporibus* (Cambridge, Mass., 1943), 6-113.

[347] J. Millàs Vallicrosa, "La introducción del cuadrante con cursor en Europa," *Isis* 17 (1932), 228.

[348] D. E. Smith and L. C. Karpinski, *The Hindu-Arabic Numerals* (Boston, 1911), 99.

[349] P. Tannery, "La géometrie au XIe siècle," *Mémoires scientifiques*, ed. J.-L. Heiberg and H.-G. Zeuthen, vol. 5 (Toulouse, 1922), 79-102.

[350] M. Folkerts, *"Boethius" Geometrie II* (Wiesbaden, 1970), ix-x.

[351] Cf. L. Mumford, *Technics and Civilization* (New York, 1963), 12-18.

Were these cultural changes the concomitants of deeper mutations in economy and society? A facile equation between material and non-material culture, as noted, is inadmissible. And parallels, where they occur, cannot be separated from their historical contexts, which include, of course, contemporary explanations for the changes themselves.

If a generalization is to be proposed, it would have to speak of a new system of exchange and communication, equally effective in economic, social, and cultural relations. Coinage appeared in quantity; markets surfaced in nascent commercial centres; prices began more and more to be determined by supply and demand; and men gradually distinguished between inherited status and contractual obligations. Money, in other words, or commodities with a monetary value, emerged as the chief force for objectifying economic concerns,[352] just as, in the cultural sphere, the written text helped to isolate what man thought about from his processes of thinking.

The use of coinage grew throughout the twelfth and thirteenth centuries; it was slowed only by the protracted economic decline preceding the Black Death.[353] Similarly, written literature and other aspects of cultural life dependent on texts gradually increased their range and depth. By the end of the Middle Ages, men had begun to think of the economy as an instituted process,[354] just as they thought of cultural continuity as being preserved by records. The shift in literature can be seen in miniature in the difference between the *Chanson de Roland* and Chrétien de Troyes. In the *Chanson*, the speeches are reflections of formerly defined, often inviolable human relations, either between members of a family or within a fixed social hierarchy; in Chrétien, they are autonomous elements in their own right, reflecting personal interaction as it is conceived and interpreted in the minds of individual characters. As such, they can be divorced from their speakers, thought about independently, and made the basis for an exchange of opinions.[355] The later eleventh and twelfth centuries, it is arguable, not only saw the rise of commercial methods for dealing with goods

[352] On rates of monetization, see the contributions to *Moneta e scambi nell'alto medioevo* (Spoleto, 1961); on monetization and intellectual history, A. Murray, *Reason and Society*, part I, pp. 25-137.

[353] M. M. Postan, "The Rise of a Money Economy," *Essays on Medieval Agriculture and General Problems of the Medieval Economy* (Cambridge, 1973), 28.

[354] K. Polanyi, "The Economy as an Instituted Process," in K. Polanyi, C. M. Arensberg, and H. W. Pearson, eds., *Trade and Market in Early Empires* (New York, 1957), 253-54. Cf. M. Nash, *Primitive and Peasant Economic Systems* (Scranton, Penn., 1966), 26-33.

[355] Cf. R. Hanning. *The Individual in Twelfth-Century Romance* (New Haven, 1977), ch. 1.

and services. For the first time since antiquity Europe witnessed the existence of a disinterested market of ideas, for which the essential prerequisite was a system of communication based on texts. The logical product of the literate organization and classification of knowledge was the scholastic system, just as the market was the natural instrument for the distribution of commodities regulated by prices.

The economic did not precede or underlie the cultural transformations. Both functioned side by side, and the new was often camouflaged in the vocabulary of the old. Abstract market relations were disguised as human relations; an archaic terminology of barter and gift was retained in both feudalism and literature.[356] But, beneath the surface, the value of goods was being determined increasingly by the laws of supply and demand. Even at the upper end of the social scale, where the unlimited capacity to consume was an important proof of membership, the "censing" of the reserve, the appearance of "bannal" feudalism, and the disappearance of the nomadic way of life gradually eroded the economy of barter, gift, reciprocity, and redistribution. The old formulae retained their appeal, but they less and less accurately described everyday economic exchange. The economy, although not recognized as such, became one of producers and consumers. Through analogous principles a new type of discourse evolved for communicating between individuals. Like the economy, it was governed by a set of abstract rules, which, like prices, were largely independent of human control. Literacy, like the market, insured that an entity external to the parties in a given interchange—the text—would ultimately provide the criteria for an agreed meaning. Just as the market created a level of "abstract entities" and "model relations" between producer and consumer, literacy created a set of lexical and syntactical structures which made the persona of the speaker largely irrelevant.

As a result, a formerly qualitatively structured society began to show signs of quantitative structuring. Moral, economic, and social decisions began to appear in separate contexts. The economy was still very largely a substantive process, but formalization could be felt just beneath the surface of the increasing legalism of property relations. The power over the concrete which abstraction yields was visible in the new optimism of "conquering nature" as well as in the rise of logico-empirical rationalism in law, philosophy, and theology. On the one hand, the forces governing man's life were no longer conceived in

---

[356] Cf. G. Duby, *La société aux XI et XII siècles dans la région mâconnaise*, 2nd ed. (Paris, 1971), 348-63.

purely objective terms. Man, as a consequence, was not the passive
receptacle of natural or divine judgments; he could understand and
therefore alter the everyday world in which he lived; the weight of
decision-making was partly shifted to his own shoulders. But, as his
notion of objectivity changed, an archaic form of subjectivity also
began to wane. The transfer of effective control from the supernatural
to the more mundane world of law, institutions, and administration,
while offering new freedoms, also brought with it the knowledge that
social relations, formerly governed by subjective considerations, could
be thought of in objective terms as well. Alienation once again became a topic of discussion. Man, so to speak, not only anguished over
a new separation from the paradise of familial relations in Eden, which
were oral, intimate, and free from interpretive superstructures. Texts,
as Hugh of St. Victor suggested, or rather, where, reading, study, and meditation based upon them, offered him a technical instrument for helping to restore the lost spiritual unity with God.

II.

TEXTUAL COMMUNITIES

Et, quid dicam? Non id idiotae faciunt, sed
doctores Christianorum, rectores plebium, et ita,
quodammodo obcaecati omnium radice malorum,
pauperes Christi ad inopiam pertrahunt.

—Abbo of Fleury, *Ep.* 14

An important consequence of literacy in any human community arises
from the area of social organization. Relationships between the individual and the family, the group, or the wider community are all
influenced by the degree to which society acknowledges written principles of operation. Literacy also affects the way people conceptualize
such relations, and these patterns of thought inevitably feed back into
the network of real interdependencies.

A branch of this general field of inquiry concerns the manner in
which the rise of literacy interacted historically with the formation of
heretical or reformist religious groups. From the eleventh century such
groups began to play the role of laboratories of social organization,
attempting both to improve their own communities and to offer a
model of betterment to society at large. Heretics and reformers of
course differed in their attitudes towards authority and the official
church. But their uses of literacy were similar: in particular, both
resorted to textual precedents for justifying deviations from what were
considered to be merely customary or unwritten ecclesiastical norms.
The practices and beliefs against which they reacted were not always
as unsupported by earlier legislation, as they maintained. But that
was how they were perceived; and it was the perception of tradition
rather than objective considerations which determined the future course
of the dissenters' activities.

The present chapter is not a comprehensive survey of heresy and
reform but rather a series of case histories. The material itself is drawn
from two groups of sources: (1) a relatively isolated series of heresies
arising roughly between the millennium and 1050 and (2) the Patarene movement in the diocese of Milan between 1057 and 1075. More
specifically, the first group consists of the heresies at Orléans in 1022,

at Arras in 1025, and at Monforte in 1028, as well as episodes of dissidence involving Leutard, a Marne peasant, and Wazo of Liège. The second part of the chapter is concerned with a single reform movement, the early Pataria, as seen through the eyes of Arnulf of Milan, Landulf Senior, and Andrew of Strumi. In order to illustrate the thesis that literacy influenced group organization, it should be stressed, the examination of heresy and reform is not the only possibility. Many other movements present themselves, orthodox religious orders such as Cluny, for instance, or the communal guilds of Italy and the Low Countries. Heretics and reformers, however, provide particular advantages for this study. The texts are reasonable in length, and therefore the attitudes towards literacy can easily be compared. More importantly, the activists raise issues which are debated in other areas of eleventh-century intellectual life. A comparison of methods is thereby suggested between disciplines.

In what follows, I have drawn liberally on the work of my predecessors. However, I have also employed a type of analysis not often used in the study of heresy and reform. This demands a word of explanation.

In general, the accounts of early heresy and the Pataria are viewed simultaneously in an historical and a literary perspective. The normal historical approach is to compare differing versions of the same set of events in order to elicit a core of irrefutable fact. The text is thereby regarded as a source of information. However, the accounts are also works of narrative art. In this capacity they operate on two levels: they tell us about the narrator's point of view, and, if a movement is recorded in more than one place, they paint different pictures of how the individuals activating it looked upon each other. Of course, both historical and literary methods inform us about the uses of literacy. But in at least two respects literary analysis provides insights which a purely historical reduction overlooks. One arises from the non-factual, inconsistent, or erroneous material in an account, which, while useless for historical purposes, may shed valuable light on problems of communication, or, at the very least, on the narrator's interpretation of them. The other arises from whether the elements making up the texts themselves come from oral or written originals. In view of such issues, each account of heresy and reform in what follows is considered both as a repository of historical facts and as a rhetorically constructed text. Each is provided with a literal summary; only after a basic meaning and point of view are established are broader interpretive questions raised.

The conclusions reached through this dual approach can be put quite simply. Eleventh-century dissenters may not have shared profound doctrinal similarities or common social origins, but they demonstrated a parallel use of texts, both to structure the internal behaviour of the groups' members and to provide solidarity against the outside world.

In this sense they were "textual communities." The term is used in a descriptive rather than a technical sense; it is intended to convey not a new methodology but a more intensive use of traditional methods, and, in particular, their use by groups hitherto dependent on oral participation in religion. What was essential to a textual community was not a written version of a text, although that was sometimes present, but an individual, who, having mastered it, then utilized it for reforming a group's thought and action. The text's interpreter might, like St. Bernard, remain a charismatic figure in his own right, whose power to motivate groups derived from his oratory, gestures, and physical presence. Yet the organizational principles of movements like the Cistercians were clearly based on texts, which played a predominant role in the internal and external relationships of the members. The outside world was looked upon as a universe beyond the revelatory text; it represented a lower level of literacy and by implication of spirituality. Within the movement, texts were steps, so to speak, by which the individual climbed towards a perfection thought to represent complete understanding and effortless communication with God. Also, if a reformist group organized itself around a primitive text, let us say the words of Jesus or St. Paul, it could, by invoking precedent, demand that society as a whole abandon "customary" principles of moral conduct and adopt a more rigorously ascetic model. The inevitable result was conflict, either within religious communities or in society at large.

How do these issues relate to the broader question of literacy? In general, the chief areas affected were orality, symbolism, and ritual. No heretical or reform movement was "popular" in the sense of reflecting the orality which literates associated with illiteracy. Heretics and reformers did not as a rule come from the less educated sectors of society and represent folk or customary practices. Heretics in particular provided a cutting edge for literacy: their criticisms were directed towards the miraculous, the sacramental, and what they considered to be superstitious lore. Reformers, too, sought a textual basis for relics, the cults of saints, and liturgical practice. Although directed towards different objects, both critiques held ramifications for symbolism and ritual. Physical symbolism of the type represented by feudal *traditio* was debased, and along with it all verbalistic, formalistic, or purely ceremonial traditions. A new sort of symbolism took their place, one which, as Augustine so aptly put it, distinguished between the *sacramentum* and the *res sacramenti*, that is, between figure and truth, the visible and the invisible. Such a distinction, of course, was unthinkable without a resort to the intellectual structures of allegory, which were in turn a byproduct of the literate sensibility. For, to find an inner meaning, one first had to understand the notion of a text *ad litteram*. Ritual, too, underwent a transformation. Archaic ritualism needed no interpretation; the meaning arose from the acting out or performing of events. This sort of ritual was replaced by a complex set of interactions between members of groups which were in large part structured by texts, or, at the very least, by individuals' interpretations of them. They were rituals of everyday life, that is, the acting out of specified roles. The same general principle, say the *Benedictine Rule*, could be adapted to different situations and used over and over again.

Finally, the textual community was not only textual; it also involved new uses for orality. The text itself, whether it consisted of a few maxims or an elaborate programme, was often re-performed orally. Indeed, one of the clearest signs that a group had passed the threshold of literacy was the lack of necessity for the organizing text to be spelt out, interpreted, or reiterated. The members all knew what it was. As a consequence, interaction by word of mouth could take place as a superstructure of an agreed meaning, the textual foundation of behaviour having been entirely internalized. With shared assumptions, the members were free to discuss, to debate, or to disagree on other matters, to engage in personal interpretations of the Bible or to some degree in individualized meditation and worship. And the uses of what was so to speak a literate's orality could be extended beyond the group, mainly by preaching. If this were done, a two-tiered structure resulted: a small inner core of literates, semi-literates, and non-literates followed the interpretation of the text itself. But the literates within the heretical or reform group could also preach outside it to nonliterates whose only bond with the founders was by word of mouth. Yet, these nonliterates had already begun to participate in literate culture, although indirectly. They were made aware that a text lay behind a sermon and they were given an indirect understanding of the principles of authentication, that is, of legal precedence and legitimation through writing. Although remaining unlettered, they could thereby comprehend how one set of moral principles could logically supersede another. In a sense, it was they rather than the spectacular leaders of movements who were the real avatars of change.

1. LITERACY AND EARLY HERESY

Introduction

Before we turn to eleventh-century heresy and reform, something must be also said about the historiography of the field of medieval dissidence. Theories of heresy's "origins" in particular have been part of medieval studies for over a century. What can the study of literacy contribute to the debate?

The traditional framework for discussion—orthodoxy versus heresy—was laid down in the Middle Ages itself, along with subjective explanations of heresy's beginnings which survived the medieval period and resurfaced, little changed, in post-Reformation Catholic and Protestant thought.[1] The growth of history as a professional discipline in the nineteenth century brought with it the first scientific investigation of the documentary sources for medieval sectarianism. But the critical editing of old texts and the bringing to light of new ones did not make the origins of heresy any easier to decipher. They merely complicated existing explanations, shifting the energies of researchers away from the apparently intractable problems of interpretation into the more manageable areas of dating, provenance, and institutional association. Over a hundred years of continuous publication has succeeded in delimiting the study of heresy as a field of historical inquiry, within which the participants recognize established subspecialties and common internalist hypotheses.[2] But there have been some unwanted

[1] For a general review of early theories, see J. Russell, "Interpretations of the Origins of Medieval Heresy," *Mediaeval Studies* 25 (1963), 26-53. On Catharism in particular, see A. Borst, *Die Katharer* (Stuttgart, 1953), 1-58. More recent literature is discussed by M. Lambert, *Medieval Heresy. Popular Movements from Bogomil to Hus* (London, 1977), 3-36. (In part one of this chapter, these and other frequently cited secondary sources are referred to by author and date after the first reference.)

[2] The literature on medieval heresy is large, and no attempt can be made to summarize it fully here. Two recent reviews of eleventh-century dissidence with full bibliographies are J. Musy, "Mouvements populaires et hérésies au XIe siècle en France," *Revue historique* 253 (1975), 33-76, and, for Italy, G. Cracco, "Riforma ed eresia in momenti della cultura europea tra X e XI secolo," *Rivista di storia e letteratura religiosa* 7 (1971), 411-77. The issues are also thoroughly reviewed by R. I. Moore, *The Origins of European Dissent* (London, 1977), 1-45. An essential compilation of secondary works is H. Grundmann, *Bibliographie zur Ketzergeschichte des Mittelalters (1900-1966)* (Rome, 1967), supplemented by "Neue Beiträge zur Geschichte der religiösen

byproducts. One is the complexity of the theories themselves. It is almost as difficult for the uninitiated to study interpretations of heresy's origins as to study heresy itself. Another problem has arisen from the failure to look critically at the nature of the theories. From a philosophical point of view many of them are dramatically simple. Indeed, although twentieth-century fieldwork has moved in the direction of an enlightened eclecticism, which employs elements of earlier theories but does not acknowledge any of them as having a monopoly of truth, a single grand scheme remains the overtly stated goal of much study.

The proliferation of books and articles on the subject has also camouflaged the fact that, broadly speaking, there have been only two major approaches over the years. One concerns the possible "social origins" of medieval heretical beliefs (and, by implication, of reform as well). The other deals with sectarianism as a phenomenon more or less limited to the field of religion. The one is largely externalist in orientation, the other internalist. From time to time the two have been intelligently combined. But no reworking of the debate on "origins" as a whole or monographic study within it has succeeded in establishing a universally acceptable cultural anthropology of dissidence.

There are really two forms of the thesis on the alleged social, economic, and political origins of heresy, although the distinction is not always recognized by medievalists. A radical version, urged by Engels, Kautsky, and later Marxist writers, sees heresy as an expression of the medieval class struggle which opposed the feudal aristocracy, the nascent bourgeoisie, and the peasantry.[3] Medieval historians have generally rejected this approach as an overall interpretation, preferring

Bewegungen im Mittelalter," reprinted with additions in the same author's *Ausgewählte Aufsätze*, vol. 1 (Stuttgart, 1976), 38-92. For more recent studies, see C. T. Berkout and J. B. Russell, *Medieval Heresies. A Bibliography 1960-1979* (Toronto, 1981). Other important reviews of the issues include: Ilarino da Milano, "Le eresie populari del secolo XI nell'Europa occidentale," *Studi gregoriani* 2 (1947), 43-89; J. B. Russell, *Dissent and Reform in the Early Middle Ages* (Berkeley, 1965), 5-53; W. L. Wakefield and A. P. Evans, "A Historical Sketch of Medieval Popular Heresies," in *Heresies of the High Middle Ages* (New York, 1969), 1-55; R. I. Moore, "The Origins of Medieval Heresy," *History* 55 (1970), 21-36; and H. Taviani, "Naissance d'une hérésie en Italie du Nord au XIe siècle," *Annales, E.S.C.*, 29 (1974), 1224-52. A highly influential early synthesis was that of G. Volpe, *Movimenti religiosi e sette ereticali nella società medievale italiana, secoli XI-XIV* (Florence, 1922), esp. pp. 5-78.

[3] For a recent restatement, see E. Werner and M. Erbstösser, "Sozial-religiöse Bewegungen im Mittelalter," *Wissenschaftliche Zeitschrift der Karl-Marx Universität* 7 (1957-58), 257-82; G. Koch, *Frauenfrage und Ketzertum im Mittelalter* (Berlin, 1962); E. Werner, *Häresie und Gesellschaft im 11. Jahrhundert* (Sitzungsberichte der sächsischen Akademie der Wissenschaften zu Leipzig, Philol.-hist. Kl., 117.5, 1975).

instead to situate class conflict within a wider spectrum of causal factors and to examine each claim in the light of available evidence. Yet, they have failed to give an adequate hearing to a more subtle argument, which, while not denying heresy's essentially religious character, sees social forces in a broader perspective either as contributing factors or as unintentional byproducts. The most influential statement of this view was made by Gioacchino Volpe and was popularized outside Italy by Ernst Troeltsch, who translated from early articles portions of Volpe's study of "religious movements and heretical sects in medieval Italian society" for his widely read *Social Teachings of the Christian Churches*.[4] Troeltsch used Volpe's research to build a bridge between two different sorts of problems, one sociological and another historical, which he effectively united by speaking on the one hand of "orthodoxy" and "heresy" and on the other of "church" and "sect." The latter categories he borrowed from his colleague Max Weber, whose "ideal types" he reduced to much less flexible instruments of analysis.

Despite a somewhat anachronistic search for the roots of Protestantism, Troeltsch laid down a number of canonical distinctions between church and sect as categories of religious grouping which have in one form or another served as guideposts to research ever since.[5] In his view, the pair were both opposed and yet complementary. The church was hierarchic and conservative; it dominated the masses, usually in co-operation with the "ruling classes" whose interests it served. The sect was egalitarian and democratic; it was a smaller body, most often composed of the socially and economically underprivileged. It stressed "inward perfection" and "personal fellowship." If the church aspired to subdue the world and to use it to its ends, the sect looked upon the world with hostility, tolerance, or even indifference. The church, working downward from above, saw itself as "the objective organization of miraculous power." The sect, working from below, was a "voluntary association" based on the free adherence of its members. A person was born into a church, but he joined a sect. A church, while approving of good works, ultimately demanded only that the

---

[4] *Die Soziallehren der christlichen Kirchen und Gruppen (Gesammelte Schriften* 1, Tübingen, 1923), 383-89; Eng. trans., O. Wyon, repr. (New York, 1960), 349-58. For Troeltsch's place in German sociological thought, see C. Antoni, *From History to Sociology. The Transition in German Historical Thinking*, trans. H. V. White (London, 1962), 39-85. More recent assessments include J. P. Clayton, ed., *Troeltsch and the Future of Theology* (London, 1976) and R. Morgan and M. Pye, eds., *Ernst Troeltsch. Writings on Theology and Religion* (London, 1977).

[5] Summarizing *Die Soziallehren*, ch. 2.9, pp. 360-77; trans., 331-43.

individual acknowledge its universal capacity for administering grace. The sect by contrast compelled its members to take an active part in communal religious life, which was rich in interpersonal relations. The church embodied such relationships in an "objective" framework which stressed transcendence from the impermanent conditions of the world. It thus placed less weight on individual methods of purification and more on the status or grade of the individual within an ecclesiastical organization. The whole secular order was in fact conceived as a means of preparing for the eternal life. The contrast, Troeltsch believed, could easily be perceived in the differing attitudes towards asceticism. In the church's view, asceticism was just one of the factors capable of raising man upwards towards the divine. In the sect's view, the individual could not achieve salvation without withdrawing completely from the world. The partially world-renouncing asceticism of the church naturally led to the institution of monasticism, while the uncompromising form practiced by the sect was directed towards such antisocial activities as refusing to obey laws, to swear oaths, to govern others, to own property, or to defend oneself by arms. Despite his emphasis on social factors, Troeltsch did not argue that heresies were socially determined. He maintained that they sprang into existence when social and economic conditions created the possibility. Their ultimate origins, like their objectives, were religious.[6]

Troeltsch's views are taken seriously today only as part of the classical theory of church and sect.[7] Yet they possess one advantage over many studies of heresy by better informed professional medievalists. Like Weber, Troeltsch admitted no artificial barriers between "social" and "religious" spheres of life, a position recently vindicated in a remarkable case-study by E. Le Roy Ladurie.[8] Yet, this perspective was not widely acknowledged by early critics of the thesis on heresy's alleged social origins. As a consequence, the theory's afterlife is more complicated than it might otherwise have been. On the one hand, the initial insights were never fully pursued. What developed over time was an unofficial division of labour between historians of society and of religion. The latter concentrated their efforts on demolition: medieval dissenters were shown to have come from all strata of society,

---

[6] *Ibid.*, 370; trans., 336.

[7] Cf. B. R. Wilson, *Religious Sects. A Sociological Study* (London, 1970), 22-25.

[8] *Montaillou, village occitan de 1294 à 1324* (Paris, 1975). For somewhat different assessments of the book's value, see N. Z. Davis, "Les conteurs de Montaillou," *Annales, E.S.C.*, 34 (1979), 61-73 and L. E. Boyle, "Montaillou Revisited: *Mentalité* and Methodology," in J. A. Raftis, ed., *Pathways to Medieval Peasants* (Toronto, 1982), pp. 119-40.

and their motives, when examined in the light of their own statements, were found to be overwhelmingly religious. Criticism of earlier sociological interpretations was synthesized in Herbert Grundmann's massive *Religiöse Bewegungen im Mittelalter* (1935), which was
a watershed in the field's burgeoning literature. Grundmann started
from the position that "all religious movements of the Middle Ages
were based on religious orders or heretical sects."[9] Despite an unparalleled command of the primary sources, he thereby reasserted the
traditional division between orthodoxy and heresy, merely replacing
an intellectual with an institutional centre of focus. He said nothing
new about social organization as such. Sociologically inclined historians, while accepting the critique of determinism, were reluctant to
yield to an intellectualist position. But they had nothing to put in its
place. The fate of the Troeltsch-Weberian hypotheses was predictable.
At the first international congress devoted to heresy after World War
II (1955), the thesis on heresy's social origins was treated inconclu-
sively.[10] A similar indecisiveness emerged from the Royaumont colloquium of 1962, which was specifically concerned with "heresies and
societies in preindustrial Europe between the eleventh and eighteenth
centuries."[11]

If we turn from these general approaches to the birth of sectarianism after the millennium, the divisions of the field can be brought
into closer focus. When applied to the evidence, the theories have
above all else attempted to find some sort of coherence in the outbreak
and spread of heterodox beliefs. Many methods of organization have
been tried: simple chronology or geography, or, in more synthetic
approaches, comparisons of points of genesis, lines of communication,
and interrelationships on western soil. The accounts of medieval
chroniclers have also been scrutinized for stylistic similarities. Yet, in
imitation of the wider debate, two means of giving shape to the meagre
source material have generally been preferred above others. On the
one hand, attempts have been made to trace the social origins of the

---

[9] *Religiöse Bewegungen im Mittelalter* (Berlin, 1935), 5.
[10] *Relazioni del X Congresso Internazionale di Scienze Storiche, Roma, 4-11 sett.*, 1955, vol. 3:
Storia del medioevo (Florence, 1955), 307-541.
[11] J. Le Goff, ed., *Hérésies et sociétés dans l'Europe pré-industrielle, 11e-18e siècles* (Paris and The
Hague, 1968). For somewhat similar conclusions, compare A. P. Evans, "Social Aspects of
Medieval Heresy," in *Persecution and Liberty: Essays in Honour of George Lincoln Burr* (New York,
1931), 115; J. Russell (1963), 32-33; Wakefield and Evans (1969), 4; M. Lambert (1976), xiv;
and R. I. Moore (1977), 265-70.

dissenters; on the other, common ground has been sought in their beliefs, rites, and other practices.

Neither of these approaches, nor for that matter any combination of them, has won unanimous support. No one doubts the influence of social factors in the broadest sense.[12] The problems begin when we look for the social origins of the dissenters themselves. If the early eleventh century is used as a laboratory, the results confirm no single hypothesis. Many were peasants: Leutard was a *homo plebeius*, his converts, *rustici*.[13] But others were not. Vilgard was a student or teacher, possibly a *grammaticus*.[14] His audience was composed of townsmen in Ravenna. We know little of Wecelino, who converted to Judaism in 1005, save that he was educated,[15] and even less of similar converts at Mainz in 1012.[16] Ademar of Chabannes mentions neither the social nor economic background of the *Manichei* who were found in the Aquitanian countryside from 1017,[17] *seducentes plebem*. Those brought to light at Toulouse in 1022 he labelled the *nuntii Antichristi*.[18] The several versions of the synod at Orléans tell us little more. The heretics came, John of Ripoll states, *de melioribus clericis sive de melioribus laicis*.[19] The seeds were sown by Lisois, a canon of the cathedral of Ste.-Croix, and by Stephen, the superior of the college of St.-Pierre-le-Puellier and confessor to queen Constance.[20] The heresy was first noticed by Arefast, who was descended from the dukes of Normandy, and it was brought into his house by a *clericus* called Herbert, who claimed to have been taught by Stephen and Lisois.[21]

Even this level of information is exceptional. The heretics drawn to the attention of the bishop of Arras and Cambrai in 1025 were described only as *viri*. Their trial was conducted before a "multitude" of both *cleri* and *populi*.[22] Their leader, Gundulfo, was given no social

[12] Cf. R. Morghen, "Problèmes sur l'origine de l'hérésie au Moyen Age," *Revue historique* 336 (1966), 10.

[13] Rodulf Glaber, *Historiae* 2.9.22, ed. M. Prou, p. 49.

[14] *Ibid.*, 1.12.23, p. 50.

[15] Alpertus, *De Diversitate Temporum*, c. 1, MGH SS 4, 704; cf. Ilarino da Milano (1947), 50.

[16] *Annales Quedlinburgensis*, an. 1012, MGH SS 3, 81; cf. Ilarino da Milano, *loc.cit.*

[17] *Chronicon*, 3.49, ed. J. Chavanon (Paris, 1897), 173.

[18] *Ibid.*, 3.59, p. 185.

[19] *Vita Gauzlini*, ed. R. H. Bautier and G. Labory (Paris, 1969), 180. Cf. *Chronicon S. Petri Senonensis*, RHF, 10, 224; *Chronicon Turonense*, *ibid.*, 284.

[20] Glaber, *Historiae* 3.8.27, p. 75.

[21] *Cartulaire de l'abbaye de saint-Père de Chartres*, ed. B. Guérard, ch. 3, p. 109.

[22] *Acta Synodi Atrebatensis*, c. 1, PL 142.1271A-B.

denomination. The hill-town visited by Aribert of Milan in 1028 was "full," Glaber reports, "of people of the highest quality."[23] But Landulf Senior, who provides a more accurate narrative of the events, is less willing to lump the heretics together in one social stratum. Gerard, their spokesman, was said to bear himself "with the greatest ease or readiness."[24] But was his confidence a reflection of his social station or his religious certitude? Among the converts to the new faith was the local countess.[25] But what of the others? Theoduin of Liège is no more instructive. He complained in 1048 of heretics whom he mistook for followers of Berengar. They were apparently spreading erroneous views "among all the faithful commoners."[26] But we do not learn what sort of persons they were. In short, as far as the evidence indicates, early eleventh-century dissenters were of both sexes and all social backgrounds. And they came from both near and afar.

The question of a common doctrinal orientation is more difficult to unravel as it preoccupied medieval commentators themselves. The conspiracy theory was popular, then as now. Yet, most modern scholars are disinclined to see a single, pronounced dogmatic thread running through the various outbreaks of heresy between 970 and 1048.[27] Certain ideas and practices were obviously held in common: negation of the trinity (Orléans, Monforte); rejection of the Old Testament (Leutard, Arras); aversion to the cross (Leutard, Aquitaine, Arras, Monforte); negation of baptism (Aquitaine, Orléans, Arras) and of confession (Orléans, Arras); and abstention from meat (Aquitaine, Orléans, Monforte, Châlons).[28] Chroniclers frequently speak of withdrawal from the institutionalized church and of disapproval of the ecclesiastical hierarchy.

However, despite whatever similarities exist, the instances of dissent have more than once been accurately assessed as "doctrinally idiosyncratic."[29] In particular, it is increasingly difficult to make a case for the traditional notion of an intercommunicating network of dualism. In the heresies at Toulouse, Goslar, Ravenna, Venice, and Ve-

[23] *Historiae* 4.2.5, p. 94.

[24] *Historia Mediolanensis* 2.27, MGH SS 8, p. 65, 31-32.

[25] *Ibid.*, 69.

[26] *Contra Brunonem et Berengarium Ep.*, PL 146.1440B.

[27] E.g., R. Manselli, *L'eresia del male* (Naples, 1963), 118-38; Russell (1965), 196-99; Moore (1970), 22-31; Musy (1975), 52.

[28] R. Morghen, "Il cosidetto neo-manicheismo occidentale del secolo XI," in *Oriente ed occidente nel Medio Evo* (Rome, 1957), 89-90. Cf. Musy (1975), 39-41 and Lambert (1977), Appendix D.

[29] Lambert (1977), 25.

rona, there is little or no indication of doctrinal orientation at all. The argument for or against eastern influence, and therefore, by implication, for a theory of ideological diffusion, rests on the evidence of Orléans in 1022, Arras in 1024-1025, and Liège around 1048. Dondaine assumed that these episodes demonstrated the presence of a well-articulated Bogomilism on western soil,[30] while Morghen and others maintained that the doctrines had no clearcut pattern.[31] In the words of H. C. Puech, "neither taken by themselves, nor juxtaposed in a somewhat artificial mosaic, do the texts of the first half of the eleventh century . . . imply without doubt that heterodox groups . . . were already influenced by Bogomilism."[32] To take Orléans as an instance, historians have concluded that the laying on of hands does not necessarily point to the Cathar *consolamentum*[33] and that the heretics' terms of reference, as revealed by Paul of St.-Père de Chartres, do not suggest anything stronger than "religious illuminism."[34] The so-called eastern dualism of many eleventh-century heretics may represent nothing more than a revival of ideas from the New Testament.[35] Of course, the introduction of eastern beliefs through Slav merchants or simply by word of mouth cannot be ruled out. Yet the "state of mind" of these ascetic, world-renouncing heretics is essentially western.[36]

Neither in their social origins, then, nor their doctrinal orientations, do early eleventh-century heretics appear to form an organized network of belief. We are therefore entitled to ask what they have in common besides proximity in time. The answer as suggested above is bound up with the rise of a more literate society.[37] Literacy, it should be stressed, should not be set up as a new *deus ex machina*, merely offering to the study of heresy and reform another oversimplified holistic theory. Yet, in two areas, an examination of problems of communication can shed valuable light.

The first concerns learned versus popular culture. The advent of literacy in oral culture undoubtedly changed the atmosphere of belief, and this was reflected in new distinctions between religious literates and nonliterates. These, in turn, implied a questioning of the status of popular culture. The notion of "popular" culture is of course not

[30] "L'origine de l'hérésie médiévale," *Rivista di storia della chiesa in Italia* 6 (1952), 47-78.

[31] Morghen (1957), 84-104; *idem* (1966), 1-16.

[32] "Catharisme médiéval et bogomilisme," in *Oriente ed occidente* . . . , 80.

[33] *Ibid.*, 72.   [34] Moore (1970), 25.   [35] Puech in *Oriente ed occidente* (1957), 82.

[36] Morghen (1966), 3, 4, 9.   [37] Cf. Moore (1977), 40-41, 244-45.

entirely satisfactory:[38] too often, popular is merely equated with lay belief, and there is an inevitable bias which arises from viewing popular piety through the lens of the official church, that is, in seeing it as an essentially passive receptacle of learned tradition. Given such presuppositions, it is of course legitimate to ask with Grundmann whether there were any "popular" medieval heretics besides Peter Waldo who actually inspired substantial religious movements.[39] But the problem cannot be posed in these terms alone, since they make the consequences of scribal culture the origin of the communities which in turn depend upon it.[40] If one begins the investigation at the point at which the first so-called "popular heresies" make their appearance—that is, shortly after the millennium—another perspective is suggested. Before literacy has made a significant impact on everyday religious practices, there is little purpose in making a distinction between learned and popular at all, that is, outside narrowly restricted, educated circles. There are no "survivals" of popular culture, only living realities, which, like the "real presence" in the eucharist, are accepted without comment or interpretation, their symbolic and ritualistic capacity to convey meaning remaining intact. When literacy emerges as an issue, popular religion also surfaces, just as illiteracy is the invariable consequence of literacy itself. The change is not only in the structure of beliefs but also in the manner in which different individuals or groups perceive them to be communicated. As the written word influences behaviour in general, so it textually orients the content of faith.

As a result, the "social" factor emerges in a new context. The traditional approach is to trace the background of the dissidents, assuming that the formative experience takes place before the individual

[38] For an expression of similar views, see N. Z. Davis, "Some Themes in the Study of Popular Religion," in C. Trinkaus and H. Oberman, eds., *The Pursuit of Holiness in Late Medieval and Renaissance Religion* (Leiden, 1974), 308-09; J. C. Schmitt, " 'Religion populaire' et culture folklorique," *Annales, E.S.C.*, 31 (1976), 941-53; C. Ginzburg, *Il formaggio et i vermi*, (Turin, 1976), xii-xiv; and J. Le Goff, *Pour un autre Moyen Âge*, 13-15 *et passim*. A more general review is A. Vauchez, "La piété populaire au moyen âge. Etat des travaux et position des problèmes," *La piété populaire au moyen âge*, 27-42, and *idem, La sainteté en Occident* (Rome, 1981), 173-287. A somewhat different perspective is taken by D. Illmer, *Formen und Erziehung*, ch. 6, pp. 180-89: Religiöse Erziehung und Akkulturation; and, on the relevance of the term popular in later antiquity, see the queries raised by P. Brown, *The Cult of Saints* (Chicago, 1981), 13-22.

[39] H. Grundmann, "Hérésies savantes et hérésies populaires au moyen âge," in Le Goff (1968), 210.

[40] On the later development, see M. Aston, "Lollardy and Literacy," *History* 62 (1977), 347-71.

enters a heretical cell and that his sense of solidarity is based upon a previously developed, commonly held need. However, membership in any group proceeds in stages. The familial, institutional, intellectual, or "class" bonds of the individual before joining are only the point of departure. In many cases the process of socialization continues within the group and arises, as suggested, from patterns of interaction with the other members. This period of education helps to determine later behaviour (and may, as well, influence the reinterpretation of earlier events). Above all, it is instrumental in the decision to rejoin the world, to reject it outright, or to try to alter it by radical methods. Group interaction also illuminates doctrinal dissemination. Only rarely is an idea utilized by a small voluntary association simply because it has deep historical roots. It must also respond to a problem in the here and now: in that sense, all dissident movements, whether heretical or reformist, are contemporaneous phenomena, no matter how they historicize their origins. But, for the fundamental, institution-building activity to take place, it is arguable, previous experience, both social and intellectual, in a community developing literate sensibilities, must be rendered as a "text," which, at that point, stands at the nexus of thought and action, whether it exists in written form, or, having been internalized, is merely presented verbally. Understanding heresy and reform, therefore, as both historical and social phenomena, must go beyond doctrinal questions and come to grips with the transformative power of such "writings," together with the role of hermeneutics and interpretation. For, within the small group, one's daily activities are structured according to such precepts. Behavioural norms are existential glosses on real or putative documents. They are part of the movement which binds the text, the speech-act, and the deed.

Leutard

One of the earliest episodes of dissidence in Latin sources after the millennium foreshadows the use of texts in later heretical groups. There is only one account, and Leutard, a peasant from Vertus on the Marne, is described as acting alone. Let us first summarize Glaber's narrative,[41] then analyse its details in depth.

The story runs as follows. Leutard, worn out from his labours, one day fell asleep in a field and dreamt that a swarm of bees, entering his body through his genitals, gradually made their way out through

[41] *Historiae* 2.11.22, pp. 49-50.

his mouth, tormenting him all the while internally with their stings. After a time it seemed that the bees were trying to tell him to perform acts normally forbidden to laymen. Emotionally drained by the experience, Leutard returned home; then, as if possessed, he divorced his wife, and, proceeding to the local church, ripped down the cross and smashed the likeness of Christ. The onlookers, simple folk like himself, trembled with fear, thinking him mad. But he persuaded them he was acting in accordance with God's revelation. He told them as well not to pay tithes, and declared that in his view the biblical prophets had inserted "falsehoods" among their "useful statements." Within a short time his reputation had spread far and wide, finally reaching the ears of Gebuin, the local bishop, who had Leutard brought before him. When interrogated, Leutard denied in particular that he had interpreted Scripture for himself. But Gebuin was not fooled and pronounced him a heretic. He then recalled Leutard's followers from error and re-established their faith. Deprived of his supporters, Leutard threw himself in a well and drowned.

This episode, which has been paraphrased as far as possible in Glaber's own words, has usually been interpreted in one of two ways, either as an early instance of Cathar dualism[42] or as a sign of opposition to the nascent feudal system.[43] Neither reading does justice to the narrative's internal features. There is presumably a substratum of historical fact—the central events, perhaps, and the geographical setting. But the story, which is probably the revision of an oral account, proceeds largely in images and symbols. If its meaning is to be made clear, these must not be overlooked.

The key lies in the swarm of bees. They are of course traditional: their chastity is mentioned as early as Vergil and Pliny,[44] and recurs frequently in patristic writing.[45] The notion passed into the *exultet* of the Easter mass, which perhaps provided the story's direct inspira-

[42] Borst (1953), 73&n.

[43] R. Fossier, "Les mouvements populaires en Occident au XIe siècle," *Académie des Inscriptions et Belles-Lettres. Comptes rendus . . . 1971*, p. 259.

[44] *Georgics* 4.198-201; *Hist. Nat.*, 11.16. Contemporaneous medieval examples include Fulbert of Chartres, *Sermo* 3, PL 141.319D and, in the context of heresy, Landulf's account of Monforte, *Historia Mediolanensis* 3.26, MGH SS 8, p. 93, 47-48. The medieval interpretation was summed up by Rather of Verona, *Praeloquia* 1.8, PL 136.155A: "Et certe apes semina filiorum non coeundo concipiunt, sed tanquam sparsa per terras ore colligunt. Invisibilium enim seminum creator, ipse creator est rerum omnium."

[45] E.g., Ambrose, *Hexameron* 5.21.67-68, CSEL 32.1, 189-90; on which see Taviani (1974), 1232 and nn. 42-44.

tion.[46] But, in addition, there is another sense suggested by an earlier tale possessing similar contours. Gregory of Tours tells of a woodcutter who was likewise surrounded, in his case by a swarm of flies.[47] For two years afterwards he was mad; then, donning animal skins, he took up a hermit's life and began to deliver regular "prophecies." Shortly thereafter he left his retreat and, accompanied by a "sister" whom he called Mary, he went about the countryside around Le Puy. Before being murdered by a local priest he had created a following of over three thousand. The tale is unlike Glaber's except in connecting physical symbols with the idea of large number. In the story of Leutard, the bees, as a consequence, may at once represent (1) chastity, (2) diabolical instructions which enter the body by way of its inferior parts and proceed to the microcosm's celestial ones, and (3) the future rise of a mass movement, based in this case on erroneous doctrine. The last sense is suggested outside a heretical context by a number of contemporary analogues, which also refer indirectly to monastic *lectio* and *meditatio*.[48] For example, men were said to rush to Richard of St. Vannes "like bees flying to their hives."[49] Similar phrases were associated with Notker, the popular bishop of Liège from 972 to 1008.[50]

Should Leutard, then, be viewed as a "heretic," or, as Glaber would like us to see him, as a reviver of ancient heresies, or simply as an illumined layman, a self-styled interpreter and propagator of Scripture,[51] who is "called" to perform the Lord's work?

The case for the last view is strengthened if one looks more closely

---

[46] Cf. C. Violante, *La società milanese nell'età precomunale*, 2nd ed. (Bari, 1974), 220n30. On the variant texts of the *laus apis* in the *exultet* rolls, see J. M. Pinell, "La bendiccio del ciri pasqual i els seus textos," *Liturgica* 2 (1958), 33-35.

[47] *Historia Francorum* 10.25, PL 71.556C-557C; discussed by P. Alphandéry, "De quelques faits de prophétisme dans les sectes latines antérieures au joachisme," *Revue de l'histoire des religions* 52 (1905), 179.

[48] E.g., *Vita S. Aderaldi*, c. 3, AASS October, vol. 8, 990E: "(Aderaldus) . . . ut apis sedula et argumentosa. . . . On *lectio* and *meditatio*," see John of St. Arnulf's life of John of Gorze, c. 80, PL 137.280D. On the bee as a symbol of the word or of divine illumination, the medieval position was well put by Bernard of Clairvaux, *Sermones super Cantica* 8.4.6, *Opera*, ed. J. Leclercq *et al.*, vol. 1 (Rome, 1957), 39, 24-26: "Est Spiritus quippe sapientiae et intellectus, qui instar apis ceram portantis et mel, habet omnino et unde accendat lumen scientiae, et unde infundat saporem gratiae."

[49] *Vita S. Richardi* 2.15, AASS 14 June, vol. 3, 459A.

[50] Anselm of Liège, *Gesta Episcoporum Leodiensis*, c. 40, MGH SS 7, p. 211. Examples of later uses include Baldric of Dole, *Vita B. Roberti de Arbrisello*, c. 2.12, PL 162.1050B-C; c. 3.19, *ibid.*, 1053C; and Orderic Vitalis, *Historia Ecclesiastica*, bk. 5, vol. 3, p. 172, from the will of Peter of Maule of 1076.

[51] Cf. Moore (1977), 35, who intelligently relates Glaber's ideas on insanity to literacy.

at the oral and written elements in the account, the one being a product of hearsay, the other Glaber's attempt to fit the events into a conventional framework. The short text can in fact be divided into the two: the learned version begins with the mention of the devil's legate (line 3), an obvious interpolation by the chronicler, and terminates with the episcopal inquisition (line 26), details of which required at least a rudimentary knowledge of canon law. The popular account, which is sandwiched in the middle, speaks largely in metaphors and describes the rapport between the charismatic Leutard and his audience (lines 5-24). The two levels of the narrative also correspond to two interpretations of Leutard's actions. In the learned version they are looked upon as doctrinal aberrations. In the popular account they are seen largely as behavioural, or, at the very least, as doctrines that issue in behaviour.

A clue to the text's ambivalence is provided by the notion of "insanity," which is used to describe Leutard's activities on some four occasions. Glaber speaks at the outset of *vesania pervicatia*. After Leutard's iconoclasm, even the local peasants think him "insane, which (the narrator adds) he was." Later, he is said to build up his following "as if through the mind of someone sane and religious." And, finally, Gebuin judges this "insane man" to be "a heretic" and "recalls the common people from the madness by which in part they were deceived."

Let us look more closely at this "insanity." Within the story's learned, interpretive apparatus there are three explanations. Although he nowhere says so directly, Glaber's images hint strongly at the obduracy of the Jews before the coming of Christ.[52] If stubbornness is not the answer, he adds, then Leutard is purely and simply "the devil's emissary." To these intellectualizations must be added a third set of ideas which do not in fact appear in the episode at all. Leutard's retrogressive behaviour is the last in a series of calamities which Glaber sees as threats to public order around the millennium, including omens, famine, and insurrection. Coming just before the signs of religious revival in book three, his vision is close to the turning point after which, following the pattern of Christ's life, the earthly world tries to set itself right. Leutard occupies a minor place in this penitential and historical scheme.[53]

But the popular elements in the account tell a different story. To return to the bees: they are not primarily symbols of specific doctrines,

[52] Cf. *Historiae* 3.6.20, p. 69.
[53] For a more extensive discussion, see Ch. 5.

even though Leutard counsels against the payment of tithes[54] and questions biblical precepts. They also anticipate a number of gestural actions, and the emphasis throughout this part of the story is on textual versus verbal communication. The bees, for instance, are said to have caused him much pain and suffering,[55] "and when he had been tormented for some time by their stings, they seemed to be speaking to him, ordering him to do many things impossible for (lay)men."[56] In other words, their essential message was to proceed from thought to action. Yet, the instructions turn out to be statements normally derivable from a literal reading of Scripture. Leutard himself, although illiterate, thereby imitates behaviour patterned on textual models. His activity amounts to a re-enactment of apostolic illumination (as he understands it) in which he plays the role of *interpres* between God and man, between word and act. As far as we know, there is no actual text present when he preaches his sermon; his symbolic actions are only dramatizations. But, as Glaber makes clear, they depend on putative texts. Leutard divorces his wife *quasi ex precepto evangelico*.[57] And throughout the story Glaber ironically contrasts the proper and improper uses of the Word. For example, when Leutard has shaken off his familial responsibilities and prepared himself for pure fraternalism, he is said to leave home and to proceed to the local church "as if to pray." While there, he destroys the external and, to his mind, empty symbols of Christ's presence, the cross and the image. He then "persuades" his fellow villagers that he is acting *ex miraculi Dei revelatione*. Again, in Glaber's distorted view, the locals are uneducated *rustici*, who vacillate and are slow-witted (*mente labiles*).[58] Leutard's eloquence is mere verbiage: thinking himself wise, he speaks with the proverbial tongue of fools. Above all he handles the literate techniques of interpretation ineptly. Glaber states: "A profusion of words poured forth, totally lacking in utility or truth. He wished to appear as a teacher, but he succeeded in undoing the teachings of authority."[59]

Utility, truth, and authority: these constitute a summary of Gla-

---

[54] Less, it is arguable, a clear social revolt than a suggestion of simony.

[55] Possibly a symptom of ergotism or St. Anthony's fire; Moore (1977), 36.

[56] *Historiae* 2.11.22, p. 49, 10-11.

[57] *Ibid.*, 49, 12-13.

[58] *Ibid.*, 49, 13-18: "Egressus autem velut oraturus, intrans ecclesiam, arripiensque crucem et Salvatoris imaginem contrivit. Quod cernentes quique territi pavore, credentes illum, ut erat, insanum fore; quibus etiam ipse persuasit, sicut sunt rustici mente labiles, universa hec patrare ex mirabili Dei revelatione."

[59] *Ibid.*, 49, 18-20: "Affluebat igitur nimium sermonibus utilitate et veritate vacuis, doctorque cupiens apparere, dedocebat magistrum doctrine."

ber's understanding of the *accessus ad auctores* as a preface to interpreting *divina pagina*. By implication, Leutard's hermeneutic activity is seen as a poor imitation of higher culture: "just as other heretics, in order that they may more cleverly deceive, cloak themselves in the sacred texts they wish to contradict, so this man said that the prophets spoke of some useful matters but that on other subjects they were not to be trusted."[60] But Leutard's appeal to the common people had little or nothing to do with such amateur scholasticism. Nor was it a reintroduction of ancient heresy, or a transformation of religious activity into a conceptual form. It arose principally through a re-ritualization of religious behaviour, using as models the early prophets and the apostles. Glaber sees no contradiction between his purely doctrinal interpretation of Leutard and the fact that his reputation (*fama*) spread chiefly among the poor and unlettered (*vulgus*). So, too, Gebuin interprets his "insanity" as "heresy," that is, behaviour, including activity and belief, as doctrinal deviation alone. Leutard's real "insanity" had other roots, directly related to his nodding acquaintance with letters.[61] The source was the Word, which was internalized literally, but presumably by verbal means. His symbolic action resulted from his interpretation of its meaning. And his suicide resulted not so much from condemnation of his ideas as from loss of his popular following, that is, the audience with which he had created an informal bond of understanding.

Orléans

In 1022, a clearer challenge to established ecclesiastical authority was brought to light in Orléans. The narratives of the episode, in particular the *Gesta Synodi Aurelianensis*, provide what historians are agreed in calling "the first circumstantial description of popular heresy

---

[60] *Ibid.*, 49, 21-24: "Et sicut hereses cetere, ut cautius decipiant, Scripturis se divinis, quibus etiam contrarie sunt, palliant, ita et iste dicebat prophetas ex parte narrasse utilia, ex parte non credenda."

[61] Orderic Vitalis speaks more briefly of a peasant named Stephen who lived near the reformist hermitage of St. Judoc, with whose experience the story of Leutard may be compared. Around 997, he had a vision of a richly dressed man, which he interpreted as a sign that he should leave his wife and children and become a monk, changing his status from *rusticus* to *clericus*; *Hist. Eccles.*, 3, vol. 2, p. 158. Fantasies inspired by texts also influenced the heretic Vilgard of Ravenna around 970; *Historiae* 2.12.23, p. 50. Moore (1977), 24, notes Vergilian menaces to the faith of Odo of Cluny and Gerbert. For a more erudite version, see Anselm of Besate, *Rhetorimachia* 2.2-5, ed. K. Manitius (Weimar, 1958), 138-50. Leutard's followers were still active around 1050; for a summary of the evidence, see Moore (1977), 36-37.

in the Middle Ages."[62] But there are serious problems of interpretation. The accounts differ in length, emphasis, and accuracy.[63] Their tabulations of the heretical doctrines vary considerably. Attempts have been made at distilling a residue of verifiable fact.[64] But other questions remain unanswered. The recorders of the episode were anything but impartial witnesses: what they said was influenced as much by the facts on hand as by literary, religious, and even emotional considerations. It is not possible to draw a hard line between fact and interpretation, the observed (or recollected) and the observers. If we compare the three lengthiest sources, the *Gesta*, Ademar of Chabannes, and Rodulf Glaber, it is not only the doctrinal orientation of the heretics which remains imprecise. We also find differing attitudes towards the nature of the religious experience. The question then arises: what are the common factors, not only in the objective events, but in the subjective reactions towards them?

The fullest account of the heresy is found in the *Vetus Agano* of Paul of St. Père de Chartres,[65] who did not write, it is worth noting, until some two generations after the event, around 1078.[66] His narrative runs as follows. In 1022, a nobleman called Arefast, who was a vassal of duke Richard II, discovered that Herbert, a domestic chaplain in his house near Chartres, had been attending the meetings of a sectarian group in Orléans. He immediately informed his superior, asking him to pass the information on to Robert the Pious. The king, somewhat alarmed, invited Arefast to go to Orléans and to investigate the charge himself. On the advice of Evrard, sacristan of the cathedral at Chartres, he journeyed to Orléans and posed as a convert to the sect. He also arranged for Robert and Queen Constance to come to the city

[62] Wakefield and Evans (1969), 74.

[63] For a recent review of the sources, see R.-H. Bautier, "L'hérésie d'Orléans et le mouvement intellectuel au début du XIe siècle. Documents et hypothèses," *Enseignement et vie intellectuelle (IXe-XVIe siècle)* (Paris, 1975), 64-69. Bautier's list is in chronological order beginning with the contemporary letter of John of Ripoll; for others see Ilarino da Milano (1947), 52n25 and Russell (1965), 276-77n24, the latter emphasizing the diploma of Robert the Pious (RHF 10, 605-07). A critical discussion of major *fontes* is also provided by Lambert (1977), Appendix A, pp. 343-47. Cf. Musy (1975), 38n3.

[64] Earlier scholarship is reviewed by Borst (1953), 67-69. Major discussions of doctrinal questions are found in Ilarino da Milano (1947), 52-59; Russell (1965), 27-35; and Bautier (1975), 69-77. The possibility of dualist influence is weighed by Moore (1970), 25-28, who presents a modified (although perhaps less acceptable) view in favour of gnosis in (1977), 25-27.

[65] *Cartulaire de l'abbaye de St.-Père de Chartres*, ed. B. Guérard, vol. 1, 109-115 (= d'Achéry, *Spicilegium* [1723] 1.204f).

[66] Bautier (1975), 68.

shortly afterwards. Before an assembly of laymen and clerics in the church of St. Croix he revealed his true identity and denounced the heretics brought there for questioning. The sect, as it turned out, had at least fourteen members,[67] both lay and clerical. Its origins (in Orléans) went back at least to 1019.[68] Prominent among the members were Lisois, a well-educated canon of St. Croix, and Stephen, a schoolmaster and confessor to the queen.[69] Attempts were made to persuade the heretics to recant, and a nun and a priest finally did. But the rest persisted in their beliefs. As punishment, they were taken outside the town walls, where, to the delight of a large crowd, they were burned alive.

"Historians," Bautier remarks, "have situated the crisis at Orléans only within the context of other heresies of the period."[70] But, as Paul relates the events, they also have a political and a literary dimension. Arefast, who appears in a Norman privilege as early as 990 and is mentioned as a monk at St. Père in 1029 and 1033, clearly played a minor role in the early eleventh-century politico-ecclesiastical rivalries at Orléans, Chartres, Sens, and Fleury.[71] As for the literary aspect, the most notable feature of Paul's account is the large role given to this knight, who is mentioned in no other source. The so-called "events of the synod" form a self-contained chapter in the cartulary for 1028.[72] They are preceded by Arefast's will, leaving to the monastery parts of three *villae*, some mills, and fishing rights. These were gifts, he asserted, which were offered not only for his and his family's salvation but also on behalf of Richard II, who died in 1027.

The presence of the will provides at least one important reason for Paul's including what was by the time he wrote probably only an oral record of the original events. He saw them primarily as an *exemplum*

[67] John of Ripoll (monk of Fleury), *Ep. ad Olibam*, in André of Fleury, *Vie de Gauzlin* . . . , ed. Bautier and Labory, 18 (= RHF 10, 498).

[68] Ademar of Chabannes, *Chronicon* 3.59, p. 185, relates that a *canonicus cantor* called Theodatus, who died in 1019, belonged to the sect. On this evidence, Russell (1965), 27, dates its appearance from 1015; but Ademar does not speak of the "Manichaeans" before 1018. On Ademar as a witness, see Bautier (1975), 65-66.

[69] André of Fleury also speaks of a certain Fulcherius (*Miraculi S. Benedicti*, ed. E. de Certain [Paris, 1858], 7.20, p. 247), and Glaber is said to confuse Stephen with a certain "Herbert" (*Historiae* 3.8.26, p. 74). The opposite has not been considered, namely, that Paul's memory failed him and that Herbert was actually in Orléans. The events could easily have been confused with other "clerical" heresies of the period; on the case of Odorannus of Sens, see Bautier (1975), 82-83. Also, have historians taken seriously enough Glaber's view that the heresy was exposed not by a layman but by a cleric from Rouen?

[70] Bautier (1975), 77.   [71] *Ibid.*, 68 and nn. 19-22, for the details.

[72] *Cartulaire*, 107-08.

of lay piety and penance, "worthy of being handed down to memory."
He arranged the details so that the heretical movement became a sort
of stage for the playing out of Arefast's own religious development up
to the time of his conversion to monasticism. Arefast was the perfect
hero for such a tale. He was well enough educated to be able to weigh
the merits of orthodoxy and heresy for himself. Also, he was the
model aristocrat in search of religious ideals. As Paul boasted, "He
was of the lineage of the dukes of Normandy, a man refined in speech,
wise in counsel, blessed with good habits, . . . (and) well known for
his services as an emissary to the French king and to great nobles."[73]
Other sources suggest that Arefast may have been all these and more.[74]
But was the romantic element not too good to be resisted? Arefast
undoubtedly played some role in exposing the heretics at Orléans.
But the literary purpose of Paul's intermingling of real life and rhetorical topoi was to prepare the way for his demonstration of "right
reason," in which secular classicism and Christian reform ideas happily coincided. In order to prove his worthiness, he had first to be
tested. His temptation took the form of a cleric in his household who
had fallen under the devil's spell. Other figures appear in the drama,
but their roles are minor. It is Arefast who stands at the crossroads.
In Paul's view he was no less admirable for having denounced heresy
than for setting out on a chivalrous quest, surviving intellectual trial,
and achieving his chosen goal.

The "heresy" which, Paul notes, was spreading "through the provinces of Gaul" about this time, is curiously interconnected in his story
with the growth of personally styled hermeneutics. Herbert, who may
have given lessons in Arefast's house, ostensibly went to Orléans for
the purpose of study (*lectionis gratia*), that is, as a part of the normal
training in theology. He became a heretic "while he busied himself
seeking out the authoritative sources of truth (*veritatis auctores*)." As a
half-educated student of Scripture he fell easily into "the pit of total
heresy." In other words, the process by which he became a "heretic"
paralleled the development of his own capacity for interpretation. His
spiritual guides were two *clerici*, Stephen and Lisois, who were widely
acclaimed for their wisdom, holiness, piety, and charity. They also
appear to have had a popular following. Herbert became their "docile
disciple"; he was misled by their "sweet words," inebriated by their
"deadly draught," trapped by their "madness and error." "Although
unskilled in theology," Paul adds, "he believed himself to have as-

[73] *Ibid.*, 109. [74] See Bautier (1975), 68, 80-81.

cended the pinnacle of wisdom" on his own. Thus illuminated, he hastened back to Chartres, where, with equally "subtle words," he attempted to persuade Arefast, to whom he was personally devoted, that Orléans outshone all other centres of learning in *sapientia* and *sanctitas*.[75] But Arefast saw through this simple-minded evangelism. In Paul's view, he had already set off on a journey of a different sort. He knew the *via justitiae*.[76] What trial by heresy essentially did was to teach him the difference between appearance and reality, which was required for the perfection of his intellectual and moral faculties. This is evident in the subsequent scenes.

Robert the Pious, widely known for his reformist ideals, ordered Arefast and Herbert to go to Orléans in person, and promised his full support. But, at this point, Herbert drops out of sight. The reason is evident: in Paul's scheme, he had already served the purpose of setting Arefast off on his quest after truth. Within the narrative there was little left for him to do. Arefast turned to the bishop of Chartres for spiritual guidance, but Fulbert had gone to Rome "to pray." Quite aside from local political considerations, the detail is perhaps significant: Arefast, who had won the support of the secular authority, now sought it from the religious. Embodying the two, he became Paul's *miles christianus*. When Evrard, the sacristan at Chartres, learned of the plan, he craftily advised Arefast what sort of arms to take into battle "against the many arts of diabolical deception." Evrard's counsel too needs to be scrutinized. Besides the eucharist, it was devoid of mention of dogma. Instead, he told Arefast to protect himself with prayer, "to fortify himself with sacred communion," and to shield himself with the *signaculum sanctae crucis*.[77] It follows that Paul, who put these words in Evrard's mouth, sees heresy in large part as magical ritual. He even links it elsewhere to the orgiastic practices of ancient sects.[78] But intermingled with these thoughts is also the idea that the evil can be overcome by the educated intelligence.

That is clearly indicated by the next scene. Arefast journeyed to Orléans. Paul relates that, although informed (*edoctus*), he sought out sectarian teaching (*eorum doctrina*) and, although literate, he acted like an untaught pupil (*ad instar rudis discipuli*).[79] He then underwent the normal initiation. Finding his way to the meeting-place, he made room for himself in the last row of seats, at first observing the group

---

[75] Summarizing *Cartulaire*, 109.   [76] *Ibid.*, 110.   [77] *Idem.*   [78] *Ibid.*, 112.

[79] *Ibid.*, 110: "Igitur Aurelianis deveniens, uti edoctus fuerat, cotidie sacra communione ac supplici oratione munitus, ad eorum doctrinam veniens, ad instar rudis discipuli, ultimus, intra domum herroneorum, ultimus adsidebatur."

without participating in it. Later, Paul adds, he was given instruction, first by *exempla*, that is, by stories with morals, and then by *similitudines*, by abstract analogies with other moral principles. Among these Paul recounts the allegory of the transplanted tree.[80] As a disciple, Arefast was told, he was like a tree that had been taken from the forest wilds to an orchard. First it was watered and put down roots; then, pruned of thorns and deadwood, it was grafted onto a domestic species in order to bear fruit. Similarly, Arefast was transported from the sinful world at large to their *collegium*, and, refreshed with the water of wisdom, was being stripped of his intellectual thorns "by the sword of God's word."[81] Only after this initiation via moral experience was the sect's theology made clear. As Paul puts it, when they were sure Arefast was a sincere convert, they presented as dogma what had hitherto been "covered" by allegory. Christ, they said, was not born of a virgin, did not suffer for humanity, was not buried, and did not rise on the third day. Baptism did not wash away one's sins. The consecration of bread and wine was not a sacrament. And one's chances of being saved were not affected by entreaties to martyrs and confessor saints.[82]

This adds up to a rationalistic interpretation of Scripture through an elimination of its sacral, miraculous, and historical elements. Arefast was somewhat taken aback: with many of his cherished beliefs rejected, there was little left in which he could place faith.[83] The heretics replied in illuministic fashion that, after the imposition of hands, he would receive an infusion of divine truth. He was nearing the summit; and, when the ritual was completed, he would be "filled with the gift of the holy spirit," whose charisma would reveal to him "the profundity of all scriptures and their true identity, without reserve." On this heavenly food he would be nourished; through this spiritual satiety he would be renewed. He would then experience angelic visions, which would transport him anywhere he wished; he would lack nothing, "for the God of all men, in whom resides the treasuries of wisdom and riches," would be his faithful companion.[84]

---

[80] *Loc.cit.*: "Cumque primum divinorum voluminum exemplis eum et quibusdam rerum similitudinibus informarent, atque, more perfecti discipuli, subdita aure intentum viderent, inter alias similitudines silvestri arboris similitudinem ei proferunt."

[81] *Ibid.*, 110-11.   [82] *Ibid.*, 111.   [83] *Loc.cit.*

[84] *Loc.cit.*: "Nunc vero erectus in culmine totius veritatis, integrae mentis oculos ad lumen verae fidei aperire coepisti. Pandemus tibi salutis hostium, quo ingressus, per impositionem videlicet manuum nostrarum, ab omni peccati labe mundaberis, atque Sancti Spiritus dono repleberis, qui scripturarum omnium profunditatem ac veram divinitatem, absque scrupulo, te docebit. Deinde coelesti cibo pastus, interna sacietate recreatus, videbis persepe nobiscum vi-

Despite Paul's disparaging asides, the programme of the Orléans sect speaks for itself. First, it shifted the weight of religious commitment away from objective elements such as "tradition, priesthood and the sacraments"[85] and onto the shoulders of ordinary believers themselves. The priest's natural extension of the idea of incarnation was replaced by the "performance of moral demands which, at bottom, was founded only upon the law and the example,"[86] either of Christ or the sect itself. These demands were largely experienced subjectively, whence Arefast's alarm at the withdrawal of the standard supports for faith. Moreover, the change in emphasis from the impersonal to the personal aspects of belief made itself felt differently at the level of the individual and the group. In the one, it resulted in mysticism; in the other, in collective interaction around a text. Throughout, literacy played a large if somewhat diffuse role. The sect rejected the written traditions and dependent institutions of the official church. In their place it put a rationality based on simplified textual criticism and on one's capacity for reflection. The implantation of God's word in man was represented in mystical language. Wisdom, so to speak, merely descended when the time was right; but this time coincided with the moment when the recruit, having absorbed scriptures through others' interpretations, suddenly began to understand them for himself. He was thereby led upwards in the fashion of all mystics towards a selfless identification with God. But he and his brethren can also be described as byproducts of a lay literacy detached from an institutional framework which would have tended to desubjectivize the experience. For it is easier to believe that one's awareness of a text's inner meaning is divinely inspired among a group of personal devotees than in a grammarian's crowded classroom. The sect tried to give its values a coherent shape and some principles of accountability. The result was not a "religion": it was a morality, to which were added textual, visionary, and otherworldly elements.

While Paul describes Arefast's initiation, the reader has at least a glimpse of the sect at Orléans as an autonomous religious group. The remainder of the account deliberately contrasts the dissenters' views with the position of the church. We admire the courage with which the heretics go to their doom. But emphasis shifts back to the spir-

---

siones angelicas, quarum solatio fultus, cum eis, quovis locorum, sine mora vel dificultate, cum volueris, ire poteris, nichilque tibi deerit, quia Deus omnium tibi comes numquam deerit, in quo sapientiae thesauri atque divitiarum consistunt."

[85] Cf. E. Troeltsch, *The Social Teaching of the Christian Churches*, vol. 1, 335.

[86] *Ibid.*, 336.

itual reawakening of Arefast. When he exposes the heretics before an assembly of his peers, the reader is led, as he was, in gradual, didactic steps from "appearance" to "reality." Arefast is also taken one step farther along the road to what Paul considers to be an acceptable form of participation in the religious life.

The manner in which the "inquisition" proceeds is instructive. Robert and Constance came to Orléans on Christmas Eve. The heretics, Arefast among them, were brought before them in chains. When Arefast protested that he was actually the vassal of the duke of Normandy, Robert asked him what he was doing in Orléans. From these carefully planned stage cues the drama of exposure then unfolded.

In the first scene, Arefast, maintaining "appearances" for the moment, replied that he came to the sectarians seeking *sapientia* and *religio*.[87] He wished to follow the example of their good works and to return to Chartres a better man. As he describes it, the pattern of participation was as follows: physical and spiritual exile (*de patria exire*), teaching by example (*exemplum bonorum operum*) together with doctrine (*doctrina*), and return as a renewed person (*ut . . . melioratus redirem*).[88] A comparison is naturally suggested between these classic gestures of reform, carefully implanted by Paul, and the sect's actual performance.

Arefast then asked them to disclose their teachings before the royal assembly in order that they be judged praiseworthy or meretricious. Their reluctance to do so marks the beginning of the second scene. Arefast continued: they claimed, he said, to be teachers of truth, not error. They would even go to death for their beliefs. Yet, abandoning these lofty principles, they were apparently willing to let an innocent disciple like himself stand in their place. In contrast, he added, a forthright statement by them would enable everyone present to understand what was "contrary to Christian piety." He concluded with mention of their two chief tenets, denial of the sacraments and of Christ's divinity.[89]

But his appeal was irresistible for other than doctrinal reasons. For Arefast had effectively challenged the sect's principles of unity. The ascetic purity of the high priests, he implied, would be sullied if a raw recruit, even a fifth columnist, to whom they had pledged themselves, had to bear the entire burden of moral responsiblity which was in their view a collective obligation. He did not question their ideas; this came later in the episcopal inquiry. He compelled them to reaf-

[87] *Cartulaire*, 113.   [88] *Loc.cit.*   [89] *Loc.cit.*

firm the solidarity of the bonds uniting them in the present, the "interaction ritual"[90] which bound priest and believer together. The argument was all the more persuasive because it came from an ideal convert. This fact, of course, was not wasted on Paul, who arranged the scene to coincide with a stage in Arefast's quest for penance and ultimately the monastic life.

Stephen and Lisois then came forward and admitted to Guarin, the bishop of Beauvais, that Arefast's charges were substantially correct. On further questioning they confessed to numerous doctrines unacceptable to Christianity. An example of the quality of their beliefs is provided by their reply to the prelate when he referred to Christ's virgin birth, incarnation, and resurrection. We ourselves were not present, they answered, and therefore cannot believe such events really took place.[91] A distinction was made, in other words, between the historical and theological understanding of biblical narratives. From their clerical education the pair clearly grasped the meaning of authority and of verification through textual precedents. They merely took these ideas in a new direction, rejecting traditional interpretations, which they did not think out for themselves, in favour of a truth born of actual, historical, and thereby sensible reality. As later and more significantly in Berengar of Tours, their isolation of the observable was related to their understanding of the relationship between texts and reality.[92]

Their sophisticated awareness of problems involving written tradition also influenced their other replies to the bishop. Guarin then asked: If you believe in ordinary parenthood, why can you not by analogy accept God's generation of another God, who needed no earthly mother?[93] To which they answered: What nature denies is out of harmony with the creator.[94] Nature, in their view, was a system governed by laws, presumably written and analysable by reason, with which the "word" of God had to agree. Then Guarin asked: Before nature brought anything into being, did God not make everything through the Son? Their answer raised the larger issue of divine illumination and earthly understanding. You, they said, can account for these events in stories suited to terrestrial wisdom and the fictions of carnal men. But we have the holy spirit's law written inside us and

[90] Cf. E. Goffman, *Interaction Ritual* (New York, 1967), 5.

[91] *Cartulaire*, 114: "Nos neque interfuimus, neque haec vera esse credere possumus."

[92] See below, ch. 3, pp. 275-81.

[93] *Cartulaire*, 114.

[94] *Loc.cit.*: "Quod natura denegat, semper a creatore discrepat."

no other wisdom than that of God, who made all things. Therefore, your arguments serve no purpose: they are unnecessary and inconsistent with divinity.[95] This statement neatly pulled together their views on the uses of literacy. What they rejected were the "stories," or, as we should call them, the myths, whose only sources of verification were unquestioned accretions of traditional lore. In their eyes, this heritage, which was a mere record, had the status of popular culture, even of superstition. In its place they preferred a form of the divine message which as they said was written in their hearts by God. This was a text with a meaning immediately apprehensible to the interior understanding, a byproduct, presumably, of study, discussion, and meditation. Traditional "literacy," or what they took it to be—the ink, glue, and parchment holding together the church's teachings—was a symbol of alienation, that is, of an uncomprehended or incomprehensible text imposed upon man from without.

To summarize: Paul of St. Père sees the outbreak of heresy in Orléans as part of a more general awakening of lay piety, to which local political rivalries and reformist instincts are vaguely appended.[96] That is why the chief role in his compelling tale is played by a lay nobleman who eventually converts from the secular to the religious style of life. However, within Paul's account, we learn much of the sect's principles of operation. The central element was a set of texts, which were used as organizational and as teaching instruments by the higher priests and which were learned, first in allegory and later as dogma, by the converts. Deductions based on their logic also influenced the sect's views on other subjects, causing the members to reject Christian doctrine and to ask searching questions about the relationship between texts and reality. Despite the narrative's brevity, we observe an internally developing set of methods, an unmistakeable if rudimentary hermeneutics.

Neither of the other two main descriptions of the heretics at Orléans provide us with insights into the internal workings of the group. But both Ademar of Chabannes and Rodulf Glaber help to establish typologies of interpretation. In Ademar, we return to the world of popular culture, pagan cults, and superstition. In Glaber, popular and learned culture are openly contrasted as he once again weds a foreign

[95] *Loc.cit.*: "Ista illis narrare potes, qui terrena sapiunt atque credunt ficta carnalium hominum, scripta in membranulis animalium; nobis autem qui legem scriptam habemus in interiori homine a Spiritu Sancto, et nichil aliud sapimus, nisi quod a Deo, omnium conditore, didicimus, incassum superflua et a Divinitate devia profers."

[96] On these issues, see the elegant synthesis of Bautier (1975), 69-77.

theological apparatus of explanation to an oral account of the events. Heresy is one threat among others to universalism, for which he is an active propagandist.

For Ademar, two features of the dissidence at Orléans stand out. The heretics were part of a conspiracy stretching northwards from Toulouse, and educated clerics were led into error by magical and religious practices involving the occult. Above all, Ademar, in attempting to explain heresy, stresses the deceptive gap between appearances and reality.

He first provides some bare details.[97] In 1022, he states, ten canons of the church of St. Croix, "who appeared to be more devout than the others, were proven to be Manichaeans." The educated priests were deceived by a *rusticus*, who is thought to have come from the Perigord.[98] This countryman said he could work wonders, and carried about with him the ashes of dead children, through which he soon made a Manichaean of anyone to whom he could communicate them."[99]

Ademar's imagination is obviously less sophisticated than Paul's. Like the monk of St. Père, he sees the origin of heresy in a ritual experience. He also refers to the transfer of a physical object in which the concrete stands for the abstract. Nor can he resist adding lurid details of orgiastic practices, which were standard fare in many accounts of medieval sects.[100] But he differs from Paul in one important respect: the deception in his view passes from popular to learned levels of society. Misled by a "rustic," the canons of Orléans are portrayed as worshipping the devil, who appeared alternately as a "black and white god" and gave them money in return for their homage. Those in the heresy's thrall were unable to distinguish between spiritual and material values, that is, in Ademar's eyes, between reality and appearances. They also showed a lack of unity between their public and private lives. Outwardly they seemed to be Christians, but inwardly they had adopted a new form of piety. Typical was Theodatus, a late canon of St. Croix, who "seemed to be religious," but, "as trustworthy men declared," died a heretic.[101] In other words, the root of the problem for Ademar lay in the contrast between external and internal types of devotion. But it could be viewed from two perspectives. For the heretics, the hiatus evidently arose between the empty, ceremonial mannerisms of inherited tradition and the vitality of inner, private, and personal spirituality. What happened *in occulto* could no longer

[97] *Chronicon* 3.59, p. 184.   [98] *Ibid.*, 184 and n.   [99] *Loc.cit.*
[100] Cf. Moore (1975), 10.
[101] *Chronicon*, 185.

be reconciled with what one experienced *in aperto*. Ademar saw the same issues in reverse. For him, the final irony came at the end of the anecdote. Believing in appearances, the heretics considered themselves invulnerable to physical harm. The illusion was shattered by their own burning flesh. In sum, Ademar not only feared and distrusted the heretics; he was also somewhat in awe of their rites. After their bodies were burnt, he notes, there were no ashes left. Were they taken back by the devil to be redistributed anew?

Glaber's account of the same episode is a little more detailed but no more substantial. Yet, more than Ademar, Glaber is in some respects the antithesis of Paul. The latter saw heresy primarily as a local affair. Although vaguely connected to manifestations of dissent elsewhere, it was chiefly explained against the background of lay piety and monastic reform in France and Normandy. For Glaber, by contrast, a particular heresy derived its importance from being part of a more widespread phenomenon. In a traditional metaphor, he likens it to a disease spreading northwards through Gaul, or to seeds, which, having germinated secretly over a long period, suddenly bring forth evil fruit.[102]

As in Ademar, its foreignness to established patterns of order is symbolized by its source, an outsider, a vagabond, and, what is worse, a woman. Coming from Italy, he states, she was full of the devil: she "seduced whomever she wished, not only the illiterate and uneducated (*idiotae et simplices*), but also quite a few more learned persons (*doctiores*) from the clerical order."[103] Like Ademar's canons, this archetypal Eve appeared to be one thing but was in reality another. She remained for a time in Orléans, where she managed to spread her message into various corners of lay and ecclesiastical society. Glaber then recapitulates parts of Paul's version, adding inaccuracies of his own. Two of the town's most knowledgeable and well-born clerics, he continues, Stephen (whom he calls Herbert) and Lisois, became heretics. They were favorites at the feudal and royal courts, which enabled them, in the chronicler's words, to more effectively corrupt the minds of those who were not united by the *amor fidei universalis*.[104] In his view, independent interpretation of Scripture acted as a threat chiefly by undermining the traditional principles of order, which comprised society's only source of universal values. Therefore, appropriately, it was not a layman like Arefast but a priest from Rouen who was instru-

---

[102] *Historiae* 3.8.26, p. 74. On the metaphor, see R. I. Moore, "Heresy as Disease," in *The Concept of Heresy in the Middle Ages* (Louvain, 1976), 1-11.

[103] *Loc.cit.*   [104] *Loc.cit.*

mental in exposing the sect. Emissaries from Orléans apparently approached him as a potential convert, claiming that within a short time the new faith would be embraced by all (*universus populus*). It was the clear challenge to established order which made him act. He told Richard II, then residing in Rouen, and through Richard word reached the king. Robert, fearful for "the homeland's ruin," hastened to Orléans, where a large body was assembled and a formal inquiry undertaken. Stephen and Lisois, having long concealed their views, now made them known to all, as if they were only waiting for the right occasion. And once exposed, they repeated the "prophetic" message that was delivered in Rouen, a message whose apocalyptic overtones coincided happily with Glaber's millenarianism. Glaber then lists their errors: they viewed signs, prodigies and other "witnesses" in the Bible as nonsense; they thought the world eternal, not created in time by God; and, like the "Epicureans," they did not think fleshly sins warranted punishment. Christianity's work on behalf of piety and justice was to their minds wasted effort.[105] Glaber concluded with a lengthy defence of the Christian scheme, possibly drawn from Augustine, Maximus, and Eriugena.[106] God, he argued, mindful of man's falling away from the divine image, provided "signs" for his instruction and betterment. His semiotic textbook is the Bible: "The whole book or written text of divine matters is the witness or documentary evidence of this fact."

There is a certain irony in the fact that the heretics at Orléans were burned on the feast of the holy innocents, 1022. For, innocent they may well have been of devoting their major efforts to the formation of the type of sect of which they were accused by most medieval and many modern commentators. The "seductive spirituality" of their "language of ritual initiation"[107] and their "simple and holy life"[108] have been noted. But these factors have been discussed mainly as an introduction to dogmas, beliefs, and ideas. There is strong evidence within all three examined accounts that the group also directed its activities towards other areas of experience, notably, for instance, natural philosophy. The summaries of doctrine presented by the sources are about as broad a survey of ancient heresies as one would expect for the time: rejection of the mass, of the trinity, of the sacraments, of confession and penance, of marriage, of ordination, of the saints, and

[105] *Ibid.*, 3.8.26-27, pp. 74-76.   [106] *Ibid.*, 3.8.28-30, pp. 76-80.
[107] Ilarino da Milano (1947), 54.   [108] Russell (1965), 28.

of divine creation in time.[109] We shall never know how many of these were actually professed, nor in what combination. Moreover, what the various tabulations have in common are two features which lie outside the field of doctrine itself. In most cases, the heretics were said to deny the sacral, miraculous, and historical elements in Christianity, along with the ecclesiastical hierarchy, which in their opinion was their logical outgrowth. What was similar in the reports was not the doctrine or practice being invalidated but the principle by which it was done. This consisted of a highly developed if somewhat personal style of "rationality" which depended on the individual interpretation of theological texts. As a result of his hermeneutic and often mystical endeavours, the interpreter was "illumined."[110] But the consequences were not only intellectual. An older ritualism, linked to oral culture, was replaced by rituals of human interaction. What ultimately held the sect together, and, incidentally, broke it up, was the set of bonds between the members themselves. The heresy, like the lay piety which grew up with it, was inseparable from the gradual formation of literate and semi-literate communities after the millennium. André of Fleury is categorical on this point: the sectarians in his view were all "educated in holy religion from childhood, imbued with divine as well as secular letters."[111]

Recognition of these facts leads us to look differently at the function of doctrinal discussions in the original sources. Certainly the heretics had specific beliefs, and these are partly revealed by the different accounts. But the careful arrangement of their ideas as the antithesis of Christianity within the writings of Christians whose positions are clearly defined also suggests that the references to doctrines have the status of evidence-documents in oral culture: they are confirmations, interpretations, and contextualizations. Like the pleasant narrative of Arefast's quest, they attempt to fit a new, troubling experience, for which there is only a verbal record, into an acceptably conventional framework involving texts, precedents, and standard hypotheses about behaviour. The terms of reference are not only assumed to be familiar to the audience for which they are written; they are also attempts to reconstitute that audience through an artistic and artificial rebuilding of its foundation for continuity over time, which is textual. This activity may have begun with the heretics themselves, who, as

[109] Ilarino da Milano (1947), 54-58; confirmed by Bautier (1975), 69-77, Lambert (1977), 344-45 and Moore (1977), 26.
[110] Cf. Moore (1970), 26-27.
[111] *Vita Gauzlini* 56a, p. 98.

educated clerics, could easily have historicized their position. It could also have taken shape as resistance to their endeavour crystallized into the full-scale *perscrutatio* organized by Robert the Pious. But its chief source was undoubtedly the medieval commentators, who believed, as they remind us, that "there is nothing covered that will not be uncovered, nothing hidden that will not be made known."[112] For the heretics, the hidden meaning emerged as they themselves interpreted biblical texts, patristic writings, and their own maxims. For the orthodox, the deception was exposed as the allegorical surface of their activities yielded under inquiry to their true, diabolical motives. And, so, what began as an opposition of methods curiously finished as an opposition of methods. Through the logic of texts the heretics challenged accepted tradition. Through textual reconstruction they were made part of a widespread, historically evolving conspiracy against the church, of which they had no knowledge and to which they were little if at all related.

Arras

The examined accounts of heresy at Orléans in 1022 provide insights from essentially two directions. In the *Vetus Agano*, we learn a little about how the group actually functioned. But in all three sources consideration must also be given to the narrator's attitude and concerns. The latter include the cultural level at which heresy is placed, the threat it posed to social and ecclesiastical polity, and how the heretics communicated their beliefs.

The same may be said of the *Acta Synodi Atrebatensis*, the unique source of information about a sectarian group active about the same time in the united diocese of Arras and Cambrai.[113] The actual synod was held on the 10th or 17th January 1025,[114] but the record, which was later revised by an unknown third party,[115] consists of two parts: the *epistola*, which is a brief letter from Gerard I, bishop of Arras-Cambrai, to an unnamed "R," and the *Acta*, which is a lengthy ac-

---

[112] Matt 10:26; *Vita Gauzlini, loc.cit.; Miracula S. Benedicti* 6.20, p. 247.

[113] The *Acta* were first edited by Luc d'Achéry, *Spicilegium* (1677), vol. 13, 1-63. On the subsequent editions, which were all based on this original, see E. van Mingroot, "Acta Synodi Atrebatensis (1025): problèmes de critique de provenance," *Studia Gratiana* 20 (1976), 228n182. On the manuscript (Dijon, Bibl. mun. 582), see pp. 208-09. All quotations in what follows are from Migne's reprinting of d'Achéry, PL 142.1269B-1312D.

[114] J. B. Russell, "A propos du synode d'Arras en 1025," RHE 57 (1962), 70, 73.

[115] Possibly the author of the *Gesta Episcoporum Cameracensium* and the *Vita S. Gaugerici*; Mingroot (1976), 225-27.

count of the alleged interrogation and conversion of the heretics. The *Acta* also comprise three basic elements, a verbal interchange, in which the heretics defend their views; a sermon by Gerard, which is intended to refute them; and a concluding scene, in which the converts make a profession of faith.[116]

Historical evaluation of the *Acta* has been chiefly preoccupied with two issues, the identity of "R," together with questions of dating, and the possible links between the Arras sect and other, early eleventh-century dissidents.[117] Little attention has been paid to Gerard's "sermon." Because his list of the heretics' errors differs on important points from their own account,[118] the longest and most informative part of the *Acta* has been dismissed as a "harangue" or an irrelevant "polemic."[119]

But Gerard's defence of the principles and practices of the church may contain the key to the meaning of the episode as a whole, and, in particular, to the role heresy played as "popular culture" in galvanizing a learned, historicist response to dissidence. As an historical record, its chief disadvantage, as noted, is that it was almost certainly written sometime after 1025. At the end of chapter one, which concludes the debate with the heretics and the discussion of baptism, Gerard remarks that much more could be said, but, as the day is declining, he must move on. Identical observations occur in the last chapter, in which the heretics reconvert.[120] Clearly the sun set more than once on the synod: much material between chapters one and seventeen, as well, presumably, as the *epistola*, were written later, either before the death of Gerard in 1051, or, if he was the letter's recipient, that of Roger I of Châlons-sur-Marne on 5th November 1042.[121]

The revision was undoubtedly intentional and served a number of literary purposes. It effectively took sectarianism out of the local realm and, by placing it in a broader context, aimed the sermon's message

[116] Cf. Moore (1977), 10, who distinguishes no less than five sources of information in the *Acta*.

[117] On the former question, early bibliography is summarized ably by J. M. Noiroux, "Les deux premiers documents concernant l'hérésie aux Pays-Bas," RHE 49 (1954), 842-43n3 and by Mingroot (1976), 205n10. On the latter issue, see Dondaine (1952), 59-60 and *passim*, Puech (1957), Morghen (1966), and, succinctly but well analysed, Moore (1977), 9-18.

[118] Wakefield and Evans (1969), 84, following Russell (1965), 22-26.

[119] Russell (1965), 22, and Moore (1970), 28n34.

[120] *Acta Synodi Atrebatensis*, c. 2, PL 142.1278B: "sed quia dies, ad occasum declivior . . . ; c. 17, 1311B: "Jam dies ad occasum declivior erat. . . ."

[121] Mingroot (1976), 223.

at a larger audience than those actually present. Also, by echoing the purely intellectual defences of orthodoxy by patristic bishops, it provided an eloquent statement of Gerard's view, archaic, perhaps in his own day, that the ideals of universalism were achievable within the episcopal administrative unit.[122] But, in order to broaden the episode's appeal, the reviser had to situate it within a recognizable theological framework. His choice was the church's legitimacy and more specifically the validity of the sacraments. The language and images of sacramentalism recur again and again: in the *epistola*, which refers to appearance and reality; in the discussion of baptism, through which "visible" water demonstrates the holy spirit's "invisible" operation; in the chapter *De Corpore et Sanguine Domini*, which is a virtual textbook of eucharistic orthodoxy; in the treatment of churches, altars, incense, images of the cross, and even bells, which are viewed both as *signa* and *sacramenta*; and in the heretics' profession of faith, which, besides being a denial of their own views, is concerned with acceptance of the "real presence."

Of course, this underlying unity may be accidental. But, if it is not, it sheds new light on the *Acta*. Gerard's "sermon" was not directed mainly against the heretics at Arras. This was merely its occasion. It reflected upon dissident theses in groups as widely dispersed as the Orléans cell and the alleged followers of Berengar. It thereby opened a broader ecclesiastical, theological, and political debate.

The literary structure of the revised synodal record may be more clearly revealed if we look in turn at the *epistola*, the *procès-verbal*, the sermon, and the conversion scene.

The letter is a reproof.[123] Considering "R's" intelligence and discretion, Gerard writes, he is at a loss to explain how "impious men, spellbound by the spirit of error, conspired in such senseless, depraved teaching" within his diocese. He is even more shocked to learn that they were able to conceal their real motives and to deceive the local authorities. For, as he subsequently demonstrated, these same men had been living for some time within "R's" jurisdiction, uncondemned. Thus, they all the more easily enthralled the common people. Missionaries were sent to Arras and, when they were apprehended, they too tried to dissimulate their intentions. No amount of torture could make them confess. Gerard finally learned of their beliefs from parishioners to whom they had apparently preached but whom

---

[122] On this theme, see in general G. Duby, *Les trois ordres ou l'imaginaire du féodalisme* (Paris, 1978), 35-61.

[123] Summarizing *Gerardi Ep.*, PL 142.1269B-70C.

they had not yet converted. Having been exposed, the heretics then confessed to a number of aberrant doctrines. Baptism, they maintained, was not a "mystery" and the eucharist not a "sacrament"; penance and marriage were useless institutions, contributing nothing towards one's eventual salvation. Their other beliefs, Gerard concludes, are outlined in the *Acta*, which he sends to "R" to prevent him from being misled further by their cunning and artifice.

What do we actually learn from this letter? First, it is a communication between two bishops, the one, Gerard, accusing a neighbour of not effectively stamping out heresy in his own diocese, whence it spread to Arras-Cambrai. Gerard was the first to learn of the heretics' existence. He apparently informed "R," who started an investigation. But the dissidents slipped through the latter's hands, and, having grown more audacious, now posed a threat to the otherwise vigilant diocese of Gerard. Gerard, for his part, takes credit for having discovered the evil force and for having exposed it for "R's" benefit. But he admits no responsibility for the unwanted consequences.

The statement cannot be accepted on its face value. The first indication of a distortion of the real events comes when we compare Gerard's prefatory account with what the heretics later tell us themselves. Gerard assumes that heresy spread from one diocese to another by means of *missi*.[124] The heretics later testified that they were converted by a certain Gundulfo, who came from Italy. Gundulfo presumably travelled about and could have been active in Liège, Châlons-sur-Marne, and Arras-Cambrai.[125] But he is mentioned nowhere else, and the heretics do not speak of links with groups outside Arras. In other words, despite local proselytizing, the sect sees itself as isolated. Again, Gerard claims that, fearing torture, the heretics lied to "R" about their true beliefs. Yet, in his diocese torture apparently had no effect on them.[126] He had to rely on the ability of his parishioners to resist their enticements. Gerard also presents within the letter somewhat different perspectives on the nature of their beliefs. In the opening lines he puts behaviour before doctrine. The heretics are virtually criminals (*nefarii homines*), deluded by magic (*magicati*), conspiring together in folly (*dementia*).[127] But towards the end he speaks of them in doctrinal terms. They are made to confess to specific deviations on

---

[124] *Ibid.*, 1270B.

[125] Cf. Mingroot (1976), 219.

[126] *Ep.*, 1269B: "quia terrore supplicii speciem religionis mentiebantur"; and 1270B: "ut nullis suppliciis possent cogi ad confessionem."

[127] *Ep.*, 1269B.

penance, marriage, and the other sacraments, deriving their aberrant ideas *ex evangelica et apostolica doctrina*.[128]

Such inconsistencies are a clue to Gerard's major intention, which is not only to expose the heresy but to reveal what was concealed from "R." He does not criticize his neighbour because deviations from orthodoxy arose in his diocese. He is more alarmed that "R" did not recognize the evil for what it was. "R" himself was misled by appearances.[129] The heretics were able without much effort to conceal their true identity. Gerard also drops the hint that "R's" inquisitors were not up to their task, for what eventually reached the ears of the *simplices* was a message especially contrived for subverting their innocent powers of reason.[130] What was really needed was a higher state of acumen and training; one could not deal with heresy effectively unless one had the requisite equipment. Further, when the "missionaries" came from "R's" diocese to Arras, they carried on the same sort of "dissembling." But they were caught, exposed, and reconverted.[131] In Arras, converts to heresy were not so easy to make; on interrogation, the wayward reaffirmed their faith. By implication, there was a loftier level of spiritual life in the diocese. But, even if that had not been the case, Gerard was rather better prepared than "R" to deal with the problem. The reasons, he implies, are contained in the *Acta*: a transcript is sent to "R" to prevent him from being further deluded by the heretics' feigned devotion (*simulata religio*) and artful language (*composita verba*).[132]

In sum, beneath a complaint about the spread of heresy, we find a comparison of the spiritual preparedness of two dioceses. The idea most often mentioned in the letter is not heresy but *dissimulatio*;[133] the central issue is how to distinguish between appearance and reality. Concealment is linked to power over words, while exposure depends on law, scholarship, and procedure. Indirectly, a literate, higher religious culture is already advocated: for, just as illiteracy allows the innocent to be deceived, so education prepares the laity to defend the faith.

But what is the precise nature of the sect? What are its real sources of inspiration? We learn as much as we know of these matters from the first paragraphs of the *Acta*, in which the heretics answer Gerard's

---

[128] *Ibid.*, 1270B.

[129] *Ibid.*, 1269B: "sed ad inquisitionem vestram qualiter dissimulare potuerint, ut vos fallerent, vehementer stupeo."

[130] *Ibid.*, 1269B-70B.   [131] *Ibid.*, 1270B.   [132] *Ibid.*, 1270B-C.

[133] E.g., 1269B, "dissimulare," 1270B, "dissimulatio, simulatio, simulata."

charges in their own words. Let us first summarize the text,[134] then approach these questions.

The synod, we are told, took place sometime early in January 1025. As was the custom in the joint diocese, the bishop celebrated Christmas and Epiphany in Cambrai and then spent several days in Arras. While performing his normal duties he was informed that men from Italy had formed a new sort of heretical association (*quaedam novae hereseos secta*).[135] They apparently rejected "evangelic and apostolic teaching" and preferred what is called their own sort of "justice,"[136] through which, they claimed, and not through the sacraments, men could alone be cleansed. Gerard ordered that they be brought before him. They tried to flee but were apprehended. Gerard was too busy to ask them more than a few routine questions, but, realizing that they harboured dangerous ideas, he had them held for three days, during which time all local monks and clerics were asked to fast in the hope of divine illumination.

On the following Sunday Gerard convened a synod in St. Mary's in Arras. The procession into the church was resplendent: Gerard took the lead, followed by his archdeacons, bearing crosses and Bibles, they in turn followed by the lower clergy and townsmen. They all sang the psalm "Let God arise," after which the bishop, seated in his consistory, asked the offenders: "What is your teaching, law and observance (*doctrina vestra, lex atque cultura*), and who is its author (*auctor*)?"[137] They were followers, they replied, of a certain Italian called Gundulfo, who had personally instructed them in the gospel's principles (*evangelica mandata*). He enjoined them to adhere literally to this text (*haec scriptura*) and to practice it in word and deed (*verbo et opere tenere*).[138] But other beliefs, the narrator adds, had been drawn to Gerard's attention: rejection of baptism and the eucharist, denial of penance, of the church's authority, and of the utility of marriage, invalidation of confession, and veneration of no one save the apostles and the martyrs.[139]

Mindful of these reports, Gerard then asked: How is it you say you follow biblical teachings but preach just the opposite? He cited the case of Nicodemus, who, converted by mere "signs and miracles,"

---

[134] *Acta Synodi* . . . , c. 1, PL 142.1271A-72C.

[135] *Ibid.*, 1271A. [136] *Loc.cit.* [137] *Ibid.*, 1271C.

[138] *Ibid.*, 1271C: "At illi referunt se esse auditores Gundulfi, cujusdam ad Italiae partibus viri, et ab eo evangelicis mandatis et apostolicis informatos, nullamque praeter hanc scripturam se recipere, sed hanc verbo et opere tenere."

[139] *Ibid.*, 1271C-D.

was reminded by the Lord that no one enters the kingdom of heaven unless "he be born again through water and spirit."[140] To accept the words of the gospel is to admit "the mystery of regeneration." But the accused replied: If anyone carefully examines our law and conduct (*lex et disciplina nostra*), he will see that it contradicts neither "evangelical decrees" nor "apostolic sanctions."[141] For it consists essentially of this: to abandon the world, to refrain from carnal desires, to earn our daily bread by the labour of our hands, to endeavour to harm no one, and to be charitable towards all who share our principles. This is the full justification for our activity:[142] within its teaching one finds the entire range of the Lord's precepts. Further, there is no need for customs like baptism, to which, as a sacrament, three arguments can be opposed. First, the minister may be corrupt and the mystery thereby contaminated. Then, although sins are disavowed at the font, they are repeated later in life. And a child who has no wish to co-operate nor a true understanding of the faith cannot be saved by another's confession.[143]

This is virtually the last point at which the heretics speak for themselves before their reconversion at the end of the *Acta*. The remainder of the synod consists of Gerard's reply and his general defence of the church's institutions, as revised, of course, by his narrator.

Within the summarized passage there are three separate accounts of the heretics. The bishop, we are told, was informed of their presence in his diocese and was given a rough outline of their ideas. He then questioned them briefly himself. Three days later he formally interrogated them at the synod. There is also evidence of a fourth intervention made on his behalf but not in his presence.[144] It was presumably from this inquiry that he learned of their specific objections to orthodoxy.

The most striking feature, as noted, is the discrepancy between Gerard's (or his narrator's) description of the heretics' beliefs and their own account of their activities.[145] Gerard, following the question-and-answer procedure of the episcopal inquisition, attributes to them a

---

[140] Jn 3.5.   [141] *Acta*, c. I, 1272A.

[142] *Ibid.*, 1272A-B: "Haec [lex et disciplina] namque hujusmodi est: mundum relinquere, carnem a concupiacentiis frenare, de laboribus manuum suarum victum parare, nulli laesionem quaerere, charitatem cunctis, quos zelus hujus nostri propositi teneat, exhibere. . . . Haec est nostrae justificationis summa. . . ."

[143] *Ibid.*, 1272B-C.

[144] *Ibid.*, 1271C: "ad notitiam episcopi pervenerat. . . ."

[145] Russell (1965), 22-24; Wakefield and Evans (1969), 84; Moore (1970) 28 and 28n34.

number of contradictions of Catholic teaching. But the heretics merely claim to be following an ascetic, world-denying way of life in accord with the gospels. At least, that is their interpretation of the New Testament. Clues to their guiding principles are found later in the *Acta*; on three occasions Gerard tells us they call themselves followers of St. Paul.[146] But what does this mean? Literal adherents to Pauline tenets would presumably have been in Gerard's camp. There is a suggestion in their own statements that they were obedient not to the letter but the spirit; in other words, that they derived from St. Paul's occasional statements on interpretation the justification to glean meaningful precepts from the gospel for themselves,[147] and, in the Pauline fashion, to preach them to small groups in foreign places.

This lay piety was neither superstition on the one hand nor a point-by-point rejection of orthodoxy, the two extremes that Gerard's letter to "R" suggests. It was the expression, in thought and action, of what the heretics took to be a direct acquaintance with the Word. Gerard's narrator de-emphasized this aspect of the episode and took pains to reinforce the traditional ceremony of the church, whence Gerard's magnificent entrance into St. Mary's. But the nature of the sectarian experience remains clear. It was not only a reaction against the official church, although it may have been that as well. It was an autonomous association. The converts were disciples of a single teacher, Gundulfo, about whom we learn only one fact: he based his instruction on a literal interpretation of certain passages of the New Testament, which he called the *evangelica mandata*. The members of the sect were probably not literate; in a significant phrase, they referred to themselves as *auditores*.[148] But they nonetheless participated directly, or so they thought, in higher religion.[149] Gundulfo asked that they accept the gospel, that is, his reading and interpretation of it, without comment (*nullamque praeter hanc scripturam se recipere*). He also insisted that they implement Christ's moral precepts "in word and deed." The ultimate objective, in other words, was not an intellectual system but an informed lay ethic, something which the adherents could take back with them and utilize in everyday life. True, when questioned further, the heretics denied the efficacy of baptism, calling into question by implication the other sacraments. But they appear to have been provoked by Gerard or his inquisitors, and their defence of their views did not

[146] *Acta*, c. 1, 1276B; c. 7, 1295B; c. 12, 1304B.
[147] Cf. Moore (1977), 12.
[148] *Acta*, c. 1, 1271C, quoted above p. 125n; c. 8, 1296D: Evangelii auditores.
[149] Cf. Ilarino da Milano (1947), 62, 66-67.

add up to an alternative theology. In fact, all three examples of invalidation—the bad priest, the unrepentant sinner, and the unwilling or uncomprehending child—were related to the same idea, the development of the inner moral conscience. In their view, one was personally responsible for one's sins, even one's intentions.[150] The precepts, moreover, were meant to be practiced, not just thought about: they spoke of *lex* and *disciplina*. And what Gundulfo taught did not in their eyes deny the church's *decreta* or *sanctiones*. It augmented them by taking the members back to the principles of primitive Christianity. Literalism went hand in hand with a return to the sources.[151]

We may think of the cycle as follows: first, the interpretation of biblical texts through a literate, charismatic leader; then, the formation of a social and religious association stressing the interaction of the individual members; and, finally, the emergence of principles of "justification" which could be opposed to the established order. This last they called *justitia* (or, as is probable, a vernacular equivalent). They meant not only ethical justice but the principles of legitimate authority on which they rested their case. This *justitia* was *lex*, to distinguish it from *usus*, the church's ceremonial accretions.[152]

With the *epistola* and the heretic's words as preface, we may profitably turn to Gerard's sermon, the longest section of the *Acta* (chs. 1-17). As noted, the text is a summary of Christian practices, with the idea of the sacraments as a unifying principle. The range of topics covered is wide, touching in turn on baptism, the eucharist, churches, altars, incense, bells, ordination, burial, penance, prayers for the dead, marriage, confession, the office, the cross, holy images, and the notion of justice. This is an impressive list for its period, especially as it is underpinned by a reasonably consistent theological position.

The "sermon" may be described in narrative terms as the conclusion of the drama; of which the letter and the *procès-verbal* are the beginning and the middle. It is also the section in which the third party who revised the *Acta* most clearly reveals his perspective on the events. There are several indications that the material has been reworked. The "sermon" is far too long to have been read aloud to those assembled and its learned references would have meant little to the lower clergy or the common people. As for the heretics, we are told that they were "stupefied" and "struck dumb" by Gerard's eloquence, which they

---

[150] *Acta*, c. 1, 1271C, 1272A-B; c. 16, 1309A-1311A (where admittedly we only hear from Gerard). Cf. Moore (1977), 12.

[151] *Ibid.*, c. 1, 1272B.

[152] *Ibid.*, 1272A (lex), 1272B (baptismi usus).

thought "divine."[153] But there is no evidence that they understood what he was saying. Even the simple Latin profession of faith at the *Acta*'s end had to be translated into French.[154] Of course, there may well have been a shorter sermon preached in the vernacular. But the intended audience of the Latin version was not primarily the laymen and clergy assembled at St. Mary's. It was a wider circle, possibly including others involved in the growing debate over reform. In order to serve this purpose, the events of the episode had to be transformed.

This took place in two stages. The doctrinal issues, somewhat amplified, were placed in a systematic framework, thereby allowing Gerard to respond in purely dogmatic terms. The behavioural primitivism of the heretics, that is, their alleged return to the sources, was thus answered by the literalism of the orthodox, both parties claiming affiliation with the gospel's true spirit. If the heretics are portrayed as revivers of ancient cults, Gerard appears as a new Ambrose or Augustine, a classical bishop defending a highly rational faith against rival pagan claims.

In this guise Gerard achieves the second broad aim of the *Acta*, which is to present the Christianity of his own day within a continuum of higher religious culture. In order to accomplish this goal he oversystematizes both the heretical and orthodox positions. Although many of the practices he describes depend on ritual, custom, or the spoken word, they are all "justified" by law, precedent, and Scripture. The purpose is not only to win an ideological victory but to fit both heresy and orthodoxy into an intellectualist mode of thought. The heretics call themselves followers of St. Paul, but he sees himself fulfilling the goals of the maxim *oportet ut haereses esse*. And, through the sermon, the *Acta* raises the general theological question of how God's word is to be legitimately communicated to man.

Gerard's authority, then, like that of the heretics, is based on a concept of *justitia*: within this notion the bishop frames his defence of the sacraments and ecclesiastical practices uniting the popular and the learned. In his opening statement he attempts to establish universalism through "justice"; in his conclusion he returns to a similar notion by arguing that salvation depends not on one's merits but on God's "just" grace. These ideas are worked out as the "sermon" proceeds.

The heretics, Gerard states, claim to be following "evangelical and apostolic teaching." But they are really like those Jews of whom Paul

[153] *Ibid.*, c. 2, 1284A.   [154] *Ibid.*, c. 17, 1312C-D.

so eloquently spoke, who adhered to the law's letter rather than to its spirit. For there is a difference between "law" and "God's justice."

He means, in effect, that one must distinguish between uninterpreted and interpreted law, the latter incorporating the institutional and intellectual development of the church. God's justice, Gerard argues, through Jesus, is in all men who believe in him: all have sinned, all are without light, all are justified through grace and redemption.[155] In this sense "Jesus alone is just and justifies everything."[156] His justice did not arise from an external source; it resided by substance and necessity in him alone. He did not participate in justice; he was justice. As James said, "All good giving and every perfect gift comes from above. . . ."[157] This means that what descends from the father also descends from the son. For "I and the father are one,"[158] Jesus said. Such justice cannot be increased, diminished, or compared to anything else.[159]

Justice, then, and not mere law, is the justification for the church's practices. Christ was not bound by the old law; he represented a new beginning. Therefore, returning to the text's letter fails to capture the spirit which animated it. In "justifying everything," Jesus opened the door to the founding of the institutional church and to the gradual evolution of its rite. Baptism provides a good example. When Jesus came to John the Baptist in Galilee, John first refused to baptize his lord. "Do you come to me?" he asked. "I need rather to be baptized by you." But Jesus replied: "It is fitting that we fulfill every justice (*omnem justitiam implere*)."[160] The question Gerard poses to the heretics is: why did Christ, the incarnation of justice, undergo the justificatory ritual of baptism at all? The answer is that it was not essential for him but for us: he sought "to implement" not his own justice but ours.[161] From the *summa plenitudinis*—an idea neatly incorporating for Gerard both theological and canonical precedence—justice flowed down to us. For the restoration of mankind remains forever in God's inner thoughts. In classically sacramental terms, Gerard states that this fu-

---

[155] Rom 3:22-24; *Acta*, c. 1, 1272C.

[156] *Loc.cit.*: Paul, of course, stated a somewhat different case when he wrote at Rom 3:22: "Justitia autem Dei per fidem Jesu Christi in omnes et super omnes qui credunt in eum," adding at 3:26 "justificans eum qui est ex fide Jesu Christi." Gerard's phrase *justificans omnia*, which is repeated seven times (1272C-73B) is supported elsewhere in Paul, but not in a specifically legal and sacramental sense.

[157] Jac 1:17.   [158] Jn 10:30.   [159] *Acta*, c. 1, 1272C, 1273A.
[160] Matt 3:13-15; *Acta*, 1273A.   [161] *Acta*, c. 1, 1273B-C.

ture promise is held out "visibly" through the minister and "invisibly" through the holy spirit's operation.[162]

These ideas are reiterated and amplified in Gerard's second discussion of justice in chapter sixteen, where, as noted, the question is whether grace or one's merits insures salvation. Once again he presents a strong case for the traditional view, beginning with two quotations. John said, "A man can receive nothing but what is given to him from heaven,"[163] and Paul asked, "Miserable as I am, who will liberate me from this body of death?"[164] To Gerard the meaning of such declarations is clear: "In the disobedience of the first man we lost our innocence and natural potential; and no one can lift himself up from the depths of ruin through his free will unless he is also raised up by merciful grace."[165] Man's personal striving after salvation is not considered useless; but, no matter what "holy thoughts," "pious counsels," or "good motives" we have, we cannot further our chances for restoration to paradise without God's help.[166] As John said, "Without me you can do nothing."[167]

Grace, moreover, Gerard argues, is a kind of foreknowledge, which takes account of individual merit in advance. It does not preclude leading a holy, ascetic life, for the gospels explicitly state, "Forgo impiety and vain desire that we may live soberly, justly, and piously in this world."[168] But, at the same time, Christians ought to recognize that grace's source lies "neither in nature's forces nor in legal precepts but in the enlightening of the heart and the freely offered gift of divine will."[169] Therefore, in the last analysis, it is God himself who inspires us to "good works," which, to that extent, are a preparation for his judgement and for salvation.[170] For "he predestined what divine equity would give back, not what human iniquity lost."[171] In other words, he readied man for a positive, not a negative, judgment. The heretics' justice in Gerard's view turns its back on such possibilities. Once again he refers to St. Paul, speaking of those who, "ignorant of God's justice, try to set up their own. . . ."[172] True justice, represented by Jesus's words, was handed down to the apostles, whence it spread to the original bishoprics of christendom and later to the many churches of the holy see.[173]

At the sermon's beginning and end, then, we find the principle of

---

[162] *Ibid.*, 1273C.   [163] Jn 3:27; *Acta*, c. 16, 1309A-B.   [164] Rom 7:24; *ibid.*, 1309B.
[165] *Acta*, c. 16, 1309B.   [166] *Ibid.*, 1309B-C.
[167] Jn 15:6; *ibid.*, 1309C.   [168] Tit 2:2; *ibid.*, 1309D.
[169] *Acta*, c. 16, 1310A.   [170] *Ibid.*, 1310B.   [171] *Loc.cit.*
[172] Rom 10:3; *ibid.*, 1310D.   [173] *Acta*, c. 16, 1310D-11A.

legitimacy. The intervening chapters deal with the sacraments as underlying foundations for the church's practices. But the method of proceeding is similar: first Gerard imputes to the heretics the rejection of the institution in question; then he establishes its "justice" through scriptural and patristic authority.

The results are threefold. Obviously, an ideal of the church is projected which is founded on legislation and respect for precedent; in other words, Gerard adopts the typical reformist strategy of justifying customary practices wherever necessary by written law. As a consequence, a distinction grows throughout the sermon between "popular" and "learned" traditions, which curiously parallels the thinking of the heretics themselves. Finally, the heretics are deprived of their group vitality and become identified only with disobedience and error. This, in turn, is viewed as a byproduct of their theological illiteracy.

The most impressive pieces of theological reasoning are devoted to the sacraments of baptism and the eucharist. Like later defenders of orthodoxy against Berengar, Gerard takes the Augustinian view that in baptism one thing is experienced through the senses but that another really takes place.[174] Greek *baptismum* means Latin *tinctio*, through which "man is changed through the spirit's grace into something better. . . ."[175] The mystery is called a "sacrament" from its secret or sacred powers, which, Gerard adds, do not depend for their efficacy on the minister's moral qualities.[176] He can neither increase merit nor diminish vice: for the gardener only plants and waters, while the creator makes things grow.[177] The baptizing priest does not say, "I, omnipotent God . . . bestow upon you the balm of eternal life."[178] Otherwise we could not accept the baptism of a Judas.[179] Moreover, emphasizing realism, Gerard insists that "the material water" baptizes, for the Lord decreed that invisible reality be meted out in a palpable form.[180] As it washes the body, so it cleanses the mind: with the invocation of God, mere water is sanctified and, like healing medicine, acquires the capacity for expurgation. . . .[181] In Pauline terms, the immersion is the death of the "old man" and the birth of the "new," thereby re-enacting Christ's crucifixion and resurrection. "Administered carnally, it works spiritually."[182]

Baptism's symbolic powers were foreshadowed in Genesis when "the spirit of God hovered over the waters."[183] It is also the starting point

[174] *Acta*, c. 1, 1273C, 1274D.   [175] *Ibid.*, 1273D.   [176] *Ibid.*, 1273D-74A.
[177] 1 Cor 3:7; *ibid.*, 1274A.   [178] *Acta*, c. 1, 1274A.   [179] *Ibid.*, 1274A-B.
[180] *Ibid.*, 1274D.   [181] *Ibid.*, 1274D-75A.   [182] *Ibid.*, 1275B.
[183] Gen 1:2; *ibid.*, 1275B.

of that earthly "justification" which Matthew said his successors were to accomplish.[184] Its legitimacy, moreover, is supported by many acts of Jesus and the apostles.[185] But, Gerard emphasizes, the real source of mystery is divine. The living fountain of purification is God himself. Through him, the son of the devil re-emerges as the son of God, the son of prevarication, the son of reconciliation. In Eden the first man was nourished directly by this fountain. Had he not sinned, it would have made him immortal. For, from one and the same fount of divine reason (*ex . . . fonte divinae rationis*), the same spirit descended, both creating man capable of immortality and later reforming him from his state of sin.[186] True, all this might have been foreseen by God. But it was man himself who sinned, and, by a single act, transmitted sin to all of human posterity.[187] Regeneration can be achieved through the sacraments, beginning with baptism. Finally, to the heretics' allegation that children cannot be saved through the sacraments, Gerard replies that sin is the condition of all human beings, whether adult or child.[188] In rejecting baptism, therefore, the dissidents are hardly following "evangelical and apostolic precepts."[189]

Gerard has similar thoughts on the eucharist, which he claims the heretics likewise reject. Human beings, he maintains, can no more fathom its mysteries than can the senses understand the soul. Nor can it be described by *humana facundia*.[190] Once again, the sacrament unites exiled man with his celestial homeland.[191] The eucharistic sacrifice is literally a *sacrum factum*, which, through prayer, commemorates the lord's passion. The bread and wine, although earthly in appearance, are sanctified and sacramentalized by the holy spirit's operation. The sacrament in turn is a viaticum to contemplating eternity.[192] What could serve the purpose better than Christ's own body and blood? Christ said, "Take the bread . . . ,"[193] and added that the rite was to be perpetuated "in his memory." Of course, objections can be raised. For instance, one can argue that, if Christ's body went entirely to heaven, nothing would be left on earth to be eaten. But the mystery must not be interpreted so "carnally." Without his "nourishment," men live physically, not spiritually, as numerous passages of the Bible illustrate.[194] In this vein Christ himself said, "I am the living bread."[195]

---

[184] *Acta*, c. 1, 1275C.   [185] E.g., Jn 3:22, 1 Jn 5:7-8, *Acta* 2.37f., *ibid.*, 1275C-76B.
[186] *Acta*, c. 1, 1276C-D.   [187] *Ibid.*, 1277A-C.
[188] On children, *ibid.*, 1277C-D.   [189] *Ibid.*, 1275D-76A, 1277D-78A.
[190] *Acta*, c. 2, 1278B.   [191] *Ibid.*, 1278B-C.
[192] *Ibid.*, 1278C.   [193] Matt 26:26-28; *ibid.*, 1278D-79A.
[194] *Acta*, c. 2, 1279B-D.   [195] Jn 6:35; *ibid.*, 1279C.

Again, one may argue that Christ's fleshly covering could not be broken up into little bits and distributed. For this would amount to cannibalism. That is to repeat the same error. Christ said, "The sermon is difficult."[196] He meant that experiencing the eucharist required mental exertion. Grace "is perceived by the palate of the interior man, that is, by the mind's reason and intellect."[197] Therefore, paradoxically, while "Christ rose with his own body, he left us the *sacramentum* of his own body."[198] By the same mystery, he who eats of his flesh will be raised up on the last day. Finally, it is erroneous to argue that Christ was circumscribed at all. Only man is limited by the body and by time. God knows no place or time: "just as his essence always exists, it always exists everywhere."[199]

The defence of the sacraments lays the foundation for Gerard's description of the utility of the church's other practices. The heretics, he claims, assert that churches are only heaps of stone and mortar. One can as easily worship in one's own house.[200] Gerard replies that a distinction must be made between the material out of which the church is made and the sacred rites which take place within its walls. Before Christ, men went into "churches" to learn about the law; after him, about grace.[201] Moreover, the spiritual element the heretics fail to attribute to places of worship they also deny to altars, incense, bells, penance, and marriage. The altar is the appointed place of sacrifice and sanctification, recalling the offering of the "true lamb" and "holding out the image of Christ's body and sepulchre."[202] In incense, too, as Augustine notes, the visible oil is a sign, the invisible a sacrament.[203] Bells recall the warning at Jericho and foretell of the last day.[204] Churches, moreover, need officials, who must be clearly distinguished from laymen,[205] a point which, Gerard holds, the heretics also dismiss, maintaining, or so he says, that all religious functions can be carried on in woods, in brief informal gatherings, and through simple incantation.[206] Nor do they see any value in Christian burial, through which man normally proceeds from the temporal to the spiritual church,[207] or in penance, which, like baptism, helps to heal the wounds of original sin.[208] They also reject marriage, even though the Bible indicates that men in lawful wedlock have no less a chance of

---

[196] Jn 6:61; *ibid.*, 1279D.
[197] *Acta*, c. 2, 1280A. [198] *Ibid.*, 1280B. [199] *Ibid.*, 1281A.
[200] *Ibid.*, c. 3, 1284C.
[201] *Ibid.*, 1286B-C. [202] *Ibid.*, c. 4, 1287D. [203] *Ibid.*, 1289C.
[204] *Ibid.*, c. 5, 1291A-B. [205] *Ibid.*, c. 6, 1294C.
[206] *Ibid.*, 1294D. [207] *Ibid.*, c. 7, 1295A-C. [208] *Ibid.*, c. 8, 1296B-D.

TEXTUAL COMMUNITIES

being saved.²⁰⁹ In each case their error in his view is the same: a
failure to differentiate between the carnal, physical, and material, on
the one hand, and the sacred, commemorative, and spiritual.

For Gerard, the legitimacy of these accumulated customs is affirmed by biblical texts. Written law as opposed to custom is repeatedly invoked as a source of authority. Anna, who never left the temple, correctly prophesied Christ's arrival *ex evangelica lectione*.²¹⁰ Whenever
Christ came to a town, he entered the local church *secundum consuetudinem*,²¹¹ but this custom became an official rule. The Jews frequented
their places of worship *ex antiqua traditione*, the Christians, *ex Novo
Testamento*:²¹² both were equally indebted to written commands. Le-
viticus "bore witness" to the use of the altar by Moses and God.²¹³
We know that incense was used by the "old and new fathers . . . on
the authority of divine teaching."²¹⁴ The imposition of hands is an
antiqua institutio.²¹⁵ To those who reject Christian burial, Gerard ex-
claims, "You, who are ignorant of the law, why do you not study
Scripture?"²¹⁶ In some cases he also distinguishes between stages of
legal development. When the prodigal son returned home, he was
given the coat he lost: the first (*prima stola*), that is, the ancient (*antiqua*), not the new (*nova*).²¹⁷ By the same token penance does not
merely cure present spiritual ills but restores our primal innocence.
The scholastic bent of the discussions is evident from the literary
manner in which the authorities are often cited.²¹⁸ Evidence for genuine saints after the age of the martyrs is furnished by "volumes of
miracles."²¹⁹ The church is allegorically called the *mater credentium*.²²⁰
The list of earlier commentators is long, including Augustine, Eusebius, Jerome, the pseudo-Denis, Isidore, the life of St. Martin, and
Gregory the Great.²²¹ Gerard's point is that, in following up the text
"He is just and justifies" with written authority, it is the orthodox
who really play the part the heretics claim to be theirs as the *imitatores
sancti Pauli*.²²²

Paradoxically, the more Gerard tries to underpin the customs of
the church with a textual basis, the wider the gap becomes within

²⁰⁹ *Ibid.*, c. 10, 1299C-1300B.   ²¹⁰ *Ibid.*, c. 3, 1284D.
²¹¹ *Ibid.*, 1285D; Luc 4.16.   ²¹² *Ibid.*, 1286C-D.   ²¹³ *Ibid.*, c. 4, 1287C.
²¹⁴ *Ibid.*, 1288C.   ²¹⁵ *Ibid.*, c. 6, 1294A.   ²¹⁶ *Ibid.*, c. 7, 1296A.
²¹⁷ *Ibid.*, c. 8, 1297A.   ²¹⁸ *Ibid.*, c. 4, 1289A; c. 10, 1299D.
²¹⁹ *Ibid.*, c. 11, 1303A.   ²²⁰ *Ibid.*, c. 7, 1295B.
²²¹ E.g., Augustine, 1287A, 1289C; Eusebius, 1297C-D; Jerome, 1302C; pseudo-Denis,
1307D; Isidore, 1278C, 1289B, 1293C; St. Martin, 1303B-C; Gregory, 1282A-83D, 1299A,
1308A-C.
²²² *Acta*, c. 12, 1304B.

the sermon between popular and learned religious culture. For, in providing a historical account of why the institutions were adopted in the first place, he has by implication to explain why they should now be adhered to by the common people, who have little understanding of ecclesiastical precedent. Gerard's answer is to redefine popular culture as all that is not official culture.

His position is complex, not wholly consistent, and composed of three elements. The first is the recognition of the heretics as dangerous *litterati* among his unlettered parishioners. They spread false doctrines (*confusio*,[223] *tenebrae infidelitatis*);[224] they "invent fables."[225] Their dialectical sophistication, or so he would have us think, is to be both respected and distrusted. However, this picture of the heretics as diabolical ministers, whose efforts are primarily directed towards the common people, is invented in part to provide a contrasting role for the church as defender, even protector, of religious communications with less learned, ordinary believers. Gerard stresses Christ as preacher:[226] *ecclesia* means *populus convocatus*;[227] the role of the bishop and the priest is "to instruct the people."[228] In other words, inherited belief is oral, just as God speaks through the Word. But specious erudition must be combatted by proper interpretation.

As a consequence, the third element in Gerard's thought is a new separation within the church of popular and learned culture, through which the spoken is both part of God's design and yet unable to stand without an interpretive gloss. Like physical symbolism in feudal law, it retains its functional orality while acquiring evidential documentation. On the one hand, the older vocabulary is reiterated: in the eucharist, "he who does not embrace the unique gage (*pignus*) of faith doubtless excludes himself from the constitution (*compago*) of Christ's body."[229] The link arises between the Word and the physical sign; in understanding sacramental mysteries, reason, that is, textual discussion, has a limited role.[230] But God's orality is not the same as man's. Discussing Christ's image on the cross, Gerard clearly distinguishes between the lettered and the unlettered. The wood, he points out, is not divine in itself. "But if you diligently search for the reason behind the mystery,"[231] it may be summed up as follows: "the less educated (*simpliciores*) and illiterate (*illiterati*) in the church, who cannot understand written biblical texts, form a mental impression of them through

[223] *Ibid.*, c. 2, 1278B. [224] *Ibid.*, c. 3, 1284B. [225] *Ibid.*, c. 4, 1287C; c. 7, 1295A.
[226] *Ibid.*, c. 3, 1285D-86A. [227] *Ibid.*, 1287A. [228] *Ibid.*, c. 6, 1293A.
[229] *Ibid.*, c. 8, 1295C. [230] *Ibid.*, c. 2, 1278B. [231] *Ibid.*, c. 13, 1305A.

the painting's delineation."[232] Thus, artistic form (*species*) provides a means of experiencing Christ's crucifixion.[233] Similarly, "interpretation is permitted of saints' images," not for worshipping likenesses but for arousing the inner man to imitate their way of life.[234]

Beginning then with means of "justification" and proceeding through a welter of ecclesiastical practices, the sermon effectively changes the direction of the *Acta*. The heretics' admission of their own beliefs, together with their infiltration into neighbouring dioceses, is replaced with a complex defence of the church's control of religious literacy. This perspective is confirmed in the final conversion scene. Needless to say, the overall impression the reader takes away from the *Acta* is not altogether harmonious. Instead, it would appear that somewhat incompatible viewpoints are maintained at once. As noted, in the final episode, the heretics, who are, with respect to Latin at least, almost unlettered, are made to acknowledge the persuasiveness of Gerard's "sermon," which they can hardly be expected to have understood. To round out this inconsistent picture, the bishop also bases their profession of faith on sacramental realism. Those who reject all physical symbols are therefore made to reaffirm the very rituals from which they derive their meaning. And, as the heretics are pushed towards one end of literacy's scale, the orthodox position moves towards the other.

Let us look a little more closely at the final scene. To these supposed followers of St. Paul, Gerard offers one final Pauline quotation, which is drawn from 1 Timothy. In the final days, Paul predicted, some Christians would leave the faith under diabolical influence. They would preach lies and forget the obligations of conscience. They would forbid marriage and the eating of flesh, even though God intended the faithful to profit from both.[235] The heretics, are then said to be rendered speechless by Gerard's cumulative wisdom, which comprises a virtual "summa of Christian salvation."[236] Gerard invites them to denounce their conspiracy: together the assembly rejects the heretics'

---

[232] *Ibid.*, c. 14, 1306B-C: "Est vero alia hujus ratio: simpliciores quippe in ecclesia et illiterati, quod per Scripturas non possunt intueri, hoc per quaedam picturae liniamenta contemplantur, id est, Christum in ea humilitate, qua pro nobis pati et mori voluit." For similar texts, see L. Gougaud, "Muta Praedicatio," 168-70.

[233] *Ibid.*, 1306C.

[234] *Ibid.*, 1306C-D: "Similiter de imaginibus sanctorum ratiocinari licet, quae ideo in sancta ecclesia fiunt, non ut ab hominibus adorari debeant, sed ut per eas interius excitemur ad contemplandam gratiae divinae operationem, atque ex eorum actibus aliquid in usum nostrae conversationis trahamus."

[235] *Ibid.*, c. 17, 1311B-C; 1 Tim 4.1-4.   [236] *Ibid.*, 1311C.

beliefs on baptism, the eucharist, penance, the church, marriage, and allegations of widespread simony and materialism among priests.[237] These denunciations are backed up by quotations from the Bible, which summarize some of the sermon's main points.[238] The heretics, it is important to reiterate, knowing no Latin, did not entirely understand what was being said, and so their excommunication and profession of faith were translated into the vernacular. However, they chose freely to reaffirm the faith and signed their declarations with a cross.[239] Then, repentant, they returned to their homes.

If we look more closely at this scene, its puzzling features all appear to be related in some way to Gerard's ambivalence before the problem of literacy. Before his sermon, the heretics thought themselves, or so he says, *insuperabiles verbo*; they were unable to be constrained by any sort of language (*nec ullo verbi genere constringi*).[240] Yet, to believe the *Acta*, they were stopped cold by the gravity of Gerard's words and the power of God they evidently represented. The purpose of this statement in part is to sidestep an important issue in communications, namely the gap between the heretics' mode, which was, although a byproduct of literacy, oral, vernacular, and unofficial, and the bishop's, which is textual, Latin, and institutionalized.

What the narrator is saying in effect is that the charisma which the heretics associated with Gundulfo has passed without much explanation to the bishop. The lack of commentary underlines all the more emphatically the obvious similarities between the theoretical message of the sermon and the actual profession of faith. Like the biblical texts which Gerard cited, the *professio* was a written document which the dissidents were asked to sign.[241] The crosses which they wrote on the parchment constituted a legal witness which could presumably be presented in their case's favour on judgment day. In other words, as the *Acta* has it, these virtuosi of oral culture, who appear to have been unlettered, committed themselves to a written authority. The message was embodied in the text; the bishop was only its medium. The declaration, moreover, had two parts, a list of actual (or putative) offenses and a minor defence of orthodoxy. The *professio*'s structure thereby repeated the order of the *Acta*, which began with the *procès-verbal* and continued with the "sermon"; that is, like them, it proceeded from words to texts. This, in turn, helped to systematize the

---

[237] *Ibid.*, 1311C-12A.   [238] *Ibid.*, 1312A-C.   [239] *Ibid.*, 1312C-D.
[240] *Ibid.*, 1311C.   [241] *Ibid.*, 1312D.

heretics' beliefs, from which vantage point a coherent rebuttal could be framed.

Realism also played a role in undermining the function of literacy in the original group. In this sense, both sides used literacy to their own ends. Rational interpretation of the gospels taught the heretics to reject the ritualistic, symbolic, and customary practices of the church. Their hermeneutics resulted logically in a system of belief understandable at an intellectual level alone. The orthodox view was the other side of the coin. The heretics were first accused of the physicalism they abjured. They reaffirmed that churches, altars, bread, and wine were more than "what is seen by corporeal eyes." No one could be saved but by "the water of regeneration," which represented forgiveness and future grace. The eucharist was "the gage" of our redemption and salvation, and so forth. The purpose of such statements is to suggest that the heretics' literacy was really a kind of illiteracy. This notion is even supported by the obvious contradiction at the *Acta*'s end: the heretics, understanding no Latin, make their choice *per interpretem vulgarem*;[242] it follows that they could hardly have repeated the *professio fidei* aloud with the "abbots, archdeacons, and clergy."[243] What is perhaps most remarkable about the *Acta* is what it never says directly, namely, that oral and written, vernacular and Latin, have become serious issues in religious communication.

Monforte

The gap between the popular and learned interpretations of heresy by contemporary witnesses widens in the case of Monforte. The events took place in 1028[244] not far from Turin. There are two accounts, one by Rodulf Glaber, which is roughly contemporary, and another by Landulf Senior written some seventy-five years later. Historians have tried to reconcile the two, but this has raised as many problems as it has solved.[245] The Burgundian monk and the Lombard cleric have little in common. For Glaber, Monforte is not only an episode of heresy but also a means by which group solidarity among Christians can be strengthened after the millennium. Landulf tells us much about the group's beliefs and principles of organization. But the story also plays a role in the historiography of Milan, as Aribert, the city's

---

[242] *Ibid.*, 1312C.   [243] *Ibid.*, 1311C.

[244] On the dating, see Ilarino da Milano (1947), 68n37, Borst (1953), 70n1, and C. Violante, *La società milanese nell'età precomunale*, 2nd ed. (Bari, 1974), 220.

[245] E.g., Ilarino da Milano (1947), 71, Violante (1974), 220-31.

renowned archbishop, attempts to regain religious and political control over the ancient see of St. Ambrose.

Once again, we will summarize the accounts before commenting on them. Glaber's tale[246] has two parts, one historical, one moral. The first is dealt with rather briefly. There was, he relates, a certain *castrum* called Monforte, located in Lombardy, which was filled with heretics, many of noble origins. Among other pagan practices they were said to worship idols and to engage in ceremonies reminiscent of Judaism. The heresy was so endemic that on one occasion Manfred, marchese of Asti, or perhaps his brother Alric, the praesul, was obliged to invade the region, accompanied by other knights. They rounded up the heretics and gave them the choice of recanting or of being burned at the stake.

The second part of Glaber's account concerns a certain Hugh, a knight on his deathbed in a neighbouring, unheretical town. When news of his illness reached heretical circles, an attempt was made to convert him before he died. The emissary was a woman who claimed to be paying him only a customary goodwill visit. But disturbing apparitions accompanied her. Hugh saw her arrive at the head of a sinister band, all of whose members were dressed in black. She passed her hand over Hugh's forehead, felt his pulse, and, after declaring that he would soon be well, took her leave. But the ominous band remained. A globe then appeared near the group's apparent leader, who asked Hugh whether he recognized him. When Hugh replied negatively, the figure announced portentously that he was "the most powerful of the powerful and the richest of the rich."[247] In veiled phrases he suggested affiliations with Conrad I, the duke of Carinthia, whom, he maintained, was now emperor in the West, and Michael IV, who had succeeded Basil II (in reality Roman III) in the East.[248] Hugh, he added, could regain his health if only he would make the sign of the cross in his presence. Frightened, Hugh did just the opposite: he professed his faith in Christ and disavowed "the fallacious devil." Then a voice was heard saying, "I beseech you, do not raise your arm against me."[249] At this divine sign the terrifying band vanished.

"No one doubts," Glaber adds moralistically, "that the vision was intended for us as well as for him."[250] But historians have paid little attention to this admonition, or, for that matter, to the charged lan-

---

[246] *Historiae* 4.2.5, pp. 94-96, which I summarize.
[247] *Ibid.*, 95.
[248] *Loc.cit.*   [249] *Loc.cit.*   [250] *Ibid.*, 96.

guage of his account. There are some four episodes of heresy related in the *Historiae*, all of which play a part in his overall scheme of sin, penance, and millenarian renewal.[251] In the case of Hugh, he effectively superimposes political material onto an oral record of supernatural forces. He thereby unites popular and learned forms of prognostication. The facts, it is worth noting, are hardly mentioned. Manfred and Alric are mere names, as are the disreputable Conrad I and Michael IV. The two parts of the narrative are really brought together by the popular elements. The heretics, although noble, are ritualistic in their approach to religion. They engage in external ceremonies *more paganorum* or in *inepta sacrificia* in the manner of the Jews, for whom Glaber elsewhere voices his dislike.[252] Hugh's female visitor gives the same impression. Her laying on of hands may weakly reflect dualistic origins, as some have argued.[253] But Glaber's setting for the interview is theologically unsophisticated. What Hugh witnesses on his deathbed is a simple contrast between God and the devil. Faith battles against the forces of darkness. The dissembling of the female missionary makes sense only within this stark framework of interpretation. The focal point of the story is not the sorceress, but Hugh. He is the one who is tested. The moral purpose of the vision is to reinforce lay piety (including the reader's). There is no evidence in the scene itself that the female heretic is aware of the presence of the "numberless army." On the contrary, what is invisible to her is visible to Hugh because of his faith, which, in permitting the dying knight to see what is really present, also provides a bridge to Glaber's sacramental realism. In sum, although learned details crop up, they are not central to what Glaber wants to say. He is opposing not theologies or political prophecies but last rites. The heretical female goes through the motions of a purificatory ritual; Hugh's rejection is a verbal profession of faith. The essential elements in the scene belong to a nonliterate world.

The twenty-seventh chapter of book two of the *Historia Mediolanensis* provides a rude contrast to Glaber's account. Landulf relates the same episode as follows.[254] Aribert, who had visited almost all the suffragans of the archdiocese of Milan, arrived at length in Turin, accompanied by a great many knights and clergy. While preaching there he heard of an unusual heresy in a *castellum* above a locality called Monforte. He asked that a member of the sect be brought before him.

---

[251] See below, Ch. 5 pp. 456-72.   [252] E.g., 3.6.20; p. 69, 71.

[253] Violante (1974), 223; but see Borst (1953), 70n1.

[254] Summarizing *Historia Mediolanensis* 2.27, MGH SS 8, p. 65, line 23 to p. 66, line 36.

The man who came was called Gerard. He bore himself well, seemed willing to answer questions, and did not fear suffering or even death on behalf of his beliefs. Aribert questioned him on the way of life, religious customs, and faith of the sectarians. Gerard, granted permission to speak, made the following statement: "I thank the father, the son and the holy spirit that you have taken pains to question me so thoroughly. May He, who knew you in Adam's loins, grant that you live with him, die with him and reign forever with him in glory! I shall set forth the way of life and faith of my brethren in the same spirit in which you have made your inquiry. We pride virginity above all else, although we have wives. He who is a virgin among us remains so; he who is corrupt, with the permission of an elder, remains chaste from that time on. None of us enjoys his wife carnally but cherishes her like a mother or sister. We never eat meat. We fast and pray continually. Our elders pray day and night, one after the other, so that prayer may never cease. We hold all possessions in common. We believe in the father, the son, and the holy spirit, as well as in those who have the power of binding and loosing. We follow the Old and the New Testaments, together with the sacred canons, which we read daily."

Many were amazed at these statements, but Aribert, recognizing an attempt at dissimulation, asked for further clarification. In particular, he demanded that Gerard explain what the sect understood by "father, the son, and the holy spirit." Gerard replied cheerfully: "The father is the eternal God, who created everything in the beginning and in whom all things exist. The son is the spirit of man, beloved by God. The holy spirit is the understanding of divine matters, by which individual things are governed." Aribert asked a further question: "What do you say of Christ, the word of God, born of a virgin?" Gerard answered: "The Jesus of whom you speak is the spirit, born sensibly (*sensualiter*) from the virgin, that is, from sacred scripture. That same holy spirit is the understanding of sacred scripture." Aribert turned to another matter. "Why," he asked, "does one have a wife except to produce children?" Gerard replied: "If the entire human race would unite in uncarnal unions, then it would experience procreation without sex like the bees." Aribert: "In whom lies the responsibility for absolving our sins, the pope, the bishop, or the priest?" Gerard: "We do not acknowledge the Roman pontiff but another, who daily visits our dispersed brethren throughout the world. When God acts as minister through him, remission from our sins is devoutly granted." Aribert: "Is it true that you end your lives violently?" Gerard: "If we die through the torture of evil men, we rejoice; but if nature brings any of us near death, his neighbour kills him before he yields up his soul." Aribert mulled these matters over. Finally he asked Gerard whether he believed in Catholicism, the church, baptism, virgin birth, and the eucharist. Gerard replied: "There is no priest beyond our priest, although he lacks tonsure and mystery."

Aribert was now convinced that what had been said about the heretics of Monforte was correct. Soon afterwards he sent an armed force to the locality and took everyone prisoner, including the area's countess. Then he brought them all to Milan, where, with the aid of his clergy, he attempted to reconvert them, lest the heresy spread to other parts of Italy. But wicked men, Landulf adds, who, unrecognized, had come to the region from elsewhere, proselytized the humble folk who came daily to the city to see them. When the elders of Milan learned of this, they built a huge pyre and set up a cross nearby. Over Aribert's protests they led the heretics out and asked them to choose between orthodoxy and death. Some came to the cross and were saved, but many, covering their faces with their hands, leapt bravely into the flames.

Landulf's account is undoubtedly based on the record of a *procès-verbal*,[255] and the questions and answers give the impression of a sectarian movement highly involved with doctrinal issues. Were it not related to Glaber's account by common historical details, one would be hard pressed to find any similarity between the two narratives.

There are two sides to the heresy as outlined briefly by Gerard. One is the list of actual beliefs. The other is the method by which the sectarians arrived at them. Historians have generally focused on dogma in an attempt to link the sect at Monforte to other eleventh-century heresies.[256] But Gerard gives an equally lucid account of their processes of reasoning, which appear to have been undertaken, elaborated, and made the basis of religious practices within the group itself. Gerard himself was reasonably erudite. He was presumably literate and had the benefit of a good lay or clerical education.[257] His technical terms often appear to echo the vocabulary of patristic theological de-

[255] Cf. C. Violante, *La pataria milanese e la riforma ecclesiastica. Le premesse (1045-1057)* (Rome, 1955), 108; Taviani (1974), 1225, 1228.

[256] Violante, *La società milanese . . .* , (Bari, 1953), 176-86 (= 2nd ed., 1974, 220-31. The second edition repeats the first, whose pagination I retain for the Monforte episode). Cf. Cracco (1971), 465, Taviani (1974), *passim*.

[257] Taviani (1974), 1241-42, argues that he was a *clericus*, but there is no evidence to support the claim. On the education of the laity in general during the period, see the review of P. Riché, "Recherches sur l'instruction des laïcs du IXe au XIIe siècle," CCM 5 (1962), 175-82.

bate.[258] Also, he is happy to demonstrate his rhetorical abilities for Aribert. He first praises the bishop; then, possibly in an effort at dissimulation,[259] fits his deviant views into an apparently orthodox framework, beginning with a reference to Adam's sin and redemption and ending with a commitment to the Old and New Testaments. Yet the manner in which he "declares" (*edico*) his beliefs is concise and moderately abstract, as if memorized from a written summary.

His explanation of the sect's allegorical method confirms the impression of erudite influences. Sensing artful deception, Aribert asks Gerard to discuss in greater detail his conception of the trinity. Gerard replies with an example of both allegory and heuristic method. In his view, the father, the son, and the holy spirit are not to be taken literally. God is eternity;[260] in him all things exist. The son is the *animus hominis*,[261] the spirit in man. The holy spirit (*spiritus sanctus*) is the *divinarum scientiarum intellectus*, the understanding of divine knowledge. It follows that Jesus was not literally born from a virgin. Gerard states that Christ is the same *animus* of which he just spoke, born *sensualiter* from the virgin Mary, that is, born *ex sacra scriptura*.[262] He equates the reality of Christ's birth with authentication in the sacred text, and adds that the "spirit" of the same sacred scriptures is nothing more than the intellect itself acting with devotion.[263] The holy spirit, then, is identical with the ordered intelligence of man,[264] which

[258] Taviani (1974), 1231-41, who, in my view, overinterprets; Violante (1953), 177-81, is more moderate.

[259] Ilarino da Milano (1947), 68-69; Violante (1953), 179.

[260] *Historia Mediolanensis* 2.27, p. 66, 1-2: "Quod dixi Patrem, Deus est aeternus, qui omnia ut ab initio, et in quo omnia consistunt." On interpretation I follow Violante (1953), 177n31 against Ilarino da Milano (1947), 69, although the text admits both possibilities.

[261] Translating *animus* as spirit and not as soul, *contra* Violante (1953), 177 and Wakefield and Evans (1969), 87-88; on the background of *animus* and *intellectus*, see Taviani (1974), 1234-39.

[262] A difficult statement, 2.27, p. 66, 5-6: "Iesum Christum quem dicis est animus sensualiter natus ex Maria virgine, videlicet natus est ex sancta scriptura." For eucharistic speculation on *sensualiter*, see Taviani (1974), 1237-38 and below, ch. 3; on general interpretation, see the useful comments of Violante (1953), 177 and Wakefield and Evans (1969), 669n9.

[263] *Historia* 2.27, p. 66, 6-7: "Spiritus sanctus sanctarum scriptuarum cum devotione intellectus," where the genitive, of course, may be read with either *spiritus* or *intellectus*.

[264] *Ibid.*, 66, 2-3: "Quod dixi Spiritum sanctum, divinarum scientiarum intellectus, a quo cuncta discrete reguntur." This may be the earliest example of an increasing tendency in the later eleventh and twelfth centuries to look upon the holy spirit as a creator not only of divine understanding but also of the manner in which it is communicated. A century and a half later the notion was neatly summed up in a Cistercian sermon on one of St. Bernard's favorite texts, Psalm 44.2: " 'Lingua mea calamus scribe.' Scriptor velociter scribens est Spiritus Sanctus, lingua predicatoris est calamus vel penna. Sicut penna nil facit sine manu ita predicator sine Spiritu Sancto cooperante non potest proficere. . . . Pergamenum scriptoris est cor hominis, in

faithfully adheres to its maker's intentions to the degree that it relies on biblical texts and *sacri canones*. Texts are the justification for eliminating any intermediary between God and man. Man achieves salvation not through God's love, sacrifice, and goodwill but through reason, understanding, and illumination.[265]

Rationality, as inspired by literate pursuits, is also the foundation of the sect's world-denying way of life.[266] Its members give up all carnal relationships, whether through food, sex, or possessions, for carnality is associated with the letter rather than with the spirit. Communication with "spirit" is maintained by continual prayer. Natural death is looked upon as a contamination of the divine spirit in man; mortification of the flesh contributes towards its upward movement back to God. All material generation and corruption are denied validity: if man had not sinned, Gerard reminds his listeners, he would still be able to procreate without sexual contact. The sect has no need of priests: the pontiff who visits the dispersed communities is none other than the spirit of interpretation itself. This *animus*, being within man, needs no tonsure or aura of mystery.

Aribert grasped immediately that the heresy at Monforte was a highly intellectual affair. His method of combating the sect was accordingly based on theology and argument. But among the capitanei and vavasours of Milan it was understood either as a form of primitive superstition or as a politico-religious conspiracy. Possibly anticipating the Pataria, the *rustici* from the surrounding countryside crowded into the episcopal court where the heretics were discussing their ideas, attracted, it would appear, as much by the doctrines as the idea of interpreting Scripture for themselves.[267] To the lay nobility the heretics were therefore perceived as a threat to established authority. If they did not recant, they had to be destroyed.

The Making of "Heresies"

The period between 1028 and 1052 saw a number of recurrences of heresy in the West. Although widely scattered in space and time,

---

Spiritu Sancto cooperante non potest proficere. . . . Pergamenum scriptoris est cor hominis, in quo debet scribere verbum Dei." The sermon is edited with a commentary by D. Richter, "Die Allegorie der Pergamentbearbeitung," in G. Keil, et al., eds., *Fachliteratur des Mittelalters. Festschrift für Gerhard Eis* (Stuttgart, 1968), 83-92; quoted passage, p. 83.

[265] Cf. Violante (1953), 177, 179.

[266] Cf. Ilarino da Milano (1947), 72-73.

[267] *Historia*, p. 66, 27-30: "At ipsi nefandissimi et a qua orbis parte in Italia fuissent eventi inscii, quasi boni sacerdotes cottidie tamen privatim rusticis, qui in hac urbe eos videndi causa convenerant, falsa rudimenta a scripturis divinis detorta seminabant."

the dissidents reiterated beliefs that were revealed in the better-known episodes at Orléans, Arras, and Monforte. They were also brought together by a bias in the sources in which they were described. As the frequency of heresy increased, the conventions for portraying it also became more familiar. They began to fit into a minor historiographical tradition of their own, in which, invariably, an attempt was made to see sectarianism in a coherent framework interrelating the past and the present. The result was "the making of heresies," that is, the placing of relatively isolated events in a literary format of shared assumptions among authors and readers. This approach confirmed the orthodox view that heresy was something well known and therefore curable with ancient remedies. But it militated against an analysis of the principles of group organization.

The notion of heresy itself became more and more a term of interpretation. Between 1030 and 1046, for instance, Gerard of Csanád wrote of dissidents in unchristianized Hungary who reminded him of similar movements in France, Greece, and Italy. He even spoke suggestively of three towns, Verona, Ravenna, and Venice, which lay on the trade routes between Byzantium and the West.[268] The possibility of dualist influence should not be ruled out: Csanád, located roughly on a parallel with Venice at a point midway between the Adriatic and the Black Sea, "abutted the cradle of Bogomilism in Bulgaria."[269] But what is most remarkable in the anti-dialectical[270] Gerard's vague account is his use of *haereses* itself, which brings together in his mind events and beliefs that were only loosely related or perhaps not related at all. A similar picture emerges from various centres in the north. Around 1048, as noted, Theoduin of Liège consciously or unconsciously confused the "popular" heretics who refused baptism and marriage for followers of the "learned" Berengar of Tours.[271] The council of Reims of 1049 created a literary context in a different way. Leo IX complained of many "illicit practices" by the local clergy, among which he included simony, lay priests, the misuse of churches,

---

[268] Lambert (1977), Appendix A.2, p. 347, based on G. Silagi, *Untersuchungen zur "Deliberatio supra Hymnum Trium Puerorum" des Gerhard von Csanád* (Munich, 1967), 97-98. On Gerard's monastic connections, see J. Leclercq, "S. Gérard de Csanád et le monachisme," *Studia monastica* 13 (1971), 13-30.

[269] Lambert (1977), 35.

[270] J. A. Endres, *Forschungen zur Geschichte der frühmittelalterlichen Philosophie* (Münster, 1915), 51-64.

[271] *Ep. contra Brunonem et Berengarium*, PL 146.1439B-42C, discussed by Russell (1965), 41, and O. Capitani, "Studi per Berengario di Tours," BIS 69 (1957), 125-26. Cf. *Gerardi Ep.*, PL 142.1269B-70C, ed. and discussed by Mingroot (1976), 215-18. For a discussion of Berengar, see below, Ch. 3, pp. 273-81.

incest, adultery, the abandonment of vows by monks and clerics, out-
rages against the poor, "and other heresies."[272] He later excommunicated those whom he called the *novi haeretici*, who were apparently
spreading nefarious doctrines about France.[273] Similarly, the dissidents
brought before Henry III at Goslar in 1051 were hanged for their
"Manichaean" beliefs.[274] Such instances illustrate that the conspiracy
theory died hard, and, once established by literary conventions, that
it played a cumulatively important role in subsequent discussions.
The "new heretics" were consistently viewed as revivers of older forms
of disobedience. The accounts in turn were used as confirmations of
the ancient origins of later dissidents. And the contemporary relevance
of the movements was largely obliterated.

A good example of historiographical typologies with which we may
conveniently bring this discussion of heresy to a close is provided by
an exchange of letters, as recorded by Anselm of Liège, between Roger
II of Châlons-sur-Marne, and Wazo, the reformist bishop of Liège
between 1042 and 1048. The letters also offer a bridge from the
isolated outbreaks of heresy in the first half of the century to the more
general issue of literacy and reform, to which we shall shortly turn.

For reasons that are not entirely clear, Roger, on finding heretics
in his diocese, turned to Wazo for advice. Certain *rustici*, he said,
were regularly attending the secret meetings of local "Manichaeans,"
who engaged in a number of perverse and idolatrous practices. They
maintained that they received the holy ghost through the laying on
of hands, for Mani, their founder, was "none other than the holy
spirit," sent to earth by God. They actively recruited new members,
teaching them to avoid marriage, and, as an interpretation of God's
directives, to abstain from eating meat or killing animals. They also
transformed their uneducated disciples into models of erudition, who
surpassed the faithful in eloquence. Roger was not overly concerned
about the sect itself, which was limited in numbers. But he did not
want heretical ideas to infect the whole diocese. He concluded by
asking Wazo whether he should summon the secular authorities.[275]

Wazo's reply[276] is interesting both for its content and for the man-

[272] Mansi, 19, 737; P. Fredericq, *Corpus Documentorum Inquisitionis Haereticae Pravitatis Neerlandicae*, vol. 1 (Ghent, 1889), no. 4, p. 8.

[273] Mansi, 19, 742.

[274] Lambert of Hersfeld, *Annales*, an. 1053, MGH SS 5, 155; for other texts, see Russell
(1965), 279n46 and for various interpretations, Borst (1953), 71n4.

[275] *Gesta Episcoporum Leodiensis*, c. 62, MGH SS 7, 226-27. A. Fliche, *La réforme grégorienne*,
vol. 1 (Paris, 1924), 113-14n2, notes no difference in the accounts; but see Russell (1965),
278-79n36.

[276] *Gesta*, c. 63, *ibid.*, 227-28.

ner in which it conceives the problem. He questioned the heretics'
interpretation of "Thou shalt not kill." He also counseled Roger not
to resort to extremist methods. But, above all he put the question of
heresy on an entirely intellectual plane.

The errors, he stated, are not new: they were refuted long ago by
the fathers. Appropriating the holy spirit to themselves, the heretics
merely misinterpret the true meaning of the Bible. The commandment *"non occides,"*[277] he continued, clearly refers to men alone; otherwise, human beings would be forbidden the constructive use of grain,
vegetables, and wine. All things grow to maturity from seeds, but in
order to be useful to man, certain plants and animals must be cut off
in their prime. Christianity abhors such "Arian" sacrilege; nonetheless, following Christ's example, it must be endured with meekness
and humility. As Gregory says, Abel's grace required Cain's malice:
to produce wine, the grape must be trodden underfoot.[278] In general,
behaviour towards heretics ought to be guided by the parable of the
wheat and the tares.[279] Who are the "servants" of whom the Lord
spoke but preachers, whose task it is, so to speak, to winnow? Yet, a
distinction must be observed between preliminary separation and final
judgment. The Lord intended that the church be patient with those
who have fallen into error, for today's tares may be tomorrow's wheat.
The spirit of the biblical text does not call for the death or suffering
of sinners but for their conversion. He therefore advised Roger not to
invoke the secular arm, which would inevitably lead to violence.

Anselm of Liège adds that Wazo reasoned through Christian law,
not irrationally, as some have, in dealing with contemporary dissidents. The French, he alleges, were so bloodthirsty that they judged
and slaughtered heretics according to "the pallor of their skin." Those
accused at Goslar fared no better. As far as he could tell, their only
crime lay in refusing to kill a chicken at the order of the local bishop.

This anecdote from the *Gesta Episcoporum Leodiensis* illustrates the
two sides of heresy as interpreted by early eleventh-century commentators. In most respects Roger's is the standard complaint: the dissidents are *rustici*; they meet in secret (*furtiva conventicula*); they revive
pagan excesses (*nescio quid obscena et dictu turpia*).[280] But, beneath such
typical details, one also perceives the emergence of a textual community. The *spiritus sanctus*, that is, the spirit in man through which
divine wisdom is reflected, is transferred by the imposition of hands,

[277] Ps 77.47.   [278] *Moralia* 2.75.   [279] Matt 13.37-39.
[280] *Gesta*, c. 62, p. 226, 34-36.

presumably after the novice has passed through the various stages of initiation. Mani, the sect's founder, received this same rational spirit from God. Like other sectarians they are celibates and vegetarians. But what worries Roger most is their uncanny ability to propagate their ideas. So successful is their instruction, he maintains, that *idiotae* and *infacundi* become "more persuasive than the faithful. . . . The sincere eloquence of the wise seems scarcely able to overcome mere loquacity."[281]

The major danger, then, as Roger sees it, is the effectiveness of the heretics' means of communication, especially among the uninstructed. This point is hardly touched upon in Wazo's reply, which views the heresy from an essentially scholarly standpoint. His letter is inserted into the *Gesta* between two better-known assertions of a division of labour between secular and religious authorities, both involving the reform ideals of Henry III.[282] His statement is also part of the picture of enlightened reformism painted by Anselm of Liège. Bishop Notker, the author tells us, encouraged the education of children and curtailed the activities of priests who were *rudes et illiterati*.[283] Wazo was Notker's chaplain and later *magister scholarum* in the cathedral school.[284] Wazo's approach therefore is hardly surprising. For him, heresy is a "manifest error"; the "Arians"[285] must simply be "refuted." His defence of legal principles takes him in two different directions. It interrelates the notions of precedent, reform, and innerworldly activity: within the overall plan of salvation, we may "licitly"[286] utilize the beasts of the field, as witness official comments (*secularium scripta*) on the commandment "*non occides*." Also, the precedence unites the life of Christ with the contemporary function of the *praedicatorum ordo*, to which he and Roger belong. That, in part, is the point of the parable of the wheat and the tares. True, heresy is "diabolical fraud."[287] But

[281] *Ibid.*, 226, 44-47.

[282] On which see R. L. Benson, *The Bishop-Elect. A Study in Medieval Ecclesiastical Office* (Princeton, 1968), 207-09.

[283] *Gesta*, c. 28, *ibid.*, 205.

[284] *Ibid.*, c. 40, 210-11. For further details, see E. de Moreau, *Histoire de l'Eglise en Belgique*, 2nd ed. (Brussels, 1945), vol. 2, 34-52; E. Amman, "Wazo de Liège," DTC 15.2, 3520-24.

[285] A frequent twelfth-century label for dualism, used here perhaps for the first time; see R. Manselli, "Una designazione dell'eresia catara: 'Arriana Heresis,' " BIS 68 (1956), 233-46; Y. Congar, " 'Arriana haeresis' comme désignation du néomanichéisme au XIIe siècle," RSPT 43 (1959), 449-61.

[286] *Gesta*, c. 63, *ibid.*, 227, lines 9 and 18.

[287] *Ibid.*, 227, 42-43.

the role of the effective priest in Wazo's view is not to deliver final judgment. He must reconvert those who have been misled.

To return to our point of departure: we began by reaffirming the well-established scholarly conclusion that early heretics in the West did not share common social or doctrinal origins. The search for "origins" moreover directed energies away from the analysis of heresy's functional interdependency with the rise of a more literate society. For, if the heretics came from different backgrounds, they nonetheless underwent a similar experience within the group. And, if the sects varied in actual beliefs, they employed comparable intellectual methods.

The common denominator was texts, and attitudes towards texts provide a leitmotif which runs through the handful of case histories we have examined. In Leutard the contact with literacy was indirect. His story's value is chiefly symbolic: it recounts the way in which man, by becoming the Word's interpreter, acquires a formerly divine charisma. Again, at Orléans in 1022, the mainspring of heresy was the study of the Bible and of religious maxims directly or indirectly derived from it. This was also true of Arras in 1025 and of Monforte in 1028. In each case, the sacral, mystical, and miraculous accretions of older tradition were discarded in favour of a rationalistic ethic based on the principles of the New Testament. Rationality in turn was a byproduct of the literate mentality, since the various interpretations of texts were subsequently codified into a set of written rules governing conduct. These norms structured the behaviour of the individual in the group and resulted in a set of interactions between the members which were designed to break down the barriers between the literate and the nonliterate.

The sources admittedly present different views of these isolated outbursts of heresy, and the bias of the narrators must be taken into account. However, the varied perspectives often amount to no more than altered perceptions of the members' status on the spectrum of popular and learned culture. For Ademar of Chabannes and Rodulf Glaber, heretics belonged to the world of pagan superstition and idolatry. But the question of initiation, education, and theological discussion did not escape the attention of Paul of St. Père or the anonymous reviser of the *Gesta Synodi Atrebatensis*. In both, a group experience based on the interpretation of texts and organized as sectarian behaviour was framed within a larger political and theological debate. Heresy, so to speak, was reinterpreted to serve the needs of monastic and episcopal reform. At Monforte, the gap between popular and learned perceptions was patent. There was no place for the astute, self-assured

Gerard in Glaber's tale of the supernatural and of political prophecy, elements which, needless to say, Landulf Senior found superfluous. In the exchange of letters between Wazo of Liège and Roger of Châlons we see how far an interpretive framework for understanding heresy had been built up by the middle of the eleventh century. Roger was concerned about itinerant preachers who undermined the ministerial labours of the regular clergy. Wazo, in effect, ignored the practical problem and limited himself to proving that the heretics' doctrines were indefensible. And thus movements and theology parted ways.

2. LITERACY AND REFORM: THE PATARIA

Magna et modernis temporibus inaudita confusio facta est
Italiae propter coniurationes, quas fecerat populus contra
principes.
—Wipo, *Gesta Chuonradi imperatoris*, c. 34.

Introduction

The case histories of early eleventh-century heresy which we have examined present an unusually clear picture of the interaction between literacy and group experience. By and large the dissident sects were isolated, even though they occasionally saw themselves as parts of larger movements and were so regarded by their commentators. While sharing in common a number of doctrines, each cell re-enacted the experience of interpretation anew.

In the period after 1050 this sort of activity did not diminish. But, in general, the social, political, and intellectual context of both dissent and reform became more complex. Throughout the later eleventh, twelfth, and even thirteenth centuries sectarians continued to be found in small independent groups following charismatic leaders like Eon de l'Etoile. But more frequently they belonged to religious movements, that is, to larger bodies which might be dispersed over a wide geographical area yet shared beliefs, practices, principles of organization, and above all common goals. As time went on and, in particular, after the impetus of the Gregorian reforms waned, the church began to distinguish more and more precisely between such movements and legitimate religious orders. However, the legalism obscured the fact that, with respect to communications, "orthodox" and "heretical" associations often employed analogous methods to achieve somewhat different ends. Before 1050, dissenters stand out in relief against the background of a largely immobile regular clergy. For that reason, they provide a weathervane for reformist tendencies inside and outside the church. During the later eleventh and twelfth centuries, movements within the church became increasingly active: Cistercians, Carthusians, Premonstratensians, and Augustinian canons all demanded a return to Christian roots.

To what degree did the rise of a more literate society affect such reform movements? Were they, like the early heresies, "textual communities" on a larger scale? And do factors of communication, if separated from a dogmatic context, offer a basis for comparison between the internal organization of heretical and orthodox groups?

Of course, the two sorts of communities shared a number of attitudes towards the uses of literacy. The leaders engaged in interpretation, either of the Bible, the fathers, earlier legislation, or, in the case of heretics, texts from other sources. The groups' members frequently had two principles of organization, a formal, articulated "rule" and an inner set of beliefs which, while not violating its dicta, nonetheless channelled energies towards certain aspects of the ascetic, meditative, and otherworldly life. The associations were understood by those participating in them to be authentic, even literal re-enactments of earlier Christian or dualist communities. And, as time went on, there was an increasing attempt by both heretics and orthodox to spread the word along a continuum from literate to illiterate. Therefore, within each side, learned and popular sensibilities emerged.

Even more than social organization, the rise of a more literate society influenced the bias of the sources. Commentators, who had from the first a tendency to intellectualize dissidence, responded to the new complexities by extending and deepening the historical context. As more became known about ancient heresies and the early church, chroniclers also became more inclined to characterize both heterodox and orthodox groups as offshoots of movements in the distant past. Dissatisfaction, in a sense, with contemporary events was a mainspring of intellectual progress, inspiring research into ecclesiastical history. But the information produced, instead of liberating interpretation from past models, often led medieval authors to account for unprecedented changes with patently inadequate explanatory mechanisms. Two phenomena existed side by side: on the one hand the beliefs of the participants that ancient heresies were actually being reborn or that reformers were imitating the *exemplum primitivae ecclesiae*, and, on the other, the interpretations of external observers, which linked the *antiqui* and the *moderni* in internal evolution. In other words, wherever there was a movement, there was also an attempt to interpret it. *Ressourcement*—the return to the sources or the rediscovery of one's alleged roots—was no longer an abstract category: it became a functioning reality, interrelating the sectarians' subjective view of what they were doing with the larger field of hermeneutics.

The purpose of this essay is to examine one reform movement, the Milanese Pataria, and its interpretive context. The events surrounding the upheaval are not always easy to follow; therefore, before we turn in detail to the three main accounts, a few words of introduction are required.

We shall limit our discussion of the Pataria to the diocese of Milan before the turn of the twelfth century. Although overflowing into politics, the movement was essentially religious; it arose among laymen and the lower clergy and was directed against simony, nicolaitism, and the worldliness of the church. Originating in Milan, it gradually spread to Cremona, Piacenza, Lodi, and later to Brescia. In Florence, the similarly inspired Vallumbrosans under John Gualbert opposed the simoniacal bishop Peter Mezzabarba.[1] Patarenes were still active in the twelfth century, when they allied themselves with the archbishop and the promoters of the commune.[2] But the major period of development was the half-century after 1045, within which it is possible to distinguish three successive phases: the beginnings, from 1045 to 1057; a generation of activism after 1057; and the movement's decline following the death of its lay leader, Erlembald, in 1075.

The Pataria was a perhaps inevitable consequence of social and religious pressures in Milan, under whose hegemony Lombardy had undergone a slow but steady renewal of commercial activity from as early as the ninth century.[3] Prosperity and population grew in both

---

[1] See S. Boesch Gajano, "Storia e tradizione vallombrosane," BIS 76 (1964), 99-215.

[2] P. Zerbi, "Alcuni risultati e prospettive di ricerca sulla storia religiosa di Milano dalla fine del secolo XI al 1144," *Problemi di Storia religiosa lombarda, Atti* (Como, 1972), 18.

[3] C. Violante, *La società milanese* 2nd ed. (1974), 19. A full bibliography of Milan's medieval history cannot be attempted here. For the standard account, see the contributions of G. Bognetti and E. Besta to the *Storia di Milano*, vol. 2: *Dall'invasione dei barbari all'apogio del governo vescovile (493-1002)* and of G. Barni to vol. 3: *Dagli albori di comune all'incoronazione di Federico Barbarossa (1002-1152)*, both published in Milan, 1954. A briefer, more recent study is G. Dilcher, *Die Entstehung der lombardischen Stadtkommune. Eine rechtsgeschichtliche Untersuchung* (Aalen, 1967); but, on social structure in particular, see the comments of H. Keller, "Die soziale und politische Verfassung Mailands in den Anfängen des kommunalen Lebens: Zu einem neuen Buch über die Entstehung der lombardischen Stadtkommune," *Historische Zeitschrift* 211 (1970), 34-64. The same author puts the issues in broad perspective in "Pataria und Stadtverfassung, Stadtgemeinde

countryside and town. The abolition of hereditary labour services, the freeing of *servi* and *coloni*, the transformation of leaseholds into private contracts, the breaking down of the lord's reserve into smaller tenures, and the fluctuating price of land all contributed to the revitalization of agrarian life. Trade in exports and imports quickened, and new wealth flowed into local markets. Long-distance commerce, passing from Islamic lands via Byzantium, also increased the need for *portus, xenodochia* for travellers, and *pacta*, such as that granted to Venetian merchants in 840, permitting them "to cross land and sea where they wished."[4] Professional merchants, documented from the eighth century, grew in numbers and wealth throughout the ninth. Unlike their northern counterparts, they began to acquire permanent possessions, usually in land, as, from the tenth century, did artisans. Such merchants, living in Milan and investing in the countryside around it, were different from the older *negotiatores majores*, whose status in public law was that of servants of seigneurial courts. Of course, bureaucrats of this type still existed in monasteries, bishoprics, and at the royal court in Pavia. But the new breed were free agents whose contractual obligations were private agreements. They worked not so much for the lord's profit as for their own. Although still beneficiaries of feudal protection, they largely obeyed the impersonal laws of supply and demand.[5] The influx of merchants, artisans, and notaries to Milan succeeded in reconstituting a stable, urbanized middle class for the first time since the later empire.

Following the lead of the moneyers, one by one the arriving groups

und Reform: Mailand im 'Investiturstreit,' " in J. Fleckenstein, ed., *Investiturstreit und Reichsverfassung*, 521-50; for bibliography, see p. 324n9. Other general articles of note include A. Bosisio, "Prospettive storiche sull'età precomunale e comunale in Milano negli studi più recenti," ASI 94 (1936), 201-16, and *idem*, "Nuovi problemi e studi sull'alto medioevo milanese e lombardo," ASI 113 (1955), 443-81; G. Fasoli, "Che cosa sappiamo delle città italiane nell'alto Medio Evo," *Vierteljahrschrift für Sozial- und Wirtschaftsgeschichte* 47 (1960), 289-305; *idem*, "Gouvernants et gouvernés dans les communes italiennes du XIe au XIIIe siècle," in *Gouvernés et gouvernants*, 4e partie (Brussels, 1965), 47-86; G. Fasoli, R. Manselli, and G. Tabacco, "La struttura sociale delle città italiane dal V al XII secolo," in T. Mayer, ed., *Untersuchungen zur gesellschaftlichen Struktur der mittelalterlichen Städte in Europa* (Stuttgart, 1966), 291-320; G. C. Mor, "Gouvernés et gouvernants en Italie du VIe au XIIe siècle," *Gouvernés et gouvernants*, 2e partie (Brussels, 1968), 395-420; and H. Keller, "Das Gerichtsort in oberitalienischen und toskanischen Städten. Untersuchungen zur Stellung der Stadt im Herrschaftssystem des Regnum Italicum vom 9. bis 11. Jahrhundert," *Quellen und Forschungen aus italienischen Archiven und Bibliotheken* 49 (1969), 1-72.

4 MGH Capit. Reg. Franc., vol. 2, no. 233, pp. 130ff.; Violante, *La società milanese*, 7 and 7n18.

5 Violante, 76-85, 143-59.

became *cives Mediolanenses*.[6] But their new prestige and political clout rose in the shadow of the church. Religious institutions owned most laymen's houses within the walls as well as forests and farmlands outside. Ecclesiastics were also proprietors of the *stationes* which merchants and artisans rented in the central market.[7] The real guarantor of the merchants' rights was not the count but the archbishop, who, through infeudation, had usurped many of his prerogatives. For instance, in Landulf Senior's words, archbishop Aribert was "the father of orphans, the clergy's ornament, and the protector of widows, paupers, and merchants."[8] By the early eleventh century upward mobility was causing particular difficulties for two classes within the social hierarchy, the capitanei and the vavasours. The capitanei were nobles whose estates lay in the countryside just outside the city. Vassals of the archbishop, they monopolized decision-making in Milan through an intricate network of marriages, property transactions, and religious alliances. Although claiming investiture as *milites majores* by archbishop Landulf II in 983,[9] their group had in fact originated in the lesser nobility and wealthier merchants of the tenth century.[10] They were feudal creations of the archbishopric, upon whose stability their real authority rested. The vavasours were often self-made men whose chief responsibility was to organize and to run their estates. They in turn felt pressure from ordinary citizens and smaller leaseholders. At the top of the pyramid was the archbishop: all changes in status among laymen were by implication new relationships with him. What went by the name of "feudalism" in Milan was in fact the city's "normal social framework."[11]

Social and political tensions came to a head under archbishop Aribert of Intimiano. The son of wealthy parents in Como,[12] he was

[6] Y. Renouard, *Les villes d'Italie de la fin du Xe siècle au début du XIVe siècle*, ed. P. Braunstein (Paris, 1969), vol. 2, p. 383.

[7] Violante, *La società milanese*, 80.

[8] *Historia Mediolanensis* 2.32, MGH SS 8, p. 69; cf. below, p. 188f.

[9] Arnulf of Milan, *Gesta Archiepiscoporum Mediolanensium* 1.10, MGH SS 8, p. 9; Landulf, *Historia* 2.17, pp. 53-54; Violante, *La società milanese*, 178.

[10] A. Visconti, "Ricerche sul diritto pubblico milanese nell'alto medioevo," *Annali della Università di Macerata* 3 (1928), 101-229; *idem*, "Negotiatores de Mediolano," *ibid.*, 5 (1929), 177-96. Cf. Violante, *op.cit.*, 270-71, and, in broader perspective, G. Tabacco, "Il regno italico nei secoli IX-XI," in *Ordinamenti militari in Occidente nell'alto medioevo* (Spoleto, 1968), 783-84.

[11] Y. Renouard, *Les villes d'Italie*, I, 384-85. Cf. G. C. Mor, "Gouvernés et gouvernants," 416, and, for a brief review of the social classifications, H. Keller, "Pataria und Stadtverfassung . . . ," 327-28.

[12] See C. Manaresi, "Notizie sulla famiglia dell'arcivescovo Ariberto da Intimiano," *Archivio storico lombardo* 49 (1922), 394-96.

elected by the cardinal clergy, which the capitanei dominated, on 18th March 1018. He died a broken, disillusioned man in his native city on 16th January 1045. His achievements were principally three-fold. He extended and consolidated the patrimony of St. Ambrose, winning from Henry II the monasteries of St. Filinus and St. Gratian and from Conrad II the rich prize of Nonantula.[13] He prevented successive emperors from interfering in Milan's internal affairs, allying himself with Conrad between 1024 and 1034 and frustrating his attempts to crush the city after 1037. His powerful leadership was also capable of overriding class tensions: when threatened by Conrad, cives, vavasours, and capitanei momentarily buried their differences to face a common foe.

But for these accomplishments Milan paid a high price. Too many people were dependent on the archiepiscopal see. The more the church tightened its grip over tenants demanding property rights and privileges, the more it ensnared itself in the net of simony and nicolaitism, thus laying itself open to later charges of ecclesiastical abuse. Also, Aribert's successes with imperial authority were more apparent than real. Up to 1034, Conrad needed his support against the aristocratic Italian families who preferred a French monarch. When Henry II's confidant, Leo of Vercelli, died in 1026, Aribert became Conrad's chief apologist in Italy. In 1027, Leo's successor and Aribert's chosen man, Arderic of Milan, presented Conrad for coronation to the pope: to the chroniclers it seemed that Milan had finally displaced Aquileia and Ravenna as the second see of Italy.[14] And, in 1034, Aribert led Lombard troops alongside Germans in Conrad's bid for the crown of Burgundy. But Aribert stayed in favour only as long as it suited the emperor's purposes. Their long-range goals were opposed. Both sought political control over northern Italy, Conrad by winning over the disgruntled vavasours, Aribert by striking an alliance against them between the capitanei and the cives. When the vavasours finally revolted in 1035, both parties appealed to Conrad. The subsequent imprisonment and escape of Aribert and the "miraculous" deliverance of Milan by Conrad's unexpected death during the siege of 1039 did not erase the important gains made by the vavasours in the *Constitutio de Feudis* promulgated by the emperor at Pavia in 1037.[15] The tract not only defended the right of vavasours to inherit their fiefs. It also attempted

[13] H.E.J. Cowdrey, "Archbishop Aribert II of Milan," *History* 51 (1966), 4.

[14] *Ibid.*, 3, 7.

[15] MGH Diplomata 4, no. 244, pp. 336-37; Cowdrey, *art.cit.*, 10-11, and, in greater detail, Violante, *La società milanese*, 245-55.

to "unite" and to "mobilize" all ranks of lay society in the imperial cause.[16] The compromise struck by Conrad was recognized by Henry III and ratified by a reluctant and increasingly isolated Aribert on his return from the coronation at Ingelheim in 1040.

Even at a personal level, Aribert's episcopate is open to misinterpretation. A resourceful and charismatic leader, he nonetheless suffered from stubbornness, a lack of diplomacy, and a hunger for personal power. Historians have viewed him from extreme positions: the eighteenth century saw in him a champion of civil liberties, the nineteenth, a feudal opponent of empire and papal reform.[17] Yet, can Aribert really be judged outside the society which produced him? He was, as Violante notes, one of its "new men,"[18] whose political strength derived in part from Milan's sense of itself as an urban entity but whose popularity was bound to wane when the bases of legitimate authority began to shift from the personal to the institutional sphere.

The decisive stages took place after the Burgundian campaign of 1032. Aribert's hitherto universal appeal declined: his former magnetism, in Arnulf's words, began to be looked upon as egotism, even tyranny.[19] In particular the political influence of the capitanei, whom he alone truly represented, was judged by all below them to be too great. It was they after all who had arbitrarily sentenced and burned the heretics from Monforte. Aribert appeared to the capitanei as the saviour of the patrimony of St. Ambrose. But to the vavasours he was only the defender of the status quo. By all accounts the archbishop had too much personal power. After Conrad's death and the destruction by fire of the imperial palace at Pavia, the *magistri* of the corporations of skilled craftsmen like the minters came to depend less on royal authority and more and more on his patronage. Even the viscount became a vassal of the Milanese church, as were the sixteen *boni viri* who acted as custodians of the cathedral.[20]

Yet, for all that, Aribert did not represent a "feudal" reaction against "progressive" change. He was merely a pivotal figure in the quicksand of Milanese social loyalties, in which the class structure of the precommunal era was slowly but surely engulfed.[21] Capitanei, vavasours, and cives were in any case locked in conflict. The predictable consequence

---

[16] Cowdrey, *loc.cit.*; Violante, 249-50.

[17] For a review, see Violante, 267-74.

[18] *Ibid.*, 277.

[19] *Gesta* 2.10, p. 14: suum considerans, non aliorum animum.

[20] Landulf Senior, *Historia*, 2.35, p. 76; see below, pp. 189f.

[21] Cf. Violante, *La società milanese*, 237.

of Henry's ratification of the *Constitutio de Feudis* was a new alliance between the two uppermost groups which permanently upset the delicate balance that Aribert had struck between the capitanei and the cives. Aribert's power never rested on a firm juridic base; the accession of a new group to official status could not help but erode it further. The cives too demanded greater freedom. Landulf Senior romantically pictured them as returning to a lost state of *libertas* before the capitanei's infeudation.[22] But they had more immediate concerns. Lanzo, their leader, did not attempt like Aribert to transcend his own class origins and to satisfy the needs of all Milanese. He represented the interests of only one political faction. When in 1040 Aribert and the older nobility were driven out of the city and Henry called upon to arbitrate, like Conrad the emperor pursued the traditional policy of pitting the lower orders against established local authority.[23] The result was a victory for the cives. Yet, at this point in time, their ranks were less homogenous than the category suggests, and included many merchants, artisans, and farm labourers. Technically speaking, many of them were not cives at all, since they did not live *infra muros*.[24] According to an assessment made in 1067, they really comprised the *reliqui* left behind by the gradual legalization of other classes.[25] Like them, they began their corporate existence with property but with no official position. Doubtless, class conflict played a large role in their growing self-consciousness. But they were brought into being as part of a larger process by which all social groups began to be designated not by inherited status but through law and social function.

After Aribert's death the cardinal clergy lost its monopoly of the archiepiscopal election. A combination of laymen and ecclesiastics presented four names to Henry. However, contrary to Milanese custom, the emperor imposed his own candidate, Guido da Velate. Henry was undoubtedly motivated by both political and religious considerations. Milan was a more complex city than in Conrad's day. Henry could not hope to perpetuate the imperial strategy of controlling Italian cities through their bishops. But he could divide and rule. The older class divisions between capitanei, vavasours, and cives had given way

[22] *Ibid.*, 257-58.

[23] Violante, "La politica italiana di Enrico III prima della sua discesa in Italia (1039-1046)," in *Studi sulla cristianità medioevale. Società, istituzioni, spiritualità*, ed. P. Zerbi (Milan, 1972), 250-90.

[24] *La società milanese*, 261-65.

[25] *Constitutiones quas legati sedis Apostolicae mediolanensibus observandas praescripserunt* (1067), *Rerum Italicarum Scriptores* 4.1, p. 32; Violante, *op.cit.*, 262f.

to a set of tensions between town and country. As a rural deacon, Guido represented the interests of lesser vassals, small proprietors, and *rustici* against all those who lived in the city and who exploited holdings in the surrounding countryside.[26] Moreover, in choosing Guido, Henry kept all his options open. The new archbishop came from a family of vavasours and was thereby linked to a rising stratum of society. But there was no danger of his becoming another Aribert, who might threaten imperial designs throughout the *Regnum Italiae*. The changed atmosphere could be felt as early as September 1045. Adalbert Azzo, marchese and count, who had been forced to flee Lanzo, re-entered the city and established higher justice in the emperor's name. His judge, Arioaldo, even took the ancient title of *missus domni regis*.[27]

Yet, the political aspects of the choice must be weighed against Henry's religious motivations. Unlike Conrad, he was a serious reformer, who had contacts with Cluny[28] and good rapport with such figures as Guido of Pomposa and Peter Damian.[29] He disapproved of the arrest on purely political grounds of Aribert's supporters, the bishops of Vercelli, Cremona, and Piacenza.[30] But he was not above meddling in episcopal elections when it suited his purposes: on Damian's advice and over the protests of Wazo of Liège, he removed Widger of Ravenna. As a general policy he favoured monasteries against their local bishops,[31] granting an undesignated Milanese house autonomy as early as February 1045.[32] Of course, Milan was not a typical diocese. In contrast to Ravenna and other north Italian towns, it had been virtually uninfluenced by outside reformers, including Cluniacs.[33] The patronage of monastic houses depended on the archbishop: St. Celso was founded by Landulf II in 996, St. Victor by Arnulf II in 1004, and St. Dionysius by Aribert in 1023. Under Aribert, reform was limited to obliging canons to take meals together and to preventing the alienation of church property, particularly through the marriage of infeudated clerics to free women.[34] By contrast, in

[26] Violante, *La pataria milanese*, 28-29; *idem*, "Hérésies urbaines et hérésies rurales en Italie du 11e au 13e siècle," J. Le Goff, ed., *Hérésies et sociétés*, 176-77.

[27] *La pataria milanese*, 34.

[28] H.E.J. Cowdrey, *The Cluniacs and the Gregorian Reform* (Oxford, 1970), 158-59.

[29] Violante, *La pataria milanese*, 6, 30.

[30] Violante, "Aspetti della politica italiana di Enrico III . . . ," 252.

[31] *Ibid.*, 278.

[32] *La pataria milanese*, 3.

[33] P. Zerbi, "Monasteri e riforma a Milano," *Aevum* 24 (1950), 176.

[34] Violante, *La società milanese*, 291-301; Cowdrey, "Archbishop Aribert II," 4-5.

Henry's eyes, monastic *libertas* was a byproduct of *ius regni*. The appointment of Guido da Velate was part of a broader reform programme: it increased the emperor's real influence in Italian ecclesiastical circles while retaining the ideological advantage of his "sacral" role in affairs of church and state.[35] In naming Guido to the see of Milan, Henry thus furthered his own designs as well as a process of evolution which was already at work in Aribert's time. The lowest echelons of society moved upwards, while the outsider effectively declared the freedom of the Milanese church from its internal hierarchy.

The Pataria, then, had its roots in the social conflicts of pre-communal Milan as well as in the growing contest between empire and papacy. The election of Guido da Velate brought the issues into the open. The cives opposed him as just another representative of the capitanei. The vavasours and upper clergy disliked him because he had been chosen by the emperor over the people's will. A "reformist" alliance was struck between laymen and the lower clergy: it was backed by a wealthy moneyer called Nazario and led by three disenchanted clerics, the deacon Ariald, the notary Landulf Cotta, and Anselm of Baggio, an educated canonist and the future pope Alexander II. Acquitted of simony at the Roman synod of 1050, Guido attempted to re-establish calm by having Henry appoint Anselm bishop of Lucca. But the agitation continued, even worsened. Ariald began preaching openly at Varese early in 1057; later in the same year he was joined in Milan by the more eloquent Landulf. Initially their words were directed against clerical marriage, but gradually their criticism was extended to cover other lay abuses of the sacraments, especially simony. On 10th May 1057 there was a riot at the Roman forum where the pair had come to preach. Afterwards, the Milanese commoners crowded into the city square and unanimously approved a set of canons on the moral obligations of the priesthood. Married priests and nobles began to leave the city, and, at the synod of Fontaneto in November 1057, the suffragans of Guido da Velate declared themselves official enemies of the Pataria. Ariald and Landulf were excommunicated. But the two journeyed to Rome, and, in response to their appeal, Hildebrand and Anselm of Baggio, then en route from Germany back to Italy, were sent to Milan as papal legates. The apparent

---

[35] G. Tellenbach, *Church, State and Christian Society at the Time of the Investiture Contest*, trans. R. F. Bennett (Oxford, 1940), 85-88, 97-112; G. Ladner, *Theologie und Politik vor dem Investiturstreit*, 60-70; Violante, "Aspetti . . . ," 252-53n20, 270-71; and, for a more recent review of the issues, O. Capitani, *Immunità vescovile ed ecclesiologia in età "pregregoriana" e "gregoriana." L'avvio alla "restaurazione"* (Spoleto, 1966), 84-113.

support of the papacy only further encouraged the Patarenes and deepened the already wide gulf separating the archbishop and the reformers. On his election in 1059, Nicolas II sent Anselm and Peter Damian on another mission. Guido panicked and raised a large crowd in defence of Ambrosian autonomy. But the sincerity and goodwill of Peter Damian prevailed, and the Milanese church agreed to penance and compromise.[36]

A new chapter was opened in 1061 when Anselm was elected pope in defiance of the imperial faction, which, acting on behalf of Henry IV, named Honorius II anti-pope. As Alexander II, Anselm appointed Erlembald, the brother of the deceased Landulf Cotta, as his personal representative in Milan, while the archbishop looked more and more to the emperor and to the feudal aristocracy for support. Two churches existed, the cathedral and the Canonica: the people, alternately incited by both sides, attacked the houses of both married priests and reformers. The Pataria spread to other centres, including Pavia itself. In 1066, Erlembald went to Rome and presented his view of the situation to Alexander, who responded by excommunicating Guido. On hearing the news, the archbishop summoned a great throng at Pentecost and presented his fate as an insult to the venerable traditions of the Milanese church. In the ensuing tumult Ariald was gravely wounded. The mob attacked Guido's palace, seeking revenge, but was driven back by his mercenaries. Guido then forbad all "reformist" preaching in the city. Ariald and Erlembald left Milan for Rome, but were attacked once again en route. Ariald was murdered shortly afterwards near lake Como by Guido's niece and her henchmen. His body was subsequently recovered and returned to Milan on 17th May 1067 in a hugh procession led by Erlembald.

With Ariald martyred, Guido had few friends left. Along with many nobles he fled the city. Erlembald assumed complete power. In a lengthy address he appointed thirty laymen to oversee the conduct of the Milanese clergy. The pope, naturally uneasy over lay control, decreed by way of compromise that Ariald was to be canonized, Guido reinstated, and the sins of simony, nicolaitism, and violence condemned. Further, he emphasized, the church of Milan was henceforth to be subordinate to Rome. Unfortunately, the admonitions did not correct Guido's ways. Wishing to retire, he recommended as his successor the palace chaplain, Godefrey. Henry IV named him arch-

[36] See C. Somigli, "San Pietro Damiano e la Pataria (Relazioni e amicizie)," *San Pier Damiano nel IX centenario della morte (1072-1972)*, vol. 3 (Cesena, 1973), 193-206.

bishop, but Erlembald once again directed his followers not to recognize a simoniac. As papal gonfalon he seized the material goods of the church, while Godefrey, unable to enter the city, took up residence in nearby Castiglione Olona. Fearing that the imperial faction would be strengthened, Erlembald attacked. The ensuing battle had no clear victor, and, to make matters worse, on 19th March 1071 a huge fire devastated the city. An immense crowd then acclaimed Erlembald's candidate, Azzo, but a group of nobles, clerics, and cives nonetheless compelled him to decline. As Henry refused to abandon Godefrey, the issue seemed to be at an impasse. Gregory VII attempted to bring about a compromise at the Roman council of March 1074. Godefrey refused to attend and was excommunicated; Azzo was consequently recognized as legitimate head of the Milanese church. Emboldened by Gregory's strong stand on reform, Erlembald publicly crushed a chalice containing the chrism consecrated by Godefrey; then, on 28th June 1075, he led an ill-advised attack on the archbishop's noble supporters in which he met his death. His removal from the scene brought the Patarene movement to a standstill. From this point, the social and political issues gravitated around the communal movement and the quarrel between emperor and pope took its place in the larger conflict over investiture. By the first decade of the twelfth century a somewhat weakened archbishopric was allied with the papacy and the commune against the intrusions of the German emperors, opposing Conrad of Hohenstaufen after 1125 and Barbarossa after 1152.

There are three main accounts of the Patarene movement and the accompanying civil disturbances in Milan during the third quarter of the eleventh century. The shortest and most authoritative is the *Liber Gestorum Recentium* of Arnulf of Milan, completed by 1077,[37] which records events witnessed by the author after the accession of Aribert in 1018.[38] Lengthier, more colourful, and less accurate is the *Historia Mediolanensis* of Landulf Senior, who was born around 1045 and was still writing as late as 1110.[39] The third major source is the *Vita Sancti Arialdi*,[40] an idealized account of the martyrdom of the movement's founder written sometime late in 1075 by Andrew of Strumi. Among other contemporary chronicles special mention should be made

---

[37] M. Manitius, *Geschichte der lateinischen Literatur des Mittelalters*, vol. 3 (Munich, 1931), 507-09; C. Violante, "Arnolfo," *Dizionario biografico degli italiani* 4, 281-82.

[38] *Gesta* 2.1, p. 11: "ea quae ipsi videndo cognovimus"; cf. 3.10, p. 18: "cum res nostris adhuc versetur in occulis. . . ."

[39] Manitius, *op.cit.*, 509.

[40] P. Lamma, "Andrea da Parma (da Strumi)," *Dizionario . . .* , 3, 111.

of books six and seven of Bonizo of Sutri's *Liber ad Amicum*, composed no later than 1085,[41] in which one finds important details of the Milanese involvement in the controversy between Henry IV and Gregory VII.

Adhering to the format of part one of this chapter, each of the three main accounts is treated separately in what follows, despite the obvious sacrifice of economy entailed. As previously, this approach is intended to serve two broad purposes: it allows one to isolate the relationship of literacy to the inner workings of the sect and it permits independent treatment of three rather different perspectives on the events. Arnulf, for instance, saw the Pataria largely in historical terms, while Landulf envisaged it as a socio-religious movement, and Andrew focused on its founder and its canonical structure. A lengthier analysis is also desirable for another reason. In the episodes of heresy at Orléans, Arras, and Monforte, the brevity of the sources and the relative autonomy of the sects made the problem of literacy easy to pinpoint and to discuss. In the case of the Pataria, as in all later, better-organized heretical and reformist associations, the social, political, and intellectual context is more diffuse.[42] A balanced picture of the movement must be presented before the issue of communications can be analysed on its own, especially if the sectarian uses of literacy are to be compared, as subsequent chapters intend, to parallel developments in philosophy, theology, and other branches of interpretation.

Arnulf of Milan

In Arnulf of Milan, the point of view of the author and the inner workings of the sectarian community are relatively easy to isolate. Let us look at each in turn.

Arnulf himself was the grand-nephew of Arnulf I of Arzago, who was archbishop from 970 to 974. He was born in the late tenth century and came of age along with the emergent class of capitanei to which he belonged. His "history of recent events" is largely the story of the consolidation of their interests. His terse style is rich in biblical images of self-righteousness and fulfilment.[43] Books one to three in particular defend the Milanese nobility and higher clergy against a

[41] W. Berschin, *Bonizo von Sutri* (Berlin, 1972), 22-23.

[42] Cf. O. Capitani, "Storiografia e riforma della chiesa in Italia (Arnolfo e Landolfo seniore di Milano," *La storiografia altomedievale* (Spoleto, 1970), 564: *"un problema . . . essenzialmente culturale."*

[43] E.g., *Gesta* 1.5, citing Gal 5.26 and Prov 16.11, 1.6; Mt 10.36.

variety of perceived threats to stability: simony, implying the alienation of church property, disorder, whether proceeding from above as in the case of Landulf II or from below in the Patarenes, and, above all, the encroachment of external principles of written law upon the customary privileges of the local church.[44]

Arnulf's ambivalence towards the present speaks out clearly through the preface's rhetoric and subsequent legalisms. He marvels that more authors do not venture into "the forest of the present age," where "the diverse leaves of novel events" are budding.[45] For so remarkable a period for writing, he asserts, never existed in the city's past, either for the learned or the unlearned.[46] Although book one deals with the period between 925 and 1018, whose events he knows only at second hand, he remains very much a *gestorum scriptor praesentium*.[47] Throughout, he vindicates the role of the capitanei, justifying their prerogatives through both ancient precedent and contemporary usage. When Hugh of Burgundy thought of appointing a new archbishop in 925, he recognized Milan's *prisca consuetudo*, by which the election was the responsibility of the *cardinales* or *ordinarii*.[48] In 948, again, he describes the capitanei as the main institutional bulwark against the *perniciosa seditio* which pitted archbishop Arderic against his rivals Manasses and Adelmann.[49] And, after 979, when the count deserted the city in another civil disturbance, Landulf II enfeoffed the nobility with church lands, thereby, in his view, defeating the insurrection of the cives at Carbonaria and re-establishing *pax perpetua*.[50]

Arnulf's unwavering commitment to the capitanei helps to explain his nuanced attitude towards Aribert. He claims only to be narrating the events of his episcopate, not to be judging them.[51] But he is too shrewd to be misled either by the archbishop's egocentrism or by allegedly reformist tendencies from below. Of course he is proud of Aribert's positive achievements, especially when they are underpinned by lay authority. It was Conrad himself, he notes with satisfaction, who reproved the bishop of Ravenna for taking Milan's rightful place in the coronation procession of 26th March 1027.[52] And when Conrad invaded Burgundy in 1032, Aribert and Boniface of Tuscany rode side by side at the head of their troops, *duo lumina regni*.[53]

[44] Cf. Violante, *La pataria milanese*, 21; H.E.J. Cowdrey, "The Papacy, the Patarenes and the Church of Milan," *Transactions of the Royal Historical Society*, 5th Series, 18 (1968), 33-35.

[45] *Gesta* 1.1, pp. 6-7.   [46] *Ibid.*, 7.   [47] *Ibid.*, 1.8, p. 8.   [48] *Ibid.*, 1.3, p. 7.

[49] *Ibid.*, 1.5, p. 8.   [50] *Ibid.*, 1.10, p. 9.

[51] *Ibid.*, 2.1, pp. 11-12: "quae quidem narranda, non iudicanda suscepimus."

[52] *Ibid.*, 2.4, p. 12.   [53] *Ibid.*, 2.8, p. 14.

Yet Arnulf is equally sensitive to the forces that brought about Aribert's downfall. In part these were changes in the *status urbis et ecclesiae* which were beyond his control.[54] But Aribert also overstepped the functions of his office as conceived by the cardinal clergy. The turning point in his view was Lodi, whose right to replace its deceased bishop was usurped with Conrad's support. When the people resisted, Aribert besieged the town and compelled them to accept an oath of fidelity. Hard feelings did not die: the Milanese continued to plunder the vineyards and fields surrounding the town, and the men of Lodi, although fewer in number, strenuously resisted the intrusions into their civic affairs.[55] Aribert, Arnulf notes, appeared mindless of the cost: "Encouraged by his success (i.e., in Lodi and Burgundy), our protector began to govern . . . immoderately, taking himself mainly into account, not others."[56] Trouble at the top of Milanese society was soon matched by uprisings from below. First the vavasours "conspired seriously against him."[57] His power was preserved by a miracle—not, as the Milanese thought, by the sudden death of Conrad in the winter of 1037, but, as one reads between the lines, by the emperor's improvident attack on Milan, which served to rally the otherwise conflicting social classes around their archbishop as never before. But for the last time: Aribert's *carroccio*, the chariot symbolizing Milan's civic consciousness, not only provided a sense of urban unity[58] before a common external foe. It was also a monument to a waning institutional order. Aribert was partly motivated out of fear:[59] "whatever the battle's outcome," Arnulf noted, "the Milanese might derive a little comfort" from it.[60] The other attack on the archbishop's power was made by the cives. Aribert never really recovered from Lanzo's onslaught, and Arnulf is at a loss to give a precise explanation why

[54] *Ibid*, 2.18, p. 16; 3.1, p. 17.   [55] *Ibid.*, 2.7, pp. 13-14.
[56] *Ibid.*, 2.10, p. 14.   [57] *Idem.*
[58] According to Arnulf, Aribert ordered all ranks of society to take up arms, 2.16, p. 16: ". . . iubet ilico convenire ad urbem omnes Ambrosianae parochiae incolas armis instructos, a rustico usque ad militem, ab inope usque ad divitem, ut in tanta cohorte patriam tueretur ab hoste." Y. Renouard, *Les villes d'Italie*, 390, saw this as a manifestation of *"une passion commune," "une émotion collective."* But it is worth noting that Arnulf uses the same rhetorical topos elsewhere, for example, when Aribert was taken captive by Conrad (2.12, p. 15: "Ecce Mediolanensis attonita inhorruit civitas, proprio viduata pastore dolens ac gemens a puero usque ad senem)," and when he escaped to Milan (*ibid.*: ". . . cui venienti tota occurrit civitas ita ylaris, ut servus domino, mulier non cederet viro prae gaudio cursitantes)." Cf. Landulf, *Historia* 3.9, p. 80, 13-17; Andrew of Strumi, *Vita S. Arialdi*, c. 25, MGH SS 30.2, 1071, 7-14.
[59] *Gesta*, 2.16, p. 16: "praevidens autem archiepiscopus futuram oppressionem. . . ."
[60] *Idem.*

the uprising took place. He falls back on topoi: the return of peace brought prosperity and, inevitably, iniquity; the Milanese, no longer beset by enemies on the outside, began to quarrel among themselves. The whole issue, he would have us believe, boiled down to a squabble between a commoner and a knight.[61]

In sum, the only class whose motives Arnulf considers natural and legitimate are the capitanei. All other social changes are disruptions, or, as he terms them, *audaciae*.[62] His principal example is the Pataria, the *civile iurgium* to which he devotes book three. Whether the changes the movement brought about were "for better or worse," he reflects, "it is not necessary to say." He would even "prefer not to know."[63] But his account of the tumultuous years following the election of Guido da Velate leaves little doubt where his sympathies lay.

His analysis proceeds simultaneously along three axes: literacy versus illiteracy, precedent versus custom, and town versus country. The Pataria in his view was chiefly brought about by the election of an archbishop who was "an illiterate coming from the countryside (*idiota, a rure veniens*)."[64] When the movement came out into the open, it attempted, in opposition to Guido's simoniacal practices, to impose its own legal authority, which was based on a literal reading of the Bible, over and above the inherited customs of the Milanese church. This activity, Arnulf concludes, was instrumental in creating a new form of religious association.

Two features stand out in Arnulf's subsequent analysis of the Pataria. One is his conception of the movement as a classical sect; the other is his sensitivity to the Patarene capacity to raise a following through preaching.

Arnulf first sketches the external events that took place before and during the agitations; then he focuses on the movement itself. In appointing Guido, he reasons, Henry III was indifferent to the social station and collective wisdom of the cardinal clergy. He thereby allied himself with the cives and the vavasours against the capitanei. Even so, Guido won acceptance only because of fear of the emperor and of internal dissension (3.2). Also, during the fifties, the political situation in Italy became increasingly complicated. Boniface of Tuscany died (3.5); Henry was preoccupied on his eastern front (3.6); and a

---

[61] *Ibid.*, 2.18, p. 16.

[62] *Ibid.*, 2.7, p. 13; 2.10, p. 14. Cf. 3.20, p. 23, 24.

[63] *Ibid.*, 3.1, p. 17.

[64] *Ibid.*, 3.2, p. 17. Cf. Bonizo of Sutri, *Liber ad Amicum* 6, MGH Libelli de Lite 1, 591: "vir illiteratus et concubinatus et absque ulla verecundia symoniacus."

new force, the Normans, began to make its presence felt in Apulia
(3.4). Papal reforms progressed in fits and starts (3.3-4). Worst of
all, long-standing differences between Milan and Pavia had burst into
the open (3.7-8). In these "stormy times," when much that the capitanei had worked for was threatened from outside, the very foundations of the Ambrosian clergy were shaken from below. The guilt
was shared by the archbishop and the Patarenes: both "sinned and
were deprived of God's glory."[65] But the chief blame for the insurrection lay with the rebels. Guido, he notes, first bestowed favours on
their leader, Ariald. But his kindness was answered by criticism of
the established clergy. Along with Landulf Cotta, Ariald usurped "the
office of preaching" from the regular priests (3.10).

The purpose of these chapters is to provide a context for the Pataria,
first historically (3.1-9) and then culturally (3.10). The sudden tran-
sitions of the opening episodes prepare the reader for what Arnulf
describes in chapter ten as a *horror*, that is, a trembling, upsetting,
or even reversal of the normal state of affairs.[66] In his view, the Patarene disturbance had two chief characteristics, the interpretation of
Scripture and preaching the Word. In his own words, first, accepted
doctrine was altered; then, spread about, it gave rise to error in many
minds.[67] For Arnulf there was no separation of the social and cultural
aspects of the problem: he speaks simultaneously of "the people, rising
anew against the archbishop,"[68] and of the reading and preaching of
the gospels. He contrasts *populus* and *clerus* not only as lay and clerical
but as unlettered and lettered.[69] Ariald's rebellion in his opinion was
founded on scholastic legalism: "Devoting himself to the study of
letters (*litterarum . . . studium*), he became a most severe interpreter
of divine law (*divinae legis . . . interpres*) and subsequently pronounced
harsh judgments (*dura . . . iudicia*) on clerics alone."[70] His relationship
to Landulf Cotta is also seen primarily in terms of eloquence and
education. Playing ironically on their different places in society, Arnulf says that the nobler Landulf nonetheless became Ariald's mouthpiece and camp follower.[71] Ariald was *interpres*, Landulf, *dux verbi*.[72]
And together they preached a new order, *contra morem ecclesiae*.[73]

[65] Rom 3.23.
[66] *Gesta* 3.10, p. 18: "horror"; "hic horror."
[67] *Idem*: "Verum talis hic horror mutata cum aspiratione littera multorum concepit errorem."
[68] *Idem*: ". . . insurgente populo noviter in eum" (= clerum).
[69] Cf. C. Violante, "I laici nel movimento patarino," in *Studi*, ed. P. Zerbi, 164ff.
[70] *Gesta* 3.10, p. 19: ". . . dum litterarum vacaret studio, severissimus est divinae legis factus interpres, dura exercens in clericos solos iudicia."
[71] *Ibid.*: ". . . familiaris eius factus assecla."   [72] *Ibid.*   [73] *Ibid.*

Arnulf, then, does not see the Pataria as a popular movement but as an example of sectarianism. It was only "popular" in its consequences, which permitted a new form of communication between the lettered and the unlettered. If we adopt his perspective, the difference between the Pataria and the sects discussed earlier in this chapter arises chiefly from its size, urban environment, and more extensive use of public preaching. In the heretical groups at Orléans, Arras, and Monforte, interpretation of texts and communication among the members were closely linked. In the Pataria a comparable result was achieved, but the methods employed were not the same. There was a division of labour between *lectio* and *praedicatio*, which Arnulf neatly recapitulates by speaking of Ariald's charisma and Landulf's oratorical skill.[74] Interaction among the members, moreover, was augmented by a relationship, structured by levels of literacy, between those inside and those outside the movement. In literary terms the *cleri* were the readers, the *populi*, the audience. This type of organization conferred a new flexibility onto the Pataria. Although based like earlier sects on written rules and norms for conduct, the movement was able to give at least a superficial collective unity to a far larger number of members by means of the spoken word.

Arnulf provides us with an illustration of how the relationship between *cleri* and *populi* worked through one of the sermons which, he asserts, Landulf daily preached "in plebeian ears."

The text can be paraphrased as follows.[75] First Landulf excuses his youth, inexperience, and unpolished speech. But God, he adds, often reveals to the humble what he denies to the great. Then he asks his listeners to make a verbal pledge of faith to "the triple and single God." Some stark biblical images come next.[76] Delighted as he is by their piety, he foresees Milan's imminent ruin. For the saviour has not walked in their midst for many a day. The Milanese have been wandering in error: no divine "footprint" shows them the way. In place of light they have darkness. The blind lead the blind. Landulf sees abuses everywhere in the priesthood, but he speaks out most fiercely against simony and nicolaitism. If the Milanese cherish any

[74] Cf. Bonizo of Sutri, *Liber ad Amicum* 6, p. 591: "Landulfus ex maiorum prosapia ortus, vir urbanus et facundissimus. . . ."

[75] Summarizing 3.11, p. 19. G. Miccoli argues that the sermon was probably late; "Per la storia della Pataria milanese," in *Chiesa gregoriana* (Florence, 1966), 147n109. For a more extensive discussion of Ariald's sermons, see below, pp. 217-27.

[76] For an analysis of Arnulf's and Landulf's scriptural references and their relations to canonical sources, see O. Capitani, "Storiografia e riforma della chiesa in Italia," 572-611.

hope of salvation, they must rid themselves of corruption among the clergy. Today, the sacraments are like dung, the churches like stables. Goods must be confiscated, evil works undone. Not that he himself is free of sin: but Milan's church has committed unforgivable offences against God himself. Landulf concludes by asking his auditors to imitate his reformed way of life.

What can we learn from this sermon? Arnulf maintains that Landulf's preaching was deliberately "arranged" for the persuasion of the unsophisticated (*concionatur in populo*).[77] While his point of view is undoubtedly biased, it cannot be denied that the text, at least as he presents it, exhibits careful organization. It contains three sections, an introductory sentence, a short exhortation to the audience, and a lengthier didactic message.

Above all, his statement is personal, individualistic and affective. "I cannot," he says, "any longer hold back the sermon conceived in my heart."[78] The phrase *sermo in corde conceptus* suggests a charismatic gift closely allied with the activity of interpretation. The words which follow are the result of his own reflection on the gospels and on the moral state of the clergy. Landulf takes pains to hide his individuality behind two rhetorical topoi: as a young man (*adolescens*), he appeals to his elders (*seniores*), and, as one untrained in public speaking (*imperitus*), he asks indulgence for his lack of style. But, having thus distanced himself by this introductory flourish, he immediately involves the audience in the discourse and in the progress of his inner thoughts. He reaches out to the people on their own level, making himself a bridge between the lettered and the unlettered. "Tell me," he asks, "do you believe in the one and threefold God?" They answer, "We believe!" "Then make the sign of the cross." They do.[79] Both oral and gestural, this revivalist give and take between preacher and audience, which the reduction of the text to Latin undoubtedly tended to suppress, has the effect of welding the two into a single unit. It also establishes a bond, if somewhat impermanently, between the members of the audience, who, despite Arnulf's perception of them as a mass, probably represented different economic and social strata. Through Landulf's words they all participate in the same religious event.

Once the rapport is established, Landulf is free to deliver his message, which has two parts, one prophetic, the other penitential. The Milanese, he claims, are headed for ruin. They wander aimlessly, un-

---

[77] *Gesta* 3.11, p. 19.

[78] *Ibid.*, 19: ". . . conceptum in corde sermonem ultra non valeo."

[79] *Idem.* On the cult of the cross, see Violante, *La pataria milanese*, 119-20.

aided by the *vestigia veritatis*. In order to find the right pathway they must take the lead in correcting ecclesiastical abuses and above all *haeresis illa symoniaca*. Landulf recognizes that the problems relate to both the countryside and the town: the bad priests in his view must be deprived of their goods whether they are found *in urbe vel extra*.[80] He is not afraid of street language: the violations are *stupra*, the forms of worship *canina stercora*, the churches *iumentorum praesepia*. But nowhere does he suggest that the sacraments themselves are inefficacious. Finally, his harsh words are deeply personalized. Although he is not one of the people, he speaks to them as if he were. He delights in their piety and suffers in their sins (*delectior . . . compatior*). He too has sinned: *ego plectenda plura commisi*. And, through dramatic New Testament images of darkness and light, he takes upon himself an apostolic role, asking like St. Paul that his listeners imitate him (*imitatores mei estote*), following not so much specific doctrines but an entire way of life (*forma nostra*).[81]

From the sermon Arnulf turns to the movement itself, which, as he saw it, was largely composed of laymen who rallied around Ariald and Landulf either for religious or materialistic reasons.[82] In subsequent chapters he increasingly identifies this lay association with an innovative legalism which easily crosses the fluid boundary between heresy and reform.[83] Social and cultural factors are intermingled: on the one hand, "the people, always eager for novelty, were aroused against the clergy . . ."; on the other, they were drawn together by the preaching of Ariald and Landulf, who incited their minds, "always proposing new and unheard of ideas through subtle discourse."[84] The winds of change blew in the leaders' direction and they wasted no time in pandering to the people's tastes (*vulgi mos*). On numerous occasions legalism worked the other way and the cathedral clergy opposed the reformers with *scripturae et sanctiones canonicae*, but to no avail.[85] Association finally led to sworn agreement and to violence. After the clash at the Roman forum on 10th May 1057, Landulf set

---

[80] *Gesta* 3.11, p. 19.

[81] *Ibid.*, 19: "Igitur imitatores mei estote, carissimi, et ita ambulate, sicut habetis formam nostram."

[82] *Ibid.*, 3.12, p. 19.

[83] On this complex question, see O. Capitani, "Storiografia e riforma della chiesa in Italia . . . ," 567-624.

[84] *Gesta* 3.12, p. 19.

[85] *Idem.*

up his own *leges* for the diocese, which were subsequently enforced by lay vigilantes.[86]

The ideological separation between clerics and laymen was completed at Fontaneto in November of the same year. "There, Landulf reviled the bishops, especially the archbishop of Milan; he raged furiously against the clerics but warmly approved of laymen as his brethren." Arnulf's language for describing the heresy is reminiscent of Gerard of Cambrai: Landulf, in his view, was merely a master of "simulation and dissimulation," adept at manipulating a popular crowd. And the people responded by swearing "a common oath," which was later enjoined upon the entire lay and religious community. From within the movement one also feels that boundaries were being fixed. For example, "from that period a band of men and women accompanied (Landulf), stayed by him, and guarded him day and night."[87] Arnulf's distaste for the lay element resurfaced after Landulf's death, when admittedly Erlembald took up his brother's cause out of personal conviction and fraternal devotion.[88] But what was good for laymen was bad for the clergy: "while a layman judged, the clergy was punished."[89] It follows that Arnulf sees the lay community of eleventh-century Milan as a popular mob, impermanent and unstable in composition,[90] abruptly bringing about changes without reference to Milan's past.[91] He describes the people as a *turba, turbo,*[92] or *tumultus;*[93] *pataria* in his view means *perturbatio.*[94] He also thrusts onto laymen's shoulders the responsibility for opposing the ancient custom (*prisca consuetudo*) of the diocese.[95] In other words, he justifies the status quo by transforming the customary privileges of the Ambrosian church into a legal ideology. The capitanei, who were no less than the cives

---

[86] *Ibid.,* 3.13, p. 20.   [87] *Idem.*   [88] *Ibid.,* 3.16, p. 21.   [89] *Ibid.,* 22.

[90] E.g., in the riot of Pentecost, 1066, 3.20, p.23: "Sed more suo populus non diu statu permansit eodem."

[91] E.g., 3.12, p. 19: populus semper avidus novorum; 5.6, p.30: Susceptus est praesul ille (= Gotefredus) a clero et populo, utpote novarum rerum usualiter avido.

[92] *Ibid.,* 3.14, p. 20; 3.20, p. 23; cf. 2.18, p. 16; 2.19, p. 17; 3.25, p. 25.

[93] *Ibid.,* p. 21; 3.20, p. 23; cf. 2.3, p. 12; 2.12, p. 15.

[94] *Ibid.,* 4.11, p. 28. Arnulf agrees with later commentators in deriving "Pataria" from some aspect of the life of the lower classes of Milan. For a general review of the question, see C. Thouzellier, "Patarins," *Hérésies et hérétiques* (Rome, 1969), 204-21. Particularly valuable among earlier studies is A. Frugoni, "Due schede: 'Pannosus' e 'Patarinus,' " BIS 65 (1953), 129-35. But even this derivation throws little real light on the Patarenes' social origins; cf. Violante, *La pataria milanese,* 198n2. Muratori, it seems, was close to the truth when he spoke of the followers of Ariald as *viri inliterati*; G. Cracco, "Pataria: *opus* e *nomen* (tra verità e autorità)," *Rivista della storia della chiesa in Italia* 28 (1974), 357-58.

[95] *Ibid.,* 3.25, p. 25. Cf. 1.3, p. 7.

a byproduct of historical evolution, are looked upon as a bastion of permanence in a sea of populist instability. This bias strongly colours his attitude towards reform. Simony, as a consequence, is less a general ecclesiastical abuse than a point of litigation between opposed factions, between old and new. Change has the same status as Ariald's introduction of *novitates* into the liturgy.[96]

Arnulf's analysis, then, opposes tradition to change. His overall perspective on the Pataria is not social but cultural and religious:[97] this, in turn, has a large influence on how he views the process of social change throughout the *Gesta*. Terms such as *cives, laicus*, and *clerus* recur again and again; but only as the story proceeds is Arnulf's idea of how Milanese society works clarified. Book one is almost devoid of the term *populus*.[98] Events are shaped by personalities. Even in chapter ten, in which archbishop Landulf enfeoffs the capitanei in order to quell an insurrection among the cives, the archbishop himself is perceived as the motivator of change.[99] Book two is similarly dominated by the personality of Aribert. For instance, during Conrad's coronation, he does not protest his improper place in the procession "lest on a festive day there be a popular uprising."[100] Again, at Lodi, the cives may be identified as a group, but only in opposition to Aribert and his nominee, Ambrose. In 1036, when Conrad triumphantly entered Milan, the people as a whole are said to come to greet him, young and old (*a puero usque ad senem*);[101] and, when Aribert was obliged to defend the city against the same emperor, the archbishop was said to levy his forces from rustic and knight, poor and rich (*a rustico usque ad militem, ab inope usque ad divitem*).[102] Even the revolt of the vavasours can partly be understood in these terms.[103] Aribert, in other words, is looked upon as both the leader and the father of his

[96] *Ibid.*, 3.17, p. 22.

[97] Preferring "religious" to Capitani's "*morale*," with its too restrictive associations in English; "Storiografia e riforma della chiesa in Italia," p. 560, 560-61n2, *et passim*.

[98] Its use is restricted to the formula *a clero et populo*, 1.8, p.9; 1.19, p. 11.

[99] *Ibid.*, 1.10, p. 9: "Iam enim successerat Gotefredo Landulfus archiepiscopus, qui propter nimiam patris ac fratrum insolentiam, gravem populi perpessus est invidentiam. Instabant enim prae solito, civitatis abuti dominio."

[100] *Ibid.*, 2.3, p. 12.

[101] *Ibid.*, 2.12, p. 15.

[102] *Ibid.*, 2.16, p. 16. For a discussion, see above, p. 165n58.

[103] *Ibid.*, 2.10, p. 14: "Multis igitur prosperatis successibus praesul Heribertus immoderate paululum dominabatur omnium, suum considerans, non aliorum animum. Unde factum est, ut quidam urbis milites, vulgo valvassores nominati, clanculo illius insidiarentur operibus, adversus ipsum assidue conspirantes."

diocese; in Arnulf's classical if somewhat ominous image, he is *patro-cinante in omnibus*.[104] The citizenry is seen as an ideological unit in relation to individual authority.

One sees the first signs of a different attitude in the revolt of the cives under Lanzo in 1040. As Arnulf himself succinctly puts it: *im-mutatus est status urbis et ecclesiae*.[105] The major shift, as noted, is from personal to institutional forms of authority and government, bringing in its wake the notion of rule by written law as opposed to custom, as well as the nebulous byproduct of class consciousness. The cives are now viewed as an autonomous group: the essential conflict involves the common people moved against the knights (*plebs commota contra milites*).[106] Association among the rebels first appears as "oaths";[107] only later, in the Pataria, do the *iuramenta* crystallize into written precepts.[108] The revolt crosses social boundaries: Lanzo, "a well-born knight of the city, nonetheless preferred the plebeian mob."[109] And, indignant at his action, the nobility became united as a knightly class.[110] The blood spilt on Milan's street corners and back lanes fore-shadows the Pataria, but by 1057, when Ariald begins preaching, the insurgents have anchored their aspirations in the firm bedrock of ec-clesiastical reform.

In book three, sectarian rivalry based on articulated institutional differences replaces the cult of personality, only to be superseded in books four and five by the legal authority of the papacy. Written legislation has thereby worked its way up Arnulf's historical scale from the lowest social to the highest ecclesiastical sphere. Individuals re-main important: as Arnulf sees it, the Patarene agitation began with Henry III's wilful decision to appoint Guido da Velate to the see of Milan over the heads of the cardinal clergy. But other conflicts are just beneath the surface. The *primus ordo* of the clergy is described as *nobilis* and *sapiens*; it is socially and culturally identified with legiti-mate authority and the monopoly of institutional literacy. Guido, as noted, is by contrast both unlettered and a countryman. Throughout Arnulf's account of the Pataria, the gulf widens between the town and

[104] *Ibid.*, 2.6, p. 13.

[105] *Ibid.*, 2.18, p. 16.   [106] *Loc.cit.*   [107] *Loc.cit.*

[108] *Ibid.*, 3.13, p. 20: "Unde potestate accepta, commune indicit (Erlembaldus) omnibus laicis iuramentum, quasi impugnanda proponens sacrorum ordinum stupra et venales consecra-tiones." On proceeding from "oath" to "decree," see the elegant analysis of Capitani, "Storio-grafia e riforma della chiesa in Italia," 614-25.

[109] *Gesta* 2.18, p. 16.

[110] *Loc.cit.*

the country and between the upper and lower cultural and social strata.[111] Arnulf himself begins to distinguish between the abstract civic virtue embodied in Aribert and the *causae civiles*,[112] the opposed interests of the capitanei, the vavasours, and the cives. But he also recognizes that increasingly the Patarene and archiepiscopal factions ground their claims to legitimacy in *lex*, the archbishop as upholder, the heretic as usurper. Legal authority from Rome is similarly Erlembald's basis for taking up the *vexillum sancti Petri*.[113]

It follows that for Arnulf agitation can be brought to a permanent halt only when a cultural equilibrium is re-established between *clerus* and *populus*, an ideal which he holds out at the *Gesta*'s end but which never emerges as a historical reality. After Erlembald's death in 1075, he notes with some relief that "the offices of clerics and laymen were divided"[114] once again. The prestige formerly invested in Aribert and the capitanei is now associated with the putative alliance between the city's establishment and the papacy.[115] Hildebrand, as a consequence, whom Arnulf criticized in book three for anti-Milanese sentiment,[116] is presented as a symbol of order. Yet this return to conventional patterns of interpretation leaves us in the end unsatisfied. Arnulf's genuine insights are overshadowed by his ideological commitments. His description of Patarene preaching takes the reader to the brink of a deeper understanding of sectarian uses of literacy. But the threshold is not crossed.

Landulf Senior

Landulf Senior's *Historia Mediolanensis* is longer and more detailed than Arnulf's *Gesta*. The first book describes the founding of the Milanese church by St. Ambrose; the second follows the story from the early sixth century down to the death of Aribert; the third begins with the preaching of Anselm of Baggio and moves dramatically through the Patarene agitations, concluding a decade after Erlembald's death. The intentions of the two authors are also different. Arnulf's interpretation of the Pataria develops as he himself deepens the social and ecclesiastical context. Only when these are established do we gain insights into problems of communication. Landulf, by contrast, speaks to the reader on social and cultural levels at once. The problem of communication is placed at the centre of the stage from the outset.

In comparison with Arnulf, Landulf is less accurate and objec-

[111] *Ibid.*, 2.15, p. 16; 3.24, p. 24.   [112] *Ibid.*, 3.8, p. 18.   [113] *Ibid.*, 3.17, p. 22.
[114] *Ibid.*, 3.14, p. 21.   [115] *Ibid.*, 5.7, p. 30.   [116] *Ibid.*, 3.17, p. 22.

tive.[117] Also, if Arnulf defends the interests of a single class, Landulf is committed to a sectarian position, namely, the legitimacy of a married clergy. Not surprisingly, historians since Muratori's time have differed widely in their estimates of the *Historia*'s value.[118] During the heated political debates of the Risorgimento, Landulf was frequently portrayed as a defender of liberalism and democracy. Carlo Romussi, a Lombard archivist, saw him among Italian chroniclers as "the first to sense . . . the oppression of the capitanei and the vavasours"[119] on the common people. He was even pictured as a "plebeian" who had courageously taken up the cause of Milan's downtrodden masses.[120]

No reader of the *Historia* can doubt Landulf's sincere interest in the fate of the lower strata of Milanese society during a period of political and religious upheaval.[121] But Landulf himself was no commoner. He was described in what is probably his will, dated 1073, as a cleric and notary of the higher Milanese clergy.[122] He was married, and he wrote his *History* in old age around 1110 as a last, somewhat despairing attempt to defend the vanishing nicolaitan priesthood of Milan. His general purpose was not to provide an account of social conflicts but to frame what he thought to be the decline of religious integrity in his own time within the larger story of the Ambrosian church. In doing so, he wilfully distorted existing sources for the city's early history and occasionally invented new ones[123] in order to hold out to his age a personalized model of reform.[124]

Clues to the nature of this design are found in the dedicatory letter to an unnamed "L" with which he prefaced the work.[125] In Landulf's view, the tribulations of his own day were brought about by a twofold evil. The church was weakened from outside by the Patarenes' *falsae praedicationes*. But many of its own number entered the clergy for personal rather than vocational reasons, thereby rendering themselves

[117] Cf. W. Wattenbach, *Deutschlands Geschichtsquellen im Mittelalter*, 6th ed. (Berlin, 1894), vol. 2, p. 242.
[118] For a brief review, see the introduction to A. Cutolo's edition, *Rerum Italicarum Scriptores* 4.2, iii-viii; and, on views of Aribert in particular, Violante, *La società milanese*, 267-79.
[119] *Milano e suoi monumenti* (Milan, n.d.), vol. 2, p. 45; quoted by Cutolo, p. v.
[120] Romussi, *loc.cit.*; cf. Cutolo, vii.
[121] Cf. Violante, *La pataria milanese*, 24.
[122] A. Columbo, "Il testamento di Landolfo Seniore?" *Archivio storico lombardo* 57 (1930), 140: "clericus ac notarius de ordine maiore sancte mediolanensis ecclesie."
[123] L. A. Ferrai, "I fonti di Landolfo Seniore," BIS 14 (1895), 7-13.
[124] Cf. O. Capitani, "Storiografia e riforma della chiesa in Italia," 557-67.
[125] *Epistola Ystoriografi ad Archipresbyterum missa*, MGH SS 8, 36-37.

incapable of conveying the sacraments.[126] Rome's powerlessness, or lack of resolve, only served to fuel the sectarian fires.

For Landulf, then, there is not one sect by two, the Patarini and the Nicolaiti. And the church of St. Ambrose in his fanciful reconstruction hovers between being a "church" and a favorably disposed "sect." Like a church, it has a hierarchy, a fixed set of ecclesiastical institutions, and, within its diocese, it is the unique dispenser of grace; but, like a sect, it has a charismatic leader, an intense, inward-turning spirituality, and a disdain for outsiders.

Landulf tailors his portrait of St. Ambrose to fit this dual perspective. The founder of the Milanese church is described both as a builder of institutions and as a dynamic teacher.[127] More to Landulf's point, he is the sort of leader who would naturally have defended the right of Milanese priests to choose freely between celibacy and marriage. There are numerous images of sectarianism. For instance, while Ambrose's learning is stressed, he is said to have used preaching as a means of transforming thought into action,[128] thereby anticipating the Patarene debate over the control of literacy and the means of ecclesiastical communication. Honey, too, flowed from Ambrose's lips; thereby the holy spirit descended:[129] like earlier heretics Landulf establishes a relationship between the cognitive and expressive aspects of interpretation. Again, the bishop tended his flock not under compulsion but of his own free will, not for gain but out of devotion[130]—virtues which, if transposed in time, neatly sum up Landulf's ambivalence towards the established clergy and reform. As in other religious movements, unity of purpose was achieved by normative rules, whose chief monuments were the church hierarchy and its liturgy.[131] These were directly inspired by God: similarly, Ambrose, granted charisma, brought his talents to perfection through meditation, writing, reading, and preaching.[132] He thus personified the original descent of wisdom from God through Christ, a capacity, of course, claimed by many sectarian leaders. Not by accident, moreover, he decided to set up the church

---

[126] *Ibid.*, lines 25-35.

[127] *Historia Mediolanensis* 1.1, MGH SS 8, p. 37, line 30: "verus magister et doctor ecclesiae"; *ibid.*, 1.2, p. 38, line 44: "scientia divina imbutus, spiritu sancto repletus."

[128] *Ibid.*, 1.1, p. 37, 34-35.

[129] *Ibid.*, lines 38-39.   [130] *Ibid.*, 40-43; 1 Petri 5.2.

[131] On the rite's development, see in general P. Lejay, "Ambrosien (rit)," DACL 1.1, 1373-1442, with bibliography, 1439-42.

[132] *Historia* 1.1, p. 37, 57-p. 38, 2: "In principio erat verbum. . . ." (Io 1.1); "Sic beatus magister et doctor Ambrosius inter ceteros doctores eximius ecclesiam Dei . . . die ac nocte meditando, scribendo, legendo, praedicando exaltavit. . . ."

of Milan on the day after he defeated the Arians. It was a literate affair: first, he thoroughly studied the writings of the patriarchs and the prophets in order to find a suitable model. Then he decided to build a church in fulfilment of David's prophecy.[133]

The identification between the inspired word of St. Ambrose and the autonomy of the Milanese church is pursued in other chapters of book one, in which Landulf carefully rearranged material from his two major sources, the *Annals* of Datius, who was bishop from ca. 530 to 552, and the *Vitae Pontificum*.[134] The resulting explanation of Milan's ecclesiastical hierarchy is largely a justification of the status quo before the Patarene agitations. Particularly important, he maintained, was Ambrose's position on married priests, in defence of which he distorted a well-known statement from *De Officiis*.[135] The bishop is pictured as an advocate of tolerance: he knew the frailties of the senses and that all men were prone to sin, especially from incontinence. No one, he argued, could attain chastity or virginity except through God. The Lord did not want forced servitude. And, in this respect, the Milanese and Greek churches were one: a man could enter the priesthood single or married, but from that point he could not change his status; and, if his wife died, he was not permitted to remarry.[136] Of course Ambrose had made no such statements. Landulf's arguments merely repeat with minor variations the standard responses of married priests to papal reform efforts. The clue is his characterization of the Patarenes as Rome's agents. They were, he said, *pseudochristi* or *pseudoprophetae*, who were "about to subvert the church of God and his people through false doctrine."[137]

In Landulf's mind, then, we find a utopian conception of the early Milanese church, against which *falsi fratres* are attempting to erect a new religious order. Both are pictured *in abstracto*: they are models around which the *Historia* is organized, providing, in part, a theoretical backdrop for the events of books two and three. As a consequence, the rise of social and religious conflict is not seen as a contest between

[133] *Ibid.*, 38, 8-26.

[134] L. A. Ferrai, "I fonti . . . ," 10-11; *idem*, "Gli Annali di Dazio e i Patarini," *Archivio storico lombardo* 19 (1892), 539ff.

[135] *De Officiis* 1.50.247, PL 16.97A. The possibility of different texts among the "Arialdini" and "Nicolaiti" is rejected by Ferrai, "I fonti," 37. Ambrose in fact argued that men who have married twice, even if the marriages took place before baptism, cannot become priests. Thus, it is a law (*lex*) that priests whose wives have died are not to marry again. However, in his view, continence was preferable for all religious.

[136] *Historia* 1.2, p. 38, 44-54, quoting Jerome, *Ep.* 82 and 1 Petri 2.9.

[137] *Ibid.*, p. 38, 58-p. 39, 19.

literacy and illiteracy. The question for Landulf is: whose erudition is historically justified, and for what ends?

BOOK TWO. These issues are brought into focus in book two, which has two broad themes, the vicissitudes of the Milanese church in the early Middle Ages (chs. 1-15) and the history of more recent bishoprics, culminating in Landulf II and Aribert (chs. 16-35). Landulf also moves from folklore to history. The early chapters, which intermingle fact, legend, and popular tradition, are almost entirely his own invention. Yet, however untrustworthy in actual detail, they provide an accurate guide to Landulf's inner preoccupations. These resurface little disguised in his explanation of events nearer in time.

The early chapters in particular illustrate Landulf's notion of the value of learned as opposed to popular culture. In his view, the Milanese church derived a large part of its prestige from its role as a centre for high religious thinking throughout the Dark Ages. One legend had it that Charlemagne tried to stamp out the Ambrosian liturgy on returning from Rome after his successful campaign against Desiderius in 774.[138] But bishop Eugenius pleaded eloquently before pope Hadrian, and, when the liturgical works of Ambrose and Gregory the Great were placed beside each other on the altar of St. Peter's, they apparently burst their bindings and gave forth a terrifying sound. Then, spread apart by God's finger, both opened in such a way that the pages of the one could not be read in isolation from the other.[139] Throughout book two, miracles, legends, and fictive documents rise to the defence of Milan's autonomy from Rome. Landulf was equally fearful lest unruly monarchs and bishops upset the delicate balance of forces within the church itself. There are as a consequence pointed references to the activity of laymen in religious affairs.

The ideological character of this material is well exemplified by the story of Honoratus and Lambert, which took place in the sixth century.[140] According to Landulf, during the episcopate of Honoratus, "king Lambert" usurped the Italian throne. Under Rome, Milan had been well known for its theatres, baths, and public buildings. Lambert wanted this rich prize for himself, but as Hilduin, the local count, resisted, he gathered a force of "Saxons, Normans, and Teutons" and besieged the city for some ten years, although to no avail. Then, one day, with a "rustic" as intermediary, a treaty was proposed by which a few chosen knights could come and go through the city

---

[138] *Ibid.*, 2.10, p. 49.   [139] *Ibid.*, 3.11-13, pp. 49-50.   [140] *Ibid.*, 2.2, pp. 45-46.

gates at will. The Milanese readily agreed. But Lambert betrayed their trust: on the third night after signing the agreement, he entered the city, overwhelmed its defences, and brought much destruction to life and property. The prayers of the unfortunate Milanese were heard by their patron saint, who appeared before Lambert on the feast of St. Severus and told him that he would die miserably and leave no heir. Lambert fled Milan in fear for Parma, taking with him Hilduin's son, Azo, as hostage. Some three years later during a hunt he found himself in a deep wood accompanied by only Azo and a servant. He suddenly felt tired and lay down in Azo's lap. The boy, urged on by the servant, slew his captor with a sharp thorn and, mounting the royal steed, hastened back to Milan. Some three days later Lambert's henchmen found the remains of his body.

The story of course is almost pure fiction. Honoratus was archbishop only from 566 to 568, and Landulf confused the Gothic invasion of 539 with the emperor Lambert's struggle against the otherwise unknown Maginfredo in 896.[141] Yet the manner in which he tells the tale clearly reveals the issues which he perceived as threats to the integrity of the Milanese church. The episode takes place against the background of greater events, the passing of the later empire and the arrival of the Langobards, who compel Honoratus to flee to Genoa with the church's treasure.[142] The story contrasts the old and the young: the ancient monuments of the church, the repositories of tradition, are saved by Azo, who, although a *juvenculus*, is a loyal and courageous defender of civic values. The tale involves two deceptions. Lambert conquered Milan through treachery and was slain by Hilduin's son as he slept, a symmetry reinforced by the parallelism of "three nights" and "three days." Further, Lambert's invasion and defeat are described in terms reminiscent of the formation of a sect. His effect on the city is called a *clandestina pestis*, that is, an unhealthy influence from outside. His entry into the urban sanctuary was made possible by a *rusticus nequissimus*, through whose wicked mouth, Landulf adds, the devil evidently spoke. Finally, the story juxtaposes not only the learned and the popular but also the bishopric, as the embodiment of the Word, and the uneducated world beyond. The essential contrast is not as in the ancients between town and country as interdependent opposites of a coherent world but more simply between town and forest, that is, between civilization and chaos. The

---

[141] L. A. Ferrai, "I fonti . . . ," 54.
[142] *Historia* 2.2, p. 46, 43-45.

geographical and spatial metaphor also interrelates the old and new secular orders: the *augustales imperatores* are set against the *barbarorum multitudo*; the cultivated leisure of the *situs Mediolani* against the aggressivity of the medieval hunt; the ancient ruins, with their noble reminders of Milan's past, against Lambert's worm-eaten bones, whose flesh has been "gnawed off" by ravens and vultures.

If we move forward in time to the accession of archbishop Walpert in 953, history would seem to be repeating itself. For, just as Honoratus rescued the church from Lambert, so Walpert saved it from the irrational Albert and placed it under the tutelage of Otto I.

Walpert's bishopric re-enacted many scenes from the early Milanese church.[143] The threat came from outside: Albert, born and raised in France, successfully drove out the Goths and Hungarians, then descended through the Alps to Milan. He too was attracted to the city for its ancient splendour, beloved by Hadrian, Trajan, and even the cruel Maximian. He prepared to enter Milan "ignoring (or so he later claimed) that no king had done so since the time of St. Ambrose, under whose protection the *civitas Mediolanensis* was decreed free from intrusion by the emperor. . . ."[144]

But, with God's approval and Ambrose's intervention, the same forces which saved Milan from Lambert protected it from Albert. What is different in the two accounts is the analytical depth of the scene. The Milanese, he informs us, feared lest the city be disturbed by an attack (*hostium incursio*), a civil uprising (*civium perturbatio*), or some other depraved inventiveness (*alium pravum ingenium*):[145] that is to say, they feared an enemy without, an enemy within, or, presumably, a form of political or religious sectarianism. Albert had dreams of grandeur but in time gave them up: "Eventually perceiving the people's will, he made out as if he were reasonably content . . . ; yet he bore a wound greater than anyone imagined in his heart."[146] Once again there is a contrast between the old and the young: Albert's ambition of imitating the emperors is frustrated, while Walpert, although still a *iuvenis*, is described in matters of statecraft as *conscilio venerandus*. The working out of the story reiterates the inequalities between the secular and religious leaders. Walpert, Landulf says, served the king loyally for several years, but one day was falsely accused by the "palace dogs" who hung around Albert's court. Albert, believing the charges true, decided to march on Milan. Walpert, however, knowing Albert to be "moved irrationally," acted not with "the power

---

[143] *Ibid.*, 2.16, pp. 52-54.   [144] *Ibid.*, 53, 13-15.   [145] *Ibid.*, 53, 16-17.
[146] *Ibid.*, 53, 19-21.

of arms" but with "strength of mind." Under the pretext of ecclesiastical business he journeyed over the Alps to Otto I to ask for help.
But, even when the new alliance emerges victorious, Landulf takes
pains to emphasize the submission of the secular to the spiritual forces.
Otto "was elected . . . by all with triumph." Yet, before Walpert
and his suffragans, he deposited on the altar of St. Ambrose "all his
regalia, his lance, containing the Lord's key, the royal sword, his
battle-ax, his sword-belt, his imperial vest, and all other regal garments."[147] Walpert even had the honour of presenting Otto to the
pope.

The portrait of Landulf II is more nuanced. If under Walpert the
ancient heritage of St. Ambrose was threatened by a lay lord, Landulf
was the instrument by which the patrimony of the Milanese church
fell irrevocably into secular hands. The chronicler had a difficult task:
he had to retain the dignity of the archbishop's office while expressing
his disapproval of the alienation of the church's landed wealth. His
portrait of Landulf II is therefore something of a compromise. On the
one hand, the archbishop is described as *iniquus velut scorpio*;[148] on the
other, he enfeoffs the capitanei only after sober reflection, in which
personal ambition is weighed against larger ethical issues.[149]

Chapter seventeen, in which Landulf's career is outlined, also deals
with two separate but interrelated sets of events. The one treats the
emergence of the archbishop's family into a prominent role among the
nascent capitanei.[150] In this sense it tells a small part of the story of
the rise of an agrarian nobility which has as yet no urban jurisdiction.[151] The other concerns Landulf II's negotiations with the emperor,[152] who was anxious to stabilize his authority in both countryside and town, as well as with the existing urban nobility, who resented
the intrusion of rural landowners but were helpless to prevent it.[153]
The chronicler takes the side of the older urban aristocrats. The archbishop, in his view, acquired the see through "the wicked designs of
his father" and handed over the benefices of the clergy in turn to "wild
and even savage laymen."[154] And thus the seeds that eventually grew
into the Pataria were sown.

---

[147] *Ibid.*, 53, 42-45.   [148] *Ibid.*, 2.17, p. 54, 33-34.
[149] *Ibid.*, p. 55, 15-24.   [150] *Ibid.*, p. 54, 41-p. 55, 4.
[151] C. Violante, *La società milanese*, 184-86.
[152] *Historia* 2.17, p. 55, 4-12.   [153] Violante, 190-96.
[154] *Historia* 2.17, p. 54, 37-40: "Enim ut archiepiscopatum, quem ipse duris et malis artibus
patris aquisierat, retineret, universos ecclesiasticos honores atque dignitates, quas ordines supradicti per multa ad honorem ecclesiarum et beati Ambrosii tempora rexerant atque tenuerant,
feris et saevissimis laicis tradidit."

Landulf perceptively distinguished between the economic and political forces that brought about the new order.[155] Under Otto I, Bonizo, the archbishop's father, governed Milan as ruthlessly "as a local count overseeing a *castrum*." During the seventies of the tenth century there was a great penury of knights or, for that matter, of well-qualified citizens, for military service owing to a wave of intestinal disease. The poor times also saw inflation: wine, grain, wood, sheep, pigs, and smaller animals rose in price "beyond what could be believed." To make matters worse, the good archbishop Godefrey died on 19 September 979. Bonizo, who was, as he puts it, *dignitatum avidissimus*, wasted no time in installing his son in the archbishop's palace "against the will of every order of cleric." Later, Bonizo was murdered in bed by a slave and Landulf was forced to flee to the court of Otto II. He reminded the emperor that his father had been a *fidelissimus miles* and implored him to help maintain order in the city. "Aroused like a lion," the chronicler notes, Otto marched on Milan accompanied by Landulf and a large force "of barbarians." On the evening of their arrival the archbishop saw a vision of heaven and hell. Touched by the fear of God and by reverence for St. Ambrose, he determined to prevent a needless slaughter of the city's citizens. He met with a group of nobles outside the walls and promised them in return for their personal loyalty "all the common people, all benefices and hostels"[156] which belonged to the *maiores ordinarii* and the *primicerius decumanorum*. A secret oath was sworn; when Otto heard of it, he reluctantly agreed. Landulf rejoiced at the display of civic unity and the emperor, somewhat appeased, withdrew to Liguria.

The details of this episode, like those which precede it, are carefully arranged to produce the desired effect. Landulf Senior agreed with Arnulf in seeing the capitanei as a form of external authority forced onto the city in a time of need. Moreover, Bonizo, who procured the see, was aided by other *milites*, "who, like him, in all probability came from the countryside."[157] But, aside from the coercive aspect,

[155] Summarizing in what follows 2.17, pp. 54-55.

[156] *Ibid.*, 2.17, p. 55, 25-26: . . . omnes plebes omnesque dignitates atque xenodochia. . . . Violante, *La società milanese*, 183, argues that two sets of concessions were made, one to the *nobiles in urbe*, the other to the *milites maiores* from the countryside who were instrumental in aiding Bonizo and later Landulf; *Hist.*, 2.17, p. 55, 31-33. But the later statement may merely be a generalization of the former. A similar double statement occurs at 2.17, p. 54, 33-40, where Landulf first denominates each order affected by infeudation, then refers to the loss of *universos ecclesiasticos honores atque dignitates* by the *ordines supradicti*. Cf. Arnulf, *Gesta* 1.10, 32-33.

[157] Violante, *La società milanese*, 183.

the two accounts differ in interpretation. Arnulf accepts the arrival of the capitanei without trying very hard to explain it. He has nothing to gain from embarrassing details, which can only detract from his image of stability imposed from above. He speaks of a divinely inspired *pax perpetua*, even taking pains to praise the moderation of both sides.[158] In Landulf's eyes the conflict is more profound, opposing town and country, emperor and citizenry and, indirectly, learned and popular culture. To his mind, Bonizo was given power, took over a defenceless city, and proceeded from protection to political control. The infeudation of the archbishopric and the establishment of *districtus* within Milan for the capitanei were correctly viewed as a continuous process.[159] Although conscious of personal machinations, Landulf looks upon this development as a necessary evil, the better so to speak of two potentially unsatisfactory courses for events, the destruction of the city by Otto or the wholesale loss of archiepiscopal authority. His strongest resentment is reserved once again for the violation of the Ambrosian church's ancient status. Milan, in his opinion, returned from civilization to savagery. A renowned ancient site and its historic traditions were handed over to barbarians. The ideological betrayal went hand in hand with physical degeneration: the *milites maiores*, now infeudated, despoiled the riches of the church.

In this atmosphere of new social forces threatening older ideals, the reader passes through the beneficent episcopate of Arnulf II and the untimely revolt of the Crescentii in Rome, arriving in chapter twenty at the accession of Aribert. In an unabashedly biased portrait, Aribert is pictured as striving ceaselessly to uphold the model of an autonomous church against his foes on the outside, the heretics from Monforte and Conrad II, and his enemies from within, the vavasours before 1037 and popular insurrection afterwards.

He entered the scene in strength, Landulf reports, but even stronger, perhaps uncontrollable forces were pitted against him. Equally versed in divine and worldly affairs, he strove "to restore everything which the archbishopric had lost through others' wrongdoing."[160] In Landulf's eyes he was chiefly a reformer: the key descriptive terms from his early career are *restauro, recupero,* and *redintegro,* together with adjectives such as *viriliter, assidue,* and *strenue*.[161] As in Arnulf, Aribert personifies Milan's urban unity and its sense of its past. His bad side

---

[158] *Gesta* 1.10, p. 9.
[159] *Historia* 2.17, p. 54, 41-44, p. 55, 2-4.
[160] *Ibid.,* 2.20, p. 57, 38-39.   [161] *Ibid.,* 2.20, pp. 57-58.

is overlooked;[162] he is put not so much in a political as in a narrative and religious context. Landulf wanted to tell a good story, whose moral is the successful fulfilment of spiritual ends through temporal means. This was a message which accorded well with his tolerance for other "ancient customs."

The groundwork then is laid in the outline of Aribert's early episcopate. He is said first to have organized a war on poverty during a famine of suspiciously long duration,[163] compelling bakers to increase productivity, enjoining economies upon cooks and servants, and even giving away garments from his sumptuous wardrobe from time to time.[164] He then emerged as the *bonus pastor oves restaurans*. He "reconstituted" the archbishopric's properties and became the trusted ally of two emperors;[165] He reasserted Milan's independence from Pavia, turning away from her gates by both word and sword all who were in his words *obliti legis paternae*.[166] Heresy is handled in a similar fashion: it is not so much a threat to the faith as to the archbishop's jurisdiction over it. The free-thinkers at Monforte are rooted out with the help of the local nobility and the *milites maiores* in Milan.[167] Yet these triumphs are minor in Landulf's eyes compared to Aribert's victory over Conrad II. The romantic episode of his escape from the hands of his enebriated "Teutonic" captors with the aid of a faithful servant and the abbess of St. Sixtus is calculated to portray him as the only figure capable of uniting the different political and religious forces in the city.[168] On his imprisonment "all Milan's citizens, priests, clerics, and even pious dames put off their finery and donned ashes and sackcloth,"[169] devoting long hours to fasts, prayers, and vigils. The tremors of his reversal were felt throughout Italy;[170] and, on his escape, he returned to a tumultuous welcome from all, *a clero et a populo universo*.[171]

Unlike Arnulf, who saw Aribert as the capitanei's express agent, Landulf does not elaborate upon the archbishop's ability to reanimate Milan's flagging civic ethos. Instead, he emphasizes Aribert's mental agility in eluding his oafish jailors and the city's courage in forcing Conrad to a showdown. For, in Landulf's eyes, there was a good deal more than personal honour at stake. The *Constitutio de Feudis* of 1037 gave ecclesiastical benefices to all those who had simply claimed pos-

---

[162] Cf. Violante, *La società milanese*, 259-60.

[163] *Ibid.*, 212n3.   [164] *Historia* 2.20, pp. 57-58.

[165] *Ibid.*, 2.20, p. 58 (Henry I) and 2.22, p. 59 (Conrad II).

[166] *Ibid.*, 2.21, p. 58, 20-21.   [167] *Ibid.*, 2.27, 65-66.   [168] *Ibid.*, 2.23, p. 60, 46-48.

[169] *Ibid.*, 2.22, p. 59, 24-27.   [170] *Ibid.*, p. 59, 21-24.   [171] *Ibid.*, 2.23, p. 60, 45-46.

session of (*invaserunt*) church property, first in Milan and later in other parts of Italy.[172] It also gave rise to a hoard of ambitious claimants who rushed to the court at Pavia "like water into a bilge."[173] Landulf took a certain satisfaction in the utter arbitrariness of Conrad's judgments. For the emperor was acting consistently against God and St. Ambrose, attempting to uproot the ancient customs of the church *secundum legem . . . humanam.*[174] He too, therefore, played his part in the sectarianism undermining the original ideals.

Successful against Conrad, Aribert was nonetheless defeated by factionalism at home. Landulf was no better than Arnulf at isolating the actual causes of the civil disturbances of the 1040s. Yet their explanations differed in significant ways. Arnulf, as noted, saw the *populi* principally as rebels against the legitimate order of church and state. Landulf subtly adapted his notion of decline from a golden age of Ambrosian polity to the needs of a secular controversy in which the people by accident emerged as the court of last appeal. The chief *casus belli* was the division of the responsibilities of government among the older nobility, the recently arrived capitanei, and the upcoming vasours. In Landulf's view, the ideal was the period before the enfeoffing of the capitanei, when the counts administered the city's affairs from their palace near the church of St. Protaxius:

". . . Whatever was honorable they performed with care on the city's behalf. If any ordinance was imprudently violated, they settled the matter with zeal and wisdom. If an unjust act was committed against anyone, they immediately saw to a trial for making amends and giving satisfaction. They helped orphans, assisted the suffering, aided widows, and nourished the homeless. . . . All merchants, peasants, fieldhands, and herdsmen looked after their affairs and derived a sure living from their own commerce. Universally prosperous, solicitous of the rights of churches and of clerics, all lived in peace. . . ."[175]

But this harmonious state of affairs did not last. From "evil sources," whose origins Landulf could not trace, the older nobility little by little ceded their honours and privileges to "the novel capitanei," until at length, "stripped of their highest offices and mindless of reverence for the ancients as well as their own forebears,"[176] they had their functions reduced to mere ceremonial. The loyalty and respect which the common people were accustomed to give to the nobility fell to

---

[172] *Ibid.*, 2.22, p. 58, 41-49.   [173] *Ibid.*, p. 59, 1.
[174] *Ibid.*, p. 58, 45.   [175] *Ibid.*, 2.26, p. 62, 46-p. 63, 6.
[176] *Ibid.*, p. 63, 13: ". . . maximis nudati honoribus, antiquorum et suorum parentum reverentiam obliti. . . ."

the "few capitanei" whom they had created. As the older aristocrats still held the most influential consultative posts, the capitanei, wishing to strengthen their own authority, delegated responsibilities in turn to the vavasours, who could be counted on for support.[177] Each new division of labour, Landulf argues, brought increasing hardship to the commoners. They found the government of their "fellow citizens more difficult to bear than that of their former lords." Matters came to a head during Aribert's episcopate. In order to escape from this "lordship" and to recover their lost "liberty," the *populi* elected to take its chances in open struggle.[178] Aribert, after all, had succeeded in bringing great princes, even the emperor, to heel; similarly, "the people battled against the nobles in order to acquire the liberty which of old their ancestors . . . had lost."[179]

For Landulf, then, it was an economic, political, and religious turmoil at once.[180] The new menace to Ambrosian polity was not a wilful individual but class disharmony. Arnulf saw diverse social coalitions rising against an unquestioned standard; Landulf looked upon all novelty since the Ottos as a decline from a lost state of unity. By a curious irony the only group in society capable of asserting the pristine ideals was the proletariat, which, Landulf notes romantically, found it "preferable to die rather than to live in dishonour."[181] So they revolted, and, in doing so, provided Landulf with the occasion for introducing two new considerations into the already heated debate on reform, namely, the role of a semi-educated laity, and, with respect to the Patarenes, the uses of literacy.

Landulf's record of the street fighting is among the most vivid of its kind in eleventh-century historical writing.[182] The capitanei and vavasours roamed the streets, butchering the *populi* at will. Mustering their inadequate arms, the common people retaliated as best they could. Eventually outnumbered, the nobility abandoned their city dwellings and conducted forays from well-protected fortifications outside the walls. They tortured captured prisoners and left their bodies in the gutters to rot. The commoners, Landulf notes, fought with better strategy but no less cruelly. No day passed without brutal confrontations within the city or just outside the gates. In time, the

---

[177] *Ibid.*, p. 63, 14-17.

[178] *Ibid.*, p. 63, 17-19.

[179] *Ibid.*, p. 63, 22-24: ". . . populo adversus maiores pro libertate acquirenda proeliante, quam olim parentes eius ob nimiam hominum raritatem amiserant. . . ."

[180] *Loc.cit.*; cf. 2.17, p. 54, 45ff.   [181] *Ibid.*, 2.26, p. 63, 26.

[182] The following summarizes 2.26, p. 63, 24-p. 64, 5.

urban area was cut off from the surrounding countryside and its food resources dwindled. Landulf observes: "If you had seen the city from within its deserted *palazzi* and now fallen towers, you would have concluded that you were amidst the ruins of Babylon, not Milan, that once noble kingdom's seat."[183] The comparison was apt: for, in the chronicler's view, the *populi* were superior both in arms and in morality. A key term is *dedecus*: "They thought it sweeter to face death than to lead a long life with nothing but shame."[184] In other words, they had a growing sense of their collective worth, a sentiment which Landulf sums up in a single sentence whose multiple images seem to follow the formation of the popular coalition itself. When the nobles finally deserted the city, he relates, the common people saw that their lives were largely in their own hands. Salvation, if it were to come, would come from arms rather than from outsiders. Feelings ran high: night and day they were tormented with the desire for war and other inventions of their minds. They were strong in poverty, but stronger in their will to freedom, concerned over their material goods, but more eager for liberty. In such a state of mind they took to battle with every available form of weapon, and became through their courage the most formidable of enemies.[185] This is the first point in the *Historia* in which the *populi* are characterized as a popular movement. They are not merely deviants from a norm, as in Arnulf: they think, feel, and act on their own. The movement does not arise spontaneously; it is a byproduct of the vacuum in leadership after the nobility's departure. And thus the people become a new fluid force in the unruly sea of Milanese loyalties.

What do they really represent for Landulf? They are a secular element, foreshadowing the role the laity plays in the Pataria.[186] Also, at this point at least, they are an elect. They thereby embody the respectable traditions of the Milanese church in bad times and reaffirm older values that were once the unique prerogative of the lay and ecclesiastical *maiores*.

The role of the laity, now firmly established, is further emphasized

[183] *Ibid.*, p. 64, 5-7.

[184] *Ibid.*, p. 63, 27: ". . . dulcius iudicans mortem videre quam vitam summo cum dedecore ducere longam. . . ."

[185] *Ibid.*, p. 63, 32-36: ". . . populus videns vitam in manibus fore, magis armis sperans salutem quam ullis beneficiis, studio bellorum et ingeniis animorum curiose diu noctuque exardescens, paupertate fortis, pro acquirenda libertate fortissimus, divitiis anxius, sed studiosior libertate. . . ."

[186] See in general, C. Violante, "I laici nel movimento patarino," and below, pp. 235-37.

in the remaining chapters of book two, first in the contrast between Lanzo and Aribert, then in Landulf's outline of the *ordinationes* of the Ambrosian clergy in 1045.

Attention is drawn to Lanzo's leadership of the *populi*, while Aribert recedes into the realm of hagiography. Lanzo is described as the people's *ductor atque . . . protector*.[187] Yet, he does not so much advocate the *populi*'s interests, as romantic historians maintained,[188] as offer the sort of leadership expected of a member of the capitanei. When he negotiates with Henry III, he speaks on behalf of both sides;[189] and when he returns to Milan afterwards, he offers the peace plan to the *nobiles* before sounding out the *populi*.[190] He appears to be a happy blend of ethical virtue and practicality. For the people he is "provident in mind, strong in body, prudent in combat," etc.[191] Yet, he is also a reflective leader, who is capable of remaining loyal to the populist cause while recognizing the necessity of compromise. He has some of Aribert's charisma: supported by God and St. Ambrose, Landulf boasts, and taking counsel with his faithful vavasour, Alberius, he decides alone to undertake a peace mission to the imperial court;[192] and this same *vir concilio discretus* accepts the emperor's generous terms, conveying them personally to the embattled Milanese nobility.[193]

Meanwhile Aribert, aging and in ill health, slips into the background, less and less an active three-dimensional figure. According to Landulf, who naturally wished to put him above factional quarrels, "he neither aided the knights who daily threw the city into turmoil nor attempted to harm the besieged citizens."[194] The remaining episodes of his life narrated in book two are carefully arranged to present him once again as the ideal archbishop, who was prevented from being a typological fulfilment of Ambrose himself by events beyond his control. The list of his achievements recapitulated from Landulf is impressive. He fought heresy;[195] during famine he aided the poor;[196] he brought about a *treuga Dei* on hours of work and commerce for merchants and artisans;[197] a miracle restored his ornamented staff after a

---

[187] *Ibid.*, 2.26, p. 63, 37.

[188] For a review of the early literature, see E. Werner, *Pauperes Christi* (Leipzig, 1956), 155-65.

[189] *Historia* 2.26, p. 64, 11-14.   [190] *Ibid.*, p. 65, 5-8.

[191] *Ibid.*, p. 64, 10-11. He was probably literate; for his signature, see Milan, Archivio di Stato M.D. n. 670, December, 1044, reproduced in the *Storia di Milano*, vol. 3, p. 105.

[192] *Ibid.*, p. 64, 14-18.   [193] *Ibid.*, p. 65, 2-14.   [194] *Ibid.*, p. 64, 29-33.

[195] *Ibid.*, 2.27, pp. 65-66.   [196] *Ibid.*, 2.28, pp. 66-67.   [197] *Ibid.*, 2.30, p. 67.

TEXTUAL COMMUNITIES

domestic stole it;[198] and, on passing away, he left most of his worldly goods to the clergy.[199] Above all, Landulf stresses, he was the spiritual leader of men and women from different walks of life. The famine of the 1030s touched *gentes notae et ignotae*; his charity was extended to *omnes fideles et infideles*.[200] Well, the chronicler added, he merited chancellor Ubertus's parting words, which spoke of him on his deathbed, as noted, as the protector of orphans, clerics, priests, widows, merchants, and the poor.[201]

Landulf concluded book two with his well-known description of the church of Milan at the time of Aribert's death. His first literary purpose was undoubtedly to provide a sequel to the ecclesiastical survey of book one. But he also wanted to pause momentarily and to review the Ambrosian polity at a high point of development before turning to the disruptive forces of the Pataria. For, he notes, had the bishop returned to Milan, he would not thereafter have recognized his native clergy or his city.[202]

Chapter thirty-five above all reaffirms the special character of the Milanese church in allowing for a high degree of lay participation in ecclesiastical affairs and in permitting a married clergy. In Landulf's view, the charismatic authority descended through God, St. Ambrose, and later bishops, working its way through the centuries by means of both laymen and clerics.[203] The lay element is stressed in the overall setup of the church as well as in obedience, self-discipline, and asceticism. For instance, if someone in the choir performed inadequately, he was invariably taken for correction to the archdeacon. "Nor did anyone dare to snatch him from his hands, since this overseer was from the marcheses, counts, or capitanei."[204] Similar lay support ran through the hierarchy of twenty-four high priests, seven deacons and subdeacons, notaries, lectors, and decuman priests. Religious discipline was enjoined upon all: no changes in grade were tolerated, no verbal irrelevance, no *laicalis habitus* in cap, vest, or shoes while in church.[205] (These customs of *longa vetustas*, Landulf adds, were widely known throughout France and Germany!)[206] The highest lay authority was the viscount, *laicus laicos et ipse regens*,[207] who may have been

---

[198] *Ibid.*, 2.31, pp. 67-68.   [199] *Ibid.*, 2.32, pp. 68-69.
[200] *Ibid.*, 2.28, p. 66, 41 and 44-45.
[201] *Ibid.* 2.32, p. 69.   [202] *Ibid.*, 2.34, pp. 69-70.
[203] *Ibid.*, 2.35, p. 70, 12-17.   [204] *Ibid.*, p. 70, 45-47.   [205] *Ibid.*, p. 70, 49-53.
[206] *Ibid.*, p. 71, 2-4.   [207] *Ibid.*, p. 71, 7-8.

infeudated to the archbishop.²⁰⁸ The twelve decuman deacons were *viri boni testimonii bonaeque famae*,²⁰⁹ the sixteen custodians, *boni viri ac in omnibus ecclesiasticis officiis curialiter eruditi*.²¹⁰ Both, in other words, were drawn from the lay nobility. Also, aging laywomen, "transformed" by religious dress, aided the ten clerics in the *scola sancti Ambrosii*,²¹¹ which, in all probability, had secular *magistri*²¹² and educated the sons of the same nobility. The church's hostels admitted not only wandering clerics but also poorer women and orphans.²¹³ The *primicerius* was described as *de populo natus*.²¹⁴ And many clerics were married. Prospective candidates for the priesthood, whether *urbani* or *plebes*, were examined for their understanding of the office and questioned as to their general morals. But they were also asked to remain *virgines* or to become *unius uxores viri*.²¹⁵ Those who through human frailty could not remain continent were forced to marry. For, while a cleric living in sin could not be promoted, a properly married priest could become an archbishop, a custom (*usus*), Landulf points out, practiced in both the Latin and Greek churches.²¹⁶ Charity ran through society and marriages were faithful: Landulf concludes by very nearly reconceiving the society before 1045 in the image of his ideal church as an *aetas integra et sana*.²¹⁷

BOOK THREE. The relevance of the Ambrosian ideal for Landulf's historiography becomes even clearer as we pass from book two to three. Broadly speaking, the subject of book three is the Pataria between the election of Guido da Velate and the death of Erlembald. Yet, the book is also divisible into four thematic sections, each climaxing in a mass demonstration. Chapters one to thirteen deal with the formation of the movement and the early preaching of Anselm of Baggio, Ariald, and Landulf Cotta, culminating in the latter's impassioned speech at the Roman theatre in 1057. Chapters fourteen to eighteen turn to the events surrounding the council of Novara in November of the same year, reaching their high point in the confrontation between Guido and Erlembald, which also took place in the theatre before a large crowd. In chapter nineteen we move forward to the bishopric of Godefrey, the papacy of Alexander II, and the reign

²⁰⁸ Violante, *La società milanese*, 236.
²⁰⁹ *Historia* 2.35, p. 71, 10-11. ²¹⁰ *Ibid.*, p. 71, 12-13. ²¹¹ *Ibid.*, p. 71, 14-15.
²¹² This is suggested by the fact that the archbishop has "for a long time" paid them a stipend; *ibid.*, p. 71, 25.
²¹³ *Ibid.*, p. 71, 28-32. ²¹⁴ *Ibid.*, p. 71, 34-35. ²¹⁵ *Ibid.*, p. 70, 20-23.
²¹⁶ *Ibid.*, p. 70, 31-32. ²¹⁷ *Ibid.*, 2.35-36, pp. 71-73.

of Henry III, a section which concludes with a fictive dramatization of sermons for and against reform allegedly preached before Erlembald and the citizens of Milan (chs. 23-28). The last part, while carrying events forward to 1085, deals essentially with the martyrdom of Ariald in 1066 and the death of Erlembald in pitched battle in 1075.

The book, in other words, has two different principles of unity, one following the narrative, although, as it turns out, not accurately, another, Landulf's own sense of thematic development, which remains understated.

Landulf claims to be turning from the *antiqui*, whose accounts of earlier bishoprics he gleaned from archival *cartulae*, to the events of his own day, which he simply arranged in sequence from experience.[218] Yet there is another type of transition at work. In book two, the romanticized Ambrosian church forms a cultural backdrop for a popular movement whose origins are largely social and political. The effectors of change are the enfeoffing of the capitanei in 979, the *Constitutio de Feudis* of 1037, and the ensuing struggle of the common people *pro libertate acquirenda*. In book three, purely social tensions recede; the rival parties in the Patarene dispute are opposed chiefly for cultural reasons. Although Landulf refers from time to time to the primitive Milanese church, there is no need for him to stress a decline from a supposedly golden age. The reformist and traditionalist factions now speak for themselves. The change is not from one to another phase of social revolt, to which religious issues are loosely tied; it is to the cultural as contrasted with the social articulation of dissent itself. And this is a byproduct of the reading, teaching, and preaching of the Bible. Although the Patarenes frequently took to the streets, they were capable of defending themselves eruditely before Nicolas II, Alexander II, and Gregory VII. Also, it is clear that for Ariald, Landulf, and Erlembald reformist principles came before everything else. Their rejection of Milan's infeudated clergy was not a social rebellion in disguise; it was an intellectuals' movement, which gradually worked its way downward through various social strata.

The interconnection between the revolt of the *populi* under Lanzo, the rejection of Guido by the capitanei, and the rise of the Pataria was therefore complex. The link was not a common philosophy, but, in Landulf's view, different forms of disrespect for the inherited authority of the Ambrosian church. In contrast to Arnulf, Landulf did not believe that the Pataria was a direct consequence of Guido's elec-

[218] *Ibid.*, 3.2, p. 74.

tion. But his centre of focus remained the archbishop. During the 1040s, he reasoned, the *populi* rebelled under Lanzo chiefly because the nobility refused the responsibility of providing government. Similarly, after 1045, the vacuum of power was again a critical issue. True, the emperor had gone back on his word: instead of choosing as Aribert's successor one of the four recommended *maiores ordinis viri* he picked a man whose primary loyalty was to the imperial faction,[219] proof enough, if the already insecure capitanei needed it, that Henry would invariably put his own interests before Milan's. The cardinal clergy hardly expected their collective will to be so easily brushed aside.[220] Yet, in Landulf's eyes, Guido was nonetheless a reasonably good archbishop.[221] He was acquitted of the charges brought against him at the Lateran synod of April, 1050. If he awoke late to the Patarene challenge, he was nonetheless described by Landulf as "ruling the Ambrosian archiepiscopate . . . with care and devotion."[222] The real problem was the *ordinarii*: he was unable to appease their wrath; they in turn slandered him daily, though, for fear of the people, in secret.[223] On one occasion they even left him alone at the altar during mass.[224] For Landulf this was too much. Although perhaps indecisive, Guido was the legitimate vicar of St. Ambrose. In exposing him to the people's scorn and to the devil's temptations, Landulf concluded, the capitanei well merited the anger of God.

But punishment took an unprecedented form, namely, reformist preaching, underpinned by a conspiracy among three members of the clergy. Landulf's reworking of these critical events, which occupies chapters five to seven, is echoed in no other account. As a piece of fiction, it takes us to the heart of the chronicler's perception of the issues. Let us first summarize the story,[225] then discuss its meaning.

In 1057, Landulf relates, a priest named Anselm of Baggio,[226] whom Guido had only a short time before ordained, demanded "obedience" from both higher and lower orders of the Milanese clergy for ill-defined reasons possibly connected to family interests. Guido took Anselm to the emperor, who settled the disagreement by awarding

---

[219] *Ibid.*, 3.3, p. 74.   [220] *Ibid.*, 3.3, p. 75, 1-2.

[221] *Ibid.*, 3.4, p. 75. For a sifting of various interpretations, see Violante, *La pataria milanese*, 88-101.

[222] *Historia* 3.3, p. 75, 11-13.   [223] *Ibid.*, p. 75, 15.   [224] *Ibid.*, p. 75, 19-26.

[225] Summarizing 3.3, pp. 76-79.

[226] Landulf distorted Anselm's involvement in the Pataria. For a full review of his early years, see T. Schmidt, *Alexander II* . . . , 1-67, and, more briefly, C. Violante, "Alessandro II," *Dizionario biog. degli italiani*, vol. 2, 176-83.

him the see of Lucca. Anselm, it turns out, was a highly articulate person, who occasionally preached polished but forthright sermons in local churches. On his leaving, Guido appointed seven deacons to administer the diocese. Each Sunday of Advent one of them was called upon to preach a sermon in S. Maria Yemale. When word of their brilliance reached Anselm, he was apparently speechless with jealousy and rage. He returned secretly to Milan on Christmas Day and, unobserved, found his way to the church, where one of the deacons, Ambrose Biffus—so called because he was *bifarius*, that is, bilingual in Greek and Latin—was speaking with "angelic eloquence." At the mass's end Anselm returned to his family home, angry, distraught, and confused. The clerics who accompanied him, ignorant of his state of mind, tormented him further with praise for the youthful priest. Anselm retorted angrily that, if the city's clergy, both high and low, had no women, no harm would come to the pursuit of their offices, especially preaching.[227] His companions protested, but to no avail.

Anselm, tired, infuriated, and driven by dark thoughts, Landulf continues, waited until nightfall, when he called to his side the two well-known dissidents, Ariald and Landulf Cotta. Landulf, the chronicler adds, was the ambitious offspring of a powerful family desirous of the archbishopric. Ariald was a mere "levite" from the countryside whom Guido had favoured with ordination. Born in Cucciago, a mere hamlet, he rose to the level of master of arts, only to inflict his erudition afterwards on the undeserving Milanese clergy. He was proud of his humble origins: lately, he had been charged and convicted by Guido before a large number of urban priests for being improperly dressed and for officiating illegally in town. Ariald retaliated by denouncing the local clergy's "concubines." Anselm, Landulf adds, knew their views. He called them to his house by night and congratulated them on their exploits. Further, he suggested that they form an association to oppose clerical marriage. The three swore an oath, and Anselm promised material aid.

The morning after, Anselm withdrew "like a serpent" from the city, without so much as a greeting to the archbishop. Landulf Cotta remained, and spread the word publicly and privately among potential converts. They too were sworn to allegiance. Ariald returned to his rural parish, where he did the same. Guido, Landulf observes, knew of their activities, but gave the matter little thought. Unopposed, Ariald dared to preach a sermon to ordinary "rustics" advocating strict

[227] *Historia* 3.5, p. 76, 30-32.

clerical celibacy. The peasants were somewhat astonished, but, or so
we are told, they reaffirmed the view that no one was truly chaste
unless so created by his maker. Then they banded together with other
outraged clerics and laymen and went to Guido as a group. The archbishop thereupon summoned Landulf and Ariald and admonished them
not to stir up a senseless mob. The ancient customs of the Ambrosian
church, indeed those of Latin and Greek christendom, might be
threatened. However, the pair remained adamant. Guido then provided them with scriptural *exempla*. A good Christian, he noted, should
look after his own troubles before turning to those of his fellow men.
But this too failed.

If we recall once again that these chapters are almost entirely a
literary fabrication, there are three ways in which they may profitably
be understood. Landulf's own reading of events provides one logic.
Another is suggested by outside witnesses who do not share his point
of view. A third impression is created not so much by the sequence
of events as by the thematic arrangement of Landulf's inner concerns.

On the surface, Landulf presents the reader with a conspiracy theory
typical of many accounts of heresy's "origins." The bearer of evil doctrines, although perhaps once an insider, comes from outside and
leaves when his perfidious work is done. He is a thinly disguised
diabolical agent, and compels those under his influence to swear an
oath of loyalty against their best interests. Landulf undoubtedly sub-
scribed to the theory; for him, the "heresy" was clerical celibacy. But
he adapted it to his own ends. Anselm, using his family's powerful
contacts, he argues, tried to win the clergy's loyalty away from the
archbishop, engaging "in many evil acts and confrontations."[228] The
troubles, one suspects, had gone on for some time; they antedated his
ordination, which probably took place in 1056,[229] and perhaps perpetuated factional rivalries following Guido's appointment. In Landulf's view, such agitations represented another attempt by the nobility to seize control of the Milanese church: the Pataria, in other
words, like earlier revolts, had as its primary cause nothing more or
less than class ambitions. Even Anselm's promotion to the see of Lucca
is so construed. Landulf Cotta, who also rose *de magna prosapia*,[230]
"panted" similarly after Milan's episcopal seat.[231] Ariald, a person of

[228] *Ibid.*, 3.5, p. 76, 1-4.

[229] Violante, *La pataria milanese*, 153-54.

[230] Cf. Bonizo of Sutri, *Liber ad Amicum*, c. 6, p. 591: "Landulfus ex maiorum prosapia ortus, vir urbanus et facundissimus. . . ."

[231] *Historia* 3.5, p. 76, 36-38.

slight influence within the city walls, became the urban rebels' mouthpiece in the countryside, for Landulf the traditional stronghold of illegitimate dissent. And so, in his view, the stage was set.

Is there any accuracy in this account? The *Historia*, it should be noted, virtually leaps from 1045 to 1057: we learn little of the rivalries of the intervening years. Surely ecclesiastical politics did not vanish. Landulf informs us of the lingering resentment of the *ordinarii*; one may assume that seditious thoughts also spread among the disappointed capitanei. For, in place of a gentleman's agreement with the emperor, the latter's express agent was installed in the chair of St. Ambrose. Yet Landulf goes too far in linking the failures of one generation's governing class to the problems of the next. Times had changed: Milan, like other north Italian towns, was increasingly exposed to reformist influences from outside. An internalist reconstruction of its religious history was less and less plausible. Arnulf, for his part, does not associate Anselm of Baggio with the founding of the Pataria; he is merely mentioned along with other promoters of new doctrines.[232] He was undoubtedly among those Milanese clerics, whose numbers included Godefrey, the future abbot of St. Dionysius, and Anselm "the peripatetic," who had undertaken *litterarum studia* north of the Alps.[233] His name is even associated, perhaps erroneously, with Lanfranc of Bec. He was also for a time chaplain at the imperial court. In any case, reformist ideas were in the air: it would have been unusual if the Milanese Pataria was motivated by forces radically different from those bringing about similar agitations in Florence, Piacenza, Cremona, Asti, and Pavia, namely, a severer discipline among the clergy, the elimination of simony and nicolaitism, and a restriction on lay interference in church affairs, especially through investiture. Landulf, it would appear, was indulging his habit of personalizing the roots of change. But Anselm was perhaps too obvious a target. His family may well have profited from the imperial connection. But it is more likely that his journey was inserted in order to dramatize the external sources of opposition to clerical marriage. With hindsight Landulf could see the future Alexander II in one of two unpopular roles, either as an avatar of the papal cause or as a betrayer of Milan's ecclesiastical autonomy.

A quite different perspective emerges if we look at the text of

---

[232] He is first mentioned in 1059; *Gesta* 3.14, pp. 20-21.

[233] Violante, *La pataria milanese*, 151-52; H.E.J. Cowdrey, "Anselm of Besate and Some North-Italian Scholars of the Eleventh Century," *Journal of Ecclesiastical History* 23 (1972), 115-24.

chapters five and six in the light of their own thematic development. First, Landulf has more in common with Arnulf than their political differences would suggest. Arnulf, as noted, saw Ariald and Landulf Cotta as communicators of false ideas. Landulf Senior's conception of Anselm is similar, but there is more emphasis on the means of communication. In the section of chapter five in which he first appears there is an abrupt change of subject. After speaking of Anselm's dispute with Guido over jurisdiction, Landulf introduces what would seem to be a *non sequitur*. "For Anselm," he adds, "was a man powerful in speech, . . . who was in the habit of delivering polished sermons personally. . . ."[234] The contrast in phrasing is instructive: on the one hand, Anselm asserts the *vis . . . communis parentum et sui* (his own and his family's public power); on the other, he is described in the translated clause as *in sermone potens . . . sancta Dei euangelia . . . reserando*. The shift, in other words, is from his social to his cultural function. And the contrast is extended. When Anselm left for Lucca, Guido is said to have appointed seven deacons of good family *ad opus ministerii Dei et praedicationis*. They enraged Anselm by preaching brilliantly (*singulo . . . lucidissime praedicante*). Clearly, then, in addition to the personal rivalry between Anselm and Guido, there was also a conflict of principles.

From this point, moreover, Landulf's account becomes more and more concerned with the uses of literacy, proceeding alternately, as is his fashion, by images and direct statements. Appropriately enough, Anselm's anger made him tongue-tied: *verba non intelligibilia fundebant*;[235] and he returned to Milan, not, one suspects, by accident, when the text of the Sunday sermon was *In principio erat verbum*.[236] Incognito, he came face to face with the gifted young preacher Ambrose Biffus. Again, Landulf's symbolism is transparent. Ambrose is a figure of renewal, whose name partly recalls the Milanese church's founder and partly suggests co-operation with the Greek-speaking east. Biffus, so to speak, replaced Anselm as official interpreter of Scripture, "expounding the Greek of the gospel texts themselves in Latin in patristic fashion." He reasserted the church's apostolic and prophetic mission: "He did not so much discourse (*tractabat*) like a man as made pronouncements (*nuntiabat*) like an angel."[237] Anselm's lack of clear thought and speech at this point contrasts sharply with Ambrose's: to the latter's *rationes* and *exempla* he replies *balbutiendo verbo* (with stut-

[234] *Historia* 3.5, p. 76, 8-10.
[235] *Ibid.*, p. 76, 15.   [236] *Ibid.*, p. 76, 17-18.
[237] *Ibid.*, p. 76, 19-23.

tering or incorrect speech).[238] Landulf Cotta provided a diabolical counterpart to Ambrose's eloquence: "Now pouring forth a sweet, now a bitter draught . . . he hardened the hearts of his listeners like stone."[239] Ariald was equally destructive, despite his lowly origins. Like Landulf, he first spread his ideas among *scolares*.[240] But he also turned towards the unlettered, preaching at large to the *plebes rusticanorum*.

With these thoughts in mind, let us turn to chapters eight to thirteen, which take the story from the episcopal palace through several stages of escalation to the audience of the rival factions before Stephen IX in 1057.[241]

Ariald and Landulf were unmoved by Guido's words. They left the episcopal palace in a huff, the chronicler reports, and made their way back through the city, encountering en route a group of pious men and women celebrating the translation of St. Nazarius. Words were exchanged: a priest called Anselm threatened Ariald and demanded to know whether what he had heard of him was actually true. Ariald replied that it was: "What I have said, I still say; what I say, I hold to be true; and what I hold I can prove with arguments."[242] Anselm raised his hand as if to strike Ariald, but instead he made a lengthy speech, accusing the young preacher of questioning the value of the priesthood, of turning the common people against their pastors, and of placing himself above Old and New Testament prophets. It was not his place to reprimand priests publicly.

Landulf Cotta was angered by the exchange and summoned a large crowd to the Roman theatre, where first Ariald and then he made lengthy, inflammatory speeches criticizing the clergy's laxity. The common people, already miserable through poverty, were sufficiently stirred up by their rhetoric to plunder the houses of many urban priests and to force them to give up their wives. Defenceless, the priests submitted. The nobility for their part either fled the city or laid low, awaiting the right moment to strike back. The rioting soon spread from Milan to nearby villas, *castelli*, and larger towns. Finally, Landulf reports, the question was taken to Rome, where each side put its case before pope Stephen. A Roman priest named Dionysius is alleged to have made an impassioned speech on behalf of the status quo. But the pope refused to take a strong position one way or the

[238] *Ibid.*, p. 76, 26-30.   [239] *Ibid.*, p. 76, 41-43.
[240] *Ibid.*, p. 76, 21 and 24; possibly the students at the local parish school.
[241] Summarizing chs. 8-13, pp. 79-82.
[242] *Ibid.*, 3.9, p. 79, 37-38.

other. He sent Anselm of Baggio and Hildebrand to Milan to arrange a settlement. But they too were unsuccessful.

Landulf greatly distorted the events described in these chapters. All sources are agreed that matters came to a head on the feast of the translation of St. Nazarius, which took place in the Ambrosian calendar on 10th May. But from that point accounts of Ariald's activity differ widely. Andrew of Strumi and Bonizo of Sutri place him in the country;[243] Arnulf credits him with instigating reformist preaching on his own.[244] Reports of the interview before Stephen IX also vary considerably.[245] But what most sets Landulf apart from other witnesses to the early Pataria is the fictive presentation of opposite sides as an intellectual debate.

The speeches of Anselm and Dionysius are found nowhere else. Using these orations as fixed points, Landulf oriented his version of the first signs of dissent not so much around the principles as around the communication of ideas of reform, thereby providing a thematic link between this section and the earlier contrast between Ambrose Biffus and Anselm of Baggio.

Ariald and Landulf are once again portrayed as typical heretics, diabolically inspired by "some highly evil force, whose spirit . . . brought forth wicked words. . . ."[246] As in Arnulf, they represent calculated misinterpretation: in Landulf's words, they would not be silent as long as their spirits breathed and their lips moved. Also, the street scene clearly set the stage for the papal audience, as the chronicler's simplified images reveal. Ariald and Landulf are described as attempting to inflict their "false chastity" on a group of pious devotees "of both sexes." The pilgrims are on their way to celebrate a saint whose body was discovered by St. Ambrose himself, the saint's day for both being the same. The putative reformers were therefore in reality sullying venerable traditions, "debating with vain words" alone.[247] Anselm by contrast rose to the faithful's defence. He saw that evil "novelties" had artificially sweetened the atmosphere and "tainted" the city. Significantly, he did not ask Ariald the specific points of his doctrine but whether what had been spread about (*diffamatum*) could really be attributed to him—incidentally informing the reader on the large role which hearsay played in the controversy. True to his heret-

[243] *Vita S. Arialdi*, c. 2, MGH SS 30.2, p. 1050; Bonizo of Sutri, *Liber ad Amicum*, c. 6, p. 591. Cf. Violante, *La pataria milanese*, 176-77.

[244] *Gesta* 3.10, p. 18.

[245] For the differing accounts, see Violante, *La pataria milanese*, 193-205.

[246] *Historia* 3.8, p. 79, 11-13.   [247] *Ibid.*, p. 79, 18-24.

ical stereotype, Ariald is said to have replied "like an insane man to an insane charge." In his own speech, Anselm emphasized the illicit spread of false ideas. He accused Ariald of inciting the people against the clergy *per execrabilem pataliam et . . . sacramenta prava*, phrases which neatly combine orality and illegitimacy. Ariald was, in sum, a hypocrite: he followed no recognized *sanctorum via*; instead, he eroded the foundations of the *ecclesia primitiva*, which, under traditional leadership, "had always flourished." Finally, not only had he dared to criticize the clergy, he had done so *publice*.[248]

But public scrutiny was just what the reformers wanted. Landulf's response to Anselm's tirade in Landulf Senior's account was to organize the Pataria's first mass demonstration. Bells were rung, women went about the streets, and notices were circulated. In Landulf Cotta's opinion, what had hitherto been whispered among the shadows was now to be shouted from the rooftops: the martyrs were no longer to be venerated and devotion to the ancients was to be stopped.[249] All assembled at the Roman theatre—the wise and the foolish, the old and the young, the upright and the sinful—eagerly seeking "edification" and "salvation." Ariald, the chronicler notes, spoke first, his eyes blazing, his words flooding over the "laughing populace" like "a filthy torrent."[250] Then the more eloquent Landulf, in "a more dignified style," finished the job.[251] To describe the ensuing popular uprising, the narrator reverts to a now familiar topos, the overthrow of civilization by savagery and chaos. When Ariald and Landulf had finished spreading (*pandere et divulgare*) their poison, he relates, the people, thirsting after blood, moved en masse (*commovebant*) against the established clergy.[252] The forces of change were essentially cultural insofar as they involved the spread of new ideas. But the words fell on eager ears: "suddenly many . . . whom dire poverty had ravaged saw a chance to resuscitate and to sustain their miserable sons and wives. A deafening cry was raised: the simple uneducated souls (*simplices et idiotae*) were aroused as if they had heard the very words of Peter and Paul."[253]

At the critical moment in the uprising, therefore, we find another paradigm for communication between *litterati* and *illitterati*. Landulf describes the common people as bewitched (*fascinati*). Image follows image: the rebels broke over the dikes of reason like a raging sea; they were "starved dogs," "mad bears in search of their cubs," "wolves

[248] *Ibid.*, 3.9, pp. 79-80.   [249] *Ibid.*, p. 80, 10-13.
[250] *Ibid.*, 80, 18-22.   [251] *Ibid.*, 3.10, p. 80, 37-39.   [252] *Ibid.*, 80, 39-41.
[253] *Ibid.*, 80, 41-46.

slaughtering calves." The resident clergy, relatively ignorant of what had transpired, was simply overwhelmed. And the sudden return to barbarism, in Landulf's view, recalled earlier periods of Milan's history with good reason, for similar conditions now seemed to exist. The nobility, when threatened, looked to its own interests as it had in the past, and left the endangered clergy to fend for itself.[254] The people, always a volatile, irrational force, now abandoned the Ambrosian ideals, just as, in Lanzo's time, they had defended them without really knowing why. On this occasion Landulf finds few redeeming qualities. Forgetting, he notes caustically, who nourished and clothed them,[255] the people turned to mundane rather than to spiritual pursuits, *non Deum sed pecuniam amantes.*[256] The reformers also acted without proper authority. Their only "licence" was "the words already spoken"[257] by Ariald. Landulf was even more horrified that they seemed to take up arms *per apostolicam licentiam.*[258] The priest Dionysius summed up his own point of view in his fictive address before pope Stephen. He denounced the *inaudita patalia.*[259] Only *viri inliterati*, he affirmed, preferred the sword and cudgel to patience and humility. The Patarenes were merely trying to put laymen above priests. The social consequences would be disastrous: dead children, murdered unbaptised; and young men, forbidden marriage, seeking less savoury outlets for their desires; all, he added, in clear contradiction of Milanese custom. Landulf Senior's position derived support from the fact that his eloquence was to no avail. Stephen sat on the fence; Anselm of Baggio and Hildebrand, "fearing the people's fury,"[260] satisfied themselves by stating that pearls should not be thrown to swine. The calculated taunt to popular culture insured that the movement would prosper.

In the third scene of book three, comprising chapters fourteen to eighteen, Landulf departs still further from the historical record and rearranges events to suit his own narrative purposes. In his time scheme, we begin "about seven years" after the events of 1057, while in reality the principal episodes are consequences of the synod of Fontaneto which Guido organized in November of the same year. Landulf jumps from the synod to Alexander II's confirmation of Erlembald as secular leader of the Pataria sometime after 1061. We then turn to the showdown between Guido and Erlembald at the Roman theatre, following which

[254] *Ibid.*, 81, 3-5. Yet others armed themselves, 3.11, p. 81.
[255] *Ibid.*, 81, 6-7.   [256] *Ibid.*, 81, 1; cf. 81, 7-8; 81, 14-15.   [257] *Ibid.*, 81, 16.
[258] *Ibid.*, 3.11, p. 81, 19.   [259] *Ibid.*, 3.12, pp. 81-82.
[260] *Ibid.*, 3.13, p. 82, 35-36.

the archbishop resigns in favour of Godefrey, actually sometime after 1067.

Seven years passed,[261] Landulf states, in which both factions knew success and adversity. Ariald and Landulf Cotta felt at length that they should appoint a temporal chief of the movement from among the capitanei or the vavasours. About this time, he continues, Landulf's brother, Erlembald, appeared on the scene, lately returned from a pilgrimage to the holy land. Erlembald was not sure he wanted to be involved, and accordingly sought advice in Rome. The pope was indecisive: a former ally of Ariald and Landulf, he nonetheless hesitated to provoke further civil disturbance. Ariald, the narrator would have it, personally accompanied Erlembald and persuaded Hildebrand that their cause was just. Hildebrand in turn won over Alexander. Publicly consecrated, the pair returned satisfied to Milan, where, through a combination of bribery, cajoling, and promises, Erlembald finally organized a militia. From that point there was no peace for the married clergy. Guido found his own position impossible: he had refused to aid his own priests; now he could hardly muster the strength to defend himself. With papal permission he called a synod of his suffragans at Novara. The assembled bishops first heard the Milanese clergy. Then they invited Ariald, Landulf, and Erlembald to meet with them in the hope of reaching a settlement. But the three greeted their overture with derision. As a consequence, the synod had them excommunicated. Next, Landulf relates, Leo of Vercelli made a lengthy speech in which he condemned the dissenters' *falsa justitia*. Guido, he pointed out, had tried to recall them from error, but to no avail. His unpopularity was understandable, but the see of Milan would undoubtedly survive. Somewhat encouraged, Guido returned home. But, when the Patarene leaders learned of their proscription, they decided to take matters into their own hands. They gathered a large, volatile crowd at the Roman theatre. After much shouting of slogans, Guido himself made an appearance. Erlembald gave the archbishop a simple choice: either to withdraw his sentence or to resign his office. The mob went wild; Guido's vestments were literally torn from his back. The people then rushed through the streets, crying out the news. The nobility were enraged. They were urged by the prominent Guido Landrianensis either to avenge the archbishop's dishonour or to leave the city altogether. Guido, perhaps ignorant of their support, re-

[261] Summarizing chs. 14-18, pp. 82-87.

turned disconsolate to his palace. Soon afterwards he handed over his staff and ring to Godefrey in a private ceremony.

These dramatic chapters reiterate some of the same distortions found earlier in book three.[262] Once again attention fluctuates between scenes of mass violence and intellectual discussion. Fictive roles are also invented. Landulf Cotta died sometime in 1061.[263] Yet the chronicler has him on hand for all the significant events of the sixties. Leo of Vercelli died in 1026; the speech attributed to him was probably made by a successor, the fervently antireformist Gregory.[264] Of course, Leo's ties with the emperor made it imperative in Landulf's view that he speak on behalf of the Milanese. In contrast, Anselm of Baggio, who became Alexander II in 1061, was portrayed as the Patarene's firm ally, even if, to reanimate his flagging reformist spirits, a persuasive nudge from Hildebrand was required. Finally, the synod of Fontaneto or Novara of November 1057 was projected to an undefined time just before Erlembald's confrontation with Guido da Velate in 1066: all of which violated chronology but made good literary sense.

Yet, if some distortions were accidental, others revealed more serious purposes. In this section of the *Historia* the Pataria developed and stabilized its internal makeup, becoming more precisely identifiable with pre-existing social and familial alignments in Milan. It acquired a secular and temporal arm, and thereby the capacity to challenge the administrative as well as the religious authority of the archbishop. And it adopted officially sanctioned warfare as opposed to occasional demonstrations of violence as a legitimate means of achieving reform.

These three objectives came together in the figure of Erlembald, with whose arrival, in Landulf's view, the Pataria was given a virtually new beginning. He became leader of the movement in two stages: first, he was singled out by Ariald and his brother as a nobleman with appropriately spiritual concerns; later, through Hildebrand's influence, Alexander conferred on him the *vexillum sancti Petri*.

Seven years passed, or so the narrative goes, which was, as it turns out, an important symbolic as well as temporal interlude. The enthusiasm for reform was possibly on the wane.[265] Ariald and Landulf

[262] Cf. Violante, *La pataria milanese*, 203-04.

[263] Arnulf, *Gesta* 3.16, p. 21; Landulf Senior 3.29, p. 95.

[264] *Historia*, p. 84n12; cf. Violante, *La pataria milanese*, 204.

[265] *Ibid.*, 3.14, p. 82, 45-46. Cf. H.E.J. Cowdrey, "The Papacy, the Patarenes and the Church of Milan," 35.

began actively to seek secular protection for their preaching.[266] Erlembald was invited to change his status from a *saeculi* to a *Dei et catholicae ecclesiae miles*;[267] in Rome, Ariald asked the pope to provide the movement with a *protector beati Petri*, the bearer of the *vexillum victoriae*.[268]

We also learn something of Erlembald, both his motives and his manner of fulfilling his sacred duties. In Landulf Senior's view, he was an important figure in two senses. He played a role in the Pataria analogous to that of Lanzo in the time of Aribert; that is, he took over and became responsible for religious burdens which ecclesiastical figures could no longer shoulder. But in this function he nonetheless represented a role directly opposed to the chronicler's interests. While personifying lay participation, which, in principle, Landulf approved of,[269] he was at the same time undermining the very order which allowed a healthy division of labour to exist. No wonder, then, that the portrait is somewhat ambivalent. On the one hand, Erlembald is a repository of ideal qualities: bearded, handsome, and courageous, yet cautious, experienced in battle, and wise in counsel, he appears to have been a happy union of natural aptitudes and *usus antiquus*.[270] He reflected seriously on the consequences before joining the Pataria.[271] Yet, he was also an embittered convert to religious purism who first turned to asceticism and reform and later to authoritarianism.[272] According to Landulf, he had recently returned from Jerusalem and chosen his bride. But, "on learning from irrefutable evidence that she had been dallying with a certain cleric,"[273] he dropped the idea of marriage. The chronicler further maintains that all the Cotta brothers were illegitimate. Aribert, he alleges, tried in vain to separate their parents.[274] Both details may be apocryphal, but they suggest that emotional and familial questions may have played as large a part as religious idealism in Erlembald's decision to join the movement.

---

[266] *Historia* 3.14, p. 82, 47-49.

[267] *Ibid.*, 3.14, p. 83, 11-12. C. Erdmann, *The Origin of the Idea of Crusade*, trans. M. W. Baldwin and W. Goffart (Princeton, 1977), 142n85, argued that Landulf might have redrafted two sets of interviews in order to bring them into line with the ideology of the First Crusade. But Landulf nowhere shows an acquaintance with the events or histories of the crusade and his support of other papal positions is weak.

[268] *Ibid.*, 3.15, p. 83, 39-40.

[269] Cf. Violante, "I laici nel movimento patarino," 164-65.

[270] *Historia* 3.14, pp. 82-83.

[271] *Ibid.*, 83, 18-20.

[272] *Ibid.*, 3.29, p. 95; Cowdrey, "The Papacy, the Patarenes and the Church of Milan," 35; Violante, *La pataria milanese*, 188.

[273] *Historia* 3.14, p. 83, 2-5.   [274] *Ibid.*, 83, 5-7.

Landulf's description of his activities on his return from Rome supports this conclusion. "Secretly, day and night, he had brought to him the city's youths, popular and noble; . . . enticing them with gifts and promises, he forced them to take the same oath as Ariald and Landulf and to pledge faith to the Pataria (*pataliae placitum tenere*)."[275] In other words, he created the same sort of feudal *conventio* or *pactum*[276] which bound the capitanei to the archbishop. After the successful "reform," claims to property and to offices would presumably be honoured. One regime would replace another. In short, beneath the papal alliance, crusading rhetoric, and reformist zeal, the other social tensions were resurfacing. In licensing a formal, temporal force, the Pataria broke the dikes that had hitherto separated the secular from religious interests and unleashed a tidewater it could not control.

The next act of the drama deals with the synod of Novara, the fictive speech of Leo of Vercelli, and the subsequent confrontation between the Pataria's leaders and Guido da Velate at the Roman theatre. The events range widely, as noted, over the decade after 1057. But the contrasting scenes also focus the narrative on the growing hiatus between the activist and intellectualist sides of the controversy.

There was in effect a split within each faction. Among the Patarenes, change had always been underpinned by canonical authority and worked out by a hard core of educated clerics. Structures inevitably appeared: the three leaders now met "like bishops in a synod"[277] and condemned Guido as a simoniac. This, within Landulf's account, represented an escalation of conflict, which, up to that point, was largely based on the issue of clerical marriage.[278] Guido's response was the synod of Fontaneto, which, Landulf fantasizes, took place *ex concessione Alexandri apostoli*.[279] In reality, the chronicler merely wished to balance the claims of the autonomous Milanese church against the authority of Rome. What the Patarene and archiepiscopal "synods" really meant was that the controversy now had two clearly defined sides. Thus, while a naked struggle was carried on in the streets, reviving and breathing life into Milan's older class tensions, an intel-

---

[275] *Ibid.*, 3.15, p. 84, 11-15.

[276] Du Cange, *Glossarium*, s.v., placitum. Cf. *Historia* 3.21, p. 89, 22 (novum placitum); 3.20, p. 89, 2; 3.29, p. 95, 2. For other examples, see O. Capitani, "Storiografia e riforma della chiesa in Italia," 613n40.

[277] *Historia* 3.16, p. 84, 28.

[278] Cf. Violante, *La pataria milanese*, 182-86.

[279] *Historia* 3.16, p. 84, 30; cf. Violante, *La pataria milanese*, 203.

lectual debate was carried on over the legality and theological justification for the so-called reforms.

During the 1060s, and, in particular, after Erlembald's arrival, action and theory moved farther and farther apart. Emphasis among the Patarenes shifted in part from religious idealism to feudal alliances; the proponents of the old order increasingly sought their *raison d'être* in custom, urban history, and arid theologisms. In this perspective, it is instructive to contrast the words put into the mouth of Leo of Vercelli with the violent degradation of Guido at the Roman theatre. Leo reasserted the paternity of the archbishop over the city's secular and religious affairs.[280] Guido was *pater amande*, the Milanese church, a *chorus . . . linguae Latinae instructus*. The revolt was a typical "schism" in which *falsa justitia* was pitted against *veritas*. Leo had "collected from ancient volumes" many examples of secular assaults on the Milanese church, all of which were eventually quashed. Every attempt should be made to rescue the heretics. In particular, Leo drew attention to the necessity of correct canonical procedures for discussing Catholic doctrines on simony.[281]

Yet, if one turns to the following scene, it was precisely the *canones conscripti*[282] from Novara which drew the Patarene intellectuals into the street. Landulf called the mob at the Roman theatre unaffectionately a *populi turba*, a vulgar crowd "whose minds were moved like leaves by the wind."[283] But how "vulgar" were they? True, a majority may have come from the lower orders. But the leaders as well as *aliquantuli clerici et sacerdotes* were educated and possibly from better families.[284] Erlembald's militia, although unmentioned, must have been represented, and it moved no farther down the social scale than the capitanei and the vavasours. The meeting's "kindling wood" was Leoprand, an educated and recently ordained urban priest. Finally, although the subject, excommunication, had practical and popular consequences, it too framed the conflict in intellectual terms. In other words, while a plurality of the participants was plebeian in origin, the crowd constituted a *vulgus* chiefly in being manipulated by Patarene preaching. The vividness of the scenes of violence—the rending of Guido's vestments or the people careening through the streets "grunting" the news of his downfall—is apt to blind one to the importance of the episode in transferring the Patarene message from the more to the less lettered levels of the movement. The catalyst for the

---

[280] The following summarizes 3.17, p. 85.
[281] *Ibid.*, 85, 32-36.
[282] *Ibid.*, 3.18, p. 86, 30.   [283] *Ibid.*, 86, 31, 39-40; p. 87, 6.   [284] *Ibid.*, 86, 31-36.

riot was "several long speeches," which transformed the doctrines into a vehicle of social action. And thus the Pataria took on a new and uglier form.

In the remaining two thematic sections of book three, the gap between the theoretical and practical issues widens. The events of chapters nineteen to thirty fall roughly in the sixties and the early seventies. Once again, historical accuracy is subordinated to polemics. According to Landulf, about twenty Patarenes, allied with the heretics from Monforte, made a further visit to Rome. They were prevented only by the influence of their most powerful patron, Hildebrand, from trying to unseat Alexander II as a simoniac.[285] Returning to Milan, Ariald was overcome with the desire for penance and made a speech to the assembled clergy in which he repudiated his erroneous ways. But his confession only served as a reminder of the injustices he had committed, and the two sides remained farther apart than ever before.[286] Anselm, Milan's viscount, also went to see the pope, who was by this time weary of Patarene intrigues. As a consequence, Landulf asserted, he declared invalid the *placitum* with the rebels which he had so imprudently created.[287] Finally, Erlembald, ignorant of Alexander's withdrawal of support, expelled the capitanei from the city and ruthlessly stripped all unreformed priests of their wives, their offices, and their worldly goods.[288]

In this increasingly litigious atmosphere the reader arrives at chapter twenty-two and the series of sermons which brings to a head the intellectual side of the controversy over a married clergy. Although, in theory, Erlembald is in charge of the proceedings, it is Ariald and Landulf who are on the defensive throughout. Three of the four speeches are made by the archbishop's men, the archdeacon Guibert, Ambrose Biffus, and a decuman priest named Andrew.[289]

The debate's literary purpose is twofold. It gives Landulf Senior an opportunity to summarize the various arguments against reform which he develops throughout the *Historia*. These reach their high point in the lengthy, eloquent statement of Andrew. The interchange also exhausts the possibilities of rational, theological, or canonically approved methods for dealing with the opposite side. When Ariald,

---

[285] *Ibid.*, 3.19, pp. 87-88.
[286] *Ibid.*, 3.20, p. 88.   [287] *Ibid.*, pp. 88-89.   [288] *Ibid.*, 3.21, 89.
[289] *Ibid.*, 3.22, p. 89. Landulf once again stresses Milan's historic relationship to the Greek church. Guibert is *utriusque linguae magister*, as is Ambrose Biffus. Andrew is described as *in divinis et humanis Graecis et Latinis sermonibus virilis seu decorus*. Needless to say, no direct knowledge of Greek is revealed by their sermons.

Landulf, and Erlembald meet their respective fates shortly afterwards, the Ambrosian church, in the chronicler's view, achieves another victory over lay and ecclesiastical forces attempting to divert its historic and apostolic course.

The sermons of Guibert and Ambrose are a pastiche of quotations from St. Ambrose allegedly supporting the traditional state of affairs. Ariald and Landulf, by contrast, rely chiefly on passages of the New Testament, by and large unadulterated by commentary. Andrew's speech rises considerably above the others in passion and persuasiveness. He seems to speak with the voice of Landulf Senior himself.

Despite the reiteration of previous positions, the fictive confrontation is instructive. Both sides lay claim to the usages of the *primitiva ecclesia*. But, whereas the Nicolaitans think of themselves as part of an unbroken tradition going back to St. Ambrose, the Patarenes insist that the original purity of the church can be restored only when "old things have passed away and everything is made new."[290] Guibert and Ambrose Biffus present different sides of the same argument. Guibert stresses the naturalness of the bond between man and woman. As St. Ambrose points out, in creation, Adam and Eve were *in uno corpore et in uno spiritu*.[291] A layman does not cease to be a good Christian by marrying; nor are priests intended to be a caste apart. "All laymen and clerics, to the degree that they are the church's sons, are its priests."[292] Ambrose adds that only God embodies perfect charity, chastity, and goodness. We know, Paul said, that the law is spiritual but that we are not.[293] Marriage, far from inhibiting spiritual existence, prevents the occurrence of worse sins. Not only, therefore, do the Patarenes erect rigid barriers between lay and religious in the church. They also attempt to apply to this world standards evidently only intended for the next. Their only means of achieving their ends is by force. Their *placitum* is not with God but with other men. In their misused idealism they try to replace St. Ambrose as the church of Milan's true *apostolus*.[294] By implication, they usurp the *licentia* granted to bishops to interpret Scripture for ordinary believers.[295]

The reply of Ariald and Landulf indicates that these charges were

---

[290] *Ibid.*, 3.22, p. 89, 38-40: "Arialdus et Landulfus proclamare coeperunt dicentes: Vetera transierunt et facta sunt omnia nova (2 Cor 5.17). Quod olim in primitiva ecclesia a patribus sanctis concessum est, modo indubitanter prohibetur."

[291] *Ibid.*, 3.23, p. 90, 5; Ambrose, *Exameron* 5.7, PL 14.215-16.

[292] *Ibid.*, 90, 9: "Omnes tamen laici et clerici, quicunque sunt filii ecclesiae, sacerdotes sunt."

[293] *Ibid.*, 3.24, 91, 1-3; Rom 7:24.

[294] *Ibid.*, p. 91, 6-18.   [295] *Ibid.*, 91, 43-45.

partly correct. Real charity, they argued, does not consist in allowing one's brethren to persist in error. Unreformed priests had to be set straight by their *ratio*,[296] that is, their reading of apostolic doctrine, which was elitist, hierarchical, and stressed the separation of the lettered and the unlettered. True, they granted, Paul says that we cannot all perform all tasks. But some of us are singled out through our knowledge of divine and human affairs to lead others through Scripture's tortuous paths.[297] Just as Christ bore the cross,[298] we must bear the responsibility for interpretation. The priest by definition was a member of a purist sect. His obligation was to fulfill ascetic ideals unattainable by ordinary mortals. Neither marriage nor otherworldly involvements were tolerable. Of course Paul tells his listeners not to dissolve marriage needlessly nor to look needlessly for a wife. But it is also written that "no one fighting for Christ will involve himself in worldly affairs."[299] The Patarene position was summed up in a rephrasing of Pauline ideas: "Just as death awakens the soul from the carnal sense, so charity brings it back from the desires of the flesh."[300]

The Nicolaitan position, then, as Landulf presents it, can be described as integrationist. Religious institutions and social organization are mutually supportive, apostolically sanctioned structures, in which theory and practice are united from the outset. The reformist position stresses the contrast between contemporary practice and past theory, the latter defended by rationality, legitimacy, and a literal reading of biblical texts. The Patarenes thereby achieve their utopia of the spirit through radical opposition: flesh versus spirit, custom versus law, and, by implication, the written versus the merely oral.

Andrew, for his part, attempted to refute the Patarene programme on essentially three grounds: it was intolerable to society; it lacked clear biblical and canonical precedents; and it was incompatible with the previous history of the Milanese church, whose continuity, in his view, was a better witness to sincere piety than their hasty, ill-conceived arguments.

What was undertaken with charity ought to be concluded with charity, not with empty rhetoric. The Lord wanted mercy, not useless sacrifice.[301] Whose example were they following in thus assuming the

---

[296] *Ibid.*, 3.25, p. 91, 60.

[297] *Ibid.*, 92, 16-17: ". . . sed unusquisque nostrum, gratias Deo, ita scientia in divinis et humanis superpollet, ut viae verae tramitem sive devium aut tortuosum sacris in scripturis longo exercitio exercitatus cognoscere. . . ."

[298] *Ibid.*, 92, 21-22; Gal 6:14.

[299] *Ibid.*, 92, 27-29; 1 Cor 7:27.   [300] *Ibid.*, 92, 26-27.

[301] *Ibid.*, 3.26, p. 92, 50-51; Exod 33:19.

spiritual responsibilities of the clergy and the people?[302] Milan had known peace and prosperity before they arrived on the scene. They fomented civil war, despite God's rejection of *coacta servitia*.[303] If they were not persuaded by words alone, a stronger argument arose from the homicides, conspiracies, perjuries, and from the children who died unbaptized. Had they not seen the bodies of murdered infants in the theatre cistern or the city's sewers?[304] Perhaps they cherished illusions about human nature: in forbidding one wife they created dozens of adulterers and prostitutes.[305] Perhaps as well they misunderstood the nature of chastity, which, as Ambrose observed, is a state of the mind, not of the body. As such, it may be revealed either *in opere* or *in habitu*.[306] But, quite aside from social considerations, Andrew believed that Patarene preaching was harmful, even corrupt:

"You defame us and our order with bittersweet words both in Rome and in our home town in order to show off your arid learning and verbosity. . . . Some of your number, avid for lucre, seek the wages of ruin: they commercialize through speaking what ought to be cloathed in silence. Others, in order to appear to know much and to vaunt their learning, state openly what they ought to keep to themselves, and, speaking without discretion, make statements which, once enunciated, cannot be recalled. . . ."[307]

As a consequence, the Patarenes in his view justified themselves not before God but before other men.[308] Yet, even God had not "commissioned them to bring everything to perfection"[309] on their own. If they wished truly to imitate the Lord, they had to accept weaker men, not just to consider themselves. They could not think themselves "juster than the apostle, holier than the prophets, purer than the patriarchs." Men were driven from their lawful wives by the lance, the cudgel, and the fist.[310] Was this the law? To his mind the *lex Domini* made it clear that no man should separate those whom God had joined. That is what St. Ambrose meant when he spoke of God's law: namely, "that a man shall leave his father and mother and live with his wife, and that they shall be two in one flesh."[311] Is it fair to call those who have been lawfully wed for twenty years "fornicators" and "adulterers"? Perhaps, he added, the Patarenes were infected with

---

[302] *Ibid.*, 92, 54.   [303] *Ibid.*, 92, 56; Rom 14:4.   [304] *Ibid.*, 92, 58-60.

[305] *Ibid.*, 92, 62.   [306] *Ibid.*, 93, 3-5; *De Bono*, cc. 25-26.

[307] *Ibid.*, 93, 10-12.   [308] *Ibid.*, 93, 12-13; Luc 16:15.   [309] *Ibid.*, 93, 14.

[310] *Ibid.*, 93, 35-37.

[311] *Ibid.*, 93, 40-41; cf. 3.23, p. 90, 40-44. Guibert's sermon is used as a reference point by both Andrew and Ariald, and by Landulf; cf. 3.25, 92, 98.

the Monforte heresy and believed that men should have no commerce with women at all.[312] But the Lord said, "No one can be clean and holy, free from sin."[313] A married priesthood, therefore, is supported by both reason and canonical authority.[314]

The speeches had scarcely ended when Landulf leapt to his feet in a wild rage and stormed out towards the theatre, where he proceeded to whip up a volatile crowd against the clergy. When he was finished, Erlembald, who stood by, as Landulf forewarns, *adorante et tamquam rex imperante*, ordered a general rout of the regular clergy. From that point, anyone who did not show proper "reverence" was put to the sword.[315]

The narrative next turns to a series of events rearranged from the years 1061 to 1075: in order, Godefrey's unsuccessful attempt to re-enter Milan from Castiglione Olona, where he was besieged by Erlembald in March 1071; the election of Azzo, the Patarene candidate for the see of Milan, in S. Maria Yemale, on 6th January 1072; the death of Landulf Cotta, which probably took place, as noted, in 1061; the flight, mutilation, and murder of Ariald on 27th and 28th June 1066; the return of his remains to Milan in May of the following year; and Erlembald's death in battle in 1075.

These events are telescoped into a few brief scenes of vivid and chilling detail.[316] Godefrey is pictured as an ineffectual figure, who is simply born along by a tide he cannot control. Erlembald's alleged collaboration with Gregory VII on Azzo's election is denounced by Landulf, now firmly committed to the imperial faction. For, in his view, Hildebrand was the original catalyst in the *placitum* between Erlembald and his secular supporters. Azzo's election was therefore "illicit"; Erlembald won only by effectively buying votes. The Patarene leader, the chronicler notes, had become a virtual dictator, judging priests "like a pope" and laymen "like a monarch." He had finally overcome the proud city through steel, gold, and conspiracies. No one could any longer offer resistance.[317]

But "God's anger" was not so easily thwarted. In Landulf's view, one by one the heads of the Pataria met appropriate fates. Landulf, frustrated in his efforts to secure the archbishopric, grew despondent,

---

[312] *Ibid.*, 3.26, p. 93, 46-48.
[313] *Ibid.*, 93, 49.   [314] *Ibid.*, 93, 62.   [315] *Ibid.*, 3.27, p. 94.
[316] Summarizing 3.29-30, pp. 94-97.
[317] *Historia* 3.29, p. 95, 11-13: "Interea cum Herlembaldus quasi papa ad iudicandum sacerdotes, rex ad conterendas gentes, urbem iam iamque ferro et auro et iuramentis multis et diversis superasset. . . ."

fell ill, and died. He was buried like a common criminal, with his legs broken.

Ariald's end was more painful, and gave Landulf an opportunity to explore the story's mythical levels. Around the end of May, 1066, he was said to have entered into a violent dispute with a number of clerics over whether St. Ambrose had stipulated a three-day fast for the Easter litanies. Accustomed now to polemics, Milan was soon divided for and against. In the ensuing skirmishes, six lives were lost. Public indignation mounted against Ariald and he prepared to flee. But, on the night of his escape, he was caught near Legnano by some men in the service of Guido da Velate's niece, Olive. She had him first taken to the isolated Rocca di Arona and later, secretly, to an island in Lago Maggiore. There she attempted to force him to acknowledge Guido as legitimate archbishop. He is said to have replied: "As long as I have a tongue in my mouth, an unimpaired mind, and a serene disposition, I shall neither consider nor recognize him as archbishop."[318] On these words, Landulf maintains, a servant proceeded to tear out his tongue. He was then left to die; however, the following day, Olive, fearing Erlembald's reprisals, had the body taken to the cellars of St. Ambrose at Travallio. After a few days the stench of rotting flesh was so great that Ariald's captors could not remain upstairs in the fort and they filled the cellar with water.

Word of these events eventually reached Erlembald, Landulf continues, and he threatened Olive with siege unless the body was immediately returned. Then, his legates, camped in the Rho valley, heard a voice by night telling them to run to the banks of the Ticino, where Ariald would appear. At the appointed place they came upon his mutilated, scarcely recognizable body. Erlembald had his remains born solemnly with prayers and litanies to the monastery of St. Celsus, where he was buried. In 1075, the chronicler adds, archbishop Anselm had the bones transferred to the convent of St. Dionysius. That, as it turned out, was also a fateful year for Erlembald and his lieutenant, Leoprand. The capitanei, loyal to Godefrey, had begun to re-enter the city and to renew their feudal alliances. Around Easter, the *ordinarii* assembled to consecrate a chalice containing the chrism for the baptism of catechumens. Weary of harassment by Erlembald's militia, they prepared a confrontation at the Roman theatre on Easter Sunday. Erlembald was in no mood for compromise; he snatched the chalice and crushed it underfoot. He then readied his troops to assault

318 *Ibid.*, 3.30, p. 95, 44-45.

the capitanei. The nobility and their popular followers prepared without enthusiasm for another civil disturbance. Erlembald, confident of victory, promised his supporters rich rewards and rode arrogantly into battle, bearing the standard of St. Peter. But, on this occasion fortune turned the other way, and he was killed in the first attack. The battle was won by the capitanei. Later, Leoprand, who had carried the cross on his behalf, had his nose and ears cut off.

Each of the three major leaders of the Pataria thus met a fate appropriate to his offence. Landulf died with his tongue hanging out. Ariald, who refused to recognize the elected archbishop, was cruelly murdered by his niece. Erlembald was slain in battle on behalf of the *vexillum sancti Petri*, which, in the chronicler's view, he had usurped. The deaths of Ariald and Landulf also take the reader close to his conception of the Pataria's real offence. In both cases he stands back momentarily from the action and comments on their misdeeds.[319]

Both meet their ends around Easter and both attempt to interfere with the liturgy, which, in Landulf's opinion, is the most tangible link with the past of the Ambrosian church and with the Word itself. Taking Erlembald's case first: Landulf, on hearing of the crushed chalice, contrasts the godless feudal union (*placitum sine Deo*) with the divinely consecrated sacrament (*sacramentum . . . per verbum Dei consecratum*).[320] We return, in other words, to two types of oral discourse, one evil, the other good. Further, the beneficent verbal union, underpinned by the authority of Ambrose, is linked ritually to the past. Erlembald's principal offence is to have criminally interrupted the ceremony of paschal baptism.[321] He thereby interceded in the church's rites of purification. The public nature of his fault was matched in the narrative by his public downfall.[322]

So, too, Ariald's intellectualism broke the sacred continuity of Ambrosian rituals, and the byproduct was civil disorder. He interjected himself into the *solempnia* of the Easter litanies, "preaching and squabbling with clerics."[323] He asserted that meat and wine could not be eaten *legaliter* and that fasting was nowhere specifically enjoined by St. Ambrose. Landulf Senior's response was more nuanced than in the

---

[319] *Ibid.*, 3.30, p. 95, 27-36, and p. 97, 2-10.

[320] *Ibid.*, 97, 2-4. Cf. Bonizo of Sutri, *Liber ad Amicum* 7, MGH Libelli de Lite 1, 605, who nowhere mentions the chalice and attributes Erlembald's death to Patarene unpopularity after the fire of 30th March 1075.

[321] *Ibid.*, 97, 8-9: "sancto baptismo sancti pascae criminose interrupto. . . ."

[322] *Ibid.*, 97, 9-10.

[323] *Ibid.*, 95, 21: "praedicando ac cum clericis rixando. . . ."

case of Erlembald. At one level he attempted (not altogether successfully) to disprove Ariald's allegations by quoting the gospel of Luke
and St. Ambrose's inscription on the gates of Milan.[324] But it is clear
from the style of Ariald's death that he had something else in mind.
Like Landulf Cotta, Ariald was finally overcome by his misuse of
verbal cleverness. If we are to follow the chronicler's interpretation,
Ariald saw that the people had turned against him, not only for his
present mischief but also for his former misdeeds. He too had offended
word and ritual with textual legalisms.

Landulf combined these themes with a typical story of family
vengeance. His captors were Guido's relatives; his tongue, the source
of his "evil," was ripped out. Yet the symbolism does not end there.
His body was then taken to the *apotheca* of St. Ambrose, where its
continuing stench is a reminder that its message and influence had
not yet died. Not by accident, the murderess is described as "steeped
in almost all the magical arts, especially in the art of incantation."[325]
She has the cellar filled up midway with water, superficially, to drown
the odour, but, at a more abstract level, as a type of ritual purification, a conscious or unconscious antidote to baptism. As in the death
of Erlembald, Landulf sees one type of oral discourse being answered
by another. The legates of the Patarene chief, who were camped in
the Rho valley, thought they heard an "angelic voice."[326] They rushed
to the Ticino's banks, where, as the narrator puts it, Ariald was *re-
praesentandus*.[327] There they found their hero's body: cut up by Olive,
it had rotted for days in foul water, and its sexual members, significantly, were shrivelled up.[328] Thus, it would appear, in Landulf's
imagination, the verbal deceptions of Ariald were countered by the
black magic of Guido's niece: evil for evil, man for woman. It was to
his mind a fitting end to a controversy which attempted to drive
lawfully wedded men and women apart.

Landulf Senior's characterization of the Pataria is too complicated
to be summed up in a few words. Unlike Arnulf, he did not look
upon the movement as an unjustified revolt from below against the
legitimate authority of the infeudated Milanese church. No single
class held for him the position of Arnulf's capitanei. Instead, he measured all social, political, and religious disruptions against an image
of the *primitiva ecclesia* as founded by St. Ambrose and perpetuated
despite difficulties by Milanese archbishops as late as Aribert of Inti-

[324] *Ibid.*, 95, 29-36, on which see the text's notes, p. 95nn26-27.
[325] *Ibid.*, 96, 9-10.   [326] *Ibid.*, 96, 15.   [327] *Loc.cit.*   [328] *Ibid.*, 96, 16-19.

miano. This idealized church had much in common with sectarian movements, or, as he believed, with the individualized communities of the Greek East. If it lacked other sects' voluntarism, it nonetheless promoted active lay participation in religion, a positive rather than a passive role for women, and an intense fraternalism intermingled in his case with civic nostalgia. Above all, it permitted, even encouraged, a married clergy. In his view, the Nicolaiti represented the traditional values of the Milanese church. The Patarini were innovators and misguided heretics.

If Landulf was more conscious than Arnulf of the purely religious divisions, he also offered, despite occasional exaggerations, a more perceptive analysis of both the social and cultural aspects of the conflict. He distinguished between the revolts of the nobility of the 1030s, the commoners of the 1040s, and the reformers after 1057. To his mind the rebellions had at least one common feature: given the opportunity, first the capitanei and vavasours, then the cives or *populi*, and finally the Patarenes tried to destroy the Ambrosian ideal, which he saw as the principal instrument of social cohesion. The most serious threat to order did not arise from class warfare, which he nonetheless vividly portrayed, but from the series of dishonours suffered by the church of St. Ambrose. No historian of the period has failed to be struck by Landulf's characterization of the common people under Lanzo's leadership, preferring to die rather than to live dishonourably (*magis mori diligens quam vivere inhoneste*).[329] But few have noted that he describes the capitanei in 1075 in almost the same terms: *parati mori quam inhoneste vivere*.[330] The key concept is honour, which he sees as both a civic and a religious virtue. The relation between the social and reformist components in his interpretation is therefore not easy to unravel. Familial and political rivalries, he thought, survived Guido's election and poisoned the atmosphere of the 1050s just as the reform platform was taking shape. But the Pataria was not only a social movement. The religious element was amalgamated onto the social, forming a new alloy. The Patarenes cut across older boundaries with a new cultural ideal: both the process and the content were equally unprecedented. When enthusiasm inevitably waned, older rivalries were quick to reassert themselves. What gave the movement its strength and paradoxically made it so vulnerable was its use of the

[329] *Ibid.*, 2.26, p. 63, 26. For a review of the attitudes of earlier historians, see Violante, *La società milanese*, 267-79, especially for the period up to the episcopate of Aribert. For a review of later developments, see Y. Renouard, *Les villes d'Italie*, 398-411.

[330] *Historia* 3.30, p. 96, 29-30.

letter and the word. The letter organized the élite; the word was communicated to the masses. Within the Pataria's ranks the division between noble and commoner was momentarily suspended in favour of that of *litteratus* and *illitteratus*.

Andrew of Strumi

Landulf Senior does not describe the inner workings of the early Pataria in detail. This task was left to Andrew of Strumi, who died in 1106. A devoted follower of Ariald, Andrew left Milan sometime after 1067 to join the expanding Vallumbrosan Order, becoming abbot of Strumi, near Arezzo, some fourteen years after the death of John Gualbert in 1073.[331] He was in a good position to look back on a quarter-century's successes and failures in attempts at reform.

His two principal works are the *Vita Sancti Arialdi*, written in 1075, and his *Vita Gualberti*, in 1092.[332] In both, stress is laid on penance, asceticism, and the need for strong leadership among reform communities.[333] The *Vita Arialdi* may be divided into three parts, the first dealing with the Pataria's early phases and with Ariald's preaching (chs. 1-18), the second with the saint's martyrdom, during which Andrew was in Milan (chs. 19-25), and the third with a possibly apocryphal[334] exchange of letters between Andrew and a Patarene priest called Sirus, who was, he claimed, an intimate of Ariald's and the author of a lost *vita prima*.[335]

Andrew begins in a sense where Landulf Senior left off, namely,

[331] On Andrew's relationship with John, see S. Boesch Gajano, "Storia e tradizione vallombrosane," 99-112 *et passim*. Andrew became abbot of S. Fedele di Strumi on 10th October 1087; *ibid.*, 112n1.

[332] F. Baethgen, *Vita Sancti Arialdi*, MGH SS 30.2, p. 1048.

[333] P. Lamma, "Andrea da Parma (da Strumi)," *Dizionario biog. degli italiani*, vol. 3, 111; in greater detail, see S. Boesch, "Giovanni Gualberto e la vita comune del clero nelle biografie di Andrea da Strumi e di Atto da Vallombrosa," *La vita comune del clero nei secoli XI e XII* (Milan, 1962), 228-35.

[334] Baethgen, *Vita*, p. 1047, thought Sirus's letters spurious. Miccoli however argues that he may have written them after reading Andrew's life; "Per la storia della Pataria milanese," in *Chiesa gregoriana*, 105n16. Violante also argues for their authenticity; "I laici nel movimento patarino," 150n13, 172, 229-31. For a recent review of the evidence, see G. Spinelli, "Il sacerdozio ministeriale nella predicazione della Pataria milanese," *Benedictina* 22 (1975), 92-93n2.

[335] *Vita S. Arialdi*, c. 26, p. 1072. Not to be confused with the *vita anonyma* of the twelfth or thirteenth century poorly edited by Puricelli (1658). For a comparison of the two lives, see C. Pellegrini, "Fonti e memorie storiche di S. Arialdo," *Archivio storico lombardo*, anno 27, vol. 14 (1900), 209-36.

with Ariald's martyrdom.[336] But, whereas Landulf sought to portray Ariald as the co-founder of a heretical sect, Andrew is replete with hagiographic conventions. A happy combination of intelligence, discipline, and austerity, Ariald is said to have committed himself early to both celibacy and monastic reform.[337] His followers were marked men: Landulf Cotta was converted by his preaching;[338] Nazario is compared to Cornelius, who sheltered Peter.[339] Erlembald was "lately returned from Jerusalem" and "wished to flee the world."[340] Seeking the pope's approval, he journeyed to Rome like a pilgrim, stopping at monasteries and hermitages on the way. He was given the *vexillum sancti Petri* as an extirpator of heretics and as a potential martyr.[341] Ariald, like Christ, was betrayed by one of his own, a priest who, like Erlembald, had recently returned from the holy land, and who visited him during the vigil of John the Baptist.[342] Ariald combined fortitude and charity. Andrew himself heard him say, "Whoever is ready to die with me for Christ, let him come to my side. Whoever is not, let him leave."[343] Yet, when wounded in a skirmish with Guido's henchmen in 1066, he admonished his followers "to love their enemies."[344] In the end, Andrew relates, he was murdered by two clerics, since secular jailors refused to lay hands on him.[345] Olive played the part of Jezebel or Herodias, and, wherever she tried to conceal the corpse, a divine light shone above it from the heavens.[346] Humble folk aided Andrew in his search for the place of assassination.[347] Algisius, who finally found the body, learned of its whereabouts from shepherds who followed an eagle along the shores of Lago Maggiore.[348] Ariald was as strong in death as in life. Returned to Milan by Erlembald, his remains drew all classes of society together in grief.

Andrew recalls the scene, which he witnessed himself: "From the towns, in which they had shut themselves up out of fear, countless numbers came forth, the old, the young, the women, bearing crosses, candles, and urns. . . . Each in his manner rendered thanks to God with an exalted voice. Bells rang out, and some climbed trees in the hope of catching a glimpse of the saint. As we approached Milan, we were met by virtually the whole city. . . ."[349]

[336] *Vita*, prologue, p. 1049.   [337] *Ibid.*, cc. 3-4, p. 1051.   [338] *Ibid.*, c. 5, p. 1053.
[339] *Ibid.*, c. 6, p. 1053; Actus 10.   [340] *Ibid.*, c. 15, p. 1059.
[341] *Loc.cit.*   [342] *Ibid.*, c. 21, p. 1067.   [343] *Ibid.*, c. 21, p. 1066, 34-35.
[344] *Ibid.*, c. 20, p. 1065, 20-21; Mt 5.44.
[345] *Ibid.*, c. 22, pp. 1068-69.   [346] *Ibid.*, 1069.
[347] *Ibid.*, c. 21, pp. 1067-68.   [348] *Ibid.*, c. 23, p. 1070.   [349] *Ibid.*, 1071, 7-13.

Ariald, in other words, is to Andrew what Aribert was to Landulf, a charismatic figure, capable, if only in death, of knitting the diverse social and religious threads of Milan into a single fabric. Yet, Andrew almost never analyses the social background of the Pataria in depth. Even Guido's forces are conceived as necessary stages in the saint's eventual martyrdom.[350] Andrew, unlike Arnulf and Landulf, cannot therefore be called a commentator on the political aspects of the Pataria. However, of the three, he is by far the most informative on the interior structure of the movement itself.

His analysis begins in chapter four, which we may first summarize[351] and then discuss. According to Andrew, the entire *ordo ecclesiasticus* was living in error. Scarcely a priest could be found in his proper functions. Some had taken up frivolities like hunting; others had become shopkeepers, bailiffs, or usurers. Many had wives, and all were "implicated" in the buying and selling of offices. Ariald came to Milan to expose vice, and preached the following sermon: "Let me begin," he said, "with what you know, and then proceed to what you do not know. The human race was blind until Christ came, worshipping mere objects of stone, wood, or metal.[352] God found this insufferable, assumed flesh himself, and underwent crucifixion. While on earth he also chose a certain number of spokesmen to spread his word. His illumination descends to earth through two means, therefore, through his own word and his teachers' way of life.[353] The teachers' light, however, is not the same as yours. Theirs is the understanding of Scripture and their lives are so to speak a text for those who cannot interpret the Bible for themselves. Yet, by implication, if they lose their guiding light, you too will be enveloped in darkness. That is just what has happened. Your present clergy give you not reality but appearances. In place of the truth they offer you lies. Do you wish to advance towards the true light? If you would serve Him, you must follow me.[354] For these are not Christ's true servants. He extolled meekness, humility, and poverty; they revel in worldly goods and sexual depravity. Indeed, Christ demands such purity in his followers that he even condemns the sins in their hearts." Ariald concludes by saying that he has tried to lead the wayward priests back to the light

[350] Erlembald's death is looked upon in the same terms; for corroboration, see Bonizo of Sutri, *Liber ad Amicum* 7, p. 605: Glorioso Erlimbaldo pro nomine Iesu martirizato. . . .

[351] The following recapitulates *Vita* c. 4, pp. 1051-52.

[352] Deut 29:17; cf. Arnulf, *Gesta* 3.11, p. 19.

[353] Mt 5:16.   [354] Jn 12:26.

but has failed. And so he has turned directly to the people: "I shall lead you back or perish by the sword for your salvation."

Despite its straightforward message, the context and meaning of Ariald's first sermon require reflection. Although appearing as a separate unit in the *Vita*, it is in fact carefully integrated with Andrew's own thoughts. Therefore, one assumes, it was not only translated from the vernacular but probably also reworked. The pair's statements, moreover, stand as a summary of Patarene doctrine as interpreted by Andrew. The author paints a picture of laxness, sexual licence, and simony with a few black and white strokes. Ariald adds the greys of deeper moral principles.[355] Andrew is the disciple, Ariald the teacher. Andrew condemns the entire clergy; none, he suggests, was "truly" ordained.[356] What disturbs him most is their wayward life-style: they have betrayed not only a spiritual but a public trust; that is, they bought and sold offices on the open market and paraded their women in the streets.[357] Ariald, by contrast, has come to restore public confidence: as Sirus puts it, *ad predicandum publice*.[358] He is thereby conceived by Andrew as a viaticum from learned to popular, from interpreter to pupil, from literate to nonliterate.

But is he? The sermon itself presents a more nuanced picture. Ariald's starting point is a series of New Testament contrasts: ignorance and knowledge, blindness and sight, the body and the mind, and, finally, darkness and light. Familiar opposites: they are phrased and rephrased in an unsophisticated fashion, Ariald leading his listeners into his sermon gently, as if he were feeling his way through the texts for the first time.

What do the Milanese "know"? That humanity was "blind" before Christ, not, however, through their eyes but through their hearts and minds.[359] This "blindness" was an inability to distinguish between the physical and the spiritual, the inanimate and the divine. The various images then coalesce into a little allegory. The highest and eternal Light, Ariald states, through which all things were created

---

[355] Ariald's actual statement on reform is framed by two denunciations of the Milanese clergy, one by Andrew, p. 1051, 16-25, the other in the latter half of his sermon, p. 1052, 17-46.

[356] *Ibid.*, 1051, 17. On the connection between "truth" and ordination, see Miccoli, "Per la storia della Pataria . . . ," 106n22.

[357] *Vita*, c. 4, p. 1051, 19-20: "Cuncti fere aut cum publicis uxoribus sive scortis suam ignominiose ducebant vitam; p. 1052, 37-38: En ipsi, ut cernitis, sicut laici palam uxores ducunt. . . ."

[358] *Ibid.*, c. 26, p. 1073, 24. Cf. Bonizo of Sutri, *Liber ad Amicum* 6, pp. 591, 596, who emphasizes that Ariald preached *in populo*.

[359] *Ibid.*, 1051, 28-32.

TEXTUAL COMMUNITIES

and exist,[360] so suffered at mankind's blindness and misery that it sent
not an angel but descended itself from on high, assumed the flesh,
and, in order to expel darkness from man's heart, freely suffered death
on the cross. From this metaphorical descent derive the two key elements in the sermon's subsequent development, the relation between
the lettered and the unlettered and the imitation of the divine by
earthly priests. First, the birth of Christ becomes an allegory of the
birth of interpretation. Light, which is the Word, descended itself.
Then, Ariald adds:

"In the days of his flesh he elected as many men from the world as
he foresaw to be necessary for universal illumination before the end of
the world. Having driven all the shadows of falsehood from their
hearts, he illuminated them with eternal light and sent them throughout the world; and he ordered the light which they had received to
shine forth everywhere and to return to the Father from whom it had
come. This lofty, eternal, and living light left two means on earth
through which all who are to be enlightened should be brought to its
radiance and through which they should remain bright up to the end
of the world. . . . Do you wish to know what they were? The word
of God (*verbum Dei*) and the life of teachers (*doctorum vita*). . . . The
same Lord placed one of these before them, the other before you. But
they to whom he gave the understanding of Scripture and elected to
his ministry in order that they might live eternally for the light of
his translucent word were constituted and ordained so that their way
of life might be a text (*lectio*) read to you who are ignorant of letters."[361]

For Ariald, then, the Patarenes are contrasted to the archbishop's
clergy as a beneficial, even a prophetic sect to a fallen church. The
genuine priesthood is an elect, whose activity of interpretation reiterates the platonized descent of the Word itself through Christ. The

[360] *Ibid.*, 1051, 34-35: "Cuius cecitati et miseriae in tantum summa lux et eterna compassa
est, per quam omnia facta sunt et in qua universa consistunt. . . ."
[361] *Ibid.*, 1052, 1-9, 14-17: "Qui in diebus carnis suae homines tot de mundo elegit, quot
sufficere ad universitatis illuminationem ante secula posse previdit. Quos omnibus falsitatis
tenebris ab eorum cordibus expulsis eterna luce illuminavit eosque per mundum universum misit
et lucem, quam acceperant, ubique deferre precepit, sicque ad patrem, a quo venerat, rediit.
Haec quippe summa et eterna vivaque lux duas in terra causas reliquit, in quibus omnes, qui
erant illuminandi, illuminarentur et usque in finem seculi semper permanerent lucidi. . . .
Vultis nosse, hae res quae fuerunt? Verbum scilicet Dei et doctorum vita. . . . Ex his itaque
unam idem Dominus posuit ante illos, aliam ante vos. Hii vero, quibus scientiam scripturae
dedit sibique ad ministrandum elegit, ut ad lumen verbi sui lucidi semper viverent, constituit
et ut eorum vita esset vestra lectio, qui litteras nescitis, ordinavit."

elect receive his charisma and deliver his message. The word is "the precept illuminating my eyes";[362] the teachers should be "the light of the world."[363]

But the Milanese clergy is far from such an ideal. As there is one wellspring of illumination, so there is one *inimicus humani generis*.[364] If the chosen priests lose their light, mankind falls back into darkness.[365] In order that the enemy delude the unlettered, he takes on a "similitude of holiness."[366] In the latter half of the sermon Ariald turns the images around one by one, painting a picture of clerical ignorance and blindness. The silence before the coming of the Word is even linked to the present educational state of the clergy: ". . . for, just as those who were deceived by stones and bits of wood thought them gods, so you think your priests true when it is clear they are wholly false."[367]

But, in order to attain salvation, the common people must first be considered illiterates. This somewhat startling conclusion emerges naturally from both Ariald's statements and Arnulf's and Landulf's comments on them. The two chroniclers accused the young preacher of disturbing a customary state of affairs, one in which relations between lay and clerical life-styles were harmonious and in which communication between the clergy and the laity paralleled other familial and civic institutions. Ariald by contrast promises change. His vehicle is not only a reform which he considers to be based on a literal return to first principles. It also involves a separation between the elect, whose task it is to interpret God's word, and, by implication, a non-elect, who are "ignorant of letters." It thereby transforms the distinction between lay and clerical into literate and illiterate. As a consequence, what had up to now been primarily an institutional difference, in which laymen and clerics belonged to "orders," has as well become cultural. A paradoxical choice is therefore placed before the laity. It can participate in a renewed church, but only by accepting a strict division of labour between interpreter and audience. Laymen thus become part of a new learned culture by being reduced to a popular level within it. And this, as Ariald's critics pointed out, is sectarianism.

A similar conclusion results if we examine Ariald's idea of knowledge. The sermon, as noted, begins with a distinction between two states of human understanding, which turn out to be enlightenment

---

[362] Ps 18:9.   [363] Mt 5:14.   [364] *Vita*, c. 4, p. 1052, 17, 19.
[365] *Ibid.*, 18-19.   [366] *Ibid.*, 20-21.   [367] *Ibid.*, 25-27.

and ignorance. Enlightening knowledge is of two types: one is the *liberalium (et) divinarum litterarum . . . scientia* which Ariald acquired in the schools; the other is illumination, which passes from the word incarnate to the chosen few and via *ministri* to the laity.[368] From the outset, therefore, the latter are both lower on the scale of literacy and, perhaps by implication, of divine understanding. The sermon's paired metaphors and their stark images underline these uncompromising positions. Further, as the sermon proceeds, Ariald refines his conception of enlightening knowledge until finally it comes to mean the understanding of inner truth. For example, he speaks of the Milanese clergy as wolves, not *veri pastores*, whose perversity must be uncovered (*detegenda*),[369] just as true meaning is sought beneath a text's allegorical appearances. Again, Ariald's wisdom, like Gerard of Monforte's, derives directly from God, the *lux eterna*, "through whom everything was made and in whom everything exists."[370] No intermediary (*angelus*) is placed between the word and its interpreter.[371] Christ's ministers, spread throughout the globe,[372] are empowered to relieve the *falsitatis tenebrae*, to defeat the enemy lurking beneath the *sanctitatis similitudo*. Like Eriugena, with whose writings he may well have been acquainted, Ariald sees knowledge arising from God, descending (*descendit*) through Christ to man and returning (*rediit*) to the source whence it came.[373] Its appearance on earth is described in mystical terms reminiscent of a theophany: in the *doctorum vita*, "which ought to be light itself, this very truth (*veritas*) manifests itself openly in its own words."[374] The circularity of the word thus intersects the linear course of human history in the sacred text.

However, if divided by the written word, men are nonetheless reunited through the byproducts of understanding, which relate man's

[368] Cf. Miccoli, "Per la storia della Pataria . . . ," 111-13 and 113n33.

[369] *Vita*, c. 4, p. 1051, 26.

[370] *Ibid.*, 1051, 34-35. Cf. Landulf Senior, *Historia* 2.27, p. 66, quoted above p. 144n260.

[371] *Vita*, c. 4, p. 1051, 35-36; Cf. Landulf, *loc.cit.*: Praeter nostrum pontificem non est alius pontifex. . . .

[372] *Vita*, c. 4, p. 1052, quoted above p. 219n. Cf. Landulf, *loc.cit.*: "Pontificem habemus non illum Romanum, sed alium, qui cottidie per orbem terrarum fratres nostros visitat dispersos."

[373] *Vita*, c. 4, p. 1051, 37 and 1052, 5. On the possible use of Eriugena by the Monforte heretics, see H. Taviani, "Naissance d'une hérésie . . . ," 1232ff., and my doubts, above, p. 144n258. The same objections do not apply to the use of the ninth-century philosopher by Ariald, who was well educated.

[374] *Vita*, c. 4, p. 1052, 11-12: "De vita vero doctorum, quod esse debeat lux, in verbis suis ipsa per se veritas aperte manifestat."

intentions to the *imitatio Christi*. Although trained in the schools, Ariald nowhere refers to the accumulation of facts. For him, useful knowledge is a force influencing the minds and hearts of men. Before Christ, men were blind, *non oculis corporis sed cordis*.[375] God accordingly sent Christ to dispel the darkness *ab cordibus hominum*.[376] His *ministri* were chosen "after all the shadows of falsehood were expelled from their hearts."[377] The laity must follow them;[378] but the reform movement consists not of theory but of individuals re-enacting the life of Christ under their guidance. They must be pure not only *in exteriori habitu*,[379] as the Milanese clergy presumably are not, but also in inner contrition.[380] His thoughts can be summed up in the notion of *veritas*, which is repeated at key points.[381] Andrew, as noted, complained that scarcely any of the regular clergy could be found *in suo loco veraciter*.[382] Ariald said that he "truly believed" the populace knew all men were blind until the word's coming: "what was false they believed true."[383] Through Christ, "truth is openly manifested."[384] The people, he argues, must combat the devil, "who took holiness's truth from them."[385] And he concludes with the admonition, "Return and take up truth and learn to repel falsehood."[386] As the word returns to God, the people must find their way back to a reformed piety.

Ariald's sermon, of course, was calculated to appeal to laymen dissatisfied with the clergy's moral state. But, as noted, it also set the lay community apart from the priesthood, both in *ordo* and *officium*. Miccoli notes that the speech was full of good sense. It invited men and women to think about the sacraments' meaning.[387] It also emphasized moral as opposed to theological concerns. Landulf Cotta complimented the speaker. But an even more eloquent testimony came from Nazario, whose way of life, Andrew notes, "was praiseworthy in all things, even though he was married."[388] If Ariald placed laymen

[375] *Ibid.*, 1051, 32. [376] *Ibid.*, 37. [377] *Ibid.*, 1052, 2-3.

[378] *Ibid.*, 29-30: " 'Qui mihi ministrat, me sequatur' (Jn 12.26). Quod est aperte dicere: nemine quippe mihi ministratur, nisi ab eo, qui me sequitur." Cf. Spinelli, "Il sacerdozio ministeriale," 97-99.

[379] *Vita*, c. 4, 1052, 20.

[380] *Ibid.*, 40-41: "Christus autem in suis econtra ministris tantam munditiam querit et exoptat, ut non solum in opere, verum etiam stupri scelus damnet in corde. . . ."

[381] Cf. G. Cracco, "Pataria: *opus* e *nomen*," 363-69.

[382] *Vita*, c. 4, p. 1051, 17. [383] *Ibid.*, 31, 33. [384] *Ibid.*, 1052, 12.

[385] *Ibid.*, 20. [386] *Ibid.*, 43.

[387] Miccoli, "Per la storia della Pataria . . . ," 113.

[388] *Vita*, c. 6, p. 1053, 14.

in a lower category of participation in divine mysteries,[389] Nazario expanded the characterization, drawing attention nonetheless to the specific needs and expectations of his own class.[390] In his view, what Ariald said was both "true and useful"; it both revalidated the sacraments and placed them in a suitable moral framework. But he added: true and useful not only for the wise (*sapientes*) but also the foolish (*vecordes*), that is, by analogy, to those who had understanding and those who did not.[391] Nazario then reiterated Ariald's statement in his own words. For who, he asked, is so ignorant (*insipiens*) that he cannot clearly understand that those whom I personally call to my residence for blessings ought to be different from me and higher on the scale of perfection? But, at present, that is not the case. The regular clergy is not purer (*mundior*) but less clean (*sordidior*).[392]

Ariald's acceptance of Nazario's offer of hospitality not only reiterated New Testament events in Andrew's eyes but also symbolically united laymen and clerics in a programme of reform. As Landulf Cotta observed, lay people were eager to become their followers.[393] Yet, as it grew, the movement remained structured between an upper, literate, priestly caste and a great many ordinary believers.[394] Encouraged by popular support, Ariald and Landulf began to preach more and more openly. Andrew records a second major sermon which Ariald delivered around 1057. Its chief themes, simony and nicolaitism,[395] are the same as in the first. But he develops somewhat further his notion of "order" and adds observations on the uses of literacy.

His bare thoughts may be summarized as follows:[396] "Let us give thanks to God," he says, "for the idea of reforming the clergy, which both you and He desire, and which, therefore, we carry out not by volition but necessity. For it is not only married priests whom we

[389] *Ibid.*, p. 1052, 37.

[390] Cf. R. S. Lopez, "An Aristocracy of Money in the Early Middle Ages," *Speculum* 28 (1953), 41-42.

[391] *Vita*, c. 6, p. 1053, 15-16.

[392] *Ibid.*, 16-21.

[393] *Ibid.*, c. 5, p. 1053, 6-11: "Nunc vero, domne Arialde karissime, quia Dei donum te dedit mihi, scito me ab ipso collatum tibi. . . . Populus namque iam fidelis haec audiens in Dei laudem crescens illarescit."

[394] *Ibid.*, c. 6, p. 1053, 36-37.

[395] Violante, "I laici . . . ," 176-78, argues that "preaching against simony began at a later date," which appears logical. But the evidence is contradictory. The two sermons recorded by Andrew from 1057 deal with both offences. Arnulf speaks only of simony (*Gesta* 3.11, p. 19), while Landulf of course emphasizes clerical marriage.

[396] *Vita*, c. 10, pp. 1055-57; outstandingly analysed by Miccoli "Per la storia della Pataria . . . ," 117ff.

223

oppose. Who would care if heretics took wives? A far greater sin is
committed by those who buy and sell holy offices, as is well illustrated
by the story of Simon Magus.[397] Peter forgave those who wronged
him 'seventy-fold,' but he took pains to condemn Simon. For he sinned
not only against man but also against God. The gospels explicitly
state that one must not traffic in God's gifts: 'Freely you received;
freely give.'[398] Moreover, simony is not only an exterior fault; it strikes
at the heart of the inner purity with which we must approach all the
sacraments, as Ambrose and Gregory bear witness. Gregory indicates
that there ought traditionally to be three orders continually combat-
ting simony. A heavy burden in particular falls upon preachers, for
they must enlighten the uninstructed. Unless they do, others will.
And their words must cut like swords, dividing the faithful from the
unfaithful."

The important element in the sermon occurs in the final section.
Having spoken at length on the notions of *donum Dei, scire*, and *necessitas*, which reiterate ideas from his first sermon, Ariald then turns to
the obligations of each class of Christians within a reformed church.
His words are as follows:[399]

"The passage of Gregory's sermon in which it is set down how each
person should strive to combat simony with respect to his own station
is perhaps unclear; therefore, it is only fitting that a lucid explanation
be provided for your benefit. In fact, the holy church has three orders,
one of preachers, a second of continents, and a third of those who are
married. The first ought to be roused against simony through tireless

---

[397] Actus 8:18ff.   [398] Mt 10:8.

[399] *Vita*, c. 10, p. 1056, 25-42: "Quoniam locus ille in hoc beati Gregorii sermone, ubi
precipitur unicuique pro sui officii consideratione contra symoniacam ardere debere, non omnibus forsitan plene patet, vobis lucide nos explanare condecet. Tres quippe ordines in sancta
ecclesia habentur, unus predicatorum, alter continentium, tertius coniugatorum. Primus namque
debet contra hanc ardere indeffessa exortatione, continentes autem assidua oratione, vos vero,
qui coniugati estis et de vestrarum labore manuum vivitis, ut Deus omnipotens hanc ab ecclesia
sancta repellat et disperdat, cotidie ardenterque operibus elemosinarum instare debetis. Quisquis
igitur nunc ex his tribus ordinibus contra symoniacam cum his iustitiae operibus ardenter minime pugnaverit, iuxta dicta Spiritus sancti, qui haec dixit per os beati Gregorii, penam, quam
Simon magus nunc habet, . . . nullo modo credat. Si enim hii, quibus est scientia officiumque
predicandi commissum, qualibet ex causa tacuerint, non solum continentes, quorum predicatio
tanto esse debet liberior et veracior, quanto constat, quia sunt ab omni re seculari expedit et
sacrae legis meditatione assidua edocti, verum etiam vos, qui estis idiotae ignarique scripturae,
communibus verbis, quibus valetis, invicem vos cautos ab hac nequitia reddere debetis. Unde
Dominus dixit: 'Si homines tacuerint, parietes loquentur.' Nonne de hac re dicit propheta:
'Maledictus, qui prohibet gladium suum a sanguine'? hoc est ab interfectione huius nequissimae
beluae."

exhortation and the second through incessant prayer: but you, who are married and who live from the labour of your hands, ought to pursue the same end daily, eagerly, through works of alms-giving, so that omnipotent God may repel this (heresy) and drive it out of the church.

"On that account, if any of these three orders refuses to fight ardently with the works of justice which are in accord with the sayings of the holy spirit put into the mouth of Gregory, he does not believe that Simon Magus now suffers punishment. For, if they, to whom the knowledge and office of preaching have been committed, remain silent, no matter what the reason, not only the continent, whose preaching ought to be freer and truer to the degree that they are released from worldly cares and instructed through ceaseless meditation on sacred law, but even you, who are illiterate and ignorant of Scripture, ought to give each other protection from this iniquity, as much as you can, through each others' words. Whence the Lord says, 'If men are silent, the walls will speak.'[400] Does the prophet not add, 'Cursed be the one who keeps blood from his sword,'[401] that is, from the slaughter of this most wicked monster?"

The implications of this text are far-reaching. Ariald states that there are three *ordines*, which he calls *predicatores, continentes*, and *coniugati*.[402] Each order has a specific *officium* on the scale of communication between man and God, namely preaching, praying, and alms-giving. But, in interrelating order and function, Ariald broadens the standard schema of the *ordines*, that is, of monks, clerics, and laymen, into a more general description of ways of life in which personal merit and individual moral commitment play a large role.[403] He emphasizes the active side of each office: *indefessa exhortatio, assidua oratio*, and *opera elemosinarum*. Even the continent are involved: as they are more otherworldly, so their preaching ought to be *liberior et veracior*. And, if those who possess the *scientia officiumque predicandi* remain silent, others must speak out.

Are these laymen? The role is called for, even if it is not fulfilled. Ariald justifies his position as a member of the prophetic elect, but,

---

[400] Cf. Lk 19.40.

[401] Jr 48.10.

[402] The distinction first arises in Gregory the Great, *Homiliarum in Ezechielem Prophetam*, 2, hom. 4, c. 5, PL 76.976A-B. For brief discussions, see H. de Lubac, *Exégèse médiévale*, vol. 2 (Paris, 1959), 571-72 and Y. Congar, "Les laïcs et l'ecclésiologie des 'ordines' chez les théologiens des XIe et XIIe siècles," *I laici nella 'societas christiana' dei secoli XI e XII*, 97-98.

[403] Miccoli, "Per la storia della pataria," 128, 137.

more than in his first sermon, attempts to build a bridge between preacher and layman. He retains the traditional distinction between those who work with their hands and those who work with their minds. But he unites all the *fideles* in one *opus*.[404] This moral obligation is underpinned by legalisms: Gregory's words were decreed (*precipitur*); as a reflection of the holy spirit they are *iustitiae opera*, and so forth. And the legalism is linked to reform through images of active combat, even warfare. All orders are to fight (*pugnare*); the laymen give alms to repel (*repellere*) and to destroy (*dispergere*) simony. In his quotation from Jeremiah, Ariald may even parallel the vocabulary of more famous statements by Gregory VII.[405] But these motifs are also woven into a pattern of communication from high to low. The *primus ordo* is the preachers; the *ignotae ignarique scripturae* receive the message from above; or, if the preachers do not fulfill their proper function, they are enjoined to discuss sacred matters with each other in ordinary language. In order for the Pataria to exist as a religious movement, in Andrew's eyes, both sides are clearly necessary. Through the *coniugati*'s active participation, therefore, lay spirituality is effectively transformed into a vehicle of religious and social change.

At this point it may be useful to reflect briefly on Ariald's intellectual techniques. What strikes one about all the descriptions of his activities is the new uses to which he puts oral discourse. Of course, he widely utilized biblical and patristic texts and generally outshone his opponents in erudition. Examples include his contribution to the debate between the Patarini and the Nicolaiti in Landulf Senior, as well as the sermon he preached against the observance of a three-day fast before the Easter litanies.[406] But, on most occasions, it was his words rather than his thoughts which tipped the scales in his favour. Andrew, who was close to events, dates his influence *ab exordio suae praedicationis*.[407] Sirus similarly speaks of the irresistible *verba veri famuli Christi*.[408] In a brief *résumé* of his preaching style, Andrew states that he personally never heard a more powerful speaker: more saints' names dropped from Ariald's lips in a day than he ever read in learned tomes. Whenever he had to engage in a public debate, moreover,

[404] Cf. c.7, 1. For the use of *fideles* by Alexander II, see Violante, *La pataria milanese*, 149 and "I laici . . . ," 174. On the Gregorian usage, see P. Zerbi, "Il termine 'fidelitas' nelle lettere di Gregorio VII," *Studi gregoriani* 3 (1948), 129-48.

[405] See A. Stickler, "Il 'gladius' nel registro di Gregorio VII," *Studi gregoriani* 3(1948), 94 and 94n14.

[406] *Vita*, c. 17, 1061-62.　　[407] *Ibid.*, c. 13, p. 1058, 30.　　[408] *Ibid.*, c. 26, p. 1074, 22.

Ariald took care to discuss matters beforehand with his other brethren.[409] The three qualities which come to light in this succinct portrait—oratorical skill, a prodigious memory, and intellectual comradeship—are all related to oral discourse, and, perhaps not accidentally, recall the alleged virtuosity of the heretics at Orléans, Arras, and Monforte.

Andrew adds one further instructive detail. So humble was Ariald in the deployment of his vast learning that "he put no greater store in his knowledge than if he had not known a single letter."[410] The statement, although exaggerated, unites preaching with poverty[411] and humility, suggesting between the lines that Ariald, as a country priest, avoided the pride traditionally associated with city erudition. A story with just such a meaning is told by Sirus and echoed by Landulf Senior.[412]

Sirus reports that when Ariald first addressed an "ordinary group of clerics" at Varese in 1056 his listeners taunted him with the following words: "You speak to us in this manner because you know we are uninstructed. If you wish your teaching to inspire true confidence, go and make the same statements in the city."[413] Ariald subsequently came to Milan: thus, symbolically, the countryside invaded the town; the simple, pure of heart overcame the sophisticated and hypocritical. But, at the same time, a new form of interpretation based on "direct" illumination replaced the accretions of customary theory and practice. A single, unavoidable truth was said to take the place of the "divided spirit."[414] The picture, moreover, is corroborated by other incidents in the *Vita*. Andrew, for instance, recalls a number of dramatic gestures in which the saint imitated the language and behaviour of Christ.[415] There were memorable personal attacks on simoniacs, as when he dispossessed a certain Lanfranc of his income at St. Celsus with the words, *Heri clericus, hodie abbas* (yesterday only a cleric, today an abbot)![416] Yet the Pataria was held together by a combination of legalo-moralistic doctrine and the spreading of the word among its members.

[409] *Ibid.*, c. 18, p. 1062, 31-40.   [410] *Idem.*
[411] Cf. Miccoli, "Per la storia della pataria," 134-37.
[412] *Historia* 3.6, pp. 77-78.
[413] *Vita*, c. 26, p. 1073, 26-29.
[414] *Ibid.*, c. 10, p. 1057, 16; Jm 1:8.
[415] Perhaps the most dramatic of these took place when Ariald was gravely wounded and taken to the church of Rozone. His followers, led by Erlembald, wanted a vendetta, but he held them back, recalling that they should "love their enemies"; c. 20, p. 1065. For other examples of Ariald's conscious imitation of the life of Christ, see Violante, "I laici," 219-30.
[416] *Ibid.*, c. 16, p. 1060.

Andrew speaks of the common people being activated by hearing a ceaseless repetition of basic principles.[417] And when he looked back on a decade of successful reform in the diocese of Milan, he spoke of "so many benefits in both words and deeds."[418]

The same uniting of learned and popular influences that one sees at work in Ariald's sermons crystallized at an institutional level. At the learned end of the spectrum there were two results, the setting up of the *vita communis* in a church appropriately named the Canonica and the winning of implicit papal approval under Hildebrand and Alexander II for the *nova militia* of Erlembald. At the popular end, Ariald gradually raised the level of awareness of the less instructed on matters of reform. He also insisted on a literal identification between the *vita* and *passio* of Christ. He and his followers mobilized support among the poorer masses by regularly visiting the churches of the different Milanese saints for devotions.

The rise of the *fideles* as a cohesive movement went hand in hand with the growing attempts of the Patarenes to dissociate themselves from simoniacs and to expel them from the body of the church. The first stage of the *vita communis* was in fact enacted under the roof of Nazario. This was also the most primitive form of institutionalization of the bridge between the hierarchy and the laity which was a characteristic feature of the mature Pataria. After Ariald's first trip to Rome in the autumn of 1057, the struggle against the married clergy was subordinated to efforts to combat the more serious "heresy" of simony. Popular awareness of the issues was raised; expectations were created. In a sense, Ariald's *necessitas* had already come to mean *ius gladii*.[419] The absoluteness of Peter's condemnation of Simon Magus gave him evangelical authority to take an uncompromising stand. Even those not directly implicated in the buying and selling of offices were now required to fight actively against *simoniaca haeresis*.

The previously adumbrated ideas of canonical authority, personal moral obligation, and election through purification come together in chapter eleven immediately following Ariald's second sermon. Ariald, Andrew reports, "divided" the *fideles* from the *infideles* "by the sword" of which Christ spoke when he said, "I have come not to bring peace but a sword."[420] As a consequence of his preaching, every class of

---

[417] *Ibid.*, 1053, 36-37.   [418] *Ibid.*, c. 12, p. 1058, 8.

[419] Miccoli, "Per la storia," 118; cf. Anselm of Lucca, *Collectio Canonum* 13.4, quoted from MSS by Miccoli, 118: "Quod militantes etiam possunt esse iusti et hostem deprimere necessitas non voluntas debet." Cf. Violante, "I laici" 203-04n210.

[420] Pp. 1056-1057, 2; Mt 10.34.

Milanese society was in theory at least required to make a choice. Guido da Velate, the majority of clerics and knights, and many of the *populo minuto* saw the reformer as their mortal enemy. "For what is our way of life (*vita*)," they asked, "if not church benefices, which we continually buy and sell?" Naturally, they pledged to die fighting against the *nova doctrina*.[421] For serious Christians of various backgrounds the choice was more difficult. Their priests might be simoniacs, but they did not wish to be deprived of the sacraments.[422] Ariald was just as inflexible with them, demanding that they "segregate themselves completely from the company of false priests."[423] There could be no compromise: all simoniacs were "unclean."[424]

The ramifications were felt at all levels. Men and women, Andrew notes, were incited to condemn the activities of simoniacal priests and even to avoid praying with them in the same oratory. The argument grew so heated that the city was literally divided into *fideles* and *infideles*. "No wonder, since one house might be faithful, another unfaithful. In still another, the mother might be a believer (*credula*) along with one son, the father an unbeliever (*incredula*) along with another."[425] Priests, as well, left the archbishop's service and joined Ariald's ranks.[426] But the culmination of his reform efforts was the setting up of a community of priests, laymen, and women living under one roof and a common rule, a move which coincided with the creation of houses of canons elsewhere in northwest Italy.[427] As to their *Rule*, Andrew provides a number of details. The cloister, which Ariald apparently paid for from family resources, was built next to a church later called the Canonica. A wall ran around the choir, separating the clerical and lay sections, which communicated through a

[421] *Ibid.*, 1057 4-8.

[422] *Ibid.*, 11-13: "Nos autem, quia christiani dicimur, absque Christi sacramento vivere nullatenus valemus. Quod si ab istis sumpserimus, potius dicitis nos sumere damnationem quam salutem."

[423] *Ibid.*, 17-21: "Ideoque qui veritatem cupit veraciter invenire, constanter omnem debet falsitatem respuere. Quapropter ut veritate, quae Deus est, perfrui perfecte valeatis, per ipsum vos obsecro, ut a falsorum consortio sacerdotum penitus vos segregetis, quoniam luci cum tenebris, fidelibus cum infidelibus, Christo cum Belial nulla esse debet conventio aut pars sive societas."

[424] *Ibid.*, 21-22: "Sic enim scriptum est: 'Exite de medio eorum et separamini et inmundum ne tetigeritis, et ego recipiam vos, dicit Dominus' " (2 Cor 6:17-18).

[425] *Ibid.*, 26-32.

[426] *Ibid.*, c. 11, p. 1057, 34-35.

[427] C. Violante and C. D. Fonsèga, "Introduzione allo studio della vita canonicale del medioevo," in *La vita comune del clero*, vol. 1, 502-03. On the foundation, see Miccoli, "Per la storia," 136-37 and Violante, "I laici," 156-60 and notes.

small door.[428] The brethren were required to live together under a single roof and to take meals in common. Secular tales and idle conversation were not permitted; instead, each day a different person offered *sancta lectio*. Andrew adds that the recitation of the seven hours was particularly important. Despite the image conveyed to the outside world, moreover, the chapter appears to have enjoyed inner tranquillity. Ariald, Andrew states, was very happy to have found a place where the reformers could "live in common." The *fideles* were equally content to be "where they could hear the Lord's words with a free mind."[429]

The college of canons established by Ariald attracted men and women not only from the city itself but also from nearby villages and *castelli*. The Canonica was filled to overflowing.[430] But the *aptus locus*, as Andrew called it, institutionalized the firm separation of clerics and laymen. This barrier, in turn, was the precondition of understanding between the *litterati* and the *illitterati*, not only through preaching, but, less obviously, through the daily ritual of the reformers' lives. In numerous ways the Patarini distinguished themselves from the regular clergy and by implication from the laymen who fulfilled priests' functions. They led lives of absolute poverty and renunciation. Ariald combined the hermit and the canon: he had a church built in St. Ambrose's honour at Nemus where he "fled the people's tumult" and carried on vigils and meditations; yet, he insisted on the communal life for all his followers, never dining without the company of *pauperes clerici* or leaving the cloister without his companions.[431] The poorer masses came into contact with the Patarenes' discipline through the *cura animarum*, which supplemented the possibly inadequate pastoral care of the archiepiscopal clergy.[432]

Communication of a nonverbal kind also took place through ritual, an aspect of Patarene activity to which Andrew turns in chapter eighteen. The subject is the manner in which the man of God expressed his devotion to the saints, which is conceived as another facet of his struggle on behalf of the *vita apostolica*. He not only knew their lives well; he also combined pious remembrance with archaeological research, thereby authenticating the cults while reviving liturgical prac-

---

[428] On this feature of canonical architecture, see J. Hubert, "La vie commune de clercs et l'archéologie," *La vita comune del clero*, I, 106-10.

[429] *Vita*, c. 12, p. 1058; cf. E. Cattaneo, "La participazione dei laici alla liturgia," *I laici nella "societas christiana*," 399-400.

[430] *Ibid.*, 24-26.   [431] *Ibid.*, c. 17, p. 1061, 9-14.   [432] *Ibid.*, c. 12, p. 1058, 20-24.

tices.[433] Andrew has left us a brief but vivid picture of his local pil-grimages:[434] "Daily, surrounded by his shield of brethren, he went round to the various saints' resting-places, arranging in each a small, tearful service on their behalf. We would leave the house singly and separately, so as to avoid the people milling about. Once past the crowd, we followed his lead and chanted psalms until reaching the doorstep of the chosen shrine. Then, from memory, Ariald would recite chants and hymns devoted to the saint in question. He always sang in a slow, sweet voice, which we were able to follow word by word. In this atmosphere of sacred music we approached the altar, where, if it was not a holy day, he knelt, opened his arms, raised his eyes, and, thus representing the cross, prayed for the pope, for peace, for the church's salvation, and for his enemies' conversion. We too prostrated ourselves and repeated what he said. We all prayed silently for a while, after which he said, 'Lord our God, give us the angel of peace and grace.'[435] We then departed from the church reciting the same psalm with which we had entered, and passed on to another."

In the minds of the unlettered these rituals made much sense. They were public in character: the Patarenes marched through the streets, patently united in spirit. Also, they provided visible and tangible links with physical relics whose influence on the popular imagination was more powerful than theological arguments. And they offered an outlet for sympathetic emotion, binding the sufferings of past martyrs to those of the present.[436] Even, therefore, to the uninstructed, Ariald appeared to be in apostolic succession from the early Christian saints whose hagiography was so intimate a part of Milan's civic ethos.

Conclusion: Preachers, Heretics, and Reformers

The reader has had to work his way through lengthy discussions of the three major accounts of the early Pataria. He is therefore entitled to ask what relation they have to the issues raised in the first part of the chapter and in particular to the problem of textual communities.

At a general level, many preachers, heretics, and reformers in the later eleventh and early twelfth centuries voiced concerns similar to those of the Patarenes.

[433] *Ibid.*, c. 18, 38-41.
[434] Summarizing c. 18, p. 1062, 40-1063, 14.   [435] Cf. Is 33:7.
[436] Cf. Sirus, *Vita*, c. 26, p. 1073, 30-31: "Nam in ipso exordio suae predicationis tam diu cum aliquantis fidelibus per venerabilia loca sanctorum, flagitans suffragia, nudis incessit pedibus. . . ." Cf. Violante, "I laici," 218-19.

Gerard II of Cambrai, for instance, who visited Lambres shortly after his election in 1076, was informed of the preaching of a certain Ramihrd in the nearby village of Schere. According to the *Chronicle of St. André of Castres*, this layman had spread doctrines unacceptable to the faith and had already drawn many disciples into the orbit of his teaching. His following consisted in the main of common people of both sexes.[437] Virtually repeating the course of action of his illustrious predecessor, Gerard had Ramihrd taken to Cambrai for questioning by his abbots and "learned clerics."[438] Ramihrd stated, like former heretics, that his claim on truth was "sanctioned"; and, refusing to participate in the sacraments, he accused the bishop and his party of committing simony together with "other forms of avarice."[439] The tone inevitably mounted: the bishop pronounced him the founder of a heterodox sect; and, when the meeting was adjourned, his cohorts placed Ramihrd while he prayed in a small hut, which was then set on fire. His followers, mainly weavers, collected his ashes and carried on his work.[440] And Gregory VII firmly condemned the *symonaici et presbyteri fornicatores* who had among other things dared to prefer investiture of their bishop by the emperor rather than by the pope.[441]

Again, a generation later, between 1112 and 1114, Tanchelm was accused by the canons of Utrecht of spreading his "poison" throughout the coastal regions of The Netherlands near Antwerp. Preaching first in secret to small groups, and later openly and publicly, they claimed, he seduced the common people, "as if he were the angel of God." Churches, he said, were brothels, priests worthless, and the sacraments mere *pollutiones*.[442] Like Gerard of Monforte, but perhaps in a

[437] *Chronicon S. Andreae Castri Cameracensii*, 3.3, MGH SS VII, p. 546: "Ubi cum ei a narrantibus intimatum esset, hominem quendam nomine Ramihrdum, apud proximam villam quae est Scherem manentem, multa preter fidem dogmatisare, et iam sub doctrina sua multos discipulos maximamque utriusque sexus plebem sibi consentaneam adquisivisse."

[438] *Ibid.*

[439] *Ibid.*: "Cumque ad hoc confirmandum dominici sacramenti particeps fieri ab episcopo moneretur, refugit, dicens a nullo abbatum nec sacerdotum nec etiam ab ipso episcopo hoc se percepturum, quod aut symoniae aut alicuius avaritiae noxa adstricti tenerentur."

[440] *Ibid.*

[441] Gregory VII, *Registrum* IV, 20, ed. E. Caspar, MGH Epistolae Selectae (Berlin, 1920), p. 328, ll. 22-25. On Ramihrd as a reformer, see Russell, *Dissent and Reform*, 1-2, 43-44, 239-40. The involvement of heretics in early communes is reviewed by Lambert, *Medieval Heresy*, 39-43.

[442] *Epistola Trajectensis Ecclesiae ad Fridericum Episcopum Coloniensem de Tanchelmo seductore*, c. 2, AASS June I, 832C-D: "In maritimis primum locis rudi populo et infirmioris fidei, venenum perfidiae suae miscuit. . . . Necjam in tenebris vel cubiculis, sed super tecta praedicare incipiens, in patentibus campis late circumfusae multitudini sermocinabatur. . . . Audiebat illum populus seductus, sicut angelum Dei."

more egocentric manner, he evidently associated the holy spirit with a likeness of divinity in himself.[443] The canons alleged that he deceived a witless populace through coercion, carnal displays, and empty ceremonial. But their disparaging words have been variously interpreted.[444] On the one hand, reformist sentiments possibly lay just beneath the surface: Tanchelm, in fact, aided by a defrocked priest named Evaerwacher, perhaps tried to obtain for the Gregorian count Robert II of Flanders a part of the bishopric of Utrecht, which was then in imperialist hands.[445] On the other, even the exaggerations of the canons' account suggest that accepted rituals were being challenged.[446] Did Tanchelm really reject transubstantiation, or was he questioning the legitimacy of unworthy priests? Did the "marriages" and Marian imagery of his rites signify sexual libertarianism, or was he trying through symbolism to recall ordinary women from luxury and vice? And did Manasses, who formed a "fraternity" or "guild" in his honour, truly engage in a systematic deformation of the gospels, or was he, like other unlettered members of clerical sects, attempting to lead those like himself towards some form of participation in the Word?

The matter of communication in such groups remained fundamental, as it did among the Patarenes. The point is well illustrated by the sermon which Bernard of Tiron preached at Coutances sometime before 1105, defending the right of hermit monks to preach, despite the potential opposition of the local hierarchy.[447] His occasion was an archdeacon who possessed a wife and children yet was considered more worthy to convey God's word than himself. Utilizing simplified alle-

[443] *Ibid.*, c. 3, 832E: "Talibus nequitiae successibus misero homini tanta sceleris accessit audacia, ut etiam se Deum diceret, asserens, quia, si Christus adeo Deus est, quia spiritum sanctum habuisset, se non inferius nec dissimilius Deum, quia plenitudinem spiritus sancti accepisset. In qua praesumptione adeo illusit, ut quidam in eo divinitatem venerarentur. . . ."

[444] For a brief review, see Lambert, *Medieval Heresy*, 55-57, and, for a fuller discussion, Russell, *Dissent and Reform*, 56-68. The sources are fully listed by Russell, pp. 265-69.

[445] The interpretation was first suggested by H. Pirenne, "Tanchelin et le projet de démembrement du diocèse d'Utrecht vers 1100," *Académie royale de Belgique, Bulletins de la Classe des lettres et des sciences morales et politiques*, série 5, 13 (1927), 112-19. But objections have been raised; see, in particular, Russell, *Dissent and Reform*, 56-68, 267-68.

[446] Cf. W. Mohr, "Tanchelm von Antwerpen. Eine nochmalige Überprüfung der Quellenlage," *Annales Universitatis Saraviensis, philosophie-lettres* 3 (1954), 234-47. Mohr's view is supported by Lambert, *Medieval Heresy*, 57, but not wholly by Russell, *Dissent and Reform, loc.cit.*

[447] On the sermon's occasion, see G. G. Meersseman, "Eremitismo e predicazione itinerante dei secoli XI e XII," in *L'eremitismo in occidente nei secoli XI e XII* (Milan, 1965), 168-71 and E. Delaruelle, "Les ermites et la spiritualité populaire," *ibid.*, 215-17. On Bernard's *imitatio Christi*, see the enduring study of J. von Walter, *Die ersten Wanderprediger Frankreichs*, 2. *Teile* (Leipzig, 1906), 43-52; on the sermon at Coutances, pp. 53-54.

gory like Ariald and Landulf Cotta, Bernard replied by retelling the
biblical story of Samson and the ass's jaw. The dead ass, he maintained, was the *simplex populus*, the jaw in its head, the preacher,[448]
who, by "chewing up" Scripture, rendered it palatable for the common people's "digestion."[449] Like the Patarenes, Bernard moved from
the recognition of vice to the need to speak out publicly against it;
but he went beyond them in deriving the right or permission to
preach from the spiritual integrity of the individual. If, he argued,
the preacher "teaches well but lives badly," he does not "instruct"
but merely "corrupts." Therefore, just as he distinguishes the historical, allegorical, tropological, and anagogical senses, so his own spiritual development must proceed from taste through various modes of
understanding to the pursuit of eternal goals.[450] Moreover, if the
Christian people, represented by the dead ass, ought to be dead to
the world, how much more must be the preacher, the ass's jaw, who,
in Paul's words, ought to imitate the process of mortification undergone by the Lord.[451] And, just as Christ was reviled by the multitude,
so the preacher, who rejects the world, is condemned by the common
people.[452] Thus, he concluded, the licence to preach was really attained through the virtue derived from his personal commitment to
otherworldliness.[453]

The Pataria, in short, looked back to smaller lay groups at Orléans
and Arras as well as to the conflicts over the reform of monks, canons,
and bishoprics. But it also looked forward to a wide range of developments in the following century: the further struggle to apply the
ideas of Gregory VII and contemporary canonists; the increasingly
litigious rivalries between emperors and popes over investiture; the
rise of public preaching in such diversely motivated figures as Robert
of Arbrissel, Peter the Hermit, Henry of Lausanne, and Peter of Bruys;
the growing involvement of the papacy in the propagation of holy
wars and the crusading ethos among the lay nobility; the intensive
search for individual salvation through monastic and canonical expressions of the *vita communis*; the communal movement, which engulfed
the Pataria in the twelfth century and led to the downfall of Arnold

---

[448] *Vita Beati Bernardi . . . de Tironio . . . auctore Gaufrido Grosso*, c. 6.52-53, PL 172.1398B:
". . . Asinus mortuus, simplicem populum (significat). . . . Mandibula, ossium robur habens
. . . , instrumentum mordendi et mandendi in capite asini, praedicatorem designat Ecclesiae."

[449] *Ibid.*, 6.53, 1398B-C.

[450] *Ibid.*, 1398C-99A.   [451] *Ibid.*, 6.54, 1399A-B.   [452] *Ibid.*, 1399B.

[453] *Ibid.*, 1399C: "inde consequens hoc trahitur, quod per virtutem mortificationis pervenitur
ad licentiam praedicationis."

of Brescia, who was, as John of Salisbury notes, "eloquent in speech, and a vehement preacher against the vanities of this world," but also "factious and a leader of schism, who wherever he lived prevented the citizens from being at peace with the clergy;"[454] and, finally, the demagogues, millenarists, and false prophets, who, like Raoul the Monk, whipped up anti-semitic crowds in towns along the Rhine, or Eon de l'Etoile, who, William of Newburgh notes, although *illiteratus et idiota*, thought himself brought to earth to judge both the living and the dead.[455]

Despite their differences, the three major commentators on the Milanese Pataria leave no doubt that the movement stood at the crossroads of eleventh-century dissent and reform. Above all, the Pataria served as a vehicle for the concentration of issues surrounding the spread of literacy. It brought the controversies over simony, nicolaitism, and the sacraments out of the classroom and into the parish church, even into the streets; and it produced a hybrid religious movement possessing an inner core of clerics and a wider circle of ordinary believers. Both of these achievements were made possible through preaching, that is, through a method of communication ultimately dependent on texts.

Cinzio Violante has demonstrated in a series of remarkable studies that the Pataria derived much of its vigour from new and more intense forms of interaction between clerics and laymen. The beginnings were undoubtedly clerical and literate. The romantic Landulf saw the Pataria as a conspiracy originating in the family interests of Anselm of Baggio. But Arnulf and Andrew recognized the founder to be Ariald, who, from the outset, not only demanded a moral restructuring of the clergy but also invited laymen to play an active role in reform. From 1057 to 1061 Ariald was assisted by Landulf Cotta, who, as a notary of the cathedral, had strong links in higher lay as well as ecclesiastical circles. The degree of lay as opposed to clerical elements in the original movement is diversely interpreted. Sirus maintained that the *famulus Christi*'s benign admonitions were rejected by the local clergy at Varese.[456] Andrew also stated that Ariald first preached to *sacerdotes* and only later to laymen.[457] Landulf Senior tells another story: returning to the countryside after sealing his pact with Anselm, Ariald is said to have preached openly against the married clergy

---

[454] *Historia Pontificalis*, trans. M. Chibnall (London, 1956), 63.
[455] *Historia Rerum Anglicarum*, bk. 1, c. 19, ed. R. Howlett (London, 1884), p. 60.
[456] *Vita*, c. 26, p. 1073, 26.   [457] *Ibid.*, c. 4, p. 1052, 44-46.

"arousing the common people with the vile expressions of rustic-ity."[458]

Furthermore, it was both *rustici* and *sacerdotes* who went to Guido da Velate for support. Guido in turn accused both Ariald and Landulf not only of professing erroneous doctrines but of inciting the laity against the clergy. Landulf undoubtedly exaggerated. But we are ill informed on how many priests actually joined the movement. Neither Ariald nor Landulf Cotta were ordained at the outset. Peter Damian spoke of two priests, Rodulf and Vitale, among the more advanced Milanese reformers,[459] and, after Ariald's death, the recently ordained Leoprand became Erlembald's official voice. Nor, among later follow-ers, should one forget Andrew of Strumi himself or the "several cler-ics" who, on hearing Ariald preach, left the *consortium clericorum pra-vorum*.[460] One such priest renounced a church recently acquired through simony and handed it over to Ariald for the founding of his chapter.[461] Other churches eventually came into the fold.[462]

But, if clerics led the movement, laymen made up the vast majority of the membership,[463] and the Pataria could not have functioned with-out them. What was the social composition of the laity? The three commentators are agreed that the most volatile element came from below, but each perceives the lower classes' function differently. Ar-nulf thought them a rabble. Landulf recognized their potential for shaping events: under the educated Lanzo's leadership he saw in the *populi* a last refuge for the Ambrosian ideal. He was less enthusiastic about the "popular" following of Erlembald. For Andrew, in contrast, real and voluntary poverty were difficult to distinguish. Bonizo of Sutri similarly intermingled social and ethical categories. He de-scribed the Patarenes as *maxime pauperes quos elegit Deus ut confundat fortia* (especially the poor, whom God elected to confound mighty forces).[464] But this was hardly a sociological classification. A wealthy bourgeois like Nazario was "elected" by his repudiation of the estab-lished clergy and its worldliness.

Of course, there is no doubt that the real poor were represented on

[458] *Historia* 3.6, p. 77, 51.

[459] *Epistolae* 5.14, PL 144.367-69; cf. Violante, "I laici," 153-54.

[460] *Vita*, c. 11, p. 1057, 34.

[461] *Ibid.*, c. 12, p. 1058.

[462] Namely S. Trinità *"di Rozone,"* S. Ambrose *"ad nemus,"* S. Victor *"ad ulmum"* and perhaps S. Maria Secreta; *Vita*, cc. 11, 14, 17, 21.

[463] Cf. Violante, "I laici," 164-65.

[464] *Liber ad Amicum*, 6, p. 591. Cf. 1 Cor. 1:27: "Sed quae stulta mundi elegit Deus, ut confundat sapientes; et infirma mundi elegit Deus, ut confundat fortia."

both sides. Landulf is eloquent on the *pauperes* who swelled the Patarenes' ranks. But he also mentions that Guido counted for support on
a part of the nobility and many of the common people (*pars nobilium
ac de populo multi*).[465] All three narrators were conscious of the fragility
of popular loyalties. As Andrew put it: *Popularis turba cito mutatur et
in diversis partibus facile inclinatur* (A popular mob is quickly aroused
and easily shifted in different directions).[466] In other words, while
there was mass action, it was only rarely if ever socially motivated.
Instead, there were simply masses on both sides. They had no juridic
status as classes, unlike the capitanei, vavasours, and cives. But Patarene preaching, together with the archiepiscopal rebuttals, galva-
nized their self-consciousness as a group and gave them a means of
articulating common material and spiritual goals. As for those higher
up on the social scale, the appeal of the reformers seems to have varied
from person to person. True, in the countryside Ariald had a more
naturally receptive audience among the economically depressed *rustici*
and small landowners like his parents, just as, in Milan, his individualistic message had an undeniable attraction for the newly constituted "middle class."[467] But Andrew notes perceptively that his sharp
words often divided members of the same family.[468] Among the laity
there were undoubtedly differing appreciations of what Patarene teaching
actually meant and what moral obligations it entailed. Only a small
number of clerics and laymen stayed constantly with Ariald, guarding
his person, joining in vigils, and, as Sirus put it, following him "with
bare feet" on his daily pilgrimages. In ordinary believers ascetic devotion was mitigated by family loyalties, economic and political interests, or simply by fear, hatred, or the desire for revenge. Arnulf
and Landulf both suggest that laymen usurped the *officium praedicationis*. But there is little evidence that they went beyond the "discussions" recommended by Ariald. The upper levels of the laity were
chiefly useful in providing secular support for the Pataria's coercive
activity and in judging, perhaps too harshly, unrepentant members of
the regular clergy.[469]

If we turn from the social origins of the members to the organiza-

---

[465] *Historia* 3.11, p. 81, 16.

[466] *Vita*, c. 21, p. 1065, 31-32. Cf. Arnulf, *Gesta* 3.20, p. 23, 18-19: "Sed more suo populus
non diu statu permansit eodem."

[467] Cf. Violante, "I laici," 169-70, and, more generally, E. Werner, *Pauperes Christi*, 111-
64.

[468] *Vita*, c. 10, p. 1057, 30-32.

[469] Violante, "I laici," 180-202, treats these questions in detail.

tion of the movement, another set of relationships comes to light. The Patarenes effectively brought to maturity the type of religious movement we have described as a "textual community," that is, a movement based on a literate inner core, a set of written legislation, and a wider, unlettered membership united orally to the same norms. The leaders were educated: Ariald was *artis liberae magister*, Landulf a notary of the church, and Anselm of Baggio a student of canon law. Even Erlembald's intense piety reflected a possible acquaintance with monastic texts. From the outset, moreover, the movement was rife with legalisms which each of the three commentators emphasized in a different way. Arnulf records that the *maiores* of the Milanese church opposed Ariald with *sacrae scripturae* and with *sanctiones canonicae*.[470] Ariald responded by drafting his *phytacium de castitate servanda*, which cited a Justinian *novella* from the preface of the synod of Pavia of 1st August 1022 to the effect that priests, deacons, or subdeacons who married after ordination were to be stripped of their offices and reduced to *servi* in the city's curia.[471] The legally trained Arnulf recognized this to be a "revolutionary" document and accused Ariald of "usurping ecclesiastical laws."

Oaths, too, were frequent throughout the movement's history. Landulf Senior recalls a possibly fictive *iuramentum* between Ariald, Landulf Cotta, and Anselm of Baggio.[472] But similar obligations were also enjoined upon lay members: Ariald swore a *sacramentum* with Nazario;[473] Arnulf spoke of a *commune . . . omnibus laicis iuramentum*.[474] Landulf Senior described as a *placitum* the feudal oath which bound the Milanese youth to his service[475] and used the same term to speak of Erlembald's receiving the *vexillum sancti Petri*.[476] Andrew of Strumi saw legal authority primarily from within the movement. He called Ariald's followers *fideles*, a term which aptly summed up their partly

---

[470] *Gesta* 3.12, p. 19, 33-34. Ariald is mentioned in an eleventh-century canonical collection and enumeration of the diocese as a violator of church discipline (*ecclesiarum Dei violatorem Arialdum . . .*); A. Ambrosioni, "Il più antico elenco di chierici della diocesi ambrosiana ed altre aggiunte al Decretum di Burcardo in un codice della Biblioteca Ambrosiana (E 144 sup). Una voce della polemica antipatarinica?" *Aevum* 50 (1976), 301; for the milieu, see pp. 312-17.

[471] Violante, *La pataria milanese*, 184-90; cf. "I laici," 175. On the scriptural and canonical origins, see in particular O. Capitani, "Storiografia e riforma della chiesa in Italia," 578-611.

[472] *Historia* 3.5, p. 77, 15.

[473] *Vita*, c. 6, p. 1053, 28.

[474] *Gesta* 3.13, p. 20, 18. For similarities with other Italian communal movements, see G. Fasoli, "Gouvernants et gouvernés . . . ," 63-68.

[475] *Historia* 3.15, p. 84, 14.

[476] *Ibid.*, 3.29, p. 95, 2.

canonical, partly moral responsibility.[477] *Fidelitas* was the principle by which lay interference in ecclesiastical affairs was justified.[478] But "faith" was also a bridge between the unlettered and the lettered, between cleric and layman. It bound the latter not to their masters in relationships of personal service but to a set of impersonal, written principles, equally applicable to all. Its chief monument was the reformed *Rule* laid down at the Canonica. Andrew also pointed out that Ariald was juridically sophisticated in his conception of the various *ordines'* obligations. This acquaintance with earlier tradition is equally revealed in the intellectual debate through sermons recorded in book three of the *Historia*. In general legalism was a potent force: it gave the Pataria continuity and institutional shape, allowing it to develop from a "sect-like" to a "church-like" structure. Yet the movement never really freed itself from the charisma of personal leadership. After Ariald's death in 1066 it lost its spiritual direction. When Erlembald passed from the scene in 1075, it ceased to be a substantial power in Milanese ecclesiastical politics.

But, if the Pataria did not create a lasting foundation, it permanently altered the perception of social and religious realities in Milan. The transition can be seen most vividly in comparing the movement to the cives' revolt. The rebellion against Aribert was largely a by-product of internal class tensions; it was an attempt on the ordinary citizens' part to break down inherited ties and to achieve the same legally guaranteed status as the capitanei and the vavasours. The Pataria by contrast transcended class relationships and placed conflict itself in the arena of universal morality. Although it never entirely freed itself from the older social problems and was gradually engulfed by them after 1066, the decade of Ariald's public preaching in Milan greatly raised the level of awareness of moral questions and of their interdependence with other areas of life. It made public what had so long been private. It asked men of all backgrounds to abandon a life of darkness, blindness, and thoughtless routine and to carry a great deal of weight for ethical decisions on their own shoulders. Ariald armed men only with the "sword" of the Word. But that proved quite enough: as the word passed from the text via his lips to their waiting ears, it kindled for the first time the light of self-conscious reflection, not only on the specific issues of nicolaitism and simony, but, by implication, on a whole range of matters whose content had hitherto

[477] Cf. Miccoli, "Per la storia della Pataria . . . ," 122.
[478] Cf. Violante, "I laici," 203-06.

lacked an appropriate form. It was the birth not only of "reform" but also of a pragmatism which took it out of the sphere of theological abstraction and reapplied it to real life situations. Landulf Senior spoke of the *simplices et idiotae* who were roused as if they had heard Peter or Paul. He correctly perceived the crucible of the new form of communication to be the Roman theatre, the ancient seat of the communal parliament. Even Arnulf grudgingly recognized the Patarenes' power over words. Andrew saw the issue in more straightforward, religious terms. For him, new life was suddenly breathed into the gospels themselves. And perhaps, for a few brief moments, it was.

III.

THE EUCHARIST AND NATURE

The rise of heretical and reformist movements went hand in hand with a number of purely ideological issues, such as simony, clerical marriage, and the meaning of the sacraments. No less than in group organization, the growth of a more literate society played a part in the timing of the debates, as well, indirectly, as the evolution within them of parallel types of argument.

The subject of this chapter is the issue most consistently dealt with by a wide range of theologians between the ninth and the twelfth centuries, namely, the nature of the eucharist. However, our interest is not limited to the discussion of one sacrament. As often happens in the history of thought, a specific controversy gave rise to more general problems; methods developed for handling one set of questions eventually turned up in other areas of inquiry. The eucharistic debate in particular opened two broad subjects to systematic study by medieval thinkers. One was the status of symbol and ritual in a theory of religion that was increasingly preoccupied with explanation in literate terms. The other was the beginnings of reflection on observable nature, or, more precisely, on the relation of phenomenal appearances to an inner reality whose logical properties coincided with those of texts.

The eucharist, the rebirth of intellectualism, and the idea of nature are not normally looked upon as parts of the same historical canvas. The suggestion that they are related therefore demands a few words of preface.

To return to our point of departure: in the eucharistic debate, there did not arise, as was the case in early medieval law, one position obviously indebted to oral culture, the other to written. From the outset the discussion took on a predominantly theoretical character in which matters like spoken rites and even the liturgy were pushed to the background. After the initial exchange between Paschasius Radbertus and Ratramnus of Corbie, the chief question in the participants' minds was whose interpretation of patristic teaching on the subject was correct. As other voices began to be heard, and, from the tenth century, as lines of division emerged between two distinctive approaches, each side gradually assumed that it had a monopoly of truth. The "true" meaning of the eucharist became associated in turn with the most erudite response to the issues.

By implication, each group asserted that the other's ideas constituted a "popular" debasement of higher culture. While there was much rhetoric involved in the mutual accusations, a classic rift opened between an intellectualist position, which, of course, both claimed to represent, and what was as a consequence considered to be erroneous, unreflective, or simply illiterate. Our concern is not whether the shift in modes of understanding actually illuminated the structures of medieval beliefs—it is arguable, in the light of recent anthropological research, that it did not[1]—but with the transformation of attitudes which it epitomized. The result can be stated in general terms as a historically evolving distinction between modernity and tradition. The *moderni*, that is, the more recent thinkers, began not only to perceive their own common assumptions but to look upon aspects of contemporary religion as something inherited from a less lettered society. Such attitudes inevitably called into question all aspects of physical symbolism and ritual.

The problem of nature evolved out of the same debate but developed along different lines.

If a solution were to be found to the enigma of the eucharist within the intellectualist position, it had to involve logic, argument, and precedent. Yet, central to the process of deduction lay an issue which fell, strictly speaking, outside the bounds of religious thought. This was the status of observable reality in the ritually consecrated bread and wine which were said to recall the actual body and blood of Christ. From this specific question it was a short step to the idea of nature itself. Was nature what one saw before one's eyes, to which the categories of human understanding were simply subjoined? Or was reality the inner core, a formal truth for which phenomenal appearances were merely a kind of allegorical covering? The question had of course been posed and reposed in the ancient world. But, as the eucharistic debate gained momentum, it was tô patristic and even early medieval answers that thinkers most frequently returned. The critical texts were found in Augustine. As the bishop of Hippo had never

---

[1] See in general J. Skorupski, *Symbol and Theory. A Philosophical Study of Theories of Religion in Social Anthropology* (Cambridge, 1976), and S. F. Moore and B. G. Myerhoff, "Secular Ritual: Forms and Meanings," in the same editors' *Secular Ritual* (Assen, 1977), 3-24, with a bibliography, 283-93.

systematized his thoughts on the sacraments, diverse interpretations were possible. The chief issue which surfaced on both sides of the debate was the meaning of "nature" and of "reality," and the degree to which such concepts could be understood using tools derived from logical and textual research. The various solutions proposed constitute the first stages in the later medieval association of nature and texts, which scholastic philosophy developed in a profitable direction for science, literature, and theology.

Like the resolution of the eucharistic controversy, the naturalism of the later eleventh and twelfth centuries can be described as a compromise. As literate science was re-established through the trivium and the quadrivium, conceptual schemes for understanding and interpreting nature gradually took over the field. Physicalism and naive symbolism, although persisting in unofficial "sciences," were more and more rejected from the classroom and regarded as uneducated empiricism. The science of one generation thereby became the superstition of the next. But naturalism also involved a process of acculturation. As it was articulated in the first quarter of the twelfth century, it was anything but a pure science of nature. It could best be described as a new attitude of mind which cut across otherwise unrelated disciplines and united them in a common approach to the comprehension of the existing world. At bottom it had only two irreducible features. The senses were the starting point of all inquiry. But verification or, to be more precise, authentication did not take place through measurement or experimentation. It was produced by examining the inner workings of the human mind, which, in the medieval context, meant the interconnections between words, thoughts, and things. The material and the immaterial were thus brought together within the same intellectual programme but represented in fact different perspectives. The insistence on the heard, the touched, and the seen may well have echoed ancient doctrines; but, for the vast majority unacquainted with them, it also expressed in writing the normal, concrete appreciation of the phenomenal in nonliterate society. The higher categories of thought which comprised the other point of view arose from no single tradition of thought. Logic, grammar, rhetoric, and theology all had a try at unravelling the "secrets of nature." What such erudite approaches had in common was the use of texts, or of methods derived from them. And, although claiming affiliation with the *antiqui*, in medieval terms their emphasis on script made them unmistakeably modern.

1. GUIBERT AND "POPULAR" CULTURE

At the centre of the abovementioned issues—namely, the growth of religious intellectualism and of scientific naturalism—one finds a single problem, the status of a physical object having religious associations during an age of increasing literacy. Does it retain its preliterate symbolic status? Or does it now derive its meaning from being interpreted through a text?

Some remarkable insights into these questions are provided by Guibert of Nogent's *De Pignoribus Sanctorum*, which was completed by 1125.[2] The treatise was Guibert's last work, and was hailed by early historians as a synthesis of "undiluted skepticism"[3] in a unique "critical and scientific spirit,"[4] which in part it is. Yet, while discrediting false relics, Guibert also proposes a set of standards for assessing their claims. This, in turn, involves a certain ambivalence towards the oral and the written. For, while relics are accepted throughout as physical objects having symbolic content, their validity is nonetheless judged by a variety of textual proofs.

The relic in question was the tooth of Christ claimed by the monks of St. Médard of Soissons. However, more general matters appear as early as the dedicatory letter to the erudite Eudes, abbot of St. Symphorien near Beauvais. Several questions, Guibert states, were addressed to him regarding the venerable tooth. But, as some argued from popular associations (*vulgariter*), he thought it worthwhile to put his thoughts in writing (*in litteris*) and to explain (*edicere*) what he knew to be others' well-meaning intentions.[5] The remainder of book

---

[2] J. F. Benton, *Self and Society in Medieval France. The Memoirs of Abbot Guibert of Nogent* (New York, 1970), 238-39.

[3] A. Lefranc, "Le traité des reliques de Guibert de Nogent et les commencements de la critique historique au moyen âge," *Etudes d'histoire . . . dédiées à Gabriel Monod* (Paris, 1896), 289.

[4] B. Monod, *Le moine Guibert et son temps (1053-1126)* (Paris, 1905), 302. For a more moderate view, see J. Chaurand, "La conception de l'histoire de Guibert de Nogent," CCM 8 (1965), 390-91. Critical attitudes towards Guibert are briefly reviewed by Benton, *Self and Society*, 8-9. On the *De Pignoribus* in particular, see K. Guth, *Guibert von Nogent und die hochmittelalterliche Kritik an der Reliquienverehrung* (Ottobeuren, 1970), 72-103.

[5] *De Pignoribus Sanctorum, Ep. Nuncupatoria*, c. 1, PL 156.607D-08D. On Guibert's autographs, see M.-C. Garand and F. Etcheverry, "Les manuscrits originaux de Guibert de Nogent," *Codices manuscripti* 1 (1975), 112-22 and M.-C. Garand, "Le scriptorium de Guibert de Nogent," *Scriptorium* 31 (1977), 3-29. I regret I was unable to benefit from the critical text of MS B.N. lat. 2900 announced by M.-D. Mireux, "Guibert de Nogent et la critique du culte des reliques," *La piété populaire au moyen âge*, p. 301.

one transforms this statement into a confrontation between popular and learned culture. In sum, through a diversity of practices, Guibert maintains, the church nonetheless displays a unity of teaching.[6] Baptism and the eucharist are preconditions for the Christian life. But only faith is truly indispensable. Other customs, among them the cult of relics, are permissible. But they are not necessary for salvation.

How does Guibert reach these conclusions? He begins by distinguishing between practice and theory, that is, between the church's customs and its teachings (*quae ecclesiastice aut tenentur aut docentur*). In his view, the two must be kept in harmony to prevent schism. Some types of worship are carried on but not taught, such as the customs (*consuetudines*) for fasting and chanting psalms. Despite a "diversity of offices," the church attains a "similar faith." Other devotions are both maintained and taught (*quae tenentur et docentur*), chiefly the sacraments of baptism and the eucharist. In these instances, Guibert argues, there exists throughout Christendom the same teaching (*paris formae doctrinae*), since what is spoken (*oratio*) conforms to instruction's objectives (*id docentium*), as the examples of ancient martyrs and saints reveal. Similarly, one may distinguish from among the church's precepts. The Bible occasionally suggests that salvation can be achieved by both faith and works. But this is only a figurative way of speaking. Works normally lead to faith, in which theory is guided by practice and vice versa. Moreover, some practices, although useful guides in life, "are not counted," and, although preached in church, are not among the essential preconditions of salvation. Such is the cult of saints' relics.[7]

In such cases, the only criterion of validity is authenticated reason (*sola authentica ratio*). This consists of reason based on texts: it is not hearsay (*opinio*), but the firm tradition of verified ancient sources (*vetustatis aut scriptorum veracium traditio certa*). For how can an individual be considered holy if no one recalls the basis for his claim (*auctoritatis memoria*)? Such a reputation is defended neither by texts (*litterae*) nor by the clear demonstration of miracles (*aperta miraculorum experientia*). Even letters, he adds, are no absolute guarantee. For hagiography is not yet a high art. Often, saints' lives are mere recitations (*preconia*), which damage rather than uplift the faith. At other times, even when the facts are correct, the style is so lacklustre that the lives have little credibility. Such so-called lives are really just trifles (*nenia*). With such *figmenta* he contrasts the *notitiae* of the gospels. What, he asks, can be

---

[6] Cf. Anselm, *Epistola de sacramentis ecclesiae*, c. 1, ed. F. S. Schmitt, *Opera Omnia*, vol. 2 (Rome, 1940), 240, lines 10-15.

[7] *De Pignoribus*, 1.1, PL 156.612C-13D.

said on behalf of those who forsake proper witnesses, whose texts obscure the facts, and whose narratives have no beginning, middle, or end?[8]

Not only must the written version be right. The claim to holiness must also be examined. Errors are easily made: Guibert cites the case of St. Pyron, revered under different names by both the French and the Bretons. After researching the matter, he discovered that the supposed holy man ended his days by falling drunk into a well. His conclusion casts another shadow over oral tradition: it is "profane" to worship a saint whose status is supported "by the memory of no one living." If a competent religious authority has not established the birthdate, life and times, and style of death of the alleged saint, "the wind of vulgar rumour" will continually circle around his unfortunate corpse. For, lacking "testimonies," the credulous "stain him with false and sacreligious words." A prelate is the "protector of God's people" insofar as he adjudicates such matters *secundum scientiam*, that is, according to fact. Moreover, if someone skilled in the art of interpretation disproves a case, what salvation can arise from actions which "neither sight, hearing, texts, nor miracles affirm"?[9]

Guibert's ambivalence extends to external signs. He does not doubt their efficacy: he himself, or so he maintains, witnessed the magic touch of Louis VI. Men can be used as "channels" for divine forces without implying particular merit on their part. Moreover, the varied nature of such signs—double meanings, forewarnings, *prognostica*, comets, prodigies, and prophecies divine or human—provides examples in "modern" times of the continuity of God's activity. He lists them not for their "novelty," but to indicate their different causes (*pro causarum . . . diversitatis ratione*).[10] Such signs can be corroborated by verbatim accounts and by eyewitnesses. They cannot be rejected on purely factual grounds. Yet, he adds, word of mouth alone cannot be relied upon. He gives the example of a boy born to a well-connected knight in the Beauvaisis who died on holy Friday. Word of the event spread quickly among the peasantry, who flocked to his grave with candles and offerings. A monument was soon erected and pilgrimages begun; the local monastery's abbot was seduced by the gifts and turned a blind eye to the fraud.[11] In another instance, a vagabond proposed to Guibert that he had born witness personally

[8] *Ibid.*, 613D-14B.
[9] *Ibid.*, 614D-15A.
[10] *Ibid.*, 1.1, 615D-1.2, 616C.   [11] *Ibid.*, 2.5, 621A-C.

"in word and text" to possessing a piece of bread actually chewed by Christ.[12]

What, then, of the real saints? Among their number, of course, Guibert includes the apostles and martyrs, whose "texts" were written in blood.[13] Yet, if the church is agreed on a figure like St. Martin, what can be said on behalf of a putative holy man whose reputation "mere rumour has spread from village to town"? He is clearly a local invention, for "nowhere do you find anything written about him but his name." What is worse, if the clergy remain silent, "old maids and simpleminded women" will spin out a contrived account of events (*commentata historia*). Their narrative is valueless if uncertainty torments the worshipper's mind. For a prayer dedicated to a saint about whom one knows nothing for sure is a sin. Nor can prayer in doubt please God.[14] And Christ stated that an *interpres . . . falsitatis*[15] would certainly perish.

Of course, there are instances in which reason merely supports faith, as, for example, in the resurrection of the virgin. The event itself cannot be established "by necessary arguments." Elsewhere in biblical study reason alone suffices (*ratio sola conveniat*). On occasion, the events of Scripture provide their own rationale. In Mary's case, since probatory evidence (*evidentia probamenta*) is not available, one is all the more praiseworthy for a display of faith. Similarly, in the authentication of saints' remains, *ratio* underpins *fides*.[16] However, that does not mean that one believes everything one reads in the often misleading saints' lives produced for his own age. Where the facts remain unsubstantiated, he prefers a prudent silence. A learned falsification, he adds, is even worse than a popular trifle. Some authors of local lives attribute great antiquity (*summa antiquitas*) to their heroes, demanding that the narratives be recorded for the present age (*moderno tempore . . . vitas scribi*). Guibert himself was asked to compose such lives but refused. For what "truth" could he profess about saints whom no one had ever seen? If he transcribed the verbal accounts, he would in effect be giving them his personal attestation.[17] For, even when authenticity is not in question, errors and disputes can arise, as was the case, for instance, of the skull of John the Baptist claimed by both Angers and Constantinople.

Guibert's mentality cannot be summed up in a single term like critical or rationalistic. Like the unearthers of relics in his accounts,

---

[12] *Ibid.*, 2.6, 621C-D.   [13] *Ibid.*, 3.1, 622A.   [14] *Ibid.*, 622D-23A.
[15] *Ibid.*, 623C.   [16] *Ibid.*, 623C-24B.   [17] *Ibid.*, 623B-C.

he is fascinated by the possibility of a tangible link with the past. He participates in the recreation of tradition which the writing down of oral saints' lives represented. Moreover, he equates local and oral, universal and written, thereby giving textual evidence and logical proof a position of prominence in his thoughts. Like Rodulf Glaber and Bernard of Angers, he also attests to the widespread eleventh-century movement of religious archaeology, underpinned by the recording of spoken accounts. Yet he cannot accept all that he observes without doubt. He is aware of his period's distinctiveness (*noster tempus, nostra aetas*),[18] but he sees discontinuity as often as continuity in the *exempla moderna*.[19] He separates custom and law, *tenere* and *docere*. Also, he sees in the moderns a frequent disjunction between outer action and inner motivation, and this in turn becomes a way of distinguishing purely popular from factual support for a saint. The most obvious type of externality is the local habit of surrounding saints' remains with precious objects.[20] More subtle is his rejection of many contemporary holy men whose commitment amounted only to formalism. In such observations Guibert singles out the special capacity of his own generation, which he sees as nascent literary activity. Yet he stands, so to speak, above the fray and attempts to transcend the uneducated use of letters. What is really new in the *De Pignoribus* is not the manner in which the divine operates but the consciousness with which its activities are interpreted.

The link between the past and the present is the physical, the tangible, and the objective. Throughout book one Guibert insists on the physicality of saints' remains and of relics before turning to their mystical, spiritual, or divine qualities. Of course, the one leads to the other. Paul, Guibert notes, refers to the holy spirit as *pignus*[21] (gage), but means *splendor gloriae* or *imago Dei*.[22] The physical is frequently referred to as the spiritual's *vicarius*.[23] He refers to the transformation which takes place after the spirit leaves the body (*ab integumento corporis exuto spiritu*).[24] Men pierce through (*transigere*) to heaven;[25] a pyx covers (*contegere, retegere*) a saint's remains.[26] The relics, therefore, while associated spiritually through the resurrection,[27] retain their status as evidence; claims for and against validity are based on the equation between existing artefacts and historical literalism. Similarly, the water

---

[18] *Ibid.*, 4.1, 626D, 628B.   [19] *Ibid.*, bk. 4, c. 1.4, 668A.

[20] Bk. 1, c. 4.1, 626A-D.   [21] Eph 1:14.   [22] *Ep.* 1, 609B; Hebr 1:3, 2 Cor 4:2.

[23] *Loc.cit.*; cf. bk. 2, c. 1, 630B: ". . . vicariam identitatem."

[24] *Loc.cit.*, 2, 611A.   [25] *Ibid.*, bk. 1, c. 1, 613D.   [26] *Ibid.*, 4.1, 627B.   [27] *Ibid.*, 1, 611C.

of baptism and the wine of the eucharist are physical symbols, literal *sacramenta*.[28] His position can be described as a version of St. Paul adapted to the needs of his own age. All earthly works are mere representations of "spiritual gifts."[29] Paradoxically, although the physical is verified by the textual, the text is also the means of transcending "the letter." Moreover, in weighing a claim for sainthood, it is not only the written record but contemporary interpretation of the subject's intentions which counts.[30] The task of hermeneutics is to impute or deny holiness to the candidate's subjective meaning.

If Guibert thus unites the physical and the spiritual, he sees the bad side of crude naturalism in externality. At the outset, as noted, he distinguishes between customs practiced at random involving nothing essential to the faith and the sacraments, where, despite a physical presence, there is "a doctrine of like form." Similarly, although a "body" covers a relic's "spirit," which is then interpreted by a text, the spirit of a text can also have a purely interpretive function, as, for instance, when Paul speaks of Abraham's unaccomplished work "figuratively"[31] or when, in a negative sense, falsifying rhetoric discredits genuine sainthood.[32] Merely external signs therefore cannot be relied upon as evidence unless situated in a textual continuum relating the individual *vita* to larger theological concerns.[33] And this requires an interpreter. Thus, while acknowledging the outer realm of causality, Guibert's explanatory mechanisms are invariably led towards the inner and reflective. The real purpose of relics, he notes in his dedicatory epistle to Eudes, is interior penance.[34] As the letter leads to the spirit, so the *pignora, reliquiae*, and even *sacramenta* signify the ultimate return of man from his present miserable state "of alienated conscience."[35]

Physicality, therefore, is ambivalent: popular culture utilizes physical symbolism without an interpretive context; sacramental theology places the same tangible objects in a framework of learned culture. Guibert interprets rather than rejects the physical awareness of things, which he himself associates with uneducated attitudes and ultimately with oral tradition. The *pignus* is thereby a *repraesentata memoria*,[36] recalling early medieval legal imagery. Mary, by contrast, is the sub-

---

[28] *Ibid.*, 1, 613B.   [29] *Ibid.*, 1, 613C.

[30] *Ep.* 2, 610B-11A; bk 1, c. 1, 615A-C; for a discussion, see DTC 13.2, 2356-57 and Guth, *op.cit.*, 77.

[31] *De Pignoribus*, bk. 1, c. 1, 613C.   [32] *Ibid.*, 614A.   [33] *Ibid.*, c. 2.1, 616B.

[34] *Ep.* 2, 610D.   [35] *Ibid.*, 611B.   [36] *Ibid.*, 1, 609B.

ject of naturalistic allegory as both *materia essendi* and *mater omnium*.[37] Yet, as book one proceeds, Guibert gradually forms a picture which equates the oral, the popular, the inauthentic, and the disreputable. Good customs do not vary from the sense of faith (*a fidei sensu*);[38] there is an identity between the spoken (*oratio*) and the taught (*doctrina*).[39] Texts, moreover, pass from higher to lower cultural levels. Erlebald, thought to be a holy man, gained credibility by preaching *ad populum*.[40] Textual rectitude is associated with God's intentions (*certitudo fidei*),[41] unreliability with *rusticitas*. The popularly venerated son of the Beauvaisis knight is described as a *vulgaris puer*. His cult is spread by rustics desirous of novelty (*rustici rerum novarum cupidi*). The local abbot, although "very wise," condones the "infected miracles," the bogus pilgrimages, and the profane multitude.[42] Similarly, merely local saints' lives are those which the populace creates in villages and towns.[43] The body of St. Exuperus was falsely discovered by a *rusticus*.[44] In all such cases, Guibert argues, there is a replacement of common bones for holy relics (*ossa vulgaria pro sanctorum pignoribus*).[45]

The theological framework for these observations is elaborated in book two.[46] Christ's physical presence and the sacraments were experienced "without any understanding or contemplation."[47] Invisible matters were thereby taught by visible signs, the object (*res*) presented without allegory (*sine typis, sine figurarum velaminibus*).[48] On the other hand, Christ migrated wholly to heaven afterwards, leaving no physical remains on earth. The *memoria* of which Paul spoke was not *sensualitas* but *intellectualitas*.[49] There were not two bodies but one; by implication, no one can claim to have a relic of Christ himself. Putting the part for the whole, i.e., synecdoche, is found in the Bible, but it is also used indiscriminately by the unlettered (*illiteratos et vulgares hac figura sermonum uti*).[50] Similarly, one must not dwell on the physical aspects of the bread and wine of the eucharist and forget the spiritual meaning: "which is to say, he who eats me exteriorly, that is, who eats my flesh and blood, lives by him who gives life

[37] *Ibid.*, bk. 1, c. 4, 626C.
[38] *Ibid.*, c. 1, 612D.   [39] *Ibid.*, 613A-B.   [40] *Ibid.*, 2.4, 619C.   [41] *Ibid.*, 3.2, 624C.
[42] *Ibid.*, 2.5, 621A-B.   [43] *Ibid.*, 3.1, 622C.   [44] *Ibid.*, 3.3, 625C-D.   [45] *Ibid.*, 626A.
[46] For a different view, see A. Lefranc, *art.cit.*, 304-05.
[47] *De Pignoribus*, bk. 2, c. 2.1, 631A.   [48] *Ibid.*, 631B.
[49] *Ibid.*, 631C. For a more detailed exposition of the "historical" and "sacramental" elements in Guibert, see J. Geiselmann, "Die Stellung des Guibert von Nogent (†1124) in der Eucharistielehre der Frühscholastik," *Theologische Quartalschrift* 110 (1929), 67-84; 279-305.
[50] *De Pignoribus*, bk 2, c. 2.1, 632A.

through the illumination of the interior man."[51] This cannot be done *ad litteram*; that is, each of us cannot "eat" all of him in any sense. Each of us imbibes a little of this "manna" and shares the spiritual benefits, *pars pro toto*. Extreme literalism, Guibert concludes, is a vice of the *simplices*.[52] One does not "believe" in "bread": for, in such a misconception, he asks, where is the worshipper's intention, the *memoria, notitia*, or *ratio* of the holy?[53] In truth it lies beneath the "shadow" of the bread and wine.[54]

The tooth claimed by the monks of St. Medard must therefore be false. If Christ is wholly risen, he reiterates, he could not have left a tooth behind.[55] The monks are *falsarii*:[56] for the alleged tooth "is a thing about which one can read nowhere, a thing proven by no testimonies."[57] What, he asks, is more infuriating than to have such nonsense "in the church's ears."[58] Who would believe it unless he were rude and untaught (*nisi rudis et inscius*)?[59] The monks' arguments amount to hearsay evidence (*opinio, assertio*), not rational thought (*ratiocinatio*).[60] Christ's only real souvenir was the events of the last supper, a *memoria sacramenti* which is "a figure to the wise man."[61] No such profundity can be derived from mere flesh or a tooth.[62] Faith, by implication, ought not to concern itself with external things, but ought to be something "substantive," a grey matter so to speak within the mind (*quasi aliquid solidum intra mentem*).[63] If faith exists in this spiritual realm, then the material presence of something promised by God may be considered an afterthought or confirmation.[64] The inner life quite simply arises from the text: "On a given page, if one seeks the deeper meaning, one reads the letters containing the sense with one set of eyes but one contemplates the reality produced by reason alone with another."[65] A spiritual sense, in other words, is adaptable to all physical manifestations of divinity: to biblical visions, which are *aenigmata* or *allegoriae*;[66] to the sense of interior contemplation in the gospels;[67] and to the human pronouncements of the prophets, which are merely concessions to human communication (*consuetudo lo-*

[51] *Ibid.*, 2.2, 632C.   [52] *Ibid.*, 632C-D.
[53] *Ibid.*, 633B: "Quo enim orantis intentio, imo memoria aut notitia quidem nulla porrigitur, qua ratione sacrari posse creditur?"
[54] *Ibid.*, 3.1, 634C.
[55] *Ibid.*, bk. 3, c. 1.2, 651B-D.   [56] *Ibid.*, 1.3, 652C.   [57] *Ibid.*, 653B.
[58] *Ibid.*, 1.4, 654A.   [59] *Ibid.*, 1.5, 655A.   [60] *Ibid.*, 2.1, 655B.
[61] *Ibid.*, 2.3, 656A.   [62] *Ibid.*, 2.4, 656C.   [63] *Ibid.*, 3.1, 658B.
[64] *Loc.cit.*   [65] *Ibid.*, bk. 4, c. 1.1, 665B-C.   [66] *Ibid.*, 1.2, 665D-66C.
[67] *Ibid.*, 667A; Apoc 1.10.

cutionis humanae)[68] and to matter already familiar to us (*in corporalia et nostris usibus familiaria*).[69]

2. INTERPRETING THE EUCHARIST

Guibert attacked the uncritical acceptance of relics from essentially two directions: the physical remains had to be authenticated, and the saint in question had to be guaranteed holy. Although referring to the past, both activities involved the interpreting subject in the present. Like the transition from oral to written tradition as a whole, the change in mentality shifted the criteria of belief from the community to the individual. For, in the last analysis, it was he who read, considered, and judged the probative text.

But written culture did not replace the oral. Unlike Reformation critics of relic worship, Guibert did not reject all *pignora sanctorum* along allegedly rational grounds. His position involved the more typically medieval association of orality with a written mode. While accepting physical symbolism at face value, he tried to underpin its authority, where warranted, with textually established evidence. The oral element thus survived the utilization of writing and was itself transformed. For, as literate standards were applied to relics, the adjudicating prelate had a simple choice. Either the concrete object was authenticated and thereby assimilated into learned culture, or, with its validity questioned, it was reduced to the status of popular hearsay.

Guibert's mind shifted back and forth somewhat uneasily between two mentalities, which, for simplicity's sake, we may call the symbolic and the hermeneutic. The achievement of philosophical theology in the later eleventh and twelfth centuries was to bring the two elements together in harmonious union. The *De Pignoribus Sanctorum* applied to a new area a critical methodology observable in other religious conflicts of the period, namely simony, clerical celibacy, the eucharist, and investiture. It is not surprising therefore that Guibert's comments echo ideas which we have earlier discussed: custom versus law; a diversity of spoken forms within a unity of written doctrine; the equation of truth, rationality, and textuality, supported by historical and archaeological research; the distinguishing of the local from the universal, the popular from the learned; and, above all, the association

---

[68] *Ibid.*, 2.2, 670B.   [69] *Ibid.*, 670C.

of reform, modernity, and canonical correctness with the document, the written verification, and the educated uses of literacy.

Yet Guibert goes beyond his predecessors like Bernard of Angers in one important respect. For him, criticism of relics forms part of a larger theological framework based upon a learned understanding of the sacraments. He thereby provides a convenient bridge to the two major problems of this chapter, namely, the rise of an intellectualist theology and the concommitant growth of empirical attitudes.[70]

For these issues, as will be evident, intersected the debate on the eucharist at a critical point. The eucharist was by definition a *sacramentum*, an oath or oral commitment, intimately related to the historical re-enactment of the last supper and the crucifixion. Also, the bread and wine on the altar were physical reminders of the body and blood of Christ. But interpreting the eucharist demanded, as did the criticism of relics, a contrast between differing modes of perception: the visible and the invisible, the material and the spiritual, and the external and the internal. The rival positions developed during some two centuries of active discussion have long had their place in the doctrinal history of transubstantiation and in the broader evolution of scholastic techniques of argument. But the analysis of the eucharist's meaning was also a watershed in dividing popular from learned tradition and in the use of logic for reflecting on the problem of nature.

The theological history of the eucharist can be traced from Paschasius Radbertus and Ratramnus of Corbie through Berengar and Lanfranc to the syntheses of Guitmund of Aversa, Alger of Liège, Hugh of St. Victor, and St. Thomas. It is more difficult to say why the issue arose when it did. The answer, to the degree that any complex intellectual movement can be traced to a starting point, is that the debate called into question the meaning of "sacrament" itself, or, more precisely, the Latin *sacramentum*, at a critical phase of its evolution from the later classical to the medieval world. The crossroads was reached at the point at which customary, unwritten, or genuinely oral elements in medieval theology were also being challenged by the logic of written texts.

There were as a consequence two possible approaches to *sacramentum*. Either it could mean the outward and visible sign of an inward and spiritual grace or the inner and spiritual meaning of an external sign, symbol, or ritual. As such, these sides of the same theological

---

[70] The term "empirical" is occasionally used in this chapter in a descriptive sense. Connections with later empirical thought are not necessarily implied. For a recent discussion of the idea, see A. J. Ayer, *The Foundations of Empirical Knowledge* (London, 1940), 58-135.

coin fitted neatly into the presuppositions of two different mentalities. In the one, emphasis was placed on the objectivity of the sacrament as a sacred sign, that is, a visible, tangible affirmation of future grace. In the other, while the physicality of the sacrament was not denied, emphasis was placed on interpretation. The sacrament became an object of thought, the physical, as Guibert suggested, leading to the spiritual. The first notion had parallels in the process of acculturation which affected other areas of oral tradition, as for instance the ceremony of investiture, in which objects physically represented the binding of the participants in a contractual agreement. The interpretive aspect of the eucharist was just as clearly a part of written tradition. For, in order to interpret the eucharist or, for that matter, any sacrament, one left the realm of experience and entered that of the text. The precondition of such activity was literacy.

"Sacramentum" - history of term

Before we turn to the debate on the meaning of the eucharist, it may be useful to elaborate these distinctions a little further. For a part of the problem as analysed by medieval theologians arose from the multiple senses of *sacramentum* itself.

All students of the somewhat obscure early history of Christian usage of *sacramentum* recognize two distinct (although probably interrelated) streams of meaning: (1) *sacramentum* in classical Latin, meaning an oath, a solemn engagement, the caution money pledged in support of a claim, or a civil suit itself; and (2) *sacramentum* as the translation of Greek μυστήριον, meaning not only the modern "sacrament," but any ritual observance of the church or, more generally, any spiritually significant object or action.[71]

One of the unsolved and perhaps insoluble problems in the word's history is the manner in which the notion of verbal commitment became wedded to that of religious mystery. Early students of the question provided an answer which stressed the continuities between pagan *mysteria* and Christian *sacramenta*. But in 1952, A.D. Nock, summarizing his own and others' investigations, reversed this trend and stated categorically: "Any idea that what we call the Christian

---

[71] A third phase may perhaps be added, namely, the restitution of a part of the original oral significance during the Reformation. For a survey, see F. Clark, *Eucharistic Sacrifice and the Reformation* (London, 1960). On early scholastic approaches, see A. Landgraf, "Das Sacramentum in Voto in der Frühscholastik," *Mélanges Mandonnet* (Paris, 1930), vol. 2, 97-143; for the later period, D. van den Eynde, *Les Définitions des Sacrements pendant la première période de la théologie scolastique (1050-1240)* (Rome, 1950).

sacraments were in their origin indebted to pagan mysteries or even to the metaphorical concepts based on them shatters on the rock of linguistic evidence."[72] Similar conclusions were reached by philologists. Hans von Soden acknowledged the important range of meanings attached to *sacramentum* / μυστήριον, but stressed that the primary sense derived from the ritual legitimation of obligations through the spoken word.[73] A similar view was taken by Christine Mohrmann. Christians, she argued, took over *sacramentum* from secular usage; thus, the notions of "oath" and "devotion" were equally balanced so as to produce the idea of *"engagement religieux."* This in turn implied three elements: a ritual of initiation into a community of believers; an oath, giving juridic status to the ceremony; and a subsequent uniting of the legal and the religious bonds.[74] In other words, the link if any between the pagan and the Christian senses lay in the spoken word and its sacral function, either for initiation or consecration. Later, the idea of "mystery" was added; but the etymological route remains obscure. One possible avenue was the symbolic as opposed to real value of the legal deposit in a lawsuit.[75] The religious formalities of Roman law could easily have been adapted to new uses in Christian communities. But it is more probable that there was a slow infiltration from the Greek, a parallel to the adaption of other abstractions to the philosophically weak vocabulary of Latin. Of that popular fusion (or confusion) of *sacramentum* as sworn pact and occult symbol we perhaps catch a glimpse in Pliny, who wrote in A.D. 93 or 94 of the Christians' habit of assembling for prayer and of "binding themselves through sacrament" (*seque sacramento . . . obstringere*) against temptations of evil.[76]

Between Tertullian and Augustine, *sacramentum* underwent a transition in two senses. The notion of oath or pledge was gradually aban-

---

[72] "Hellenistic Mysteries and Christian Sacramenta," *Mnemosyne*, 4th Series, 5 (1952), 200.

[73] "Μυστήριον und sacramentum in den ersten drei Jahrhunderten der Kirche," *Zeitschrift für die neutestamentliche Wissenschaft* 12 (1911), 188-227; summarized by J. de Ghellinck, *Pour l'histoire du mot "Sacramentum" I. Les anténicéens* (Louvain and Paris, 1924), 47-51.

[74] "Sacramentum dans les plus anciens textes chrétiens," *Etudes sur le latin des chrétiens*, vol. 1 (Rome, 1958), 237. On *sacramentum* as "religious engagement" in the first five centuries after Christ, see C. Capelle, *Le voeu d'obéissance des origines au XIIe siècle. Etude juridique* (Paris, 1959), 33-65. For a discussion of *mysterium* in medieval texts, see H. de Lubac, *Corpus Mysticum. L'eucharistie et l'Eglise au moyen âge* (Paris, 1954), 45-64.

[75] For a discussion of *sacramentum* in Roman law, see M. Kaser, *Das römische Zivilprozessrecht* (Munich, 1976), 60-97.

[76] *Ep.* 96, ed. J. B. Lightfoot, *The Apostolic Fathers*, vol. 2.1 (London, 1885), 51 and 51-52n11. Cf. Tertullian, *Apol.* 2, CCSL I, pp. 87-91.

doned; and sacrament as an aspect of religious conduct, either as a rite or a sacrifice, was balanced, if not overbalanced, by sacrament as an object of contemplation.[77]

Tertullian, who was converted in A.D. 195 or 196, utilized *sacramentum* somewhat more often in the sense of oath than of religious mystery (134 examples versus 84).[78] He spoke of the *sacramentum militiae*, that is, the formula of response by soldiers to the *praeiuratio* read aloud by the head of each legion.[79] Baptism was conceived as a type of military service. He also called it a *signaculum fidei*, a physical sign of the faith which recalled the imperial *insignia* and looked forward to the Christian *vexillum*, the Lord's banner.[80] *Sacramentum* thus became a synonym for *signaculum* or *signum*. Commenting on I Corinthians 5, Tertullian referred to the incestuous of Corinth as having been released from their "sacrament," never again to return to the "camp" of the faithful.[81]

The notion of a legal pledge was eventually interrelated with other meanings, of which one of the most important was initiation. In parallel with μυστήριον, *sacramentum* meant a particular rite or initiation itself, *sacramenta*, a whole group of initiations.[82] *Sacramentum* thus came to mean *sacrum*, a sacred or consecrated thing. The initiated was *sacratus*: he was both sworn to obedience and introduced to religious secrets.[83] Tertullian also used *sacramentum* in more general senses, such as that of religious devotion expressed verbally.[84] It stood for *veritas, disciplina, doctrina*, or *fides*.[85] Such matters could be communicated only to the initiated, usually through revelation, parable, or in ecstasy.[86] Again, *sacramentum* meant rite or sacrifice: Tertullian con-

---

[77] Cf. H. de Lubac, *Corpus Mysticum*, p. 55, who speaks more generally of two "zones" of meaning for *mysterium* and *sacramentum*: "d'une part, la zone que . . . nous appellerons rituelle ou cérémonielle, et, d'autre part, la zone que nous qualifierons de scriptuaire, entendant par là non l'Ecriture elle-même, mais le domaine—si vaste—des spéculations sur l'Ecriture. . . ."

[78] E. de Backer, "Tertullien," in J. de Ghellinck *et al.*, *Pour le mot "Sacramentum* . . . ," 143.

[79] *Ad Martyres* 3.1, CCSL I, p. 5, 11-13.

[80] de Backer, "Tertullien," 67.

[81] *De Pudicitia* 14.17, CCSL 2, p. 1308, 67-71.

[82] *De Corona* 15.3-4, CCSL 2, p. 1065, 17-27 and *Apologeticum* 2.6, *ibid.*, I, p. 88, 23-30. For Greek equivalents, see A.D. Nock, "Hellenistic Mysteries," 185. But the "adaptation before the fourth century" was less "slow and slight" than he assumed, p. 203. See de Backer, "Tertullien," section 2, pp. 115-42, and, among earlier studies, the parallel remarks of V. Gröne, *Sacramentum oder Begriff und Bedeutung von Sakrament bis zur Scholastik* (Brilon, 1853).

[83] de Backer, "Tertullien," 75.

[84] *Apol.*, 15.8, CCSL I, p. 114, 39-45.

[85] *Ibid.*, 47.14, p. 165, 60-66.

[86] *De Praescriptione Haereticorum* 26.2, *ibid.*, p. 207, 5-7.

trasted the *sacramentum diuinorum* of the Christians with the *idolorum mysteria* of the pagans.[87]

Of course, it is a short step from the symbolic associations of such meanings to symbolism itself. Tertullian used *sacramentum* in a full range of metaphorical senses. One of his favorites was to indicate prefiguration: Moses, who prefigured Christ,[88] or the cross, a sacrament of future salvation.[89] In such contexts, *sacramentum* was a prophetic or figural type in itself.[90] On other occasions, figural typology was united with other sorts of symbolism: Abraham's son born of a free woman represented the nobility of Christianity (to come), while his son born of a slave stood for the legalistic attitude of the Jews towards spiritual matters.[91] *Sacramenta* in the widest sense were all *figurae, allegoriae,* or *aenigmata,* whose true inner sense was veiled to the uninstructed. The range of meanings was broad enough to include symbol, figure, allegory, symbolic virtue or power, a symbolic object or person, as well as the *ordo* or *dispositio* of which the symbols were a part.[92] All were *sacramenta.*

Tertullian was the father of sacramental terminology in the West. His broad division of *sacramentum* into "oath" and "symbol" was followed by Cyprian and a number of pre-nicene fathers. But, by this time there was already a tendency to reverse the priorities. In Cyprian, the notion of verbal commitment waned; in Lactantius, Irenaeus, and the Donatists, it virtually disappeared.[93] In its place a new division appeared between *sacramentum* as a ritual and as a symbol. The most eloquent examples of sacramental rites are found in the sermons for catechumens which St. Ambrose published under the title *De Sacramentis.*[94] The most elaborate development of *sacramentum* as a symbol took place in Augustine.

There is no simple way to summarize Augustine's use of the term.[95]

---

[87] *Ibid.,* 40.2, p. 220, 2-4.

[88] *Adversus Iudaeos* 9.21-22, *ibid.,* II, p. 1370, 149-p. 1371, 161.

[89] *Ibid.,* 13.11-12, p. 1387, 64-73.

[90] *Adv. Marcionem* 4.40.1-2, *ibid.,* I, p. 655, 26-p. 656, 22.

[91] *Ibid.,* 5.4.8, p. 673, 13-28.

[92] de Backer, "Tertullien," 129, 134f.

[93] de Ghellinck, *ibid.,* 311.

[94] Dom B. Botte, ed., *De Sacramentis, Des Mystères* (Paris, 1950), 24-32. See L. Lavorel, "Oblats et corps du Christ sur l'autel d'après saint Ambroise," *Recherches de théologie ancienne et médiévale* 24 (1957), 207-24: on the eucharistic transformation, pp. 207-10; on *similitudo,* 217-21.

[95] For a tabulation, see C. Couturier, " 'Sacramentum' et 'mysterium' dans l'oeuvre de saint Augustin," in H. Rondet, M. le Landais, A. Lauras, and C. Couturier, eds., *Etudes augustiniennes* (Paris, 1953), 161-332. For an earlier defence of Augustine primarily as a "realist," see K. Adam, *Die Eucharistielehre des hl. Augustin* (Paderborn, 1908), 64, 146-61.

He nowhere wrote a special treatise on the subject. His usage must be pieced together from innumerable references scattered throughout his works and embracing the entire range of his theology.[96] Of seminal importance are two letters written around 400 to a layman, Januarius, treating fasts, communion, the eucharist, and other topics connected with the Christian rite. Among other things, Augustine took the occasion to say "many things about the sacraments." He stated that a *sacramentum* was both a sacred rite and a mystery at once.[97] In his view, Christ left as evidence of the forthcoming age of *novi populi* a group of observances, later sanctioned by the church, which were "few in number, easy to follow, and rich in meaning."[98] These sacraments were equally part of action and of thought. And while one could discuss the ultimate meaning of any sacrament, one could not dispute the manner in which it was to be carried out.[99] Sacraments, in other words, formed an essential part of the Christian cult, but they could nonetheless be understood according to the *intellectus spiritualis*. They were therefore a subject of interpretation.

This double view of the sacraments was incorporated into the definition which Augustine offered to Januarius in his second letter. A sacrament, he said, is a sacred rite (*celebratio*), commemorating a past deed or act (*rei gestae commemoratio*), in order that something else, which is to be received sacredly, is understood as signified (*ut aliquid etiam significari intelligatur, quod sancte accipiendum est*).[100] Here, the ritual and the symbol were united more successfully than in Tertullian or in Ambrose. Augustine was also more philosophical and theological in his interpretation of sacramental symbolism. His meaning for *sacramentum* was "inseparable from the spiritual interpretation of Scripture" itself.[101] To put the matter another way, the sacraments were viewed as symbolic actions in which interpretation formed an integral part of enactment. In this way, *sacramentum* was made to fit into one of Augustine's main theological tenets, namely that objects in the created world are signs (*signa*) representing realities (*res*) which are

[96] For a brief review of early studies, see P.-Th. Camelot, " 'Sacramentum.' Notes de théologie sacrementaire augustinienne," *Revue thomiste* 57 (1957), 429-30 and nn., on whose excellent summary I have drawn.

[97] Cf. P.-Th. Camelot, "Réalisme et symbolisme dans la doctrine eucharistique de saint Augustin," RSPT 31 (1947), 398.

[98] *Ep.* 54.1, PL 33.200.

[99] *Ep.* 6, PL 33.202.

[100] *Ep.* 55.2, PL 33.205.

[101] Camelot, " 'Sacramentum' . . . ," 434.

obscure, hidden, and often divinely inspired.[102] The holy spirit, he maintained, guides the faithful from the visible to the invisible, from the imitative to the genuine, from this world to the next. *Sacramenta* are both the outward symbols of inner reality and the inner reality itself. They are given to us *per allegoricam significationem.*[103] The link between the oral and the written aspects of *sacramentum* is provided by the performance of the sacraments themselves: the essential element is the Word.[104] The priest is the *dispensator verbi et sacramenti.*[105]

Paschasius Radbertus and Ratramnus of Corbie

Four centuries separate Augustine from the revival of his views represented by Paschasius Radbertus's *De Corpore et Sanguine Domini,* the first version of which appeared between 831 and 833.[106] The subsequent controversy over the meaning of the eucharist is usually divided into two major phases. The first consists of Radbert's treatise and the reply of Ratramnus of Corbie, together with a number of disparate contributions from the later ninth and tenth centuries. The second begins in the eleventh century and is generally agreed to have reached a climax in the Roman council of 1059, which condemned the doctrines of Berengar of Tours. The replies of Lanfranc, Guitmund of Aversa, and Alger of Liège effectively ended the intellectual development of the second phase. But, during the twelfth century, the issues were raised by a large number of both heretical and orthodox writers before the solution known as transubstantiation was declared *de fide* at the Lateran council of 1215.[107]

The two phases also represent different stages in the development of an interpretive solution. Radbert and later Lanfranc insisted on an understanding of the eucharist stressing the spoken, the physically symbolic, and the performative, while Ratramn and Berengar emphasized the written, the allegorical, and the search for meaning beneath

[102] See R. A. Markus, "St. Augustine on Signs," in R. A. Markus, ed., *Augustine* (New York, 1972), 61-91 and B. D. Jackson, "The Theory of Signs in St. Augustine's *De Doctrina Christiana,*" *ibid.,* 91-147.

[103] *Ep.* 54.29, PL 33.214.

[104] Camelot, " 'Sacramentum' . . . ," 435f; 440-43.

[105] 1 Cor 4:1; Aug., *Ep.* 228.2, PL 33.1014; *Ennarratio in Psalmos* 119.1, PL 37.1445; cf. Camelot, 436n1.

[106] B. Paulus, ed., *De Corpore et Sanguine Domini,* CCCM 16, p. viii.

[107] For a checklist of the main contributions, see J. de Montclos, *Lanfranc et Bérenger. La controverse eucharistique du XIe siècle* (Louvain, 1971), 27-29n2. For a brief account of the development, see H. Jorissen, *Die Entfaltung der Transsubstantiationslehre bis zum Beginn der Hochscholastik* (Münster, 1965).

the formalistic surface. As noted, what had been a set of distinctions between the oral and the written re-emerged in an intellectualized form. In Radbert, the idea of hermeneutics was introduced by acculturation. The central meaning of the eucharist did not need interpretation: it simply was. For Ratramn and later symbolists, the physical element in the eucharist could only derive meaning from being situated in an interpretive framework. In other words, it had to be allegorized. For them, to admit the existential dimension of the ceremony on its own was to descend to popular culture and to ritualism. This meeting of opposites, moreover, laid the groundwork for the second phase, in which essentially the same conflict was expressed in more sophisticated terms. Beneath the abstractions and logical exercises the old issues could easily be discerned. But now the entire question was intellectualized and the rival positions were dignified by the participants and later commentators as "realism" and "symbolism." The doctrine of transubstantiation worked out in the twelfth century was in fact a compromise between the two.

Radbert therefore occupies a position in the eucharistic controversy similar to Guibert of Nogent on relics. He insists on the physical reality of the *pignus* or *sacramentum* and makes a literal identification with their antecedent historical events. Yet he deepens human understanding of the ceremony in which the eucharistic mystery occurs through Pauline and Augustinian allegory. As in Guibert, the two sides of the question, the material and the spiritual, form an uneasy union.

His point of departure is not the eucharist itself but the principle of causality by which its mysteriousness is explained. There is no doubt, he argues, that the bread and wine are the true body and blood of Christ. For any Christian who believes that God created something out of nothing should not be astonished if he merely changed one thing into another, even "against nature."[108] For "natures" do not exist in themselves; nor do they truly give birth to what is produced from them. Their source is God's will: this is the unique *causa rerum*. What appears to be in disaccord with nature may in fact be in harmony with his wishes. Nothing lies beyond his power: in sum, *nihil extra uel contra Dei uelle potest.*[109]

Accepted as fact, the eucharist must, however, be explained. Although appearing "in the figure of bread and wine," God arranges

[108] *De Corpore et Sanguine Domini* c. 1, CCCM 16, p. 13, 3-7.
[109] *Ibid.*, p. 13, 7-14, 43.

that "there is nothing at all after the consecration but the flesh and blood of Christ."[110] This same flesh was born of the virgin, died on the cross, and was resurrected on the third day. Like the miracles of the Old Testament, these events were "against nature's course." They must be both acknowledged and interpreted: acts performed against nature but in accord with divine will take place "for the utility of rational beings."[111] So it is with the flesh given on the world's behalf: it is a token of the whole church (*pignus totius ecclesiae*), which brings about the interior mystery of salvation.[112] Radbert adds that nothing more remarkable takes place in the world of matter or appearances. A single mystery, therefore, confirms all Christ's other miracles, which are like the eucharist operations from within.[113] For instance, in the case of the tree of life, the potency did not arise from the nature of wood. Rather, an invisible power operated by means of a visible object.[114] Similarly, Christ's flesh is "nourishment for the mystery." The mind bows before the rock of faith. For the factual truth (*facti ueritas*) lies beyond human reason.[115]

But, if God's law is not natural law, what sort of law is it? Radbert clarifies the matter in chapter three by recalling the two sides of the patristic concept of *sacramentum*. A sacrament, he states, is "whatever is handed down to us as a gage of salvation in a divine celebration, in which a visible deed acts from afar and from within upon something invisible and is therefore to be understood in a spiritual manner."[116] Whence, he adds, *sacramenta* are etymologically derived from *secreta*: the divine works secretly either through a perceptible change or a form of sanctification.[117] The "divine power" prefers to lead the believers' minds toward the invisible, proceeding as Paul suggested "by faith, not by sight."[118] But *sacramentum* may also be understood as a type of legal oath (*sacramentum iuris*), in which, after sides have been taken, "each and every party swears what is stipulated by the agreement."[119] In this sense, it is a sacrament through verbal commitment, "since invisible faith is held secretly through the consecration of God or some other sacred person by what the swearer's voice

[110] *Ibid.*, p. 15, 1-2.   [111] *Ibid.*, 17, 100.   [112] *Ibid.*, 17, 114-19.

[113] *Ibid.*, 18, 119-24.   [114] *Ibid.*, 19, 143-48.   [115] *Ibid.*, 19, 165-66.

[116] *Ibid.*, c. 3, p. 23, 2-5: "Sacramentum igitur est quicquid in aliqua celebratione diuina nobis quasi pignus salutis traditur, cum res gesta uisibilis longe aliud inuisibile intus operatur quod sancte accipiendum sit."

[117] *Ibid.*, 23, 5-24, 10.

[118] 2 Cor 5.7; *ibid.*, 24, 10-14.

[119] *Ibid.*, 24, 19-20: "Est sacramentum iuris in quo post electionem partium iurat unusquisque quod suo pacto decreuerit."

senses exteriorly through sight or sound."[120] *Sacramentum* then is both Greek "mystery" and Latin "oath," the latter arising in Scripture whenever the "sacred spirit" works on something from within by means of the speaking voice (*loquendo*).[121] And it follows, for Radbert, in order to unite the two senses, that God's divine power is not a text but a word.

Is the eucharist, therefore, *figura* or *ueritas*? Both. On the one hand, the Bible attests that the bread and wine are "nothing but the true flesh and blood," although understood mystically. On the other, if they are a "mystical sacrament," they must also constitute a figure.[122]

But, if a figure, how can they really be true? The answer Radbert proposes is not altogether satisfactory and provides a basis for his critics' attacks. He states that "every figure is the figure of some thing and invariably refers back to it." Of course, a figure may be only "the shadow of truth." By implication, the bread and wine would have to be either reality itself or an imitation. But the eucharist, he adds, is not this sort of illusion. The bread and wine appear to be a figure only when they are broken up, that is, when in visible appearance they seem to be something other than what the senses recognize as flesh and blood.[123] But they are really a "sacrament of faith": a truth, because the body and blood of Christ are made (*efficere*) from the substance of bread and wine by the spiritual power of the word, and a figure because the priest acts as if he were providing something from the outside in order to recall sacred events.[124] In other words, the eucharist is a "figure" or "mark" (*caracter*) of truth because it is sensed exteriorly and truth itself by what is understood interiorly or believed.[125] This is the case, moreover, with a number of biblical figures. When for instance Paul spoke of the *splendor gloriae et figura substantiae*,[126] he meant the *figura uel caracter substantiae eius*, that is, the "human nature" in which the whole of divinity corporeally dwelt.[127]

[120] *Ibid.*, 24, 28-30.

[121] *Ibid.*, 24, 28-25, 33.

[122] *Ibid.*, c. 4, 27, 3-28, 26. Radbert restated essentially the same position in reply to Ratramnus in his letter of 856 to Fredugard of St. Riquier, *Epistola Radberti Pascasii ad Fredugardum*, CCCM 16, p. 148, 92-102: "Nec igitur mirum, si figura hoc mysterium est et huius mysterii uerba tropica locutio appellatur, cum ipse Christus ab apostolo Paulo 'caracter uel figura' dicitur, quamuis ipse sit Veritas [Hbr 1:2-3]. . . . Ecce, ut audis, ipse summa Veritas caracter appellatur et figura. Tamen in eo nihil fictum fuit, nihil uacuum a ueritate, sicut nec caracteres uel figuras uacuas esse dicimus litterarum a ui et potestate earum, cum easdem figuras tropice litteras uocamus." Here, the connection between truth, the letter, and the physical is striking.

[123] *Ibid.*, 28, 34-36.   [124] *Ibid.*, 28, 37-43.   [125] *Ibid.*, 29, 43-46.

[126] Hbr 1:3.   [127] *De Corpore*, 29, 52-55.

The *figura* or *caracter* is sensed outside, while the whole truth without penumbra is understood within.[128]

In subsequent chapters Radbert completes his outline of the theology of the eucharist. But his opening statements lay before us the essentials of his approach. Putting the matter simply, he sees one set of links between the material, the spoken, and the ritualistic, another through the spiritual, the thought, and the signified. At times he seems to be writing for two sorts of audience at once, both *illitterati* and *litterati*. He attempts to bring the pair into harmonious union, but the difficulties and oversights in his exposition leave us unconvinced.

Why is this so? To answer the question, we must go briefly beyond his actual words and examine the *De Corpore*'s intellectual context. A first consideration is the varying educational backgrounds of the monks at Corbie, where Radbert was abbot from 841 to 853.[129] As part of his pacification programme for the Saxons,[130] Charlemagne relocated some of their unlettered soldiers at Corbie, where they were placed under Adalbert, the emperor's erudite cousin. Adalbert founded a sister house, Corvey (*Corbeia Nova*), in unsettled territory. The original monastery was not a success, and with the aid of Wala, his brother, he moved it to a more propitious site on the Weser, some twenty-five miles from Paderborn, in 822. In 826 he named as abbot Warin, who was also part Frank and Saxon. Radbert was present at Corbie during the eventful years between 822 and 826. He authored the *Vita Walae* and dedicated both the *De Corpore* and his *De Fide, Spe et Caritate* to Warin. One of the chief opponents of his eucharistic doctrines was Fredugard, a monk of Corvey.[131] Like the new foundation, the *De Corpore* was a pioneering effort. It was the first post-patristic synthesis of the views of Ambrose and Augustine on the subject,[132] and, through theology, it attempted to articulate the ideal of a higher culture implicit in Alcuin's reforms.[133]

[128] *Ibid.*, 30, 73-81.

[129] Cf. M. Jacquin, "Le De Corpore et Sanguine Domini de Pascase Radbert," RSPT 8 (1914), 81-84.

[130] See A. Hauck, *Kirchengeschichte Deutschlands* (Leipzig, 1912), vol. 2, 371-424, and E. Amman, *L'époque carolingienne* (Paris, 1937), 104-05, 188-90.

[131] On these connections, see H. Wiesemayer, "La fondation de l'abbaye de Corvey à la lumière de la *Translatio Sancti Viti*," in *Corbie, abbaye royale* (Lille, 1963), 127-28.

[132] Cf. G. Gliozzo, *La dottrina della conversione eucaristica in Pascasio Radberto e Ratramno* (Palermo, 1945), 4.

[133] Cf. O. Capitani, "Studi per Berengario di Tours," BIS 69 (1957), 72-73; M. Cristiani, "La controversia eucaristica nella cultura del secolo IX," *Studi medievali*, 3rd Series, 9 (1968), 221-33.

Radbert's consciousness of the difference between popular and learned tradition is more clearly revealed in the prefaces to the twelve books of his *Expositio in Matthaeum*, which was composed during the 830s. Once again the task was related to the needs of his own monks, who, despite their devotion to "the highest eloquence" in prayer, demanded of him an orderly exposition of the text (*textus narrationis per ordinem*) so as to put an end to disputes about its meaning.[134] He saw his role like Matthew's as spreading the word to all; the gospel's aim was didactic. Aware, perhaps, of his uneducated audience, he both excused himself for his lowly style and yet drew attention to its advantages over "Vergilian flowers."[135] He also delimited the role of *humana ratio*: through "the simplicity of ignorance" man could easily deceive himself with falsity. Yet he praised "the simple faith" of uncluttered minds; that, surely, is the proper context of his "Anselmian" statement of faith's ability to grasp where reason fails.[136] In the preface to book three, which was presumably written after the publication of the first version of the *De Corpore*, he reversed his earlier, tolerant views and took an uncompromising stand against the pagan classics,[137] speaking of "some of our number, who, because of inadequate understanding," turn to distortions: "Although their vain eloquence is polished . . . , their discourse is so uncultivated that it smacks of rusticity."[138] He became from that point an unflinching critic of what he termed the *tragodiarum naenia* and the *poetarum figmenta* of the ancients, reserving a small role in theology for "human eloquence" or for "secular philosophy."[139]

But the contrast was not only between pagan and Christian. In place of ancient learning he proposed the divine Word—a word, however, which was both oral and written. For, the biblical message was too complicated for ordinary readers and therefore required an accompanying explanation. His images as a consequence retain a flavour of oral delivery while his intention is literary and explicative. His exposition, he maintained, was an attempt to enlighten through the ear (*auribus explanare*).[140] Scripture's obscurities could be revealed by sim-

---

[134] *Expositio in Evangelium Matthaei, prologus*, PL 120.31B-C.

[135] *Ibid.*, 32C.

[136] *Prologus libri secundi*, 103A-04B.

[137] G. Mathon, "Pascase Radbert et l'évolution de l'humanisme carolingien. Recherches sur la signification des Préfaces des livres I et III de l'*Expositio in Matthaeum*," in *Corbie, abbaye royale*, 145-48.

[138] *Praefatio libri tertii*, PL 120. 181D-82D.

[139] *Ibid.*, 183A and *Praefatio libri octavi*, 556B.

[140] *Praefatio libri tertii*, 184A.

ple eloquence (*simplex eloquium*). The holy spirit inflated the "inner ears" like sails in order that the ship of reflection could steer a straight course.[141] The gospel was to his commentary as word to text: "For the divine discourse (*sermo divinus*) . . . depicts not with the brush or reed but through reason (*ratio*) and celestial instruction, in order that the whole man may be reformed within."[142] Human explanation can decode biblical parables, "which are veiled to the common people."[143] But it is the light of the Word which penetrates our hearts. He even graced his novices with a metaphor which aptly summed up their own situation. Theological education, he said, was little different from the martial passage from boyhood to maturity. With one's initiation completed (*expleto tyrocinio*),[144] it helped one to recover from the errors of youth (*juventus errores*).[145] In sum, "the power of holy scripture is not so dimmed by mysteries that the less educated (*simpliciores*) are unable to understand it."[146] But, implicit in his division into higher and lower culture is the assumption that *illitterati* and *litterati* each appreciate the Bible on their own level.

A similar doctrine informs the *De Corpore*. Historians who have studied the treatise have been concerned almost exclusively with tracing the origins of the notion of the "real presence."[147] This approach presumes that there was an "unreal" presence, that is, an already existing basis for allegory and interpretation, which there was not. In fact, Radbert's tract is just the opposite of what it is often taken to be. It did not only revive and consolidate a rather oversimplified view of patristic teachings on the eucharist. It introduced them into an intellectual milieu in which any sort of hermeneutics was regarded as superfluous. For the unlettered, still largely attached to oral traditions, the concrete representation of the eucharist and its associated rituals were the norm. The idea that one could "interpret" the eucharist was something new. Moreover, Radbert's innovation lay less in his actual statements than in the relevance he saw for earlier instruction for both the lettered and the unlettered. His achievement can be described as a compromise. He retained the essential physicality which nonliterates saw as part of oral tradition; yet he placed it in a theo-

[141] *Prologus libri quarti*, 267B-C.   [142] *Praefatio libri septimi*, 481D.

[143] *Ibid.*, 483A.   [144] *Praefatio libri noni*, 644A.   [145] *Praefatio libri sexti*, 396B.

[146] *Praefatio libri primi*, 37A.

[147] J. Geiselmann, *Die Eucharistielehre der Vorscholastik* (Paderborn, 1926), 145-70; A. J. Macdonald, *Berengar and the Reform of Sacramental Doctrine* (London, 1930), 324-49 (summarizing previous positions); J. de Montclos, *Lanfranc et Bérenger*, 448-52; and, more generally, F. Vernet, "Eucharistie du IXe à la fin du Xe siècle," DTC 5.2, 1209-33.

logically acceptable interpretive framework. To do so, he had to emphasize the historical element in his patristic sources to the detriment of the philosophical, as his critics pointed out. But what was remarkable was that traditional thinking actually supported his position. For he effectively went back over the heads of the fathers and recreated the original senses of *sacramentum* on his own.

The two sides are evident throughout. On the one hand, Radbert treats the material aspects of the eucharist with a certain awe. His unsophisticated notion of divine causality is less an explanation of how things came about than a justification of what they are. Augustinian vocabulary is present, but its richness is greatly diminished. His notions of *ueritas* and *figura* are two-sided. The truth is latent in the configuration, just as reality lies behind appearances. Yet, *figura* is a synonym for *caracter*, a mark or sign.[148] Ritual, too, has an ambivalent status. The oral commitment of the sacrament is confirmed by the consecration of the priest, but the inner meaning of the eucharist is a product of reflection alone.[149] Thus, formalism is both adhered to and denied. But above all Radbert reveals his dual perspective in his attitude towards interpretation. As part of the search for inner meaning, he admonishes his brethren not merely to accept inspired events but to make sense out of them, to decipher why an act against the *ordo naturae* is nonetheless in accord with God's will. But one proceeds from sense to spirit as one advances from oral to written: "Just as an infant gropes slowly towards literacy through signs or configurations of letters, then advances to the spiritual sense and understanding of holy texts, so one reaches from the humanity of Christ to the divinity of God." As a consequence, the one is called the *figura* or *caracter* of the other.[150]

The comparison is apt, suggesting not only a process of education but that interpretation is an addendum to what is seen, heard, and performed,[151] an idea which received indirect support from Am-

[148] See N. Häring, "*Character, Signum* und *Signaculum*. Die Entwicklung bis nach der karolingischen Renaissance," *Scholastik* 30 (1955), 481-512; on Carolingian authors, 506-12.

[149] Cf. Dom O. Casel, "Das Mysteriengedächtnis der Messliturgie im Lichte der Tradition," *Jahrbuch für Liturgiewissenschaft* 6 (1926), 180: Ein Ausfluss davon ist auch die offenbarung durch das Schriftwort.

[150] *De Corpore*, c. 4, p. 29, 58-62.

[151] On the continuity of the oath uniting *fides* and *res sacra*, see M. David, "Le serment du sacre du IXe au XVe siècle," *Revue du moyen âge latin* 6 (1950), esp. chs. 2-3, pp. 66-157; on the earlier intermingling of Roman and Germanic vows, see C. Capelle, *Le voeu d'obéissance . . .* , 219-37.

brose.[152] Moreover, the parallelism of the material and the spiritual is carried over to the notion of *sacramentum*. The term *pignus* is absent from Isidore's definition, on which Radbert heavily relied, although it occurs elsewhere in Augustine, Isidore's chief source.[153] But Radbert also took the words of the bishop of Seville a little out of their context. The sacraments were dealt with in a book six of the *Etymologiae*, under the title *De Officiis*. As a subtopic, Isidore compared the ceremonies of Greek, Hebrew, and Christian tradition.[154] In his opinion, all *caerimoniae*, *sacrificia*, and *sacramenta* were alike. The eucharist was at once a ritual, a sacrifice, and a mystery, for the body and blood of Christ, although material, were "sanctified and made sacred through the invisible power of the holy spirit." Echoing Augustine, Isidore defined *sacramentum* as the celebration of one thing so that another might be signified, the latter bearing a "spiritual" sense. In reworking Isidore's definitions, Radbert emphasized the physical through such terms as *pignus*, *figura*, and *caracter*. He also distinguished more clearly than his mentor between the oral, ritualistic, and performative side and the cognitive, intellectual, and interpretive.[155] It is difficult to imagine that he did this without some knowledge of his audience in mind. Nor was his initiative isolated. For "ritualism is one of the most notable features of the period's religious life."[156] As the immediacy of the sacraments was threatened by the implicit division of popular and learned culture, "the conscious participation of the community" was lost. The mass gradually became a mystery which one had to "wonder at and contemplate from afar."[157] The theological controversy, in other words, was a symptom of a more widespread hiatus between theory and practice.

Once the *De Corpore* became well known, it acted as a reference point in all subsequent discussions. It also raised the issues to a new

---

[152] On Radbert's Ambrosian sources, see Cristiani, "La controversia," 169-71.

[153] E.g., *Sermo* 334, 2, PL 37.1469: ". . . Tene pignus mortem Christi. . . . Promisit, cautionem fecit, pignus dedit. . . . Noli desperare, qui vivis ex pignore. . . ."

[154] *Etymologiae* 6.19.35-39, ed. W. Lindsay (Oxford, 1911). For an exposition of Isidore's view, see J. Geiselmann, *Die Abendmahlslehre an der Wende der christlichen Spätantike zum Frühmittelalter. Isidor von Sevilla und das Sakrament der Eucharistie* (Munich, 1933), 165-68; on Isidore's patristic sources, pp. 169-79.

[155] For analogies in Carolingian legal thought, see M. David, *art. cit.*, 66-96, and F. L. Ganshof, "L'origine des rapports féodo-vassaliques," *I problemi della civiltà carolingia* (Spoleto, 1954), 29-42.

[156] A. Vauchez, *La spiritualité du Moyen Age occidental, VIIe-XIIe siècles* (Paris, 1975), 14; cf. 16-17.

[157] J. A. Jungmann, *Missarum Sollemnia*, Eng. trans. (New York, 1910), vol. 1, p. 84.

level of complexity. Occasional explications of biblical texts would no longer do.[158] One had to agree or disagree with Radbert with reference to an internally developing tradition of patristic writing.

The first negative vote was cast by Ratramn, also a monk of Corbie, whose own *De Corpore et Sanguine Domini* was written around 859. Like Radbert's treatise, it was dedicated to Charles the Bald, who asked for answers to two questions: whether the bread and wine were the flesh and blood of the historical Christ and whether the eucharist presented them *in mysterio . . . an in veritate*.[159] To the first question Ratramn gave a flat no;[160] to the second he was inclined to reply "both."[161] He disagreed with what he considered to be Radbert's crude physicalism, and restored the spiritual element to the thought of Ambrose and Augustine. But the significant difference between the two did not lie in the realm of ideas alone. Radbert's starting point was the concrete. His treatise was the authentication of an historical and, to his mind, ever-present reality. Ratramn did not deny what appeared before the senses. But he considered the eucharist an intellectual problem soluble with the help of grammar, logic, and allegory. In his explanation of the eucharistic "mystery" there is less that is genuinely mysterious.

His approach lay in the mainstream of patristic commentary, and, had it been written two centuries later, might well have passed without criticism.[162] The essential issue in his view was whether the eucharist represented the body and blood under a figure (*figura*) or veil (*obvelatio*) or whether it was the unadorned manifestation of truth (*veritatis nuda manifestatio*).[163] Radbert, he argued, had drawn attention only to the realistic element in Augustine. But the bishop of Hippo clearly distinguished between *figura* and *veritas*. A figure, in Ratramn's

---

[158] No attempt can be made here to trace relations between eucharistic theory and liturgical practices. For the eleventh and twelfth centuries, the question is discussed by F. Holböck, *Der eucharistische und der mystische Leib Christi in ihren Beziehungen zueinander nach der Lehre der Früh-scholastik* (Rome, 1941), 36-85; for early monastic practices, see A. A. Häussling, *Mönchskonvent und Eucharistiefeier* (Münster, 1973), chs. 2-6.

[159] *De Corpore et Sanguine Domini*, c. 5, ed. J. N. Bakhuizen van den Brink (Amsterdam, 1954), 34 (= PL 121.129B-30A); using this text in preference to the author's 2nd ed., 1974, on which see J. P. Bouhot, *Ratramne de Corbie. Histoire littéraire et controverses doctrinales* (Paris, 1976), 107.

[160] *Ibid.*, c. 57, p. 48 (PL 150A-51A).

[161] Cf. Vernet, DTC 5.2, 1214-15.

[162] For a somewhat schematic analysis, see R. Béraudy, "Les catégories de pensée de Ratramne dans son enseignement eucharistique," *Corbie, abbaye royale*, 158-80. The author's assertion that "Ratramn does not speak of an intellectual understanding" (p.159) is contestable. On the same theme, cf. Cristiani, "La controversia," 192-94 and nn.

[163] *De Corpore*, c. 2, p. 33 (PL 128A).

view, was a kind of obscurity (*obumbratio*). It concealed truth beneath wraps or covers (*velamina*), as, for example, when speaking of the Word, we say "bread" in the Lord's prayer, or, when Christ himself said at John 6:52 "I am the living bread which descended from heaven. . . ." In such expressions, one thing is said, another is meant. Truth, by contrast, is the clear designation of a thing (*rei manifesta demonstratio*), veiled by no clouds, shadows, or images.[164] An example is Christ's birth, crucifixion, and resurrection, where there are no concealing figures.[165] The truth of the matter is stated in plain language and nothing is understood but what is said. In figurative discourse, of which the eucharist is an instance, there is no such *nuda et aperta significatio*.[166] One thing is presented exteriorly to the senses while another is called forth interiorly to the minds of the faithful.[167] Outside, there are colour, taste, and other sensations; within, the spiritual significance of the rite. Clearly, the latter are given "figuratively."[168]

In sum, Ratramn did not deny the real presence, but he refused to affirm it alone.[169] For, if everything in the eucharist was accomplished *secundum corpus*, there could be no role for faith or any basis for mystery.[170] Nor, he added, would there be any means of transformation (*permutatio*). If we believe only what is before our eyes, there is nothing out of which change may arise nor anything into which something can be changed. To put the matter another way, if nothing is changed in the eucharist, nothing could have existed before.[171] For Ratramn the way out of such difficulties lay through the traditional method of allegory. Under the covering (*velamentum*) of corporeal bread and wine there exist spiritual body and blood.[172] These pairs, he asserted, are not different; they are "one and the same thing" viewed in different perspectives. Corporeally, they are physical things, but in potential they are the mysteries of Christ's body and blood.[173] As for Radbert's notion of *pignus*, that too may be dispensed with. In the mass after the eucharist, Ratramn maintained, the faithful are said to receive "the gage of eternal life." This again is both *pignus* and image, both reality and symbol.[174]

We may perhaps be able to frame the distinction between Radbert

---

[164] *Ibid.*, 7-8, pp. 34-35 (130A-C).   [165] *Loc.cit.*   [166] *Loc.cit.*

[167] *Ibid.*, 8-9, pp. 34-35 (130C-31C).

[168] *Ibid.*, 11, pp. 35-36 (131C-32A).

[169] For a view similar to my own, see M. Gibson, *Lanfranc of Bec* (Oxford, 1978), 75-76.

[170] *De Corpore*, c. 11, p. 36 (132A).

[171] *Ibid.*, 12, p. 36 (132A-B).

[172] *Ibid.*, 16, p. 37 (134B-35A).   [173] *Loc.cit.*

[174] *Ibid.*, 86, p. 56 (163A).

and Ratramn more precisely if we return momentarily to the legal analogies of an earlier chapter. For Radbert, the eucharistic rite itself was "dispositive"; the interpretive material supporting it had only the status of evidential documents. For Ratramn, the authenticity of the eucharist was inseparable from the texts which related its meaning. Although the presence was "real," its reality had to be consonant with grammar and logic. To understand the eucharist, therefore, was to apply grammar and logic—in short, to allegorize it.

Radbert did not wholly deny the value of interpretation, nor did Ratramn deny the real (as opposed to historic) presence of Christ in the ceremony. But they differed in the manner in which they approached the issue of *figura* versus *veritas*.[175] For Ratramn, the distinction arose within the logic of human understanding. In order for the bread and wine to be the body and blood of Christ *in veritate*, Christ had to be experienced in the flesh and blood by the bodily senses. This was obviously not the case. The eucharist was apprehended by the senses as bread and wine; it was the body and blood of Christ only *in figura*. Put in other terms, the bread and wine were symbols of the body and blood of Christ.

If Ratramn interrelated *figura* and *veritas* as categories of understanding, Radbert did just the opposite. For him, *veritas* inhered in the physical, the historical, and by implication the ontological. Truth or falsehood could not be verified by human logic alone. A thing was "true" when in reality it was what it was affirmed to be; it existed *in figura* when, while really being what is was, it also signified, evoked, or represented something else. There was to Radbert's mind no incompatibility between the two: the eucharist was the sacramental body and blood of Christ *in veritate*, no matter what else it signified *in figura*. The link between experience and reality was provided by the Word, the affirmation of reality, or, more precisely, by the Word as authenticating text, since Radbert accepted the gospels as a simple transcription of God's verbal intentions and commands. The distinction between *veritas* and *figura* was nothing more than that between the original word and/or text and subsequent commentary.

If we step aside from the eucharistic controversy for an instant, it is possible to see Radbert and Ratramn as contributors to the two problems with which this chapter began. First, both distinguished between what they saw as popular and learned approaches to the ques-

[175] J. Lebon, "Sur la doctrine eucharistique d'Hériger de Lobbes," *Studia mediaevalia . . . R. J. Martin* (Bruges, 1948), 67n2.

tion. In Radbert's case, this involved a partial rehabilitation of the oral, the symbolic, and the performed; in Ratramn's, a reconceiving of the whole question within the framework of higher religious culture alone. More significantly, both threw into relief the phenomenal aspects of reality, although once again from different perspectives. For Radbert, the physical implied the spiritual: human interpretation merely amounted to underwriting. For Ratramn, sense data were also the starting point of all genuine understanding of reality. But oddly, by questioning the nature of reality as it appeared before him, Ratramn was further able to distinguish what was apprehended by the senses from what was understood by the mind. This byproduct of textual research was exploited in the eleventh century by Berengar, as later by twelfth-century philosophers, who applied it to scientific rather than to theological questions.

To conclude this brief discussion of Radbert and Ratramn, we may turn briefly to the summary of the two ninth-century positions in Heriger of Lobbes, who died in 1007. He was distant enough from the original participants in the debate to distinguish confidently between the *antiqui*, that is, the fathers, and the *moderni*.[176] He was also the first contributor to make selective quotations from patristic sources to suit his own design.[177] He therefore offers a bridge between the first phase of the eucharistic discussion and the techniques which became fashionable in the eleventh century.[178]

His short treatise, in fact, marked a new stage in the development of an interpretive tradition. It presupposed that the reader was familiar with Radbert's ideas, and, while fundamentally realist in orientation, it tried to effect a union between opposed positions. Heriger had read earlier attempts at compromise: he knew of Ratramn's letter to Heribald of Auxerre and the letter (also perhaps by him) to Egilo, both of which criticized Radbert.[179] He also quoted Gezo of Tortona, who paraphrased Radbert around 950, and through him Rémi of Auxerre,[180] as well as lengthy statements by a *quidam sapiens* who authored a *Responsio* defending the realist approach.[181] With such con-

---

[176] *De Corpore et Sanguine Domini*, c. 1, PL 139.180A; c. 4, 182B, 182C.

[177] For differing views, see Geiselmann, *Die Eucharistielehre*, 274-75, and Lebon's reply, "Sur la doctrine eucharistique," 70-75.

[178] Geiselmann, *Die Eucharistielehre*, 277-80.

[179] The evidence is summarized by Macdonald, *Berengar and the Reform*, 241n4.

[180] See J. Geiselmann, "Der Einfluss des Remigius von Auxerre auf die Eucharistielehre des Heriger von Lobbes," *Theologische Quartalschrift* 114 (1933), 222-44.

[181] Ed. d'Achéry, *Spicilegium*, vol. 1, p. 149; on its use, see Lebon, *art. cit.*, 66-70.

temporary discussion in mind, Heriger attempted to fit the ancients and the moderns into a coherent tradition of thought. Overlooking patristic differences on the meaning of *sacramentum*, he argued that the fathers presented an essentially unified outlook.[182] Some writers of the "modern age" had once again raised the spectre of heresy. In his view, it was impossible to "categorize" Christ or to "dogmatize" whether the eucharist existed *in veritate vel in figura*.[183] Yet patristic teaching on the question was reasonably clear. While admitting the possibility of interpretation, Ambrose, Augustine, Basil, and Gregory unequivocally stated that the bread and wine were the actual body and blood of Christ.[184] Indeed, he added, the doctors of the church spoke so eloquently that "the simplicity of Radbert could perhaps be excused."[185] By implication, the purely allegorical approach of Ratramn rested on a misinterpretation of earlier views. The authors most frequently quoted, namely Jerome, Augustine, Fulgentius, and Eusebius, did not deny the reality of the sacraments. Heriger also claimed, following the fathers, to put more confidence in "simple words and prayer" than in "dialectical argumentation."[186] Perhaps he did: but his treatise placed the eucharistic debate on an intellectual level which made those simple words an increasingly remote ideal.

Eleventh-Century Authors

The lines of inquiry laid down by Radbert, Ratramn, and their successors were pursued in greater depth during the major phase of the debate on the eucharist. The protagonist was Berengar of Tours.[187] Among his early theoretical (as opposed to conciliar) opponents were Hugh of Langres, Durand of Troarn, Lanfranc of Bec, and Guitmund of Aversa.

The renewed controversy went far beyond the specific arguments of the central figures. For canonists and other spokesmen on behalf of

---

[182] *De Corpore et Sanguine Domini*, c. 1, PL 139.180A.

[183] *Ibid.*, 180B.   [184] *Ibid.*, c. 2, 180B-81B.   [185] *Ibid.*, 180C.

[186] *Ibid.*, c. 5, 183C; c. 7, 185A.

[187] For a brief review of the circumstances surrounding the debate, see M. Gibson, *Lanfranc of Bec*, 63-71; for the papal connections, C. Erdmann, "Gregor VII. und Berengar von Tours," *Quellen und Forschungen aus italienischen Archiven und Bibliotheken* 28 (1937-38), 48-74 and the revisions of O. Capitani, "La lettera di Goffredo II Martello conte d'Angiò a Ildebrando (1059)," *Studi gregoriani* 5 (1956), 19-31, and, *idem*, "Per la storia dei rapporti tra Gregorio VII e Berengario di Tours," *ibid.*, 6 (1959-61), 99-145; also, R. Somerville, "The Case Against Berengar of Tours: A New Text," *ibid.*, 9 (1972), 55-75.

the increasingly reformist papacy, the issue was universal authority versus particularistic innovation; for students of the liturgy, mysticism, or theology, it was the degree to which intellectualism was permissible in the fideistic, ritualistic, or participatory areas of religion. Although differing on much else, the two sides had a similar response to such questions. As the number of contributions swelled and positions hardened, it was clear that the eucharist had become an object of cognition to be discussed by experts on the legal, philosophic, and even diplomatic meaning of texts. After Berengar, Christians may still have been divided on how the eucharist was to be interpreted, but only a tiny minority opposed the use of hermeneutics itself.

Berengar of Tours

Berengar's intellectual development can be divided into four stages: the early correspondence, including the letters to Ascelin the Breton and Adelmann of Liège; quotations from a lost treatise written shortly after the council of Rome of 1059 and preserved in Lanfranc's *De Corpore et Sanguine Domini* from ca. 1065; the *De Sacra Coena*, the lengthiest statement of his position, which can be dated around 1067; and a *mémoire* on the Roman councils of 1078 and 1079, probably composed in 1080.[188]

The various treatises do not illustrate a linear growth of ideas. Instead, rather similar notions recur again and again amid carefully calculated replies to those holding other opinions. Yet, throughout the often excited, tendentious repetition of his position, Berengar makes one point clear: his belief in the value of logically defensible systems of interpretation. On a number of occasions he was forced to retract his doctrinal views. But he never really denied his faith in rationalistic exegesis; and the rigidity of the confessions he was compelled to make betray that it was this rather than his specific tenets which was looked upon with such alarm. He does not appear to have thought out his

[188] On the division I follow Macdonald, *Berengar and the Reform*, 254; on the dating, Montclos, *Lanfranc et Bérenger*, 3-5. The essential scholarship on Berengar is listed briefly by O. Capitani, "Studi per Berengario di Tours," 67-71. I have not considered the problem of Berengar's supporters, since, by and large, the little we know of them suggests that they merely repeated his doctrines. For an interesting example, see M. Matronola, *Un testo inedito di Berengario di Tours e il concilio del 1079* (Milan, 1936), 109-21 and the critical observations of J. Geiselmann, "Ein neuentdecktes Werk von Tours über das Abendmahl?" *Theologische Quartalschrift* 118 (1937), 1-31, 133-72.

doctrinal position with care before the council of Vercelli of 1st September 1050,[189] but long before that date he was widely known as a successful teacher committed to a philosophical methodology. After the Roman council of the same year he was more and more frequently called upon to defend the content of his views. But what evidently interested him most was the logic by which they were reached. Legislation and administrative coercion were partially effective in silencing his voice. Yet, the final irony of the affair was that his opponents overcame his position only through an often less sophisticated adoption of the methods he himself pioneered.

Of all the contributors to the eucharistic debate, Berengar also speaks to us most clearly as an individual. His unusual lecturing style, his involvement in Anjou politics, and his subsequent appearance at papal councils made a deep impression on the thinkers of his own day and have coloured historical interpretation ever since. Nothing he wrote was free of polemics: it is not always easy to separate his own reflections from his reaction to the ideas of others.

Yet, despite the difficulties of his style, his deliberate use of innuendo, and the fragmentary character of his works, there are several strands of thinking which pervade Berengar's entire *oeuvre*. They surface for the first time in the letter he wrote to his friend Ascelin towards the end of 1050 and perhaps after the council of Vercelli.[190] Ascelin accused Ratramn (whom he mistook for Eriugena) of heresy. If the report is true, Berengar observed, then his friend is an unreflective, impious, and even unworthy priest. For, to have accused "Eriugena" of heresy is to put oneself in the camp of Radbert and Lanfranc.[191] This, in turn, implies an incorrect notion of the eucharist and, more generally, of the philosophy of change. Berengar replied that it is contrary to the gospel, the apostles, and the rules of nature (*omnis naturae rationes*) to believe "that the bread's substance is entirely withdrawn from the sacrament of the Lord's body."[192] But it is also unreasonable to forbid interpretation, since the gospel of John clearly stated that religious mysteries are not often evident to the senses. To oppose this is genuine heresy.[193] For the material bread no more rep-

[189] *De Sacra Coena*, c. 9, ed. W. H. Beekenkamp (The Hague, 1941), 13.

[190] R. Heurtevent, *Durand de Troarn et les origines de l'hérésie bérengarienne* (Paris, 1912), 150n1.

[191] *Ep. Berengarii ad Ascetinum*, ed. R.B.C. Huygens, in *Texts and Manuscripts. Essays presented to G. I. Lieftinck*, vol. 2 (Amsterdam, 1972), 18-19 (= PL 150.66A-B).

[192] *Ibid.* (66B).

[193] *Ibid.* (66B-C).

resents the whole sacrament than the bishop's staff the cure of souls.[194] Berengar confesses he has not read the whole of "John the Scot," but he warns Ascelin not to take a position against interpretation for its own sake. He who holds the keys of knowledge, if not passing the threshold, should not bar the way to others.[195]

Here, in a nutshell, we find two of Berengar's major tenets, namely, the commitment to logical discussion of religious issues and the rejection of all forms of naive physicalism, even if guaranteed by faith.

Similar thoughts were voiced in a letter which Berengar wrote to Adelmann, a fellow student at Chartres, who became bishop of Brescia in 1048. Although difficult to date precisely, it was probably written between the councils of Tours in 1054 and Rome in 1059.[196] Nowhere, Berengar protested, had he advocated the "Manichaean" position whereby the historical Christ was just an image of reality. "I have held and still hold," he maintained, "that the true and human body of Christ is present on the altar during the mass."[197] He "conceded" that the bread and wine were made (*fieri*) into the body and blood of Christ after the consecration and was willing to allow that this very (*ipsum*) bread and wine actually became the verifiable (*verum*) body and blood of the Lord.[198] Yet, he continued, to leave the matter there was to misunderstand the nature of the sacraments as outlined in the Bible and as developed in patristic thought. *Sacramentum*, as Augustine taught, means *sacrum signum*. There is a difference between *res* and *signum*, that is, between the object itself and the "sign" by which it is consecrated.[199] Thus, while the reality of the eucharist is not denied, neither is its inner spiritual significance minimized.

The fathers in Berengar's view were agreed on this matter. When terms like *figura, pignus, signum*, and *similitudo* are used in patristic texts, reference is not made to the true body and blood of Christ but to its spiritual significance.[200] For the body and blood are one thing, the sacrament of the body and blood another. The one is visible, the

[194] *Ibid.* (66C). For a similar attitude on biblical texts, see the glosses attributed to him by B. Smalley, "La Glossa Ordinaria. Quelques prédécesseurs d'Anselme de Laon," *Recherches de théologie ancienne et médiévale* 9 (1937), 391-92.

[195] *Ep., ibid* (66D).

[196] Macdonald, *Berengar and the Reform*, 256; Montclos, *Lanfranc et Bérenger*, 125-26.

[197] *Berengarius in purgatoria epistola contra Almannum*, ed. Montclos, *Lanfranc et Bérenger*, 531.

[198] *Ibid.*, 531-32.

[199] *Ibid.*, 533. Montclos, p. 133, pushes the distinction too far. On the difficulties of Augustine, see P.-Th. Camelot, "Réalisme et symbolisme . . . ," 394-410; on symbol and sacrament, pp. 405-06.

[200] Montclos, *loc.cit.*

other invisible. The statements "This bread is my body" and "The bread which we break is Christ's body" do not mean that the *substantia* was consumed.[201] Radbert, he continued, pandered to popular taste: he produced not *sententia* but *insania*. Unfortunately, Lanfranc followed his lead; they both urged that somehow a little portion (*portiuncula*) of the actual body and blood was produced by the transformation of the bread and wine.[202] But his argument, or, as he put it, that of Scripture, was as follows: "the bread and wine . . . are converted into Christ's body and blood not sensibly (*sensualiter*) but intellectually (*intellectualiter*)." It is not "consumed" but rather "assumed"; it is not changed in small parts but entirely.[203] For a crude materialist "conversion" is denied by both the senses and reason. Whenever one thing is changed into another—as, for instance, when Moses's rod was made into a serpent, Loth's wife into a statue of salt, or the water at the Cana wedding feast into wine—the second state cannot be said to exist (*existere*) before the first has ceased to do so.[204] Using this criterion, the bread and wine on the altar cannot be transformed "sensibly" into Christ's body and blood. For Christ exists wholly in eternity.[205] Berengar claims, moreover, that this approach unites *ratio* and *auctoritas*, a theme to which he turns in the last section of the letter. Through a judicious selection of texts, he illustrates that Augustine both accepts the sacraments as divinely inspired mysteries and interprets them using logical methods.[206]

The letter to Adelmann, then, not only presented a clear statement of Berengar's position. It also grouped a number of Augustinian texts into a self-conscious tradition for the first time since Isidore and Radbert. Essentially the same framework for understanding the sacrament was employed in his lost *Opusculum*, which, as noted, was written shortly after his condemnation in 1059 and quoted in large part by Lanfranc.

The treatise is not only a list of authorities or a *scriptum contra synodum*,[207] as his opponents would lead us to believe. It also marks a new stage in the articulation of Berengar's ideas. Between the synod of Tours in 1054 and the Roman council of 1059 his teaching had become well known in many European centres, both in France and Italy. His followers were singled out less for their conception of the

[201] *Loc.cit.*   [202] *Ibid.*, 533-34.
[203] *Ibid.*, 534.   [204] *Ibid.*, 534-35.   [205] *Ibid.*, 535.
[206] *Ibid.*, 536; for an analysis, see Montclos, 139-41.
[207] Montclos, 181.

eucharist than for their advanced methods of scriptural exegesis.[208] Not surprisingly, principles of interpretation became a major issue in 1059 in Rome. Present at the council were Hildebrand, Lanfranc, and Humbert of Silva Candida. Berengar, by his own report, came voluntarily to the meeting and hoped for Hildebrand's support. He was bitterly disillusioned by the whole affair. According to his account of the proceedings, he was not even allowed to state his case.[209] The assembly made it clear that it was opposed not only to his specific tenets but also to his methods. At the very mention of the word "spiritual," he said, they stopped up their ears.[210] In the end, a humbled Berengar was compelled to repeat an oath eschewing not only his eucharistic "heresy" but even the possibility of higher criticism. The "confession" effectively eliminated the distinction between the appearance and the reality of the sacrament.[211] Both were one: therefore, a deeper, reflective understanding through the comparison of relevant texts disappeared. Berengar's *Opusculum* was a reply to the council, and, in particular, to Humbert's excessive literalism. It reaffirmed his own position virtually unchanged. The view of Radbert and Lanfranc, he reiterated, was a "vulgar error."[212] The *substantia* remained on the altar after consecration.[213] The slow-witted Humbert had even proposed a logical contradiction.[214]

The doctrinal elements of the *Opusculum* were incorporated without alteration into Berengar's *De Sacra Coena*. This work, discovered only in 1770,[215] is known from a single manuscript possibly annotated in the author's hand. Its repetitions and stylistic imperfections suggest that Berengar intended to revise it at a later date. It presupposes a reader already familiar with the eucharistic controversy up to the ap-

[208] Macdonald, *Berengar and the Reform*, 120.

[209] *De Sacra Coena*, c. 18, p. 30; cf. Lanfranc, *De Corpore et Sanguine Domini*, c. 5, PL 150. 415B-C, who says that Berengar was granted the *respondendi licentia* but refused to take advantage of the opportunity. Was the curia against Berengar before the Roman council of 1050? The evidence is weighed by O. Capitani, "Studi per Berengario . . . ," part 3, pp. 129-53. For a comparison of the texts of 1059 and 1079, see L. Hödl, "Die confessio Berengarii von 1059. Eine Arbeit zum frühscholastischen Eucharistietraktat," *Scholastik* 37 (1962), 370-82.

[210] *De Sacra Coena*, c. 18, p. 30. Berengar's use of the term in this context was of course not new. For the growth of the equation *spiritualitas = incorporalitas*, see J. Leclercq, "Spiritualitas," *Studi medievali* 3rd Series 3 (1962), 282-83.

[211] Quoted by Lanfranc, PL 150.410C-11B.

[212] *Ibid.*, 4, 412D.   [213] *Ibid.*, 4, 412D and 5, 414D.

[214] *Ibid.*, 7, 416D; 8, 418C, 418D-19A.

[215] G. E. Lessing, *Berengarius Turonensis oder eine Ankündigung eines wichtigen Werkes desselben* . . . (Brunswick, 1770). For a discussion of the manuscript (Wolfenbüttel, Herzog August Bibliothek, Weissenburg 101), see R.B.C. Huygens, "A propos de Bérenger et son traité de l'eucharistie," *Rben* 76 (1966), 133-39.

pearance of Lanfranc's *De Corpore et Sanguine Domini*, including the decisions of the councils of Vercelli and Rome as well as much unrecorded discussion.[216] Despite its weaknesses, it is also Berengar's most self-conscious literary product. No one who has worked through its confused, labyrinthine periods has been able to avoid taking a position for or against his subsequent fate. But the *De Sacra Coena* also contributed in several respects to strengthening the case in favour of hermeneutics. Its erudition is impressive: precise biblical and patristic quotations occur throughout, and the views of Berengar and earlier writers are fed into a logically interdependent train of thought.[217] It refines and develops an already sophisticated notion of allegory, and for the first time Berengar's mind comes to grips with the purely philosophical question of language versus reality. Finally, it reasserts the primacy of reason and of textual methodology, not, as some maintained, against authority,[218] but in opposition to unrigorous habits of mind which Berengar associated with the popular imagination. The *De Sacra Coena* thereby became the eleventh-century's most forceful statement on behalf of serious biblical criticism and its implications for the educated Christian life.

Its chief originality, as noted, does not arise from stating a radically new thesis. By and large, Berengar repeats what he proposed elsewhere. But the framework for discussion is greatly expanded. He refuses to admit anything which is denied by the evidence of the senses or by simple logic. The bread and wine, he repeats, despite their sacramental value, remain on the altar after consecration, for they can be felt, seen, and tasted. Radbert, Humbert, and Lanfranc, in his view, approach the eucharist in too fundamentalist a fashion, accepting a crude equation between the letter of the text and events in the real world. If the eucharist is to have any genuine meaning, one must get beneath the surface senses and therefore employ methods of interpretation. This was the approach of Ambrose, Jerome, and Augustine, which now, he feels, needs to be reinstated.

However, Berengar is not content as were the fathers with separating the logic of texts from that of reality. He claims that the one can be imposed upon the other. His philosophical method is essentially a series of deductions based on the relations between words, phrases, and syntax. This logic in turn is assumed to apply to the realities

---

[216] Montclos, *Lanfranc et Bérenger*, 198-200.

[217] Esp. chs. 29-46, pp. 62-166.

[218] Cf. Macdonald, *Berengar and the Reform*, 304, quoting Harnack, *History of Dogma* 6, 46, against Reuter, *Geschichte der religiösen Aufklärung im Mittelalter*, 1, 97.

which lie behind the verbal arrangements, whose formalistic and conventional qualities he nonetheless recognizes. He thus reasons from
texts to reality, that is, from words to things. His separation of the
literal and the allegorical also leads as did the cruder formulation of
Ratramn to a radical isolation of the world as perceptible to the senses.
Yet this comes about in a different way. For the dualism of words
and things as he understands it implies that things themselves cannot
simply be broken down into substances and qualities. To put the
matter another way, he takes the ancient distinction between substance and quality and reapplies it by analogy to words and things.
He then denies that it applies to things alone. One cannot sum up
this position as "grammatical," as "nominalistic," or even as an anticipation of the distinction between particulars and universals. Despite authorities, the implications of his thinking are largely his own.
The *antiqui* are important chiefly as reference points for the individual
in his search for meaning. The book purports to reassert a pre-medi-
eval position, but it is really a statement on behalf of modernity.

In Berengar's mind, then, the distinction between sensible and
spiritual is based on the analogy of text (or textual sign) and interpretation. Biblical and patristic writing on the eucharist is a kind of
figurative speech, in which the concrete stands for the abstract, the
particular for the universal. On "mysteries" like the sacraments, Scripture
cannot stand alone. It must be interpreted, preferably with the aid of
reason. Reason, in turn, cannot be employed in a haphazard way; it
must be engaged logically, that is, according to pre-established rules.

The flavour of the discussion can perhaps be caught by paraphrasing
a few passages of interest. Early, for instance, Berengar insists that
his position on interpretation has biblical and patristic precedents.
"The light shines in the darkness," John wrote, "and the darkness has
never quenched it."[219] It even illuminates the "obscurities" of this
world, but Lanfranc's "beclouded mind" is not able to perceive it.
His opponent's chief error arises from overestimating his personal ability to interpret the Bible and from assuming that what he teaches is
always in accord with God's will.[220] There is a more positive basis for
hermeneutic science which begins in the Bible, is handed down through
the fathers, and has been revived in his own teaching. He did not
read the heretical opinions of "Eriugena" in public.[221] He only asserted that the eucharist was "a *similitudo*, *figura*, or *pignus* of the
Lord's body and blood," notions which were fully defensible *secundum*

---

[219] Jn 1.5; *De Sacra Coena* 3, p. 3.   [220] *Ibid.*, 3.   [221] *Ibid.*, c. 9, p. 12.

scripturas autenticas.[222] Had the authorities taken a serious interest in his work, they only had to follow John's advice "to read the scriptures diligently"[223] and to compare what they found to his own understanding. But, he added, one had "to read in order to understand."[224] Without an attentive perusal of the texts, Humbert refused to acknowledge what was "before his eyes" and merely spouted "words without order."[225] Among the many possible guides to the Bible's correct meaning he might well have glanced at Augustine, who, on numerous occasions, clearly distinguishes between reality and symbol. For example, speaking of the transformation of snow into ice, the bishop referred to the crystals as "snow." But he never called snow ice, "unless by that manner of speaking (*locutionis modo*), by which the thing produced (*res effecta*) is conventionally called by its material name (*materialis nomen*)."[226] Similarly, in the Bible, when man is said to be made of earth or Christ is said to be a cornerstone, the text employs a similitude (*similitudo*).[227] Moreover, putting bread and wine for the body and blood of Christ is no different from any other biblical example of one thing standing for another.[228] Ambrose, when he interpreted the sacraments for catechumens, was well aware of this. The water of baptism is not baptism; the bread and wine are not the eucharist.[229] Radbert, Humbert, and Lanfranc, he concludes, are guilty of the fundamental error of mistaking the particular and the universal.[230] "For everything which exists is one thing in that which it is, another thing in being some [particular] thing."[231] In the eucharist there is real bread and wine; there is also "mystical," "tropical," or "figurative" meaning.[232] The two must not be confused.

Nor should the word be put before the text. The primacy of textual analysis based on logical principles is the basis for Berengar's attack on the unreasonable abuse of authority and on all forms of oral, popular, or crudely realist thinking.[233] It is questionable, he asks, who is the more dangerous allegorist, he who utilizes rational methods to elucidate biblical texts or he who confuses them through needless "obscurity."[234] Radbert, in his opinion, reduced important theological

[222] *Loc.cit.*
[223] Jn 5.39, c. 9, p. 12.   [224] *Ibid.*, c. 16, p. 28.   [225] *Ibid.*, c. 16, p. 29.
[226] *Ibid.*, c. 19, p. 32.   [227] *Loc.cit.*   [228] *Ibid.*, c. 20, pp. 33-35.
[229] *Ibid.*, c. 39, p. 122.   [230] Cf. Macdonald, *Berengar and the Reform*, 317.
[231] *De Sacra Coena*, c. 16, p. 29.   [232] E.g., c. 41, p. 137.
[233] Cf. *Ep. contra Almannum*, ed. Montclos, p. 534: Ratio, consulta intus veritate, quae menti humanae sola supereminet. . . .
[234] *De Sacra Coena*, c. 3, p. 3.

issues to the level of *fabula*.[235] The sacrament is not merely a form of participation (*communio*). It is also a form of communication (*communicatio*),[236] and as such must be interpreted. In searching for the right meaning, no one has a monopoly of truth: a "friend" like Humbert, who asserts that he has the whole truth, is really truth's enemy.[237] Moreover, a refusal to consider the real questions has led to a number of "vulgar errors," like the accusation that he holds Manichaean views.[238] Only a radical oversimplification of his teaching could lead to the unsupportable conclusion that Christ's earthly presence was only a phenomenal appearance. He had never been tried by approved legal procedures, which, once again, would have necessitated a careful examination of his writings, not the emotional unanimity of a "mob."[239] "For a crowd of the unlearned in the church does not constitute the church."[240] As it turns out, he was convicted largely by hearsay.[241] His appointed defenders were hardly acquainted with his work.[242] He desired to prove his case "more by sacred authority than by argument"; he was ruined "by the stain of depraved rumour."[243] Authoritarianism and crude realism, he felt, went hand in hand. "What would be more normal for these simpletons than to assert that a man was made in God's image according to his bodily delineation? What would be more typical of an uneducated rabble than that God had made three parts of himself?"[244] Humbert's faction evidently thought that it could approach a mystery like the sacrament by merely breaking bread with the hands and grinding it up with the teeth.[245]

Early Criticism

Beneath the sarcasm, of course, Berengar was affirming his positive belief in the value of interpretive logic. This, in turn, helped to make a case for distinguishing between popular and learned approaches to the eucharist, and, as a consequence, between appearances and reality.

His ideas elicited a wide variety of responses, mostly negative. Although his opponents shared a dislike of his methods and doctrines, their own writings do not fit into any easily definable tradition of thought. Berengar's first detractors were his former student friends, whose appeals were made on their own behalf. Only later did orthodox

[235] *Ibid.*, c. 7, p. 9.   [236] *Ibid.*, c. 8, p. 10.   [237] *Ibid.*, c. 4, p. 5.
[238] *Ep. contra Almannum*, p. 531; *De Sacra Coena*, c. 6, p. 6, following Augustine.
[239] *Ibid.*, c. 6, p. 7.   [240] *Loc.cit.*   [241] *Ibid.*, c. 5, p. 6.
[242] For Vercelli, c. 10, p. 14; for Rome, c. 18, pp. 30-31.
[243] *Ibid.*, c. 6, p. 8.   [244] *Loc. cit.*   [245] *Ibid.*, c. 9, p. 14.

spokesmen become aware of commonly held assumptions. As literary genres, the various contributions to the debate can be classified roughly under three headings: correspondence with old friends like Drogo of Paris or new enemies like Lanfranc; councils, including the major assemblies at Rome in 1050 and 1059 as well as at Vercelli (1050), Paris (1051), and Tours (1054), with which may be included the recantation of 1079 requested by Gregory VII; and major treatises, which begin as early as 1049 with Hugh of Langres and develop through Durand of Troarn (1053), Lanfranc (ca. 1065), Guitmund of Aversa (1075-1078), and Alger of Liège (1110-1121).[246]

Historians have in general arranged the orthodox replies to Berengar so that opposition culminates in the work of Lanfranc, whose *De Corpore* was used by both Guitmund and Alger. But there is another way of looking at the evidence. Early orthodox writers, following Radbert, not only displayed a lack of technical expertise in logic. The views often amounted to authentications of an existing state of affairs, in which texts merely served an evidential function. When opposition to physical symbolism resurfaced in Berengar and his followers, orthodox writers were compelled to develop an interpretive tradition of their own. Thus, as noted, by the century's last quarter, we find a set of differing doctrines but a gradual fusing of methodologies. This meant that the interpreting of the eucharist had become a question for higher culture alone. The essential debate was over conceptual schemes and the degree to which linguistic philosophy was an admissible tool. Even when ritual and symbol were introduced into later discussions, as they were in Lanfranc's case, they formed part of an intellectualist position.

The poles of interest of early replies to Berengar are well conveyed by two writers, John of Fécamp and Adelmann of Liège. For simplicity's sake we may call them monastic and early scholastic approaches to the theme. In John, hermeneutics is considered to be largely superfluous. In Adelmann, interpretation takes its first steps towards grappling with the issues which later philosophers thought important.

John of Fécamp (ca. 990-1078) was the nephew of William of Volpiano, the founder of St.-Bénigne in Dijon. His principal work appeared in three successive versions, the last of which, called the

---

[246] On Guitmund, see Montclos, *Lanfranc et Bérenger*, 462-64 and below, pp. 309-17; for Alger, see N. Haring, "A Study in the Sacramentology of Alger of Liège," *Mediaeval Studies* 20 (1958), 51-56, and, Montclos, 461-62n2.

Confessio Fidei, began to circulate after 1050.[247] Although primarily a mystical treatise, John's "confession" makes its opposition to Berengar clear. In his view, the eucharist was to be experienced, not interpreted, seized by faith, not grasped by reason.[248] Of course, the sacrament is a *res divina*; as such, it can be understood "divinely" or "spiritually."[249] Yet, even this approach, as Gregory the Great illustrates,[250] is less textual than mystical. The transformation of the bread and wine into the body and blood of Christ is brought about by our participation in the mass. One sees the priest before one's eyes at the altar, but the mystery can be seen only through the intuition (*intuitus*) of faith and the heart's introspection (*inspicium*).[251] "Through this mystery we are all participants in Christ: we are all in him." Divine unity is conveyed through "the sacrament's communication"; the mystical bond is thereby subsumed within a verbal pact.[252] And, just as there is one faith, so there is one body and blood of Christ. On the one hand, the real presence is before us; to deny this is to be guilty of heresy.[253] But the universal instrument of communication and contemplation is the Word. "What is seen has a corporeal appearance; what is understood is spiritual. . . . Christ is eaten and yet does not die, he is chewed up but not broken into small bits, he remakes but is not unmade. . . ."[254] Like Radbert, John refers these mysteries to God's limitless power. If they were comprehensible through reason, they would hardly be remarkable.[255]

John's approach, being mystical, is of course irrefutable. That was not the case with the arguments of Adelmann of Liège, who composed one of the lengthiest early critiques of Berengar. On learning of the latter's aberrant doctrines, Adelmann asked Paulinus of Metz, a common friend of both parties, to intervene on his behalf.[256] Paulinus wrote two letters to Berengar, the first towards the end of 1050 or early in 1051, the second sometime later in 1051. Despite Berengar's replies, Adelmann claimed that Paulinus had "left him in suspense"

---

[247] J. Leclercq and J.-P. Bonnes, *Un maître de la vie spirituelle au XIe siècle, Jean de Fécamp* (Paris, 1946), 31.

[248] *Confessio Fidei* 4.1, PL 101.1087A.

[249] *Ibid.*, 1087B. As this would suggest, John was not entirely "mystical" in his approach. On the philosophical element, see the corrective to Leclercq by G. Mathon, "Jean de Fécamp, théologien monastique? (Notes de lecture de *Confessio Fidei* III, 36-40)," *La normandie bénédictine au temps de Guillaume le Conquérant (XIe siècle)* (Lille, 1967), 487-88; and, on the eucharist, 490.

[250] *Dialogi* 4.58; *ibid.*, 1087A-B.

[251] *Ibid.*, 1087B.   [252] *Confessio* 4.3, 1088B.   [253] *Ibid.*, 4.4-5, 1088D-90C.

[254] *Ibid.*, 4.3, 1088D.   [255] *Ibid.*, 4.6, 1090C.

[256] Montclos, *Lanfranc et Bérenger*, 126-29.

and, after a certain period had elapsed, undertook to write Berengar himself.[257] His letter is extant in two versions, one composed at the beginning of 1051, the other, "a little more detailed,"[258] towards the end of 1052. Adelmann's letter has "the dimensions of a true treatise"[259] and may be divided into two parts, the introduction and conclusion, which put the eucharistic controversy in a wider cultural context,[260] and the middle sections, which treat in order christology,[261] baptism,[262] the eucharist, and the range of possibilities for interpretation within the orthodox position.[263]

Adelmann's treatise is written in a refined style, and the rhetoric is deliberate. For he is really presenting two sorts of argument at once. His specific case is directed against Berengar's ideas, or, more particularly, his use of logic. But his juxtaposition of images from the Bible and the classics helps to frame his arguments as a more general contrast between the ancients and the moderns.

Berengar proposed that the Bible could not be accepted without interpretation. He also opposed the unsophisticated methods of many predecessors and contemporaries. What was called for in his view was a clean break with uneducated tradition. Adelmann, too, saw problems in biblical criticism. But, whereas Berengar expressed differences as conflict, he preferred to emphasize continuity. His view was close to that of Fulbert,[264] and, to look forward to the following century, Bernard of Chartres. He asked Berengar to reflect not only upon the memory of their common master, a "modern Socrates," but on the nature of tradition itself.[265] The best way to insure religious truth was to avoid "those who, deviating by heresies and schisms, break the Catholic peace. . . ."[266] He advised his friend to desist from his pointless "vagaries," which had already spread dangerous ideas "into French and German ears."[267] There were in fact precedents for the present situation. The martyrs fought to preserve the integrity of the *respublica christiana*. No "new enemy" should now be introduced.[268]

[handwritten marginal note: part of "Bible meaning" controversy wh. continue in 15c (= translation debates)]

[257] *Ep. ad Berengarium*, ed. R.B.C. Huygens, "Textes latins du XIe au XIIIe siècle," *Studi medievali*, 3rd Series 8 (1967), 477, lines 41-47.

[258] *Ibid.*, 488, line 413.

[259] Huygens, 459. On the literary history, see H. Silvestre, "Notice sur Adelman de Liège, évêque de Brescia (†1061)," RHE 56 (1961), 866-71.

[260] *Ep. ad Berengarium*, pp. 476-78 and 487-88.

[261] *Ibid.*, 478-80.   [262] *Ibid.*, 480-81.   [263] *Ibid.*, 481-87.

[264] On Fulbert's role as an opponent of Berengar, see Capitani, "Studi per Berengario di Tours," 89-103.

[265] *Ep. ad Berengarium*, 476, lines 3-10; 478, 58-59.

[266] *Ibid.*, 477, 27-28.   [267] *Ibid.*, 477, 32-35.   [268] *Ibid.*, 478, 60-66.

Further, the lessons of history were reasonably clear. All the early battles were won by the church. Where, he asks, are the Manichaeans, the Arians? "Even their memory has rotted away, while Augustine, Jerome, and the other opponents of those arena beasts are alive today and flourishing. . . ."[269] Young thinkers should take shelter under their collective authority. As for new ideas, they are very often wrongheaded. The history of pagan philosophy is filled with "monstrous" notions that were refuted not only by logic and reason but by faith, humility, and worship.[270]

Such an introduction, of course, could lead only to the exposition of traditional views. Yet Adelmann's argument is highly developed. Speaking of the eucharist, he maintains, Christ said, "I shall give this bread, that is, my flesh, on the world's behalf." Note, Adelmann adds, that he said "I shall give," not "I gave."[271] When did he begin to give? At the last supper, to which there were numerous eyewitnesses.[272] His statements on that occasion had the same status as the word of God in Genesis, "*Fiat lux.*"[273] The essential instrument of validation, in other words, was the communication of God's power through the Word. Naturally, one may ask whether a single man, even if divine, was capable of what was impossible for all others. The answer again is found in Scripture. When Christ was still mortal, he said, "Without me you can do nothing,"[274] and just before he attained immortality, he added, "I am with you always."[275] Echoing but developing Radbert, Adelmann explains the connection of time and eternity as a neoplatonic paradox. From two natures, he states, one circumscribed, the other uncircumscribed, a harmony was struck. Through the one, Christ transmigrated from one place to another; yet, through the other, he remained with the apostles. In his uncircumscribed nature he is "wholly everywhere and yet lacking locality" (*inlocaliter ubique est totus*).[276] In this way God assured that the *filius Dei* was not separated from the *filius hominis*.[277]

Evidence of Christ's simultaneous participation in two worlds at once is furnished elsewhere in the Bible and helps to underpin Adelmann's realism.[278] It may be asked, he states, why "the appearance of the flesh and blood is not visibly transformed."[279] For Paul said, "We are led about by faith, not by what we see (*species*)"; and elsewhere he

[269] *Ibid.*, 478, 68-70.   [270] *Ibid.*, 478, 78-479, 104.   [271] Jn 6:51-52.
[272] *Ep. ad Ber.*, 479, 97-102.   [273] *Ibid.*, 479, 109-10.
[274] Jn 15:5.   [275] Matt 28:20.
[276] *Ep. ad Ber.*, 480, 120-23.   [277] *Ibid.*, 480, 123-24.
[278] E.g., Actus 9.4 and 1 Cor 15.8.   [279] *Ep. ad Ber.*, 481, 171-72.

defined faith as "the substance of things to be hoped for, the argument of non-apparent things."[280] Paul had good reasons: for, if the sacraments displayed outwardly what they signify within, then faith, by which a just man lives, would serve no purpose. "For who actually sees what he hopes for?"[281] Clearly, faith is an exercise of belief in what is non-apparent, "the vital sacrament beneath the bodily appearance," just as, with equally good reasons, the incorporeal soul lies hidden beneath the form of the body.[282] Similarly, commenting on the *res sacramenti*, Adelmann asks: does baptism seem to be anything but water to those seeing but not understanding the mystery? Does the baptized man seem to be anything but what he was before? Of course not: even the "bath of regeneration" cannot change black into white or educate an illiterate.[283] To think such thoughts is to be "drunk with carnal phantasies rather than wine," to believe in "the illusions of sleep or the reflections produced in mirrors and still waters."[284]

We can understand this activity better, Adelmann continues, if, instead of dividing man's "compact of human nature and power" into "the sense of the body" and "the intellect of the soul," we more carefully examine the characteristics of each. For there are many things which occupy only the senses, like seeing and hearing; others, like writing and reading, which are administered by the senses and the intellect in common; and several matters to which access is not possible through the senses at all, such as the relations between numbers, the harmonious proportions of sound, and all conceptions of incorporeal things. Here, even the purest and most polished mind has difficulty.[285] But "no human faculty," even with God's good will, is sufficient in itself for understanding sacramental mysteries, which pertain to the eternal salvation of Christ.[286] For example, what can sense and reason really understand of baptism? The water can be touched, seen, and tasted; beyond this sense cannot go. Reason can comprehend the physical qualities of water, its mobility, obtuseness, humidity, and its relationship to air, fire, and earth.[287] But neither can unfold the "inscrutable secret" by which water prepares the way for the remission of sins.[288] And yet we maintain that the incorporeal soul is reborn (*renasci*) through corporeal water, restored, so to speak, to the

[280] 2 Cor 5:7; Hebr 11:1.
[281] *Ep. ad Ber.*, 481, 174-482, 177.
[282] *Ibid.*, 481, 177-79. [283] *Ibid.*, 481, 179-82. [284] *Ibid.*, 481, 185-86.
[285] *Ibid.*, 481, 193-201. [286] *Ibid.*, 482, 204-483, 208.
[287] *Ibid.*, 483, 208-17. [288] *Ibid.*, 483, 217-21.

state in which Adam was before he sinned.[289] By similar means we "know" the trinity, that divine "enigma," by which God, as noted, is "wholly everywhere and yet nowhere."[290] In other words, beyond sense and reason, there is really only faith, the "mediator between God and man, bearing in itself all nature, both created and creating."[291] With faith as guide, as Cicero says, we are led over "the sea of this tempestuous period, surrounded as we are on all sides by the densest cloud of error."[292]

Hugh of Langres and Durand of Troarn

Adelmann of Liège was typical of early opponents of Berengar in stating that reason's limitations could be overcome by "simple" faith: simple, above all, because nothing is more odious to our maker than "excessive scrutinizers."[293] The human mind is always bubbling with contradictory philosophies, he maintained, passionately tearing apart the *causae* and *rationes* of everything.[294] "Pompous didacts" invariably follow a train of thought "from the sensible to the intelligible, but avoid the question of faith alone."[295]

His point of view was echoed in less sophisticated responses by such writers as Ascelin the Breton, Anastasius of Angers, and Theoduin of Liège. However, the orthodox could not hope to vanquish Berengar's followers from such a weak position. Accordingly, a more rigorous approach was taken by Hugh of Langres, who wrote his *De Corpore et Sanguine Christi* before the council of Reims in October, 1049, and after having a lengthy interview with Berengar.[296] Like Adelmann, his realism is linked to the will and word of God, which has the power to change (*mutare, transformare*)[297] the bread and wine. Yet, although written a little earlier than the latter's treatise, his argument opens up more philosophical possibilities. His short work therefore provides a bridge between the early critics of the master of Tours and the lengthier replies of Durand of Troarn, Lanfranc, and Guitmund.[298]

Berengar's position, Hugh states, is a veil of error (*erroris involu-*

---

[289] *Ibid.*, 483, 221-24. [290] *Ibid.*, 483, 225-27. [291] *Ibid.*, 483, 233-34.
[292] *Ibid.*, 483, 235-37; Cicero, *Aratea* 40, ed. Muller (Leipzig, 1910), 361.
[293] *Ibid.*, 483, 246-50. [294] *Ibid.*, 483, 252-55. [295] *Ibid.*, 483, 258-59.
[296] *De Corpore et Sanguine Christi contra Berengarium*, PL 142.1334A. On the dating, see Capitani, "Studi per Berengario . . . ," 112n1.
[297] *De Corpore*, 1328C.
[298] Cf. Macdonald, *Berengar and the Reform*, 273-75.

crum).[299] If he had carefully examined "the nature of existing things" and "the teachings of the fathers," it would have appeared to him illogical to describe Christ's body at once as "corporeal" and "incorporeal."[300] For Berengar, he argues, states that "the nature and essence" of the bread and wine is not changed, and hence, the body of Christ, although truly crucified, had only an "intellectual" existence.[301] For if, after consecration, the "primary reality" of the bread and wine persist, nothing can be said to be "transformed"; and, if what is added is only a product of the mind, the nature of Christ's body—which, up to that point, cannot be said to exist—is not clearly understood.[302] "For the intellect is the examiner, not the author, of essences, the judge, not the inventor." Although it "delineates" or "configures" the images of things, it produces no body by creating it from matter.[303]

Hugh, of course, misunderstands Berengar's actual position, which did not deny the intellectual production of categories in the mind, but insisted nonetheless that the sacrament's material reality could not be understood without interpretation, which ultimately depended on them. He thereby attributes to Berengar a more radically symbolist stance than the latter was prepared to defend.

Through the same logic Hugh also adopts an interpretive position himself. If in their *essentia vel natura*, he argues, the bread and wine are only what one has before one's eyes, then they do not contain the potential for bringing about salvation. They remain "impotent." Therefore, in his opinion, one has a choice: either the bread and wine are simply material, and not sacraments at all, or they are in some mysterious way transformed into Christ's body and blood.[304] In separating the *res* from the *signum*, Hugh thus rejects Ratramn's allegorism. For a Caesar, he says, cannot be judged by those beneath him.[305] But a more radical symbolism, as he conceives it, is really a straw man. His approach makes an intellectualization of *res* itself unavoidable. His shift in thinking can be thought of as the conclusion to a long previous tradition of interpretation, which resulted in the orthodox adoption of a genuinely reflective focus.

His argument, in fact, unites the realism of Radbert and, in particular, its explanation of physical symbolism,[306] with a prescholastic conception of essence and change. Reality, for Hugh, is *essentia* or *natura*. If Berengar argues that the bread and wine retain their "reality" and yet are powerless as sacraments, he proceeds "against rea-

---

[299] *De Corpore*, 1328D.   [300] *Ibid.*, 1327A.   [301] *Loc.cit.*   [302] *Ibid.*, 1327A-B.
[303] *Ibid.*, 1327B.   [304] *Ibid.*, 1327C.   [305] *Ibid.*, 1327B-C.   [306] *Ibid.*, 1331A-32D.

son."[307] For a thing's nature or essence cannot be separated from its qualities. If water turns to wine, in no sense is it any longer water.[308] Berengar, he adds, also mistakes superficial for elemental change. A thing, after all, may appear to change before our eyes but in reality remain the same. "Air does not suffer from the arrow's flight."[309] In order to have essential change, which the eucharistic mystery requires, one needs divine intervention. For "stable Nature," veiled for eons by appearances, must first relax firmly established bonds and become once again the elemental force out of which she is made.[310] To suggest that this can be done without God's assistance is "unreasonable."[311] Berengar, he states, takes the side of those who assimilate God's power to nature.[312] But mysteries like the sacraments cannot really be explained in this way. The word was made flesh; similarly, the bread and wine are transformed.[313] Those who have faith are "free men," those who require a hermeneutic veil, "slaves."[314]

Hugh's explanation amounts to a reaffirmation of God's essential stability in a material world of fluctuating forms. "This is especially appropriate in the sacrament's case. For the created form (*creatura*) of bread and wine prove they serve God while he changes nature's constancy with invisible speed, transfiguring (*transfigurans*) himself into everything. . . ."[315] Like Berengar, he opposes those who take the sacrament for granted "ignorantly."[316] A crude physicalism is therefore unacceptable. But, in addition to his own naturalism, inspired doubtless by the Latin Plato, he returns to the notions of divine power and to reliving ritual. The one relates the visible and the invisible, the other, past reality and present re-enactment. The last supper, he argues, is not an allegorical story but a sacrificial reality.[317] The central mystery is the word made flesh. Christ's birth moreover was not "terrestrial"; that is not the meaning of *caro facta carnem*. Similarly, the rebirth brought about by the sacraments is not earthly.[318] "For God's changeless word, humbly made flesh . . . , is carried over to a renewed creature. . . ."[319] Just as the word of God was invisible in the flesh, which was nonetheless a product of creation, so that very flesh exists already in the word, somehow created invisibly and only concealed by qualities.[320] "But this reality of the flesh is not denied to spiritual eyes."[321]

[307] *Ibid.*, 1327C.   [308] *Ibid.*, 1327C-D.   [309] *Ibid.*, 1327D.
[310] *Ibid.*, 1328A-B.   [311] *Loc.cit.*   [312] *Ibid.*, 1328B-C.   [313] *Ibid.*, 1328C.
[314] *Ibid.*, 1329A-B.
[315] *Loc.cit.*   [316] *Ibid.*, 1329D.   [317] *Ibid.*, 1329D-30A.
[318] *Ibid.*, 1330B-C.   [319] *Ibid.*, 1330C.   [320] *Ibid.*, 1330D.   [321] *Loc.cit.*

Hugh, in short, asks, from a scholastic viewpoint, the right sort of questions, even if he does not provide adequate answers. His line of attack was pursued at greater length by Durand of Troarn, whose *De Corpore et Sanguine Domini* appeared in 1053. Durand was the first author to direct a theological tract against Berengar personally, and no one previously had defended the orthodox position with so wide a selection of biblical, patristic, and early medieval texts.[322] Yet Durand was also caught uneasily between two worlds: his treatise is a hybrid of mystical anti-intellectualism and interpretive realism. He perpetuated the approach of Radbert, emphasizing the absolute transcendence of God's will through the word, and placing religious enactment and participation before forms of understanding. But he also presented traditional authority as an intellectual position in its own right, a summation, so to speak, of various writings.

His task, he announces, is to inquire into all the early Christian teachings in order that the "substance" of divine truth, concealed (*operta*) beneath the bread and wine,[323] might be revealed, and that heresies and schisms, which are making their way "through Frankish lands,"[324] should be countered by a brief presentation of authorities. It is not only the beliefs of Berengar which he questions but also the methods by which they are established. The eucharistic opinions of his opponents are consequently viewed as a classical heresy, a *veternus hostis*, an *antiqua mortalium pestis*.[325] Its diffusion (*diffudere*) is an intellectual phenomenon. Like the literary portrayals of heresy which we have already examined, Berengar's ideas are regarded as a revival of ancient errors, which then infiltrate Christendom like poisons spreading through the body.[326] Placing Berengar's position in a historic context of course allows it to be attacked using the same technique. Durand quotes *antiqui* like Cyril, Hilary, Basil, Leo, John Chrysostom, and, above all, Ambrose and Augustine, as well as *moderni* like Hincmar, Amalarius, Radbert, and Fulbert of Chartres. He also calls as witnesses the pseudo-Isidorian decretals, an apocryphal letter of Clement of Rome, Eusebius of Emesa, Cassiodorus, and Bede.[327] Moreover, he puts past teaching into three categories, *doctrina, sanctae vitae exempla*, and *miracula*.[328] But, at bottom, his realism is not philosophical or theological. It depends on faith and oral experience. More

---

[322] Heurtevent, *Durand de Troarn*, 244, 249.
[323] *Liber de Corpore et Sanguine Christi, proemium*, lines 1-4; PL 149.1375.   [324] *Ibid.*, 1376.
[325] *Ibid.*, 1.1; 1375, 1377A.
[326] *Ibid.*, 1.1; 1377A.
[327] Heurtevent, *Durand de Troarn*, 244-45.   [328] *Liber de Corpore* 2.2; 1378C.

than Hugh, he returns to an essentially non-intellectual point of view, rejecting entirely the "crass similitude and figure"[329] which attempts to explain away the last supper's reality. The events of the Bible, he argues, happened literally. They depended on the Word, which engaged directly in creating, becoming flesh, and performing miracles. The eucharistic mystery re-enacts the original scenes of Christ's sacrifice.

Berengar's error, in his opinion, is not only to have thrown accepted teaching to the winds and to have overinterpreted the sacrament.[330] It is to have mistaken the ritual aspects of Christianity for structures of words. For Durand, religion is *professio*.[331] He does not adhere to a negative literalism, which sees the eucharistic sacrifice as "true" because Christ actually lived.[332] He gives a positive evaluation to the Lord's symbolic behaviour. This is clear from his exegesis of John 6:52. Christ, he argues, affirmed two things: the bread which he gave was his true flesh and this flesh was the world's life.[333] Christ, in other words, passed from the corruptible to the changeless;[334] similarly, the sacrament on the altar "is immediately transformed from its visible appearance into that which only He understands. . . ."[335] Also, when Christ referred to the eating of his flesh and the drinking of his blood, he was not speaking of "the impurity of digestion" but the external sign of divine mystery.[336] The form of the sacrament is visible, the operation invisible;[337] the means of transformation is the holy spirit, acting through the Word. From the visible, even earthly substances, that is, from bread and wine, the true body and blood of Christ are made by means of "the incomprehensible artifice (*opificium*) of the spirit" and from "mystical words."[338]

The link between the last supper and the eucharist is therefore provided by re-enactment. The visible form is directed by means of a "celestial commerce" towards the invisible "in the minister's hands."[339] Word and ritual act together: the interpretation goes beyond Augustine, whose *De Trinitate*, quoted at length,[340] limits itself to conceptual issues, and takes its meaning from the liturgy itself. Penance is also stressed. Christ, Durand reminds his readers, gave himself on the

[329] *Ibid.*, 3.4; 1383A; cf. 1.1; 1377A.
[330] *Ibid.*, 1.1, 1377B-C; 5.12, 1393A; 9.32-33, 1421B-24B.
[331] *Ibid.*, 1.1, 1378A; 2.2, 1378C.   [332] *Ibid.*, 2.2; 1378D.
[333] *Ibid.*, 2.2; 1379A.   [334] *Loc.cit.*   [335] *Ibid.*, 1379B.
[336] *Ibid.*, 2.2, 1379B.
[337] *Ibid.*, 1380A.   [338] *Loc.cit.*   [339] *Loc.cit.*
[340] *De Trin.* 3.4.10; *Loc. cit.*, 1379C-D.

world's behalf twice, once during the last supper, a second time on the cross. The first sacrifice was a prefiguration of the second,[341] and the eucharist relives the memory of those events. Christ "signified beforehand," just as we "taste beforehand" the bread's "visible substance."[342] Durand's exposition makes use of Hilary's conception of the incarnation,[343] as well, perhaps, as Eriugena's notion of Adam's sin as the fall of *humana natura*.[344] But the core of his thinking revolves around the mass itself, and he tolerates no interpretive vehicles as intermediaries between the priest and his audience.[345] The identity of the two ritual events also transcends, to his mind, any possible logical contradictions. The sacraments are communicated equally by acts (*facta*) and words (*verba*).[346] "What I have done through my power," said Christ, "you do through my authority, I by example, you by imitation."[347] To do what? To fashion (*conficere*) his body and his blood through his words, not only to preserve his memory but to see him spiritually, to sense his presence.[348]

Ritual, then, is vitalized by the Word, and Durand's central problem is how to move from word to text. His attitude towards written tradition is understandably ambivalent. He is convinced that the eucharistic heresy is the consequence of false *documenta*.[349] But faith cannot be called into question by such "broken figures of the truth."[350] On the other hand, he is aware of the pitfalls of physical symbolism, as evidenced in his discussion of the psalm "Extol the lord our God; worship at his footstool. . . ."[351] On the surface, he remarks, we would seem to be asked to display reverence towards a concrete object. But, as in the sacrament, one thing is before us, another is meant.[352] Reality is present *in pignore*.[353] Natural processes are subordinated to the word along lines suggested by Ambrose, in which the examples illustrate not what "nature formed" but what "the benediction consecrated."[354] The word of Elias was sufficient to bring fire from heaven. Could Christ's word then not bring about a change in "the elements' appearance"?[355] Further, if Christ was able to invent what did not exist, surely he could change already existing things into those which did not yet exist.[356] For first creation is more remarkable than simply changing essences (*mutare naturas*).[357] The same principle of explana-

---

[341] *Ibid.*, 3.3, 1381B-C.   [342] *Ibid.*, 1381B.
[343] *Ibid.*, 1382B-C; 3.4, 1383A.   [344] *Ibid.*, 2.2, 1380C.
[345] *Ibid.*, 3.3, 1381C.   [346] *Loc.cit.*   [347] *Loc.cit.*
[348] *Ibid.*, 1381D.   [349] *Ibid.*, 1382C.   [350] *Loc.cit.*
[351] Ps 99:5; 1383B.   [352] *Ibid.*, 3.4, 1383B-C.   [353] *Ibid.*, 3.5, 1384A.
[354] *Ibid.*, 4.7, 1385A.   [355] *Loc.cit.*   [356] *Ibid.*, 1385B.   [357] *Loc.cit.*

tion is used in a number of analogous cases. For instance, was the *naturae usus* not suspended in Christ's birth, which, if the natural order had been followed, would have resulted in an ordinary human being?[358] Yet, Christ's birth, crucifixion, and resurrection also involved his "true flesh," which, as a consequence, is a *sacramentum* brought to life for us during the mass by the priest's words.[359] Therefore, "what speech sounds out, affection senses."[360] By the same token, just as Christ's *corpus* was both material and spiritual, so the words of the Bible have both a literal and a figurative sense.[361] Christ's spiritual body can be the subject of figurative expression in the same way that manna means "the angels' bread."[362] In both cases there is not merely an image which conceals reality. A latent meaning is also revealed in the course of time.[363]

While not denying the power of the word, then, but by building on it, Durand arrives at the necessity of texts and interpretations. The antinomy of word and text is never completely resolved; the operative power of the word is continually reiterated. But the possibility of hermeneutics is also admitted. One thing may be seen by the eyes, another signified by means of *ratio typica*.[364] This, he adds, is the meaning of *similitudo* and *figura* in Ambrose and Augustine.[365] But why did Christ resort to figures of speech at all? First, to demonstrate that through the power of his word he could alter *genera instituta*; secondly, because his disciples no less than his later communicants would have been shocked to see his real blood.[366] Yet the bread and wine are not on that account mere figures. The word became flesh and the bread descended: those who receive "the flesh" are "participants" in the mystery "through the food of his substance."[367] Rather than calling a figure of this type a mere appearance of reality it should be termed *supersubstantialis*, as Augustine suggested and Radbert confirmed.[368] Expressions like *figura* and *similitudo corporis et sanguinis* are frequently found in the fathers.[369] But they do not diminish the sacrament's "reality," which simply hides beneath the surface of the grammar and rhetoric. When Paul, for instance, speaks figuratively of the body and blood, he does so to celebrate the mystery of the

---

[358] *Loc.cit.*   [359] *Ibid.*, 1385B-C.   [360] *Ibid.*, 1385C.

[361] *Ibid.*, 4.8, 1386D.   [362] *Ibid.*, 4.8, 1386A-C.

[363] *Ibid.*, 4.9, 1387B; 4.10, 1389D-90B.

[364] *Ibid.*, 4.8, 1387C.

[365] *Ibid.*, 4.9, 1388B-89C; 5.11, 1392C-D.

[366] *Ibid.*, 4.9, 1388B-C.

[367] *Ibid.*, 1388C.   [368] *Ibid.*, 1389B-D.   [369] *Ibid.*, 5.11, 1391C.

eucharist, not to create a circumlocution.[370] "The similitude or figure
is full to the brim of truth and grace."[371] The eucharist therefore is
at once a real sacrifice and a symbol.[372] What is more, in reading
figurative expressions in the Bible and the fathers, one must watch
out for "subtle distinctions of words." The apparent sense is not always the meaning, contrary to what the Manichaeans, the Arians, and
more recent heretics have taught. In a *figura* they often see only *fig-
mentum*, not *veritas*.[373] But, when God made woman, he did not change
humanity's essence, as a cursory reading of Genesis might suggest.[374]
Nor, in his letter to the Hebrews, did Paul oppose *figura* to *veritas*.[375]
Even the figurative expressions of Ambrose, on which Berengar relied
heavily,[376] can be reconciled with Christ's words.[377] No one denies
that there are figures of speech in their own right, but these are just
"figures of figures." The sacrament is a *figura substantiae*.[378] Needless
explanation is to be avoided,[379] but only an "illiterate" could fail to
see the Bible's deeper sense.[380]

Durand concludes with a number of miracles drawn from Radbert,
Gregory of Tours, Rufinus, and John the Deacon. These illustrate that
he has in general two answers to the problem of why Christ spoke in
figurative expressions. One relates to higher culture, is based on the
fathers, and is seen as a reply to Berengar himself. The other is a
paradigm for communication among the less well educated. Here his
chief biblical text is once again the sixth chapter of John. The scene
is the Sea of Galilee, where "a large crowd" was seeking out Jesus.
There follows the miracle of the loaves and the fishes, after which
Jesus walks across the rough sea towards Capernaum. On the following morning, Durand reminds his readers, Christ told the assembly
to "work not for this perishable food, but for the food that lasts, the
food of eternal life." The people asked for a sign like manna, which
descended for Moses in the desert. Jesus answered that this was not
the true bread; he alone was the "bread of life." And he alone would
raise the dead on the last day. To the ensuing incredulity among the
ranks at how someone could offer "his flesh to eat" Durand responds
in largely allegorical terms. The uneducated, he argues, failed to appreciate the symbolic nature of Christ's words. Jesus used everyday

---

[370] *Ibid.*, 1392A-B.   [371] *Ibid.*, 1392B.   [372] Heurtevent, *Durand of Troarn*, 228.
[373] *Liber de Corpore* 5.12, 1393A.
[374] *Ibid.*, 1393B.   [375] Hebr 1:3.
[376] Cf. Heurtevent, *Durand of Troarn*, 229.
[377] *Liber de Corpore* 5.14-15, 1395A-98A.
[378] *Ibid.*, 5.13, 1394B.   [379] *Ibid.*, 6.17, 1400C-D.   [380] *Ibid.*, 5.15, 1395C.

phrases so that his message would be acceptable. He said bread but meant flesh, attracting his listeners with a novel expression but not shocking them with the naked truth. However, to his disciples he revealed that only the spirit has life: this, Durand says, is the spiritual sense of the text.[381]

Lanfranc

Only roughly a decade elapsed between the appearance of Durand's treatise and Lanfranc's *De Corpore et Sanguine Domini*, which was composed between 1063 and 1068.[382] Lanfranc's ostensible reason for writing was the request of Thierry of Paderborn that he answer the *Opusculum*, in which Berengar attacked the council of Rome of 1059. Lanfranc did not take part in the actual debate,[383] but he cast his epistle to Berengar in the form of a fictive dialogue before an ecclesiastical tribunal with the council clearly in mind.

His work marked an important phase in the eucharistic discussion. It was a defence of the orthodox position at a high philosophical level and, significantly, the first that depended almost entirely on an internally developing tradition, including the writings of Berengar himself. If Durand's interpretive technique was unsure, Lanfranc, like Berengar, wrote within a tradition of commentaries laid down by the fathers. He thereby united the *antiqui* and the *moderni* in a continuous body of theory. After Lanfranc, discussions of the eucharist's meaning became almost exclusively the responsibility of professional canonists and theologians. Oral experience, liturgical practice, ritual participation, and popular appreciations of the sacraments were afterwards of less interest than the internal philosophical evolution within the treatises themselves.

Lanfranc's *De Corpore et Sanguine Domini* can be divided into two major sections.[384] In the first (chapters 2-17), he answers Berengar's *Opusculum* point by point, dealing in turn with the charges against Humbert of Silva Candida, the use and abuse of dialectic in theology, and the legitimate manner of interpreting the eucharist. In the second (chapters 18-23), he refines and elaborates his own conception of the sacrament, first according to *auctoritas*, then according to *ratio*. In the

---

[381] *Ibid.*, 1380B; 5.13, 1394A-B.

[382] Montclos, *Lanfranc et Bérenger*, 249.

[383] Macdonald, *Berengar and the Reform*, 128 and n3.

[384] Cf. Montclos, 272-73, whose detailed exposition (part II) provides an outstanding guide to the development of Lanfranc's ideas. For a briefer but acute analysis, see M. Gibson, *Lanfranc of Bec*, 84-91.

introduction and chapters sixteen and seventeen he also reviews the events which, in his opinion, led to the condemnation of 1059.

The summary content of Lanfranc's treatise is reasonably well known. Less often discussed is his attitude towards popular and learned tradition and the manner in which orality is transformed as part of a systematic approach to interpretation.

In the introduction, he explains how, in his view, the controversy arose and what its real significance is. He was, he says, initially disposed to a public debate on the eucharist with Berengar. But, as no appropriate occasion presented itself, he decided at length to put together a "compendium" refuting the essential errors. He accuses Berengar not only of maintaining doctrinally incorrect ideas but of forming a sectarian movement ultimately destined to subvert the faith. When the works of Augustine, Gregory the Great, and other authorities were brought before him, he purposefully deformed their meaning through *falsa et depravata ratio*. He therefore came to the holy city not out of love but fear. Rather than adopt an authoritative exposition of the texts, he engaged in "clandestine meetings" with his followers. As a result they all had to be silenced.[385]

Clearly, more than a single controversy was at stake, for Lanfranc suggests political, sectarian, and larger interpretive issues. Further, he argues, Berengar's "diabolical fallacy" easily seduced "minds ignorant of divine mystery." In thus sinning against his less well educated brethren, the master of Tours sinned against Christ.[386] Specifically, he ensnared those who, "not knowing how to resist, contemplated things visible rather than invisible." He preached such errors, committed them to writing, and sent his envoys "into diverse regions." His opinions were justly examined by Nicolas II, but, "bending his body rather than his heart, he reignited them." Replying to all Berengar's theses would be a thorny business, he concludes, since, through verbal cleverness, the master of Tours colours his apparitions "black and white at will." But, if ordinary believers (*populum Dei*) are to have any peace, an attempt must be made.[387]

Berengar, then, stands accused of forming a heretical sect based on intellectualism. Beyond this, what Lanfranc says simply turns Berengar's views of his opponents back on himself. Berengar claimed that the realists merely pandered to popular taste and to illiteracy. He also alleged that the uneducated masses and their theological spokesmen

[385] *De Corpore et Sanguine Domini*, c. 1, PL 150.407A-09C.
[386] 1 Cor 8.12.
[387] *De Corpore*, c. 1, 409A-09C.

like Humbert trusted appearances and physical changes alone. This is precisely Lanfranc's argument. Through interpretive techniques, he states, Berengar overcame those least capable of resisting; and he did so by focusing their attention on superficial linguistic questions at the expense of deeper mysteries. The important point is not the actual case presented by either side; it is the independent recognition by both of a hiatus between popular and learned culture.

However, if that assumption is shared, other views are not. In Lanfranc's opinion, Berengar is a "heretic" because his teachings are not consistent with orthodoxy and because he dares to contradict the church's legislation.[388] The handling of Humbert's case is illustrative. Humbert, Lanfranc argues, was anything but the uncouth "Burgundian" that Berengar alleged. He was a *vir religiosus*; his place of origin was Lotharingia (well known for its venerable educational institutions). Equally capable in "faith" and "science," he was appropriately made archbishop and later cardinal by Leo IX.[389] Further, he did not draw up Berengar's confession on his own authority but at the request of the entire assembly at Rome in 1059.[390] Copies of the text were circulated and everywhere met with approval.[391] Berengar thus stands twice convicted: he not only opposed inherited authority but affixed his signature to tenets he believed contrary to Catholicism.[392]

Needless to say, this approach is different from Berengar's. Lanfranc's argument is from authority to understanding: the capacity of the church to legislate is the criterion of the belief's legitimacy. If one sees the church in an apostolic role, the responsibility for making legal and theological decisions is also the criterion of truth. For Berengar, the ultimate court of appeal is the human mind and reason. Legislation and inherited doctrine play a secondary part. Lanfranc thus presupposes an institutionalized church, without which the continuity of ecclesiastical thought and action is inconceivable. Berengar sees the church primarily as a community of believers, onto each of whose shoulders devolves a certain responsibility for subjective commitment and logical thought. The two views are not mutually exclusive. Lan-

---

[388] *Ibid.*, c. 2, 410B. Cf. Montclos, *op.cit.*, 280. Estimates of Lanfranc's mastery of canon law vary. For a positive view, see Z. N. Brooke, *The English Church and the Papacy* (Cambridge, 1931), 57-83; for a more accurate assessment, J. Gilchrist, *The Collection in Seventy-Four Titles: A Canon Law Manual of the Gregorian Reform* (Toronto, 1980), 8-9.

[389] *De Corpore*, c. 2, 409D-10A; c. 16, 426B. Humbert was from either Lyons or somewhere in the Lorraine; on the former, see Bonizo of Sutri, *Liber ad Amicum*, MGH Libelli de Lite I, 598, 18-20.

[390] *De Corpore*, c. 2, 411B, D.   [391] *Ibid.*, 411D-12A.

[392] *Ibid.*, 410B.

franc reserves a large function for reason within traditional teaching and Berengar sees no incompatibility between individualism and membership in the church.[393] Yet, their respective conceptions of literacy's uses remain far apart.

So, by implication, does their attitude towards "popular culture," which is essentially negative in both but exploited for different polemical ends. In calling Humbert a "Burgundian," Berengar meant that he adopted the position, or, as he would prefer, the mad view of the common crowd (*vecordia vulgi*); this, in turn, he equates with Radbert's and Lanfranc's teaching, namely, that, after the consecration, the "substance" of the bread and wine "does not at all survive."[394] Lanfranc points out that Berengar argues *ad hominem*,[395] i.e., against the cardinal rather than the church or theology, and he adds that he would prefer to be thought a *rusticus* or *idiota* rather than a supporter of such specious erudition.[396] For neither, then, is the question "for" or "against" interpretation: it is whose interpretation is correct, and why. Popular culture has become merely a metaphor for describing the arguments of the other side.

The debate between Lanfranc and Berengar thus brought the question of the eucharist to an important crossroads. It not only specified which interpretive positions could be reconciled with the church's teaching. It also drew into focus more sharply than before the status of appearance and reality, and, by implication, the criticism possible of traditional ritual and symbol.

This is clear from chapter five, in which Lanfranc takes up Berengar's criticism of the orthodox view of the sacraments. Inherited ideas, he repeats, are hardly Humbert's invention. Berengar accuses him of stating that the bread and wine are only sacraments. This, he retorts, is not Humbert's but Berengar's own view. Berengar also attributes to the cardinal the notion that the bread and wine are only the true body and blood of Christ. This, Lanfranc says, is the view of no one.[397]

Both authors, of course, distort each other's position, which does not advance either side but illustrates their attitudes towards interpretation. Berengar puts Humbert and Lanfranc in the position of asserting one of two ridiculous extremes: either the bread and wine are only what appears on the altar, or they are only flesh and blood, that is, what they evidently appear not to be.[398] He thereby pictures

[393] Montclos, *Lanfranc et Bérenger*, 282; 441-44. Cf. *De Corpore*, c. 16, 426C-D.
[394] *Opusculum, ibid.*, 412D.   [395] *De Corpore*, c. 3, 412C.   [396] *Ibid.*, 414B-C.
[397] *Ibid.*, 415A.   [398] *Opusculum, ibid.*, 414D.

them as excluding the possibility of higher understanding, which, paradoxically, he insists is essential for making sense out of the sacrament. In reality, Humbert's criticism of Berengar made the potential for further dialogue minimal. Nor was Lanfranc correct in stating that the cardinal's opinions were shared by all previous commentators.[399] What, it is arguable, the latter had in common was a faith in the *magisterium*:[400] the institution rather than the individual was conceived as the instrument of interpretation. In the end, Lanfranc is compelled to misrepresent Berengar's position in his turn. Berengar, he states, not the church, wishes to consider the eucharist "only a sacrament."[401] It is he who refuses to admit anything but appearances, etc. In fact, both authors' point of departure is Augustine's notion of *sacramentum* as a visible manifestation of an invisible reality which requires the mind's interpretive activity in order to be understood. Lanfranc as much as admits this when he advances the idea that the bread and wine are the true body and blood in "no man's" opinion, yet maintains in the same breath that Berengar denies all realism.[402] For his part, Berengar sees Lanfranc's "heresy" as a simple denial of the value of the human mind as an intermediary between the eucharist's external and internal meaning. Neither is wholly correct; both in part are wrong.

In chapter six Lanfranc counters with an interpretation of his own. Berengar, he informs us, argued that, in calling Christ the "chief corner-stone," Christ, as logical subject of a sentence, is not removed (*aufert*) but entirely retained (*omnino constituit*). Similarly, he would argue, when one says "The bread on the altar is only the true body of Christ," the bread on the altar is not denied. Logically speaking, the bread and wine are confirmed to exist (*esse confirmat*) in the Lord's meal.[403] In commenting on the set of statements Lanfranc has no quarrel with a neutral methodology.[404] He is merely against its misapplication to reality and to change, especially if words are mistaken for things. He replies: "You would string out the truth (*verum*) if someone inexperienced with it maintained the first part of the proposition (i.e., bread and wine), unless by chance he put forward the other words (i.e., body and blood) in a figurative manner (*figurato*

[399] Macdonald, *Berengar and the Reform*, 131.

[400] *De Corpore*, c. 4, 413A-14A; c. 5, 415A; c. 18, 427A.

[401] *Ibid.*, c. 5, 415A.   [402] *Loc.cit.*

[403] *Opusculum, ibid.*, 415D-16A.

[404] *De Corpore*, c. 6, 416A; cf. c. 17, 129B. On the pair's use of dialectic, see J. A. Endres, *Forschungen zur Geschichte der frühmittelalterlichen Philosophie*, 43-47, 114-19.

locutionis modo)."[405] But that, he adds, is just playing with words. Anyone knows that on occasion we call things out of which other things are made by their former names, even if they are physically transformed into something new. Berengar himself pointed out that Augustine refers to ice as the crystals out of which it is made. But the master of Tours wants to accept the first part of the equation without necessarily admitting the second, that is, as he sees it, to take the figure of speech without the reality. However we wish to name it, there is still a reality to contend with.[406]

Here, again, Lanfranc misrepresents Berengar's intentions. Reality was not denied: Berengar merely said that interpretations dealing with it belong essentially to the realms of logic and language.[407] Lanfranc proposes that "names" are only useful in describing realities and does not see any a priori value in a science of interpretation. In his view, expressions like bread and wine keep the appearance and the names of the realities they once were, but, after consecration, they are really transformed into body and blood.[408] He concludes by putting into Berengar's mouth words very like those Berengar put into his. "You," he says, "who deny the flesh and blood, do not accept the latter half of the (abovementioned) proposition, whereas we, who affirm both halves, nowhere deny the existence of a sacramental figure for many celestial things." This *similitudo*, he adds, which impedes Berengar's ideas, advances his own.[409] If we peel away the rhetoric, the difference between the two may be stated as follows: Lanfranc asserts that names (*nomina*) are always attached to realities (*res*), while Berengar maintains that, while realities exist, they tell us little about what names mean in expressions, which must be investigated through the behaviour of language. In other words, both Berengar and Lanfranc agree that "when *divina pagina* calls the body of Christ bread, it is a question of *sacrata ac mystica locutio*."[410] But Lanfranc says that the figure describes a pre-existing reality, while Berengar asserts that what comes first is the linguistic description, from which inner reality can perhaps be inferred.

Lanfranc adds that, in his view, as noted, there can be no purely logical solutions to theological problems.[411] For the historical or spiritual realities are given and cannot be explained away. He prefers

---

[405] *De Corpore*, c. 6, 416A; cf. c. 18, 427A.

[406] *Ibid.*, c. 6, 416A-B.

[407] See above, pp. 278f.   [408] *De Corpore*, c. 6, 416B-C.   [409] *Loc.cit.*

[410] *Ibid.*, 416C.

[411] *Ibid.*, c. 1, 408A-B; c. 3, 412B; c. 7, 416D-17A.

sacrae auctoritates to *dialecticae rationes,* not only because of the inherent limits of human reason,[412] but also because he fears that philosophically sophisticated *periti* will invariably deceive faithful but less well educated *imperiti.*[413] The argument is two-sided: in spiritual matters, realities come before intellections, and, when popular culture is involved, authority, affirmed by faith, is better than a poorly understood rationality. No less than Berengar, he takes the Augustinian position that philosophy is a useful aid to exegesis. Yet he would limit its function to the explication of a given text in accord with traditional teaching. His position is considerably more sophisticated than Radbert's evidentialism, in which the text was a mere memorandum for the Word. But he sees little role for new interpretations as independent texts.[414] In particular, he appears to have limited the use of formal logic to the *materia disputandi.*[415] In short, his conception of hermeneutics moves from grammar and lexicography through syntax and rhetoric and finally to theology, while remaining within the orbit of the original text.

But, as Berengar caustically noted, Lanfranc did not adhere strictly to his own principles.[416] He put forward two irreconcilable statements, namely, that the bread and wine are only sacraments and that they are only Christ's body and blood. He then attempted to dismiss the master of Tours through an error of logic, the very abuse to which he took most serious exception. The method was inappropriate; nor was Lanfranc a real match for Berengar in philosophical analysis.[417] Berengar, in fact, affirmed that, if any term of a proposition were suppressed, the existence of the whole was thrown into doubt. Thus, if one asserted, on the one hand, that the bread and wine were only a sacrament, and, on the other, that they were only the body and blood of Christ, a refutation could only come about by negating one of the two. In his reply, Lanfranc does not deal with the logical issues but confines himself to inessentials.[418]

The further, in fact, Lanfranc moves onto Berengar's ground, the more clearly he reveals his own weaknesses. An example is provided in chapter nine. Berengar argued that, through consecration, the bread and wine became a *sacramentum religionis.* They did not cease to be

---

[412] *Ibid.,* c. 7, 416D.   [413] *Ibid.,* c. 8, 418D.
[414] *Ibid.,* c. 7, 417A.
[415] Montclos, *Lanfranc et Bérenger,* 289 and 289-90n7.
[416] *De Sacra Coena,* p. 50, 26-28; p. 51, 17-19; p. 53, 7-54; Montclos, 291n2.
[417] Montclos, 291-93. For a similar conclusion, see M. Gibson, *Lanfranc of Bec,* 84-88.
[418] *De Corpore,* c. 7, 417D-18A.

what they were: while remaining that, they were also changed into something else.[419] In other words, while remaining physical objects apprehensible to the senses, they acquired a religious value perceptible to the mind. His authority was Ambrose's *De Sacramentis*.[420] Lanfranc, in replying, once again distorts Berengar's sense, accusing him of maintaining simultaneously that the bread and wine do not cease to be what they were and of their being changed into something which they were not.[421] His own interpretation of Ambrose is less sophistical, but it convinces only to the degree that he abandons Berengar's statement and strikes off in a direction of his own. Ambrose, he correctly observes, did not propose that the manna from heaven was like the mystery of the eucharist: the one was *umbra et figura*, the other *lux et veritas*.

Berengar did in fact take Ambrose out of context.[422] But Lanfranc did not answer his critique. Berengar, following the fathers, argued that all divine mysteries consist of two parts, *res* and *signum*. That Christians interpreted manna as *figura* and the passion as *res*—using the distinction so to speak as a figure of speech—did not change the methodological significance. However, Lanfranc added, Ambrose also said that the mystery consists "not of what nature formed but of what the benediction consecrated."[423] Here he struck close to the weak link in Berengar's chain of thought. Both Ambrose and Lanfranc were referring to the transformative power of the Word; both considered the change to be "real." For Ambrose, it was inseparable from the mass (which, neither of his later students recalled, he was elucidating for recent converts). Lanfranc sees the Word in a larger context as the principle behind all "mysterious" change.[424] His interpretation, as it turns out, no less than Berengar's, is an expansion of the original's meaning. But Lanfranc incorporates orality, which Berengar does not,[425] and returns to the idea in his later discussion of eucharistic change.

While there are genuine differences of position, then, there are more evident points of conflict arising from the pair's mutual distrust of each other's methods, a distrust, it should be added, which is based as much on hearsay as on the opinions each claims to be refuting. This is evident from chapters ten, eleven, and twelve. In ten, Berengar states that the eucharist consists of two elements, one visible, one invisible, that is, in Augustinian terms, *sacramentum* and *res sacra-*

---

[419] *Opusculum, ibid.*, 419C.   [420] *Loc.cit.*; *De Sacramentis* 4.4.15.

[421] *De Corpore*, c. 9, 419C.   [422] Montclos, *Lanfranc et Bérenger*, 297.

[423] *De Corpore*, c. 9, 420A; *De Sacramentis*, c. 9.

[424] *De Corpore*, 420A-B.   [425] *Ibid.*, 420C-21A; *De Sacramentis*, c. 4.

menti.[426] Lanfranc's view is a slightly altered version of the same statement. In eleven, he is compelled to seize upon Berengar's minor grammatical errors in an effort to put some distance between them. In twelve, he argues that Augustine's definition of *sacramentum* as *sacrum signum* is taken out of its ritual context and used simply as an analytical tool[427]—which is correct enough, but hardly a reply to Berengar's substantive ideas. Nor does Lanfranc actually trust that "the mystery of faith can be safely believed but not usefully investigated."[428] For many of his difficulties stem from his advocacy of a non-interpretive position by means of interpretation. The further he moves into the field of logic, the more he is forced to adopt the same terms of reference as his opponent.

Lanfranc sounds a more original note in the following three chapters, in which he presents the core of his own thinking on the eucharist. He extends his analysis of Augustine's concept of *sacramentum*, distinguishing it from Berengar's. He also develops the links between word, ritual, and experience mentioned in chapter nine.

Chapter thirteen opens with two quotations from Augustine by Berengar. In the first, Augustine states that, if the sacraments did not contain the image of the things of which they were the sacraments, they would not be sacraments at all. In the second, he says that signs of divine realities are visible but that invisible things are glorified in them.[429] Lanfranc "situates the sacramental resemblance on an entirely different basis."[430] In his view, without a "resemblance" between the eucharistic reality and the body of Christ there can be no sacrament, that is, no rapport between reality and sacred sign. But he does not establish this simply by following the bishop of Hippo.[431] Instead, while a certain intellectualism is retained, the ideas progress by analogy with ritual, oath, and custom. It is true, he allows, that the sacraments bear the image of their inner realities. But this philosophical relationship cannot be isolated within the rite. "When the host is broken and the blood poured . . . , what else is designated (*designatur*) but the sacrifice of the Lord's body on the cross . . . ?"[432] In other words, what constitutes the sacrament is not only its resemblance to something else but its confirmation of a sacred reality through

[426] *Opusculum, ibid.*, 421A-B.

[427] *De Corpore*, c. 12, 422C-D.   [428] *Ibid.*, c. 10, 421D.

[429] *Opusculum, ibid.*, 422D-23A, quoting, respectively, Augustine, *Ep.* 98.9, PL 33.364 and *De Catechizandis Rudibus*, c. 2, PL 40.311.

[430] Montclos, *Lanfranc et Bérenger*, 404.

[431] For the opposite view, see Montclos, 406-07.   [432] *De Corpore*, c. 13, 423A.

a verbal commitment (*jusjurandum*).[433] Historical precedents are recalled. Gregory the Great, writing to Justinus, is said to have employed *sacramentum* in this sense. Elsewhere it is called *sacratio*; its relation to *res* is similar to the type of argument which gives verbal assent to a fact or "rhetorical support" to a cause. Augustine, after all, was not writing dry philosophy; he was preaching in the quoted passages "to the uninitiated." When he said that the invisible glorifies the visible he was not merely dividing things as they appear into the categories of sanctified and unsanctified. He was referring to a reality made evident by ritual. "For we see in the appearance of the bread and wine, which are before our eyes, invisible realities; that is, *we* glorify the flesh and blood of Christ." It is not a question of dividing the matter into two "appearances," one before consecration, the other after. Moreover, Augustine, in speaking of the eucharist, was also thinking of the other sacraments, which are not obedient to intellectual principles alone but also to accepted custom (*consuetudo*).[434]

The sacrament, then, is considered both as word and text, that is, both as oral communication (*jusjurandum, consuetudo*), involved in rite (*immolatio, sacratio*), and as an object of cognition (*sacramentum/similitudo*). In sum, Lanfranc sees the eucharistic ceremony as the subjective attempt to recall an objective fact through ritual.[435]

A further integration of these elements is attempted in chapter fourteen. Berengar quotes Augustine, who states: Just as the sacrament of Christ's body is "in a certain fashion" Christ's body, and the sacrament of his body is in the same fashion Christ's blood, so the sacrament of faith is faith.[436] Lanfranc's interpretation is this: "The body of Christ's sacrament, insofar as he was actually sacrificed on the cross, is his flesh, which, hidden under the bread's form, we receive in the eucharist, along with his blood as wine; that is, flesh is the sacrament of flesh, blood of blood. Thus, by flesh and blood, at once invisible, intelligible, and spiritual, is signified (*significetur*) the redeemer's body, visible, palpable, full of grace, virtue, and majesty."[437] The essential transformation takes place during the rite: "The bread, when broken, is divided up for the people's salvation; the wine, when poured, is taken up by the lips of the faithful." Thereby, "his

---

[433] *Ibid.*, 423A-B.

[434] *Ibid.*, 423B-D.

[435] Cf. O. Casel, "Das Mysteriengedächtnis der Messliturgie . . . ," 113-15; 188-89. R. W. Southern records Lanfranc's gloss on *pignus* as *filius vel consanguineus*, with its legal implications; *St. Anselm and his Biographer* (Cambridge, 1963), 20.

[436] *Opusculum, ibid.*, 423D.   [437] *De Corpore*, c. 14, 423D-24A.

death on the cross, as well as the spilling of his blood, is represented (*figuratur*)."⁴³⁸

Gregory the Great, he adds, referred to just such a ritual transformation when he said that eating the bread and drinking the wine re-enacted (*imitatur*) Christ's crucifixion and brought about our absolution and purification.⁴³⁹ Gregory, he notes, said *imitatur* not *operatur*:⁴⁴⁰ he meant the reliving of an experience through the rite, including its intellectual significance, not a physical or intellectual change alone. He also used the concrete rather than the abstract. In this sort of realism, the eucharist, as a visible process, is integrated into the processual changes of Christ's birth, crucifixion, and resurrection. And, in this sense only does the linguistic interplay to which Berengar alludes actually become relevant. "Flesh and blood, by which we are nourished daily towards obtaining the clemency of God for our sins, are called body and blood, not only because they remain essentially the same, but also by that manner of speaking by which the signifying thing (*res significans*) is accustomed to be called by the term of the thing signified (*significatae rei . . . vocabulo*).⁴⁴¹ In the Bible, when a relationship between symbol and reality is established, it is integrated into the overall mystery of change by means of typology. An example occurred after Christ rose from the grave. Two men on their way to Emmaus met him but did not know who he was. His appearance, as Augustine noted, signified that he would soon rise into heaven.⁴⁴² The episode, in Lanfranc's view, was not only part of the gospel narrative; it also attempted to present the events in a mysterious form, far from the common experience (*communis vita*) of men.⁴⁴³

The discussion of the eucharist as ritual is brought to its culminating point in chapter fifteen. Once again the analysis begins with a quotation from Augustine by Berengar. In his letter to Boniface, the bishop of Hippo made the following statement: "Christ is sacrificed once in himself; and yet he is sacrificed in the sacrament not only during each Easter ceremony, but, for the ordinary people, every day as well."⁴⁴⁴ Lanfranc proposes this interpretation: Christ, it is true, was sacrificed once in himself. The "true man" and the "true God" hung at once on the cross, the man offering himself as a living victim for the father, suffering, dying, bringing remission of sins to both the living and the dead.⁴⁴⁵ In the eucharistic ceremony the church com-

---

⁴³⁸ *Ibid.*, 424A.   ⁴³⁹ *Loc.cit.*; *Dialogi* 4.58, PL 87.425D.   ⁴⁴⁰ *De Corpore*, c. 14, 424B.
⁴⁴¹ *Loc.cit.*   ⁴⁴² *Ibid.*, 424B-C; Lk 24.13ff.   ⁴⁴³ *Ibid.*, 424C.
⁴⁴⁴ *Opusculum, ibid.*, 425A-B; Augustine, *Ep.* 98.9, PL 33.363-64.
⁴⁴⁵ *De Corpore*, c. 15, 425B.

memorates this act. The Lord's flesh is sacrificed daily; it is divided and eaten, and his blood is poured from the chalice into the mouths of the faithful. Both enactments are "true"; both have their origin in the incarnation. Yet neither could take place without a rationale of certain mystery (*sine certi mysterii ratione*). Thus, when it said that the whole Christ is eaten "after a manner of speaking," what is intended is that eternal life, which he represents, whets the appetite of spiritual desire, recalling his sweet commands and inspiring fraternal charity, reigniting the memory of his crucifixion and spilt blood.[446] There is a meeting of the actual physical and philosophically material aspects of the eucharist: the one complements the other.[447] Berengar, therefore, argues to no purpose that, "if Christ suffered once in himself, he suffered only once in his own body, since his body cannot in any way be separated from himself."[448] For a logician he is not reasoning very logically. "For there are many things which exist in reality which cannot be brought together simply through their constituent parts. Since the Lord was at once true God and true man, just as every man is made of rational soul and body, neither his soul nor his body alone can rightly be called man or God."[449] In other words, there is an answer to Berengar's methodology.[450] The ritual of the bread and wine re-enacts a historical reality originally bringing together the human and the divine.

This is the ultimate source of the "mystery," the subject to which he turns in chapter seventeen after once again defending Humbert against Berengar's charges.[451] Berengar, recalling the cardinal's words, is reported to have said: "For who can concede that the bread is miraculously broken into pieces of Christ's body, since, after the resurrection, he will reappear intact, and since, moreover, he remains up to that point wholly unrecallable?"[452] Lanfranc replies that such processes cannot "be investigated by argument or conceived by reason." To such celestial mysteries one simply adds faith, so that in the end one attains one's just reward instead of merely confusing oneself attempting to understand what is unfathomable. "For it is not necessary for one to see things which are veiled from one's eyes" and are brought about "through the operation of divine power." Then as now, God's true nature is concealed under wraps (*tegumenta*). Heretics and over-interpreters are babes: "Laughing at faith and wishing to understand everything rationally," they are ignorant of genuine reason. They are

---

[446] *Ibid.*, 425B-C.   [447] Montclos, *Lanfranc et Bérenger*, 414.
[448] *Opusculum*, 426A.   [449] *De Corpore*, c. 15, 426A.   [450] *Loc.cit.*
[451] *Ibid.*, c. 16, 426B-D.   [452] *Opusculum*, 426D.

like horses or mules, which react without thinking. They are unconvinced of divine truths not by understanding but by poor exposition
(*male exponendo*).[453] The Bible furnishes many examples of things which
were consumed and not diminished, to say nothing of mysterious
comings and goings on the Lord's part.[454] The essence of good interpretation is the ability to distinguish between "things to be taken
literally and things to be understood spiritually."[455]

So ends Lanfranc's point-by-point refutation of Berengar's *Opusculum*. From chapter eighteen, he focuses his attention on the eucharistic
conversion itself, arguing from *auctoritas* (chs. 18-19), *ratio* (chs. 20-
21), and from objections to the master of Tours (chs. 22-33).[456] There
is little that is genuinely new in part two, in particular on the question of transubstantiation and the real presence. But formal distinctions between his and Berengar's views are more sharply contrasted.
Lanfranc reiterates that he and Berengar are separated as church (*fides*)
and sect (*secta*).[457] The one is universal, spreading doctrines held "from
earliest times,"[458] uniting the *antiqui* and the *moderni*.[459] The other,
although claiming to return to the apostolic church,[460] is particularist;
its ideas are spread about by his "disciples" and "followers," who win
their shortlived victories by replacing "light" with "shadow."[461]

In repeating patristic and more recent ideas on the eucharist, Lanfranc's fundamental tenet remains that the eucharistic conversion of
terrena substantia comes about with the aid of divine power, "ineffably,
incomprehensibly, and marvellously."[462] He adds the evidence of miracles, which, for him, involve not only suspension of natural laws
but, very often, the numinous power of words in a ritual context.[463]
He also purges naturalistic language so far as possible from the vocabulary of conversion, utilizing most frequently the terms *operor* (to work,
labour, or toil) or *converto* (to convert or change).[464] He thereby emphasizes the activity's concreteness and reaffirms the original biblical
phrasing. In avoiding naturalism, he once again implies an analogy
with the ritualized *instituta* of customary law.[465] In other words, if
there is a parallel with the eucharistic ceremony in another area, it

[453] *De Corpore*, c. 17, 427A-C.   [454] E.g., III Reg 17.15; *Loc. cit.*, 427C.   [455] *Ibid.*,
429B.

[456] Cf. Montclos, *Lanfranc et Bérenger*, 320-21.

[457] *De Corpore*, c. 18, 430A.   [458] *Ibid.*, 430C-D.   [459] *Ibid.*, c. 19, 435C.

[460] *Ibid.*, c. 9, 420C.

[461] *Ibid.*, c. 20, 436A; cf. c. 9, 420C.

[462] *Ibid.*, c. 18, 431B-C. On eucharistic miracles in general, see P. Browe, *Die eucharistischen
Wunder des Mittelalters* (Breslau, 1938).

[463] *Ibid.*, 431C.   [464] *Ibid.*, 432B.   [465] *Loc.cit.*

does not arise from abstraction alone but as well with the codes of conduct in oral culture. God's intervention and the sacraments function within the same mode. As Christ said, "You have the words of eternal life."[466] The fathers, he adds, while aware of the physical transformation, never adopted a fully symbolist position.[467] Augustine, for his part, underlined the ritualistic associations, and, like Gregory after him, preferred real images for representing real changes.[468]

Lanfranc's position, of course, is a subtle interweaving of interpretive and non-interpretive approaches, as is clear from his reply to Berengar's "objections." Certainly Augustine, whom the master of Tours quotes, asserted that his own words on the eucharist were to be understood *spiritualiter*.[469] But that was not a denial of the real presence. It is necessary, to recall his words, "that one thing be celebrated visibly and another understood invisibly."[470] *Spiritualiter* is a synonym for *invisibiliter*.[471] Similarly, terms like *species, similitudo, figura, signum, mysterium*, and *sacramentum* are employed on behalf of a real entity.[472] *Species, similitudo*, and *figura* refer to realities that have disappeared;[473] *signum, mysterium*, and *sacramentum*, to Christ's actual suffering on the cross.[474] Berengar, Lanfranc concedes, comes close to a deeper understanding from time to time, but it is always conflated with verbiage.[475] Further, Berengar seems dumb to the inner meaning of the rite. When *species* is used in the canon of the mass, it refers, not to appearances as Ratramn suggested, but to a "manifest vision" under which truth is hidden.[476] Ritual meaning moreover is specific. Berengar errs in too facilely comparing the eucharist with baptism.[477] True, there is no death of Christ in baptism, but that does not mean there is no real blood in the eucharist. One cannot simply compare rituals, which are enactments of lived situations, by means of *verborum intelligentia* or *similitudinis identitas*.[478] Not to recognize such different senses, he concludes, is to class oneself as an *idiota* or *imperitus*.[479]

But interpretation, as Lanfranc sees it, is based ultimately on *auctoritas*, which, as noted, is universal.[480] On the surface his argument appears to be a tautology: the church legislated certain norms, and these are the basis for placing *auctoritas* above *ratio*. But the matter goes deeper than that. Berengar asserted the value of the text over the

---

[466] Jn 6.69; 432C.   [467] *Ibid.*, 432D-33A.   [468] *Ibid.*, 433A-C.
[469] *Ibid.*, 433C.   [470] *Ibid.*, 434A-B.   [471] Montclos, *Lanfranc et Bérenger*, 312.
[472] *De Corpore*, c. 20, 436A.   [473] *Ibid.*, 436A-B.   [474] *Ibid.*, 437C-38A.
[475] *Ibid.*, 436A.   [476] *Ibid.*, 436B.   [477] *Ibid.*, 438D-39B.
[478] *Ibid.*, 439A.   [479] *Ibid.*, c. 22, 440C.
[480] *Ibid.*, 440D-41D.

word. The individual, as interpreter of the text, thereby supplanted
what he considered to be uneducated ways of thinking. Textual criticism, moreover, has its own rules; once adopted, the system could
not be suspended arbitrarily to avoid embarrassing consequences.
Lanfranc did not accept the autonomy of hermeneutics. For him, the
essence of Christianity resided in God's word, which is expressed in
textual form only to facilitate communication. It is a record of events
alone. Legislation, therefore, and commentary, indeed, all forms of
ratio, are appendages,[481] which can in part explain the word, but
which do not take its place. The proof of the word's efficacy is not its
interpretability but its consistency of meaning for the entire Christian
community. Latins, Greeks, and even Armenians, in Lanfranc's phrase,
"bear witness with one mouth to the faith."[482] The unity of God's
word reproduces itself in the unity of the church's members. Heresy,
by implication, of which Berengar stands accused, is not only a doctrinal error; it is an attempt to undermine universalism.[483] For that
reason, rather than its cleverness, it is considered to be the devil's
work.[484]

Guitmund of Aversa

Lanfranc's views were put into a naturalistic context by his pupil
Guitmund, whom Urban II named bishop of Aversa in 1088. Like
his master, Guitmund argued that Berengar misinterpreted Augustine
on the real presence. But he went further than his teacher in reflecting
the genuine tenets of his opponent and in anticipating scholastic discussions of the sacraments in such thinkers as Alger of Liège. He not
only provides a bridge between the unperfected sacramental vocabulary of the eleventh century and later, official doctrine. He also takes
up a number of issues of central importance to twelfth-century thinkers on scientific naturalism.

The three books of the *De Corporis et Sanguinis Christi Veritate in
Eucharistia* are framed as a dialogue between the author, who takes
the orthodox position, and a certain Roger, who appears bemused by
the Berengarian "heresy."

Guitmund first gives us a pen-portrait of Berengar, whom he sees
as a pompous autodidact. The mixture of fact and fiction is instructive. When Berengar was a schoolboy, witnesses report, he was so
impressed by his own brilliance that he paid little attention to anyone

---

[481] Cf. Montclos, *Lanfranc et Bérenger*, 311, who limits the contrast to doctrine.

[482] *De Corpore*, c. 20, 439A.   [483] *Ibid.*, c. 23, 439A.   [484] E.g., c. 1, 409A.

THE EUCHARIST AND NATURE

else. France was then lacking in guides to "higher philosophy's secrets." So he amused himself by wrenching novel senses (*novae . . .
interpretationes*) from what he knew, thereby appropriating to himself
a unique science (*singularis scientia*). This, in turn, he vaunted publicly: "Simulating the style of a master instead of following the matter
of instruction, he covered his head with a hood, and, deep within its
recesses, pretended to meditate, deceiving many through the rasping
of his scarcely audible voice." He was set straight by Lanfranc, Guitmund continues, but, unable to bear the humiliation and the loss of
his students, he turned to dissecting the sacraments, a subject obviously beyond his adolescent range. "He preferred to remain a heretic
and to enjoy shifting public admiration rather than to live privately
as a Catholic under God."[485]

These are strong words. Yet, pruned of their rhetoric, do they not
present Berengar somewhat as he saw himself, that is, as an individual
interpreting Scripture in his own manner through logic? Guitmund
concludes by accusing the master of Tours of two beliefs he did not
hold, namely denying the sacraments of marriage and of baptism. The
former, he adds, enabled him to prostitute women, the latter to condemn infants to perdition. In both cases he was the devil's mouthpiece.[486] The central issue as Guitmund elsewhere puts it is *haeretica
fallacia* versus *catholica veritas*.[487] These are familiar details. Berengar,
like earlier heretics, becomes a stereotype, someone long ill "with the
heretical plague."[488] Moreover, he achieved his ends only by employing the distorted logic (*ratiuncula*) common to all subverters of orthodoxy, to which were added the "sweet but corrupt" words of his
supporters. And so, little by little, "the disease was spread about."[489]

The establishment of the conspiracy theory is the preface to Roger's
pinpointing of Berengar's chief offence in Guitmund's eyes, which is
to maintain that the eucharist is not substantially (*substantialiter*) Christ's
body and blood. It is only so named by the voice alone (*sola vox*),
signifying its shadow and figure (*umbra et figura*).[490] Even though the
senses normally deceive the mind, Berengar insists on reasoning through
the flesh (*carnaliter*), evidently distorting his patristic sources. Guitmund proposes to dispute his logic and his authorities on whether
nature does not permit such a change (*natura hanc mutationem non
patitur*).[491]

Not all Berengar's followers err in the same way. All *Berengariani*

[485] *De Corporis et Sanguinis Christi Veritate in Eucharistia*, bk. 1, PL 149.1428A-C.
[486] *Ibid.*, 1429A.   [487] *Ibid.*, c. 2, 1445B.   [488] *Ibid.*, 1462A.
[489] *Ibid.*, 1429D-30A.   [490] *Ibid.*, 1430A.   [491] *Ibid.*, 1430A-B.

agree that the bread and wine do not change essentially (*essentialiter*). But they differ on much else. Some assert that virtually nothing of Christ's body and blood is present and call what is on the altar only "shadows and figures." Others, yielding on some points, say that the eucharist truly represents the body and blood but contains them secretly (*latenter continere*) in order that they may be imbibed (*sumi*), or, as their leader prefers to say, made bread (*impanari*). And they affirm that this is Berengar's "more subtle view." Still others, opposing Berengar, nonetheless make use of his arguments, stating that the bread and wine are changed in part and remain unchanged in part. Finally, there are those who do not find the Lord's straightforward words adequate and prefer to seek meanings on their own. Among other things they state that, while the bread and wine are wholly transformed, they revert to mere flesh and blood when the unworthy come to receive communion.[492]

But all *Berengariani* oppose orthodoxy with the same idea, that there is no essential change of bread and wine.[493] Guitmund's reply is to extend the notion of God's omnipotence to what Berengar regards as the realm of nature. His opponents maintain, or so he affirms, that nature cannot permit such a transformation. But, "whatever the Lord pleases, he does"—a verse of the Psalms, he adds, they quote but do not understand.[494] If they did not believe God omnipotent, they could not argue that he violated nature. And, if not omnipotent, then he is not God at all. Nature can permit such a change if he wills it. For this "nature," which in itself is literally nothing, is brought into being and forms species through his volition. How can mere bread and wine resist? Further, Berengar's followers, who think they defend nature, are really ignorant of its forces. If physical proof were necessary, it is furnished by physiology. The "nature" of the bread and wine which we eat and drink every day is "transformed naturally into flesh and blood." If such nourishment is normally changed into flesh and blood in our stomachs, how can the same power be denied to God's word? These new pagans should perhaps concede as did Plato that "the nature of things is what God wishes."[495]

As for "eating" Christ's body and blood, that too is in harmony with God's will, as the Bible bears witness. After all, Thomas doubted

[492] *Ibid.*, 1430C-31A.　　[493] *Ibid.*, 1431A.

[494] Ps 134.6: Omnia quaecunque Dominus voluit fecit. Cf. J. Leclercq, "Passage authentique inédit de Guitmond d'Aversa," Rben 57 (1947), 214: "Si placet ita Deo nulla contra eum natura esse potest, sed quod ei placet ilico simul naturale est, et proprie si ita est locutus sum."

[495] *De Corporis* . . . , 1431A-D.

the resurrection until he had before him the visible and tangible Christ.[496] If he was able to touch the Lord with his hand, or, for that matter, his whole body, why could he not "touch" with his teeth? And, if Thomas, the apostles, and the holy women had this experience in the past, why can the faithful not have it in the present? "No reason is opposed." Nor is it undignified, as some assert, for Christ to be "bitten into." For the faithful are saved by this physical act, just as He saved all mankind by suffering death on the cross. It was necessary that he die in reality; similarly, it is necessary that he be eaten "in truth." What is more: in the Old Testament, man "died," not by eating the shadow but the fruit of the forbidden tree; so the "new men" avoid death and receive life by eating not the figure but the reality of Christ, who also died from the limb of a tree. All this, Guitmund adds, is prophesied by Isaiah 25:6-7, where the Lord spoke of "a feast of wine on the lees." Corroboration is found in Paul, who speaks of Christ, in whom lives the fullness of divinity corporeally (*in qua habitat plenitudo divinitatis corporaliter*).[497] One can argue that teeth are in themselves unworthy instruments for divine acts. But remember Titus 1:15: "To the pure all things are pure." The argument concludes with a parallel: "It is natural for flesh to be touched; it is its infirmity to be wounded." Therefore, Christ, as flesh, was and is "touched," was and is "wounded." And in his *humilitas* lies our redemption.[498]

What, then, of the meaningful element in the eucharistic rite? Guitmund assigns this too to God's intentions, once again adding physical analogies. A good example is provided by the problem of division. When Christ's faith is "divided among the people," it is not diminished by division (*partiendo minuatur*). This seems to be the case only on account of an image of breakup (*propter similitudinem fractionis*).[499] For his body is not distributed through division but through participation. The host cannot be divided any more than the trinity, which, appearing as three, is really one. Division in fact is brought about by the office of the priest, which celebrates the eucharistic mystery of the many in the one. Moreover, the mystery, Guitmund argues, transcends physical reality just as thought assimilates words. For we know through "everyday experience" that our understanding, that is, "the word of our inner being," when clothed with sound, allows what was known to us alone and hidden in our hearts to be made manifest to others through the voice and at the same time to

[496] Jn 10.25-28; *loc.cit.*   [497] Col 2.9; *loc.cit.*   [498] *De Corporis*, 1432A-33C.
[499] *Ibid.*, 1434A.

remain wholly within the mind. If a thousand men hear the sound, the same paradox is observed: they hear the words all at once, yet each one keeps his thoughts for himself.[500] If, then, God offers so great a mystery through the human word, he too is able to reach a thousand ears. He too therefore is "clothed" by his voice. And no one ought to think the mystery of him, his coeternal word, or his flesh incredible, even though it appears to us in the form of words, "since one is never able to seize a meaning fully from man's fragile, transitory speech or his shortlived, momentary sounds, even though, as a rule, one retains something of the sense."[501]

But what one "grasps" also involves interpretation. Committed to a revalorization of the tangible, Guitmund nonetheless incorporates the idea of inferiority. On the one hand, he despises over-interpretation. Even Solomon could not explain everything. How, then, can man?[502] On the other, he clearly distinguishes between sense and thought. Roger asks how something can be divided before our eyes and yet remain whole in essence.[503] Guitmund replies that one must see with the eyes of the mind or of faith. There is no equation between what Christ wishes to effect (operari) and what is apprehensible to sense (carnalis aestimat sensus). Scripture furnishes numerous examples of the senses' inadequacies. Mary Magdalene saw Christ as she wept outside his tomb, but she did not at first know who it was.[504] Similarly, Luke says, "Their eyes were kept from recognizing him."[505] The analogy can be pushed further: since it was Adam whose spiritual eyes were shut and whose carnal eyes were open, it is fitting that Christ close our carnal eyes and open those of the mind, by which truth is apprehended. No one considers a man healthy whose palate judges sweet to be sour; likewise, no one mistakes the external for "the medicine of interior light." The sacrament, therefore, works contra visum. For the senses often deceive, as ancient philosophy and everyday experience plainly teach.[506] They are particularly prone to error, Boethius notes, on the greatest and the least matters. In general, the exterior senses cannot be trusted on their own. Even a harlot seems beautiful to her lover! One's ears are no better: the love song which attracts the lascivious is a trifle to the sober man. The real challenge is to escape the senses: striving spiritually, we exert faith; exerting, we grow learned; learned, we are nourished; nourished, we grow; and, growing, we reach towards spiritual perfection. It is inconceivable,

[500] Ibid., 1434A-35B.   [501] Ibid., 1435B-C.   [502] Ibid., 1436A.
[503] Ibid., bk.1, 1436B-C.   [504] Jn 20.11.   [505] Lk 24.16.
[506] De Corporis, 1438B-C.

therefore, that the eucharist's "miracle" be revealed to the senses, for the faithful and the unfaithful would then be on an equal footing.[507]

But what, then, is the status of sense data? Some reject the eucharist because they believe no such transformation has ever occurred during the course of nature.[508] But the Bible does report other substantial changes, as, for example, when Moses's rod became a serpent.[509] The human mind is limited: it cannot "grasp how that which is wholly in one place at one time can also be in another." But such a mystery is no stranger than the voice that is heard by all but emanates from one place, or the soul, which is one but which is spread throughout our limbs. The best example is creation itself: all men believe it, although none can explain it. Furthermore, with respect to the creative process, who is capable of understanding what has been done after it is done? For, what was not by definition was not done, and, having been done, is already brought into existence. When it exists, it is no longer being made: it just is. And that which has been made cannot be anything midway between being and non-being. For, if it lies between two states, it has nonetheless already been brought into being. Indeed, when can we say that what has already been made has been in the process of making? For that which lacks a beginning can in no way be said to exist. How marvellous, then, that what is made is by necessity believed in and yet understood by no form of thought. Moreover, if anyone thinks this line of reasoning confusing, Guitmund adds, let him conduct an inquiry into the beginnings of things in words or thoughts.[510] The same relationships will be seen to hold.

As a consequence of this train of thought, Guitmund concludes book one with a purely logical solution to the problem of change. The Bible, he states, narrates the creation of man in one of four ways: from neither man nor woman, like Adam; from both man and woman, the contrary; woman from a virgin man, like Eve; and man from a virgin woman, like Christ. No one thinks the birth of man from man and woman extraordinary because it happens every day. But, it is also logically possible to generate a contrary from a contrary, as for example man from non-man or Eve from virgin Adam. Such was the birth of Christ: the whole world rose against it in contradiction. And it was no less "against the customary course of nature" than the birth of Eve from Adam's side. More abstractly, Scripture speaks of a "fourfold substantive or effective principle of change." One principle is that by which all things were made into what they are from nothing. A

---

[507] Ibid., 1438C-39B. [508] Ibid., 1440B. [509] Exod 7.10. [510] De Corporis, loc.cit.

second is the opposite, which is a product of thought rather than of experience, by which whatever exists on its own can return to nothing. A third operation takes place when substances become non-substances, either through natural or miraculous change. The fourth is the case of the eucharist, in which one existing thing becomes another.[511]

Are the "sacraments of the altar," then, *figura* or *veritas*? As in Radbert, but with greater philosophical sophistication, the answer again is "both." Without abandoning the tangible, Guitmund admits an interpretive framework. He opposes Berengar not so much with authority as with textuality. Also, like Lanfranc, he reserves a special place for ritual.

Augustine, he argues, did not state, as Berengar assumes, that the sacraments were only a *signum* or *figura*. He spoke of them as a *celebratio*, "in which and through which we commemorate his death." In other words, the eucharist is a recollection and re-enactment. Relating the passion signifies the passion itself; in that sense, the celebration of the body and blood is the *signum* of the passion. The sign, by implication, is both physical and spiritual, physical in reanimating, spiritual in meaning. For, unlike the sacrifices of the Old Testament, the eucharist must not be understood "servile and infirm according to the letter." When we say *"Christus immolatur,"* we refer to a signifying commemoration of an act already completed (*jam peractae significativa commemoratio*). Augustine often speaks in such *figurata locutio*. But that does not mean the sacrament is a mere figure. The reference is to the spiritual meaning of physical events. The *"Umbratici,"* who assert that the eucharistic body is only the shadow of the historical, misinterpret his words. The purpose of the eucharistic ceremony is to recall the crucifixion to mind (*recolendum in memoria*). The eucharist is a *signum* or *figura* in the sense of a *sacrum signum*, that is, a *sacra oblatio*.[512] Isaiah said, "Where is the lettered?" (*Ubi est litteratus?*), that is, the "judge of words."[513] The *grammatici* and *dialectici* may ridicule ordinary usage (*quotidianus usus*).[514] But that same experience ultimately gives the eucharist its meaning.

3 . NATURE AS TEXT

Guitmund of Aversa brings the discussion of the eucharist to questions similar to those treated in Guibert's treatise on relics, with which

---

[511] *Ibid.*, 1444A-44C.   [512] *Ibid.*, 1454C-58A.
[513] Isaiah 33.18; *loc. cit.*, 1463B.   [514] *Ibid.*, 1436C.

we began. In both, the central problem is not so much verification as authentication.

Like Guibert, Guitmund uses interpretive techniques within a limited context. He provides an adequate foundation for the orthodox position, but he fails to explore the wider connections of hermeneutics with logic and language. In these spheres he is no match for Berengar, whose views he disingenuously represents as both "popular" and "learned" heresy at once: popular, insofar as he and his followers are said to focus on the carnal alone, acknowledging in the eucharistic sacrament only *umbra, figura*, or *signum*; and learned, since, despite these allegedly uneducated attitudes, they are said to manipulate words with diabolical logic.

As in Guibert, there are in Guitmund two sides to the question: on the one hand, there is the physical, the tangible, and the concrete; on the other, a method of proof involving the quotation and discussion of texts. The two, as noted, are only loosely united in his mind. Convincing evidence of this is furnished by his argument that the bread and wine are not really "consumed" but only appear to be so, a view whose radicalism leans logically towards his opponents and was therefore reversed by later commentators.[515] But, owing to his relative imprecision, Guitmund, rather, say, than a more canonically oriented theorist like Alger of Liège, offers a convenient focal point for the analysis of attitudes towards naturalism as they appeared on the eve of two large intellectual movements, the scholastic solution to transubstantiation and the rebirth of scientific empiricism. The subject is too large for full treatment here, and would in any case require a departure from the study's main theme. By way of conclusion to this chapter, we may summarize Guitmund's reflections on the problem; then, if only briefly, turn to parallel ideas in William of Conches, Alan of Lille, and Hugh of St. Victor.

Guitmund, first of all, insists on a serious consideration of what appears before the senses as his starting point. Thomas, he argues, believed in the resurrection only when he actually saw the risen Christ. The sacrament's phenomenality is not a sign of physical baseness but of spiritual humility; that is, it constitutes the preparatory stages of redemption. The eucharist is thus aptly designed by God as the change of one substantial thing for another. Commenting on Hilary of Poitiers, he adds that one should speak of the sacrament not *substantialiter*

[515] *Ibid.*, 1440n10; cf. R. Grégoire, "Guitmond of Aversa," *New Catholic Encyclopedia*, vol. 6, 859.

but *naturaliter*.[516] The role of the senses in appreciating the eucharist is also emphasized by analogies with everyday experience. Through *quotidianum experimentum*, Guitmund maintains, we learn that the eu-charistic mystery is similar to the relations between thoughts and words. Would Berengar not have agreed? Guitmund evidently did not think so. The senses, he adds, often fail, and Berengar, in his view, erred in trying to disprove sacramental signs through material experiment alone.[517]

However, such adaptations of "experience" must be seen against the background of Guitmund's search for biblical authority and prec-edent. Book three of the *De Corporis* is a virtual checklist of previous authorities, including the lives of the early saints and the fathers. Moreover, Guitmund's approach to interpretation is not a blind fidel-ity to traditional doctrine. It depends on the educated individual's ability to work through inherited ideas for himself. Employing a eu-charistic analogy, he remarks that every person is capable of holding an image (*figura*) of himself in which there is nothing of his own substance (*substantia*).[518] Similarly, the physical presence in the eucha-rist is not the same as God's intended meaning. Understanding the mystery, as Ambrose suggests, is seeing it without anything to cover it up (*absque ullo velamine*).[519] Therefore, nothing is beyond nature (*praeter naturam*) in Christ's being represented by objects like a stone, a lamb, and so forth. But the sense of such figures must be confirmed by Scripture.[520] Even miracles, to the degree they are recorded, are admissible as evidence.[521]

Not surprisingly, the issues raised by authors like Guibert and Guitmund found an echo in twelfth-century treatises dealing with more scientific aspects of nature. One can of course propose that stu-dents of the eucharist and of the natural world utilized similar sources for their doctrines on subjects like appearance and reality. However, an argument can also be made for parallel modes of thought. For, in many areas of twelfth-century natural philosophy, criteria of validity

[516] *Ibid.*, bk 3, 1476B-C.

[517] *Ibid.*, bk 2, 1452C-D: "O haeretica malitia, hoccine experimento ausa es probare. . . . Quam immanissima audacia, nec praesentis Dei tremendam majestatem in experiendo perti-muisti. . . ."

[518] *Ibid.*, 3, 1471A: "Omnis quippe homo figuram sui, in qua nihil de substantia sua est, ferre potest."

[519] *Ibid.*, 1472D.

[520] *Ibid.*, 1473A.

[521] *Ibid.*, 1479A: "Non solum praedictis auctoritatibus, sed et multis quoque miraculis evi-dentissimis, rationabiliter confutantur."

were textual. Guitmund makes liberal use of medical doctrines in analysing how the eucharistic bread and wine are converted in the body. Writers on nature did just the opposite: they imported to discussions of the elements, the humours, and the world's origin the same concerns which motivated the debate on the sacraments. Twelfth-century naturalistic thought could in theory have reanimated its classical *fontes* and progressed without intersecting the rise of other interpretive traditions. But in practice it did not. Its vitality derived not only from treatises newly translated from the Greek and Arabic but also from a changed attitude towards factual knowledge. The growth of a more literate society did for naturalism what it had done for the eucharist: it placed the whole matter on an intellectualist plane and dismissed as rustic, popular, and irrational all that did not accord with a *ratio* synonymous with the inner logic of texts. The interest in empirical reality already evident in discussions of the sacrament was consequently supported by a genuine appreciation of science.

To establish this point, there is no need to review the numerous studies of the idea of nature,[522] together with its ramifications in law,[523] sculpture, and art,[524] in the first half of the twelfth century. The point under discussion can be illustrated by a few key passages from William of Conches, Alan of Lille, and Hugh of St. Victor.

For a criticism of symbolism and an interest in language, few better examples can be found than the first book of William's youthful *Philosophia Mundi*, a work almost contemporary with the *De Pignoribus Sanctorum*. Although the subject is declared "scientific," the concerns

---

[522] See, in general, H. Liebeschütz, "Kosmologische Motive in der Bildungswelt der Frühscholastik," *Vorträge der Bibliothek Warburg 1923-24* (1926), 83-148; J.M. Parent, *La doctrine de la création dans l'école de Chartres* (Paris and Ottawa, 1938); E. R. Curtius, "Rhetorische Naturschilderung im Mittelalter," *Romanische Forschungen* 56 (1942), 219-56; M.-T. d'Alverny, "Le cosmos symbolique du XIIe siècle," AHDLMA 20 (1954), 31-81; T. Gregory, *Anima mundi* (Florence, 1955), ch. 4, and "L'idea di natura nella filosofia medievale prima dell'ingresso della fisica di Aristotele il secolo XII," in *La filosofia della natura nel medioevo* (Milan, 1966), 27-65; N. Häring, "The Creation and Creator of the World According to Thierry of Chartres and Clarenbaldus of Arras," AHDLMA 22 (1956), 137-216; M.-D. Chenu, "La nature et l'homme. La renaissance du XIIe siècle," in *La théologie au douzième siècle*, 19-51; B. Stock, *Myth and Science*, chs. 3-4; and P. Dronke, *Fabula. Explorations into the Uses of Myth in Medieval Platonism* (Leiden and Cologne, 1974).

[523] See B. Tierney, "Natura Id Est Deus: A Case of Juristic Pantheism?" *Journal of the History of Ideas* 24 (1963), 307-22; G. Post, *Studies in Medieval Legal Thought* (Princeton, 1964), 494-561; P. Weimar, "Die legistische Literatur . . . ," in H. Coing, *Handbuch der Privatrechtsgeschichte*, 214n1.

[524] See L. White Jr., "Natural Science and Naturalistic Art in the Middle Ages," *American Historical Review* 52 (1947), 421-35.

are not so very different from those of Guibert or the students of the sacraments.

Even a brief perusal of William's habits and expressions of thought reveals a number of similarities. Existing things, like the perceptions of the eucharist, are divided into the seen and the unseen.[525] Man has only an imperfect knowledge of God, who cannot be circumscribed by categories of understanding.[526] His wisdom is manifested in the world's "daily disposition,"[527] a phrase which neatly captures both the notion of phenomenality and of ideal order. For, if "disposed," it displays evidence of "wisdom"; and, if disposed wisely, witnesses *divina sapientia*, which "makes things live and speak." Thus, through daily disposition one arrives at divine wisdom, and, through this in turn, at *divina substantia*, which, to recall the physical side of signs, is just another way of indicating the mark and icon of God (*signaculum et imago dei*).[528]

Other parallels with discussions on the sacraments are not difficult to find. One arises from the power of abstraction and the idea of a higher scientific culture. In making the universe, William asserts, God utilized his *potentia, sapientia,* and *voluntas,* which, he adds, "the saints, adapting from ordinary usage (*a vulgari*) . . . have called the three persons."[529] Less erudite personification is by implication a popular habit. But an essentialist position demands greater precision, since the father gave birth to the son "not by doctrine or usage but from his own nature."[530] Analogies from written, i.e., learned, language occur elsewhere. Elements, he argues, are like letters, that is, the indivisible parts of syllables.[531] And, just as the individual letter loses its character in the syllable, so the elements are intermingled in the body's composition.[532] As in the eucharist, the physical both persists and is consumed. Only *rustici*, he adds, rely for their knowledge of the world on what they learn through their senses.[533] Again, he discusses at length whether elements are unseen or seen: the one he names *elementa*, the other *elementata*.[534] Elements are the principal building blocks of things, but they retain their identity primarily as do words and are perceived by the senses only in combinations of

[525] William of Conches, *Philosophia Mundi* 1.1-3, ed. G. Maurach (Pretoria, 1980), 10, 25-35.

[526] *Ibid.*, c. 4, pp. 10-11, 42-55.   [527] *Ibid.*, c. 5, p. 12, 80.

[528] *Ibid.*, 12, 81-82.   [529] *Ibid.*, 12, 89-90.   [530] *Ibid.*, c. 8, p. 13, 104-06.

[531] *Ibid.*, c. 22, p. 19, 61.   [532] *Ibid.*, 20, 287-89.

[533] *Ibid.*, 20, 289-92. Cf. c. 22, p. 32, 577-78: "sed et rusticos nos credere. . . ."

[534] *Ibid.*, 21, 299-300; on the term, see T. Silverstein, "Elementatum: Its Appearance Among the Twelfth-Century Cosmogonists," *Mediaeval Studies* 16 (1954), 156-62 and Stock, *Myth and Science*, 143&n and 270f&n.

sounds or syllables. When earth, for instance, dissolves in water, the irreducible element does not disappear but is only decreased by a small amount, the proportion being comparable to the relationship between adjective and noun.[535] Reason, William declares, is to be sought in all things.[536] Yet, like the more sophisticated theorists of the sacraments, his *ratio* is inseparable from the logical, linguistic and meaningful relations of texts. Even the story of creation is a myth whose kernel of truth is a byproduct of interpretation.[537]

Similar ideas were reiterated and developed in his *Glosae super Platonem*, which, Jeauneau notes, "occupy a central place in his philosophical *oeuvre*."[538] William's assumption throughout is that one can unravel the secrets of nature by deciphering the code of the *Timaeus* as translated and interpreted by Calcidius. Plato's original task is seen as positive rather than natural justice;[539] as such, he deals with manmade knowledge and permits an intellectual equation between creation and interpretation. The simple definition of philosophy in the *Philosophia Mundi* is thereby expanded into a full division of the sciences.[540] The world is known through the knowable, that is, the *rationes* of each science in its ordered place.[541] The *Timaeus*, he adds, was difficult for the early commentators, not because Plato wrote obscurely, but because his readers were ignorant of the disciplines needed to interpret it. For, when dealing with the problem of creation, the author made mention of many sciences "according to the properties of each, adding proofs."[542] Each "art" therefore has its method, and the whole confirms the structure of existing reality. Nature is not one book but many books at once: there are as many "readings" as disciplines and controlled interpretations. Conversely, finding out about the world is tantamount to reconstructing Plato's inner meaning. Just as in nature one proceeds from sense data to understanding, so in interpretation one is led from the seen to the unseen, from surface to inner meaning.

William equates theory with divine and practice with human knowledge. These in turn become the bases for distinguishing be-

---

[535] William of Conches, *Philosophia Mundi*, c. 22, p.22, 348-50.

[536] *Ibid.*, p. 32, 580-81: "Nos autem dicimus in omnibus rationem esse quaerendam, si potest inveniri."

[537] *Ibid.*, p. 31, 63-64: "Non enim ad litteram credendum est deum excostasse primum hominem."

[538] *Guillaume de Conches, Glosae super Platonem* (Paris, 1965), 15.

[539] *Accessus ad Timaeum* 3, ed. Jeauneau, p. 59.

[540] *Ibid.*, 5, pp. 60-61. [541] *In Timaeum* 29b, c. 45, p. 113. [542] *Accessus* 7, p. 63.

tween the abstract and the concrete. A somewhat different version of such relationships was presented in the *De Planctu Naturae* of Alan of Lille. Students of this work have traditionally focused on the "Platonic" quality of the personifications, that is, the manner in which the allegorical goddesses symbolize inner abstractions.[543] But, from the outset, Alan emphasizes the interdependence of structures of reality and of texts. The prostituting of Nature's laws is due to "magical art":[544] the learned is contrasted with the pagan, the sanctioned with the blasphemous. The natural is the normative: where, the dreamer asks, have fled "the grace of nature, the form of customs, the precepts of decency"?[545] Grammatical error represents sexual deviance. The sex of the active degenerates into the passive genus. Man "becomes both predicate and subject." Grammar's laws are "over-extended." Later, types of unnatural sexuality are even catalogued according to grammars of love and of logic. And man's denial of his own manhood is looked upon as a "barbarism," thus interconnecting written law (*lex*) and his correct image of himself. Again, as a fornicator, man is not pleased by genuine art (*ars*) but by a mere trope (*tropus*), which is in reality a degraded figure. As such, he is only a manipulator of words (*modo logicus*). And "the simple conversion of his art brings about the loss of nature's laws."[546] Thus, his "hammer of invention" deforms its own anvil; the form in the womb is imprinted upon no waiting matter. Alan returns again and again to such parallels. For instance, when the dreamer, first overcome by Nature's appearance, clears his head, Nature is said to depict for his mental understanding the image of a material voice and to produce vocally the sounds of ideally preconnected verbal archetypes.[547]

Alan also reflects an aspect of the orthodox position in the eucharistic debate not normally discussed by twelfth-century philosophers of language, namely, the rehabilitation of the physical, the spoken, and the performed. When Nature first appears in the *De Planctu*, the details of her appearance and dress are elaborately described. We view

[543] For a general introduction to the subject, see W. Wetherbee, *Platonism and Poetry in the Twelfth Century* (Princeton, 1972), and, with respect to Alan in particular, the still useful study of G. Raynaud de Lage, *Alain de Lille, poète du XIIe siècle* (Paris and Montreal, 1951), I, chs. 2-3. For a recent review of twelfth-century allegorical language, see H. Westra, *The Commentary on Martianus Capella's "De Nuptiis" attributed to Bernardus Silvestris: A Critical Edition*, diss., Toronto, 1979.

[544] *Magistri Alani Enchiridion de Planctu Naturae*, metre 1, ed. N. Häring, *Studi medievali* 19 (1978), 806 (= PL 210.431A).

[545] *Loc.cit.* [546] *Ibid.*, ed. Häring 806-07 (PL 210.431B).

[547] *Ibid.*, prosa 3, p. 825 (442B).

her arrival through the eyes of the mortal narrator whose understanding is limited to the sensual world. In other words, we have the same perspective as the observer of the eucharistic rite who is as yet not initiated into its deeper mysteries. We are struck by the rhetoric with which the poet portrays her hair, forehead, skin, eyes, nose, lips, teeth, cheeks, and chin. But in each case the visible and tangible come first.[548] And, although intricate mechanics of appearance and reality accompany her diadem, gown, and tunic, the concrete provides the ground for the various devices. Nature herself shares the ambivalence of eucharistic realism, both visible and invisible. Although, as the poet invents her, she is an abstraction based on earlier allegory, she is also a creature who communicates by means of the spoken word. Moreover, she not only interprets and explains; she also performs. Her moral and scientific instruction is delivered orally. And, as the drama unfolds, ritual plays an increasingly important role. The purely philosophical issues gradually yield the stage to mythical stories. Venus deserts her lawful bed with Hymen and takes up with Antigamus; in the last act, Genius, the *alter* of Nature, makes his appearance with Truth and Falsehood, excommunicating all who deviate from legitimate forms of love. The ending may be poor philosophy and weak narrative, but, despite the otherworldly air which pervades the allegory, we are actually led as in the sacraments from ritual towards meaning.

Again, Alan is not so much indebted directly to the eucharistic debate as he is aware of many of the same issues. Such new readings of nature implied a different approach to reading itself. The period's finest compendium of reflections on this question was undoubtedly Hugh of St. Victor's *Didascalicon*.

Hugh's point of departure is not nature in the eucharist but nature in man, which, as it turns out, is placed in a similarly theological framework. In a fallen world, Nature has left men "so destitute of inventiveness" that even simple matters lie beyond their grasp. Some men, although conscious of their limitations, nonetheless pursue knowledge ceaselessly, their will to learn outstripping their capacity for achievement. Others, knowing that the highest matters are too difficult for them, pay no attention even to lesser ones. But not knowing (*nescire*) and not wanting to know (*nolle scire*) are not the same: the one springs from infirmity, the other from an impaired will. Nature has endowed another sort of man with the facility for approaching

548 *Ibid., prosa* 1, pp. 808-19 (432A-39A).

truth; but even among the talented, one finds differences of ability and dedication. Most worthy, in Hugh's view, are those who labour "in hunger, in thirst, and unclothed." Yet, all who desire to advance in knowledge must follow the same route, which consists of reading and meditation (*lectio et meditatio*).[549]

Beneath the schoolmaster's exhortations and the plea for a learned monastic culture, an important point is made. What is essential for the advancement of personal knowledge is not only natural endowment but one's consciousness of its uses. Not only is man's inner nature identified with the ability to think and to interpret. The degree to which his reason is an "image and likeness" of the divine depends on the exercise of the will. Subtly adapting Augustine, Hugh thereby allows for the possibility of progressive knowledge, or, more precisely, man's progress through knowledge. "Wisdom illuminates man in order that he may know himself."[550]

Man's dignity, in other words, both personally and cosmologically, is related to self-consciousness and self-knowledge. The original patterning of formless matter is microcosmically imitated by the cognitive activities of man, who proceeds from the concrete to the abstract, and, through reading and meditation, gradually repairs his fallen nature. Entelechy is endowed with the ambivalence of consciousness: becoming, it knows what it is, and, knowing what it is, it becomes. Like the eucharistic mystery, it incorporates both the visible and the invisible within the permanence of eternal change. Similarly, in Hugh's view, the human soul is imprinted not physically but ideally: it reflects the tangible but has the intangible potential to be all things at once. This dualism is reiterated in the structure of knowledge itself. For Hugh, *philosophiae* consist of organized knowledge. But wisdom, which worldly knowledge imperfectly reflects, is plan, pattern, or idea (*ratio*): it is an ur-text, the Word which has the potential to become all written texts.

All human activities and pursuits, Hugh continues, are intended either to improve our nature or to moderate the defects of our present life. Imperfections moreover are repaired through knowledge and virtue (*scientia et virtus*). From these two alone arises our likeness to divine substance. For, although man is composed of mortal and immortal elements, he "truly exists" through the second alone.[551] And

[549] *Hugonis de Sancto Victore Didascalicon de Studio Legendi, praefatio*, ed. C. H. Buttimer (Washington, D.C., 1939), 1-3.

[550] *Ibid.*, I.I, pp. 4-5.

[551] *Ibid.*, c. 5, p. 12.

the bridge between them is the text. *Scientia* is absorbed by reading and study; once internalized, it becomes virtue, the potential for right action. Not only, therefore, through applied knowledge, but also through the process of applying it, man helps to undo the wrongs of Eden.

Hugh devotes special attention to the origin of the arts and the beginnings of logic.[552] Boethius, he states, traced the manner in which the ancients first began to distinguish between words and intellections (*voces et intellectus*). But logic, since it is derived from *logos*, can mean one of two things, either discourse (*sermo*) or reason (*ratio*), that is, either *sermocinalis sive rationalis scientia*. In other terms it can refer to words or texts. Rational logic, he adds, contains dialectic and rhetoric, which are useful for written forms, while linguistic logic is a rubric for grammar as well. As one proceeds from words alone to a combination of words and texts, one also goes from mere verbal usage to disciplined language. Before linguistic logic, he adds, men used both spoken and written words (*sermones communes et litterae*), but they had no science of discourse for the spoken and the written (*ratio sermonum et litterarum*). There were no *praecepta*: "all sciences existed in use rather than art," that is, in practice, not theory. The introduction of "rules" and "precepts" based on texts changed all that: henceforth, habits which arose by change or by nature (*partim casu, partim natura*) were organized as forms of art.

Yet, if words, texts, reason, and nature are so interrelated, what is the place of things, which, it is worth recalling, Guibert and Guitmund made the ultimate source of meaning? Hugh's answer to this question provides a convenient summary of this chapter's major themes. He turns to the problem midway through the *Didascalicon*, part two of which is devoted to the study of the Bible. In divine eloquence, he states, not only words but also things have meaning (*non tantum verba sed etiam res significare habent*). This mode of communication is not found elsewhere. The philosopher, limited to *scientia*, knows only the meaning of words. But, ideally, signification through things is preferable. For usage (*usus*) relates words, nature, and things. The one is the voice of men (*vox hominum*); the other, the voice of God towards men (*vox Dei ad homines*). Mere words, once uttered, perish, but things, as created, endure.

Moreover, the voice is the physical sign of the senses (*nota sensuum*); the thing is the likeness of a divine original (*divinae rationis simula-*

---

[552] *Ibid.*, c. 11, pp. 19-21; *In Porphyrium comm.*, 1, CSEL 48, 138-39.

crum). And the sound is to the idea as time is to eternity. The pattern in the mind (*ratio mentis*) is the interior word, which is made manifest by the sound of the voice, the external word. Finally, divine wisdom, which the father "exhales" from his heart, although invisible in itself, takes on a visible form: it is known through creatures and in creatures. Thus, in biblical study, one should proceed through *vox, intellectus, res, ratio*, and *veritas*, an intellectual journey not accessible to the less learned (*minus docti*).[553] Hugh, of course, stood midway on the journey himself. The word of God was now halfway between word and text: man's earthly duty was to coordinate idea and exemplar through reading and meditation. *Ratio*, too, was contextualized, as was nature. Yet Hugh retained strong links with eleventh-century theorists of the sacraments, while, in writers like William of Conches and Alan of Lille, the idea of nature came closer to a scientific notion of empirical reality.

[553] *Ibid.*, 5.3, pp. 96-97.

IV.

LANGUAGE, TEXTS, AND
REALITY

Non est Deus grammaticae curiosus.
—Guibert of Nogent, *De Pignoribus Sanctorum*, 1.4.2.

[Grammatica] est totius philosophiae cunabulum.
—John of Salisbury *Metalogicon*, 1.13.

This study has so far looked at two different fields of activity influenced by the rise of a more literate society, namely, the appearance of
heretical and reformed communities and the debate over the nature
and meaning of the eucharist. Through the analysis of specific examples, an attempt was made to draw attention to broader issues: in
Chapter Two, the question was literacy and social organization; in
Three, the formation of religious intellectualism, the questioning of
ritual and symbol, and the emergence of empirical attitudes.

We now turn to purely philosophic and theological activity, into
which by 1150 many of the problems raised during the eleventh century by heretics, reformers, and scholastic commentators had been
channelled. For the spread of literacy not only brought about permanent changes in the interaction between popular and learned tradition.
Equally profound transformations took place in learned disciplines
themselves. What emerged as a central subject for discussion was the
relationship between language, texts, and reality, and, as a consequence, the potential uses of knowledge. Of course, thinkers had always distinguished between different functions—the active and the
contemplative, the practical and the theoretical. But the study of texts
provided a new focal point for discussion and isolated the approaches
from each other as never before.

The intellectual efflorescence may be viewed from within individual
disciplines such as law, philosophy, and theology. Yet, it is recognized, the "renaissance of the twelfth century" was a unified intellectual development in which the principles of factual organization from
one branch of knowledge were carried over without much change to

others.[1] The "scholastic method" is just what its name suggests, not a group of doctrines but a set of techniques for evaluating and reconciling opposed positions. Subjects in the arts curriculum evolved at varying rates of progress. Theology and canon law achieved coherent systems of classification long before history, natural philosophy, or literary criticism. In this respect the twelfth century continued what the eleventh began.

In comparing the two centuries, one discerns the use and reuse of familiar dichotomies, such as visible and invisible, material and spiritual, image and reality, and, of course, word and text. What was novel after 1100 was the setting, the diversity of application, and the breadth of the implications. As textual analysis emerged as a general methodology, many thinkers began to speculate along the lines of a semiotics of culture. Phenomenal manifestations of meaning were looked upon as a series of signs and symbols which could be interpreted once one broke the code of their grammar, logic, and rhetoric. One only had to search for the interior unity concealed beneath the exterior "integument." Using Latin, that is, the written, as a prototype, twelfth-century authors implicitly or explicitly developed formal languages in many areas of culture—in art, architecture, literature, music, and philosophy—against the background of which they invariably contrasted local, popular, and oral traditions. Indeed, without the emergence of such official cultures, the distinction between learned and popular would have made little sense.

Culture and nature thus parted ways, separated by a barrier which at once alienated man from the paradise of verbal, interpersonal communication with God, and yet, through education, as Hugh of St. Victor suggested, held out the possibility of reintegration at a purely spiritual level. The theological metaphors seem inappropriate to modern ears, but they aptly characterize twelfth-century man's perception of the intellectual forces creating a new cultural universe all around him. However, the "renaissance" was not achieved without strain: as the influence of textual culture spread, so did conflicts over the relationship between language, texts, and reality. Did words, as the realists assumed, describe the objective world, or were they, as the nominalists argued, merely "the breathing of the voice"? The accumulation of factual information from recordable sources and the evident need for a method of organization created another problem, namely, the

[1] M.-D. Chenu, "La nature et l'homme: la renaissance du XIIe siècle," *La théologie au douzième siècle* (Paris, 1957), 19-21, 44-51. Cf. Ph. Delhaye, "L'organisation scolaire au XIIe siècle," *Traditio* 5 (1947), 211-68.

purpose of knowledge itself. Was its proper function, as St. Bernard asserted, a meditative dialogue between one's inner self and God, or was it, as Abelard seemed to imply, the production of logically defensible statements about the knowable?

A more fundamental philosophical issue was also at stake. The twelfth century saw a great increase in the numbers of masters and students in cathedral schools and in nascent universities. As a result, there was also a rise in the circulation of independent texts treating specific themes. As the scholarly audience was reconstituted, the abstract idea of information, that is, of factual knowledge, was gradually separated from the individual understanding. A difference was recognized between the knower as inquiring subject and the knowledge which was the object of his investigations. Unlike the eastern "wise man" and the early medieval sage, the twelfth-century intellectual did not embody a subject personally: he taught it. Being an intellectual was a profession, even a social role.[2] Moreover, the century's great divide is not only along institutional lines between "monastic" and "scholastic" ways of thinking.[3] It arises as well from the attitudes of individuals towards texts. "If one wishes to characterize the *lectio* of the scholastic master in contrast to the *collatio* of the monk," notes Chenu, "we could say that it consists above all in exegesis, that is, in interpretation designed to set forth the objective contents of the text."[4] Among monks, by contrast, Leclercq reminds us, the synthesis always contains a personal, subjective element, which provides the point of departure for further reflection.[5]

The present chapter, like the two previous ones, proceeds by means of examples. However, in the figures chosen—Anselm, Abelard, and St. Bernard—a deliberate attempt is made to move away from particular issues and into the mainstream of early modern thought. The book's theme thereby shifts from individual interpretive traditions to the larger problem of interpretation itself.

In St. Anselm, two questions prominent in medieval philosophy made their appearance. The basic question was that of language versus

[2] J. Le Goff, *Les intellectuels au moyen âge* (Paris, 1962), 67-68.

[3] For a recent review of the issues, see J. Leclercq, "The Renewal of Theology," in R. L. Benson and G. Constable, eds., *Renaissance and Renewal in the Twelfth Century*, 68-87. For an accurate assessment, see G. Mathon, "Jean de Fécamp . . . ," *La normandie bénédictine . . . ,* 486.

[4] "Les *magistri*. La 'science théologique,' " *La théologie au douzième siècle*, 344.

[5] Leclercq "The Renewal," p. 77. For a brief review of positions for and against dialectic, see J. de Ghellinck, "Dialectique et dogme aux Xe-XIIe siècles. Quelques notes," *Festgabe . . . C. Baeumker* (Münster, 1913), vol. 1, 79-99.

truth. But, connected with it was Anselm's notion of "ordinary language": that is, what we do when we use words to describe situations involving things and how such everyday usage differs from logical expression. Peter Abelard took the matter in a different direction. His starting point was the medieval inheritance of later ancient grammar and logic, which had an inherently textual bias. Abelard freed the philosophy of language from its dependence on the theories of written language and proposed that linguistic change operates if not autonomously at least according to its own laws. His discoveries therefore held wide implications for the notion of meaning. In St. Bernard, a stern opponent of all he stood for, a radically different approach to texts emerged. Bernard was a master of rhetoric, whose sermons thoroughly renewed the monastic tradition of meditation and inner reflection. But he also ordered and disciplined the subjectivity of the cloister; he united its personal qualities to the larger spiritual goals of the Cistercian Order, which was the period's most successful "textual community." Above all, he transformed the sort of symbolism evolved by orthodox commentators on the eucharist into a vehicle capable of bringing together the individual, the monastic community, and the sacramental process.

1. ANSELM OF CANTERBURY

St. Anselm is perhaps the most popular medieval thinker among contemporary philosophers and theologians. His writings take us to the heart of matters interrelating faith and reason which remained under investigation throughout the Middle Ages. And, at the centre of his remarkable achievement lies the problem of texts: the concept of the text, the uses of texts, and their relation to the Word.

Anselm entered the abbey of Bec in 1060 and succeeded Lanfranc as archbishop of Canterbury in March 1093. Despite a career preoccupied with ecclesiastical business, he completed over a dozen theological treatises.[6] Grabmann called him "the father of scholasticism," but in reality he embraced both "monastic" and "scholastic" ways of thinking.[7] He fervently believed in prayer, mysticism, and supreme

[6] For a remarkable study of Anselm's career and thought, see R. W. Southern, *Saint Anselm and his Biographer. A Study of Monastic Life and Thought 1059-c. 1130*, esp. pp. 3-226.

[7] *Die Geschichte der scholastischen Methode*, vol. 1 (Freiburg-im-Breisgau, 1909), 258. The bibliography of Anselm's life and thought is abundant, and cannot be fully summarized here. The early literature is listed by J. Bainvel, "Anselme," DTC 1.2, col. 1349, and in Ueberweg-

values; yet he pursued logic, factuality, and the resolution of opposed views.

A great deal of Anselmian scholarship is devoted to a single issue, the "ontological" argument for the existence of God.[8] Less attention has been paid to his notions of language, meaning, and reality.[9] As a result, while a large literature has grown up around his dogmatic

Geyer, *Grundriss der Geschichte der Philosophie*, pt. 2 (Berlin, 1928), 698-700. An extensive bibliography of the more recent philosophical literature will be found in J. Hopkins, *A Companion to the Study of St. Anselm* (Minneapolis, 1972), 261-75, and in the same author's translation, *Anselm of Canterbury*, vol. 4 (Toronto and New York, 1976), 149-61. A general bibliography also appears in *Analecta Anselmiana* 1 (1969), 269-80 and 2 (1970), 223-24. For a guide to current themes in the discussion of Anselm's philosophy and theology, see the various volumes of *Analecta Anselmiana*, and for a summary of post-World War II interests, *Spicilegium Beccense I: Congrès international du IXe centenaire de l'arrivée d'Anselme au Bec* (Bec and Paris, 1959).

Anselm's precise influence on the formation of scholastic theology has been the subject of numerous studies. For a mid-twelfth-century summary, see H. Weisweiler, "Das erste systematische Kompendium aus den Werken Anselms von Canterbury," Rben 50 (1938), 206-21, while the connections with the school of Laon are briefly noted by Southern, *St. Anselm*, 82-87, and in greater detail by Dom Lottin, *Psychologie et morale aux XIIe et XIIIe siècles*, vol. 5 (Louvain, 1959), 9-188. General reviews of Anselm's influence on the twelfth century include A. Landgraf, "Der Gerechtigkeitsbegriff hl. Anselm v. Canterbury und seine Bedeutung für die Theologie der Frühscholastik," *Divus Thomas. Jahrbuch für Philosophie* . . . , 3rd Series, 5 (1927), 166-77; S. Vanni Rovighi, "Notes sur l'influence de saint Anselme au XIIe siècle," CCM 7 (1964), 423-37; 8 (1965), 43-58; R. Heinzmann, "Veritas humanae naturae. Ein Beitrag zur Anthropologie Anselms von Canterbury," in L. Scheffczyk *et al.*, eds., *Wahrheit und Verkündigung. Michael Schmaus zum 70. Geburstag* (Munich, 1967), vol. 1, 791-98; and G. R. Evans, *Anselm and a New Generation* (Oxford, 1980). More specific studies on twelfth-century thinkers include: A. Hayen, "Le concile de Reims et l'erreur de Gilbert de la Porrée," AHDLMA 10-11 (1935-36), 96-101; M.-T. d'Alverny, "Achard de saint Victor, évêque d'Avranches, disciple de saint Anselme," *Analecta Anselmiana* 2 (1970), 217-22; and R. D. Crouse, "Honorius Augustodunensis: Disciple of Anselm," *ibid.*, 4.2 (1975), 131-39. For a review of the thirteenth-century discussion of the ontological argument, see A. Daniels, *Quellenbeiträge und Untersuchungen zur Geschichte der Gottesbeweise im dreizehnten Jahrhundert mit besonderer Berücksichtigung des Arguments im Proslogion des hl. Anselm* (Münster, 1909) and J. Châtillon, "De Guillaume d'Auxerre à saint Thomas d'Aquin: l'argument de saint Anselme chez les premiers scolastiques du XIIIe siècle," *Spicilegium Beccense I*, 209-31.

[8] For the essential bibliography, see J. Hopkins, *Companion*, 261-65, and, for a recent historical discussion, the papers in *Analecta Anselmiana* 4.1 (1975), 59-364.

[9] For an excellent review of the question, see M. Colish, *The Mirror of Language* (New Haven, 1968), ch. 2: "St. Anselm: The Definition of the Word." Other significant discussions include: M. Grabmann, "Die Entwicklung der mittelalterlichen Sprachlogik," *Mittelalterliches Geistesleben* 1 (Munich, 1926), 106-15 (reviewing primary sources); V. Warnach, "Wort und Wirklichkeit bei Anselm von Canterbury," *Salzburger Jahrbuch für Philosophie* 5-6 (1961-62), 157-76; M. del Pra, *Logica e realtà. Momenti di pensiero medievale* (Bari, 1974) (a full, lucid exposition); R. Berlinger, "Zur Sprachmetaphysik Anselm von Canterbury. Eine speculative Explikation," *Analecta Anselmiana* 5 (1976), 99-112 (without references); and G. R. Evans, *Anselm and Talking about God* (Oxford, 1978), 17-38, 81-86, 115-25, and 138-39.

theology, certain basic issues in his work have not yet received adequate treatment. Some of these—the notion of audience, of conventional as opposed to formal language, and of interior versus exterior speech—clearly echo themes discussed elsewhere in this book. We are therefore entitled to ask to what extent Anselm can be isolated within the rise of a society whose institutional and intellectual structures are heavily dependent on texts. Of course, there can be no final, satisfactory answer to such a question. Individual thinkers of Anselm's quality are not reducible to a combination of cultural forces active at the time they wrote. On the other hand, Anselm returns so often to basic problems involving written language that they can be considered an undercurrent to his more overtly theological concerns. It is to these areas of his thought that we now turn.

The "Monologion" and "Proslogion"

The best introduction to the status of texts in St. Anselm lies through the *Monologion*, his first published work, which was completed in the second half of 1076.[10] In his preface, Anselm makes a number of observations on the oral and the written which can serve as a prologue to his *oeuvre* as a whole.

In this well-known statement, Anselm tells us that, at the request of his fellow monks,[11] he is writing down a "meditation" which formerly existed only in verbal form. His line of thinking, he adds, depends not on scriptural authority—although, he is quick to point out, he holds no opinions contrary to the Bible or the fathers, especially Augustine[12]—but on reason alone (*sola ratione*). We may make

[10] F. S. Schmitt, "Zur Chronologie der Werke des hl. Anselm von Canterbury," Rben 44 (1932), 322-50, contains the most authoritative statement of the dating of Anselm's works, which I follow throughout.

[11] *Monologion, prologus*, ed. F. S. Schmitt (*S. Anselmi . . . Opera Omnia*, Edinburgh, 1946), vol. 1, p. 7. (All quotations are from this edition.) Eadmer describes the literary composition of the *Monologion* and the *Proslogion* in virtually identical terms; *Vita Anselmi*, c. 1, ed. R. W. Southern (Edinburgh, 1962), 29-30; cf. *idem, St. Anselm and his Biographer*, 49-54. The process of interior text formation is well illustrated by *Oratio* 9, *Ad Sanctum Petrum*, vol. 3, p. 30, 8-15. While Anselm speaks of *verba* and *cor*, the thought moves inexorably towards *mens* and *intentio*. Unlike Anselm's philosophical and theological works, the prayers were widely read and imitated; on their "oral" appeal, see Southern, *St. Anselm*, 35-38.

[12] *Monologion, prol.*, p. 8; cf. *Ep. 77, Ad Lanfrancum*, vol. 3, p. 199, discussed by Southern, *St. Anselm*, 31. On Anselm's use of Scripture, see the thorough study of S. Tonini, "La scrittura nelle opere sistematiche di S. Anselmo: concetto, posizione, significato," *Analecta Anselmiana* 2 (1970), 57-116; on c. 1 of the *Monologion* and Aug., *De Trin.*, 8.3, see F. S. Schmitt, "Anselm und der (Neu-) Platonismus," *ibid.*, 1 (1969), 47-53. On Anselm's use of Augustine elsewhere, see in general K. Flasch, "Der philosophische Ansatz des Anselm von Canterbury in Monologion

the change as he sees it a little more specific. He previously discussed the themes of the meditation in ordinary language (*usitato sermone colloquendo*). While retaining their qualities as interior reflections, he now wishes to record them in writing (*meditationis exemplo describerem*).[13] In the term *exemplum* he suggests a copy, a transcript, or, in a special sense, a proof.

In addition to desiring a permanent record of the soliloquy, his monastic brethren made other demands. In writing out his thoughts Ansélm was to bring together in a single treatise and to bind by a unified chain of reasoning whatever had been revealed by his separate investigations. In other words, the final product was to be a logically coherent whole. The correctness of his position was to be established through a plain style, commonplace arguments, and straightforward debate (*plano stilo et vulgaribus argumentis simplicique disputatione*). Above all, it was to be corroborated by necessary reason (*rationis necessitas*),[14]

---

und sein Verhältnis zum Augustinischen Neuplatonismus," *ibid.*, 2 (1970), 15-43; on Augustine as a source for the ontological argument, see above all Th. A. Audet, "Une source augustinienne de l'argument de saint Anselme," in J. Maritain, ed., *Etienne Gilson: philosophe de la chrétienté* (Paris, 1949), 105-42.

[13] The literary vitality of meditation is well explained in *Orationes sive Meditationes, prologus*, vol. 3, p. 3: "*Orationes sive meditationes* quae subscriptae sunt, quoniam ad exercitandam legentis mentem ad dei amorem vel timorem, seu ad suimet discussionem editae sunt, non sunt legendae in tumultu, sed in quiete, nec cursim et velociter, sed paulatim cum intenta et morosa meditatione. Nec debet intendere lector ut quamlibet earum totam perlegat, sed quantum sentit sibi deo adiuvante valere ad accendendum affectum orandi, vel quantum illum delectat." Cf. R. Roques, "Structure et caractères de la prière Anselmienne," in H. Kohlenberger, ed., *Sola ratione: Anselm-Studien für . . . F. S. Schmitt* (Stuttgart, 1970), 121-22.

[14] The sources of Anselm's *rationes necessariae* lie in ancient logic and rhetoric. A. M. Jacquin, "Les 'rationes necessariae' de saint Anselme," *Mélanges Mandonnet*, vol. 2 (Paris, 1930), 72, draws attention to Cassiodorus's distinction between *argumentum necessarium* and *probabile*. Aristotelian and Ciceronian *fontes* are noted by J. de Ghellinck, "Dialectique et dogme aux Xe-XIIe siècles," *Festgabe . . . C. Baeumker*, 90-92. For further bibliography, see C. Vagaggini, "La hantise des rationes necessariae de saint Anselme dans la théologie des processions trinitaires de saint Thomas," *Spicilegium Beccense I*, 105n9. For a general review of the function of *ratio* in Anselm, see M. Grabmann, *Die Geschichte der scholastischen Methode*, I, 272-332; A. Schurr, *Die Begründung der Philosophie durch Anselm von Canterbury: eine Erörterung des ontologischen Gottesbeweises* (Stuttgart, 1966), 36-65; H. Kohlenberger, *Similitudo und Ratio* (Bonn, 1972), 127-71; and S. Vanni Rovighi, "*Ratio* in S. Anselmo d'Aosta," *Mélanges . . . Dom Jean-Pierre Müller* (Rome, 1974), 65-79. For a defence of God's "necessary existence," see in particular C. Hartshorne, *Anselm's Discovery: A Re-Examination of the Ontological Proof for God's Existence* (La Salle, Ill., 1965), 6-7, 10-11, and 41-47; for a review of Hartshorne's ideas, see D. A. Pailin, "An Introductory Survey of Charles Hartshorne's Work on the Ontological Argument," *Analecta Anselmiana* I (1969), 195-221, with bibliography, 219-21. For a purely logical analysis, see among others J. A. Brunton, "The Logic of God's Necessary Existence," *International Philosophical Quarterly* 10 (1970), 276-90.

that is, by the logical interrelationship of words in sentences. Finally, no objection, however unworthy it seemed, was to be overlooked, as the work was intended to serve the needs of ordinary monks. This last requirement in particular made Anselm hesitate before so difficult a task. The favorable reception the treatise had received was accordingly a pleasant surprise. To avoid unnecessary controversy, he now asked only that anyone copying it preface the book with his own statement of purpose as well as the table of contents indicating the chapters' order.[15]

Anselm's outline of his intentions must be read on two levels at once. One concerns the relationship of the completed text to its reading audience. The other deals with Anselm's own process of literary production.

Of the two, the first is by far the easier to grasp. In composing the *Monologion*, Anselm effectively replaced a living audience (*quidam fratres*)[16] with a reading public (*quis hoc opusculum voluerit transcribere* . . .).[17] The written product was intended to be of practical use, and, therefore, presumably, subject to further discussion. Yet, as a text, it comprised a statement of principles rather than a recorded interchange between a master and his students. Moreover, the monastic audience was assumed in part at least to be less erudite than the author. The treatise can therefore be assumed to have been designed to bridge the gap between the more and less learned monks.

To put the matter another way, there are two types of audience, one real, the other fictive. The real audience consists of his brethren. The fictive may once again be understood in two senses. There is a fictive dialoguer with whom Anselm engages in conversation inside his own mind, and there is a wider audience which constitutes a potential readership. The audience within the mind is in principle oral; the wider public is presumed to be dependent on writing. Through the latter, Anselm becomes one of the first authors to conceive of a reading public in the modern sense. Indeed, the assumption of an abstract audience helps to guide the presentation of his thoughts as the *Monologion* progresses.

The treatise, therefore, must be looked upon as a work of literature as well as philosophical theology. But by what steps was it actually produced? To this question Anselm provides only a partial answer. The *Monologion* arose, as he puts it, from meditations on divinity's essence (*de meditanda divinitatis essentia*). It was then written down,

[15] *Monologion, prol.*, p. 8. [16] *Ibid.*, 7. [17] *Ibid.*, 8.

meditationis exemplo. But there was more to the process of composition than this. Anselm wrote the work at the age of forty-three, when he was already a mature student of the Bible and of the fathers. In the *De Veritate,* written sometime after 1080, he even spoke of his earlier investigations as "pertaining to the study of sacred scripture."[18] Vestiges of this period in the evolution of his thinking are scattered throughout his books.[19] As a consequence, when he states, in response to his brethren's demands, that he intends to support his position not at all through scriptural authority (*auctoritate scripturae penitus nihil*),[20] we must understand, not a rejection of the Bible, but an attempt to move beyond simple reading and discussion to a more logical, abstract consideration of biblical texts. The approach is made clear in chapter six of the *Epistola de Incarnatione Verbi,* which was completed sometime before September 1092. Here, the commitment to "necessary reason without scriptural authority" in the *Monologion* and the *Proslogion* was reiterated. His intention, he adds, was not to try to improve on the ancients, but to discuss matters which had not sufficiently attracted their attention. And, it was precisely in this sense that the two works were designed as aids to those "humbly desiring to understand what they firmly believed."[21]

The essential term of this well-known expression is understanding: by it, Anselm means, in effect, to discuss, to comment upon, and to produce a new text. In other words, the text is the bridge between *ratio* and *auctoritas.* Through the interior dialogue, a summary of biblical and patristic authority becomes a "text" before actually being written down. The "cogency of reason" to which he refers is in reality this text's principle of organization. Anselm, therefore, plays the role (*persona*) of someone in conversation with himself[22] who both internalizes a textual methodology and anticipates a written product.[23] For him, this process alone gives rise to a defensible theological discourse, since it is achieved through the logic of *rationis necessitas.*

To produce theology, it follows, one must begin with a type of oral exchange. The essential contrast is between what one simply hears or believes and the persuasive capacities of logical thinking.[24] Anselm,

[18] *Praefatio,* vol. 1, p. 173.   [19] E.g., *Proslogion,* c. 1, vol. 1, pp. 99-100.
[20] *Monologion, prol.,* p. 7.
[21] *Ep. de Incarnatione Verbi,* c. 6, vol. 2, pp. 20-21.
[22] *Monologion, prol.,* p. 8.
[23] For a review of the literary problems Anselm faced, see F. S. Schmitt, "Les corrections de saint Anselme à son Monologion," Rben 50 (1936), 194-205.
[24] *Monologion,* c. 1, p. 13, 9-10. Cf. P. Vignaux, "Structure et sens du *Monologion,*" RSPT 31 (1947), 192-94; and more generally, *idem,* "La méthode de saint Anselme dans le *Monologion* et le *Proslogion,*" Aquinas 8 (1965), 110-18.

moreover, is not speaking as a philosopher, for whom such distinctions would be normal, but as an ordinary believer, who may if he wishes abandon the casualness of spoken forms of argument and adopt the rationality of texts. He need only turn his mind's eye to "the investigation" of the source of the good things which he naturally enjoys. Reason will lead the way; he has only to follow. He will eventually arrive "rationally" at an understanding of what he "irrationally" ignored.[25] Once again Anselm emphasizes that he is not superseding biblical authority. The old and the new texts are mutually supportive: the one is received, the other established truth.[26]

If this argument seems familiar, it is because we have seen it previously in other forms. Anselm effectively proposes a paradigm for theological investigation which is inseparable from his consideration of oral and written modes of communication. Just as, in general, orality became associated with illiteracy as a byproduct of literacy itself, so, in Anselm's mind, irrationality and rationality are viewed in the image of unstructured and structured language. Conventional speech, so to speak, is a kind of theological popular culture. Logical reasoning is the equivalent of learned culture. By proceeding through a verbal process towards reason, one establishes a concrete verbalization which is for all intents and purposes a text. By establishing a text, that is, a discourse modelled on written language, one proceeds towards reason.

Before we discuss the *Monologion* further, it may be useful to summarize the essentials of these relationships.

1. For Anselm, the text acts as an intermediary for discussion within his own mind; that is, words in the mind constitute a mental text, and this in turn eventually gives rise to a real written text.

2. The written text also acts as an intermediary between Anselm and his real and fictive audiences. It is a focal point for both dialogue with his brethren and, *in abstracto*, with a putative reading public.

3. While achieving these positive purposes, text production is nonetheless a reductive process.

The text, Anselm proposes, refines ordinary conversation into logically coherent discourse; that is, individual verbal investigations, which, as noted, are themselves taking shape as texts, are systematically organized into one text.

However, this articulation, which is a prerequisite of communication, ultimately leads Anselm to reassert the superiority of the oral mode. In arguing that the text producer needs "a plain style, ordinary

---

[25] *Monologion*, c. 1, p. 13, 13-14.   [26] *Ibid.*, 14, 15-18.

arguments, and simple disputation," he implicitly elevates the interior dialogue over the written product, even though the latter exhibits much of the former's rational organization. In Anselm, it follows, "literacy," at the highest level, is illustrated by speaking, by dialogue, and by other linguistic phenomena connected to the Word, that is, to an ideal rationality. Although, as he later points out, the *intima locutio* utilizes grammar, logic, and excerpts from the Bible, the text produced can never fully recapture the vitality of the original processes of reasoning. As he puts it, the *Monologion*'s written argument constitutes a record, a transcript, or an *exemplum*.

These relationships are essential for an understanding of the "proof" of the *Proslogion* and of the argument between Anselm and Gaunilo. However, before we turn to them, it is necessary to retrace our steps and to return to the *Monologion*'s opening chapters, summarizing then commenting on a few key passages.

Anselm, in effect, leads the reader through a process of reasoning similar to the one that his preface outlines. His well-studied thoughts have essentially three stages. First, he sets up a system of comparison based on the acceptance of abstractions as the highest order of reality. Then he generalizes from such concepts to the existence of a superior nature through which they derive their being or essence. Finally, he argues that the manner in which the *summa natura* creates from within itself is analogous to logically informed discourse.

Abstraction is fundamental. Anselm's example is "the good." He asks: since we experience many good things through the senses and the mind, is it not possible that there is one thing (*unum aliquid*), through which whatever is good derives its goodness?[27]

This, of course, is another way of asking whether things are good through similarity or difference. To solve the problem within the limits of grammar Anselm turns to comparison. All things, he points out, are not equally good. Some are "better," others "worse." But the capacity for comparison implies a standard against which goods can be measured; that is, goods are related to the Good as being just is to Justice.

Moreover, the language through which we describe such relations and the realities which lie behind them are closely interrelated. In particular, the standard of comparison is independent of the quality by which something is good. If one horse is strong and another swift, both are in some sense "good" horses. But a swift, strong robber is

[27] *Ibid.*, 14, 5-9.

bad. Therefore, although the measurement of the degree of goodness is a conceptual affair, good things are ultimately judged by their disposition in the real world.[28]

This sort of comparison, Anselm continues, helps to explain existence itself.[29] For, if all good things derive their goodness from a single entity (*per idem aliquid*), then, by implication, everything which exists also derives its existence from something. The opposite, namely, that something exists through nothing, is impossible. If one is to offer a logical explanation of existence, the only alternatives are existence through many things or existence through one thing. If things all existed separately, each would have the "power or nature of existing" in itself. But that is not the case: although the power works differently in each case, it is nonetheless the same *vis vel natura existendi*. It is greater than the individual forces by which things exist individually; therefore, things may be said to exist more truly through it than through them. By this sort of reasoning Anselm comes to the conclusion that the being through which all things exist is one. Although some natures are superior to others, this nature must be conceived as something pre-eminent. It is a nature beyond which, as he puts it, nothing can be greater. And there is of course only one nature of this type.[30]

The establishment of a supreme nature leads to a separation between the creator and the created. This, in turn, brings Anselm to a definition of *creatio ex nihilo* which involves the structure of language.

In what sense, he asks, may things be said to have been created by the highest nature? Verbal nuances are put aside: there is no difference, he argues, in stating that something is created from it (*ex ipsa*) or through it (*per ipsam*).[31] The only valid distinction is between creator and created. For the highest nature exists from or through itself; all other things exist from or through it.[32]

But what does this distinction really mean? Everything which exists through something else, he states, exists either through an effecting agent, through matter, or through some other form of assistance, as if by means of technical aid (*per efficiens aut per materiam aut per aliquod aliud adiumentum, velut per instrumentum*).[33] But, if something is created in this way, its existence is posterior to and in some way less than that which created it.[34] The supreme nature could not have been brought into being in this manner, since nothing is antecedent to it or greater

---

[28] *Ibid.*, 14-15.   [29] *Ibid.*, c. 3, 15f.   [30] *Ibid.*, p. 16, 18-27.
[31] *Ibid.*, c. 5, p. 18.   [32] *Ibid.*, c. 6, p. 18ff.   [33] *Ibid.*, p. 19, 1-3.
[34] *Ibid.*, 19, 3-5.

than it in creation. Therefore it must derive its existence from itself.
To describe how this takes place, Anselm reasons by analogy from the
metaphor of light. As "light" is to "to light" and "lighting through
and from itself" (*lux et lucere et lucens*), so we may speak of "being,"
"to be," and "existing" (*essentia et esse et ens, hoc est existens sive subsis-
tens*).[35] The remainder of creation, Anselm adds, exists through something else, whether the creating agent actually made things or merely
the matter out of which they are made.[36] No one doubts that the
universe is material, since it is composed of the four elements. But,
from where does the matter out of which the material world is made
derive its own existence? This primary creation, he argues, cannot be
material, since the *summa natura* creates only from itself. It follows
that all other creation takes its existence from the supreme being,
which created things without aid, that is, from nothing. Of course,
this does not mean that things were literally made "from nothing."[37]
Ex nihilo in this context really means *non ex aliquo* (not from something).[38] By way of explanation Anselm once again turns to metaphors. The *creatrix substantia* or *essentia* brings things into being "from
nothing" in the same sense that a poor man is made rich or a sick
man well. What formerly was nothing is now something.[39]

All of this brings Anselm to the meaning of creation itself. For,
when we use expressions like "it created" or "they were made," we
imply that the supreme substance created something (*aliquid fecit*) or
that things were made as something (*aliquid facta sunt*).[40] How does
this come about?

Anselm's answer interrelates words, thoughts, and things. His point
of departure is Augustine's notion of a model in the creator's mind.[41]
Nothing, he states, can be created unless there exists in the maker's
ordered thoughts (*in facientis ratione*) an exemplar, pattern, likeness,
or guide (*exemplum . . . , forma vel similitudo, aut regula*).[42] This structure
existed before the world was made; in this sense, the universe was
never truly "nothing," as the previous discussion might suggest.
Moreover, this model of things (*rerum forma*), which preceded their

[35] *Ibid.*, 20, 15-16. On Anselm's metaphors of light, see H. K. Kohlenberger, "Zur Metaphysik des Visuellen bei Anselm von Canterbury," *Analecta Anselmiana* I (1969), 15-29. General
bibliography is listed on p.15n14. Cf. F. S. Schmitt, "Anselm und der (Neu-) Platonismus,"
62-64.
[36] *Monologion* c. 7, p. 20, 22-24.   [37] *Ibid.*, 21-22.
[38] *Ibid.*, c. 8, p. 23, 23-24.   [39] *Ibid.*, 23, 26-33.   [40] *Ibid.*, 23-24.
[41] *De Doctrina Christiana* 1.7, PL 34.22; *Tract. in Joh.*, 1.16, PL 35.1387.
[42] *Monologion*, c. 9, p. 24, 12-14.

creation, is a kind of expression of them in the creator's thoughts (*rerum quaedam in ipsa ratione locutio*), similar, Anselm maintains, to the design in a craftman's mind before he fashions an object.[43] By "an expression of the mind or of reason" Anselm understands not words (*voces*) representing things but the things themselves (*res ipsae*) as visualized in present or future existence.[44]

For, he adds, we may speak of a thing in common usage in three ways: by sensible signs, that is, through the senses; by a mental consideration of those same signs; or, putting aside sensible and nonsensible signs, by forming an "expression" of things themselves in the mind, either through an image of corporeal things or a conception of them.[45] Take a man: I may pronounce the word "man"; I may think of the word "man" silently; or I may form a physical or mental image of a man in my mind. In the first two cases I am concerned only with the name (*nomen*) man, while in the last I consider the man himself (*is ipse*).[46] Following Boethius,[47] Anselm classifies the first two linguistic descriptions as being composed of words found in specific languages, which vary with time and place. But the third is "natural": ~~essence~~ it is the same among all nations. Since all other words owe their origin to these, where they exist no other term is necessary for the recognition of a thing (*ad rem cognoscendam*). Where they are absent, no word suffices for its delineation. Words, therefore, may be said to be "truer" the more they are like the things they represent or the more clearly they signify their objects. For, apart from words which merely indicate sounds (like the letter "a"), no word is so like a thing or so accurately describes it as the natural language cogitated in the mind. On that account it should be called the proper and primary verbal expression of the thing (*proprium et principale rei verbum*).[48]

Anselm next specifies what he means by "expression." Above he argued that the *intima locutio* in the creator's mind is like the design of a future object in the thoughts of a craftsman. Now he sees much

---

[43] *Ibid.*, c. 10, p. 24, 24-27.

[44] *Ibid.*, 27-30. Cf. P. Vignaux, "Structure et sens . . . ," 202-03.

[45] *Monologion*, c. 10, p. 24, 30-p. 25, 4: "Aut enim res loquimur signis sensibus, id est quae sensibus corporeis sentiri possunt sensibiliter utendo; aut eadem signa, quae foris sensibilia sunt, intra nos insensibiliter cogitando; aut nec sensibiliter nec insensibiliter his signis utendo, sed res ipsas vel corporum imaginatione vel rationis intellectu pro rerum ipsarum diversitate intus in nostra mente dicendo." On thinking in words and in images in Anselm, see in general G. R. Evans, *Anselm and Talking about God*, 22-29.

[46] *Ibid.*, 25, 4-7.

[47] *Comm. in Librum Aristotelis Peri ermeneias* 1.1, c. 1, ed. C. Meiser (Leipzig, 1879), I, 37.

[48] *Monologion*, c. 10, p. 25, 10-22.

that is "dissimilar" in this "similitude." For the highest nature took from nowhere else a model for his work, whereas the craftsman has nothing in his mind but what he takes from external objects. Unlike the creator, he needs some material form as a basis for realizing his plans. For instance, although an ordinary mortal man, through a concept or an image, may represent an animal that does not exist, he does so by drawing from memory elements from known animals. We may therefore put the difference as follows: both the *creator* and the *faber* work from mental designs of what they want to make. In the creator's case the *intima locutio* suffices in itself; in the craftman's, it is neither the first, the sole, nor the sufficient cause of the undertaking.[49] What the craftsman makes always depends on the prior existence of something else. But, if the highest being creates only from within itself and only by means of its inner expression—either through individual words or by uniting its ideas in one word—it follows that this expression of the highest nature (*summae essentiae locutio*) is nothing but the *summa essentia* itself.[50] It maintains all other forms of creation;[51] it exists in and throughout all things.[52]

But what can be said concerning its substance? Anselm takes this question up at two levels in the *Monologion*. An earlier linguistic discussion dismisses relational terms when applied to the highest nature's expression and places descriptive terminology within the realm of logic.[53] If, logically speaking, nothing is better than the supreme substance, it is superior to all the other things which it is not.[54]

A more theological analysis begins in chapter twenty-six. Anselm has devoted considerable attention to the *summa natura*'s temporal and spatial qualities. He now asks how what is in effect beyond substance in the normal sense can be called substance at all. For it is not subject to differentiation through mixing or mutation through accidents.[55] His reply is that *substantia* in this context virtually means *essentia*.[56] The highest nature does not, like other substances, separate into universals and particulars, as, for example, being a man may be distinguished from individual men.[57] A better term than substance, he adds, would be "spirit," since of all things composed of the corporeal and the spiritual it is the highest or purest. It is a unique spirit,

[49] *Ibid.*, c. 11, p. 26, 3-20. Cf. P. Vignaux, "structure et sens," 204-05.

[50] *Ibid.*, c. 12, p. 26, 26-28. [51] *Ibid.*, c. 13, p. 27. [52] *Ibid.*, c. 14, p. 27.

[53] On Anselm's use of grammar and equipollent proofs here, see in particular M. Colish, *The Mirror of Language*, 138-46.

[54] *Monologion*, c. 14, pp. 28-29. [55] *Ibid.*, c. 26, p. 44, 7-9. [56] *Ibid.*, p. 44, 10-11.

[57] *Ibid.*, c. 27, p. 45, 6-10.

which exists simply, perfectly and absolutely,[58] unaffected by temporal changes. Compared to it, other things seem hardly to exist at all: it is so to speak the *creator spiritus*, which makes them "something" from "nothing."[59]

But what is the relationship of this personified *essentia* to its own expression? If it made nothing except through itself and if whatever was created by him was made through his expression, then the two are identical.[60] After reiterating his previous argument, Anselm comes to an original conclusion on the matter. It has been proven, he states, that nothing exists except the creating spirit (*creans spiritus*) and the product of its creative activity (*eius creatura*). But the expression (*locutio*) of the spirit cannot be included among the things created, since it is created from itself. Therefore, the expression of the supreme spirit is the spirit itself; or, to be more precise, the expression is nothing but the intelligence (*intelligentia*) of the spirit, by which it understands or conceives (*intelligit*) all things. Indeed, for the creator, expressing a thing is nothing but framing it in his mind, since, unlike man, he never fails to find a suitable discourse for his inner thoughts.[61] Thus we may say that the highest spirit (*summus spiritus*) and its expression (*locutio*) are consubstantial, since the spirit, however we call it, is one and indivisible.[62] It consists of one word, through which all things were made.[63]

Anselm then turns to the nature of the divine word itself, stating that, in his view, it is not the likeness of created things but the reality of their being (*non sit similitudo factorum sed veritas essentiae*).[64] All words of the type by which we express objects in the mind are the likenesses and images of the objects to which they correspond.[65] The likeness is "truer" the more closely it resembles its object. But the word of the creator is not a likeness of this kind. If it were an image of mutable things, it itself could not be immutable.[66] One must therefore distinguish between the word of the creator, which is the true and simple essence of things, and the word in things created, which is an imperfect imitation of them.[67]

[58] *Ibid.*, c. 28, p. 45-p. 46, 3.   [59] *Ibid.*, 46, 10-31.   [60] *Ibid.*, c. 29, p. 47, 9-11.
[61] On the distinction between *cogitare* and *intelligere*, see P. Michaud-Quantin, "Notes sur le vocabulaire psychologique de saint Anselme," *Spicilegium Beccense I*, 23-25.
[62] *Monologion*, c. 29, p. 47, 12-p. 48, 5.
[63] *Ibid.*, c. 30, p. 48.   [64] *Ibid.*, c. 31, p. 48, 14.
[65] *Ibid.*, 48, 18-20: "Etenim omnia huiusmodi verba quibus res quaslibet mente dicimus, id est cogitamus: similitudines et imagines sunt rerum quarum verba sunt." Cf. c. 65, p. 57, 20-28.
[66] *Ibid.*, 48, 23-28.   [67] *Ibid.*, 50, 7-10.

However, if every word is the representation of an object, and, if between the *creator* and the *creatura*, word and object do not correspond, how can we be sure that in any given situation we have the right word? And, if nothing was created, how could we prove that there was any word at all?[68]

Anselm responds to this problem by picturing the supreme spirit in terms of a rational mind. The highest spirit, being eternal, is eternally mindful of itself and understands itself in the image of a mind that is continually thinking. But priority must be given to the *mens rationalis*.[69] If it understands itself eternally, it expresses itself eternally; and, if it expresses itself eternally, the word is eternal with the creator.[70] Does the highest nature then express itself by one word and create by means of another?[71] No: the word by which the creator expresses himself (*quo seipsum dicit*) is evidently identical with himself (*necesse est idipsum esse*). The word by which he expresses himself and the word by which he expresses creation have the same *substantia*. But there are nonetheless two words. For the creator, who speaks these words, shares substance with them, and yet is not the word himself. Identity of substance does not necessarily imply a uniformity of expression.[72] To explain this, Anselm elaborates a little further the notion of a word as a mental concept. No one, he states, can deny that when a rational mind conceives of itself in meditation the image of itself rises in its thoughts, or rather, the thought is its own image, as if formed by impression.[73] The rational mind, then, when it conceives of itself in thought, brings forth an image of itself, the likeness so to speak of its own thought, even though the mind cannot, except in thought, be separated from its image, which is its word.[74] By the same token the supreme wisdom, when it conceives of itself by expressing itself, gives rise to a likeness "consubstantial" with itself, that is, its word, which is wisdom's image, representation, or mark (*imago et figura et caracter eius*). This word, by which the creator ex-

---

[68] *Ibid.*, c. 32, p. 50, 16-21.

[69] *Ibid.*, p. 51, 12-14: "Ergo summus ille spiritus sicut est aeternus, ita aeterne sui memor est et intelligit se ad similitudinem mentis rationalis; immo non ad ullius similitudinem, sed ille principaliter et mens rationalis ad eius similitudinem."

[70] *Ibid.*, 51, 15-17.   [71] *Ibid.*, c. 33, pp. 22-24.

[72] *Ibid.*, p. 51, 24-p. 52, 6.

[73] *Ibid.*, 52, 12-15: "Nam nulla ratione negari potest, cum mens rationalis seipsam cogitando intelligit, imaginem ipsius nasci in sua cogitatione; immo ipsam cogitationem sui esse suam imaginem ad eius similitudinem tamquam ex eius impressione formatam."

[74] *Ibid.*, 52, 24-28: "Habet igitur mens rationalis, cum se cogitando intelligit, secum imaginem suam ex se natam, id est cogitationem sui ad suam similitudinem . . . ; quamvis ipsa se a sua imagine non nisi ratione sola separare possit. Quae imago eius verbum eius est."

presses the created world, is not the same as the word of the created world, since, as was previously pointed out, it is not its likeness (*similitudo*) but its principal essence (*principalis essentia*).[75]

In subsequent chapters Anselm applies his ideas to the three persons of the trinity, but he does not further elaborate the interrelationship between language, texts, and reality. We may therefore pause at this point in the *Monologion* and review his position as a whole.

Anselm nowhere explicitly refers to the contrast between the oral and the written. Yet, his defence of reason's role in theology is heavily influenced by his notion of written language. Indeed, *intima locutio* could more accurately be called a contextualization than a rationalization of the word. Not only is his literary product a written example of oral meditative dialogue. His *ratio* is also modelled along the lines of words in sentences. Just as the biblical text leads the uninitiated into the secrets of divinity, so Reason now guides his inquisitive mind into the untravelled pathways of formal theology.

The internal conversation Anselm has with himself is an anticipation of the two sides of the scholastic *questio* in which the spoken dialectic of the two parties is transformed into a written presentation of opposed positions. With one difference: in the process of inquiring into the logic of words, Anselm makes a number of discoveries which alter his perception of real theological relationships. These concern abstraction, reductive definition, natural language, and above all the disjunction between words and things. Throughout the *Monologion*, Anselm maintains that he is illuminating realities rather than forms, images, or likenesses. But his *rationis necessitas* is the imposition onto an implicitly present body of biblical material of an external logic and grammar: an exploration, as he puts it, of faith by reason. Faith, as noted, is a received text, reason, an established one.

Moreover, Anselm proceeds by analogy from words and things to the created and the creator. For God, words, which are normally the mental images of objects, are the inner realities of the objects themselves, logically and therefore temporally prior to them in the creative process. He sees in God the verbalization (*locutio*) of a perfect grammar of texts. But his deity's word is an expression with a context. He illustrates the grammatical relationship between *essentia, esse,* and *ens* by one of the commonest Joannine metaphors for the Word, *lux, lucere,* and *lucens*. It does not follow that for Anselm to exist is merely to be thought to exist. Rather, to exist is in large part to exist in

---

[75] *Ibid.*, 53, 2-6; cf. *Proslogion*, c. 23, p. 117, 6-9. On the neoplatonic elements in *similitudo, imago,* and *imitatio*, see F. S. Schmitt, "Anselm und der (Neu-)Platonismus," 60-62.

thoughts capable of logical expression, for which the model is a text. Even God speaks a word which has all the qualities of a text before it is spoken: this, in Anselm's view, is what makes it the Word and not just mere words. A clear example of this type of reasoning is found in his explanation of the phrase *ex nihilo*. Something cannot be made from nothing; therefore, creation must have developed from "not any-thing" to "something." The biblical phrase is thereby put in a logical context and then reapplied to reality as revealed in the Bible. The one text cannot function without the other. To move from faith to reason is to progress from an authentic statement about reality—the Bible— to a logically defensible interpretation of its meaning.

Anselm refined his position in the *Proslogion*, composed between 1077 and 1078, and in his reply to Gaunilo of Marmoutier, which was probably written a year later.

The notion of the text once again provides a point of comparison.[76] In the preface to the *Proslogion* he states that the *Monologion* was writ-ten as an *exemplum meditandi de ratione fidei*; that is, he took the part of someone who conducts an inquiry into what he does not know by reasoning silently with himself.[77] However, the *Monologion* was woven of different strands of thought. Could he not find a single argument sufficient in itself for demonstrating that God truly exists and that his goodness is supreme?[78] The *Proslogion*, therefore, is not only a second attempt to move from a silent text to one that is written down. It is also a reduction to *unum argumentum*.

The "ontological proof," then, is among other things a special kind of written record. It is an internally developing, logically intercon-nected exercise in reasoning; and it is the fruit of meditation on his own previous writing as well as on biblical and patristic material.[79] His earlier text, the *Monologion*, now occupies a place in a sequential tradition of writings. His formerly subjective reflections have become objects in an external world of scribal forms which provides a further stimulus to personal reflection. Anselm, as well, has created his own fictive listening audience within his mind. The "proof," he adds, came to him when least expected.[80] He hastened to put his thoughts on parchment both for his reading public and as an aid to deeper contemplation.[81] This activity retains an oral flavour, which is caught in his twin titles for the work, *soliloquium* and *alloquium*; that is, he

---

[76] Cf. A. Stolz, "Das Proslogion des hl. Anselm," Rben 47 (1935), 332-33.

[77] Cf. P. Vignaux, "La méthode . . . ," 112-13.

[78] *Proslogion, Prooemium*, vol. I, p. 93, 2-10.

[79] Cf. A. Stolz, "Das Proslogion," 340.

[80] *Proslogion, Pro.*, p. 93, 13-19.   [81] *Ibid.*, p. 93, 20-p. 94, 2.

keeps before him the model of an oral exchange even though his product is a text.[82] The final stage in the process is his acknowledgment of his own authorship, which was urged by Hugh of Lyons, and the contributions to his thoughts by his readers.[83]

The commitment to written language is maintained in the *Proslogion*'s argument. The point of departure as every reader recalls is Psalm 14:1: "The fool has said in his heart, there is no God." For Anselm, the very act of thinking about God negates any potential denial of his existence. But this involves a change from imprecise spoken to rational forms of thought and a recognition of the difference between *verba* and *res*. The same fool, he states, on hearing the words "something than which nothing greater can be conceived" understands both what he hears and what he understands is in his mind, even though, at that point, he may not understand what is in his mind to exist. For it is one thing for an object to be in the understanding, another to understand that it exists.[84]

To illustrate his point Anselm once again draws on the analogy of the artist from Augustine's *De Doctrina Christiana*.[85] When a painter thinks out ahead of time what he is about to draw, he already has the future design in his understanding; but he does not understand it to exist, since he has not yet brought it into being. However, once it is drawn or painted, he both has it in his mind and understands it to exist, because of course he made it.[86] Therefore, in Anselm's view, even a fool can comprehend the greatest conceivable thing. For, when he hears it spoken in words, he understands what he hears; and whatever he understands in this manner may be said to exist in his mind. Further, as it is "greater" to exist in reality and in the intellect than in the intellect alone, this being "than which nothing greater can be conceived" cannot both be conceived and be said not to exist.[87] Why, then, did the fool make such a philosophically irresponsible statement? Because his foolishness took the form of failing to recognize

[82] *Ibid.*, p. 93, 3f. ". . . in persona alicuius tacite secum ratiocinando . . ."; pp. 93-94: ". . . de hoc ipso et de quibusdam aliis sub persona conantis erigere mentem suam ad contemplandum deum et quaerentis intelligere quod credit, subditum scripsi opusculum." In this respect, the *Proslogion* has much in common with Anselm's other meditative prayers; see E. A. Synan, "Prayer, Proof and Anselm's *Proslogion*," in *Standing Before God*, ed. A. Finkel and L. Frizzell (New York, 1981), 270-82.

[83] *Proslogion*, p. 94.

[84] *Ibid.*, c. 2, p. 101, 7-10: "Sed certe ipse idem insipiens, cum audit hoc ipsum quod dico: 'aliquid quo maius nihil cogitari potest,' intelligit quod audit; et quod intelligit in intellectu eius est, etiam si non intelligat illud esse. Aliud enim est rem esse in intellectu, aliud intelligere rem esse."

[85] 1.7, PL 34.22.   [86] *Proslogion*, c. 2, p. 101, 10-13.   [87] *Ibid.*, 101, 12-102, 3.

the difference between existence in the understanding and in reality. A thing after all may be thought about in one of two ways, either when the word signifying it is spoken and conceived or when the thing itself is understood in the mind.[88] In the former sense God can be said or thought not to exist, but not in the latter: for, one may say "God does not exist," or think those words; yet, as God exists, the words do not correspond to reality.

Our purpose in paraphrasing Anselm's "proof" is not to provide another commentary on his theology but to suggest that his achievement depends in part on a complex sort of orality within a textual mode. Is the fool a kind of illiterate? Yes, in the Anselmian sense of failing to distinguish between *verba* and *res*. He either thinks mere words or verbalizes what logical thought will not admit.[89] Once again, however, Anselm's mystical pathway ends at the doorstep of a rationality affiliated with his notion of a standard, natural, or structured linguistic form. The understanding produced by words in the mind is in fact a kind of text. The bridge between existence "in reality" and "in the intellect" is textual production.

NB

But the fool was not so easily silenced. His case was taken up by Gaunilo of Marmoutier, who first summarized Anselm's position as he saw it[90] and then attempted a refutation.

Gaunilo argued that the highest being exists in one's understanding only because one understands what is said.[91] He thereby thrust the problem back from the level of *res* to that of *verba*. The mind, he said, retains at any moment a great many real and unreal things. How could one differentiate among them if one did not understand what they were when one heard the words by which they are signified?[92] The only exception would be a highest being that was unable to be conceived when described in words and heard, or unable to be held conceptually in the mind (*non . . . auditum cogitare vel in cogitatione habere*).[93] But this is impossible: with respect to the supreme nature,

---

[88] *Ibid.*, c. 4, p. 103, 18-19: "Aliter enim cogitatur res cum vox eam significans cogitatur, aliter cum id ipsum quod res est intelligitur."

[89] On the reapplication of these ideas in the *Cur Deus Homo*, see R. Roques, "*Derisio, Simplicitas, Insipientia*. Remarques mineurs sur la terminologie de saint Anselme," *L'homme devant Dieu. Mélanges . . . H. de Lubac* (Paris, 1963), vol. 2, 47-61.

[90] On Anselm's and Gaunilo's mutual confusion of each other's positions, see J. Hopkins, "Anselm's Debate with Gaunilo," *Analecta Anselmiana* 5 (1976), 25-53. For a full review of Gaunilo's argument, see M. del Pra, *Logica e realtà*, 47-81.

[91] *Quid ad haec respondeat quidam pro insipiente*, c. 2, vol. 1, p. 125, 14-15: "Quod hoc iam esse dicitur in intellectu meo, non ob aliud nisi quia id quod dicitur intelligo."

[92] *Ibid.*, 125, 15-17.   [93] *Ibid.*, 125, 17-20.

I must both understand it and have it in my understanding, since I cannot conceive it in any other way than by grasping the knowledge that it exists by itself (*scientia comprehendendo re ipsa illud existere*).[94] Yet, if this is the case, contrary to what Anselm proposes, having an object in the understanding does not logically precede understanding that it exists.[95] Therefore, Anselm's argument that God's existence can be denied in words but not in reality falls. Furthermore, it is not clear that what I understand, when I hear it, is already in my understanding. For there are many things in my mind which I have not heard, some of whose existence is uncertain, others which have no real existence at all. To turn Anselm's argument around: someone may say the words by which such things are represented, but that does not mean they really exist.[96]

To Anselm's example of the artist's design Gaunilo opposes Augustine's image of a craftsman, whose plan "lives" in his mind, just as his soul lives, before it is brought into being.[97] An exception may be made for pure concepts, which, on being heard and thought about, are perceived to be real. Such reality is one thing, the perceiving mind another.[98] But the being "than which nothing greater is conceivable" is by Anselm's own definition not an entity of this type. Therefore, if one follows the argument logically, Gaunilo suggests, Anselm's God is inconceivable. For, as he puts it, one cannot conceive of this being on hearing of it, nor can one simply have it in the understanding. In other words, one cannot prove whether it exists or not. For, to return to the imagery of the artist, we normally picture the less familiar by comparison with the more familiar. If a totally unknown man is described for me, how do I know that I am not being deceived? Similarly, I can form no clear mental picture of God or of *quo maius cogitari non potest*.[99] Such statements are mere words, from which alone no real object can be described. When we attempt to conceive God in this way, it is not only the real sounds of the letters which are in the understanding but also the word's significance (*vocis auditae significatio*). Yet, again, one cannot grasp the meaning of something with which one is totally unfamiliar. The mind, on hearing such a word, may attempt to form an image of the purported reality, but it will not succeed. Hence, when I merely hear the word "God," God is not necessarily in my understanding: he is present *in verbis*, not *in re*.[100]

[94] *Ibid.*, 125, 20-126, 1.   [95] *Ibid.*, 126, 1-3.   [96] *Ibid.*, 126, 8-13.
[97] *Ibid.*, c. 3, p. 126, 18-23; Augustine, *Tract. in Joh.* 1.16, PL 35.1387.
[98] *Ibid.*, 126, 23-25.   [99] *Ibid.*, c. 4, p. 126, 29-p. 127, 13.
[100] *Ibid.*, 127, 14-23.

Gaunilo replies to Anselm's other argument in a similar fashion. Anselm proposed that, if nothing greater exists, the supreme being must first exist in reality and only secondarily in the mind. Gaunilo maintains that a being which cannot be conceived prima facie with reference to an object has only a conceptual and not a real existence. It is a figment of the imagination. For Anselm did not say "greater than any object" but "greater than anything existing," which can include existence in a purely verbal form. As a result, this being cannot be in the mind in the way that real objects are.[101] Saying that God exists through these criteria is like positing the existence of an island paradise superior to all other places on earth. Its hypothetical existence is not in doubt. But how can one be sure it really exists?[102] One can in fact turn Anselm's logical solution upside down: if the supreme being is so great that negating its existence is literally unthinkable, then, by the same token, the supreme being cannot truly be understood.[103] For, if Gaunilo is correct, no real object is so grasped by the mind.

Anselm replied at length to Gaunilo. His point of departure, as in the *Proslogion*, is that God exists.[104] His logical demonstration is largely a confirmation, the text once again having the status of an evidential document. But he also takes pains to point out where Gaunilo went wrong.

The existence of a being whose reality cannot be denied, he asserts, is not the same as that of a being whose reality cannot be certainly affirmed. For if *"quo maius cogitari non potest"* can neither be understood nor conceived, then it is effectively not in the understanding or the intellect. As a consequence, God ceases to exist. This, Anselm assumes, is false; therefore, either Gaunilo's premises or conclusions must be in error.[105]

Gaunilo, in Anselm's view, maintains that, even if God existed in the understanding, it does not follow that he exists in reality. His view is just the opposite. A being "than which no greater can be conceived" can only be thought of as something which exists eternally and has no beginning. But something which does not yet exist and yet can be thought to exist must necessarily come into existence at some point in time. This cannot be the supreme being, since such a nature had no beginning.[106] Thus, if it can be thought to exist, it

[101] *Ibid.*, c. 5, p. 127, 25-p. 128, 7.
[102] *Ibid.*, c. 6, p. 128.   [103] *Ibid.*, c. 7, p. 129, 1-13.
[104] *Quid ad haec respondeat editor ipsius libelli*, c. 1, vol. 1, p. 130, 12-16.
[105] *Ibid.*, 130.   [106] *Ibid.*, 131, 2-5.

must necessarily exist. Further, if it can be thought at all, it must exist. Anselm offers the example of a being which does not exist, even though it may be conceived. It would not be a supreme being by his definition, for its non-existence, either in the understanding or in reality, would become a possibility. The same conclusion is reached: if the supreme being can be thought, it exists, and, if it can be understood, it exists in the mind.[107] It does not at any time or place fail to exist as a whole; it exists as a whole everywhere and always.[108] In fact, Anselm adds, it exists and is found in the understanding to the degree that meaningful statements about it can be made. For, just as something conceived, as it is conceived, exists in conception, so something understood, as it is understood, comes into being in the understanding. And, if it exists in the understanding alone, it can be conceived to exist in reality, which is superior.[109] One can put the same conclusion another way: if a being "than which nothing greater can be conceived" is in the understanding, it is indeed that which it is stated to be.[110]

Gaunilo's lost paradise has therefore been found. The supreme being cannot be thought not to exist because its existence has been logically demonstrated "through the certain reason of truth." Otherwise, Anselm states, it would not exist at all.[111] If anyone says that he conceives the supreme being not to exist, he either conceives something "than which a greater is inconceivable" or he does not think. If he does not think, he does not think of the non-existence of that which he does not conceive. If he thinks, he thinks of a being which cannot be conceived not to exist. For, if it could be conceived not to exist, it could be thought to have a beginning and an end. This is impossible: therefore, Anselm a third time concludes that the non-existence of God is logically inconceivable.[112]

Finally, he answers Gaunilo's argument that it would be preferable to speak of God's existence as not being able to be understood (*intelligi*) rather than as not being able to be conceived (*cogitari*).[113] Anselm disagrees. For, to substitute "understanding" for "conceiving" in this context would be to yield to one of the fallacies Gaunilo himself underlines, namely the fact that something unreal cannot truly be understood. This same objection cannot be raised against conceiving (*cogitatio*). For, although no objects which exist can be understood not

[107] *Ibid.*, 131, 6-12.   [108] *Ibid.*, 131, 18-132, 2.   [109] *Ibid.*, c. 2, p. 132, 14-21.
[110] *Ibid.*, 132, 27-28.   [111] *Ibid.*, c. 3, p. 133, 3-12.   [112] *Ibid.*, 133, 12-18.
[113] Cf. P. Michaud-Quantin, "Notes," *loc.cit.*, and, on the "transcendental-constitutive" aspects of Anselm's distinction, A. Schurr, *Die Begründung*, 73-86.

to exist, yet all objects except that which exists in the highest degree can be conceived not to exist. For all things that have a beginning, an end, and are composed of parts can be conceived not to exist. I can conceive my own non-existence, even though I am sure I exist. For we conceive of the non-existence of a good many things which exist, and vice versa, not by forming an opinion (*existimando*) but by imagining (*fingendo*) that they exist as we conceive them. In short, in Anselm's view, all things except God can be affirmed or conceived to exist or not to exist.[114]

It is clear from even so brief an outline of their respective positions that the difference of opinion between Gaunilo and Anselm was not only about how God could be demonstrated to exist but also about the manner in which meaningful statements could be made in language about reality.[115] On the latter issue the pair brought to the surface a controversy analogous to that which divided Berengar and Lanfranc. For they effectively examined opposite sides of the same insight, namely, that man's intellectual apparatus was highly influenced by the structure of language, providing him with beneficial aids to thinking such as grammar and logic but cutting him off from an ideal or inner reality whose existence he could only indirectly infer. The language in question was written language and, within its systematic framework, their debate was in large part over words, things, and meaning.

Gaunilo takes the view that what is in the mind is the conceptual equivalent of words (*quod dicitur, intelligo*). For him, therefore, the text comes first. The mere fact of being in the mind does not make words into things, since the mind, by its very nature, contains a mixture of the real and the unreal. He would argue that one can understand what is said about things of which one has no knowledge; but that does not make them real, for the simple reason that there is no evidence in the form of an object corresponding to the verbal descriptions. However, if the link between *intellectus* and *res* is broken, Anselm's conclusions become invalid. Gaunilo is willing to admit that when something is heard and thought about in the mind it may be perceived to be real. He also agrees, as noted, that the perceived reality is one thing, the understanding by which it is grasped, another. But to his mind there is nonetheless a gap between words and things. His position begins with doubt and ends in skepticism. For,

---

[114] *Quid ad haec*, c. 4, p. 133, 21-p. 134, 13. In chapters four to nine Anselm answers other objections, such as misquotation, inconsistency, and the meaning of the artist's design. But he does not add substantially to what he has said about language and reality.

[115] Cf. K. Barth, *Anselm: Fides Quaerens Intellectum*, Eng. trans. (London, 1960), 28-31.

either what one has in the mind are mere words implying no reality or a conceptual reality which has no verbal counterpart in a known object. The name "God" is conceived by Anselm, who does not have any direct knowledge of the thing to which it refers. Merely defining God negatively—*quo maius nihil cogitari potest*—does not prove that he really exists.

Anselm approaches the problem from a different perspective. He does not doubt God's existence and wait for a positive demonstration through reason, but assumes his reality and asks how one can make sense out of the fact by using language logically. Therefore, he does not argue that, because a word is spoken, an object exists *in intellectu* and *in re*. Rather, given the a priori existence of "*quo maius nihil cogitari potest*," he asks what are the logical interrelationships between words that account for it. For this reality can be discussed and thought about by humans only through the vehicle of language. Hence, for such a reality, saying that it exists is equivalent to its existing in the understanding, which, like the design in the artist's mind, implies that it is understood. From Anselm's definition of the supreme nature it follows that existence in reality is implied by existence in concept.

In the final analysis, Gaunilo and Anselm have simply a different point of departure. Gaunilo finds the hiatus between words and things insurmountable; Anselm's solution for him is a mere logical sophistry. But he is not on that account a "nominalist," just as Anselm is not a "realist."[116] Both authors stand at the threshold of medieval linguistic philosophy as it begins to come to grips with the implications of logic, grammar, and written language. Gaunilo follows up the problem of words as names of things, but he is no less interested in their objective reality. Anselm, by contrast, assumes that the reality of the highest being is revealed by the Word in textual form, the Bible. The disjunction between words and things does not negate this set of revealed truths, since, in creation, God followed a logical process of discourse and hence of text formation.

Logic, Grammar, and Forms of Expression

The issues regarding language, texts, and reality which Anselm discussed in the *Monologion*, the *Proslogion*, and the reply to Gaunilo

---

[116] Cf. D. P. Henry, *The Logic of Saint Anselm* (Oxford, 1967), 97-107. An intelligent criticism of Baeumker's *Begriffsrealismus* is offered by J. Fischer, *Die Erkenntnislehre Anselms von Canterbury nach den Quellen dargestellt* (Münster, 1911), 40-41, who adds that Anselm's realistic inclinations should not be confused with those of later scholastics. They are "at best" what he calls *erkenntnistheoretischen Rationalismus* (p. 43).

recurred in different contexts in his other writings. His belief in the value of logic for clarifying theological problems led in particular to serious consideration of when we can call a proposition "true" or "false."

He answered the question briefly in *De Veritate*, which was written between 1080 and 1085. He also put the matter in a wider and more technical framework in *De Grammatico*, which belongs to the same years.[117] Finally, he added a few purely logical insights in his *Philosophical Fragments*, which are possibly the early draft of the longer treatise on linguistic analysis promised in *Cur Deus Homo* sometime after 1094.[118]

The essentials of his position are made clear in *De Veritate* and *De Grammatico*, to which we briefly turn.

The *De Veritate* begins by recalling a passage from chapter eighteen of the *Monologion* in which Anselm reasons from the timelessness of the highest nature to the eternity of truth. The highest nature is *vera aeternitas*. But, if that is the case, there was no point in time when "truth" began, and, of course, there will be no point when it ends. His statement once again is reducible to a syllogism about the real: if God is eternal, and God is truth, then truth too is eternal.[119]

The student in the dialogue then asks the master to provide a definition of truth.[120] Anselm replies by taking up the question on a logical level. Let us first ask, he says, what truth there is in a statement (*enunciatio*), since truth or falsehood refer in fact to what is said. The student suggests that a statement is true when what it enunciates is in fact the case (*quando est quod enuntiat*), whether positively or negatively. Anselm then asks: Does it seem that the thing stated (*res enuntiata*) is the statement's truth (*veritas enuntiationis*)? No, says the student, because nothing is true except by participation in truth.[121] The truth of a true thing truly exists in that same thing, whereas the thing stated exists in a true statement (*in enuntiatione vera*). Therefore, it would appear that a statement's truth is to be sought in its language, discourse, or manner of delivery.

Anselm then asks a further question. Does the problem lie in the

[117] For a brief review of Anselm's use of logic, see S. Vanni Rovighi, "Notes sur l'influence . . . ," CCM 7(1964), 423-28; in greater detail, Henry, *The Logic, passim*.

[118] Henry, 120. On the treatise's relation to the *De Grammatico*, see Colish, *The Mirror of Language*, 110-11.

[119] *Monologion*, c. 18, pp. 32-33; *De Veritate*, c. 1, vol. 1, p. 176.

[120] *De Veritate*, c. 2, pp. 177-80, on which the following summary depends. Cf. G. R. Evans, *Anselm and Talking about God*, 81-86.

[121] Cf. Boethius, *In Categoriis Aristotelis*, 1.4, PL 64.285.

statement as delivered (*oratio*), in its meaning (*significatio*), or somewhere in the stated definition (*in diffinitione enuntiationis*)? The student thinks not, since, if any of these were correct, the truth of a statement would merely be a form of expression. For the internal logic of a proposition is not affected by external facts: it may be formally true and really wrong.

What then, Anselm asks, is the statement's truth? After a discussion of the nature of utterance, he proposes a solution himself.[122] He argues in effect that a statement may be true because as a proposition it performs a logical task, but that it is true in another sense because it signifies what is really taking place. We do not normally call a statement true when it refers to a condition which in reality does not exist. Nonetheless, the statement has a certain "truth" and "rectitude," since, as a proposition, it signifies what it should. However, when it refers to an existing state, it signifies what it is taken to signify and also what it is really signifying; that is, it achieves its meaning both through words alone and through the correlation between words and things.[123] This leads Anselm to a set of simple dichotomies between words and things which recall the theological distinctions of the *Monologion*. Words are mutable, things immutable; words derive their meaning from accident and usage, things, from essence, that is, from objects' reality. Anselm adds that the *ratio veritatis* which one finds in logically correct spoken statements (*in propositione vocis*) applies to all systems of signs (*in omnibus signis*), whether written in words or conveyed in sign-language by the hands.[124] It is not only the voice but even gestures which are reduced to a textual model.

A more systematic treatment of this problem was undertaken in

---

[122] *De Veritate*, c. 2, p. 179. On the importance of the *De Veritate* for Anselm's thought, which cannot be conveyed in so short a summary, see E. Gilson, "Sens et nature de l'argument de Saint Anselme," AHDLMA 9 (1934), 10-15, 40-42; E. Fairweather, "Truth, Justice and Moral Responsibility in the Thought of St. Anselm," *L'homme et son destin d'après les penseurs du moyen âge* (Louvain and Paris, 1960), 386; and M. Colish, *The Mirror of Language*, 112-16. On Anselm's notion of truth, see K. Flasch, "Zum Begriff der Wahrheit bei Anselm von Canterbury," *Philosophisches Jahrbuch* 72 (1965), 322-52 and on the related notion of rectitude, the full study of R. Pouchet, *La rectitudo chez saint Anselme* (Paris, 1964).

[123] *Ibid.*, 179, 2-4: "Sed cum significat esse quod est, dupliciter facit quod debet; quoniam significat et quod accepit significare, et ad quod facta est." Cf. J.-D. Folghera, "La vérité définie par saint Anselme," *Revue thomiste* 8 (1900), 413-18, who speaks of a distinction between *veritas significationis* and *veritas opinionis*.

[124] *Ibid.*, p. 179, 32-p. 180, 3. Cf. c. 9, 189, 2-4: "Namque non solum in iis quae signa solemus dicere, sed et in aliis omnibus quae diximus est significatio vera vel falsa."

the short, complex dialogue, *De Grammatico*. The question, derived
from Boethius's interpretation of the *Categories'* opening chapter,[125]
was whether *grammaticus* was a substance or a quality.[126] By providing
an answer, the student hopes, Anselm will shed light on the logical
status of other denominative terms, which were defined by Aristotle
as words "which derive their name from some other name but differ
from it in termination."[127] Included in this category are the Latin
terms referring to expertise in grammar, or, as D. P. Henry correctly
interprets Anselm's meaning, to an understanding of literacy,[128] which,
as we have noted, is inseparable from latinity and written language.
In Anselm's view, the two statements *grammaticus est substantia* and
grammaticus est qualitas are not incompatible.[129] The demonstration
however requires that one exhaust the range of logical possibilities
implied in the two propositions.

   This is essentially what the dialogue does. First Anselm takes up a
set of consequences of the statement that an expert in grammar, or,
as we shall call him, a literate, is a man.[130] Two falsifications are
proposed, which result in the nonsensical statement, "No literate is a
man." This, says Anselm, is impossible, for, while animals can be
understood without rationality, man cannot.[131] A second set of syllogisms is then constructed around the antitheses animal/non-rational
and man/rational, concluding in the statement, "No man is an animal." The student now realizes that his master's motive was to offer
him two similar sets of syllogisms in which the premises were valid
but the conclusions false.[132] In a further exercise it is shown that
premises formerly considered defensible have in fact no common term.
No conclusions therefore can be drawn from them.[133] For, Anselm
adds, the common term is less an aspect of utterance (*in prolatione*)
than of meaningful sense (*in sententia*). However, there is no objection
if the common term exists in the understanding (*in intellectu*) and not

[125] D. P. Henry, *The De Grammatico of St. Anselm* (Notre Dame, 1964), 80-82; *idem, The Logic of St. Anselm*, 36-38; 41-64. The treatise was thought by early historians to be of little value. For a history of the reassessment, see L. Steiger, "Contexe syllogismos: Über die Kunst und Bedeutung der Topik bei Anselm," *Analecta Anselmiana* 1 (1969), 107-43.

[126] *De Grammatico*, c. 1, vol. 1, p. 145, 4-6; on misinterpretations of the *incipit*, see Henry, *The Logic*, 31-36.

[127] *Categoriae*, c. 1; Henry, *The De Grammatico*, 80.

[128] I follow Henry in translating *grammaticus* as "literate"; for his reasons, see *The Logic*, 69-75; *idem*, "Why 'Grammaticus?'," *Archivum Latinitatis Medii Aevi* 28 (1958) 165-80.

[129] *De Grammatico*, c. 2, p. 146, 11-14.

[130] *Ibid.*, c. 1, 145, 15: ". . . omnis grammaticus homo et omnis homo substantia."

[131] *Ibid.*, c. 2, 147, 11-17.   [132] *Ibid.*, 148, 2-6.   [133] *Ibid.*, c. 4, 148, 12-149, 6.

in a verbal statement (*in prolatione*). The meaning, not the words, holds the syllogism together.[134]

If the student cannot prove what he wants to say, are his statements therefore meaningless?[135] No: by rearranging the evidence, Anselm comes to the "logically sound" conclusion that "literate and man are not identically defined."[136] A further series of propositions follows, after which the master concludes that, in proving that the essence of man is not the essence of literate, a common term is nonetheless implied.[137] When the student appears confused at these apparently contradictory results, Anselm tells him that he too has concentrated on words to the neglect of meaning.[138] The student confesses that he did not realize that a syllogism could mislead him by its logical structure alone. The now familiar distinction between mere verbal usage, however logical, and truth is emphasized in subsequent statements, after which the student insists on being shown the source of his initial confusion. Anselm accordingly takes him back to the examples of *animal* and *homo*. Propositions concerning them were so evidently true by their sense that they could not be logically invalidated. The master then asks if something's essence can exist in the form of a definition.[139] Thus, by their essences alone, we might know what is an animal and what a man. He rearranges the previously discussed syllogisms, arriving at an expected conclusion: if being literate is not being a man and only a man, then whatsoever is essentially literate need not on that account be essentially man. Having isolated the inner meaning of being literate from being man, he can finally state, *"Nullus grammaticus est simpliciter homo."*[140]

Anselm thus establishes by a new route the difference between the illogic of utterance and the logic of artificial language. At this point the student raises another question. Aristotle, he points out, said that

---

[134] *Ibid.*, 149, 11-14: [Master]: "Communis terminus syllogismi non tam in prolatione quam in sententia est habendus. Sicut enim nihil efficitur, si communis est in voce et non in sensu: ita nihil obest, si est in intellectu et non in prolatione. Sententia quippe ligat syllogismum, non verba." Cf. Steiger, "Über die Kunst," 127-28.

[135] *Ibid.*, c. 5, 149, 16-17.

[136] *Ibid.*, 149, 31-33: "Sed si ita intelligas: grammaticus non est homo, ac si dicatur: grammaticus non est idem quod homo, id est non habent eandem definitionem: vera est conclusio."

[137] *Ibid.*, c. 6, 150, 29-30: "Nam ad hoc probandum quia essentia hominis non est essentia grammatici, habet earum significatio communem terminum."

[138] *Ibid.*, c. 7, 151, 19-21: "Bene enim intellexi quid loquendo mihi significares, sed idipsum quod significabas non bene consideravi, quia quomodo me deciperet ignoravi."

[139] *Ibid.*, c. 8, 152, 28-30.

[140] *Ibid.*, 153, 15-20.

a literate is one of the things which exists in a subject (*in subiecto*).
Yet no man is a subject; therefore, once again, no literate is a man.

Anselm responds that this conclusion is contrary to Aristotle's intention. He asks in turn:[141] When you speak to me about a literate
(whence I understand you to be speaking), does what you signify in
speech concern the name (*de nomine*) or the things (*de rebus*)?[142] The
student replies that the words mean the things, that is, *homo* and
grammatica. But, if this is so, then, on hearing the name, I may
understand man and literate, and, speaking of a literate, I may mean
man or literacy. From this it follows that man is a substance, not a
subject.[143] Literacy is both a quality and a subject; that is, it may be
asserted that, with respect to man, literate is a substance, and, insofar
as literacy is concerned, it is a quality. The student raises a further
objection based on Aristotle, namely that every substance is either
primary or secondary, and literate appears to be neither. But Anselm
counters easily that, insofar as a literate being is not a subject, it falls
under both genus and species (i.e., animal and man) and to this extent
it is a secondary substance.[144]

The discussion then turns towards defining the nature of logical
discourse. Anselm asks the student to prove that, if literate is not
man, then literate is not literacy.[145] The student foresees an obvious
problem. If, he says, I were to assert that "Being literate is a useful
form of knowledge" (*Utilis scientia est grammaticus*) or that "Man well
knows literate" (*Bene scit homo iste grammaticum*), not only the literates
(*grammatici*) but also the uneducated (*rustici*) would laugh. Do the
authors of logical treatises have nothing better to do than to set down
in writing (*in suis libris scripsisse*) what they themselves would blush to
state in familiar conversation (*colloquentes dicere erubescerent*)?[146] In other
words, the student distinguishes between what men say in ordinary
usage (*usus omnium loquentium*) and what they set down in writing (*ubi
scriptum sit . . .*).[147] Spoken usage draws attention to literate as a

[141] *Ibid.*, c. 9, 154, 3-5. For a full discussion of Anselm's use of Aristotle and Boethius, see Henry, *The Logic*, 42-60.
[142] *Ibid.*, 154, 7-8. [143] *Ibid.*, 154, 12-16. [144] *Ibid.*, c. 10, 154, 26-155, 13.
[145] *Ibid.*, c. 11, 155, 15-16.
[146] *Ibid.*, 156, 5-11: "Quoniam nemo qui intelligit nomen grammatici, ignorat grammaticum significare hominem et grammaticam, et tamen si hac fiducia loquens in populo dicam: utilis scientia est grammaticus, aut: bene scit homo iste grammaticum: non solum stomachabuntur grammatici, sed et ridebunt rustici. Nullatenus itaque credam sine aliqua alia ratione tractatores dialecticae tam saepe et tam studiose in suis libris scripsisse, quod idem ipsi colloquentes dicere erubescerent." Cf. Henry, *The Logic*, 5; 14-15.
[147] *Ibid.*, 156, 13-14 and 19-20.

substance, not as a quality or accident. Yet the logicians never say "like literate," etc. If, in this frame of reference, literacy is both a quality and a substance, why is not man as well?

Anselm's ingenious reply takes the reader to the heart of the dialogue. The student, he says, rejects his argument that literate is both a substance and a quality because both cannot be applied to the name man (*in nomine hominis*).[148] There is a difference between the way in which *homo* signifies what makes up a man and *grammaticus* signifies what makes up both man and literate. The name "man" signifies man wholly and all at once. Its chief feature is substance, without which other qualities would not suffice. For, there is no characteristic of substance (*differentia substantiae*) in whose absence substance cannot also be found, whereas, if substance is absent, no characteristic can exist. Therefore, although all the qualities taken together signify "man," forming, so to speak, a unity with a unified meaning, the name is nonetheless principally a signifier (*significativum*) and appellative (*appellativum*) of substance. Thus, it is correct to say "Substance is man" but not "Rationality is man," or vice versa.[149] By contrast, literate does not signify man and literacy wholly and at once; it signifies literacy through itself and man through something else.[150]

Grammaticus, then, is a *nomen*, an appellative but not properly speaking a signifier. Further, although literate signifies literacy, it is not the appellative of literacy. The general rule is as follows: the appellative name of a thing (*appellativum nomen rei*) is what the thing is called in everyday usage (*usus loquendi*). Statements like "Literacy is literate" run counter to such usage.[151]

The student is not yet convinced. What, he asks, is the point of distinguishing so carefully between definition through itself (*per se*) and definition through another (*per aliquid*)? For there never was a man apart from literacy or literacy apart from man.[152] Why, in fact, is literate not definable as a man knowing grammar (*homo sciens grammaticam*)?[153] Anselm brings five convincing arguments against this position, thereby reconfirming that literate does not strictly speaking signify man.[154] It only signifies knowing literacy.[155] The student then asks that he clarify the difference between the two types of signification, that is, the significative (*significativum, per se*) and the appellative

[148] *Ibid.*, c. 12, 156, 22-23.
[149] *Ibid.*, 156, 26-157, 1.   [150] *Ibid.*, c. 13, 157, 10-11.
[151] *Ibid.*, c. 12, 157, 2-8.   [152] *Ibid.*, 157, 10-15.   [153] *Ibid.*, 157, 16-17.
[154] *Ibid.*, cc. 13-14, p. 157, 18-p. 159, 18.   [155] *Ibid.*, 159, 24.

(*appellativum, per aliud*).[156] Anselm explains how a word may name
something it does not signify by using the example of a white horse
and a black bull. If, standing before both, someone gave the order,
"Strike the white one," the hearer would automatically strike the
horse. Yet "white" in itself does not signify "horse."[157] Therefore, an
adjective may name a thing which it does not signify.[158] The student
realizes that what is true of this example is valid for all denominative
terms, both nouns and verbs.[159] The name, Anselm adds, is accidental
to significant utterance (*voces significativae*), while the signifier is substantial. Thus *vox significativa* means nothing but signification *per se*.[160]
Finally, Anselm rounds out the discussion by returning to Aristotle,
who, he argues, refers to words by the name of the things they signify, not by the names of their appellatives.[161] He then emphasizes
that this is a difference common to grammarians and logicians. Grammarians say one thing according to the form of the word, another
according to the nature of the thing.[162] Logicians write one way about
words insofar as they are signifiers, but use them in another in ordinary speech insofar as they are appellatives.

By a different route, then, we return to the problem of written
language, and, in a logical sense, to the status of oral utterance within
it. The *De Grammatico* has as its principal subject the difference between the ordinary use of language (*usus loquendi*) and logically significant statement (*voces significativae, significatio per se*).[163] The distinction parallels that between *verba* and *res* in the *Monologion*, the *Proslogion*,
and *De Veritate*, providing a "systematic unity"[164] of method which
underlies the treatment of diverse theological issues.

The *De Grammatico*, despite its specialized appeal, also marked an
important stage in clarifying the philosophical difference between the
speech habits of ordinary people (*populi*) and the technical language of
those engaged in logical discourse (*dialectici*). This was not a simple
distinction between popular and learned culture. True, for Anselm,
popular speech was spoken; its grammar was based primarily on usage
and could not be scientific or logical. Technical language, while also

---

[156] *Ibid.*, 159, 26-160, 3. Is this Frege's *Sinn* and *Bedeutung*, as suggested by S. Vanni Rovighi, "Notes . . . ," CCM 7 (1964), 427?

[157] *Ibid.*, 160, 3-161, 4.   [158] *Ibid.*, c. 15, 161, 6-8.   [159] *Ibid.*, 161, 11-13.

[160] *Ibid.*, 161, 14-18.   [161] *Ibid.*, c. 17, pp. 162-63.

[162] *Ibid.*, c. 18, 164, 7-10: "Non enim movere nos debet quod dialectici aliter scribunt de
vocibus secundum quod sunt significativae, aliter eis utuntur loquendo secundum quod sunt
appellativae, si et grammatici aliud dicunt secundum formam vocum, aliud secundum rerum
naturam."

[163] Cf. Henry. *The Logic*, 12-24.   [164] *Ibid.*, 119.

existing in spoken form, was based on grammar, that is, on the norms of written language. Its logic was a set of rules relating to the use of words in specific contexts. The contrast may be put as follows. While popular speech has rules governing its written forms, they are usually empirical generalizations based on oral usage. While, in theory, technical language is still a spoken form, or, at least, exists in a form that can be spoken, its rules are logically interconnected and independent of local or individual variation. Logical discourse can, and, at times, must be "nonsense," which *usus loquendi* never is. Anselm applied this distinction to all non-logical languages, including signs and gestures. Whenever the student of the dialogues protested that the master was violating customary usage, Anselm replied as he did in *De Casu Diaboli* that many things are "improperly expressed" in ordinary language (*Multa namque in communi locutione dicuntur improprie*).[165] This tenet, in turn, provided a basis for further analysis. We should not, he argued, cling to inappropriate words that merely conceal truth (*improprietas verborum veritatem tegens*), but rather seek to discover the proper truth of philosophical reality hidden beneath the many-faceted usages of everyday speech (*proprietas veritatis sub multimodo genere locutionum latens*).[166]

Yet, in thus distinguishing between *res* and *forma loquendi*, Anselm did not advocate the unlimited use of logic in theology. The two sides of the question were dealt with in his *Epistola de Incarnatione Verbi*, which went through some five recensions between 1092 and 1094.[167] His opponent on this occasion was the celebrated Roscelin, who had abjured tritheism at Soissons in 1092 only to lapse into heresy again shortly afterwards.[168] Anselm therefore felt compelled to embark on a lengthier refutation of nominalism than he had attempted in his occasional correspondence with John the Monk or Fulco of Beauvais.[169] In the course of his rebuttal he spoke of many of the same forces which had brought about the composition of the *Monologion* and the *Proslogion*: the entreaties of his brethren that he solve the problem (*ut*

---

[165] c. 12, vol. 1, p. 253, 19-20; cf. Henry, *The Logic*, 13.

[166] *Ibid.*, c. 1, p. 235, 8-12; Henry, pp. 13-14; 184-85.

[167] See F. S. Schmitt, "Cinq recensions de l'Epistola de Incarnatione Verbi de S. Anselme de Cantorbéry," Rben 51 (1939), 275-87.

[168] *Epistola de Incarnatione Verbi*, c. 1, vol. 2, p. 4, 19. For Roscelin's views in comparison with Anselm and Abelard, see B. Adlhoch, "Roscelin und Sanct Anselm," *Philosophisches Jahrbuch* 20 (1907), 442-56; on Roscelin's doctrines, see the useful group of texts in F. Picavet, *Roscelin philosophe et théologien* (Paris, 1911), 112-43.

[169] *Epp.* 129 and 136, vol. 3, respectively pp. 271-72 and 279-81.

solverem questionem);[170] the necessity of understanding what one believed; and the care needed in approaching *sacra pagina*, lest one fall prey to the *dialecticae haeretici*. Yet once again the crux of his argument rested on the logical defence of the previously established distinctions between words and things.

Anselm reiterated and extended his thoughts in his longest and most mature theological work, *Cur Deus Homo*, which was completed in the summer of 1098.[171] His major purpose was to illustrate through logical argument why God assumed a human form in order to redeem fallen man. The question, he claimed, was of interest both to *litterati* and to *illitterati*, both of whom had demanded a logical exposition (*ratio*).[172] The treatise's contents lie beyond the scope of this discussion. Yet, it may be noted that *Cur Deus Homo* effectively brought the reflective, theoretical qualities of eleventh-century theology to their culmination. "In the old three-cornered conflict of God, Devil, and Man," Southern suggests, "Man had played a very subordinate rôle; in the new order the rôle of Man was necessarily greater, and that of God less easily defined. . . ."[173] It has also been proposed that *Cur Deus Homo* presents a "penitential-eucharistic" as opposed to a "baptismal" theory of atonement.[174] In other words, in placing Christ's sacrifice at the centre of the stage, Anselm inevitably created a man-oriented theology: the passive acceptance of a divinely inspired historical process was in part replaced by man's own active striving after understanding within faith.[175] There was as a consequence a new place for human consciousness within the traditional framework of sin and redemption.

This transformation, we have argued, could not have been brought

---

[170] *Ep. de Incarnatione Verbi*, c. 1, p. 5, 2.

[171] See in general F. S. Schmitt, "Die wissenschaftliche Methode Anselms 'Cur Deus Homo,' " *Spicilegium Beccense I*, 349-70, and R. Roques, *Anselme de Cantorbéry: Pourquoi Dieu s'est fait homme* (Paris, 1963), 47-190. The treatise's intellectual background is ably presented by R. W. Southern, *St. Anselm*, 90-121. For a critique of approaches to the work, see J. McIntyre, *St. Anselm and his Critics. A Re-Interpretation of the "Cur Deus Homo"* (London, 1954), 117-204. On the soteriology, see J. Rivière, "Rédemption," DTC 13.2, 1942-44 (bibliography, col. 1988), and *idem, Le dogme de la rédemption au début du moyen âge* (Paris, 1934), 65-95.

[172] *Cur Deus Homo*, c. 1, vol. 2, p. 48, 5-6.

[173] *St. Anselm and his Biographer*, 97.

[174] G. H. Williams, *Anselm: Communion and Atonement* (St. Louis, 1960), 6-7, 26-62.

[175] On Anselm's middle position between early medieval "objective" and later medieval "subjective" theories of salvation, see B. Funke, *Grundlagen und Voraussetzungen der Satisfaktionstheorie des hl. Anselm von Canterbury*, I. Teil (Münster, 1903), 1-3; E. Lohmeyer, *Die Lehre vom Willen bei Anselm von Canterbury* (Leipzig, 1914), 39-41; and R. Heinzmann, "Veritas humanae naturae . . . ," 787-91.

about without a reassessment of theology's relation to written language. Anselm's dialogues all proceed from meditation to meditative text and depend upon increasingly intensive repetitions of the hermeneutic process. They oscillate like his famous prayers between word and text, between the activities of *intima locutio* and *cogitare/intelligere*. In each case the opposite numbers in the dialogues—Boso, for instance, in *Cur Deus Homo*—provide alter-egos for Anselm himself. The meditations therefore have audiences before they reach parchment. The reflection is rational not because of its rationalism, although, as Grabmann emphasized, *ratio* has a "systematic function" in all Anselm's works,[176] but because, within Anselm's mind and afterwards, it involves the playing out of a set of "speech-acts" as texts. What has been called "the Anselmic method"[177] is really a type of "proof" utilizing logic in which the human interlocutors have in part the status of means of communication.

In so reformulating the Augustinian notions of will and mind, Anselm often visualizes God as a dialoguer, as a being engaged in the original production of the text. *Ratio* is God's reason, that is, the process by which word becomes text, and, in thus becoming the Word, also authenticates itself. Creation is thereby made coterminous with "talking about creating."[178] Similarly, in his approach to ethics, "the phenomenological aspect of the moral life"—its acting out as a set of "problems" in the here and now—"predominates over the metaphysical reconstruction."[179] Ethics becomes a way of revitalizing experience, an extension, so to speak, of eucharistic and sacramental "realism."[180] Hence, for Anselm, texts, although resulting from purposeful text generation, are not in themselves dispositive; they are evidence, memoranda, aids to the recreation of the experiential process linking man and God through Christ. Scripture, no reader can forget, is excluded as "proof" on its own. In fact, Anselm refers to the Bible as

---

[176] *Die Geschichte der scholastischen Methode*, I, 272-332.

[177] J. McIntyre, "Premises and Conclusions in the System of Anselm's Theology," *Spicilegium Beccense I*, 95-96, 100; cf. *St. Anselm and his Critics*, 39: "It cannot be denied . . . that for St. Anselm the credo provides the *intelligenda*, or the *probanda*, the conclusions which he endeavours to establish by his argument." Cf. K. Barth, *Anselm: Fides Quaerens Intellectum*, 19-20, 22-25.

[178] Cf. G. R. Evans, *Anselm and Talking about God*, 21-24.

[179] S. Vanni Rovighi, "L'etica di S. Anselmo," *Analecta Anselmiana* 1 (1969), 75. The inserted phrase is my own.

[180] Cf. P. Evdokimov, "L'aspect apophatique de l'argument de saint Anselme," *Spicilegium Beccense I*, 238: "Le 'réalisme' de saint Anselme rejoint la notion liturgique et iconosophique du 'symbole'. Si un 'signe' peut 'signifier' même une absence . . . un symbole contient toujours une certaine présence du symbolisé. . . ."

scriptura, autentica pagina, auctoritas, lex, and so forth,[181] clearly indicating a distinction between *verbum Dei* and *scriptum verbi*. For God's function in part in Anselm's thought is to stimulate man to explore the limits of what he can certainly know concerning divine truth.

2. PETER ABELARD

Omnis controversia, Tullio dicente, aut in scripto aut in ratione versatur.
—*Theologia Christiana* 2.13b (and elsewhere).

Among the numerous students of the problem of language and reality during the first half of the twelfth century, the most original by common consent was Peter Abelard, who was born in 1079 in Le Pallet, Brittany, and died in the Cluniac abbey of St. Marcel on 21st April 1142.[182]

Abelard was recognized both by those who favoured his views and

[181] S. Tonini, "La scrittura," 74-75, provides a complete list of such expressions.

[182] The appearance in 1969 of two important studies of Abelard makes a full review of the bibliography superfluous. For Abelard's 'school' and its influence in the twelfth century, see D. E. Luscombe, *The School of Peter Abelard. The Influence of Abelard's Thought in the Early Scholastic Period* (Cambridge, 1969), with a bibliography pp. 316-43. On Abelard's intellectual development, see J. Jolivet, *Arts du langage et théologie chez Abélard* (Paris, 1969). A classic early account of Abelard's philosophy and theology is that of M. Grabmann, *Die Geschichte der scholastischen Methode*, vol. 2 (1911), 168-229; a good general summary of his place in scholastic thought is P. Vignaux, "Nominalisme," DTC 11.1, 718-33. A still useful review of Abelard's sources is found in E. Kaiser, *Pierre Abélard critique* (Fribourg, 1901), 19-36 (in tabular form) and 123-81 (in detail). A full introduction to the logic is L. M. de Rijk, *Petrus Abaelardus Dialectica. First Complete Edition of the Parisian Manuscript with an Introduction*, 2nd ed. (Assen, 1970), ix-xcviii; a brief but excellent survey is M. del Pra, *Pietro Abelardo, scritti filosofici . . .* (Milan, 1954), ix-xxxvi; a useful group of texts is assembled and translated by J. Jolivet, *Abélard ou la philosophie dans le langage* (Paris, 1969); more general is W. and M. Kneale, *The Development of Logic* (Oxford, 1962), 202-24. Four recent conferences which review issues under discussion are *Peter Abelard. Proceedings of the International Conference, Louvain, May 10-12, 1971*, ed. E.M. Buytaert (Louvain, 1974); *Pierre Abélard, Pierre le Vénérable. Les courants philosophiques, littéraires et artistiques en Occident au milieu du XIIe siècle*, ed. R. Louis, J. Jolivet and J. Châtillon (Paris, 1975) (in which note should be taken of the important review essay of N. M. Häring, "Abelard Yesterday and Today," pp. 341-403); *Petrus Abaelardus (1079-1142). Person, Werk und Wirkung*, ed. R. Thomas, *et al.* (Trier, 1980), esp. part II: "Abaelard Philosoph und Logiker im 12. Jahrhundert," pp. 103-79; and M. de Gandillac, *et al.*, eds., *Abélard. Le "Dialogue." La philosophie de la logique. Actes du Colloque de Neuchâtel 16-17 novembre 1979*, (Geneva, Lausanne and Neuchâtel, 1981). Among encyclopedia articles, a useful early account of Abelard's theology is E. Portalié, "Abélard," DTC 1, 36-55; also, B. Nardi, "Abelardo," *Enciclopedia italiana* 1, 54-55. For a more recent survey, see L. Minio-Paluello, "Abailard," *Dictionary of Scientific Biography* 1, 1-4, where there is a full list of earlier general histories, pp. 3-4.

by those who opposed them to have stood at a sort of crossroads in the development of medieval philosophical theology. Like Berengar, the major champion of the use of logic in *divina lectio* before he wrote, Abelard was for many generations better known as a personality than as the proponent of a consistent theological position. History in one sense repeated itself: the council at Sens in 1140 reiterated a similar injustice as took place during Berengar's various trials in pronouncing guilt on the basis of unsubstantiated quotations or mere hearsay. Only since the actual range of Abelard's teaching was revealed by D. E. Luscombe and his linguistic theories fully analysed by Jean Jolivet and L. M. de Rijk have we been in a position to undertake an evaluation of his overall achievement. Not only have the accusations of heresy withered under the relentless pressure of historical research; new dimensions have also been added to the understanding of his life, his career, the spread of his ideas, and his treatment by his contemporaries. To early historians he appeared by and large to be a thinker who fought a resolute if losing battle against the traditional values of his age. Nowadays, it would be more appropriate to speak of him as a pioneer of two notions within the field of exegesis which within a century of his death had become the norm: namely, the extensive use of reason in interpretation and the harmonization of contrary views by a "dialectical hermeneutic"[183] involving accurate quotations from patristic sources. Indeed, Luscombe argues, "the conflicts between Abelard and the two leading monastic theologians of the day (i.e., St. Bernard and William of St. Thierry) should be seen not merely as disputes between the upholders respectively of faith and reason but as the effects of the realization of structural differences between two traditions of theological analysis and reflection."[184]

The purpose of the following discussion of Abelard and Bernard is to offer a clarification of these structural differences, and, in particular, to go beyond the content of their respective positions, together with the controversies surrounding them, in an effort to contrast their views on such matters as the status of oral discourse, the subjective versus objective aspects of hermeneutics, and the more general uses of factual (i.e., textually established) knowledge in questions involving faith.

In Abelard's case, the range of interest in literacy's uses was of course very broad. His twenty or so genuine students were attached

[183] Luscombe, *The School of Peter Abelard*, 113.
[184] *Ibid.*, 111.

to him "for personal reasons,"[185] and, from his first casual audience in Laon to his setting up of the Paraclete, he continued to promote a variety of communities of study, often of dissident or reformist tendencies. His biblical commentaries, and, above all, the gloss on Romans, were "readings" of a more strictly systematic kind than those of his contemporaries, Rupert of Deutz, Anselm of Laon, and William of Champeaux. The famous prologue to the *Sic et Non*, although not as original and audacious as was once thought,[186] contains perhaps the twelfth-century's clearest statement in favour of a linguistic and referential basis for all serious theological research. Abelard asserted, as had not the collections of *flores* and *sententiae*, that *auctoritas* implied the correct reproduction and careful ordering of early Christian statements on belief. The fifty-eight groups of quotations were to be evaluated according to two criteria, external criticism, which dealt with authenticity, and internal criticism, that is, the author's intention, including all matters that might bring about a disharmony between what a text said and what it actually meant.[187] Abelard's defences of the use of dialectic were likewise inseparable from his conception of the role of a culture of written information.[188] The informal disputation, questioning, or dialogue invariably took place against the background of a putative library, a resource collection from which a logically consistent unity might eventually be forged. Indeed, he was even more conservative than Anselm in looking upon not only the Bible but also the *sancti patres* as a set of ur-texts.

However, unlike Anselm, whose ideas on language are inseparable from his theological speculations, Abelard created an autonomous theory whose relationship to the various revisions of his theology will not be fully clarified until the manuscript versions of his many commentaries are systematically sorted out. On the question of language itself, however, Abelard's views are better understood: he not only used logic to separate meaningful from imprecise forms of discourse. New perspectives also seemed to be opened onto the real. At the centre of these insights was a notion of signification in which language effectively acted as a bridge between *res* and *intellectus*.

---

[185] *Ibid.*, 7.

[186] See E. Bertola, "I precedenti storici del metodo del 'Sic et Non' di Abelardo," *Rivista di filosofia neo-scolastica* 53 (1961), 279. For a review of the question, see J. Jolivet, *Arts du langage et théologie chez Abélard*, 240-41.

[187] *Sic et Non, prologus*, PL 178.1340D-41D; ed. B. B. Boyer and R. McKeon (Chicago and London, 1976-77), p. 91, l. 54-p. 92, l. 85.

[188] Jolivet, *Arts du langage*, 263-75.

Abelard made his clearest statement on the subject in his logical works, which were written roughly between 1110 and 1127[189] in the form of commentaries on such textbooks of the "old logic" as Aristotle's *Categories* and *On Interpretation*, as translated and interpreted by Boethius, and Cicero's version of the *Topics*.[190] The commentaries, which may occasionally have originated as lecture-notes, passed through a number of overlapping stages, first appearing as literal glosses, later in the more connected versions of the *Logica Ingredientibus*, and finally in successive redactions in the *Dialectica*.

An understanding of Abelard's logic and of its relationship to his notions of the uses of texts cannot be achieved without returning to its source, that is, the old logic itself. Just as his successive theologies, it has recently been argued, departed increasingly from Boethius's views on the trinity,[191] so his revisions of the logical books developed and modified the position of the thinker whom he described as *maximus ille Latinorum philosophus*.[192] This is not surprising. The synthesis of Greek logical thinking which first passed to the Latin world and then to the early Middle Ages was put together during the late Latin period, a time during which, as noted earlier, first bilingualism and later uniform latinity were being challenged by linguistic diversity. The Latin into which the Greek logical works were rendered was becoming, even during the period of translation, a learned, bookish tongue. The interpretations of Boethius, no less than the Justinian codifications in law, had to take account of the growing distance between spoken and written forms. Boethius's solution was consciously or unconsciously to orient large portions of his discussion around the norms of written language. However, by recognizing certain disjunctions between the spoken and the written, Boethius provided one of Abelard's main points of departure for a reversal of certain late classical ideas and for a reaffirmation of linguistic considerations which he associated rightly or wrongly with Aristotle's original intentions. Above all, Boethius provided Abelard with the model of written language against the background of which spoken discourse could recreate meaning out of patterns of sound. Before taking up Abelard's

---

[189] On the dating, I follow M. Buytaert's Introduction to CCCM 11, xxiii-xxv.

[190] On the manuscript evidence of Abelard's understanding of Aristotle, see the dated but still useful survey of B. Geyer, "Die alten lateinischen Übersetzungen der aristotelischen Analytik, Topik und Elenchik," *Philosophisches Jahrbuch* 30 (1917), 25-43.

[191] C. Mews, "The Development of the Theologia of Peter Abelard," *Petrus Abaelardus*, 184; 191-93.

[192] *Theologia Christiana* 1.134, CCCM 12, p. 129 (= PL 178.1165A).

innovations, therefore, we must turn briefly to the thoughts of his mentor.

Boethius on Aristotle

For both Boethius and Abelard, Aristotle's central statement on language and meaning was contained in the opening paragraphs of *De Interpretatione*.[193] Let us first look at Boethius's translation of the text and then discuss his commentary on it.

The translation of the relevant passage runs as follows.[194] Aristotle first lays out the book's general theme, which, in order, treats the noun (*nomen*) and the verb (*verbum*), negation (*negatio*) and affirmation (*adfirmatio*), and a statement (*enunciatio*) and a sentence (*oratio*). Then Aristotle turns to the relation between the oral, the written, and meaning. Spoken sounds (*ea quae sunt in voce*) are signs of affections in the soul (*in anima passionum notae*) and what is written (*ea quae scribuntur*) represents spoken sounds. And sounds (*voces*) vary among peoples no less than written forms (*litterae*). But the signs (*notae*) stand for the same affections of the soul and the verbal likenesses (*similitudines*), the same things (*res*). Moreover, some spoken sounds, like the soul's affections, are lacking in truth or falsehood, while others are necessarily one or the other. For falseness and truth imply combination (*conpositio*) and division (*divisio*). Nouns and verbs by themselves are similar to thought (*intellectus*) without combination or division. Examples include "man" or "white" when they stand alone, the words being neither true nor false in themselves. Even the name of the non-existent "goat-stag" is a sign (*signum*), inasmuch as it signifies something (*significat aliquid*). It is neither true nor false since as yet "it is" or "it is not" has not been predicated of it, either simply or with respect to time.

Aristotle proceeds to a more detailed discussion of these matters, but what concerns us most is Boethius's commentary on his initial distinctions.

In his exposition, Boethius first turns to the physical aspects of sound (*vox*).[195] Spoken sound, he explains, is a striking of the air by

---

[193] *Peri ermeneias* 16a. On Aristotle's meaning, see in general J. L. Ackrill, *Aristotle's Categories and De Interpretatione*, 2nd ed. (Oxford, 1966), 113-14, and, on Boethius's simplification of Aristotle's σύμβολα and σημεῖα as *notae*, see N. Kretzmann, "Aristotle on Spoken Sound Significant by Convention," in J. Corcoran, ed., *Ancient Logic and its Modern Interpretations* (Dordrecht and Boston, 1974), 5 and 18-19n6.

[194] *Commentarii in Librum Aristotelis Peri ermeneias*, ed. C. Meiser, vol. 1 (1877), c. 1, pp. 3-4.

[195] *Ibid.*, vol. 2 pt. 1 (1880), bk. 1, pp. 4-6.

the tongue, through which the voice produces noise in the throat. Of course, some sounds, like coughing, are not made by the tongue, but these cannot be expressed in a written form (*scribi enim nullo modo potest*). Therefore, they are not meaningful sound (*vox*) but mere noise (*sonus*). Meaningful spoken sound can be defined as sound with a mental image for signifying (*sonus . . . cum quadam imaginatione significandi*). When such a sound is emitted, an instance of meaning (*significationis causa*) is brought forth, as is not the case with a cough. When the physical processes are complete and a meaningful sound has been produced, it may be called speech (*locutio*), translating λέξις, rather than mere *dictio*, which renders φάσις. Such speech is articulated sound (*articulata vox*); its elements are letters (*partes sunt litterae*), which, when joined together, form a single, harmonious, grammatically correct expression. Sound signifies in a number of ways: it may signify something, as does the word "man," or nothing at all; it may be put in the place of a noun which signifies something; or, while signifying nothing in itself, it may have meaning in grammatical relation to other words. All these are called types of speech (*locutiones*), since the form of the spoken expression (*locutionis forma*) consists of sound in a construction (*vox conposita*), which can be set down in writing (*quae litteris describatur*). In sum, in order for there to be speech, first the tongue must strike the air and then the emitted sound must be transcribable in written characters (*inscribi litteris possit*). For speech to have meaning, there must in addition be a mental image intended to signify (*significandi imaginatio*), through which the object (*id quod*) is brought forth in the voice or the statement. Thus, in addition to sound, speech, and a written point of reference, signification demands a certain capacity for creating images in the mind.

What is notable about these introductory remarks is the reflection upon the Aristotelian connection between the spoken and the written. Sound, in effect, achieves meaning, if not only in relation to letters, certainly with a knowledge of textual equivalents in mind. Boethius pursued this line of thinking in his subsequent discussion of *interpretatio*.[196]

At the outset he attempts to limit the subject. An interpretation, he states, is an articulated sound signifying something through itself (*vox articulata per se ipsam significans*).[197] Of course, not all *voces* and *locutiones* are *interpretationes*. Some have no meaning; in others, the sense is not established and maintained through the verbal construc-

---

[196] *Ibid.*, vol. 2.1, pp. 6ff.   [197] *Ibid.*, bk. 1, p. 6, 4-5.

tions themselves.[198] A second limitation is introduced through the place of *De Interpretatione* in the Aristotelian canon. In the *Ars Poetica*, Aristotle divided speech into letters, syllables, and other grammatical forms; in the *Categories*, he spoke of the manner in which reality was mediated to the mind via the senses and the intellect. In both cases, speech was looked upon as the union of the physical and the meaningful elements in human communication in which the latter were "superimposed" on the former.

Neither work, however, concerned itself specifically with the logical aspects of interpretation. Accordingly, Aristotle's intention in *De Interpretatione* was to deal with constructions having a noun and a verb, which, when occurring together in a simple sentence, indicate whatever arises from the mind's intellections (*quidquid est in animi intellectibus*).[199] He did not restrict himself to relations between the spoken and the written, but, with grammatical correspondences as a foundation, went on to the issue of signification. In this sense, he developed and expanded the design of the *Categories*. For the divisions of this text were originally set up to delineate things by means of intellections; that is, as there are ten types of reality in nature, so there are an equal number of potential categories of thought. The latter in turn are represented by nouns and verbs, which are the basic elements of interpretation. Further, Boethius notes, Aristotle did not deal with all five classical divisions of *oratio*, but only the last, *oratio enuntiativa*, which concerns itself with the truth or falseness of propositions. Finally, Aristotle called intellections (*intellectus*) the events, receptions, or movements of the soul (*passiones animae*), referring chiefly to their *raison d'être* and utility: for, what comes about usefully in his view must result from a purposeful mental experience.[200]

He then puts Aristotle's thoughts into his own words, somewhat altering the original. No matter how one approaches the question, he argues, *oratio* always contains three, or, as he later puts it, four essential components, namely things, intellections, and words, together with letters (that is, the written form of words). Things are conceived by the mind; words signify these conceptions or intellections; and the mental products are both conceptions of objective reality and things as signified by words.[201] Moreover, while the object and the mental

---

[198] *Ibid.*, p. 6, 6-13.   [199] *Ibid.*, p. 6, 15-p. 7, 12.   [200] *Ibid.*, p. 12, 28-p. 13, 2.

[201] *Ibid.*, 20, 15-25: "Tribus his totus orandi ordo perficitur: rebus, intellectibus, vocibus. Res enim ab intellectu concipitur, vox vero conceptiones animi intellectusque significat, ipsi vero intellectus et concipiunt subiectas res et significantur a vocibus. . . . Quartum quoque quiddam est, quo voces ipsae valeant designari, id autem sunt litterae."

configuration are one, the intellection depends on the spoken word, which in turn reflects the relationship between linguistic and scribal forms.[202] Things, that is, substances, ultimately give rise to intellections. Understanding always proceeds from things, from which, then, the significance of words arises. For, beyond the mental awareness of a thing, a word has no meaning. But, Boethius adds, where there are spoken there are also the written forms of words, that is, the written expression of the smallest linguistic elements distinguishing words from each other.

These matter-of-fact observations on a rather complicated Aristotelian text are then illustrated by a set of simple parallels.[203] If a people employ the same alphabet and phonetic system, Boethius suggests, they will also use the same nouns and grammatical constructions. It follows that they will express the same mental conceptions. And this implies that they have the same reality in mind. The conclusion, he adds, is only reasonable: for a people may share the same things and intellections and yet represent them differently in both spoken and written forms. The Roman, the Greek, and the barbarian all see the same horse, but each calls it by a different name and uses a different script to record what is spoken. Therefore, the identity of the thing with its mental image is not founded upon linguistic evidence alone. The thing precedes its conceptualization; the spoken word follows, and finally the written form.[204]

Of course, for Boethius, the one implies the other. If there were no written characters, the meaning of a word would be difficult to establish. An illiterate cannot relate the verbal and scribal forms of a name.[205] Nor, if we had only words, would understanding necessarily follow, since there are many words which signify nothing in reality.[206] And the intellect does not always have its object in a thing. There are mental images which correspond to nothing known, such as a centaur.[207] However, from the viewpoint of essences, he argues, if a thing exists, so does its intellection, if not among men, then certainly in Him whose understanding is omniscient. But, to return by a dif-

---

[202] *Ibid.*, 20, 29-31.

[203] Summarizing p. 21, 8-p. 23, 14.

[204] *Ibid.*, 21, 25-30: "Recte igitur dictum est apud quos eaedem res idemque intellectus sunt, non statim apud eos vel easdem voces vel eadem elementa consistere. Praecedit autem res intellectum, intellectus vero vocem, vox litteras. . . ."

[205] *Ibid.*, 21, 31-33: "Hominibus namque qui litteras ignorant nullum nomen quaelibet elementa significant, quippe quae nesciunt."

[206] *Ibid.*, p. 21, 31-p. 22, 2.   [207] *Ibid.*, 22, 2-5.

ferent route, if there is an intellection, there is also a word; and, if a word, also a written form, without the knowledge of which nothing could really be learned of the thing's essence.[208] In sum, *res* and *intellectus* are established by nature (*esse naturaliter constitutos*), while words and letters, which change with man's setting (*positio*), are often different.[209]

Following Aristotle, Boethius next reviews a number of ancient approaches to sounds and signs.[210] He then moves on to the interrelationship of language with sense, imagination, and understanding.

Buttressed by a passage from *De Anima*,[211] he proposes the following general scheme as a recapitulation of the original. A name like Socrates, he argues, signifies not only a mental image but also an intellectual understanding of the real man.[212] For intellections rest on the foundation of sense and imagination, like a fully coloured painting on the backdrop of a pencil sketch. In other words, they provide a substratum for the soul's perceptions.[213] When a thing is seized by sense or imagination, the mind first creates a mental image of it; later, a fuller understanding emerges as the hitherto confused pictures are sifted and coordinated. For that reason, he concludes, Aristotle insists that nouns and verbs do not reflect the sensorial or imagistic directly, but rather signify different sorts of intellections in the mind.[214]

The Peripatetics, following him, suggested that sentences (*orationes*) were of three possible kinds: one which could be written (*scribi*), a second spoken (*proferri*), and a third coordinated (*conecti*) in the mind.[215] Porphyry asked why Aristotle spoke of those things which are "in sound" or "in letters" as opposed to speaking of "sounds" and "letters" alone. But, Boethius counters, the two major components of a sentence, the noun and the verb, exist independently of whether the sentence is written, spoken, or thought. More precisely, Aristotle argues that nouns and verbs enunciated in a sentence make a vocal declaration (*denuntiare*) of the soul's affections. Similarly, what is written represents what is spoken.[216]

The relationships may be illustrated through the metaphor of a coin. For a piece of money is not only an object in metal onto which a face has been impressed. It is also an instrument of exchange which

---

[208] *Ibid.*, 22, 6-13.   [209] *Ibid.*, 22, 27, 5.   [210] *Ibid.*, p. 25, 15-p. 27, 6.

[211] *Ibid.*, 28, 3-7; *De Anima* 3.8.

[212] *Ibid.*, 28, 25-28.   [213] *Ibid.*, p. 28, 28-p. 29, 6.   [214] *Ibid.*, 29, 6-16.

[215] *Ibid.*, 29, 16-21: "Unde illud quoque ab Aristotele fluentes Peripatetici rectissime posuerunt tres esse orationes, unam quae scribi possit elementis, alteram quae voce proferri, tertiam quae cogitatione conecti, unamque intellectibus, alteram voce, tertiam litteris contineri."

[216] *Ibid.*, p. 30, 17-p. 32, 5.

represents the value of another thing. Likewise, verbs and nouns are not only physical sounds but linguistic conventions established in order to signify intellections. If a sound designates nothing, it is not a noun or a name. Just as a coin is called a piece of money and not just a metal object, so a word signifies not only a physical sound but a noun or a verb. When Aristotle speaks of "those things which are in sound," he means not only the sounds themselves but sound having specific properties: they are, so to speak, "impressed" with conventional signification.[217] What Aristotle says about written signs, Boethius adds, can be understood along similar lines. Once again, he did not intend to identify the physical object, the letters, with the written form of the verbal statement, that is, "what is in writing."[218]

In the same fashion, Boethius argues, Aristotle states that "what is in sound" represents "the signs of the soul's affections." For, as noted previously, what exists in sound signifies both things and intellections, principally, of course, intellections, and things through them. But these very products of the mind generate intellections in their wake. The process is as follows. When we experience a thing, its reality is grasped by the mind. We then try to say what it is. More precisely, we first experience the thing through a mental image, after which follows a certain affection or perception in the mind itself. A second phase of mental activity is then initiated by the will. Through the force of inner reason the original understanding is perpetuated and refined; that is, the discourse, through an effort of its own, explains and elaborates those things which first provided a foundation for understanding through the soul's activity. Or, more accurately, the development of signification and discourse proceed together in a dialectical manner.[219] This process, too, is like impressing a coin, but in a purely intellectual sense. For every reception in the soul reflects the nature of reality, and the *passiones animae* are born through likenesses to things.[220] For instance, if one sees a sphere or a square, one grasps its shape in the mind. But one also reflects on the likeness while it is in the mind, and, having experienced this mental process, readily recognizes the object when it reappears. Every image mediated by the senses is capable of generating a likeness of this type. The mind, when it engages in understanding, reasons through such forms. Whence, Boethius concludes, Aristotle's *passio* may be rendered as *rei similitudo*.[221]

Even so brief a summary of Boethius's views clearly displays the

---

[217] *Ibid.*, p. 32, 13-p. 33, 2. [218] *Ibid.*, 33, 2-24. [219] *Ibid.*, p. 33, 33-p. 34, 13. [220] *Ibid.*, 34, 13-19. [221] *Ibid.*, p. 34, 21-p. 35, 21.

thrust of his argument, which amounts to a recognition of a disjunction between the spoken and the written without necessarily following up all of the consequences. In general, he sacrifices a good deal of Aristotle's subtlety and complexity in attempting to interrelate the oral, the written, the imagined, and the understood. He does not, of course, confuse the spoken and the written. *Littera* is defined as an "inscription," the configuration of an articulated sound's smallest part (*inscriptio atque figura partis minimae vocis articulatae*), while *elementum* is the equivalent of that same inscription in physical sound (*sonus ipsius inscriptionis*).[222] Yet, in thus differentiating text and word, he nonetheless underlines his interest in the written, both as a reference point and as a framework of analysis. He maintains with Aristotle that written depend on spoken words, and these in turn on intellections of things. But he also reverses the pair, stating in one place that words "are designated"[223] by letters, while in another that letters "signify" words,[224] adding elsewhere that, above all, they "signify" verbs and nouns. His ambivalence towards written language and his corresponding lack of depth on purely linguistic phenomena are evident in his limiting of the discussion to *vox, res*, and *intellectus*, "leaving letters aside on account of those who are ignorant of them."[225]

Abelard: "Oratio"

With these reflections in mind, we may profitably turn to Abelard, whose perspective was different. Like Boethius, he saw sounds or words as "absent letters."[226] But his point of departure was a more fundamental inquiry into the basic units of speech, that is, sounds, words, and sentences. Like Boethius, Abelard based his theory of language on grammar. Yet he saw in the too rigid identification of things and ideas a problem which a properly linguistic analysis could solve.

Accordingly, Abelard's philosophy of language may be thought to consist of two interdependent parts. The first deals with the relationship between sound and sense. The fundamental question is how words, that is, meaningful sounds, signify. The second turns to the larger issue of meaning or signification. Incorporating the first theme in a broader context, it asks how words, either singly or in grammatical arrangements, relate to things and to intellections.

On the first question, Abelard's differences of opinion from Boe-

---

[222] *Ibid.*, 23, 16-18.   [223] *Ibid.*, 20, 25-26.   [224] *Ibid.*, 24, 11-12.
[225] *Ibid.*, 21, 31-33.
[226] *Super Aristotelem de Interpretatione*, ed. M. del Pra, *Pietro Abelardo, scritti . . .* , 73.

thius can perhaps best be observed in his various discussions of *oratio*, which, like his mentor, he uses simultaneously in two senses, grammatically to mean a sentence and linguistically to refer to meaningful discourse.

There are some clear parallels between the two authors. In Abelard's view, a sentence, as it is spoken (*vocalis oratio*), is nothing more than "air," that is, in Aristotelian terms, a body and a substance.[227] In his glosses on the *Categories*, Abelard treats the subject under quantity,[228] speaking of *oratio* as the name of a certain measure of the air making noise and sound. Its quantitative aspects are assessed by the sense of hearing.[229] As in Boethius, *oratio* unites the oral and the written: it represents both the divisible and indivisible combinations of elements, that is, of letters, which appear as syllables, words, or sentences.[230] The name of a sound, so to speak, is transferred to quantities bearing significance.[231] That, in Abelard's view, is why Aristotle speaks of *oratio* as sound signifying a convention of speech (*vox significativa ad placitum*).[232] Abelard does not deny the interdependence of meaningful discourse with the grammar of the written text. But, in his view, the tenor of speech does not correspond precisely to scribal norms. If, he says, I say "a" or voice some other "literal element," which Priscian calls an "individual sound," the written character does not match what is spoken or heard. The air is struck many times by the tongue, and each striking may be called an individual sound; but the sense of hearing does not distinguish any one among them. For, just as sight does not perceive invisible bodies, so the ears do not hear the individual elements of sound. These *invisibiles tenores* are the true, primary parts of discourse (*elementa orationis tamquam primae partes*). Of course, to the degree that a letter represents "invisible" sound, it too may be called a primary element. But there are elements of speech which have no equivalent in letters.[233]

A further exposition of these ideas takes place in the *Dialectica*.[234] Recapitulating his own and others' views, Abelard asserts that there is much disagreement among previous authorities on *oratio*'s mean-

---

[227] *Glossae in Categorias*, ed. M. del Pra, *Pietro Abelardo*, 65, 33-34.

[228] *Super Praedicamenta Aristotelis*, ed. B. Geyer (Münster, 1921), 173-74.

[229] *Ibid.*, 173, 7-9.   [230] *Ibid.*, 173, 25-29.   [231] *Ibid.*, 173, 29-31.

[232] *Ibid.*, 173, 33-174, 4; citing Aristotle, in *Commentarii*, ed. Meiser, vol. 1, p. 4, 5-6, p. 5, 12.

[233] *Ibid.*, 174, 15-29.

[234] *Dialectica* 1.2.2, *De Oratione*, ed. L. M. de Rijk, *Petrus Abaelardus Dialectica*, 65-71.

ing.[235] The Greeks, as Boethius pointed out, appear to have subsumed the topic under three headings: what is spoken as speech, what is written representing real things, and what is produced by the voice on behalf of what is understood.[236]

But, in his opinion, the issue cannot be so simply resolved. First, the qualitative aspects of sound, as Priscian notes, are ultimately reducible to the quantitative.[237] This *spiritus* helps to account for our reaction to sound when it is weak or loud, low or high, and so forth.[238] However, it is not true to state, as has an opponent,[239] that meaningful sound is nothing but the striking of the air. On the contrary, sound is significant whenever the waves which are sustained through the air reach the ear and create understanding. In mediating sense-data, therefore, hearing is no different from the other senses.[240] But, most importantly, sounds must not be indiscriminately identified with letters. True, the smallest particles of sound are named by analogy with the elements of the cosmos, and these verbalizations of single letters (*singularum litterarum prolationes*)[241] make up syllables, words, and sentences. Yet it is incorrect to think of the simplest parts of discourse as the spoken versions of letters (*unius litterae prolatio*). Particles of speech can more accurately be described as being in their turn made up of several parts (*ex pluribus partibus coniuncta*).[242] For, when we utter the sound of a letter, we strike the air, however slightly, in several places at once. Each vibration produces an individual sound, even though the sound waves are not perceived or uttered as meaningful sound. These minuscule motions are sound's simplest parts. Individual letters are not "indivisible"; they are related to other strikings of the air, that is, to the utterance of other letters, which make up the elements of meaningful discourse.[243]

Such sounds, words, syllables, and expressions, Abelard continues, are interconnected temporally. The tiniest parts do not have perma-

---

[235] *Ibid.*, 65, 23-66, 13.

[236] *Ibid.*, 66, 18-20: "Tribus enim modis 'orationis' nomen apud Grecos accipitur, pro vocali scilicet orationi que profertur, ac pro reali que scribitur, ac pro intellectuali que voce ipsa generatur."

[237] *Ibid.*, 66, 29-70, 2; Priscian, *Inst. Gramm.*, 2.44, ed. M. Hertz in H. Keil, *Grammatici Latini* 2 (1885), 1-2.

[238] *Ibid.*, 67, 2-4.

[239] *Ibid.*, 67, 5-8; perhaps William of Champeaux, de Rijk, 67n1. On the justice of Abelard's criticism of contemporary masters, see E. Bertola, "Le critiche di Abelardo ad Anselmo di Laon ed a Guglielmo di Champeaux," *Rivista di filosofia neo-scolastica* 52 (1960), 522.

[240] *Ibid.*, 67, 10-15.   [241] *Ibid.*, 67, 20-21.   [242] *Ibid.*, 67, 22-24.

[243] *Ibid.*, 67, 24-31.

nence, any more than instants of time. Rather, like the flow of time, the parts of discourse (*orationis partes*) make up one continuous human utterance (*prolatio continua*).[244] Although, on occasion, many words may be spoken in a given interval of time—by different men or by one man to others, either all at once or interspersed by pauses—to the degree that they cohere through meaning, they may be referred to as a single discourse (*una oratio*).[245] For, if physically divisible, the sounds nonetheless signify a comprehensible unit. Take, for instance, the statement, "A man runs." If one says "a man" and then "runs" as separate entities, no meaningful sentence (*oratio*) but only a set of words (*plures dictiones*) are spoken. Each term has its own sense; the whole is not united by coherent thought. Nor, in such cases, does the memory have a recollection of what came before and afterwards, such reminiscence, of course, being a principal aid to understanding. Still less can this random group of words be thought of as the single understanding of an utterance (*unus orationis intellectus*). In other words, the division of an utterance inevitably results in a break in meaning. For a statement to have connected meaning, the individual sounds or words (*voces*) must be joined in a single verbal statement (*continua prolatio*). No other group of sounds fulfills these conditions. Individual words are interpreted as individual meanings (*singularum significatio*). One can argue that these should be included under the rubric of *oratio*. But they do not really comprise *una vox*.[246]

At what point, then, in the utterance of a meaningful expression does meaning actually arise? Abelard's answer to this question takes him in the direction of a distinction similar to that between *parole* and *langue*. In one sense, he argues, the meaning is not established until the last instant of utterance (*in ultimo puncto prolationis*). Yet, the parts of the discourse which do not physically exist at a given instance do not on that account lack potential significance.[247] Meaning, it would appear, arises equally from that which exists in spoken sound and from that which does not.

Abelard's approach to this problem devolves from his notion of *oratio*. A single understanding, he argues, is gathered from many different words. But the two do not coincide in time. Most often, what has been said is rechannelled through the mind via the memory. In that sense, the significance of a single sound or word is not made clear until the whole sentence has been spoken. Also, it often happens that

---

[244] *Ibid.*, 67, 33-36. [245] *Ibid.*, 67, 38-68, 3. [246] *Ibid.*, 68, 3-24.
[247] *Ibid.*, 68, 25-34.

what is said is not immediately understood. We frequently need to reflect, if only momentarily, on the words and constructions we have heard. The listener's mind is always held a little in suspense while a statement is being made. Something, after all, may be added, and change the sense. As a consequence, his mind cannot really rest until the speaker's tongue is silent. For no statement is linguistically or meaningfully complete while anything which can contribute to the sense remains unsaid. Significance, then, is really a problem of the hearer's mind. The statement, "A chimaera is conjectural," derives its meaning, not from the chimaera's form, which does not exist, but from the conjecture of someone trying to picture it. Further, if by "signifying" we understand, not a formal quality of reality, but "an intellection generated through itself," then it follows that a statement has meaning just as long as any single verbal element within it makes sense to the hearer. Significance, in other words, is produced by the ordering of physical sound, but it is established and maintained by means of a conventional agreement between the speaker and the listener.[248]

In sum, in discussing the manner in which sounds signify, Abelard is much more overtly linguistic in approach than Boethius. Of course, for both, as for Aristotle, there is a significance in individual words and the written are the reflections of the spoken forms. A sentence is a group of such words in which the sense of each is transcended by the meaning of the whole. But, for Abelard in particular, a statement is also a set of linguistic conventions uniting the speaker and the hearer in a nexus of meaning independent of both. This meaning, inspired by spoken language, has a no less objective reality than the things to which the words actually refer. The union of spoken and written languages takes place in the mind, where, through the imposition of established conventions, the temporal structure of the sentence is recreated and given an intellectual context.

Abelard: "Significatio"

We are thus brought to the doorstep of the first major issue in Abelard's philosophy of language, namely signification. This, in turn, leads to two related subjects in his logic: the interrelationship of words, things, and thoughts, and the problem of universals.

Regrettably, Abelard nowhere made a single, definitive statement of his views on signification. Instead, he scattered his observations

[248] *Ibid.*, 68, 34-69, 31.

throughout his logical works, evolving his ideas as time passed and as he shifted from early commentary to later synthesis. A section of the *Dialectica* is in fact devoted to *significatio*.[249] But the lengthiest and most instructive survey of the question occurs in the opening paragraphs of his commentary on *De Interpretatione*.[250] Using this discussion as an introduction, we may approach his concept of meaning as a whole.

Like Boethius, Abelard limits the field of endeavour to *oratio enuntiativa*, and, more particularly, to the study of propositions' truth or falsehood.[251] But, from the outset, he enlarges the inquiry, distinguishing as his mentor does not between Priscian's and Aristotle's notions of signification.[252] Priscian, he points out, held that sound's sense (*significativa vox*) can be related back to the speaker's intentions, which are put forth as words.[253] Yet Aristotle, in treating nouns and verbs, refers both to things (*res*) and intellections (*intellectus*). Things, in his view, create meaning by establishing a mental awareness of their nature or properties. This understanding is the same whether it is said to come from the speaker or the hearer. In response to Priscian, Abelard notes that a dog's barking may have an intended sense, but human beings cannot comprehend it. It is only "natural sound."[254] Therefore, following Aristotle, he distinguishes between "articulated" and "signified." Signification arises only when the sense intended by the speaker and heard by the listener are agreed to be the same. As this cannot be determined from the speaker alone, he prefers, with Aristotle, to refer significance ultimately to the hearer's understanding (*ad intellectum audientis*).[255]

Abelard adds that, in dealing with *oratio enuntiativa*, Aristotle was concerned to illustrate not the variety of things but the variety of thoughts about them. In his view there are three logically interrelated reasons. First, the same thing can be signified by a noun and a verb. For example, in "a race" and "he runs a race," the reality, a race being run, remains the same but is conceived differently in the mind. Again, Aristotle deals with nouns and verbs not to study reality but the uttered sentence. A proposition is materially constructed of a noun and a verb; similarly, the understanding of it is made up of "the

---

[249] *Dialectica* 1.3.1, ed. de Rijk, pp. 111-17. Cf. 5.1.6, pp. 562-63.
[250] *Glossae super Peri ermeneias*, ed. Geyer, 307-34.
[251] *Ibid.*, 307, 1-22.   [252] *Ibid.*, 307, 24-308, 19.
[253] *Inst. Gramm.*, 1.1, ed. Hertz, p. 5, 6; Abelard, *loc. cit.*, 308, 1-4.
[254] *Super Peri ermeneias*, 308, 19-33; cf. *Dialectica* 1.3.1, p. 114, 20-23.
[255] *Super Peri ermeneias*, 308, 17-20.

intellections" of the various parts. But the same correspondence does not exist between the proposition and the words which make it up considered as things. For, as a "thing," the sentence has no other substratum. Finally, Abelard argues, while things' existence is transitory, understanding is permanent. Take a rose or a lily: even if the reality is absent, the idea remains in the mind. For this reason Aristotle argues that a statement's meaning should always be referred to the conception in the mind (*ad animi conceptionem*), not to the naming of things (*ad nominationem rerum*).[256] For the sounds which make up meaningful words and sentences do not actually make things exist but rather arouse the intellect for contemplating them. They have the function of signifying (*officium significandi*), that is, of establishing understanding (*intellectum constituere*).[257] The human invention of sound (*inventio vocis*) of which Aristotle speaks in the *Categories* has the same ends. And this meaning within the mind (*significatio intellectus*) he rightly calls interpretation (*interpretatio*): for, to interpret a word is not to reveal a thing but to open the door to understanding.[258]

But the correspondence between thoughts and things via language also depends on the operations of the mind itself. Not only do groups of sound derive their sense from cerebral activity; sounds are also the equivalent of Aristotle's *notae passionum animae* in their non-physical sense (by which Abelard later calls them *sermones* rather than *voces*).[259] Yet, do such signs, as in Boethius, stand for written characters? If not, how do they signify?

Abelard's answer is a combination of Aristotle's and his own thinking. He distinguishes more subtly than Boethius between imagination, which is a byproduct of the senses, and understanding, which is a function of reason.[260] Consistent with his earlier argument, he sees reason as the potential for seeking out and deliberating (*potentia discernendi*).[261] It is the power of grasping the nature or property of an object, whether it really exists or is only a product of the mind.

With Aristotle he agrees that we perceive only through the senses.[262] But that does not solve the problem of *imaginatio* versus *intellectus*, since, in theory at least, both can function without sense. If we are far from Rome, we can nonetheless picture the city in our minds.

---

[256] *Ibid.*, 309, 9-13.   [257] *Ibid.*, 309, 19-22.

[258] *Ibid.*, 309, 27-28; cf. Jolivet, *Arts du langage*, 80.

[259] Jolivet, *op.cit.*, 69-71.   [260] *Super Peri ermeneias*, 313, 8-9.

[261] *Ibid.*, 313, 10-11: "Est autem ratio potentia discernendi, id est attendendi et deliberandi, apud se aliquid quasi in aliqua natura vel proprietate consistens. . . ."

[262] *Ibid.*, 313, 16-31.

Both imagination and understanding, he continues, can work through insensible means, as in the case of abstractions like "the soul" and "paternity." Indeed, the mind normally operates through imaginary forms (*formae imaginariae*) which it creates at will. It thus contemplates the true nature of things, often restraining imagination or intellect. For, although Rome may be far away, our image of the city is influenced by an absent reality. To put the matter another way: the imagination and the intellect perceive through a copy or imitation of the thing (*rei effigies*), even though the reality may not be present.[263] This "copy," he adds, is spoken of in different ways by Plato, Aristotle, and Cicero, but the issues come down to the same thing. Plato's *ideae* or *exemplares formae*, for instance, are no different from Cicero's *imagines, notae*, or *simulacra*. Also, Priscian speaks of images in the mind as the plan or design of a house in the builder's head, a metaphor which recalls Plato's formula for God's creation of the world from an eternally existing archetype.[264] However, none of these "forms" are substances in themselves nor are they forms underpinned by substances.[265] If one imagines a tower which is not present, one can get a clear idea of its height and shape from the image which the mind creates, just as if it were before one's eyes. But this image has no formal or substantial reality.[266]

Above all, the words by which such images are designated must not be mistaken for their objects, as Aristotle makes clear.[267] For words are not invented on account of similitudes of things or of the intellect but rather because of things themselves and their intellections, in order to instruct us about their essences. In other terms, they are intellections of things, not images, but they function by means of images which we utilize for configuring absent things. They are so to speak signs which operate between things (*intersigna rerum*).[268]

Words, then, as signs of this type, apply the mind of the listener to the likeness of the thing.[269] Moreover, in this process, one must distinguish between *imaginatio* and *intellectus*. When one sees a statue

---

[263] *Ibid.*, 313, 31-314, 6.   [264] *Ibid.*, 314, 7-24.

[265] *Ibid.*, 314, 27-28.   [266] *Ibid.*, 314, 28-31.   [267] *Ibid.*, 315, 18-19.

[268] *Ibid.*, 315, 28-34: "Non enim propter similitudines rerum vel propter intellectus similitudinem voces repertae sunt, sed magis propter ipsas res et earum intellectus, ut videlicet de rerum naturis doctrinam facerent, non de huiusmodi figmentis, et intellectus de rebus constituerent, non de figmentis, sed tantum per figmenta quando pro rebus absentibus ipsa constituimus quasi quaedam intersigna rerum."

[269] *Ibid.*, 34-37.

of Achilles, one takes notice of it not for itself but for Achilles, whom it represents; that is, one focuses not on the statue but on the man, using the copy as a likeness rather than a thing. Therefore, the statue cannot be said to represent itself to the intellect but rather configures Achilles: while the sense perceives the statue, the same sense directs the mind towards Achilles as a thing. But, should one put the statue in place of the reality, one's attention would be directed to nothing else. In that case sense perception (*sensus*) and understanding (*intellectus*) would have the same object. Of course, this can take place if the image is a fiction, which one can understand either as an image or a reality. However, if one is speaking of a thing, there is an intellection of the thing itself through the medium of the image. Nor does it matter whether the name refers to an individual like Socrates or to a collectivity like "men."[270]

Yet, if the images of things and copies must be distinguished with respect to the understanding, the intellect itself must also be separated from image formation. For *imaginatio* is really the confused conception of the mind (*confusa animi conceptio*), common to all creatures having senses.[271] It can exist without intellection, but intellection cannot exist without it, as Aristotle and Boethius emphasize. Aristotle, Abelard points out, indicates that understanding cannot arise without prior perception through the senses. *Sensus* and *imaginatio* are, so to speak, a foundation onto which *intellectus* is superimposed, just as sketches and pen-drawings precede a fully coloured painting. *Imaginatio* may be described as the beginnings of thought (*inchoatio cogitandi*), before the mind has perceived the nature or property of a thing. *Intellectus*, by contrast, is a further stage of the mental process, whether the understanding arises through the thing, reality, substance, body, or even through qualities like "white" or names like Socrates. Through understanding the mind is finally led from disorder to order, from confusion to reason.[272]

Having outlined the functions of *sensus, imaginatio*, and *intellectus*, Abelard now turns to the problem of language and reality. The issue of written language is also integrated with that of meaning.

The nexus of the question resides in understanding. Words, he reiterates, are not products of sense or imagination but of the intellect, as Aristotle maintained.[273] Aristotle further united all sounds as

---

[270] *Ibid.*, p. 315, 37-p. 316, 16.
[271] *Ibid.*, 315, 19.
[272] Boethius, *De Interpretatione*, 28, 27; Abelard, *op. cit.*, 316, 30-317, 7.
[273] *Super Peri ermeneias*, 318, 23-25.

"events of the mind" constituting understanding; then he separated them through their different meanings. Similarly, Boethius, following the ancients, distinguished between "things which are in sound" and "things which are sound."[274] For, he recalls, among the Greeks, *voces* had a threefold meaning, either as sounds, as texts representing sounds, or as the understanding of sounds.[275]

How are these components connected? In part, Abelard's argument merely reiterates Boethius in his own words. However, once the exposition of basic relationships between sound, letters, and sense is completed, he turns to the question of why *intellectus* rather than *voces* is the same among different peoples. For, he notes, one might assume that their understanding was the same not because of identity between essences but because of a similar mode of conceptualizing (*consimilis modus conceptionis*). Thus, diverse tongues might refer to the same thing through their *modus significationis*,[276] in the way that Greek *anthropos* and Latin *homo* both mean *animal rationale mortale*. Further, why should Aristotle argue that understanding is any more permanent than words?

The answer, in Abelard's view, is that Aristotle was interested in a better comprehension of both words and intellections. But, in order to establish this position, he feels he must clarify and expand some of Aristotle's observations on unwritten and written languages. The understanding of a Greek and a Latin, he argues, is not "essentially" different on account of diverse tongues but because of their "foundations." A man who knows different languages never has quite the same understanding of a thing if the languages in fact bring into play different conceptual tools. Moreover, the intellect is not divided in its conceptualizing functions (*in officio concipiendi rem*), since it does not conceive different things or conceive things in different ways. One must recognize, Abelard insists, that the problem of linguistic communication is distinct from the identity of *res* and *intellectus*. Linguistic difference can also be looked upon simply from a phonetic or a scribal point of view.[277] For, it is not the essence of things, the essence of understandings, or the mode of conceptualizing that varies among peoples who speak different languages. Rather it is the form or office of signifying (*forma vel officium significandi*) for *both* sounds and letters which is changed. So *res* and *intellectus* are the same for all, as Aristotle asserts, while conventions of language vary, although, it would ap-

[274] *Ibid.*, 319, 16-34.   [275] *Ibid.*, 319, 23-26.
[276] *Ibid.*, 323, 18-22.
[277] *Ibid.*, p. 323, 36-p. 324, 14.

pear, not for the same reasons as were advanced by Boethius.[278] And Abelard agrees with Boethius but from a linguistic point of view that texts are less essential for the ordering of discourse (*ordo collocutionis*) than *voces, intellectus*, and *res*.[279]

Having established his own criteria for the discussion, Abelard then directs his attention towards types of understanding. A simple intellection, he proposes, has no parts, as is the case of individual words.[280] For, although, on hearing the word "man," one reflects upon several things at once—considering, so to speak, matter, form, substance, and images—there is nonetheless one simple action (*una simplex actio*), appropriately called "understanding," through which one thinks of everything at once, one's thoughts both informing the living reality and differentiating it from others.[281] If on the other hand one hears "a rational mortal animal," one grasps what was initially conceived through a single act of understanding by means of several acts. For, in expressions, individual words too have their own meanings. Although "man" and "rational mortal animal" indicate one object, the understanding of the name is simple while the definition is composed of more than one thing. In other words, the name signifies totally through itself, not through its parts. But the definition requires several acts of understanding. Whence, it follows, the understanding of words is always simple, while that of expressions is complex, although, paradoxically, the two may describe the same thing.[282]

Further, the understanding of a word can be of things united (*coniunctorum*) or divided (*divisorum*), but never at once united and divided. For, one who hears the word "man" or "non-man" grasps the term as a totality or not at all. But, one who hears "rational mortal animal" in place of "man" understands the unity through the expression's significance. For, "uniting" and "disuniting" are complex mental operations, both for language and for understanding. For instance, to the expression "rational mortal animal" we may oppose its logical opposite, "non-rational, non-mortal animal." In both, the mental unity is made by the mind in the course of understanding the expression. The significance does not arise from the individual words, for, in that case, as Abelard noted, the whole meaning would be grasped at once. A similar set of distinctions may be made with respect to understanding. It too is either simple or complex: simple, inasmuch as it unites like the word "man" several "members" in a single "person"; complex,

---

[278] *Ibid.*, 324, 23-28.
[279] *Ibid.*, 324, 29-40, quoting Boethius, *De Interpretatione*, 20, 16-21.
[280] *Ibid.*, 325, 19-20.   [281] *Ibid.*, 325, 19-23.   [282] *Ibid.*, 325, 24-37.

when the activity of understanding, while running through various images, makes a unity of them or not. Just as several people can have different understandings of the same thing, so the same understanding can exist for several things, that is, if the hearer understands a single entity through them. Logically speaking, Abelard concludes, there is one understanding which is both simple and complex, that is, which consists of a single union or disunion of things. When I say "Socrates is a man" or "is not a man," I make one union or separation of "Socrates" and "man" in the whole proposition.[283]

A related issue involves the truth or falsehood of statements. Both simple and complex forms of understanding, in Abelard's view, can be correct or incorrect, depending only on how closely their meaning conforms to the intended thing. But the situation is altered if these sorts of expressions occur in propositions in which the definition in question is true or false according to the statement's logic. The question then arises: does truth inhere in the statement or in the mind? Does verification involve the statement or reality? In Abelard's view, both. In a "definition" within a proposition, truth or falsehood is not signified according to what is to be received in the understanding but according to the statement of the proposition. And, it is the statement which is referable back to reality; its truth or falsehood ultimately depends on what exists. It follows, of course, that a "true proposition" can sometimes generate a false meaning, not, as Aristotle points out, from the viewpoint of understanding, but certainly with respect to what is said. For example, if, while Socrates sits, one hears "Socrates stood," what is said makes logical sense but creates a misleading impression. For, the mind's conception (*animi conceptio*), guided by words, does not conform to the status of reality (*status rei*).[284]

The understanding, then, judges truth or falsehood not according to the conception or disposition of images (*conceptio vel dispositio imaginum*) but according to the attention of the mind (*attentio animi*), which focuses on being or non being in the past, present, or future.[285] For, after all, Abelard adds, one does not gather mental images of what presently exists alone, but also of the past or the future. The intellect, for its part, specializes in making distinctions (*ad discretionem*), while conceptualizing is left to the part of the mind which makes images (*imaginatio*).[286] Abelard thus separates the temporal and atemporal aspects of language philosophy as they pertain to thinking.

[283] *Ibid.*, p. 325, 38-p. 326, 29.
[284] *Ibid.*, p. 326, 30-p. 328, 17.   [285] *Ibid.*, 328, 18-22.   [286] *Ibid.*, 328, 22-26.

At the point at which distinctions are actually made, the images we use and their temporal qualities do not refer back to "the intellect's truth."[287] Otherwise, no recollection of the past or prediction of the future would be a correct "intellection." Further, if, while thinking in the present, we conceive the past or future, the truth or falsehood of the intellect's understanding is not involved.[288] In that sense, truth and falseness in the intellect do not depend on the conceiving of images but on the focusing on things through images; that is, we establish images on behalf of signs not so much for signifying things as for bringing the mind to bear on them.[289]

Beginning, then, with Aristotle and Boethius, Abelard concludes by applying rationalism to the real. He is more overtly interested in linguistic or, one should perhaps say, semantic[290] phenomena than either of his authorities. Accordingly, he introduces the notion of the written, not, as in Boethius, as a stable reference point from which to interrelate words and things, but chiefly in order to comment on the structure of language itself. Language, therefore, is considered independently of things and intellections.

To create an understanding in the mind, one must signify through words. Words have a dual character: as sounds (*voces*), they affect the sense of hearing; as signs (*signa, sermones*), they are interpreted by the mind. In Abelard's view, a sentence says something through a group of words, but this something is not a real thing: it is a *quasi res*. It expresses the manner in which things relate to each other. When internalized in the mind, the same sentence represents not things said (*dicta*) but things in the form of intellections (*res in intellectu*).

In one sense, then, the ontological sphere of language is reduced. Language is what can be studied through logic and linguistics. In another sense, however, its range is increased. Words, in Abelard's view, are not created on account of images, which merely act as a bridge between the senses and the mind. They are the verbalizations of man's inner conceptions of reality. As meaningful sounds, words or sentences indicate their meaning in speech, as texts, and as thoughts.

---

[287] *Ibid.*, 328, 26-28: "Quibuscumque ergo imaginibus utamur vel quomodo eas disponamus, nil refert ad veritatem intellectus, dummodo attentio discretionis sit."

[288] *Ibid.*, 328, 28-33.

[289] *Ibid.*, 328, 33-36: "Ideo autem non ad conceptionem imaginum, sed ad attentionem rerum per imagines veritas intellectus vel falsitas pertinet, quia imagines tantum pro signis constituimus non eas quidem significantes, sed in eis res attendentes."

[290] Cf. L. M. de Rijk, "The Semantical Impact of Abailard's Solution of the Problem of Universals," *Petrus Abaelardus*, 139.

As in Aristotle and Boethius, the essential identity is established be-tween things and intellections. Language, in this sense, remained for Abelard as for his predecessors a set of conventions. However, the structure of the written, or, more particularly, of grammar and logic, led Abelard to free language from its former immobility with respect to *res* and *intellectus* and to consider it as operating potentially in ac-cord with its own laws. Language, as invented, utilized in discourse, and internalized as thought, was thereby made the official mediator between reality and mental experience.[291]

Universals

The relationship between language, thought, and reality was more systematically explored by Abelard in his exposition of the problem of universals, to which we now turn.

A bridge between universals and signification was provided in the *Dialectica*,[292] where he briefly repeated his views on words and things and more closely tied together the structures of language and think-ing. Signification, he reiterated, was not only a property of words but also of things. For written characters, when they appear before the eyes, represent verbal and linguistic elements of discourse. Aristotle, he added, therefore speaks of *significativa* as both what is written and what is spoken: together these constitute the signs of mental experi-ence. Once again he stresses that a thing's nature is revealed through a word expressly designed to perform "the office of signifying." Such signs, he says, are *voces supraposite*; they are words "placed upon" things by means of intellections.

This concept plays a large role in his theory of universals. His most important discussion of the question took place in his commentary on Porphyry's *Introduction* to the *Categories*, as translated and interpreted by Boethius. The major lines of Abelard's approach are well known. In general, he first refuted overly simplistic, realist arguments, his reasons in some cases paralleling Berengar's rejection of eucharistic physicalism. He then determined that universals were ascribable "to

[291] Jolivet, *Arts du langage*, 74. Abelard, in fact, would seem to anticipate Saussure's oft-quoted statement, *Cours de linguistique générale*, p. 98: "Le signe linguistique unit non une chose et un nom, mais un concept et une image acoustique."

[292] *Dialectica* 3.1.1, p. 111, 13-p. 112, 21. Not to forget the discussion of similar issues in a less systematic fashion in the *Glosse super Librum Porphyrii secundum Vocales*, ed. C. Ottaviano, in *Testi medioevali inediti* (Fontes Ambrosiani, vol. 3, Florence and Milan, 1933).

words alone,"[293] that is, to the nexus of words, things, and intellections presented in his idea of signification. The consequence of this seminal analysis was not only the oft-emphasized placing of universals within the realm of meaningful discourse.[294] It also completed his theory of objective reality, and how we understand it, based upon linguistic considerations. These, in turn, rested upon assumptions about the behaviour of spoken and written language in relation to each other.

Boethius on Porphyry

As previously, Abelard's achievement cannot be fully appreciated without reference to his major authorities, against whose views he was often reacting. Boethius's *In Porphyrium* did for the problem of universals what his *De Interpretatione* did for signification: it provided a language of analysis and set Abelard on the road to original insights.

Porphyry had declined to comment on universals,[295] preferring instead to give his readers a brief introduction to the categories under five headings, namely genus, species, difference, property, and accident, the standard terms which his predecessors agreed could be predicated of a subject and were therefore essential to defining its nature as a thing.

Boethius introduced the question by putting the whole matter in a broader context. He first described the three-fold power of the soul, that is, supporting life, judging perceptions, and providing a foundation for rational thought.[296] The critical functions, of course, are *sensus, imaginatio,* and *ratio* as elaborated in his commentary on *De Interpretatione*.[297] Corresponding to this triad are three intellectual ac-

---

[293] *Glossae super Porphyrium*, ed. B. Geyer (Münster, 1919), 21-22: . . . Restat ut huiusmodi universalitatem solis vocibus adscribamus.

[294] The literature has recently been reviewed by M. M. Tweedale, *Abailard on Universals* (Amsterdam, 1976), 3-12. Fundamental remains B. Geyer, "Die Stellung Abaelards in der Universalienfrage nach neuen handschriftlichen Texten," in *Festgabe . . . C. Baeumker*, vol. 1, 101-27. A brief exposition is provided by J. G. Sikes, *Peter Abailard* (Cambridge, 1932), ch. 5, pp. 89-112, and a lucid analysis by J. F. Boler, "Abailard and the Problem of Universals," *Journal of the History of Philosophy* 1 (1963), 37-51. Aspects of the problem have recently been discussed by W.L. Gombocz, "Abaelards Bedeutungslehre als Schlüssel zum Universalien-problem," *Petrus Abaelardus*, 153-64, and K. Jacobi, "Discussionen über Prädikationstheorie in den logischen Schriften des Petrus Abailardus," *ibid.*, 165-79. For more extensive interpretations, see Tweedale, chs. 3 and 4, pp. 89-211 and Jolivet, *Arts du langage*, 85-115. A recent response to Tweedale is G. Küng, "Abélard et les vues actuelles sur la question des universaux," in M. de Gandillac, *et al.*, eds., *Abélard. Le "Dialogue,"* pp. 99-104.

[295] Boethius, *In Porphyrium*, bk. 1, PL 64.82A-B.

[296] *Ibid.*, 71A-B.　　[297] *Ibid.*, 71B-72A.

tivities of the soul, namely, comprehending things present, understanding things absent, and inquiring into things unknown. In the
application of reason, Boethius continues, it is easy for the mind to
be misled into believing that what is logically correct is factually true.
But, what is encountered in the flow of words (*sermonum decursus*) is
not always established in nature (*natura fixum*).[298] In Boethius's view,
one can only proceed to a true understanding of reality after learning
the rudiments of thinking. This, in turn, implies a knowledge of
disputation, that is, of invention and judgment,[299] and of logic.

Signification is then related as in Aristotle to the five predicables
and in particular to the meaning of genus and species. Boethius thereby
orients the problem of universals around the relationship of genera,
species, and other categories to the individual forms in which things
normally exist and are perceived. Although Porphyry, he notes, refused to take a position, he framed the issues as three interdependent
questions. Boethius accordingly responds in three stages. He first re-
phrases Porphyry's well-known questions in his own terms. He eliminates what he considers to be his authority's ambiguities, and, with
the aid of Alexander of Aphrodisias, attempts to resolve the matter.

His "solution" has been criticized for its vagueness and lack of
philosophic rigour.[300] In reality, it rests less on a foundation of logic
than of common sense. Throughout book one of *In Porphyrium*, Boethius builds a case for distinguishing between things and thoughts
about them through the different mental operations appropriate to
each. His approach to universals is a specific application of these relationships, camouflaged at times under technical terminology. In a
nutshell, he proposes that genera and species, and, by implication,
other universals, appear in reality in one form, namely as individuals,
and are represented in the mind in another, namely as principles of
classification.[301]

This, clearly, was an approach which Abelard could not accept,
however broadly it influenced the direction of his own thoughts. But,
for this reason, it merits a brief exposition.

Porphyry, Boethius relates, asks of genera and species (1) whether
they subsist in reality or are brought forth as "bare ideas"; (2) whether,
if subsisting, they are corporeal or incorporeal; and (3) whether, as a
corollary, they exist separately from sensible things or are located in
them.[302]

---

[298] *Ibid.*, 72B-73A.   [299] *Ibid.*, 73B.
[300] E.g., Tweedale, *Abailard on Universals*, 63.   [301] *In Porphyrium* 1, 82A-B.
[302] *Ibid.*, 82B-C.

In reformulating these questions, Boethius puts the first into the context of his theory of signification. Are genera and species, he asks, categories of understanding, or do they exist in things in reality? In his view, this is tantamount to asking whether they are understood by the mind through the dual operations of conceiving (*intellectu concipere*) and reasoning (*ratione describere*), or whether they are a vacant, unconnected image (*vacua, cassa imaginatio*) which the mind "paints" for itself.[303] Secondly, if they exist, what is their nature? For all things are either corporeal or incorporeal.[304] Finally, do they exist in connection with bodies or beyond them? To take an example: God, mind, and the soul exist incorporeally and outside bodies, but line, surface, and number do not. The latter inhere in other things. Separated from bodies, they no longer truly exist.[305]

In short, whereas Porphyry had restricted his discussion to the categories, as evidenced, for instance, by his derivation of *subsistere* from *substantia*,[306] Boethius moves in the direction of signification, as illustrated by his continued use of the key terms *sensus, imaginatio, intellectus*, and *esse*. The questions he asks of each of Porphyry's three questions are: what does the mind understand, what really exists, and what exists through sense?[307]

These concerns are carried over to the section in which he attempts to eliminate what he considers to be Porphyry's ambiguities.[308] In his view, the basic question is, in what sense do genera and species exist? He agrees that there are two possibilities: either they exist or subsist in reality or are formed by the intellect and by thought alone.[309] But he does not look upon these as mutually exclusive alternatives, and his exposition does not so much clarify Porphyry's thinking as it points toward his own solution.

To achieve this, Boethius presents examples of the philosophic problems which arise if genera and species are assumed either to exist as, or to be byproducts of, thought alone. To exist, as he sees it, is to exist individually in concrete reality. In this sense, genera and species do not exist. Anything that is common to many things at a given moment cannot be only one thing. However many species there are, they all share the same genus, which is not present in them in

---

[303] *Ibid.*, 82C-D.   [304] *Ibid.*, 82C-D.   [305] *Ibid.*, 82D-83A.

[306] See Tweedale, *Abailard on Universals*, 64-66, who argues that Boethius's sense is different from Porphyry's. I do not find the evidence conclusive.

[307] *In Porphyrium* 1, 82B-D.   [308] *Ibid.*, 83A-84B.

[309] *Ibid.*, 83A: Genera et species aut sunt et subsistunt, aut intellectu et sola cogitatione formantur. . . .

part but in whole. Therefore, the entire genus, although distributed to individuals, cannot be one, not even in number. But, if it is not one, then, by definition, it does not exist.[310] A genus, in fact, is one and many at once: it is one, just as animals are one, in having something in common, but many, just as the same animals are many in reality. What is one is its likeness of itself.[311]

If this were not so, insoluble problems would arise. For genera cannot be only one; if so, they could not truly be common to many. A part, not the whole, would be common, and, as a part, it would be common in use or function (like a servant or a horse used by different men), not in constituting the form or substance of the things themselves. For this reason genera can be said to have no absolute existence; they cannot be derived from things alone.[312] The mind plays a role in understanding what they are. In fact, genera and species are no different from other intellections in one sense. When they are grasped as subjects representing things in the mind—whether or not the thing exists in reality—the idea of genus and species exists like other ideas, and comes into being as the thing is established in the mind, or, at least, is understood to be established. In that sense they are not only placed in the mind, but, through the mind, are placed in the reality of things. In other words, the essence of things corresponds to the inner forms of thought in the mind.[313] In Boethius's view, then, the problem of universals is both logical and ontological. In what sense, he asks, can we predicate existence of genera and species, since they neither exist absolutely nor represent a truth derivable from real things?

The answer he proposes is to separate existence in reality from existence in thought, as does Alexander of Aphrodisias.[314] We must distinguish, Boethius argues, between the truth and falsehood of things in reality and in the mind. An idea about a thing which does not conform to reality is not necessarily false, unless, of course, with respect to reality, it attempts to unite elements that do not belong together, as, for instance, would be the case in the attempted union of a man and a horse to form a centaur. Yet, if the notion of a centaur comes about by means of the mental processes of abstraction and division, whether or not a reality corresponds to it, then the idea itself, *qua* idea, is not false or devoid of meaning. Rather, it means what it means as a product of the mind;[315] and the subject established in the

[310] *Ibid.*, 83A-B.   [311] *Ibid.*, 83B-C: . . . habet sui similitudinem.
[312] *Ibid.*, 83C-D.   [313] *Ibid.*, 83D-84A.   [314] *Ibid.*, 84B.
[315] *Ibid.*, 84B-C.

mind is no less real to the mind on account of its lack of correspondence with concrete reality. To illustrate the point, Boethius takes the example of a line in a body. The line exists only through the prior existence of the body. The mind, receiving at once the intermingled images of line and body, makes a distinction between them, ultimately, of course, in order to examine things in their incorporeal state.[316] Genus and species, if not arising incorporeally, are similarly abstracted from bodies in the mind. "Things of this kind," Boethius argues, "exist in corporeal and sensible things, but are understood beyond the sensible in order that their nature be perceived and their property comprehended."[317] Genus and species are products of cogitation (*cogitare*), but a likeness is brought together (*similitudo colligitur*) from individual things. And, in this way, one proceeds from species to genus, that is, from the diversity of men to the image of humanity.[318]

The mental likeness, then, when in individuals, is sensible, and when in universals, is intelligible.[319] Boethius claims to derive these notions in large part from Aristotle,[320] but his vocabulary is influenced by several strands of later platonism. The written word also impinges on his analysis from many directions. As in his commentary on *De Interpretatione*, the logic of texts plays a distant if nonetheless discernible role in his various observations on language, thought, and reality. He refers to the need to arrive at the principle of substance (*substantiae ratio*), but the means he proposes are inseparable from his assumptions about the written mode. In *descriptio*, he sees not only "description" but "de-scribing," that is, the making of a copy or a transcript; in *diffinitio*, not merely "definition," but the setting forth of precise lexical or semantic boundaries. Description establishes property and this leads to the principle of substance; by implication, *ratio* is *ratio scripta*.[321] The notion of the text also helps him to distinguish between *descriptio* and *diffinitio*; he speaks of collecting (*colligere*) properties but of a definition being made (*fieri*),[322] relating the one to gathering lexical meanings, the other to the interdependent understanding of the essence of things. At the back of his thoughts are the connections between sense, imagination, and thought, between which, as in *De Interpretatione*, written language provides, once again, uninvestigated links.

[316] *Ibid.*, 84C-D.   [317] *Ibid.*, 85B.   [318] *Loc.cit.*
[319] *Ibid.*, 85B-C.   [320] *Ibid.*, 86A.
[321] Cf. T. Gregory, "Considérations sur Ratio et Natura chez Abélard," *Pierre Abélard, Pierre le Vénérable* . . . , 573-75.
[322] *In Porphyrium*, 79C-D.

Porphyry's tripartite question regarding universals, which was intended to be limited to the categories, thus becomes a larger issue involving reality, abstraction, and the workings of the mind.

Abelard on Porphyry

Boethius's achievement, despite its limitations, was Abelard's point of departure. His fullest account of the problem of universals is found in the opening sections of his own glosses on Porphyry. The two central themes are the limits of naive realism and the status of universals with respect to language and things.[323]

In Abelard's analysis the issue of spoken and written language reached its culminating point in twelfth-century thought. Like Berengar in the eucharistic controversy, Abelard henceforward became a standard against which other thinkers measured their positions on realism and nominalism. Abelard's "solution" to the problem of universals has long occupied a respectable place in the history of logic. Yet, it is arguable, his discussion generalizes in a philosophical format an attitude of mind which, as we have noted, was gradually emerging in other thinkers and disciplines concerning potential links between textuality, rationality, and the nature of reality. For that reason his often-studied thoughts deserve still another review.

After restating Porphyry's three questions, Abelard establishes that the ancients are divided on whether universals are words or things. Authority, he observes, seems confused. Aristotle defines the universal as predicable of many, while Porphyry refers to one.[324] Worse, both speak on occasion as if things were encompassed in the names designating universals. But the same authors also speak of universals as words. Aristotle, for instance, says that genus "determines quality with respect to substance" and Boethius, his interpreter, writes of it as "the unitary likeness of many species." Further, the verbs the pair use are *significare* and *monstrare*: the one pertains to words, the other more properly to things. Again, Boethius states that genus is a noun predicated of several other nouns, thus employing the analogy of the parts of speech in defining genus and species. In Abelard's view, he errs, for a noun and a universal are not the same thing. Universals are

---

[323] *Glossae super Porphyrium*, p. 7, 34-p. 8, 8.

[324] *Ibid.*, 9, 18-20, quoting, respectively, Boethius, *In Peri ermeneias*, ed. C. Meiser, vol. 2, p. 135, 23, and *In Isagogen Porphyrii*, ed. S. Brandt, CSEL 48, vol. 2, p. 183, 7.

words whose only function is supplying the predicate terminations of propositions.[325]

For that reason they cannot refer to things alone. Abelard therefore sees as his first task the demolition of this position.[326] However, as becomes evident, oversimplified realism is not so much a serious philosophical argument as a springboard for his own solution to the problem of universals. And this, as expected, is inseparable from his theory of language and signification.

Abelard considers three theories by which universals may be located in things alone. The first asserts that universals predicated of things are different in form (*formarum diversitate*) but are essentially the same in matter (*eadem essentialiter materia*).[327] In other words, Plato and Socrates are substantially the same but differ in accidents. The second, which Abelard finds closer to the truth, maintains that individual things not only differ in form but are also separated in essence (*in suis essentiis esse discretae*). As such, they share neither matter nor form. Yet, those who hold this position still believe that universals exist in things, as they put it, not essentially but indifferently (*non essentialiter, sed indifferenter*);[328] that is to say, Plato and Socrates, although discrete men, do not differ with respect to their humanity. The third position sees universals as individuals which are predicated of many things not because of similarity of essence but because of harmony or agreement (*non essentialiter, sed quia plura cum eis conveniunt*).[329]

Abelard plays logical havoc with these positions. The first holds that animals differing in species nonetheless share the same substance, as different statues may be made of the same wax. But therein lies the flaw: at any moment, the same wax is not found in all the statues, whereas, Boethius makes clear, the same universal is. That, Abelard adds, is why Porphyry's official commentator argues that universals exist in one sense but are understood in another.[330] By contrast, the first position allows contraries to exist in the same species at the same time, proposing, for instance, that Socrates can be both rational and irrational at once. For, if men differ only in accidents, contrary accidents may find their place in a being that still remains substantially man. Abelard proves that this is logically impossible: neither can the

---

[325] *Glossae*, 9, 22-10, 7.

[326] Inadequately reviewed by Sikes, *Peter Abelard*, 89-96 and Tweedale, *Abailard on Universals*, ch. 3, pp. 89-132: Sikes ignores the logical proofs and Tweedale treats nothing else. A full study of the matter would be useful but cannot be attempted here.

[327] *Glossae super Porphyrium* 10, 17-23.   [328] *Ibid.*, 13, 19-20; 14, 1-2.

[329] *Ibid.*, 15, 23-26.   [330] *Ibid.*, p. 10, 29-p. 11, 9.

same man harbour contraries nor can it be argued that the paradox rational/irrational refers only to words and not to things. For propositions of this type must be verified by testing against what actually exists.[331] Moreover, stronger arguments against such naive realism can be brought from other quarters. It is illogical to suppose that things can be alike in essence and different in form. As all qualities would then be the same, so would all substances. If Plato and Socrates share the same things of each category (*res singulorum predicatorum*), they would be the same person, both essentially and formally.[332] Nor, as a corollary, can it be maintained that individuals are made of their own accidents.[333] For that is to reverse the categories' logic, namely, to make individuals prior to their accidents.

Abelard illustrates similar fallacies in the second and third positions. Regarding the second, he states, there is a diversity of opinion. Some hold that the universal thing is just a collection of many,[334] while others say that a genus or species is not just a group of individuals. In this case, expressions like "The thing which is Socrates is predicated of many" is to be taken figuratively, as if to say, "Many like beings are in agreement with him," or vice versa.[335] But neither view can be defended. For the accommodation of individuals to each other is not the same as predication through a universal.[336] That would merely make Socrates a universal in himself, or, for that matter, any group of men taken together.[337] This, in turn, would lead to the general opinion that there are many abstractions of the highest order in a given group of substances. The actual difference between genus and species would thereby be blurred. For, while the part is not the same as the whole, the species is always the same as the genus. Abelard has little more patience with the third option. In his view, the proponents simply confuse universality and individuality. To be predicated of many is not merely "to agree" with many. If the man who is Socrates is the same as Socrates himself, then there is no difference between the category and the thing.[338]

Abelard thus concludes that things cannot be called universals either singly or collectively. Universality can be ascribed only to words, or, as he more specifically puts it, to certain types of nouns.[339] Once again he reasons from grammar to speech, that is, from the norms of written

[331] *Ibid.*, p. 11, 25-p. 12, 26; on the logical implications, see Tweedale, *Abailard on Universals*, 98-108.

[332] *Ibid.*, 13, 5-17.   [333] *Ibid.*, p. 13, 18,-p. 14, 6.   [334] *Ibid.*, 14, 8.

[335] *Ibid.*, 14, 18-31.   [336] *Ibid.*, 14, 35-37.   [337] *Ibid.*, p. 14, 40-p. 15, 4.

[338] *Ibid.*, p. 15, 36-p. 16, 18.   [339] *Ibid.*, 16, 19-21.

to spoken language. Grammarians, he states, call some nouns appellative, that is, designators of a class, while others are proper, that is, designators of individual things. Similarly, logicians call some uncompounded speech forms (*simplices sermones*) universal and others particular. A universal is a term (*vocabulum*) devised to be predicable singly of many things. It links a noun like "man" with particular men and is imposed upon the things which comprise its subject. By contrast, a particular noun is predicable of only one thing, as for instance, the name Socrates. Moreover, when a universal is said to be predicated "singly," the claim is made both with respect to the word's simplicity as spoken speech (*oratio*) and with respect to its unequivocal unity of meaning.[340]

This is the sense in which a universal is that which is predicated of many. But, he then asks, what is meant by this expression? For, as Aristotle makes clear,[341] universals are neither appellative nor proper nouns as Priscian later defines them. To be predicated is first of all a function of discourse; it means "to be conjoinable to something" in truth, that is, in the nature of reality, through the speaking (*enuntiatio*) of a substantive verb in the present tense.[342] Examples may be found for "man" such as "he runs" or "he walks." Such verbs have the power of copulas, even though "to be" is absent. In "of many," Aristotle also brings together names or nouns as such according to the diversity of things named. Otherwise, the name Socrates could be predicated of many, when it is said, "This man is Socrates," "This animal is Socrates," etc. That is to say: the names are different in the understanding but in reality refer to the same subject-thing.[343]

Abelard then returns to the analogy of grammar in an effort to clarify predication further. The grammarians, he notes, speak of union through constructions; the logicians refer to linkage through predication. The two in his view are not the same. According to grammar, "man" and "stone" may be joined by "is." Any two nouns may be so united and present a purely grammatical relationship: the case of the nouns and the number of the verbs are correct and the resulting sen-

---

[340] *Ibid.*, 16, 19-35. Tweedale, *Abailard on Universals*, 141-42, distinguishes between *vox* (utterance), *vocabulum* (word), and *sermo* (expression). But Abelard's terminology is not consistent. For a discussion of *vox* and *sermo*, see above pp. 372-76, and Jolivet, *Arts du langage*, 22-27 (*vox*), 70-71 (*vox* and *sermo*), and 89-90 (*vocabulum*). Abelard himself appears to have revised his thinking in the *Logica "Nostrorum Petitioni Sociorum,"* an alternative gloss on Porphyry, ed. B. Geyer (Münster, 1933), 522, 10-32, discussed in detail by Tweedale, 142-57.

[341] *Glossae super Porphyrium*, 16, 39-17, 6; Boethius, *Super Peri ermeneias*, vol. 1, p. 14, 12.

[342] *Glossae*, 16, 39-40: "Est autem praedicari coniungibile esse alicui veraciter vi enuntiationis verbi substantivi praesentis. . . ."

[343] *Ibid.*, 17, 7-11.

tence is grammatically sound. But this holds true whether or not the sentence refers accurately to a state of affairs in the real world (*ad ostendendum rei statum*). By contrast, predication pertains to the nature of the thing and to the illustration of its actual state (*ad rerum naturam pertinet et ad veritatem status*). Thus, the sentence "A man is a stone" is grammatically correct and appears to use predication through categories correctly. Yet, with respect to reality, it makes no sense.[344]

Having so described "universal" and "particular," Abelard turns to the property of universals as spoken words (*universalium vocum proprietas*).[345] Here, his objections to Boethius become clearer. Boethius, he holds, voiced doubts about their capacity to signify. Do they, he asked, have anything as their subject-thing (*res subjecta*) or any sound meaning (*intellectus sanus*)?[346] They are not directly imposed on things, because, as established above, things exist as individuals. Nor do things themselves "agree" in a manner permitting predication.[347] One might therefore conclude with certain of the ancients that universals derive none of their meaning from things, especially since, in themselves, they do not constitute things' understanding. At least, Abelard adds, that appears to be Boethius's view, both in *De Divisione*[348] and in his commentary on Porphyry. In particular, in the latter book, he maintains that every understanding devolves from a subject-thing, whether the thing is being apprehended by the mind at that point or not. For, he says, an idea cannot be created without a subject.[349]

Abelard argues that this notion, which would make universals alien to signification, is incorrect. For universals in his view signify by naming things: not by forming an understanding *arising* from them but by forming one which *pertains* to each.[350] The word "man" names individual men for the *raison d'être* which they all share, namely, being men. On this account "man" may justly be called a universal. The understanding established in the mind is not proper or specific but common; that is, it relates to the individuals whose common likeness (*communis similitudo*) it conceives.

Universals, then, as Abelard sees them, really involve three problems at once: (1) the common cause (*communis causa*) according to which the universal is imposed; (2) the mental conception of the understanding of the common likeness (*conceptio intellectus communis similitudinis*); and (3) whether the term (*vocabulum*) is called common be-

---

[344] *Ibid.*, 17, 12-28.   [345] *Ibid.*, p. 18, 5-p. 19, 13.

[346] *Ibid.*, 18, 6-9.   [347] See above, p. 392f.   [348] PL 64.889B.

[349] *Glossae super Porphyrium*, 19, 4-6; Boethius, *In Porphyrium*, vol. 2, p. 163, 7.

[350] *Glossae*, 19, 8-9: ". . . non constituendo tamen intellectum de eis surgentem, sed ad singulas pertinentem."

cause of the common cause in which things agree (*propter communem causam in qua res conveniat*), or because of the common conception (*propter communem conceptionem*), or because of both at once.[351] In other terms, Abelard wishes to investigate the cause, the likeness, and their relationship to the universal as a word.

He first turns to the common cause.[352] Individual men, he repeats, are entirely distinct from each other both in essence and in form. Yet they are united in being men. What then does "to be men" logically mean? The expression fulfills none of the requirements Aristotle sets down for substances. To be a man is not the same as "man"; that is, "not to be in the subject" is not any actual thing. Nor does "to be men" admit contraries of being greater or less. Therefore, the expression "to be man" is not anything (*nec res aliqua*). For example, Socrates and Plato are alike "in being men" in the same way that a horse and an ass are alike in being non-man.

How then are Socrates and Plato united? In the condition of man (*in statu hominis*), that is, in that they are men (*in eo quod sunt homines*).[353] The *status hominis* therefore is "to be man," which means that the expression is not a thing but the common cause of the imposition of the name onto individuals insofar as they truly agree with each other.[354] The state or condition need not refer to reality. For example, in the sentence, "He was beaten because he did not wish to go to the forum," the principal clause does not describe an existing situation. In that sense, it is a cause (*causa*) but not an essence (*essentia*).[355] In sum, Abelard calls the condition of man those things established in the nature of man, things whose common likeness he who imposes the word conceives.[356]

Universals, then, signify things by giving them names (*nominatio*). The common cause of such names' imposition is the condition of the entities themselves.[357]

But what of the intellections which they constitute? To answer this question, Abelard largely repeats Aristotle and Boethius, adding insights from Priscian and a few ideas of his own.[358] Like Aristotle, he

[351] *Ibid.*, 19, 14-20.

[352] *Ibid.*, p. 19, 21-p. 20, 14.   [353] *Ibid.*, 20, 3-4.

[354] *Ibid.*, 20, 7-9: "Statum autem hominis ipsum esse hominem, quod non est res, vocamus, quod etiam diximus communem causam impositionis nominis ad singulos, secundum quod ipsi ad invicem conveniunt."

[355] *Ibid.*, 20, 12.

[356] *Ibid.*, 20, 12-14: "Statum quoque hominis res ipsas in natura hominis statutas possumus appellare, quarum communem similitudinem ille concepit, qui vocabulum imposuit."

[357] *Ibid.*, 20, 15-17.   [358] *Ibid.*, p. 20, 20-p. 21, 26.

attributes both sense and understanding to the soul. But, whereas sense requires the physical perception of bodies, understanding is satisfied with the likeness of things (*rei similitudo*), which the mind configures for itself and towards which it directs its active thought. To return to a previous image: one may destroy a tower but retain an image of it in one's mind. The sense data pass away, but the likeness remains.[359]

Yet Abelard reconceives both sense and understanding somewhat differently than do his mentors. The sense, in his view, does not consist of the thing perceived (*res sentita*), but rather the activity of the mind directed towards the thing. Similarly, the understanding is not the form of the thing it conceives (*forma . . . rei quam concipit*). Rather, *intellectus* is a certain activity of the soul, whence it is expressible by the present participle *intelligens*.[360] The form towards which this activity is directed is an imaginary and fictive thing (*res imaginaria quaedam et ficta*) which the mind constructs for itself when and how it wishes, like the artist's model, a city seen in a dream, or any other image or copy of a thing to be formed (*instar et exemplar rei formandae*).[361] As such, it has neither substance nor accidents. Some thinkers, he adds, apparently following Aristotle, identify the image and the reality. They say that the form of a tower in the mind is somehow the physical building itself. But it is really only a likeness of the thing.[362]

In a sense, the intellection can also be called a likeness, since it conceives what is accurately called a thing's image.[363] But here too Abelard sees a problem. For, beyond the composite image of the tower there are components like squareness and height out of which the tower in turn is formed. These, in his opinion, comprise the intellection's true form (*vera forma intellectus*). Yet, he is quick to add, squareness and height cannot exist apart from bodies, for, as proven above, neither an essence nor an understanding can be created from a fictive quality.[364] Perhaps this form is like a mirror image, which is the subject of sight but is itself truly nothing. Again, if I see a stone, does my mind react to the reality or to an image?[365] In Abelard's view, when the reality is present, the mind has no need of an image. On the other hand, he opposes the view that, where there is only sense, there is no understanding. For the mind often perceives one thing and thinks of another.

---

[359] See above, p. 379. [360] *Glossae*, 20, 28-31. [361] *Ibid.*, 20, 31-36.
[362] *Ibid.*, 21, 1-5. [363] *Ibid.*, 21, 6-17.
[364] See above, p. 392f. [365] *Glossae*, 21, 18-26.

Understanding, then, as in Aristotle, is always based directly or indirectly on reality. But what does this imply for the understanding of universals and particulars?[366] Abelard's point of departure in replying to this question is to inquire into the type of image which each sort of word generates. The universal, he argues, produces a common and confused image, while the particular produces the specific or individual form. Let us compare "man" and "Socrates." When I hear "man," an image (*instar*) arises in my mind which is common to all men and proper to none. But, when I hear "Socrates," a form (*forma*) arises which expresses the likeness of an individual person. Thus, as a word (*vocabulum*), Socrates brings to mind the proper form of one thing, which it certifies and delimits (*certificatur et determinatur*), while "man" signifies neither Socrates nor any other man, since no single man is specified by the term's force (*ex vi nominis*), although, in fact, it names particulars.

Socrates, however, not only names a particular thing but also determines a subject-thing.[367] Boethius, of course, said that every understanding has a subject-thing,[368] and this applies to universals. For the thing which is the subject of understanding is either the substance of the real thing as received by sense or the conceived form of a thing when the reality is absent; and this form may be common, as in the case of many things, or proper, as in the case of one. For example, to depict a lion we may draw a picture of what is common to all lions or what is proper to one in various situations. But, if the universal or particular refer back to reality, the name also looks to the form towards which the understanding is directed.[369] This, Abelard adds, was also the view of Priscian, who maintained that universals signified both common imposition and common form.[370] And, before they come forth in bodies, they are produced in the divine mind. To illustrate the point, Abelard once again has recourse to Priscian's image of God as an artist or artisan.[371]

The *communis conceptio*, then, is ascribable to God, not to man. Such "general works" or "special conditions of nature" are not produced by a mundane craftsman. Concepts, therefore, like man, soul, or stone are proper to the deity, those like house or sword, to man: the latter are not works of nature (*naturae opera*), nor do their words refer to substances (*nec eorum vocabula substantiae sunt*). Rather, they are acci-

---

[366] *Ibid.*, 21, 27-28.   [367] *Ibid.*, p. 21, 27-p. 22, 6.   [368] See above, p. 395.
[369] *Glossae*, 22, 7-24.   [370] *Inst. Gramm.*, 17.44, vol. 2, p. 135, 7.
[371] *Glossae*, 22, 34-23, 1.

dents, and, as such, they are neither genera nor species.[372] Moreover, these ideas, Abelard proposes, are imputed to the divine mind by abstraction (*abstractio*). Men learn of most things through the senses and scarcely ever rise to such an intellectual awareness. They are prevented from knowing the natures of things in their most refined state by exterior sensation (*exterior sensualitas*). God, however, distinguishes the individual states in themselves (*singuli status in se*). Further, when ordinary mortals are deprived of the senses' evidence, all too often they reason not by understanding (*intelligentia*) but by opinion (*opinio*).[373] Similarly, men have only an "opinion" of such intrinsic forms as rationality, mortality, and fatherhood, which do not arrive in the mind via the senses. Yet, the names of existing things generate understanding because their inventor intends that they be imposed according to a selection of natures or properties, even though, as a mortal, one is not able to discover by thought alone the precise nature or property of the thing.[374]

The various ancient authorities appear to be agreed on this point. Priscian, Abelard points out, calls the common conceptions "general" or "specific," since they are so described by nouns. By analogy he thinks of universals with proper nouns. Just as they direct the listener's mind to the one thing signified, so universals act as proper nouns for common conceptions. The nouns, although confused with respect to essential significance, nonetheless direct the hearer's mind toward the conceptions.[375] Porphyry for his part seems to have conceived universals in a comparable manner, since he distinguishes between ideas made from matter and those made from their likenesses.[376] Boethius, too, speaks of genus and species as mental constructions made up of many individuals' likenesses.[377] Even Plato's and Aristotle's approaches, Abelard urges, are reconcilable. For, when Aristotle argues that universals exist in sensible things, he speaks of actuality or toward activity (*ad actum*). Plato refers to existence when the sensible thing has been withdrawn. Thus, what Aristotle denies with respect to actuality, Plato, "the inquirer into physical phenomena," assigns to the natural faculty (*naturalis aptitudo*). And, what authority affirms, reason approves: for, conceiving through nouns is nothing but signifying through nouns. However, Abelard adds, there is one matter which authority omits but reason must resolve. If such forms or images are different from understandings, there exists by implication, in

[372] *Ibid.*, 23, 1-6.   [373] *Ibid.*, 23, 6-17.   [374] *Ibid.*, 23, 18-24.   [375] *Ibid.*, 23, 24-30.
[376] *Ibid.*, 23, 30-33; Boethius, *In Porphyrium*, vol. 2, p. 267, 3.
[377] *Ibid.*, 23, 34-24, 2; *In Porphyrium*, vol. 2, p. 167, 2.

addition to the thing and the understanding, a third element in meaning, namely the signification of nouns (*nominum significatio*).[378]

Do universals, then, exist because of common cause of imposition or because of common conception? Both, Abelard replies, adding only that the common cause taken from the thing's nature has the greater weight.[379]

But how are universals formed by abstraction? And how can they be spoken of as "single, bare, and pure" and yet not be devoid of true meaning?[380]

The key in Abelard's view lies in abstraction, which he explains as follows.[381] A thing exists at once in matter and in form. But, through reason's application, the mind retains the capacity to think of the one or the other, either together or apart. Isolating the pair is brought about by abstraction, that is, by "drawing something away" from its composite state in order to reflect upon its nature alone. The opposite to this state of affairs, of course, is thinking in terms of unity. Take, for instance, a "man": he is at once body, animal, and man, and is invested with infinite forms. If one ignores the forms and concentrates on his material essence, one effectively brings about an understanding by means of abstraction. If, however, one thinks of both his essence and his body simultaneously, one thinks in terms of a unity. Yet, one can think even of these two in isolation from his other characteristics, in which case the result once again is understanding through abstraction.[382]

Such conceptions may appear to be false, since they envisage the thing in terms other than those in which it substantively exists. Not so, Abelard argues: for the abstraction does not violate the nature or property of the thing itself. It pertains to the mind's application (*attentio*), not to the mode of existence (*modus subsistendi*).[383] Otherwise, understanding itself would be devoid of meaning. After all, it is not the thing alone which possesses such an idea; rather, attention is focused on it to the degree that the form inheres in it. And, in a certain sense, as Boethius says, it is understood differently from how it is. But this otherness is not a state; it is only a mode of understanding. In other words, through the process of abstraction, one thing is understood to be separate from another, but, in truth, it is not separate at all. Thus, matter and form are not isolated in reality but in the mind, that is, in the place in which the intellectual reduction actually oc-

[378] *Ibid.*, 24, 2-31. [379] *Ibid.*, 24, 32-37. [380] *Ibid.*, 24, 38-41.
[381] *Ibid.*, p. 25, 1-p. 27, 9. [382] *Ibid.*, 25, 1-15.
[383] *Ibid.*, 25, 27.

curs. Just as sense makes such distinctions—perceiving, for instance, the gold and silver separately in a statue—so does the mind.[384] Abelard adds that abstraction can include foresight (*providentia*), in both God's case and man's. In God, present and future are one; therefore, the question of diverse understandings does not arise. In man, foreknowledge must later be confirmed by fact. The design in the artist's mind must represent the future work.[385]

Abelard now finds himself in a position to answer Porphyry's questions. Do genera and species exist in the sense of signifying things that truly exist? Yes, by naming (*nominatio*). In this sense they are no different from nouns which refer to individual things. Yet, universals also exist purely and singly in the understanding.[386] Nor should these two be regarded as mutually exclusive alternatives, as logicians might suggest.[387]

A similar reply is made to the second question. If subsisting, are genera and species corporeal or incorporeal? Following Boethius, Abelard reads "discrete" for "corporeal": for nothing, the pair argue, truly exists except in a singular form. And, in this sense, the answer to Porphyry's question again is both. Universals signify things discrete in essence and yet, at the same time, incorporeal with respect to the universal noun's mental image (*notio*), since universals, as established, do not signify discretely but confusedly. In other words, they signify corporeally with respect to things and incorporeally with respect to the manner of signification. They name things which are discrete, but they do not do so discretely or determinately.[388]

It follows, therefore, in reply to Porphyry's third question, that, while universals exist in sensible things, they designate them as separated from their things. Whence Boethius, Abelard states, proposes that universals reside in sensible things but are understood outside them.[389] In his view, the second and third questions can be merged. Universals may be said both to signify sensible things and to signify the common conceptions which Priscian locates in the divine mind.[390]

Abelard adds one further corrective to Boethius. Concerning spoken words (*voces*), he says, doubts do not arise about how they signify individual things, since the mode of signifying corresponds to the status of the thing signified. In other terms, as things exist discretely, so words actually name them.[391] But doubts exist concerning the real-

[384] *Ibid.*, p. 25, 28-p. 26-15; on Boethius, see above, p. 371.
[385] *Ibid.*, 26, 16-27, 9.   [386] *Ibid.*, p. 27, 39-p. 28, 6.   [387] *Ibid.*, 28, 7-15.
[388] *Ibid.*, p. 28, 16-p. 29, 7.
[389] *Ibid.*, 29, 8-20.   [390] *Ibid.*, 29, 28-38.   [391] *Ibid.*, 30, 6-10.

ity of universals, which nonetheless perform the same task.[392] In this respect, therefore, Boethius's account of the subject was incomplete. Although the universal's definition refers only to spoken words (*solae voces*), the names (*nomina*) are often transferred to things (*ad res*). Thus, when the word's nature is disclosed, it is found sometimes to refer to words, sometimes to things. Frequently, the names of the one and the other are transposed, and grammar and logic, if incorrectly applied, may lead to error. This, in Abelard's view, is what happened to his illustrious predecessor.[393] Boethius was correct in calling a thing a thing, and in insisting that the universal, *qua* word, is common by its nomination of many. However, he did not sufficiently emphasize that the many themselves give rise to the universal. The universality which the thing confers upon the word is something it does not have itself. For the word does not ultimately derive its meaning from the thing but from the mode of signification in the human mind.[394]

Beginning, then, with rejections of realism, Abelard finishes in an intellectualist position which combines Aristotle, Boethius, and Priscian with his own insights on the nature of language and reality. His relationship to the notion of written language is complex, and operates on several levels at once. In terms such as *abstractio* the spoken is directly infused with written linguistic norms. As in Anselm, a text appears in the mind before it is rendered as script. Again, to be predicated is essentially a function of the spoken word; in this sense, universals are imputable "to words alone." Yet, these turn out to be words in grammatical or logical arrangement; they are spoken sounds whose meaning is inseparable from the ordered discourse of texts.

Thus, for Abelard, as, in the eucharistic controversy, for Ratramn and later Berengar, the problem of universality concerns the relationship of logico-linguistic structures to the mind, and, as a consequence, to reality. His definition of the universal as a noun that can be predicated of many things is evidently derived from logic (Porphyry) and grammar (Priscian). But, from the outset, he is occupied simultaneously with words *and* things. Although *oratio enuntiativa* is his proper subject, he repeatedly asserts his interest in nouns and verbs as "substantial" elements of communication which are combined "in truth." Therefore, he does not abandon Boethius's conceptualism but rather refines and extends it. He adheres to the vocabulary of "likeness" and to the notion of the mind as the active inventor of universal concepts. Yet he clears up ambiguities in Boethius's oversimplified

[392] *Ibid.*, 30, 10-16.   [393] *Ibid.*, 30, 17-26.   [394] *Ibid.*, 32, 2-12.

explanation of how universals signify discrete things. For Abelard, as for none of his ancient predecessors, language is the chief instrument of discourse. By isolating language from things and thoughts, he is able to provide a more defensible relationship between the two.

3. BERNARD OF CLAIRVAUX

Idiota quilibet, si charitatem habet, valde doctus est.
—*Tractatus de Statu Virtutum*, 3.37

Abelard was alone in his time in weaving the various threads of interest in language into a coherent theory and in testing his hypotheses against the full range of available ancient authority. The above account says little about his pure logic, about his applications of dialectic to theology, or about internal developments within his own thought. Yet, even a synthetic representation of his ideas makes clear his belief that semantic analysis—that is, the exploration of the meanings of words in textual contexts—can aid one to understand higher theological realities.

Abelard thereby places himself at one pole of twelfth-century hermeneutic development, while St. Bernard,[395] together with other

---

[395] The early literature on Bernard is briefly summarized by E. Vacandard, "Bernard (Saint)," DTC 2.1, 784-85 and exhaustively by L. Janauschek, *Bibliographia Bernardina* . . . (Vienna, 1891). Later studies are listed by J. de la Croix Bouton, *Bibliographie bernardine* (Paris, 1958). For critical reviews, see E. van Gassel, "Bibliographie over H. Bernardus," *Sint Bernardus van Clairvaux* . . . (Rotterdam, 1953) and M. Bernards, "Der Stand der Bernhardforschung," *Bernhard von Clairvaux, Mönch und Mystiker* . . . (Wiesbaden, 1955), 3-43. More specialized bibliographical reviews include E. T. Kennan, "The 'De consideratione' of St. Bernard of Clairvaux and the Papacy in the mid-Twelfth Century: A Review of Scholarship," *Traditio* 23 (1967), 73-115; A. H. Bredero, "St. Bernard and the Historians," *Saint Bernard of Clairvaux* . . . (Kalamazoo, Mich., 1977), 27-62; and, on the manuscripts of Bernard's works, the various studies of J. Leclercq, *Recueil d'études sur S. Bernard et ses écrits*, 3 vols. (Rome, 1962, 1966, 1969).

Fundamental to the study of Bernard's life, thought, and influence on his age is E. Vacandard, *Vie de Saint Bernard*, 2nd ed., 2 vols. (Paris, 1897). Briefer encyclopedia articles include: *idem*, DTC 2.1, 746-85, A. le Bail, "Bernard (Saint)," *Dictionnaire de spiritualité, ascétique et mystique* 1 (1937), 1454-99 (with an extensive bibliography, 1498-99), F. Roch and M. Herold, "Bernhard, Abt von Clairvaux," *Realencyclopädie für protestantische Theologie und Kirche* 2, 623-39, and F. Oppenheim and K. Rathe, "Bernardo di Chiaravalle," *Enciclopedia cattolica* 2, 1423-36. In addition to the congresses listed above, important recent commemorations of Bernard include: *Saint Bernard théologien, Analecta Sacri Ordinis Cisterciensis* 9 (1953), *Festschrift zum 800-Jahresgedächtnis des Todes Bernhards von Clairvaux* (Vienna, 1953) (dealing mainly with Austrian monasteries), *Mélanges Saint Bernard* . . . (Dijon, 1954), *San Bernardo. Pubblicazioni commemorativa nell'VIII centenario della sua morte* (Milan, 1954), and *Studi su S. Bernardo di Chiaravalle* . . . (Rome, 1975). A number of studies of Bernard's mysticism will be cited in the course of this

mystical thinkers, stands at the other. Of course, it is now recognized that the doctrinal differences between them are not as great as they themselves thought.[396] Abelard wrote brilliantly of the monastic spirit in his letters to the nuns of the Paraclete, and, since Gilson,[397] there has been an increasing awareness of the "systematic" elements in Bernard's thought. However, despite points of contact in the content of their ideas, their conceptions of relations between author, text, and audience were not the same. Nor were their notions of the relationship between literary form and individual thought and action.

To describe these differences, it is nowadays fashionable to speak in terms of "hermeneutics." The word is so widely used in critical discussions that it has lost much of its ancient association with a science of interpretation. Yet, it was precisely in the definition and application of this *scientia interpretationis* that eleventh- and twelfth-century authors began to evolve differing notions of the text. Anselm, for his part, had bridged the monastic and scholastic realms by suggesting that the establishment of logico-linguistic facts was not incompatible with deep personal meditation on religious mysteries. He effectively reconciled the objectifying and subjectifying aspects of critical investigation within one literary endeavour. Abelard, by contrast, when treating similar issues, shifted the burden of inquiry to the comparison of texts. True, in the *Theologia "Scholarium,"* he emphat-

---

chapter. Important reviews of his influence on medieval thought not mentioned below are: J. Châtillon, "L'influence de S. Bernard sur la pensée scolastique au XII et au XIIIe siècle," *Saint Bernard théologien*, 268-88, A. M. Landgraf, "Der heilige Bernhard in seinem Verhältnis zur Theologie des zwölften Jahrhunderts," *Bernhard von Clairvaux*, 44-62, S. Vanni Rovighi, "S. Bernardo e la filosofia," *S. Bernardo*, 132-50, and E. Bertola, *San Bernardo e la teologia speculativa* (Padua, 1959). On the afterlife of the period's mystical thought, see in general, G. Constable, "Twelfth-Century Spirituality and the Late Middle Ages," *Medieval and Renaissance Studies* 5 (Chapel Hill, 1971), 27-60; on Cistercian ideals in comparison with other twelfth-century orders, see C. W. Bynum, "The Cistercian Conception of Community," *Harvard Theological Review* 68 (1975), 273-86.

[396] Two important reassessments are D. E. Luscombe, *The School of Peter Abelard*, 103-42, and N. Häring, "Abelard Yesterday and Today," *Pierre Abélard*, 343-55. On Abelard's theology, one still turns to the older review of J. Cottiaux, "La conception de la théologie chez Abélard," RHE 28 (1932), 247-95, 533-51, and 788-828. Important among reviews of the historical questions is A. Borst, "Abälard und Bernhard," *Historische Zeitschrift* 186 (1958), 497-526; more specialized is P. Zerbi, "San Bernardo di Chiaravalle e il Concilio di Sens," *Studi su S. Bernardo*, 49-73. A general review of Bernard's attitude towards scholasticism is S. Vanni Rovighi, "San Bernardo e la filosofia," *San Bernardo* (Milan, 1954), 132-50. For a list of the manuscripts of Bernard's attack and of successive redactions, see J. Leclercq, "Les formes successives de la lettre-traité de S. Bernard contre Abélard," Rben 78 (1968), 89-93.

[397] *La théologie mystique de saint Bernard* (Paris, 1934).

ically equated *ratio*, *logos*, and *verbum*.[398] But, when he turned to the *Sic et Non*, the various discussions of the trinity, or the methods by which moral and ethical conclusions were reached, the knowable was largely associated with the accumulation of facts that were directly or indirectly derived from texts. Although Abelard nowhere allowed a model of written language to stand on its own, the applications of his ideas generally strengthened the already prevalent medieval link between rationality and textuality.

But there was another possible approach to the meaning and function of texts, which considerably antedated the uses put to logic and grammar after the millennium. Instead of leading one to a deeper appreciation of objective reality, texts could be called upon to structure the conduct of everyday life, either of the individual or of the group. Knowledge in this sense would be related less to expanding the corpus of existing information than to influencing the use of constructs within some aspect of social experience.

One aspect of the latter problem has been discussed in Chapter Two, namely the growth of textual concerns and group organization among early heretical and reformist communities. But the issues also link up with those of Chapter Three, that is, with the intellectualist or symbolic approaches to sacramental realities and the concommitant priority given to reason or to sense. For, as Bernard of Clairvaux's sermons were circulated throughout the expanding Cistercian Order, they not only provided the century's outstanding example of a "textual community." They also brought together into one group of writings and gave a definitive stylistic imprint to feelings, perceptions, and practical ideas that were the antithesis of the scholastic, informational, or objectifying approach. In Bernard's view, hermeneutics functioned by means of a dialectical swing between the text and experience. The text therefore retained its inner meditative concentration directed towards the reform of outer action, as it did not in scholastic analysis. Physical symbolism, too, if allegorized, remained within a framework that was essentially ritualistic, although such rituals, now dependent on subjective interpretation, were, like the group interactions of earlier reformers, byproducts of an intensively literary experience. The externalization of the ascetic ideal was thus brought about by a simultaneous development of the inner, emotive, and personal aspects of hermeneutics and by a forceful restructuring of external behavioural patterns within the group. Life, in that sense, and not merely the

---

[398] *Introductio in Theologiam*, bk. 1, c. 11, PL 178.995D-997A.

words describing it, became a text, which was commented upon, discussed with oneself, and compared to established norms. In one sense, Bernard's spirituality was very old, as those searching for his Greek or Latin roots have taken pains to point out. There are no unusual sources; there are few if any innovative doctrines. But the size and nature of the literate community before which he preached his sermons irrevocably altered the context of his message. *Litterati* and *illitterati* (i.e., *conversi*) were bound together in a single historic and sacramental experiment.

The contrast in approaches between Abelard and St. Bernard was put rather bluntly in the nineteen *capitula* of Bernard and the thirteen of William of St. Thierry which were condemned as Abelard's teaching at Sens in 1140.[399] Of course these lists of alleged errors presented Abelard's theology only imperfectly. Yet, whatever their limitations for an objective assessment of his thought, they provide an accurate picture of how he was viewed by his intellectual adversaries. Not surprisingly, there are numerous connections with themes discussed earlier in this volume.

On the one hand, Abelard is accused of believing in physical symbolism. He is said to propose that the devil's "suggestions" to man come about *per physicam* (W 10), that is, "through the application of stones or herbs" (B 15). On the other, Abelard is said to withdraw the physical element from the trinity, the sacraments, and in particular from penance. Hence, his names for the triune God are *impropria* (W 2). He claims that the holy spirit does not arise "from the substance" of the father and son, nor the son from the father (B 2, W 4); and that Christ did not assume flesh merely to liberate us from the devil's mundane bondage (*a jugo diaboli*, B 4, *a jure diaboli*, W 7). The bread and wine on the altar are not wholly transformed: "the sacrament," he is said to assert, "remains in the air through the form of the previously existing substance" (W 9).

Alleged to have rejected realism, Abelard is therefore painted as an overly clever exegete, who continually seeks a rational, internal sense

---

[399] I have used the convenient summary of E. Little, "Bernard and Abelard at the Council of Sens, 1140," in *Bernard of Clairvaux. Studies Presented to Dom Jean Leclercq* (Washington, D.C., 1973), 55-71. The most recent edition is that of N. Häring, "Die Vierzehn Capitula Heresum Petri Abaelardi," *Cîteaux* 1 (1980), 35-52. The abbreviations below refer to William's (W) and Bernard's (B) lists. As my purpose is prefatory, no attempt is made to assess the degree to which the *capitula* actually discuss Abelard's teaching; on this issue, see the thorough treatment of Luscombe, *The School*, 115-42. Dom Leclercq notes ("Les formes", p. 105): "De qui sont ces capitula? On a suggéré les attribuer aux rédacteurs de Clairvaux. Il semble plus vraisemblable qu'ils soient l'oeuvre du Concile de Sens."

for religious mysteries best left uninterpreted. He is said to argue that the father is "full potential," the son "some," and the holy spirit "none" (B 1, W 3). The third person of the trinity is not the God and man who is Christ (B 5, W 8), but rather Plato's "world-soul" (W 5). In his opponents' view, Abelard granted God omnipotence, but then restricted his activity to the boundaries of dialectic. His God does not simply do what he wishes but acts in accordance with law, effecting change only at prearranged times and places (B 7). And, although all-knowing, he is not automatically "wise" and "benign" (B 13). Religion, too, in his logical reconstruction, is purged of its affective qualities. In Christ there is no "spirit of fear" (B 10) and in the future life there will not exist "even chaste fear" (B 14). Further, as God obeys laws, he provides no answer to theodicy: "he neither should nor can prevent evil" (B 17). Also, the power of binding and of loosing was given to the apostles but not to their successors (B 11). Above all, Abelard is accused of holding to the inner nature of all true religious experience. Faith is "the estimation of things unseen" (W 1). We did not inherit "guilt" from Adam but only "punishment" (B 8, W 11). By implication, the Jews were not responsible for Christ's death, "since what is committed in ignorance is not ascribable to guilt" (B 9). The precondition of sin is consciousness, for "from free choice without grace's aid we can both will and act" (W 6, B 6). Merely physical frailties like sensual desire do not represent "sin" but only "nature" (W 13). For there is no genuine culpability where there is "accord in sin" and "contempt for God" (W 12).

Abelard's theology is thus portrayed at once as crude, and, in terms of true faith, illiterate, yet, at the same time, as a heresy of grammar, logic, and textual manipulation. In that sense he is pictured for polemical purposes as a "scholastic," in implied contrast to a thinker like Bernard.

In reality, both authors are byproducts of textual culture, although in different ways. To return to our earlier analogy: if, for Abelard, the text is dispositive, for Bernard it is largely evidential. Although Abelard wrote much about the nature of language, and, although he held traditional views on most doctrinal issues, his ultimate aim was to explain how we understand objective reality. Whether a question was "philosophical" or "theological" did not matter as much as what was, in his view, a reasonable solution. In Bernard's case, as we shall see, just the opposite was true. Fact, as he saw it, was already established by the Bible and the fathers. The problem was its reassimilation back into the meditating subject's mind. In his mysticism the new text did not supplement the old, text to text: meaning, as noted, was the byproduct of religious, psychological, and hermeneutic experience. The purpose of studying Scripture was not to advance external knowledge but to try to reintegrate oneself into a previous state of spiritual awareness. In his view, the monastic community was a group of such textually informed individuals.

Bernard achieved his results by recreating in mystical language a sense of the spoken, the physical, and the performed to which this study has frequently alluded. In that sense, his sermons can be described as the acting out of an intensely personalized ritual. But Bernard also brought to perfection oral techniques utilized by earlier monastic authors. To understand them, Dom Leclercq reminds us, one must recall the meaning of "reading" and "meditation" in St. Benedict himself. For, during the Middle Ages, monks usually read "not as today, principally with the eyes, but the lips, pronouncing what they saw, and with the ears, listening to the words pronounced, hearing what is called 'the voices of the pages.' " In this "acoustical reading,"[400] *legere* had the sense of *cogitare* or *considerare*; that is, one thought about the text as one read it aloud. In the monastic environment texts also influenced "the practical or even moral order."[401] The strong psychological relationship between the reader and the textual experience produced an aural as well as visual record of what was heard. Therefore, *meditatio*, as an exercise in memorization, was inseparable from *lectio*.[402] Above all, monastic reading did not proceed by abstraction. It permitted the brethren "to picture, to 'make present,' to see things with all the details provided by the texts: the colours

---

[400] *The Love of Learning and the Desire for God*, trans. C. Misrahi (New York, 1961), 23-24. Cf. J. Rousse, "Lectio divina et lecture spirituelle," *Dictionnaire de spiritualité*, vol. 9, 481-87. A simple list of authors is provided by J. Mattoso, "A 'lectio divina' nos autores monásticos da alta Idade Média," *Studia Monastica* 9 (1967), 167-87; for a full review of the subject, see Fr. Vandenbrouke, "La lectio divina du 11e au 14e siècle," *ibid.*, 8 (1966), 267-93. On the continuity with ancient reading practices, see J. Balogh, " 'Voces Paginarum'. . . ," *Philologus* 82 (1927), 84-109, 202-40, and G. L. Hendrickson, "Ancient Reading," *The Classical Journal* 25 (1929), 182-96. On the role of the word of God, see the important study of D. Farkasfalvy, *L'inspiration de l'Ecriture sainte dans la théologie de saint Bernard* (Rome, 1964), 27-41. On Bernard's style of biblical quotation in the *Sermones super Cantica*, see J. Leclercq, "S. Bernard et la tradition biblique d'après les Sermons sur les Cantiques," *Sacris Erudiri* 11 (1960), 225-48.

[401] Leclercq, *The Love of Learning*, 25.

[402] *Ibid.*, 78. Cf. St. Bernard, *In Dedicatione Ecclesiae, sermo* 5.5, *S. Bernardi Opera*, ed. J. Leclercq, C. H. Talbot, and H. M. Rochais (Rome, 1968), vol. 5, p. 391, 10-13. All quotations will be taken from this edition and cited by volume, page, and line.

and dimensions of things, the clothing, bearing and actions of the people. . . ."[403]

In other words, as the monastic "reader" engaged his mind and his senses, he rehearsed, revivified, and ultimately relived the experience which created the initial mystical state. Sacred and profane *scientiae* might provide aids to understanding, but the grasping of the inner meaning depended largely on his ability to come to grips with what was before him on the page. The interaction took place between the text, his self, and his faith.

Bernard's intentions are confirmed by what we know of his manner of composition, delivery, and publication. Like many twelfth-century preachers, he did not circulate precisely what he said.[404] His sermons were both oral and rhetorical performances, but on different occasions. In the fifty-fourth of his *Sermones super Cantica*, which were written between 1135 and 1153,[405] he made one of his rare statements on the matter. As his text, he noted, was the same as on the previous day, there was no need for him to repeat himself. The message could not have been forgotten in so short a time. Even if it were, recovery would be easy, since his words, as was his habit, were written down (*scripta*) as they were spoken (*dicta*), that is, recorded by pen (*excepta stylo*).[406] Elsewhere, he indicated that the different stages of literary production were themselves independent. In one letter he spoke of three phases, composition (*dictare*), transcription (*transcribi*), and publication (*edidi*).[407] In another, he mentioned oral presentation in small groups (*conferre*), writing out (*scribere*), revisions for correction (*recogitare, corrigere*), and the putting out of an anthology (*legendum praebere*).[408] These rough indicators of his methods of composition are confirmed by his contemporaries, who often served as his notaries, collectors, or imitators, and may be summed up as follows: a purely verbal delivery; transcription, usually by other hands; revision and editing by himself;

---

[403] Leclercq, *The Love of Learning*, 81. These qualities are not without rapport with tribal religion; see P. Ryan, "St. Bernard and the Barundi on the Name of God," *Bernard of Clairvaux*, 203-14.

[404] Leclercq, "Saint Bernard et ses secrétaires," *Recueil* 1, pp. 3-4.

[405] *Sermones super Cantica* 1, xv. On the *terminus a quo* see J. Leclercq, "La date du 1er sermon sur le Cantique des cantiques," *Saint Bernard mystique* (Paris, 1948), 480-83.

[406] *Sermo* 54.1.1, vol. 2, 102, 12-15: "Non est opus superiora repetere, quae excidisse non arbitror in tam brevi. Si quominus tamen, scripta sunt ut dicta sunt, et excepta stylo, sicut et sermones ceteri, ut facile recuperetur quot forte exciderit." Cf. Leclercq, 7.

[407] *Ep.* 153, *S. Bernardi Opera*, vol. 7 (1974), 360 (= PL 182. 313A-B). Cf. Leclercq, "Saint Bernard et ses secrétaires," 8.

[408] Leclercq, *ibid.*, 11.

and, very frequently, correction before circulation.[409] Once published, of course, the *Sermons* were looked upon as a text (*opus, expositio*).[410] Three major redactions developed, each with its own zone of influence.[411] But his sermons never completely lost touch with the spoken milieu in which they were conceived and delivered.[412]

The following discussion is devoted exclusively to Bernard's *Sermones super Cantica*.[413] The analysis does not deal with the internal ordering of the Cistercian communities, which, it is arguable, they influenced, but rather to elements of Bernard's thought and expression which helped to make it possible. In that sense, the question of "textual communities" is taken in a different direction, that is, one which focuses on a body of texts themselves. By way of introduction, the first sermon is examined in detail. Its images and ideas can then act as a reference point for investigating the topics to which Bernard subsequently turns his attention.

Super Cantica, Sermo 1

The sermon is devoted to the title of the Song of Songs. Before its meaning is discussed, its contents may be summarized as follows.[414]

Monks, Bernard states, require other nourishment than those living in the world, and their instruction must be given in a different manner. Paul said that ordinary souls should be given "milk, not meat."[415] But elsewhere he noted, "We speak not in the teachings of human wisdom but in the doctrine of the spirit, comparing spiritual things with spiritual."[416] And he added, "We speak wisdom among the per-

---

[409] *Ibid.*, 23-24. Cf. P. Rassow, "Die Kanzlei St. Bernhards von Clairvaux," *Studien und Mitteilungen zur Geschichte des Benediktiner-Ordens* 34 (1913), 67-69.

[410] Leclercq, "Les étapes . . . ," 214.

[411] *Ibid.*, 216-17.

[412] J. Leclercq, "Les Sermons sur les Cantiques ont-ils été prononcés?" *Recueil* 1, 193-212. On stylistic questions in general, see J. Leclercq, "Saint Bernard écrivain," *Recueil* 1, 321-51 and "Aspects littéraires de l'oeuvre de saint Bernard," *Recueil* 3 (1969), 13-104. The case of Bernard's letters is equally complex; see Leclercq, "Lettres de S. Bernard: histoire ou littérature," *Studi medievali* 12 (1971), 1-74. On Bernard's Latin, see C. Mohrmann, "Observations sur la langue et le style de saint Bernard," in *Sermones super Cantica*, vol. 2 (1958), ix-xxxiii. Bernard's style is treated more generally by E. Paratore, "San Bernardo scrittore," *Studi su San Bernardo*, 261-79 and by E. Auerbach, *Literary Language and its Public*, 70-78.

[413] The following supersedes my earlier essay, "Experience, Praxis, Work and Planning in Bernard of Clairvaux: Observations on the *Sermones in Cantica*," in J. E. Murdoch and E. D. Sylla, eds., *The Cultural Context of Medieval Learning* (Dordrecht, 1975), 219-68.

[414] *Super Cantica, Sermo* 1, vol. 1, pp. 3-8.

[415] 1 Cor 3.1-2; Hebr 5.12-14.   [416] 1 Cor 2.13.

fects."[417] So it is for his brethren: they have long busied themselves with celestial matters, that is, with God's law. Now they may open their mouths to receive not milk but the bread of Solomon, that is, the message of the Song.

Ecclesiastes has taught them, he continues, to know and to despise this world's vanity, as has Proverbs. Have their lives and conduct not been informed with those doctrines? As Luke suggests, their "friend" has three loaves in his cupboard, of which they have tried two.[418] May they not now try the third? To the two above-mentioned books of the Old Testament corresponded two evils, namely, worldly vanity and excess. The one text improved our morals, the other discovered through reason the difference between vanity and truth, putting the fear of God and the observance of his rules before mundane interests. For fear is the beginning of wisdom, observance its consummation: the only true wisdom consists of avoiding evil and doing good, and no good work is possible without obeying commandments. Having thus rid themselves of worldly excess, the monks can turn to such a sacred, theoretical discourse, a text which is, as suggested, the fruit of the other two. Indeed, this "sacred reading" could not have been undertaken before the flesh was subdued and the world's vanities spurned. The blind man cannot see light; "the animal man does not perceive what is of the spirit of God."[419]

But who will break this third loaf? For, it is written, "Know the Lord in the breaking of the bread."[420] Not I, says Bernard: his brethren must "look upon" him as if to "look for" nothing from him. He himself begs for enlightenment into the Song's mysteries. He asks God to "break the bread" by his own power, if through his hands. Moreover, speaking of interpretation, he asks, of whom and to whom is it said, "Let him kiss me with the kiss of his mouth?"[421] Why this interjection at the outset? For the words are spoken as if in reply to another person. Further, why a kiss "of his mouth"? It is, after all, a charming way to begin, to entice the reader, and to lure him towards the text's hidden senses. In short, one is immediately struck, as Bernard puts it, by this "beginning without a beginning," which provides clear evidence that the work was not of human but divine inspiration.

The title too has its own meaning. In Hebrew, Solomon signifies peace. The canticle begins with a kiss, a token of peace; and only

[417] I Cor 2:6.
[418] Lc 11:5.   [419] I Cor 2:14.   [420] Lc 24:35.   [421] Cant 1:1.

those who have found peace after worldly cares have been put aside can truly understand the text. There is another "song" in the Bible which has the same meaning, that is, when Israel sang of freedom after escaping from bondage in Egypt. Judith, of course, Samuel's mother, and several of the prophets are also spoken of as "singing." Yet, such hymns all had special motives, whereas Solomon was in need of no earthly benefit which would have compelled him to compose the Song. It is a unique piece of writing, celebrating as it does the marriage of Christ and the church,[422] thereby embodying the sacred soul's desire in figurative language. No less than Moses on Sinai, Solomon veils his true countenance.

Bernard then returns to his brethren. If they re-examine their own experience, have they not too sung a "new canticle" for the Lord? He delivered them from the twin evils of worldly vanity and lack of discipline. When their penance obtained from him not merely pardon for sins but the promise of future reward, did they not sing his praises even more enthusiastically than before? For, if on occasion an obscure biblical text suddenly became rife with meaning, was it not their duty to charm God's ears in thanks for the alms bestowed?

One need not wait for such notable events. In the trials and combats of everyday life, the monks sing their gratitude for small victories—a temptation overcome, a vice eradicated, a passion quashed, or a virtue finally achieved. In all such cases we trumpet our praise, lest, on the final day, we cannot say, "Your justifications were the subject of my song in the place of my pilgrimage."[423] Bernard adds that his brethren already recognize from experience what the psalter calls not the song of songs but the song of steps. For, with every stage of the ascent towards perfection a particular canticle of praise and glory must be sung, as Scripture teaches.

But the Song of Songs surpasses all other sacred melodies. It can only be taught by grace and learned by experience. The experienced know it: others burn with desire, not so much for knowing as for feeling, since the Song is not a noise of the mouth but a jubilation of the heart; not a sound of the lips but a motivation towards joy; in short, a harmony not of words but of wills. It cannot be heard outside: only the singer and He to whom it is sung, that is, the bridegroom and the bride, can actually hear it, as is fitting for an epithalamium. Above all it cannot be heard or sung by weak and imperfect souls.

[422] For an exploration of this theme, see Y. Congar, "L'ecclésiologie de S. Bernard," *Saint Bernard théologien*, 136-90.

[423] Ps 118:54.

One must be well on one's way to maturity, "marriage," and mystical experience.

Let us now look a little more closely at the sermon's themes and modes of expression.

Its point of departure is two interrelated types of comparison. One is between the secular and the spiritual. The other is within grades of spiritual ascent. As the monks, who have left the secular routine, engage in spiritual activities, their sustenance becomes "more solid." Paradoxically, therefore, their spirituality is highlighted by the physical.

As they are *perfecti* in Paul's terms,[424] so they must be given not "milk" but "meat," that is, spiritual flesh which, we learn a sentence later, is really sacramental "bread." Bernard plays on the monks' otherness: they require "other things"; those living in the world are "the others." But, most of all, they require a different mode of communication (*aut certe aliter dicenda sunt*). And the otherness thus inspired influences not principally doctrine but a way of life. Paul holds up the model by his instruction (*formam tenet in docendo*); he teaches by example (*docet exemplo*). The text in Bernard's view plays a fundamental role in leading their minds upwards. They have long been *caelestibus occupati*, meditating day and night *in lege Dei*. Now their "mouths are open"; they hunger after the Song's "bread."

The concrete images are drawn from the Bible, the fathers, and, very possibly, the agrarian life itself. But the spiritual nature of the undertaking is also emphasized by the physicality of the milk, the meat, and the bread. As the otherworldly end becomes more evident, the tangibility of the imagery is more pronounced. The text itself is a symbol of what is performed in the sacraments: the book of the Song is "proferred"; its bread is "broken." And, for Bernard, the new text, the commentary, will undoubtedly retain some of the sensual attraction of the old.

From stages of spirituality he then turns to states of self-knowledge. There are three books and three loaves. Ecclesiastes teaches the monks to know and to condemn (*cognoscere et contemnere*) the world's vanity; Proverbs, how to regulate their lives and morals (*vita et mores*). But the knowledge to which he refers a few lines later is not simply a doctrinal message. Although it involves dogma, it works chiefly through the experience of the text and the retransformation of its principles

[424] On the Pauline element in St. Bernard's thought, one has only the outdated study of G. Frischmut, *Die paulinische Konzeption in der Frömmigkeit Bernhards von Clairvaux* (Gütersloh, 1933).

into action. In this way behaviour is both improved and reformed (*emendati et informati*), the latter term effectively combining both instruction and contemplation. The question of interpretation is not mentioned directly, but it obviously lies just beneath the surface. For both books are too large to be absorbed wholly as guides for conduct in the sense that Bernard suggests. Excerpts must be made and rules put in order. Thus, while Scripture is understood literally, the texts are not assimilated as they are: they too are subject to experience.

Also, once again the material and the spiritual are played upon. Ecclesiastes utilizes "the hoe of discipline." Proverbs is handled more subtly: by reason's light (*luce rationis*) it distinguishes worldly vanity from truth's solidity (*veraciterque distinguens a solido veritatis*). Sacramental bread and physicality are thus linked to inner truth, and the pair of Old Testament books are made steps in moral reform. Proverbs, he adds, teaches fear of God and obedience to his commandments. The one, as Psalms notes, is wisdom's beginning; the other, Bernard affirms, is its fulfilment. For wisdom, in his view, is not merely a static virtue: it actively avoids evil and practices good (*declinare a malo et facere bonum*). Here, too, Bernard's starting point is the text. For, without fearing God, we cannot avoid evil; and, without observing his commandments, we can do no good work. He thereby begins to build a case for linking textuality and innerworldliness.

The two books, then, lead to the third as stages of personal, mystical ascent. Having passed through their steps in reform, one can approach the threshold of the *sacer theoricusque sermo*,[425] which is the fruit of both. This is reserved not only for the sober "in mind" but

---

[425] Bernard's ideal of contemplation has been discussed by commentators from a number of points of view. On the Greek element, see the essays of J. Daniélou and J.-M. Déchanet in *Saint Bernard théologien* as well as the earlier investigation of J. Ries, "Die Kontemplationsarten nach der Lehre des hl. Bernhard," *Jahrbuch für Philosophie* . . . 23 (1909), 150-78 and the same author's *Das geistliche Leben in seinen Entwicklungsstufen nach der Lehre des hl. Bernhard* (Freiburg-im-Breisgau, 1906). An early phenomenological approach was J. Schuck, *Das religiöse Erlebnis beim hl. Bernhard von Clairvaux. Ein Beitrag zur Geschichte der christlichen Gotteserfahrung* (Würzburg, 1922), 58-102. E. Gilson's *La théologie mystique de saint Bernard* was the subject of a critique by A. d'Alès, "Le mysticisme de saint Bernard," *Recherches des sciences religieuses* 25 (1935), 364-84 (attempting to reassert the interesting but confused views of P. Rousselot). For an interpretation which stresses the different functions of mysticism, see my own essay in J. Murdoch and E. Sylla, eds., *The Cultural Context of Medieval Learning*, and two essays by J. Sommerfeldt, "The Epistemological Value of Mysticism in the Thought of Bernard of Clairvaux," *Studies in Medieval Culture* 1 (1964), 48-58, and "Charismatic and Gregorian Leadership in the Thought of Bernard of Clairvaux," *Bernard of Clairvaux*, 73-90; cf. E. Kennan, "Antithesis and Argument in the *De Consideratione*," *ibid.*, 91-109. Mention should also be made of the studies of P. Delfgaauw and E. von Ivánka in *Saint Bernard théologien* and the useful introduction of R. Linhardt, *Die Mystik des hl. Bernhard von Clairvaux* (Munich, 1923), 25-79.

also "in ears." Yet the oral and textual experiences are intermingled. The mystical reading of the Song is a *sancta lectio*, which cannot be undertaken before the spirit has subdued the flesh. And, as this higher state of awareness is approached, Bernard's imagery becomes characteristically more concrete. The blind eye cannot see; the *animalis homo* cannot perceive inner realities. The world's wisdom is therefore foolishness before God. His is the *veritatis . . . spiritus*; but He is also the paterfamilias who literally breaks the bread at the human family's meal.

He is therefore distant and objective, and yet near and experienced subjectively. For Bernard, the images imply authority and social cohesiveness as well as the legitimate basis for restructuring the personal moral life. At the same time, the biblical father is portrayed as the ultimate source of interpretation for the Song's message. Although, as later sermons illustrate, Bernard is the active subject of the mystical experience, he avoids the responsibility for the subjective aspects of hermeneutics. He does not shift the weight of decision-making to his shoulders. Instead, he stands aloof, and, while striving after truth, remains a passive receptacle of God's forces. He is a *mediator* and a *viator* between the Word and his brethren, whose group experience he embodies as the Song's "bread" is broken. He sums up his position in an apt contrast between the external and the internal, stating that, if his brethren look to him (*spectetis*), they can look for nothing from him (*non exspectetis*). For he too is one who waits in anticipation (*unus sum de exspectantibus*). Spiritually undernourished, he implores Him "who opens the door and closes it to no one" for this textual bread, this *profundissimum sacramentum*. What he wants is the verbal bond implied in the Song, and he thus unites the physical, the sacramental, and the text.

The image through which he combines the physical and the spiritual is the kiss, to which he next turns. The kiss confirms that his mystical experience begins with the sensual. And, from what the text suggests to the senses, one then proceeds to higher understanding.[426] The "face of the text" entices one to read further, lures one to investigate the hidden meaning. The task does not tire when the text's sweetness so charms.[427]

Bernard's interpretation of the Song's opening verses maintains this

[426] For a discussion, see D. Farkasfalvy, *L'inspiration de l'Ecriture*, 31-32.

[427] *Sermo* 1.3.5, p. 5, 11-15: "Et quidem iucundum eloquium, quod ab osculo principium sumit, et blanda ipsa quaedam Scripturae facies facile afficit et allicit ad legendum, ita ut quod in ea latet delectet etiam cum labore investigare, ne fatiget inquirendi forte difficultas, ut eloquii suavitas mulcet."

parallel by relating the physical and the oral, and the spiritual and the written. The Song, he recognizes, is a dialogue. For the words burst forth (*verba prorumpit*) as if there had been a previous speaker (*quempiam loquentem*), to whom the other participant is presented as if replying (*respondentem*). But why, he asks, does this woman ask expressly and explicitly (*signanter et nominatim*) for a kiss on the mouth? Further, why by "his own mouth," as if it were a habit?

Who, he continues, could resist this "beginning without a beginning," this novelty within the discourse of an old book (*novitas in veteri libro locutionis*)? It is proof, in Bernard's view, that the work (*opus*) is not of human invention (*humano ingenio*) but was composed by the spirit's craft (*spiritus arte ita compositum*). In other words, we have a text (*scriptura, librum, opus,* etc.), which actually speaks (*sermo, verba, eloquium, locutio,* etc.). Moreover, Solomon, as noted, means *signum pacis*: we thus move from the kiss's tactile aspects to the name as a sign and thence to genuine interpretation, which, he adds, is the prerogative of minds at peace (*ad hanc intelligendas scriptam mentes invitari pacificas*). Having reached the plane of mystical interpretation, Bernard then makes it clear that this is a unique song, that is, pure spirit or word. Solomon celebrates Christ and the church, the grace of holy love, and the sacrament of eternal nuptials. But he also expresses the desire of the "sacred soul," and, exulting in the spirit, composed the epithalamium in "sweet but figurative terms" (*iucundo . . . figurato tamen*). Like Moses, "he veils his face." So this text, whose textuality so sensitizes Bernard, has its ultimate mystery in the Word.

He asks the other monks to participate with him, to consult their own "experience." For, have they not sung "a new song"? Has their faith not "overcome the world"? Has He not worked miracles before them? Thus, the new canticle, the hymn to God, becomes identified with conversion of the spirit and reformed conduct.

The experience of the text, in fact, becomes a ritual involving the individual interpreter, the larger group, and the written. On the one hand, new songs are composed, Bernard states, whenever penance obtains not only remission of sins but promise of reward. The "song" completes the rituals of life's fulfilment. But that is not the only use. If, Bernard adds, for any among his brethren, a mysterious or obscure text suddenly becomes luminous with meaning, surely it is their duty to charm God's ears "with the voice of joy and peace, the sound of feasting." Even in the everyday battles with the flesh, the world, and the devil, we are obliged to sing daily songs for victories. As often as this happens, Isaiah teaches, should resound the *actio et vox laudis*. The "song," then, which results from experiencing the Song, is a more profound form of a quotidian dramaturgy rather than the examination of a text in isolation from monastic life itself.

Bernard therefore describes the activity as "recognition" (*recognoscere*). It is a *cantica graduum*: for every step upwards a canticle must be sung in praise of Him who is the source of their advance. The sermon ends with a remarkably concise summary of Bernard's views on ritual, experience, and self-knowledge. The Song can only be taught by anointing (*sola unctio*); it can only be learned by experience (*sola . . . experientia*).[428] The experienced, as noted, "recognize" it, the inexperienced "burn with desire," not so much for knowing as for experiencing (*Experti recognoscant, inexperti inardescant desiderio, non tam cognoscendi quam experiendi*). So the Song, which is the Word, is not merely words; that is, not the *strepitus oris* but the *iubilus cordis*. And this word, which is perceived as a text, is not heard outside (*non auditur foris*) nor sounded out in public (*nec . . . in publico personat*). Only he who sings it can hear it and she to whom it is sung, that is, the groom and the bride. As the text internalizes the word, mere sound is ritually transformed into inner thought. And thus reform is brought about.

Word, Text, and Experience

The texts quoted in the first sermon are commonplaces of monastic thought, but the manner in which they are brought together gives them new meaning. They are in fact united by Bernard's style of expression, which, in turn, is a reflection of his inner emotions and states of mind.

His exploration of relations between word, text, and experience is

---

[428] Bernard's emphasis on experience has been discussed by a number of commentators. See above all J. Mouroux, "Sur les critères de l'expérience spirituelle d'après les sermons sur le Cantique des cantiques," *Saint Bernard théologien*, 253-67; also, M. Standaert, "La spiritualité de saint Bernard," *S. Bernardo . . .*, 46-48 and E. Wellers, "Saint Bernard mystique et docteur de la mystique," *ibid.*, 67-70. Guerric d'Igny, who heard Bernard preach, speaks of initiation into Scripture as attaining the *limen scientiae; In Natali Apostolorum Petri et Pauli, sermo* 3.1, PL 185.183D. An explicit statement of Bernard's principles was made by William of St. Thierry, *Tractatus de Natura et Dignitate Amoris* 10.31, PL 184.399A-B, ably translated and discussed by M. Dumontier, *Saint Bernard et la Bible* (Paris, 1953), 91-98; cf., more generally, J. Hourlier, "S. Bernard et Guillaume de Saint-Thierry dans le 'Liber de Amore,' " *Saint Bernard théologien*, 223-33. For a full recent analysis of Bernard's "experience" of Scripture, see D. Farkasfalvy, *L'inspiration de l'Ecriture* chs. 2-3, pp. 42-91.

continued in subsequent sermons on the Song of Songs, to which we now direct our attention.

In sermon two, the sensing, thinking, and interpreting subject emerges more clearly. Bernard confesses: "Whenever I reflect on the yearning and ardent desire of the fathers for Christ's presence in the flesh, I am filled with grief and confusion."[429] There are two sets of physicalities and two yearnings. On the one hand, he speaks of the historical Christ, that is, of *Christus in carne*. On the other, we, as readers, feel, as did his monastic brethren, that same presence as active subjects (*cogitans, compungor, confundor*). The contrast is not only between the ancients and the moderns, that is, between the undiluted faith of the patristic age and the spiritual tepidness of his own "miserable times." It is also between the monks' desires and his own. Is there any among us, he asks, for whom Christ's display (*exhibitio*) of grace excites the same passionate promise (*promissio*) as it did for them? Although we rejoice in Christ's birth, how many really understand its meaning?[430]

The past and present expectations are then related to the first verse of the Song, "Let him kiss me with the kiss of his mouth." At these words, Bernard states, he feels some of the fathers' *desiderium* and *exspectatio*. Whoever was "spiritual" at that time sensed that grace would be dispensed "from his lips."[431] This train of thought brings him back once again to the physical and the verbal, to which he now adds ritual. For the fathers longed not to be deprived of participation (*participatio*) in such sweetness. A *perfectus*, he notes, of those days might have said, "Why do you offer me those babbling lips of the prophets?" The older spokesmen on God's behalf, such as Moses, Isaiah, and Jeremiah, were all tongueless (*elingues*). Their utterances contained no promises of salvation. But, he adds in a frenzy of mystical desire, "Let him, let him alone, of whom they speak, put forth his words, let him kiss me with the kiss of his mouth." He wants no interpreters between himself and that tangible presence: "No longer in them or through them, let him speak to me." The mouth is both the source of a personal embrace and the means by which Christ's grace becomes a living fountain in him (*fons aquae salientis in vitam aeternam*). The immersion in the word via the text is a sensuous ritual, a paraliturgical experience, of which he remarks: "Surely I may expect a more abundant outpouring of graces from him whom the father 'has

---

[429] *Sermo* 2.1.1, p. 8, 20-22: Ardorem desiderii patrum suspirantium Christi in carne praesentiam frequentissime cogitans, compungor et confundor in memetipso.

[430] *Ibid.*, p. 8, 23-p. 9, 1.   [431] *Ibid.*, 8, 3-4; Ps 44.3.

anointed with the oil of gladness above his fellows,'⁴³² if only he will
condescend to kiss me with the kiss of his mouth." For, he repeats,
the kiss is not just a "coming together of the lips"; it is also a *sermo
vivus et efficax*.

For Bernard, then, the physical, via the text, is apprehended tan-
gibly, but, at the same time, it represents a divine reality. He is not
so much an "interpreter" as a delver into sacramental meaning, since
his point of departure is the thing, real or imagined, rather than the
words alone. He seeks both a *revelatio secretorum* and "a marvellous,
and, in a sense, inextricable mingling of light from above and from
within the enlightened soul." In this, he adds, "He that adheres to
the Lord is one spirit with him."⁴³³ Purely intellectual understanding
therefore is put aside. Bernard rejects *visiones et somnia, figurae et enig-
mata*, even when they convey an angelic beauty. For these images all
fall short of Christ's perfection. And, it is He, not angel or man,
whom Bernard asks to kiss him with the kiss of his mouth.⁴³⁴

Variations on the theme of word and text are pursued in sermons
three and four, in which Bernard turns to the significance of the three
kisses.

In sermon three he begins with a direct appeal. Today, he says, we
are reading in the book of experience (*Hodie legimus in libro experientiae*).
He asks the monks to turn towards themselves and to examine their
consciences concerning what should be said (*quae dicenda sunt*). He
wishes to ask whether any of them has reached the point of stating as
a *sententia*, "Let him kiss me with the kiss of his mouth."

For, in his view, this progress from word to text must come from
within (*ex affectu*). The awareness of its inner truth arises in turn from
repeated experience: he who has once received it seeks after it again
and again. And "no one can know it who has not undergone it." Like
the eucharistic bread, therefore, it is "hidden manna." It is a "sealed
fountain" in which "the stranger has no part."⁴³⁵ In this sense, the
three kisses—that of the feet, the hands, and the mouth—represent
the soul's progress (*animae profectus*). By the first, in Bernard's terms,
we consecrate the initial stages of our conversion. The second is granted
to those making steady progress. But only a "rare perfection" of the
spirit experiences the third, and this state alone pertains to the Song.⁴³⁶

The first two kisses are present only to make the last's meaning

⁴³² Io 4:14; Ps 44:8.
⁴³³ 1 Cor 6:17. ⁴³⁴ *Ibid.*, 2.1.2, p. 9, 7-25. ⁴³⁵ *Sermo* 3.1.1, p. 14, 7-19.
⁴³⁶ *Sermo* 4.1.1, p. 18, 9-11: "In primo sane primordia dedicantur nostrae conversionis, secundum autem proficientibus indulgetur, porro tertium sola experietur et rara perfectio."

clear. For, Bernard argues, there must be some distinction among the metaphorical embraces. The female partner in the Song did not say, "Let him kiss me," but, "Let him kiss me with the kiss of his mouth," obviously going beyond custom and ordinary usage (*praeter morem . . . usumque loquendi*). Bernard reasons that she meant a kiss that was supreme (*summum*) but not unique (*solum*). In normal usage, he adds, the expressions "kiss me" or "give me a kiss" are frequent. No one affixes "with your mouth" or "with the kiss of your mouth." Why? Because a kiss normally requires that lips meet: there is no need to mention it. Scripture, moreover, furnishes numerous examples of this sort of embrace, which is the custom of all who write or speak (*Omnis qui scribit et qui loquitur consuevit*). Therefore, there must be a deeper meaning for the phrase, which cannot refer to anything but the three states (*affectus*) or stages of progress (*profectus*) of the soul. These are fully known only to those who have experienced them (*experti*).[437]

If Anselm saw special languages as grammatically perfect versions of ordinary speech, Bernard sees the same distinction between customary and mystical meaning in the Bible. These considerations bring him to the related problem of the word, creation, and understanding, to which he turns in sermons four, five, and six.

In sermon four, Bernard quotes John 4:24 (*Spiritus est Deus*) as witness that God is a unified substance (*simplex substantia*), lacking corporeal members. One does not literally "kiss" his feet, hands, and mouth. For God, he argues, is said to possess members through effect, not nature (*per effectum, non per naturam*). We find in him something resembling feet, before which we kneel; hands, by which our strength is renewed; and a mouth, which offers pleasant food for thought (*iucunda contemplatio*). Paradoxically, "he who governs is all things to all and yet is properly not any of them." For, as Scripture frequently tells us, he is never far away from his creatures, who are nothing without him. Yet, if there is nothing "more present" for us, there is as well nothing "more incomprehensible." As Paul says, "All things exist from him, through him, and in him." In this sense, God is the being of all he has made, not materially but causally. He has no need of the corporeal, since he created everything by his word alone (*solo verbo*). Using only his will, he derives what is necessary for creating and ordering.[438]

The emphasis on God's absolute power recalls the eucharistic theory of Radbert. But what is the place of the text and of physical reality,

[437] *Ibid.*, p. 18, 11-p. 19, 5.
[438] *Sermo* 4.3.4, p. 19, 26-p. 20, 21.

to which Bernard above referred as the starting point of all higher understanding? He turns to this question in sermon five, arguing that there are four kinds of spirits, those of animals, our own, the angelic, and the being which created the others (*pecoris, noster, angelicus, et qui condidit istos*).[439] Of these, only God can truly do without some corporality; the others are all involved with bodies to some degree. Paul, he recalls, said, "The invisible things of God are clearly seen and understood by the things that are made."[440] The latter in Bernard's opinion are *corporalia et visibilia*, which we only come to know through bodily means.[441] The sacramental process therefore begins with what is heard, seen, and touched. Although man is essentially a *spiritualis creatura*, he has need of the body, without which he could not acquire the knowledge (*scientia*) enabling him to ascend to higher understanding (*cognitio beata*).[442] Angels, too, have need of bodies; otherwise, they could not minister to those who live in bodies.[443] Moreover, Bernard asks, without bodies, how could they move from place to place? The angels in fact appeared palpably before the church fathers: they lived with them, ate with them, and had their feet washed.[444] Bernard concludes that both angelic and brute spirits have need of bodies, but to help others rather than themselves,[445] the superior out of love, the inferior out of necessity.[446]

But what benefit does each derive with respect to eternal salvation? The irrational spirit perceives bodies, but it is not led upwards through the senses to spiritual and intelligible realities. Unable to attain such understanding of itself, it aids those who transfer the use of temporal things to the fruition of eternal ones, "using this world, so to speak, as if not using it."[447] Just the opposite is true of the angelic spirit. Without bodily aid or intuition from the senses, it is capable of apprehending what is "highest" and "most intimate" by the "affinity and vitality of its nature alone." Paul, Bernard asserts, clearly intended this sense. For, while he said that the *invisibilia Dei* were comprehensible through *ea quae facta sunt*, he added, "by the creatures of the world," suggesting by implication the opposite for creatures of

---

[439] *Sermo* 5.1.1, p. 21, 9-10.   [440] Rom 1:20.

[441] *Sermo* 5.1.1, p. 21, 20-21: ". . . nonnisi per corporis instrumentum sensa in nostram notitiam veniunt."

[442] *Ibid.*, p. 21, 21-p. 22, 1.   [443] Hebr 1:14.   [444] *Sermo* 5.1.2, p. 22, 9-12.

[445] *Ibid.*, 22, 12-14: "Ita inferior superiorque spiritus propriis corporibus egent, sed tantum quibus iuvent, non etiam iuventur."

[446] *Ibid.*, 5.1.3, p. 22, 22-24: "Ille igitur ut iure serviat, iste ut pie subveniat, ambo procul dubio suis corporibus egent ut iuvent."

[447] *Ibid.*, 22, 24-30; 1 Cor 7.31.

heaven.⁴⁴⁸ This, Bernard maintains, was another way of saying that the angelic spirit needs no bodily aid to perceive objects of contemplation, while the human spirit must approach them slowly and laboriously.⁴⁴⁹ The angelic spirit in fact provides its own text. Why should it seek spiritual matters among the bodily when it can read in "the book of life" without contradiction and understand its message without difficulty?⁴⁵⁰ There is even less need for allegorization. Why should the angel "sweat" to separate the wheat from the chaff, to press wine from grapes, or oil from olives? By this manner of thinking Bernard comes to another conclusion. While lower and higher spirits utilize bodies, neither benefits from them "in acquiring what makes the spiritual creature blessed." The brute is incapable of enlightenment; the celestial spirit has no need of it.⁴⁵¹

What then of man, whom Bernard, in the traditional metaphor, sees as occupying a midpoint between the highest and the lowest?⁴⁵² His spirit needs a body both for his own advancement and for the benefit of others.⁴⁵³ Bernard asks how he could instruct his brethren without a tongue. It follows that every created spirit, and not just man's *rationalis anima*, requires the use of the body, either for others or for itself and others.⁴⁵⁴ Some living things seem to have no human use, but that belief is an illusion. Often, Bernard argues, they perform more beneficial services as objects of reflection than in fulfilling corporeal needs.⁴⁵⁵ Some in fact are harmful, like poisonous plants. But, even if they do not provide food or serve another function, they offer matter for exercising the intelligence (*ingenium exercendo*). For all who use reason (*omni utenti ratione*), they bear witness to Paul's dictum that "the invisible things of God are seen and understood through the things that are made."⁴⁵⁶

Bernard's position is not anti-rational, as his mystical ascent was portrayed by his opponents. He has only led the reader back by another route to the physical element in his theory of signs. He is aware

⁴⁴⁸ On the independence of Bernard's views of angels, see E. Boissard, "La doctrine des anges chez S. Bernard," *Saint Bernard théologien*, 114-35.

⁴⁴⁹ *Sermo*, 5.1.4, p. 23, 1-11.

⁴⁵⁰ *Ibid.*, 23, 11-13: "Cur enim inter corpora spirituales scrutetur sensus, quos in libro vitae et absque contradictione legit, et absque difficultate intelligit?"

⁴⁵¹ *Ibid.*, 23, 13-21.   ⁴⁵² *Ibid.*, 5.1.5, p. 23, 22-23.

⁴⁵³ *Ibid.*, 23, 24: ". . . ut absque eo (corpore) nec ipse proficere, nec alteri prodesse possit."

⁴⁵⁴ *Ibid.*, 5.1.6, p. 23, 28-p. 24, 2.

⁴⁵⁵ *Ibid.*, 24, 2-3: "Prosunt profecto visu, etsi non usu, utiliora cordibus intuentium quam utentium esse corporibus possunt."

⁴⁵⁶ *Ibid.*, 24, 3-9.

that his divisions of sense and spirit involve philosophical difficulties.[457] But he prefers to bypass them, and returns to the means of communication between God, spirit, and man.

No created spirit, he proposes, can of its own accord be applied to our minds in such a way that, lacking intervention on our parts, it "intermingles with us" or "overflows into us," thereby rendering us learned or virtuous. Therefore, higher truths cannot be generated by human or angelic spirits alone.[458] The prerogative is limited to "the highest and uncircumscribed spirit," who can convey knowledge to angel or to man without the use of ears or mouths. "He is infused through himself, he is made known through himself, and, being pure, he is apprehended by pure mind." Although self-sufficient and omnipotent, he nonetheless brings about many operations through his created subject, whether corporeal or spiritual. However, he "orders"; he does not "beg."[459] Bernard takes his own preaching as an example. See, he says to his brethren, how he now instructs you through my corporeal tongue, when doubtless he could inform you directly with greater facility.[460] He employs the human voice, he adds, not as a "need" but as an "indulgence." He thereby advances the monks' interests while advancing his own.[461] And, if God has no real need of men, he has even less use for creatures that lack sense or reason. He takes up lower spirits not for their "efficacy" but their "congruence," since he knows from what causes the most suitable physical results ensue.[462] Such bodies obey him, but he has no need of a body.[463]

That is how things always were, although, before Christ's coming, men were generally ignorant of the fact. Accordingly, sermon six recapitulates earlier religious history as an example for the present.[464]

In Bernard's view, the ancients "experienced" God's benefits, yet their "benefactor was concealed" from them. They lived in ignorance (*nesciebant*): they were from Him but not with Him; they lived by Him but not for Him; they had a taste of Him but not Him Himself. In short, they were *alienati, ingrati, insensati*.[465] They attributed what they were, what gave them life, and what they knew to nature rather

---

[457] *Ibid.*, 5.2.7, p. 24, 14-25.

[458] *Ibid.*, 5.2.8, p. 24, 26-p. 25, 2.   [459] *Ibid.*, 5.3.8-9, p. 25, 3-10.

[460] *Ibid.*, 25, 10-12: "En, verbi gratia, quod linguam meam corporalem assumpsit nunc in opus suum, docere videlicet vos, cum per se absque dubio facilius suaviusque id possit."

[461] *Ibid.*, 25, 13-14.   [462] *Ibid.*, 5.3.10, p. 25, 25-26.   [463] *Ibid.*, 25, 31.

[464] On the action of the Word in history, see B. McGinn, "Saint Bernard and Eschatology," *Bernard of Clairvaux*, 175-85.

[465] *Sermo*, 6.1.2, p. 26, 21-p. 27, 4.

than to their author. Even less intelligently, they often attributed their existence to chance. Many erred, Bernard continues, in ascribing to their own ability what was in fact a gift from above. God's works were credited to evil spirits, the sun, the moon, the earth, and even human artefacts. Grass, trees, and even seeds were worshipped as gods.[466] Thus did men descend even to praying to a "golden calf."[467]

To combat this idolatry, God did not appear as reason. He presented himself physically to those who understood only the corporeal so that they might more easily be led upwards to things of the spirit.[468] For, while appearing as flesh and yet working things not of the flesh, he demonstrated that he was responsible for such contradictions involving "nature," "fortune," or "the devil" even before his coming to earth. Paradoxically, he was, like the sensual message of the Song, both visible and invisible at once. Bernard concludes his brief allegory of man's desertion of pagan superstition with a list of Christ's miracles, pointing out their public character in each case. No less than scholastic theologians, he sees the religions that preceded Christianity as forms of ignorance. However, vulgarity is not attributable to a lack of understanding of God's ways but rather to a lower state of spiritual awareness. The kiss "of his mouth" accordingly becomes the "breath," of which the evangelist spoke, by which the primitive church received the holy ghost.[469]

Once again, then, Bernard equates the physical kiss, the holy spirit, and the word. That, he explains, is why the spouse so eagerly asks for a kiss. In requesting it, she effectively prays for the threefold knowledge of the trinity, insofar as a creature can possess it while still in the flesh.[470] And this knowledge, of course, which flesh promises, is really an understanding of the spirit. "It does not only illumine one with intellectual awareness but kindles one to divine love."[471] It is Paul's charity.[472] Moreover, he reiterates, it is not only necessary to know (*cognoscere*) but also to love (*amare*).[473] Otherwise, the kiss's enlightenment would only "puff up."[474]

[466] *Ibid.*, 27, 4-10.   [467] *Ibid.*, 6.1.13, p. 27, 11-12.

[468] *Ibid.*, 27, 14-15: "Obtulit carnem sapientibus carnem, per quam discerent sapere et spiritum."

[469] *Ibid.*, 8.1.2, p. 37, 7-8: " 'Insufflavit,' inquit, 'eis' [Io 20.22] haud dubium quin Iesus Apostolis, id est, primitivae Ecclesiae. . . ." Cf. M. Caliaro, "Lo spirito santo nella vita spirituale secondo S. Bernardo," *Divus Thomas* 51 (1947), 307-08.

[470] *Ibid.*, 8.2.5, p. 38, 15-16: Trinae igitur huius agnitionis infundi sibi gratiam, quantum quidem capi in carne mortali potest, sponsa petit, cum osculum petit.

[471] *Ibid.*, p. 38, 21-23.   [472] Rom 1:21.   [473] *Sermo*, 8.3.5, p. 38, 25-27.

[474] 1 Cor 8:1.

Bernard ends sermon eight with a word on the limits of interpretation. In inquiring into deeper senses (*in arcanis sensibus*), the monks should not attempt to fathom what lies beyond their modest abilities.[475] They should "walk" with the spirit, not the letter, of their own readings.[476] One should not be satisfied with "carnal senses" or acquiesce to "the inane reckonings of human curiosity." She who begs for the kiss, that is, who invokes the holy spirit, should receive both "the taste of knowledge" and "the condiment of grace." The kiss is evidence (*indicium*) of love; but it does not impart *scientia . . . sine caritate.* Along with "the light of understanding" comes "the oil of devotion." Indeed, in Bernard's terms, it is the *spiritus sapientiae et intellectus* which ignites the *lumen scientiae* and infuses the *sapor gratiae.*[477]

Another fashion in which the same contrast is illustrated is through the identification of Bernard's point of view and the bride's, as in sermon nine. He returns afresh to the Song's opening verse, he states, in order to provide an explanation (*rationem dare*).[478] But he soon surpasses the limits of reason.[479]

Rather than offer an exegesis, he recreates a spiritual setting in which the bride's and his own thoughts can merge.[480] Let us suppose, he asks his brethren, that, on successive days, the friends of the groom have come to pay tribute to the spouse. They find her out of sorts and ask what is wrong. They presume that she is returning to her former husband after a period of infidelity. They then ask her to rehearse the enactment of the three kisses. On your return, they ask, did you not importune him with tears to let you touch his feet? But, having attained this privilege, you once again grew discontented and, desiring greater familiarity, obtained a second grace, receiving many virtues from the kiss of the hand. Yet, did you not then agree to ask for nothing more?

Yes, she confesses. What then, they ask? Are you afraid that the gifts will be taken away? No, she replies. Then, they add, tell us what we can do to help you. To this she replies partly in her own words and partly in Bernard's thoughts, which can be summarized as follows: "I cannot rest," she says, "until he kisses me with the kiss of his mouth. I am grateful to have kissed his feet and hand: but, if he

[475] *Sermo*, 8.4.6, p. 39, 12-14; Eccli 3.22.
[476] *Ibid.*, p. 39, 14-15: "In spiritu ambulate in illis, et non in sensu proprio."
[477] *Ibid.*, p. 39, 16-26.   [478] *Ibid.*, 9.1.1, p. 42, 11-12.
[479] *Ibid.*, 9.2.2, p. 43, 11; p. 43, 15.
[480] What follows summarizes 9.1.1-2.2, pp. 42, 12-p. 43, 27.

really cares for me, let him kiss me with the kiss of his mouth. I am not lacking in gratitude, but I am in love. What I have received is more than I deserve but less than I desire. I am driven by passion, not reason. Do not criticize my boldness, since it is motivated by affection. Modesty asks sensibly, but love conquers! My judgement sleeps. I ask, I beg, I implore, 'Let him kiss me with the kiss of his mouth.' For, on his behalf I have led a disciplined life for many years. I have devoted myself to monastic study, resisted vice, prayed constantly, and held vigils against temptation. I have recounted my years in the bitterness of my soul.[481] I have lived in common and obeyed my superior. I have not coveted others' goods; I have given my own, and myself with them. I have eaten my bread in the sweat of my brow.[482] Yet, in place of sweetness, I have known only routine (*consuetudo*). Am I a useless servant who only obeys?[483] Is my soul to remain in thirst?"[484]

Of course not. But, as Bernard subtly shifts from her desires to his own, from the carnal to the spiritual, from the female to the male, and from drama to meaning, we, as readers, like his monastic contemporaries, also recreate in living images the theme of the soul's advancement. Many of his brethren, he adds, complain in confession of "dry souls" and "heavy minds." They do not know how to "penetrate" God's deeper mysteries. He asks: is that not the same longing to be kissed?[485] For clearly they yearn after the spirit of wisdom and understanding. With understanding as a guide, wisdom savours what it apprehends.[486]

Sermons nine to twelve take up a theme implicit in much of Bernard's erotic and mystical language, namely, *lectio* as ritual initiation and purification.

The Song's verses continue: "For your breasts are better than wine, smelling sweet of the best ointments."[487] As a parallel to the three kisses, Bernard envisages three kinds of unguent, conversion, contrition, and piety. The verse, he thinks, was spoken by the bride. As she speaks of him, he appears and gives her the kiss she desires, thus fulfilling the prophecy, "You gave her her heart's desire and did not withhold from her the will of her lips."[488] So great is the spiritual

---

[481] Is 38:15. [482] Gen 3:19. [483] Lc 17:10. [484] Ps 19:4.

[485] *Sermo* 9.2.3, p. 43, 28-p. 44, 2.

[486] *Ibid.*, 44, 2-4: "Suspirant plane, et inhiant spiritui sapientiae et intellectus: intellectus utique quo pertingant, sapientiae qua gustent quod intellectu apprehenderint."

[487] Cant 1:1-2.

[488] Ps 20:3.

kiss's power that, on receiving it, the bride conceives. Her breasts swell and milk begins to flow.[489] Bernard once again shifts from this highly sensual imagery to the monks' situation. "Those of you," he adds, "who desire to pray often know from experience of what I speak. Frequently, we approach the altar with dry and tepid hearts. Yet, by persisting in prayer, we are unexpectedly infused with grace. Our breasts swell and we are filled to overflowing with pious thoughts. Were someone to press our breasts, the milk of sweetness would surely begin to pour forth."[490]

Truly, then, the groom may say: "My wife, you received what you asked for, namely, the proof (*signum*) that your breasts are better than wine, better, that is, than the impure draught of secular knowledge (*scientia saecularis*), which inebriates with curiosity, not charity."[491]

Bernard elaborates the process a little further in describing the making of the first and second ointments. The soul, he says, trapped by sin, begins to reflect upon its ways. Collecting the "many and varied species of sin," it crushes them in the mortar of conscience. Later, when they are melted in the heart's crucible, the devout can say with the psalmist, "My heart has grown hot within me and my fire flames with inner thoughts."[492] These *conversionis primordia*, which represent the feet's ointment, foreshadow the second unguent, which is made from more precious material cultivated in the gardens of our own consciences. Unlike the first, the second is not produced by man alone, but "descends from the father of lights."[493] Crushed once again, it is applied to the head, that is, to Christ. Using the second ointment requires withdrawal, reminiscence, and the desire for spiritual advancement. Its effects begin in confusion, but proceed to an anticipation of divine goodness. Bernard sees the second unguent recapitulating man's progress from sin to the foretaste of grace.[494] Sin, he states, requires sorrow, but, in the end, gives way to clemency.[495] As man ascends, the soul's powers, reason, will, and memory, play their part.[496] But, in such matters, reason is easily deceived, the will defeated, and memory obscured.[497] Yet, God manages to penetrate the

[489] On this imagery, see C. W. Bynum, "Jesus as Mother and Abbot as Mother: Some Themes in Twelfth-Century Cistercian Writing," *Harvard Theological Review* 70 (1977), 258-84.

[490] *Sermo* 9.5.7, p. 46, 19-26.   [491] *Ibid.*, 46, 26-31.

[492] *Ibid.*, 10.4.5, p. 50, 24-29; Ps 38.4.   [493] *Ibid.*, 10.5.7, p. 51, 27-p. 52, 7; Ps 49.23.

[494] *Ibid.*, 10.5.8, p. 52, 17-22; 1 Cor 11.3.

[495] *Ibid.*, 11.1.2, p. 55, 12-20.

[496] On the soul's parts in Bernard, see W. Hiss, *Die Anthropologie Bernhards von Clairvaux* (Berlin, 1964), 89-137.

[497] *Sermo* 11.3.5, p. 57, 17-19.

human soul, communicating to reason as *plenitudo lucis*, to will as *multitudo pacis*, and to memory as *continuatio aeternitatis*.[498] Finally, Bernard adds, the third ointment, that of piety, is extracted from the miserable.[499] It is superior to the others because it is spread over the whole of Christ's body, that is, the church.[500] What the church offers us collectively, we enjoy individually through participation.[501]

Variations on these themes recur in later sermons, of which, within the framework of the present discussion, two others deserve special attention.

In sermon fifteen, Bernard speaks of the names of God and the name of Jesus. A critical attitude, he argues, is essential to any higher understanding. True, God is available to all who pray.[502] But the Song's text suggests that His name is "as oil poured out;" that is, it is a word in need of interpretation. First Bernard reduces the biblical names for God "to oil," that is, to qualities, stating his preference for two, *pietatis gratia* and *potentia maiestatis*.[503] At length he comes to the appellative "I am who am."[504] Even Moses, he argues, could not have understood its meaning had it not been poured out (*effunderetur*). Metaphors for the flow of the Word follow: it was not only poured (*fusum*) but poured forth (*effusum*), that is, poured into Moses (*infusum*) and thereby grasped (*captum*). In other words, what had been poured into the angels was now overflowing among men.[505] The verse, "Your name is as oil poured out" thereby becomes a symbol of the Word's communication.

Jesus resembles "oil" in three senses, in providing light, food, and medicine. The name gives light when preached (*praedicatum*), nourishes when thought about (*recogitatum*), and tranquillizes when invoked (*invocatum*).[506] He then examines each sense in detail. Nothing, he argues, could have spread the "light of faith" throughout the world but the preaching of Jesus's name.[507] For the light is his word, as Paul states.[508] But illumination began with the tangible: He bore his light "like a lamp";[509] He directed everyone's eyes "to the candle."[510] And Jesus's preaching, for Bernard, went hand in hand with his phys-

---

[498] *Ibid.*, p. 57, 24-26.

[499] *Ibid.*, 12.1.1, p. 60, 12-18; Mt 5.7.

[500] *Ibid.*, 12.7.10, p. 67, 3.   [501] *Ibid.*, 12.7.11, p. 67, 25-26.

[502] *Ibid.*, 15.1.1, p. 82, 7-9.   [503] *Ibid.*, 82, 4.   [504] *Ibid.*, 15.2.2, p. 83, 20; Ex 3.14.

[505] *Ibid.*, 83, 21-26.

[506] *Ibid.*, 15.3.5, p. 85, 23-27.   [507] *Ibid.*, 15.3.6, p. 85, 28-29.

[508] *Ibid.*, 86, 1-2; Eph 5.8.   [509] *Ibid.*, 86.4.   [510] *Ibid.*, 86.7.

ical death for man's sake.[511] His name, moreover, is a kind of spiritual food (*animae cibus*),[512] without which neither text nor word have meaning. For, if you write or speak, Bernard asserts, your work will not instruct me if it lacks Christ's name.[513] Finally, to turn to medicine, he states that the name enters one's heart, leaps to the lips, radiates as light, and disperses clouds of doubt. It is thus the name of life (*nomen vitae*).[514] Again, one proceeds through these images from heard sound to meaning and illumination, that is, from the *invocatio nominis* to *certitudo*.[515]

Bernard sums up this aspect of his mysticism in sermon sixteen, where he also adds a few comments on his exegetical method. The holy spirit, he proposes, causes everything to be made (*fieri*) and to be written (*scribi*). These things are done for the improvement of spirits misled by the body's "perfidious society" or mistaught by the world's "foolish wisdom." No one ought to be astonished if he scrutinizes the "storehouse" of the holy spirit, since he recognizes that "the spirit's life" resides there. Moreover, his preaching is directed equally at the quick and the slow witted. My purpose, he adds, is not so much to comment on words (*ut exponam verba*) as to imbue hearts (*ut imbuam corda*). Such instruction cannot be given rapidly; it requires "diligent treatment" and "frequent exhortation." The discussion of the mysteries (*discussio sacramentorum*), he confesses, took him longer than anticipated. He thought to pass in one day from the dark, shaded, hidden wood of allegory (*silvaque ista umbrosa latebrosaque allegoriarum*) to the open plain of the moral senses (*ad planitiem moralium sensuum*), that is, to proceed from a contemplation of the text to a state of readiness for action.[516] Christ is envisaged as one potent in both work and word (*potens in opere et sermone*),[517] providing Bernard with a model from above. The physical imagery even invades his moment of hermeneutic reflection. "I ruminate," he notes, "with delight": Christ's mysteries replenish his breast, fatten his innards, and cause his very bones to break into praise. In a sense, the church transforms everyone; but we, he says to his brethren, sense it to be activated daily in ourselves individually. The light of intelligence is offered to the heart, the word of edification to the mouth, and the work of justice to the hands.[518]

---

[511] *Ibid.*, 86.8   [512] *Ibid.*, 86.16.

[513] *Ibid.*, 86, 17-18: "Si scribas, non sapit mihi, nisi legero ibi Iesum. Si disputes aut conferas, non sapit mihi, nisi sonuerit ibi Iesus."

[514] *Ibid.*, 15.4.6, p. 86, 20-23.   [515] *Ibid.*, 86, 29.

[516] *Ibid.*, 16.1.1, p. 89, 12-p. 90, 2.   [517] *Ibid.*, 16.2.2, p. 90, 14; Lc 24.19.

[518] *Ibid.*, p. 90, 18-22.

For, through his gift, we sense faithfully, we speak usefully, and we implement efficiently.[519] In the end, his is practical advice. Reduced to its essentials, his "triple cord" consists of thinking rightly, speaking worthily, and confirming one's words through life.[520]

The Word, Interiority, and Reform

The sermons discussed so far provide a rough paradigm for reform in Bernard's theology which involves the word, the text, and experience. The starting point is the word. Enunciated by the Spirit, it is formalized as a text. And that, of course, as in the Song's case, is how it is first experienced. However, through active meditation, it is revivified as word. In the process, psychological reform is brought about.[521]

The manner in which this comes to pass is treated in detail in subsequent sermons. The question has many facets, and Bernard nowhere pulls his thoughts together as a single doctrine. Yet, if passed in review, sermons seventeen to twenty-three tell us much about his notions of interiority, self-knowledge, and reform. To these texts we now turn.

A fundamental issue for Bernard is how we understand right and wrong, which, he argues, involves the word and the heart, not the mind. This is the message of sermon seventeen, in which the text remains, "Your name is as oil poured out." Have we, he asks, penetrated far enough into the *sanctuarium Dei*? Have we sufficiently scrutinized the *mirabile sacramentum*? Or should we now proceed further in the investigation of inner truths (*ad interiora*)? For the holy spirit not only examines men's hearts but also the deep matters of God. Securely, he adds, we follow the spirit's beacon into earthly or divine regions, praying only that God keep our hearts and minds on the right course. We can remain ignorant of God's ways without imperilling our chances of salvation. But, the inability to recognize *when* he comes or goes is fraught with danger.[522]

Once again, the stressing of physical signs, both external and internal, is the opposite of the scholastic approach, which, in Berengar and Abelard, begins with man's rational capacities. To illustrate his point, Bernard refers to the last conversation between Elisha and Eli-

[519] *Ibid.*, p. 90, 22-23: "Dat sentire fideliter, dat proferre utiliter, dat efficaciter adimplere."
[520] *Ibid.*, p. 90, 24-25: ". . . si recte sentias, si digne proloquaris, si vivendo confirmes."
[521] *Ibid.*, p. 90, 28-p. 91, 2: "Os ori applicavit, iterato inspirans in faciem meam spiraculum vitae, sed sanctioris quam primo: nam primo quidem in animam viventem creavit me, secundo in spiritum vivificantem reformavit me."
[522] *Ibid.*, 17.1.1, p. 98, 7-16.

jah before the latter's spirit was taken up to heaven.[523] After the Jordan's waters miraculously parted to let them pass, Elijah asked Elisha what he could do for him before he left this life. Elisha replied, "I ask that you impart to me your double spirit (*duplex spiritus*)." Elijah said that this was a difficult task, and set the following condition. If Elisha saw him as he was being taken up to heaven, the wish would be fulfilled; if he did not, it would not.

The episode was attractive to Bernard because it once again drew a clear contrast between the visible and the invisible. The starting point was real change as evidenced by the senses: this "figure," he asserts, was "written" on our behalf. Accordingly, we must watch carefully over our own salvation (*opus nostrae salutis*), which the holy spirit activates within us (*actitat Spiritus in intimo nostri*), subtly, sweetly, and ceaselessly. In other words, although grace is invisible, it leaves visible signs, which we must acknowledge; and, although the spirit operates in mysterious ways, its action never stops. If we do not wish to be deprived of the "double gift," it can never be taken away from us. But, by implication, God must never find us "unprepared"; we must be waiting with "faces uplifted" for his benediction. We must be vigilant at all times because we do not know at what hour the spirit will come.[524]

As a parallel to the two states of knowledge with which we greet the spirit, Bernard adds a further distinction between truth and falsehood. It is one thing merely to doubt the truth (*dubitare de veritate*), another to savour falsehood (*sapere falsitatem*). We may avoid the latter by refusing to remain ignorant of our ignorance. For *falsitas* and *dubietas*, he allegorizes, are the miserable daughters of "mother ignorance." When the spirit speaks, both vanish: they are replaced not simply by truth but by *certa veritas*, that is, by the "spirit of truth," which, in the terms of our previous discussion, is authenticated truth. Above all, Bernard adds, we must especially be on our guard "when the spirit does not speak to us." For, at such moments, it is really speaking through silence.

Moreover, Bernard sees a profound difference between rashly asserting what one does not know and simply affirming what is probable. Some men, he asserts, openly say what is false; others speak of what they do not know. The former, he notes, are in good faith; the latter lie. For the former merely say what they actually believe to be

[523] 4 Reg 2.9-10.
[524] *Sermo* 17.1.2, p. 99, 3-10.

true, although it is not. The latter pretend to have certainty when they do not. Therefore, they speak falsely even when what they say happens to be true.[525] In other terms, the criterion of truth is what is; it cannot be altered by mere affirmation. As a consequence, man's moral reform cannot begin in something external to himself—a text, a set of teachings, etc. Its precondition is his inner awareness of the spirit.

Bernard, then, is interested not in factual objectivity but in a kind which, while related to facts, is also a byproduct of will and intention. What, he asks, does the holy spirit demonstrate to us about ourselves in the text, "Your name is as oil poured out"? Chiefly, the experience of his twofold operation, which fortifies us interiorly with virtues for our own salvation and adorns us exteriorly with his gifts for the salvation of others.[526] We obtain faith, hope, and charity for ourselves, and, for others, "the word of wisdom or knowledge, the grace of curing, the gift of prophecy," etc.[527] These operations of the holy spirit Bernard calls respectively infusion (*infusio*) and effusion (*effusio*). We must take care, he notes, not to give away to others what is reserved for ourselves, nor to retain for ourselves what is destined for others.[528] In metaphoric terms, he asks his brethren to be "vessels" rather than "channels" for the divine spirit. For a vessel waits until it is filled up before it gives anything away.[529] One should remember Solomon's warning: "A fool speaks all his mind (*spiritus*) at once; the wise man retains something for a later time."[530] The present church, Bernard adds, has many channels but few vessels. Many wish to pour out (*effundere*) what has not yet been poured in (*infundere*), to speak rather than to listen, to teach rather than be taught. Although unable to govern themselves, they gladly agree to rule over others.[531]

Yet true reform, Bernard maintains, requires a restructuring of experience, and, in particular, an acceptance of the physical and historical Christ. He turns to this issue in sermon twenty, where he once again identifies the reason for Christ's presence on earth as the need to enlighten the spiritually ignorant. Paul says, "If any man does not love Christ, let him be anathema."[532] But what, Bernard asks, does

[525] *Ibid.*, 17.2.3, p. 99, 22-p. 100, 12.
[526] *Ibid.*, 18.1.1, p. 103, 14-17: "Profecto, quod interim occurrit, geminae cuiusdam suae operationis experimentum: unius quidem, qua nos primo intus virtutibus solidat ad salutem, alterius vero, qua foris quoque muneribus ornat ad lucrum."
[527] *Ibid.*, 103, 19-22.   [528] *Ibid.*, 18.1.2, 104, 8-9.
[529] *Ibid.*, 18.1.3, 104, 19.   [530] Prov 29:11.   [531] *Sermo* 18.1.3, p. 104, 25-28.
[532] *Ibid.*, 20.1.1, p. 114, 7-8; 1 Cor 16:22.

this mean? Christ, first of all, is to be venerated as the source of one's being, life, and capacity to understand.[533] To be ungrateful for such gifts is to be unworthy of them. However, beyond this, he who refuses to live for Christ, as Paul states, is dead; he who has no understanding is a fool; he who does not exist for him is already nothing.[534] At the essence of man's existence is an active relationship with his maker:[535] for, "what is man"[536] but "that you are made known to him."[537] Of course, God's love is not the same as Christ's. God made everything for himself; Christ drained his "earthly chalice" to complete the "work of our redemption."[538] In making the world, God merely willed and spoke, while, in suffering on earth, Christ "laboured mightily" for our salvation.[539] He not only endured the world's disdain; He loved us before we existed, even, after creation, when we resisted.[540] And so we should love Him. To return to a now familiar image, Bernard states that, at the core of our devotion is an *amor cordis* which is also *carnalis*.

Why? Because, he suggests, it turns us toward the physical Christ, together with what he undertook to perform while in the flesh.[541] To repeat: the "invisible God" appeared visibly, so that, as a man, he might dwell among men, drawing towards spiritual truths those who only knew how to love carnally.[542] Putting the matter in human terms, Bernard proposes that Christ's *corporalis praesentia* alone caused his followers to leave worldly things behind. For, before the crucifixion, they could not bear to hear of his death, while afterwards sorrow prevented them from witnessing his ascent.[543] Thus, paradoxically, devotion to Christ's flesh is a "great gift" of the holy spirit. It is called "carnal" not with respect to the word that became flesh but with respect to the virtues which appeared as the word in Christ, who, after all, did not represent them but rather was them.[544] There are, Bernard adds, three stages of love, carnal, rational, and spiritual (*carnalis*, *rationalis*, and *spiritualis*). Carnal love, by beginning with the flesh, enables us to overcome the world. As it advances, it becomes rational and then spiritual. For Bernard, rationality is literalism; that

---

[533] *Ibid.*, 114, 8-9: "Valde omnino mihi amandus est, per quem sum, vivo, et sapio,"

[534] *Ibid.*, 114, 9-11.

[535] *Ibid.*, 114, 12: "Denique quid est homo, nisi quia tu innotuisti ei?"

[536] Ps 143:3   [537] Prov 16:4   [538] *Sermo* 20.1.2, p. 115, 3-5.

[539] *Ibid.*, 115, 7-9.

[540] *Ibid.*, 115, 14-15.

[541] *Ibid.*, 20.5.6, p. 118, 13-15: "Et nota amorem cordis quodammodo esse carnalem, quod magis erga carnem Christi, et quae in carne Christus gessit vel iussit, cor humanum afficiat."

[542] *Ibid.*, 118, 21-26.   [543] *Ibid.*, 118, 27-119, 3.   [544] *Ibid.*, 20.5.8, p. 120, 4-8.

is, love is "rational" when it adheres to all Christian doctrine without deviation and exhibits "sober moderation" in conduct. It is, in that sense, a kind of law, and rationality is once more identifiable with a text. This same love becomes spiritual when, freed from all difficulties, it adds the "strength of spirit."[545]

Again, then, in Bernard's thought, we move from the word to the text to the word: from the physical Christ, who is the Word, to doctrine and precept, which is a text, and to spirit, which is a word dependent on the other two.

This dialectical process is central to Bernard's notion of reform, as sermon twenty-one reveals. His text is, "Draw me; he will run after you to the odour of your ointments."[546] But how is one drawn to Christ? Do you not see, Bernard asks his brethren, that he who walks with the spirit is placed in a difficult dilemma? For, he can neither remain in the same state nor very easily advance much beyond it. His way, in fact, lies not through man but through the spirit, which, as manager (*moderator*), proceeds as it wishes, either slowly or quickly.[547]

Moreover, what happens from the outside, Bernard states, the monks may, if they pay attention, learn from the inside, that is, from their own experience.[548] Whenever they feel *torpor, acedia,* or *taedio,* they should simply follow the example of the spouse.[549] For, if at times of temptation or the will's failure, one shows faith in the spirit, running, so to speak, after "the odours of its ointments," then one may, despite the vicissitudes of time, exhibit an image of eternity, mirroring changelessness by the constancy of one's own soul.[550] In this sense, one attains a similarly eternal state (*perennis . . . incommutabilitatis status*).[551] In the same process, one automatically begins to renew (*renovare*) and to reform (*reformare*) oneself into the ancient, remarkable likeness of the eternal God, in which there is neither change nor change's shadow. In other words, man is capable through reform of imitating eternity himself.

Bernard thereby underlines another contrast with a more scholastic approach to the question. Man does not passively reflect his divine

[545] *Ibid.,* 20.5.9, p. 120, 22-p. 121, 5.   [546] Cant 1.2.

[547] *Sermo* 21.3.4, p. 124, 20-24.

[548] *Ibid.,* 124, 24-25: "Puto quod hoc ipsum, si attenditis, vestra vobis experientia intus respondet quod ego foris loquor."

[549] *Ibid.,* 21.3.5, p. 124, 26-27.

[550] *Ibid.,* 21.3.6, p. 125, 15-17: ". . . erisque inter prospera et adversa mutabilium temporum tenens quamdam aeternitatis imaginem, utique hanc inviolabilem et inconcussam constantis animi aequalitatem. . . ."

[551] *Ibid.,* p. 125, 19-20.

origins as his maker's image. Nor, through rational activity alone, can he fully recover the likeness he lost. He must undergo active spiritual development.[552] The *nobilis creatura*, in Bernard's terms, originally created in imitation of his maker, recovers (*receptare*) his ancient dignity to the degree that he spurns the fleeting world and, as Paul suggests, reforms his awareness (*sensus*) to the divine exemplar.[553] The essential relationship is between *reformari* and *conformari*.

Bernard's most comprehensive statement on reform occurs in sermon twenty-three. The text is the "king's storerooms" (*cellarium*), which he treats along with the "garden" (*hortus*) and the "bedchamber" (*cubiculum*) from subsequent verses of the Song.[554]

Here, he is directly concerned with the spiritual sense of the text hidden beneath the literal. In his view, the garden represents the historical reading, the storeroom the moral, and the bedchamber the secret of "theoretical contemplation."[555] The investigation however is not conducted according to the rules of the trivium and the quadrivium. Instead, he refers in each case to his own experience of the text.

The garden is history (*historia*), he argues, because, like fruit trees in the garden of the bride or in the garden of Eden, we find there men of virtue (*viri virtutum*), from whose good actions and morals we may take examples.[556] For a good man is a "tree planted."[557] Moreover, the garden has a history, which is divided into three parts, the creation of heaven and earth, the reconciliation, and the restoration.[558] To turn to the moral sense, three things are also notable, as if there were three cellars in the same storehouse, containing wine, spices, and unguents.[559] But these three subcellars also correspond to discipline, nature, and grace.[560] In the first, we learn according to ethical principles how to be "inferior"; in the second, "equal"; in the third, "superior." In other words, we learn how to live under, with, and over others.

Nature made all men equal, but, corrupted with pride, they degenerated through envy and jealousy. For that reason, in the first "cellar," our behaviour is disciplined, our obstinate wills mollified, and our pride humbled and healed. When, through "natural affection

---

[552] *Ibid.*, p. 125, 19-22: ". . . dum te coeperis renovare et reformare in insigne illud antiquum similitudinis aeterni Dei, apud quem non est transmutatio nec vicissitudinis obumbratio."

[553] *Ibid.*, p. 125, 23-27; Rom 12:2; 8:28.   [554] Cant 5:1; 3:4.

[555] *Sermo* 23.2.3, p. 140, 19-20.   [556] *Ibid.*, 23.2.4, p. 140, 21-24.   [557] Ps 1:3.

[558] *Sermo* 23.2.4, p. 141, 4-6.

[559] *Ibid.*, 23.3.5, p. 141, 15-27.   [560] *Ibid.*, 142, 1-2.

alone," we have learned to live in common with others, we pass to the second cellar, nature itself.[561] Here we experience the truth of what is written about monastic unity.[562] For, to disciplined morals (*disciplinati mores*), one now adds the *bonum naturae*, since authority and discipline "beat out and extract" the natural superiority of good precepts.[563] But there is an important distinction between these two cellars not revealed by their names alone.[564] For monks do not all possess the happy faculty of living together in peace and harmony. It is one thing to obey a superior; it is quite another to be obedient by internal willpower alone.[565] Likewise, few superiors govern well, fewer still with humility.[566]

With the cellar and the garden behind him, Bernard then turns to the bedchamber. Am I, he asks, to presume I can know what it is? Truly this "experience" belongs to the bride alone. But what understanding he has he is willing to impart.[567] As he has many cellars, the king has numerous bedchambers, each reserved for a different wife. Bernard describes three such "places," of which he has had mystical intimations.[568] The first is a place (*locus*) in the home of the groom, where, as governor (*gubernator*) of the universe, he determines his laws and arranges his counsels, constituting the physical relations of all creatures, their weight, measure, and number. Although lofty and sequestered, this place is not quiet. The groom may dispose "sweetly," but he nonetheless disposes. Here the contemplative has no place: he is pleasantly tired by ceaseless activity.[569] This is what the bride means when she refers a few verses later to "sleeping with her heart awake."[570] Similarly, every soul may wish to decline sweetness so that the appetite can rise again.[571]

A second "place" keeps watch over reprobate rational creatures. It is the home of "the righteous judge," who is "terrible in his counsels over the sons of men."[572] Here, the "timid contemplative" beholds God's just but secret judgment. He refuses to accept the good works of those whose hearts are permanently hardened or to offer to heal them. And he carries on these activities with a certain eternal rationale (*certa et aeterna ratio*), which is all the more fearful as it is immutable. Bernard in particular admonishes simoniacs and other abusers of the church's material and spiritual goods.[573] Who, he asks, would seek

---

[561] *Ibid.*, 142, 2-16.   [562] Ps 132:2.   [563] *Sermo* 23.3.5, p. 142, 17-19.
[564] *Ibid.*, 23.3.8, p. 143, 15.   [565] *Ibid.*, 143, 21-27.   [566] *Ibid.*, 144, 1-2.
[567] *Ibid.*, 23.4.9, p. 144, 19-23.   [568] *Ibid.*, 23.4.11, p. 145, 24.
[569] *Ibid.*, 145, 26-146, 4.   [570] Cant 5:2.   [571] *Sermo* 2.3.4.11, p. 146, 10-12.
[572] *Ibid.*, 23.5.12, p. 146, 16; Ps 7:12.   [573] *Ibid.*, 146, 16-147, 3.

rest in so frightening a place? The vision, he admits, is calculated to inspire "the fear of the judge," not "the security of the bedchamber." For the place is "terrifying" and totally lacking in tranquillity.[574]

But, in contrast to the first *locus*, the second is the *initium sapientiae*. Bernard's reflections so adequately sum up his thinking on the relation of theory to practice that the passage may be cited in full:[575]

"Do not yourself be disturbed then that I have bestowed wisdom's origin to the second place rather than the first. For, in the one, as in a lecture-hall, we hear *Sapientia* as a mistress who teaches all things. But in the other we take them up. In the one we are instructed (*instruimur*), in the other, affected (*afficimur*). Instruction renders us learned; affection, wise. For the sun does not light all that it warms. Similarly, *Sapientia*, which teaches many what is to be done (*quid sit faciendum*), does not continuously quicken one for doing it (*ad faciendum*). It is one thing to know of many riches, another to possess them. And it is not the information (*notitia*) which makes a man rich but the actual possession (*possessio*). By the same reasoning, it is one thing to know (*nosse*) God, another to fear (*timere*) him. It is not understanding (*cognitio*) which makes a man wise, but fear (*timor*), by which we are affected. You would not call a man wise whom knowledge merely 'puffs up.' . . . God has a taste for the soul (*animae Deus sapit*) when he affects it for fearing, not when he instructs it for knowing (*cum eam afficit ad timendum, non cum instruit ad sciendum*). For 'the beginning of wisdom is fear of the Lord.' You fear God's justice, you fear his power; and, since fear is savour (*sapor*), the just and potent God has a taste (*sapit*) for you. Just as knowledge (*scientia*) makes one well-informed and riches, rich, so this savour makes a man wise. What then of the first place? It only prepares one for wisdom. There you are prepared (*praepararis*) so that here you may be initiated (*initieris*). This preparation is the understanding of things (*rerum cognitio*). . . . In sum, in the first place we obtain access (*accessus*) to wisdom, in the second, entrance (*ingressus*)."

Bernard then turns to a third *locus*, a place of imperturbable tranquillity, a place not of the judge or the teacher but of the bride,[576] and he dwells at length on its mystical delights. It is the *arcanum . . . sanctuarium Dei*, the true "bedchamber of the king," the home of perfect peace.[577] His concluding paragraphs also provide us with a

[574] *Ibid.*, 23.5.13, p. 147, 4-7. [575] *Ibid.*, 23.5.14, p. 147, 21-p. 148, 13.
[576] *Ibid.*, 23.6.15, p. 148, 18. [577] *Ibid.*, 23.6.16, p. 149, 15-26.

convenient reference point for reviewing his central thoughts on experience and reform.[578]

We begin with the text. The place of law and discipline is where the monks learn knowledge about God. Bernard speaks of *scientia, cognitio,* and *instructio.* The first *locus* is a preparation for the second, in which one passes from theory to practice, from thought to action. The monks also proceed from *instructio* to *affectio,* that is, from looking upon the text as object to assimilating it as subject. The process is not wholly cognitive. Like a didactic ritual, it is a blend of the sensual and the spiritual which is captured in the term *sapor.* Also, in the second *locus*, as in the first, there is ceaseless activity; but they are of different kinds. The one concerns the acquisition of knowledge, the other, its application. Overlooking both is the ultimate law-giver and decision-maker.

So man, passing from discipline to obedience, blending theory and practice, attains, if only briefly, a third state, a beatific vision which is an anticipation of grace. Yet the third bedchamber is not merely a mystical vision. It comes about as an active reworking of the two previous states. Grace, by implication, while a future gift, is mystically manifested on earth. So once again we have an intimate uniting of the physical and the spiritual, that is, in Bernard's terms, of the word and the text. For one passes from discipline to nature, which internalizes discipline as obedience, and thence to grace, which assimilates both. Grace, then, as man mystically experiences it on earth, is both the final application of discipline and the appropriation of nature. We may speak of it as a kind of "praxis," that is, an identification of object and subject. For the word, appearing as text, has effectively been both internalized and re-externalized.

Man as an Image of God's Word

In these thoughts, Bernard adapts the Pauline distinction between the external and the internal man and expresses it as a mystical ideal.

But what of God? He is not conceived as in scholasticism as the "architect" of the created world. When Bernard speaks of his *dispositio,* he is thinking primarily of the monastic "plan of living."[579] To put the matter another way: God's relationship to the universe and to man

---

[578] For what follows, I draw on my earlier essay, "Experience, Work, and Planning . . . ," 244-46.

[579] Cf. Max Weber, *Die protestantische Ethik und der Geist des Kapitalismus,* in J. Winckelmann ed., *Max Weber. Die protestantische Ethik I* (Hamburg, 1973), 134-35.

is viewed, not chiefly in terms of cause and effect, but of means and ends. Bernard's notion of God's influence on man is not naturalistic but moralistic and psychological. The mediator between the divine and the earthly is not law but experience; not only everyday experience, that is, the living out of daily activities, but, more profoundly, the experience of the Bible, the energy generated by *divina lectio*, which is re-expressed in an active outlook.

The relations between God and man form a principal subject of sermons twenty-four to fifty.

Bernard's text in twenty-four, which he delivered and revised after returning from Rome in 1138,[580] was, "The righteous love you."[581] But what, he asks, are we to understand by *rectus*? Not primarily a corporeal sense, but rather a spiritual, that is, a rectitude of the heart or mind (*spiritualis, id est animi rectitudo*).[582] "For it is the spirit which speaks, comparing spiritual to spiritual."[583] Therefore, with respect to his heart or mind (*animus*), not his corruptible frame, God made man "upright."

Man's likeness to God is an image of His righteousness, and, it is in man's "spiritual portion" that God's image is to be preserved or repaired (*Dei similitudinem conservandam sive reparandam*). For "God is spirit," and those who wish to be like him must find the way into their own hearts and become active in the same spiritual business.[584] True, God also gave man uprightness of body. Perhaps, Bernard reasons, he wished that the viler exterior recommend the worthier interior part, the body's comeliness, so to speak, acting as a foil to the soul's "deformity." Indeed, he states, it is perverse that the base body should have the capacity to look upwards towards the heavens while the celestial spirit lowers its "interior senses and affections" to the ground, and, like a pig, embraces what is most earthly.[585]

"Blush, my soul," says the body in Bernard's words, "for trading a divine for a bestial image, a 'stellar' for a 'cinder.' Created upright like the creator, you have me as a helper, an exemplar for yourself. Whether you look above or below, your gaze falls on an image of your own beauty and, wherever you turn, you have advice from *Sapientia*.

[580] *Sermo* 24.1.1, p. 151; cf. Geoffrey d'Auxerre, *Vita Prima Bernardi* 4.1.1, PL 185.321.
[581] Cant 1.3.
[582] *Sermo* 24.2.5, p. 156, 10-11.
[583] *Ibid.*, 156, 11-12; 1 Cor 2.13.
[584] *Ibid.*, 157, 6-8: "Spiritus enim est Deus [Io 4.24], et eos qui volunt similes ei vel perseverare vel fieri, oportet intrare ad cor, atque in spiritu id negotii actitare. . . ."
[585] *Ibid.*, 24.2.6, p. 157, 10-p. 158, 4.

But, while I have kept my original uprightness, you have lost yours. Why should God be obliged to see his image destroyed in you, while, in me, your likeness has been carefully preserved?"[586] Bernard concludes his address by the body to the soul by observing that a *curva anima* cannot be the bride's lover, since it is essentially "of the world."[587] But here the paradox of the spiritual in the physical once again makes itself felt. *Curvitas* seeks things of this world, *rectitudo*, those above. Yet, for righteousness to be "perfect," it must affect both thoughts and actions (*si recte in omnibus sentias et factis non dissentias*). The soul's condition, invisible to man, must be "announced" by both *fides* and *actio*. And the two, Bernard advises his brethren, must not be separated.[588]

Faith, then, lives by spirit, that is, in Bernard's terms, by hearing. This is the conclusion Bernard reaches after a set of sermons dealing with the Song's reference to the bride's "blackness" and "the curtains of Solomon."

In sermon twenty-five his text is, "I am black but beautiful."[589] Bernard asks, "What is repulsive in these words?"[590] Only *simplices*, he states, fail to distinguish between colour and form: the one pertains to inner composition, the other to superficial pigmentation.[591] Therefore, not everything that is black is deformed. Black gems and hair are attractive in themselves; and, while many things are "discoloured on the surface," they are "truly beautiful in makeup." Such is the case of the bride in her "place of pilgrimage": it shall be otherwise in her "native land," where she will present herself without blemish.

Analogies like these, which, of course, merely restate traditional medieval colour symbolism, turn up in sermon twenty-eight, in which Bernard turns to the significance of the curtains.[592] They are really those of the king's tent, he proposes, which are blackened from exposure to the elements. Yet they protect the tent's inner decoration.[593] For this reason, the text does not speak of the bride's denying her blackness, merely her excusing it.[594] Indeed, Bernard adds, through solicitude, "the darkness of one makes many bright." Just as one man

---

[586] *Ibid.*, 158, 5-p. 159, 2.   [587] *Ibid.*, 24.2.7, p. 159, 5-6.

[588] *Ibid.*, 24.3.7, p. 159, 10-p. 160, 3; *ibid.*, 24.3.8, p. 161, 3-4: "Mors fidei est separatio caritatis. Credis in Christum? Fac Christi opera, ut vivat fides tua: fidem tuam dilectio animet, probet actio."

[589] Cant 1:4.   [590] *Sermo* 25.2.3, p. 164, 12.

[591] *Ibid.*, 164, 12-14: "Propter simplices dico, qui inter colorem et formam discernere non noverunt, cum forma ad compositionem pertineat, nigredo color sit."

[592] Cant 1:4.   [593] *Sermo* 28.1.1, p. 192, 18-p. 193, 1.   [594] *Ibid.*, 193, 1-2.

died for all, so one woman is discoloured for all. Yet, Bernard sees in Solomon's exterior blackness "the form of our denigrated nature," that is, the very clothing with which our first parents covered their nakedness.[595] These same garments, he adds, are full of the promise of our "inheritance."[596]

To highlight the difference between appearances and reality Bernard turns to the contrast between seeing and hearing. As in Genesis, one may, like blind Isaac, be easily fooled. But the word is heard by faith, as is illustrated by a number of examples. For instance, the centurion who stood over Christ acknowledged his divinity on the expiring of his voice. "He knew the Lord not by his face but by his sound";[597] hearing discovered what as yet escaped the eye.[598] For, to look at, Christ was weak, miserable, and mortal; but the ear recognized him to be the son of God.[599] Again, Peter cut off the servant's ear so that the truth could find its way in.[600] For "faith comes by hearing."[601] True, it would be more appropriate for truth to enter the mind via the eyes. But that is reserved for the next life, when we shall see God "face to face." Meanwhile, man's "remedy" follows the same tracks as his "disease," light travelling, so to speak, through the paths of darkness. "The ear, death's first gateway, shall open up life. Hearing, which bore life, restores sight. For, unless we believe, we cannot understand."[602]

For Bernard, then, hearing alone grasps the truth,[603] since it understands through the word.[604] But what is the relationship of the word to God in an objective sense?

The answer is bound up once again with the experience of biblical texts, as is evident in sermon thirty-one. "Word," Bernard argues, appears as "bride" in biblical texts, but not always in the same fashion.[605] In fact, among the instances of the word's mystical presence, the Bible presents several possible "visions."[606] The loftiest occurs at the end of time, when the elect shall see God "as he is." God, of course, undergoes no change; and, Bernard adds, where the *forma* is immutable, the *visio* must also remain the same.[607] But, to see God

---

[595] *Ibid.*, 25.1.2, p. 193, 6-23.   [596] *Ibid.*, 25.1.3, p. 194, 7-10; Ps 2.8.

[597] *Ibid.*, 28.2.4, p. 195, 4-7; Mc 15.39.   [598] *Ibid.*, 28.2.5, p. 195, 9-10.

[599] *Ibid.*, 195, 10-11.   [600] Actus 7:51.   [601] *Sermo* 28.2.5, p. 195, 14-18; Rom 10.17.

[602] *Ibid.*, 195, 20-25.   [603] *Ibid.*, 28.2.6-3.8, pp. 196-98.

[604] *Ibid.*, 28.2.8, p. 197, 21: "Solus habet auditus verum, qui percipit verbum."

[605] *Ibid.*, 31.1.1, p. 219, 8-9.

[606] For a discussion, see E. von Ivánka, "La structure de l'âme selon S. Bernard," *Saint Bernard théologien*, 203-06.

[607] *Sermo* 31.1.1, p. 219, 9-21.

as he is is not "for the present life": now he appears to whom he wishes and as he wishes but not as he is. Neither sage, saint, nor prophet can see him as he is while living in a mortal body; they merely see him "as he wills." In this sense, God is like the sun, which is only seen by the light it sheds in the air, on a mountain, or on a wall. And, he reasons, we could not see light at all if the human eye did not bear some resemblance to its celestial radiance.[608] But even the eye's reflection of the sun is imperfect. Similarly, the human soul perceives God to the degree that he enlightens it.[609] The real advance in our spirit is through his.[610]

The fathers, Bernard states, speak of another kind of apparition by which God makes himself manifest in sundry forms and on an intimate level while remaining essentially one.[611] But, the most important sort of vision is the kind we have of God within ourselves, which is a byproduct of meditation.[612] Bernard then puts this interior image in the context of his previous statement on the value of spoken testimony. It is not a physical vision: take care, he admonishes, to understand that he is not making "the mixture of word and soul something corporeal or understandable through graphics."[613] He merely uses human language as Paul suggests to provide an incomplete picture of what is in fact ineffable.[614] The actual union is spiritual. For the word of God is not a sounding (*sonans*) but a penetrating (*penetrans*); it is not pronounced by the tongue but is efficacious to the spirit. It does not sensitize the ears but the affections.[615]

How then, we may ask, does it differ from a text? Bernard's mystical perspective would appear to include both possibilities at once, that is, a word which is heard, and thus authenticates the reality of faith, and a word which is internal, and, while perhaps heard as well, appears in the mind as spiritual truth.

Sermon thirty-two turns to a different aspect of the question, namely, how the word presents itself to the monk who is engaged in meditative prayer. Bernard first recapitulates what he previously said about vision and address. Although their language and images may seem

[608] *Ibid.*, 31.1.2, p. 220, 5-15.

[609] *Ibid.*, 220, 21-24.   [610] *Ibid.*, 31.1.3, p. 221, 1-4.

[611] *Ibid.*, 31.2.4, p. 221, 16-18.

[612] *Ibid.*, 31.2.4, p. 221, 25-26: ". . . qui expertus est."

[613] *Ibid.*, 31.2.6, p. 223, 1-2: "Vide autem tu, ne quid nos in hac Verbi animaeque commixtione corporeum sue imaginarium sentire existimes."

[614] *Ibid.*, 223, 2-5.

[615] *Ibid.*, 31.3.6, p. 223, 14-16: ". . . quo intus, non foris. Verbum nempe est, non sonans, sed penetrans; non loquax, sed efficax; non obstrepens auribus, sed affectibus blandiens."

corporeal, their intention is spiritual. Hence, their "causes" or "sources" must be sought in the spirit.[616] But this in turn requires that we investigate the spirit in ourselves.[617]

How does one in fact perceive the spirit? For Bernard, only in a mystical manner. If one desires God night and day and meditates upon him continuously, one occasionally "receives the word" like a chance visit from the groom in the Song. At such moments, the monk feels himself "embraced within *Sapientia*'s arms" as "her love's sweetness" is infused into him. Yet this experience is short-lived. Bernard returns to the metaphor of the groom: just when we catch hold of him, he slips away; and, as we weep in remorse, he appears before us again, allowing himself to be taken hold of but not to be held. He vanishes from view, and does not reappear until our minds and hearts have reattained a sufficient level of devotion. Moreover, the groom's visit brings both pleasure and pain; for, during the meditative process, one's inner thoughts struggle with good and evil.[618]

Bernard asks his fellow monks: "Have we not often felt this tension as we prayed? Were we not both tempted by the present and tormented by the past?"[619] Some, he grants, may not have had this experience.[620] They are the "tired in spirit." But there is an answer to their problem.[621] Whenever celestial thoughts are entertained, their source must be acknowledged as the Lord.[622] The monks must think of Him as speaking within them.[623] "For the cogitations of our mind are very similar to the words of truth pronounced within." Of course, he repeats, it is not easy for one to distinguish between "what he hears" and "what the heart brings forth from within."[624] But there is plentiful evidence in the Bible that both evil and good thoughts spring up inside man. The difference is this: the evil in our hearts is our own

[616] *Ibid.*, 32.1.1, p. 226, 19-22: "Nam etsi verba illa, quibus ipsae visiones seu similitudines describuntur, sonare corpora atque corporea videantur, spiritualia tamen sunt quae nobis ministrantur in his, ac per hoc in spiritu quoque causas et rationes earum oportet inquiri."

[617] *Ibid.*, 226, 24-227, 5.

[618] *Ibid.*, 32.1.2-3, p. 226, 6-28.

[619] *Ibid.*, 228, 3-5: "Annon saepenumero sic sentimus, et sic experimur orantes, nos qui nostris quotidie adhuc excessibus tentamur praesentibus, mordemur praeteritis?"

[620] *Ibid.*, 228, 11-13; Is 61.1.

[621] *Ibid.*, 228, 13-14.

[622] *Ibid.*, 32.2.4, p. 228, 16-26.

[623] *Ibid.*, 32.2.5, p. 229, 5-6: "Tu ergo cum tibi talia volvi animo sentis, non tuam putes cogitationem, sed illum agnosce loquentem. . . ."

[624] *Ibid.*, 32.3.5, p. 229, 8-10: "Simillima enim sunt nostrae cogitata mentis sermonibus Veritatis in nobis loquentis; nec facile quis discernat quid intus pariat cor suum, quidve audiat, nisi qui prudenter advertit Dominum in Evangelio loquentem. . . ."

thought; the good is the speech of God.[625] In other words, the heart's goodness is not its own offspring but simply "God's voice."[626]

The presence of the word is a prelude to understanding oneself and God. This is the theme of sermons thirty-five to thirty-eight. Bernard's main text throughout is Song of Songs 1:17: *Si ignoras, egredere* . . . (If you are ignorant, go forth . . .). Sermon thirty-five interprets the verse as a contrast between the spirit and the flesh. Sermon thirty-six turns to the implications of knowing our own thoughts and those of our maker. The following two sermons embellish these subjects and provide a discussion of such matters as higher knowledge and despair.

In Bernard's view, the text means, "If you do not know yourself, you are commanded to go forth."[627] This is the language in which the groom appropriately addresses the bride. On the one hand, he can issue no more serious threat than the conditional ignorance of oneself; on the other, the bride must leave spirit for flesh, the heart's goodness for earthly desires, and internal peace for external cares. In other words, the spouse is bidden to seek *labor* and *dolor*. A soul that knows itself, one which "enters into itself" and "breathes after God's presence in its innermost being," would never consider experiencing the pain, chastisement, and slavery of the senses.[628] By implication, to know yourself in the Song's sense means to know that you are undeserving of "the contemplation of celestial, intelligible, and divine matters."[629] The text continues: "Go forth and feed the kids." This, Bernard says, means to go forth from God's sanctuary, that is, from your own heart, where truth and wisdom reside, in order to satisfy the external senses.[630] The "kids" represent sin or the bodily senses, which do not need spiritual nourishment. The "shepherd's tents" refer to the goods of this world, the region of bodies (*regio corporum*).[631] In short, the Song, for Bernard, speaks of the soul's exile from unity with God, of its degradation from spiritual to physical.[632] So fallen, man becomes one of the beasts.[633]

[625] *Ibid.*, 32.3.5, p. 229, 14-15: "Cum ergo mala in corde versamus, nostra cogitatio est; si bona, Dei est sermo."

[626] *Ibid.*, 32.3.7, p. 230, 19-28.   [627] *Ibid.*, 35.1.1, p. 249, 2-4.

[628] *Ibid.*, 249, 5-17.   [629] *Ibid.*, 35.1.2, p. 249, 30-p. 250, 1.

[630] *Ibid.*, 250, 1-4.

[631] *Ibid.*, 250, 6; 250, 13-14; 250, 14-15. On the "region of dissimilitude," see P. M. Standaert, "La doctrine de l'image chez saint Bernard," *Ephemerides Theologicae Louvaniensis* 23 (1947), 70-129, E. Gilson, " 'Regio dissimilitudinis' de Platon à Saint Bernard," *Mediaeval Studies* 9 (1947), 108-30, and W. Hiss, *Die Anthropologie Bernhards von Clairvaux*, 66-89.

[632] *Sermo* 35.1.3, p. 250.

[633] *Ibid.*, 35.2.3-5, pp. 251-52. Cf. C. Bodard, "La Bible, expression d'une expérience reli-

But what was the cause of man's fall? Ignorance. What did he fail to understand? The Bible does not say, but Bernard does: he was ignorant of himself and of God.[634]

This is the theme of sermon thirty-six. Before turning to it, Bernard asks whether all types of ignorance are damnable. No: in many cases, "not knowing" does not "diminish salvation." Lack of knowledge of carpentry, masonry, or other arts "useful in the present life" offers no impediment. Even training in the liberal arts is not essential. For Paul speaks of many who were saved not by *scientia litterarum* but by "a pure conscience and a faith unfeigned." They pleased their maker not through *scientia* but their *vitae merita*. Neither Peter, Andrew, nor the sons of Zebedee, he notes, were chosen from "the schools of rhetoric or philosophy." They spread "ways of life," not "sublime speech" and "the words of human wisdom."[635] Bernard does not condemn the study of letters as such, an intolerance of which he was often accused. He is aware how much *litterati* benefit the church.[636] But, he adds, such knowledge is like a picture, whose image must rest on a more solid base.[637]

In his view, there are two types of knowledge, one which inflates (*inflans*), the other which sobers (*contristans*).[638] Only the latter is "useful" and "necessary" for salvation.[639] Paul does not prohibit knowing (*sapere*), only knowing more than is necessary. But what does it mean to be wise for sobriety (*sapere ad sobrietatem*)?[640] To look carefully at one's preferences and priorities in knowing.[641] For, with respect to salvation, "time is short."[642] Of course, he reiterates, all knowledge is good, provided that it is subordinated to truth. But, in view of our earthly condition, we must concentrate on the sort of understanding which brings us closer to salvation. In this, knowledge is no different from medicine or food: the one cures disease, the other relieves hun-

gieuse chez S. Bernard," *Saint Bernard théologien*, 27-28, and, for a more explicit statement, see *In Cantica* 81.4.7-5.11, vol. 2, pp. 288-91 (on sin) and 82.2.2-8, pp. 293-98 (on dissimilitude).

[634] *Ibid.*, 35.4.9, p. 255, 2-3: "Patet ergo quia ignorans ignorabitur, sive se, sive Deum ignorare contingat."

[635] *Ibid.*, 36.1.1, vol. 2, pp. 3-4. On this theme see the thorough discussion of E. Kleineidam, "Wissen, Wissenschaft, Theologie bei Bernhard von Clairvaux," *Bernhard von Clairvaux*, 133-45 and more briefly J.-M. Déchanet, "La christologie de saint Bernard," *ibid.*, 64-65; also J. Sommerfeldt, "Epistemology, Education and Social Theory in the Thought of Bernard of Clairvaux," *Saint Bernard of Clairvaux*, 170-71.

[636] *Sermo* 36.1.2, p. 4, 15-17.   [637] *Ibid.*, 37.1.2, p. 10, 3-5.

[638] *Ibid.*, 36.1.2, p. 4, 20-21; 1 Cor 8:1; Eccle 1:18.

[639] *Ibid.*, 4, 21-24.   [640] *Ibid.*, 5, 4-5.

[641] *Ibid.*, 5, 5-6: "Vigilantissime observare quid scire magis priusve oporteat."

[642] 1 Cor 7:29.   [643] *Sermo* 36.1.2, p. 5, 7-14.

ger, but only if taken in due measure.[643] For, to his mind, Paul taught not merely a number of facts but the manner in which we should know them, that is, wherein consists the "fruit" and "utility" of knowing. By the *sciendi modus* he meant "the order, desire, and end" of knowledge, either for one's own edification or one's neighbour.[644]

By this route Bernard returns to knowledge of oneself and of God, which is the subject of sermons thirty-seven and thirty-eight. In both cases the discussion begins with interior conversion. Having passed through the first bitter stages, the individual begins "to breathe in the hope of consolation." As such, he already enjoys "the temporal fruit of his tears." He has both "seen God" and "heard his voice."[645]

The process in Bernard's view is twofold. In shedding tears, we discover knowledge of ourselves; in joy, knowledge of God.[646] But, having acquired this dual potential, we stand in danger of being "puffed up" by earthly learning or honours. For this charity which we have earned "infuses" the heart with certitude.[647] Yet, paradoxically, although our own learning furthers us little, nonetheless we cannot live in ignorance of God. For how can hope be placed in one whom one does not know? And, if we are ignorant of ourselves, how can we have true humility, which consists in denying our earthly importance?[648] We must guard against these two kinds of ignorance, the one being sin's source, the other its consummation.

A parallel occurs to Bernard with the manner in which we acquire wisdom. Just as the first of the two kinds of knowledge is the beginning of wisdom, the second its perfection, so the two kinds of ignorance stand in a similar relationship to sin. As fear of the Lord is the beginning of wisdom, so pride is the beginning of sin; as love of God is the consummation of wisdom, so despair is the end result of sin.[649] Bernard sees the stages as pride, which overvalues our worth, then ignorance of God, which leads to despair.[650] For, if someone looking inwardly at himself recalls his sinful past and hopes to convert, yet is not acquainted with God's goodness, his own thoughts will quickly drive him to desperation. And, either he will remain depressed or take up with the world again.[651] In the end, he concludes, no one can

---

[644] *Ibid.*, 36.2.3, p. 5, 15-24.   [645] *Ibid.*, 37.2.4, p. 11, 5-8.

[646] *Ibid.*, 11, 18-19: "Ubi breviter comprehensa utraque cognitio est: et nostri quidem in lacrimis serens, quae autem Dei metens in gaudio."

[647] *Ibid.*, 37.3.5, p. 11, 20-25.   [648] *Ibid.*, 11, 26-12, 3.

[649] *Ibid.*, 37.3.6, p. 12, 5-14.

[650] *Ibid.*, 12, 16-26.   [651] *Ibid.*, 38.1.1, p. 14, 9-p. 15, 3.

have knowledge of God who does not undergo conversion towards him.[652] That is the first stage of self-enlightenment. As Bernard later puts it, each monk must recognize spiritual reality in his own life history.[653] This, again, means proceeding from biblical text to meditation and to new experience. As such, the monk is both subject, reflecting on a text, and object, who becomes a "text" for further reflection.

The ultimate purpose of self-knowledge is to examine our intentions. This is the topic of sermon forty. Bernard's text is, "Your cheeks are beautiful as the turtle dove's."[654] At these words, he observes, the bride must have blushed. For the soul, which she represents, is an incorporeal and invisible substance, possessing neither members nor colour. He admonishes his brethren to try to achieve "the intuition of the spiritual by means of the spiritual." For "the face of the soul" is really "the intention of the mind."[655] Just as one's body is judged by one's face, the righteousness of a work is judged by the intentions of the doer. Moreover, these intentions involve two things, the object (res) and the reason (causa), that is, what you intend (quid intendas) and for what purpose (propter quid). By these alone can one measure the "beauty or deformity" of the soul.[656] But why compare the soul to a turtle dove? Because, Bernard replies, of its shyness and solitary life. As the bride reserves herself for the groom, the praiseworthy monk thinks only of the singular experience of God.[657] He must withdraw in mind and body from others' company,[658] striving after the exclusion of "common" and "present" things in his *mentis et spiritus solitudo*.[659] Everything, he adds, depends on one's frame of mind. For one can find solitude in a crowd and feel others' presence when alone.[660]

In sermon forty-one, Bernard relates the question of the internal life to the manner in which physical signs bespeak spiritual realities. His text is, "Your neck is as jewels; we will make you chains of gold inlaid with silver."[661] In a passage suffused with Pauline mysticism, he attempts to explain the imagery in terms of levels of experience of the divine.

---

[652] *Ibid.*, 38.2.2, p. 15, 8-9: "Ego autem dico omnes ignorare Deum, qui nolunt converti ad eum."

[653] *Sermo* 39.1.3, p. 19, 27-28: "Non ambigo quosdam iam vestrum in semetipsis recognoscere quae dicuntur, proprioque experimento commonitos ad intelligentiam praevolare."

[654] Cant 1:9.   [655] *Sermo* 40.1.1, p. 24, 19-p. 25, 1.   [656] *Ibid.*, 40.2.2, p. 25, 11-13.

[657] *Ibid.*, 40.3.4, p. 26, 20-22.   [658] *Ibid.*, 27, 5-9.

[659] *Ibid.*, 40.3.5, p. 27, 16-19.   [660] *Ibid.*, 27, 20.   [661] Cant 1:10.

We must take into consideration, he emphasizes, what sort of chains these are. Gold represents "the brightness of divinity," that is, "the wisdom from above." The physical gold is thus equated with the *signacula veritatis*, which, to extend the metaphors, the heavenly ministers fit onto "the internal ears of the soul."[662] But these, he adds, are nothing but the *spirituales similitudines*, by which the purest thoughts emanating from divinity are presented to the contemplative soul. Through them, it is permitted "to see as through a glass darkly."[663] Furthermore, these thoughts (*sensa*) are divine, and unknown to those who have not experienced them; otherwise, we, who are limited to the flesh, would never attain the sublimity of inner contemplative truth.[664] At best we might say, "Now I know in part and prophesy in part."[665] Bernard also provides some details on the nature of the experience. On occasion, he states, the soul, superseding itself, is transported momentarily to a higher state. It perceives the imagistic likenesses (*imaginatoriae similitudines*) of inferior things, which help to make the divine "more tolerable" and "more acceptable."[666] Such images, he repeats, temper divinity's pure radiance;[667] or perhaps they are part of what Paul saw as *speculum atque aenigma*.

But what happens when the bride and groom meet face to face? This possibility is briefly taken up in sermon forty-five. Bernard's text is, "Behold, you are fair. . . . Your eyes are those of doves."[668] Love, he explains, is the source of the bride's presumption as well as the groom's displeasure. But he also sees in this verse a recapitulation of the soul's threefold spiritual progress. "For presumption is followed by reproof, reproof by correction, and correction by reward."[669] All formality and ceremony are put off: the Word and the soul, like two long-standing neighbours, now enjoy *familiaris confabulatio*.[670]

Moreover, the soul is now "fair" in two senses, that of humility and innocence.[671] But what of the conversation itself? As in the case of the "gold and silver chains," Bernard continues, their words do not "adorn the body's ears" but "inform the hearing of the heart." As the soul's heart is more purified from the faith which comes from hearing, she herself is made more capable of seeing what previously lay beyond

---

662 *Sermo* 41.3.3, p. 30, 8-11.   663 *Ibid.*, 30, 11-15; 1 Cor 13.12.
664 *Ibid.*, 30, 15-19.   665 1 Cor 13.12; 1 Cor 13.19.   666 *Sermo* 41.3.3, p. 30, 21-27.
667 *Ibid.*, 30, 27-29.   668 Cant 1.14.
669 *Sermo* 45.1.1, p. 49, 24-26.   670 *Ibid.*, 50, 5.
671 *Ibid.*, 45.1.2, p. 50, 11-16; 45.2.3, p. 51, 13-15.

her.[672] The groom delights that the bride now "perceives in spirit," a fact confirmed by her "dove-like eyes." Bernard allows that the vision of Christ of which he is speaking is a mystical experience in the present and, as such, inferior to the real presence in the afterlife. But Bernard is trying to convert his monastic brethren now, and, in order to attribute value to his vision, returns to the Song's words, "Behold, you are fair, my love, and comely." The bride, he reasons, has evidently been exalted, as she now claims the groom as *her* beloved.[673] I think, he adds, that there is nothing here of images of a sensory nature, either of the flesh, the cross, or other corporeal things.[674] What is implied is simply that the groom has appeared *in visione meliori*. Like Moses of old, he speaks from mouth to mouth (*ore . . . ad os*). And she sees God openly, not through allegories or figures.[675] In fact, in Bernard's view, her words are as sweet as her vision, language, so to speak, on this occasion, transcending ordinary usage and approaching pure spirituality.

Bernard then anticipates the objections of his brethren. One might ask: how can she reply to the Word? For *we* speak with words, but the Word is not spoken. Also, the soul can speak only through the body's mouth.[676]

The doubts, Bernard admits, are justified. But they must bear in mind that the holy spirit is speaking, and that its words must be understood spiritually. The statement appears to apply equally to the content and to the linguistic form. Whenever, he adds, one hears or reads of the Word and the soul in dialogue, corporeal sounds are not exchanged any more than realities are actually speaking.[677] For the

[672] *Ibid.*, 45.3.5, p. 52, 16-20: "Et si placeat, oportet referas capitulum praesens ad id, quod paulo ante sodales muraenulas ei facere aureas promiserunt, non intendentes, ut tunc docui, ornare aures corporis, sed informare auditum cordis. Potuit itaque fieri, ut fide, quae est ex auditu, corde amplius mundato, ad videndum, quod ante non poterat, instructior redderetur."

[673] *Ibid.*, 45.3.6-4.6, p. 53, 3-10.

[674] *Ibid.*, 45.4.6, p. 53, 11-13: "Existimo enim nequaquam hac vice eius sensibus importatas imagines carnis, aut crucis, aut alias quascumque corporearum similitudines infirmatum."

[675] *Ibid.*, 53, 14-17.

[676] *Ibid.*, 45.5.7, p. 54, 5-10: " 'Qua ratione verba Verbi facta ad animam referuntur, et rursum animae ad Verbum, ut illa audierit vocem loquentis sibi et perhibentis quod pulchra sit, vicissimque idem praeconium suo mox reddiderit laudatori? Quomodo possunt haec fieri? Nam verbo loquimur, non verbum loquitur. Itemque anima non habet unde loquatur, nisi os corporis sibi verba formaverit ad loquendum.' "

[677] *Ibid.*, 54, 11-14: Quoties proinde audis vel legis Verbum atque animam pariter colloqui, et se invicem intueri, noli tibi imaginari quasi corporeas intercurrere voces, sicut nec corporeas colloquentium apparere imagines.

Word is spirit and the soul is spirit. They both have tongues, with which they communicate to each other and indicate their presence. The Word's "tongue" is the bestowing of favour, the soul's, the fervor of devotion. The impious soul is, so to speak, "tongueless"; it is "an infant," which does not possess the capacity for "conversation with the Word."[678] Moreover, when the Word wishes to speak with her, the soul is obliged to hear what is said. And when the soul speaks, the Word always hears, since, in effect, she speaks through him.[679] Therefore, the Word's speech is really an infusion of grace (*locutio Verbi infusio doni*).[680]

In sermons forty-nine and fifty, Bernard turns to the subject of charity. His text is, "The king brought me into the wine-cellar; he set charity in order in me."[681]

Of all the king's cellars, the wine-cellar is special. In Bernard's interpretation, it refers to the ecstasy of prayer, the penetration of divine mysteries, and the zeal of the burning heart. Through it, the initiate begins to appreciate "the wine of happiness." Of this sort of *contemplationis excessus* there are two species, one in the understanding (*in intellectu*), the other in affections (*in affectu*). The one acts through light, the other through fervor; the one in knowing (*agnitio*), the other in devotion (*devotio*).[682]

"He set charity in order in me," states the bride. This, Bernard argues, was necessary, since zeal without knowledge is unsupportable. The more ardent the desire to please, the greater the benefits of discretion (*discretio*), which, Bernard adds, is the *ordinatio caritatis*. It is written, "By your ordering my day goes on."[683] By "day," Bernard proposes, the psalmist meant "virtue." *Discretio*, in other words, is not so much a virtue in itself as a moderator and director (*moderatrix et auriga*) of virtues, an orderer of affections and a teacher of morals. The groom, that is, the Word, originally "ordered charity" when he created the church, giving us apostles, prophets, evangelists, pastors, and teachers. Binding them by a single bond of charity requires order. So charity, in order to provide order, must first be ordered itself.[684]

Charity, Bernard continues, exists in two forms, in action (*in actu*)

[678] *Ibid.*, 54, 14-19.   [679] *Ibid.*, 54, 19-24.
[680] *Ibid.*, 45.5.8, p. 55, 2. Cf. J.-M. Déchanet, "La christologie de S. Bernard," *Saint Bernard théologien*, 89-90.
[681] Cant 2.4.   [682] *Sermo* 49.1.4, p. 75, 14-26.
[683] Ps 118.91.   [684] *Sermo* 49.2.5, p. 75, 27-p. 76, 17.

and in affection (*in affectu*).[685] In general, action belongs to this world, affection to the next. In enjoining law upon men, God demanded action. For commands cannot be implemented by feelings alone. One can put the matter another way by stating that active charity brings about merit, affective charity, reward. Bernard does not deny that anticipations of grace occur in the present. But life's consummation remains a future ideal. Why, then, did God give man an order which he can only partially carry out? God well knew that: but he thought man should be reminded continuously of his insufficiency and presented with unattainable goals. The ultimate goal of God's actions was to increase our humility.[686]

When the Lord gave commands like "Love your neighbour," and "Love your enemies," he added that we were to make an external demonstration of charitable works. This was active, not affective, charity. For, by ordering us to obey the commandments, God effectively directed us towards works. As in the case of the law, if his love were only a matter of feeling, works would be superfluous.[687] Of course, Bernard does not advise his monks to exercise their hands and not their hearts.[688] There are, he states, three sorts of affective charity which they can practice: one which flesh instils, another which reason rules, and a third which wisdom establishes. The first is subject to no law, while the second is law's byproduct. The third, by implication, eliminates the need for the first and rewards the second. Is it then effective or affective charity which the bride "orders?" Both, *actualis* first, then *affectualis*.[689] Naturally, Bernard admits, we are normally preoccupied with "peace on earth" rather than "glory on high." We minister little to the soul, much to the body.[690] In this sense, "necessity has no law."[691] Effective charity simply pursues its course. But, for affective impulses to be released, we must demand, not the "truth of charity" but the "charity of truth." Once again, both law and text are transcended by the Word.

Bernard's "commentary" on the Song of Songs has now been followed to the point at which the central elements in his doctrine of reform are reasonably clear. The analysis has not dealt with all of Bernard's writings on the theme, but has the advantage of illustrating

[685] *Ibid.*, 50.1.2, p. 79, 5.   [686] *Ibid.*, 79, 5-20.
[687] *Ibid.*, 50.1.3, p. 79, 24-p. 80, 1.
[688] *Ibid.*, 50.1.4, p. 80, 8-10.
[689] *Ibid.*, 50.2.5, p. 80, 29-p. 81, 1.   [690] *Ibid.*, 81, 5-11.   [691] *Ibid.*, 81, 18-19.

how his thought develops as a set of meditations on an interdependent group of biblical texts.

His discussion begins with "experience," which may be understood as everyday monastic routine or, in a more technical sense, as the experience of the text, that is, as hermeneutics. In Bernard's mind the two are interrelated. Just as man's understanding begins with the perceptions of the senses, so the point of departure for the mystical appreciation of God begins with the tangible element in the sacraments. His interpretations of the various verses of the Song of Songs are all based on dramatic situations or concrete symbols, thereby creating in the listener's or the reader's mind the impression of a palpable reality being experienced by Bernard himself.

As a result, all mysticism for Bernard involves both the text and reality: it is partly sensorial, partly intellectual, or rather intellectual through first being sensorial. He continually repeats that one cannot understand a biblical text until one has "experienced" it. Only after initiation, ritualized meditation, and interiorization is one sufficiently enlightened to be able to reapply precepts, that is, new texts, to everyday activities and thereby to achieve lasting spiritual progress.[692] Behind the Song stands St. Paul, who is quoted in almost every sermon. The one text is used to give form to the other, just as the New Testament supersedes the Old. But meaning does not arise in the scholastic fashion from a comparison of different texts. Like a physical sign, the text is a given; in that sense, it is a "record" of tangible reality. Internalized, it allows formerly experienced historical events like the fall and the crucifixion to be reimposed on life.[693]

Bernard has Anselm's respect for the Word as "evidence," but uses his insights differently. If, for Anselm, God and, to a lesser degree, man, are text-producers, Bernard is more interested in distinguishing between orality as "the person who speaks" and the text as "the words pronounced."[694] In contrast to Anselm, he sees in former authorities only "mediators of the divine word."[695] It is the *sapientiae spiritus* itself which speaks poetically through the Song, as he sees it, and creates its many layers of mystical and allegorical meaning.[696] "Thus," Far-

---

[692] Cf. Y. Congar, "L'ecclésiologie de S. Bernard," *S. Bernard théologien*, 143: "De toute évidence, ce qui intéresse Bernard dans l'Eglise, ce n'est pas tant le mystère objectif et transpersonnel, c'est la réalité concrète que ce mystère a dans les âmes saintes."

[693] Cf. J. Mouroux, "Sur les critères de l'expérience spirituelle . . . ," *ibid.*, 262-67.

[694] D. Farkasfalvy, *L'inspiration de l'Ecriture*, 27.

[695] *Ibid.*, 42.

[696] For a discussion, see M. Dumontier, *Saint Bernard et la Bible*, 130-39.

kasfalvy observes, "when Bernard evokes the birth of the word in spiritual experience, it is the genesis of his own preaching and of his writings which he retraces."[697]

His focus is on the nexus "letter/spirit" with its clear links with sacramental mystery. And this in turn leads him inevitably back to the concrete: *Habeo et ego Verbum, sed in carne; et mihi apponitur veritas, sed in sacramento.*[698] Bernard defines *sacramentum* as *sacrum signum* or *sacrum secretum* in the Augustinian fashion,[699] but he nearly always illustrates sacramental realities by means of the physical rather than the abstract. Unlike later scholastics, he does not divide the sacramental process into two operations, the one consequent upon "efficient causes . . . created in the soul," the other upon "material causes," that is, "dispositive causes of sanctifying grace."[700] Instead, he maintains a position which more erudite, thirteenth-century thinkers called "sacramental causality."

For *sacramenta*, he argues, following Radbert, are signs with external manifestations. As such, they parallel the mode of operation of other rites of investiture, for instance, the normal ecclesiastical ceremonies involving the book, the staff, and the ring.[701] The "dispositive" element is oral, tangible, and conveyed by the principles of gift exchange. One may think of the sermons on the Song of Songs as Bernard's most extensive documentation of this belief, which, as noted earlier in this volume, does not consist of a simple renaissance of literacy but, in addition to that, of an acculturation of oral tradition. Therefore, although utilizing sophisticated methods of interpretation, the sermons are in fact just the opposite of an abstract separation of

---

[697] *L'inspiration de l'Ecriture*, 60.

[698] *Sermo* 33.2.3, vol. 1, p. 235, 10-11; cf. R-J. Hesbert, "Saint Bernard et l'eucharistie," *Mélanges saint Bernard*, 160-62, and, on Bernard's notion of *sacramentum*, see J. Leclercq, "Christusnachfolge und Sakrament in der Theologie des heiligen Bernhard," *Archiv für Liturgiewissenschaft* 8 (1963), 59-64, 68-71. On the place of the sermons in the liturgy itself, see H. Rochais and J. Leclercq, "La tradition des sermons liturgiques de S. Bernard," *Scriptorium* 15 (1961), 240-84.

[699] *In Cena Domini*, c. 2, *Sermones*, vol. 2 (Rome, 1968), p. 69, 11.

[700] W. J. Courtenay, "The King and the Leaden Coin: The Economic Background of 'Sine qua non' Causality," *Traditio* 28 (1972), 190.

[701] *In Cena Domini*, c. 2, p. 68, 18-p. 69, 5: "Ad hoc instituta sunt omnia sacramenta, ad hoc eucharistiae participatio. . . . Sicut enim in exterioribus sunt diversa signa et, ut coepto immoremur exemplo, variae sunt investiturae secundum ea de quibus investimur,—verbi gratia, investitur canonicus per librum, abbas per baculum, episcopus per baculum et anulum simul—, sicut, inquam, in huiusmodi rebus est, sic et divisiones gratiarum diversis traditae sunt sacramentis." For an able discussion, see W. J. Courtenay, "Sacrament, Symbol, and Causality in Bernard of Clairvaux," *Bernard of Clairvaux*, 111-18.

words, thoughts, and things. Oddly enough, Bernard's notion of sin as an interior fault correctable only through contrition and desire for improvement is not far from Abelard's moral intentionality: proof, if it were needed, that despite differences of personality and doctrine the two had in common a search for theological truth through texts[702] which merely led them in different directions.

[702] Cf. P. Delhaye, *Le problème de la conscience morale chez S. Bernard étudié dans ses oeuvres et dans ses sources* (Namur, 1957), 11.

V.

RITUALS, SYMBOLS, AND INTERPRETATIONS

Nec mireris, frater charissime, quod haec
haeresis nostro moderno tempore crevit,
quo justitia excessit terris.
—Abbo of Fleury, *Ep.* 14

The influence of literate ways of thinking has now been traced through heresy, reform, sacramental theology, and the philosophical attitudes towards texts. These changes within medieval cultural life, it was proposed, were not only produced by a renaissance of higher disciplines. They also revealed a new balance between oral and written communication, adapted, as it were, to the needs of different branches of thought. Culture, therefore, was reborn, while the forms through which it expressed itself emerged as self-conscious instruments of analysis.

As experience became richer, deeper, and more complex, it also demanded a different shape. Interpretive models evolved from texts, whether disseminated by verbal or written means, were increasingly called upon to provide explanations for behavioural patterns. Just as, for Abelard, the mind acquired the capacity through the use of language to structure the raw data of the senses, so written statements began to act as reference points for giving meaning to everyday human relations.

How did such texts operate as intermediaries between thought and action? There is no simple formula for answering this question. Nor are the techniques of contemporary literary history an infallible guide. For, by and large, the discussion of "literature," that is, of the written record, presupposes a clearcut textual tradition, which, in the case of medieval models, is rarely furnished. The final text summarizes and records events, but it omits the stages of oral and written interchange along the way.

The present chapter can be described as a series of case histories of such textual encounters. It is also an interpretive essay, which takes up themes and ideas from previous discussions and attempts to illustrate them through the patterns imposed on life by typical individuals. The point of departure in each example is the idea of modernity, that is, in medieval terms, the awareness on the actor's or the narrator's part that, for reasons difficult to specify, the present had become unlike the past, a fact which in itself demanded reflection and explanation. This, in turn, involved new interrelations between rituals, symbols, and texts.

More precisely, for the articulation of interpretive models, there had to be, if not a fully written text, at least some formalized discourse, which, if recollected by a non-literate, could, while remaining unwritten, nonetheless offer a focal point for subsequent thinking and acting, the two being progressively distinguished on his part only as the criteria of literacy were imposed on them. Texts, so utilized, inevitably structured aspects of experience which, before their advent, were not thought of as being structured at all. Moreover, as a by-product of reading, writing, and more widespread education, patterns of behaviour were not only derived more and more from established texts, although that itself was an important development. The patterns, crystallizing from symbolic action, were also contextualized; that is, while still largely existing as forms of experience, they were increasingly compared to textual exemplars or justified by them. As written language gradually reoriented man's faculties of interpretation, the models produced could not help but feed back into the network of real social relations.

Rodulf Glaber's "Stories"

Let us begin with Rodulf Glaber, who effectively represents the prehistory of the *mentalité* which we are examining. For, although Glaber is himself literate, his *Historiae* do not clearly distinguish individual from collective activity, visible from invisible causal forces, or rituals and symbols in experience from textual models of interpretation imposed upon them.

As an empirical historian, therefore, Glaber leaves much to be desired. He tells his "stories," Prou noted, "in the fashion of old men and children," in which "one idea calls others to mind";[1] that is, he writes in an associative rather than a sequential fashion. The critical

---

[1] *Historiae*, preface, vii.

mind is inclined to pry the factual content, such as it is, from its often erroneous interpretive encrustations. But that is to tell only half the story. Glaber's purpose is not just to relate what has taken place but to understand and explain it as best he can. In doing so, he reverts to what his age considered to be standard exegetical procedures.[2] More importantly, he levels types of change to a common denominator. He felt that the physical misfortunes of the world were somehow connected to the absence of stable institutions and government. But he gave no special place within his enumeration of catastrophes to plagues, poor weather, prodigies, insurrections, heresies, or invasions. He applied this homespun equivalence of causal mechanisms both to material recorded in earlier texts and to events which took place in his own day. In part he echoed the crude fatalism of many peasant and rural societies. But he was also making use of the principle of causality as he understood it. The natural, human, or supernatural agencies which periodically wrought destruction were all considered from an eschatological standpoint.

The harmonization of types of change with a mind to their long-term effects helps to elucidate a number of otherwise puzzling aspects of his imagination. Perhaps the easiest to recognize is his over-simplification of the significance of the millennium and of its symbolic associations. But there are other elements: his intermingling of the scientific, based on fact, and the superstitious, based on hearsay; his denomination of all spiritual troubles, whether heretical or orthodox, lay or ecclesiastical, peasant or noble, under the same rubric; and his reworking of collective ideas such as penance, pilgrimage, and the peace of God not merely as abstractions but as realities informing the otherwise meaningless lives of historical actors. To this notion of enactment, we may add his habit of juxtaposing local and universal events: he devotes little more space to the conversion of Hungary than to the mysterious rain of pebbles at the disputed farm of a certain Arlebaud at Joigny on the Yonne. He not only relates events which classical canons of taste would have considered inappropriate. He also refuses to separate the oral and the written record. Yet, curiously, this odd mixture of events and emotions takes us to the centre of eleventh-century fears, frustrations, and unfulfilled expectations.

[2] See J. France, "The Divine Quaternity of Rodulfus Glaber," *Studia Monastica* 17 (1975), 283-94; and, on the source, P. Dutton, "Raoul Glaber's *De Divisione Quaternitate*: An Unnoticed Reading of Eriugena's Translation of the *Ambigua* of Maximus the Confessor," *Mediaeval Studies* 42 (1980), 431-53.

To turn to the text, the *Historiae* are organized so that Glaber's personal responses to events and conditions may serve as a point of departure for understanding the history of religious experience between about 980 and 1040. Books one and two by and large record misfortunes, which are, in his view, the legacy of Adam's disreputable behaviour in the garden of Eden.[3] However, order, discipline, and spiritual progress make their appearance just before the year 1000, reaching the apogee of their development within the thirty-three years that recapitulate the life-span of Christ.[4] Book one ends by describing a number of calamities, real or imagined, in the religious life. One can sum up the contrasting themes of the two books by stating that group activity would appear to be working both for and against civilization.

In book three, despite new disasters, the religious revival foreshadowed in book two begins to take place. Its subject, and the essence of Glaber's overall message, is the appearance of a collective religious sensibility in the northwest of Europe and the growing desire of lay and ecclesiastical groups for participation, chiefly through mass movements. Men of all strata of society yearn for an articulated, externalized, even institutionalized means of expressing new values, goals, and alliances. The desire does not first appear as a set of abstract ideas advocating such clearly defined notions as "reform" or "universalism." It occurs in forms in which the actors and the author are barely conscious of inner meanings, that is, in dreams, visions, or apparitions. In other words, it is concretized before it is made abstract. Although elsewhere Glaber does not hesitate to moralize on motives or events, he is reluctant to comment at length on these exceptional occurrences. He thereby leaves the bewildered reader to fend for himself. In this

---

[3] *Historiae* 1.5.26, pp. 24-25.

[4] It is now widely recognized that the millennium's significance was exaggerated by Michelet, Sismondi, and other nineteenth-century historians. For similar conclusions, see F. Plaine, "Les prétendues terreurs de l'an mille," *Revue des questions historiques* 13 (1873), 145-64 (on Glaber, 156-59); P. Orsi, "L'anno Mille. (Saggio di critica storia)," *Rivista storica italiana* 4 (1887), 1-56 (on Glaber, 43-44); and more generally, F. Lot, "Le mythe des terreurs de l'an mille," in *Recueil des travaux de F. Lot*, vol. 1 (Geneva and Paris, 1968), 398-414. A useful collection of translations with commentary is G. Duby, *L'an mille* (Paris, 1967). The theme of eschatology, Antichrist, and empire attracted earlier German historians; see K. Grund, *Die Anschauungen des Radulfus Glaber in seinen Historien* (Greifswald, 1910) and the broader survey of E. Wadstein, *Die eschatologische Ideengruppe: Antichrist—Weltsabbat—Weltende und Weltgericht in den Haupt momenten ihrer christlich-mittelalterlichen Gesamtentwickelung* (Leipzig, 1896), 7-36. For a recent review, see P. Classen, "Eschatologische Ideen und Armutsbewegungen im 11. und 12. Jahrhundert," *Povertà e ricchezza nella spiritualità dei secoli XI e XII* (Todi, 1969), 126-62.

sense, his stories demand interpretations. Of course, care must be taken not to impose too much coherence on the various episodes. The real problem is not Glaber's lack of lucidity but that the events he understands lucidly are not always those we want to have explained. Throughout the *Historiae* one is struck by the contrast between the vividness of those scenes and the utter lack of analysis with which they are related.

In general, the place of reflection is taken by movements of people, in particular, group movements and the ideas that accompany them. The masses become an amorphous intermediary between the individual and the forces of good and evil. The roles are gradually spelled out in the episodes of books one and two.

Book one, chapter four, contains among other details three examples of this sort of interaction, each of which is taken from the reign of a different Ottonian emperor. The stories are well enough known that a brief summary of each will suffice.

With the fall of the last Carolingians,[5] Glaber narrates, the imperial responsibility fell on the worthy shoulders of Otto I, whose frontiers were unfortunately subject to Moslem incursions. On one occasion, Maieul, the abbot of Cluny, was kidnapped for a ransom of a thousand pounds. Wounded in the hand, the abbot wrote for help, and, while held prisoner in the mountains, he impressed the heathen with his saintly behaviour. He refused their bread, whereupon he was made a fresh loaf; and an Arab who trod on his Bible was reprimanded, later losing his foot in a quarrel. The ransom was finally paid, and the Arabs were slaughtered at La Garde Freinet by William of Arles.[6]

This story is followed by an episode from the reign of Otto II telling of the martyrdom of Adalbert, bishop of Prague. He had been making progress in his missionary work among the Prussians, but one day announced that he had a premonition of death. Shortly afterwards, he ordered a sacred tree by a river to be cut down and had a Christian altar built in its place. The unconverted shot arrows at him, and, when he had completed the inaugural ceremony, he died. His disciples carried his body back to Prague, where, Glaber adds, it has since performed many beneficial acts.[7]

[5] *Historiae* 1.4.8, p. 10.

[6] *Ibid.*, 1.4.9, pp. 10-12. On the events of the capture in 967, see E. Sackur, *Die Cluniacenser* (Halle, 1892-94), I, 222, 230-32; on Maieul's diplomatic journeys, 217-29.

[7] *Historiae* 1.4.10, pp. 12-13. Martyred by heathen Prussians on the Baltic coast, Adalbert

The third story, taken from the time of Otto III, concerns the ill-considered revolt of Crescentius. During the early years of the emperor's reign, the papacy was vacant. Otto nominated his cousin, Bruno, the son of the duke of Carinthia, but Crescentius, a Roman aristocrat, deposed him with the aid of a local faction and installed the bishop of Piacenza in his place. When Otto marched on Rome, Crescentius and his followers shut themselves up in the Castel Sant'Angelo. Otto nonetheless subdued the city, mutilated the imposter pope, and besieged the ancient fortress housing the rebels. Crescentius, disguised as a pilgrim, appeared before the emperor, begging for his life. Otto said to him: "How is it that . . . the judge of emperors . . . and the creator of popes enters a humble Saxon abode? Take this man back to his lofty throne until a more suitable welcome can be arranged." Crescentius was returned to the Castel Sant'Angelo, while Otto drew up his artillery. Crescentius was later thrown from the ramparts, dragged through the city's gutters, and hanged in public view.[8]

What do these grisly stories tell us about Glaber's inner concerns? First, it should be noted, he committed two errors in arranging the episodes to suit his designs. The martyrdom of Adalbert took place on 23rd April 997 in the reign of Otto III, not Otto II. The latter died in 983, by which time Otto III was three, not twelve. Consciously or otherwise, then, Glaber placed a major event in each monarch's period. And what the three narratives have in common is the skilful interweaving of historical events and ritual gestures. In each case, a single significant act on the part of an important personage effectively recreates an entire previous tradition of similar thinking

was ransomed by King Boleslas and buried at Gniezno in 1039. His remains were later translated to Prague. For a review of the evidence, see F. Dvornik, *The Making of Central and Eastern Europe*, 2nd. ed. (Albany, 1974), 131-33, and p. xx, summarizing S. Mielczarski, *Misja praska Świętego Wojciecha* (Gdańsk, 1967).

[8] *Historiae* 1.4.12, pp. 13-15. On the revolt of Crescentius, the son of Crescentius de Theodora, who was killed by Otto III on 29 April 998, see P. Fedele, "Richerche per la storia di Roma e del papato nel secolo X," *Archivio della Reale Società Romana di Storia Patria* 34 (1911), 408-23; G. Bossi, *I Crescenzi. Contributo alla storia dal 900 al 1012* (Vatican City, 1915); C. Cecchelli, *I Crescenzi, i Savelli, i Cenci* (Rome, 1942); and O. Gerstenberg, "Studien zur Geschichte des römischen Adels im Ausgange des 10. Jahrhunderts," *Historische Vierteljahrschrift* 31 (1937), 1-26. Good brief reviews of the involvement of the Crescentii in urban politics are found in B. Hamilton, "Crescentii," *New Catholic Encyclopedia* 4, 443-44 and, with earlier bibliography, M. Falco, "Crescenzi," *Enciclopedia italiana*, vol. 2, 840. On mutations in the rural history of Latium during the period of upheaval, see above all P. Toubert, *Les structures du Latium médiéval*, vol. 1, ch. 4, pp. 305-68.

and acting. In this way, a link is forged between an uncertain present and a more certain past.[9]

The scene opens with the disappearance of the Carolingian empire, and running through the entire chapter is an understated threat to public order. Maieul's capture and Adalbert's martyrdom counterbalance this impression by establishing an atmosphere of ecclesiastical universalism.[10] In both cases the models are traditional. Maieul is a pilgrim, Adalbert, a holy man. Maieul's exchange with his captors, together with the stigma on his hand, creates a situation in which the Arabs, like the ancient Romans, are virtually forced to persecute Christians against their will. Adalbert represents another familiar theme, the opposition of Christian good and pagan evil in the natural order. A primitive science still holds sway; therefore, to prove God's effectiveness, Adalbert must die. His prediction of his death is of course taken from the life of Christ and earlier passions.

The revolt of Crescentius is a different sort of story but similar motifs appear. Here the contrast is between what Glaber considers to be a defunct and a living imperialism. We never really learn why Crescentius took up arms. Glaber is more interested in reversing the customary roles of conqueror and conquered in a series of heroic exchanges. Crescentius, although authentically Roman, is portrayed as a *nouveau riche*: "The more burdened he was with money, the more prone to serve Avarice."[11] His threat is thus presented as a typical attack on traditional values by a recent entrant into proper society. The irony is that the emperor and pope are Germans, the imposters, Romans. Otto's taunt to the false pilgrim who kneels before him in the holy city is a calculated abuse of imperial clemency. The final twist is Crescentius's murder in the Castel Sant'Angelo, that ancient reminder of resistance to the barbarian hoards.

As noted, these episodes reveal an interest in the concrete, the ritualistic, and the manner in which ancient models take on new life. The stories from the reigns of the three Ottos also inaugurate a relationship between group participation and spiritual development which becomes more pronounced as the *Historiae* progresses.

Particularly significant are a set of scenes crowded together towards the end of book two. Chapter nine consists of three episodes, begin-

---

[9] Cf. E. Vinaver, *The Rise of Romance*, pp. 5, 10-11.

[10] E.g., Maieul tells the Arabs: "Ego enim, si esuriero, Domini est me pascere" (1.4.9, p. 11). Adalbert's body bestows *plurima beneficia* (1.4.11, p. 15).

[11] *Ibid.*, 1.4.12, p. 13.

ning with Glaber's justly famous recollection of the famine which
probably took place in 999. It was, as he puts it, a time of "unprecedented harshness . . . , when many of the common people were worn
by hunger and perished . . . , when men ate the flesh of unclean
animals and reptiles as well as of men, women, and children."[12] This
is followed by a scene of suffering of a different sort, namely the heroic
resistance of a certain William, called duke of Navarre, against al-
Manṣūr.[13] The juxtaposition of the two episodes allows Glaber to present an image of extreme penury among ordinary people, followed by
one of group solidarity by knights against a common external enemy.
Purification is thus made a prelude to deliverance. The second narrative also focuses more clearly on the experience of the group. As Glaber puts it, "It happened in these daily battles that many religious
among the Christians were slain. They desired to enter the struggle
not for hollow personal renown but for the love of fraternal charity
(*ob fraternae caritatis amorem*)."[14] This larger ethical concern unites the
peasant and the noble, the layman and the monk, creating a universal
brotherhood.

The notion of spiritual confraternity, together with the participation of the dead in the religious lives of the living, is more specifically
dealt with in the remarkable vision of Vulferius, which follows. A
monk of Moutiers-St.-Jean in the diocese of Langres, Glaber narrates,
he had withdrawn on Trinity Sunday to pray alone after matins, when
he saw the church fill up with men wearing white robes and purple
stoles. They seemed serious; and preceding them with a cross was one
who styled himself "the bishop of many peoples." He and the others
declared that they had been present invisibly that octave day. The
mysterious bishop then prepared to celebrate mass at St. Maurice's
altar. But at this point Vulferius asked him who he was, where he

[12] *Ibid.*, 2.9.17, p. 44.

[13] *Ibid.*, 2.9.18, p. 44. The reference is to al-Manṣūr, i.e., Ibn Abī ʾĀmir Mohammed, b.
939, a lawyer from Cordova who gradually usurped the crown of Muslim Spain after the death
of Hakam II in October, 976. He was opposed by his father-in-law, Ghālib, after 978, the
latter forming an alliance with the Christian rulers Ramiro III of Léon, Sancho II of Navarre,
and García Fernández, count of Castile. Ghālib was defeated in battle on 10 July 981. Sancho
II, who reigned from 970 to 994, is called *Willelmus dux Navarrie* (p. 44), unless, of course,
Glaber has confused him with his brother-in-law, William of Gascony, active in battle against
the Muslims in 1010. On Sancho II, see E. Lévi-Provençal, *España musulmana hasta la caída del
califato de Córdoba (711-1031 de J.C.)*, 3rd ed. (Madrid, 1967), 416-17; J. F. O'Callaghan, *A
History of Medieval Spain* (Ithaca & London, 1975), 126-28.

[14] *Loc.cit.*

came from, and why he had stopped on that particular day in Moutiers. The bishop replied that he and his brethren had born "a Christian profession," but that Arab swords had separated their bodies and their souls. They were in Moutiers because, as he put it, soon many of its inhabitants would belong to their "college." After mass had been celebrated, Vulferius was asked to follow one of the brethren. But when he tried to do so, the bishop and his followers vanished.[15]

This vision is rich in associations. The key terms are *plebs*, *professio*, *vocatio*, and *collegium*. The bishop is a mass leader;[16] his followers are laymen (*viri*) who have taken a sacred vow. Of course, the profession may simply refer to the cross which he bears before them. But, in view of their vaguely mentioned battles and peregrinations, it more likely represents a combination of penance and holy war. The brethren are united by a calling (*vocatio*): the term retains the oral flavour of the vow and yet binds the committed together as a group. The movement is given the Roman designation of *collegium*, further emphasizing its obligatory character. The vision itself is both anticipatory and penitential, thereby uniting the future and the past. It occurs a week after Whitsunday, that is, at the conclusion of the liturgical celebration of the descent of the holy ghost on the apostles. The ceremony in Jerusalem was made familiar to pilgrims after the fourth century by the Spanish nun Aetheria.[17] The death of the Catholic homeland's defenders is a martyrdom.[18] To draw attention to the point, the bishop begins the antiphon from the altar of a martyr, St. Maurice. His brethren are clearly souls departed for paradise. They have returned to earth to prophesy universal brotherhood through a similar sacrifice. On earth they are wanderers or exiles, who are compelled to move from place to place without rest. Like all pilgrims, they have at once a tangible and a spiritual goal: hence their appearance as living beings yet bearing a symbolic message. After the celebration of mass, the monks of Moutiers are forewarned that many will follow in their footsteps.[19] These strangers, then, have suddenly become strangely familiar; the "others" are now "brothers."[20] In an atmosphere charged with

---

[15] *Ibid.*, 2.9.19, pp. 45-46.
[16] Similarly, somewhat later, Bernard of Tiron's future preaching is foretold in a vision in which he sees a *multitudo monachorum; Vita B. Bernardi Tironiensis*, c. 2.17, PL 172.1379A-B.
[17] *Itinerarium Egeriae*, c. 39.1, ed. O. Prinz (Heidelberg, 1960), 48-49.
[18] *Historiae* 2.9.19, p. 45.
[19] *Ibid.*, 46.
[20] Cf. V. Turner, *Dramas, Fields, and Metaphors*, 186-90.

the unexpected, the lay and the religious, the present and the other-worldly, are intermingled.

The subsequent episode, which has two parts, reinforces the notion of collective action by introducing the external threat of the devil.

Five months after his vision, Vulferius was ordered to look after some sick monks in Auxerre, since he appears to have had some knowledge of medicine. Claiming that his death was near, he insisted on seeing the sick shortly after his arrival. The monks of Auxerre were used to his sharp wit and paid no attention. They implored him to take a day of rest. However, on the following day he fell ill, and, while in the infirmary, had another vision: a virgin, appearing before him, asked whether he harboured any doubt. She then told him to have no fear for his "forthcoming journey," as she would be at his side. Achard, an erudite member of the community, interpreted the vision as evidence that Vulferius would soon die, and this took place three days later.

While the monks were preparing for his burial, another unusual set of events took place. A pious layman, who lived nearby, heard the abbey bells, and, thinking it was time for matins, got up to go to church. About midway along the road was a small bridge. When he arrived there, he heard voices from inside the monastery crying, "Pull, pull him out," and, "If not this one, bring another." Then, above the bridge, he saw a figure resembling a neighbour, but who, Glaber informs us, was in reality the devil. It advanced towards him in a friendly manner, telling him he could cross safely. Hoping to deceive him, the devil even turned into a turret. But the layman fell on the bridge, came to his senses, and made the sign of the cross. He returned home a more prudent man, and soon he, like Vulferius, was released from the bonds of the flesh.[21]

What are we to make of these two stories? Each concerns a man given to doubt and searching for certainty as he passes through the last stage of life's journey. Both the religious and the layman are engaged in relatively straightforward activities at the moment when their faith is tested and reaffirmed. Vulferius knows that he is near the end of the road, but the monks in Auxerre will not listen to him. The pious layman takes a short journey which is both real and symbolic in order to dramatize the omnipresence of dark forces in the world. These have invaded the monastery of St.-Germain in the form of illness, which, for Glaber, is a physical manifestation of sin and of

[21] *Historiae* 2.9.20, pp. 46-47.

the need for repentance. For this reason, and not only because of Vulferius's death, the voices asking that the innocent layman be lured towards the devil come from the monastery's side of the bridge. Vulferius, for his part, is almost prevented by pain from attending mass. His physical weakness is also a sign of doubt, which is relieved by the appearance of the virgin, who reassures him and strengthens his resolve. The layman wishes to reach the church inside the monastery in order to celebrate matins. He is prevented from doing so by an apparition of the devil above a symbolic bridge which separates the lay and the ecclesiastical worlds. Throughout the two episodes, the customary is associated with religious doubt and the unusual with certainty. Vulferius, Glaber tells us, was "always"[22] known as a clever man, and so the monks do not believe him when he says he has little time left. His vision establishes security in place of doubt.[23] He is assured of a certain reward, but he must pay a certain price, his life. When he is dying, the other monks pay him a visit *secundum morem*. They perform his last rites *ex more*. And the pious layman gets up for matins *ut solebat*.[24] His vision, too, arises out of everyday experience and involves someone close to him, his neighbour. Even here the customary order of things is overturned. In Glaber's view, these are confirmations that the lay world is suffering from new religious anxiety.

Should one then conclude that, for Glaber, what is new must break violently with what is customary? Only in books one and two. Later, change acquires ethical respectability; so, in its context, does a certain amount of individuality, which is sternly condemned in the heretics Leutard and Vilgard. But the atmosphere is also different. From book three, change not only takes place in a world undergoing moral dissolution. There are also some examples of fulfilment. The line between the two sections of the *Historiae* is not hard and fast. Indeed, some of the worst catastrophes lie ahead. But the millennium is nonetheless a symbolic turning point: "From that year there appeared in Italy as well as in Gaul men of both orders, religious and lay, whose lives and activities might well serve as examples to be imitated for posterity."[25]

In books three to five, Glaber continues to be preoccupied with movement. Nor do his methods of analysis change. As previously, he does not build up a logical or sequential train of thought but links

---

[22] *Ibid.*, 46: "ut erat semper alacri mente placidus. . . ."
[23] *Loc.cit.*   [24] *Ibid.*, 47.   [25] *Ibid.*, 3.1, p. 51.

his anecdotes and *exempla* through the interlacing of subjective associations.

The groundwork is laid in the oft-quoted opening chapters of book three, where Glaber speaks of the most important historical changes occurring around the year 1000, namely, the formation of stable governments in Europe, the opening of a safe land route to Jerusalem, and the frustration of Byzantine ambitions in southern Italy.[26] On this foundation is erected a structure of collective religious revival.[27] Throughout France and Italy, he points out, ecclesiastical councils tried to resolve long-standing differences.[28] Monasticism, hitherto in decline, began to win new converts and to establish outposts in backward regions.[29] Success alternated with disaster, as was illustrated by Abbo of Fleury's murder by a Gascon mob.[30] Yet, such incidents in themselves could not dampen the overall enthusiasm for reform: "It was as if the world, rejecting its roots, cast off what was old, and everywhere put on the white gown of the church."[31]

But how does Glaber really look upon reform? We get one side of the picture from portraits of figures like Hervé Buzançais, who rebuilt the church of St. Martin at Tours,[32] or from vignettes from the lives of better-known reformers such as William of St.-Bénigne in Dijon.[33] The other and perhaps more revealing side is conveyed by *exempla* of error, doubt, and self-questioning.

A remarkable group of the latter precedes book three, chapter six, and may be summarized briefly as follows.

When the entire world, Glaber reports, was beautified by new churches, the moment came when, through diverse signs, men were able to rediscover the long hidden relics of the saints. As if waiting for a sort of resurrection, he adds, these relics were presented to the

[26] *Ibid.*, 3.1-3.2, pp. 51-56. For a critical discussion, see Plaine, "Les prétendues terreurs," 156-59.

[27] Cf. G. Duby, "Les laïcs et la paix de Dieu," *Hommes et structures du moyen âge*, 227-40.

[28] *Historiae* 3.3.12, p. 61. Plaine, p. 148f., points out that the revival is not a notable feature of other annalists and chroniclers, such as Haimo of Fleury, Odorannus of Sens, Ademar of Chabannes, Maieul of Cluny, Abbo of Fleury, or Bernwald of Hildesheim.

[29] *Historiae* 3.5.17, pp. 66-67.

[30] *Ibid.*, 3.1.11, pp. 60-61. On the assassination, see P. Cousin, *Abbon de Fleury-sur-Loire* (Paris, 1954), 172-88.

[31] *Ibid.*, 3.4.13, p. 62.

[32] *Ibid.*, 3.4.14, p. 63. Glaber is the chief source of information for Hervé; for a discussion, see G. Oury, "L'idéal monastique dans la vie canoniale. Le bienheureux Hervé de Tours († 1022)," *Revue Mabillon* 52 (1962), 4-29.

[33] *Historiae* 3.5.16, pp. 65-66.

faithful on God's signal, providing them with a source of contemplation and strength.

The first discoveries took place in the cathedral of St. Stephen in Sens, and among them the archbishop Lierri came upon a piece of Moses's staff. The news spread, and pilgrims came from near and afar. Sens, as a result, acquired great tourist wealth, but, along with it, insufferable pride. When Fromond, the good count, passed away, he was replaced by his son, Rainard, who was a poor administrator of the church's goods and often frequented the local Jewish community, at one point even calling himself their king. Under their influence, Glaber states, he became dishonest, disrespectful, unmerciful, and a threat to the faith.

Two miraculous stories confirmed this change for the worse. In the first, Rainard ordered a common thief hanged, despite pleas for his life. The man asked only that he be allowed to confess, as it was Friday. The executioners then did their work: but, after the man was suspended for a day, the rope snapped, and he was set free, alas, Glaber adds, to return to his old ways.

The second story came from the neighbouring town of Troyes. A group of thieves, having stolen a bull, turned it over to an old man when it appeared that they would be caught. He protested his innocence, but Herbert, the local count, ordered him hanged. As the execution was being carried out, a large, strong heifer came along and supported the man from below with its horns. The two remained in the same position for some three days, until some local townsmen finally cut him down. The man then explained that his rescue was appropriate, since, when newly married, he and his wife had held on the baptismal font a child to whom they had given their only heifer. Glaber adds that the custom of giving heifers to one's godsons survives. But then he returns to the moral of the story. All of this, he reasons, was a clear sign that the "judaizing mania" of Rainard had gone too far. The king was obliged to send a force to restore order. But part of the town was burned as a result.[34]

Let us now look at these anecdotes in a larger context. Robert the Pious, aided by Eudes of Chartres, actually took Sens on 22nd April 1015. Rainard was not expelled, and eventually reached an agreement with the king. Glaber argued that the attack was retribution for Sens's error and greed. But he also saw Moses's staff and the judaizing heresy as forces for change. In the case of the relics, the relation between

---

[34] *Ibid.*, 3.6.19-23, pp. 68-71.

vetus and *novum*, the hidden and the discovered, is roughly typological. In fact, the staff is the first in a series of manifestations of *antiquorum sacrorum insignia*.[35]

More particularly, within the stories Glaber draws attention to what is right by presenting a fulfilment of what has gone wrong. Rainard and Herbert are in his view men of the letter, not of the spirit. Rainard's flirtation with the local Jews even transfixes him in the preparatory stage of history under the law, as, with lesser detail, is the case with Herbert. In other words, at a time when Glaber thinks that what is young and innovative is acceptable, even perhaps beneficial, they represent a youth that is merely old age relived. Afraid of change in the present, they have retreated into archaic models of conduct. Had they guided their judgments by Christ's precepts, Glaber implies, the innocent would not have suffered. Yet the abuse of justice offers visible proof that God is working against them in the world. As it is, a guilty thief is hanged on the eve of the sabbath and an innocent man is condemned without a hearing. The old man is saved by a good deed from his younger days; and Rainard, who succeeded a respected count, is an example of unwise youth in authority. Finally, there are the Jews, who are stereotyped as being stubborn and in error. By allying himself with them, Rainard links himself to a position of historical inflexibility. For, as the relics bear witness, the message of the day is that the new has come to replace the old. Glaber himself is somewhat ambivalent on the question of custom, hearsay, and other unwritten evidence. Throughout the episodes, *fama*, which causes men to alter their ideas, is a two-sided force, both a harbinger of promise and of potential delusion: for instance, the rumour of Moses's staff brings the pious to Sens but only to have them mulcted as tourists. In sum, while, in Glaber's view, change is anticipated, it does not necessarily bring about the desired state of affairs. There is a considerable gap between what the revelations suggest and what history actually reveals. The force that creates a new religious sensibility also leads to social and political disorder. The good news of Jesus's message is once again in the air, but men persist in their old habits.

The story of Jewish influence in Sens opens the door to other issues that are interrelated in Glaber's mind, namely, Islam, Jerusalem, and heresy. The Jews, whom he sees as the source of Rainard's downfall, are associated with larger religious and political subversion. The way

---

[35] *Ibid.*, 3.6.19, p. 68. Glaber explains the prefiguration, *ibid.*, 5.1.10, pp. 121-22.

is thus paved for the destruction of the holy sepulchre in the following chapter, which is also a byproduct of Jewish intransigence. As Glaber has it, a fugitive slave called Rotbert was paid by the Jews of Orléans to bear letters to the Fatimid calif al-Hakim, requesting that all Christian influence in the holy land be eliminated.[36]

The story effectively links the idea of religious disorder at home with lack of Christian control over Jerusalem. The point is made clear in book four, chapter two, which tells the story of a Cathar *castellum* near Asti and of its leader, Manfred.[37] Here, as in the dissidence at Orléans, heresy does not only fulfil a doctrinal role in the *Historiae*. It is also employed as a vehicle for transforming Christian awareness into a form of group participation. The central incident concerns a knight whose village remained Christian despite the prevalence of Catharism in the region. Ill and nearing his end, he sent for a woman to minister to his last needs. But she only came to spread heresy. Entering his house with her, he saw a large group of men dressed in black. They remained after her departure, and their leader, possibly the devil in person, claimed affiliation with the disreputable duke of Carinthia, Conrad I, whom he said was now emperor, and Michael IV, who had murdered his predecessor, Basil, in the East. When Hugh, the knight, pledged faith to Christ, the hoard vanished.

"No one would doubt," Glaber adds, "that the vision was intended for us as well as for him." But in what sense? Its purpose was not to draw attention to a threat to Christendom but rather to awaken group obligation in living Christians. Hugh's weak lay piety is thus able to stimulate firmer resolve among Glaber's readers, who, through the invocation of Judaism, Islam, and Byzantium, can relate their spirituality to larger issues.

Scenes like this form a prelude to the chapters which may justly be viewed as the *Historiae*'s climax, book four, chapters four to six, which tell in turn of the famine of the early 1030s, the plentiful harvests marking the anniversary of the crucifixion, the movements towards the peace of God, and the upsurge of pilgrimages to Jerusalem, together with their attendant signs, omens, and tribulations.

As the year 1033 approached, Glaber relates, the whole of the Christian world experienced a severe famine. Several illustrious men passed away as the date came near, as if to warn of the impending doom. They included Benedict VIII, Fulbert of Chartres, and Wil-

[36] *Ibid.*, 3.7.24-25, pp. 71-73.
[37] *Ibid.*, pp. 94-96. Basil II is mistaken for Romanus III.

liam of St.-Bénigne, who died respectively in 1024, 1029, and 1031.[38] The ensuing famine was so severe that it was thought the whole human race would perish. Drought alternated with floods; blights, arising in the East, spread through Greece and Italy to France. Inflation pushed food prices beyond reason, when, that is, nourishment could be found at all. Men had to survive on reptiles, carrion, roots, weeds, and even other humans. Glaber recalls several instances of cannibalism. Travellers were murdered by their hosts; children were lured to remote places, butchered, and devoured; and graves were regularly robbed of the dead. Cooked human meat was sold for beef in an open stall at Tournus; and, not far from Mâcon, a wild man was found living in a hut with the bones of some forty-eight victims. In desperation, men mixed flour with earth; and the treasures of many churches were simply sold. The normal rhythm of the seasons seemed to have been arrested, and the universe, Glaber adds, to be returning to primeval chaos.[39]

However, in 1033 the torrential rains ceased. The earth once again was blessed: famine disappeared, food became plentiful. First in Aquitaine, then in diverse regions, abbots and other clergy began to meet in groups. The bodies of saints and their relics were transported to the meeting places. The purpose of these councils, in Glaber's words, was "to reform the conditions of peace and to re-establish the Christian faith." When news of the gatherings spread, lords, middling persons, and even those of lower rank also came together. Their support for their pastors was for once wholehearted,[40] for the disasters of the previous few years had left them apprehensive. A document was drawn up listing the legal conditions for peace: clerics and laymen were henceforth to bear no arms; thieves were to be rigorously punished; churches were to become sanctuaries for anyone seeking refuge; and monks and nuns were not to be harmed under any pretext. Miracles, Glaber adds, contributed to the atmosphere of goodwill. But in any case it did not last: the great lords soon returned to exploiting the less fortunate; the middle and lower orders, misled by their superiors, fell into similar vices. Incest, adultery, and concubinage once again became common. A child was even said to have been made pope. The one lasting result was the new interest in pilgrimages to

[38] *Ibid.*, 4.4.9, p. 99.
[39] *Ibid.*, 4.4.10-13, pp. 99-103.
[40] For a discussion, see G. Duby, "Les laïcs et la paix de Dieu," *loc.cit.*

Jerusalem, which continued to bring together men and women from all social classes and walks of life.[41]

Unlike Glaber's anecdotal tales, the logic of these scenes presents no serious problems. The famine is for him a time of testing, sacrifice, purification, and group cohesion. The year 1033 partially fulfils God's promise within the design of Christian history, at once restoring plenty, creating universal institutions, and inspiring men to demonstrate their faith through pilgrimages.

But, if need is answered by physical plenty, the working out of history also demands asceticism and discipline. The church and the monasteries show the way; but self-denial on so large a scale also implies a common religious goal. In a sense, physical need, as produced by famine, has its fulfilment in the tangible Jerusalem, just as mystical self-abnegation finds its reward in the heavenly Jerusalem. Both images work side by side in Glaber's imagination, subtly interpenetrating each other.

Also, the famine is foreshadowed by the deaths of eminent reformers, those who were, in his words, among the chief models for conduct "in the present age." Glaber himself had written a little treatise celebrating the merits of William of St.-Bénigne.[42] The famine suggests the idea of anarchy in two classic images from the Old Testament: original chaos and the flood. Just as chaos preceded order in Genesis, so natural disaster precedes the anniversary of the passion. God therefore appears as an avenger of sins, his wrath entering France by the same eastern route as the diabolically inspired heresies and political threats. The lesson of the famine also has its spiritual side: "There was no refuge from God's anger, unless towards himself."[43]

The abundance of the years following 1033 repeats another Old Testament theme, the jubilee of Moses, while the peace of God echoes the images of the coming of the law to the Jews. For Glaber, both established universal principles. Of course, these years too were not without their problems. Man, ever sinful, soon returned to his old ways. But a new collective conscience had in his opinion made its appearance, manifesting itself chiefly in the desire to visit the holy land, uniting men and women, rich and poor, in a common quest. One concludes book four in a mood of restrained optimism. The deeper conflicts of the West have not vanished, but there is a new spirit of cooperation in the air. Again and again men have been wrenched from

[41] *Historiae* 4.5.14-17, pp. 103-06.
[42] *Ibid.*, 4.4.9, p. 99.
[43] *Ibid.*, 4.4.10, p. 100: "non ergo aufugium ire ultionis Dei, nisi ad semetipsum."

their customary practices, or, to employ the vocabulary of nascent feudalism, thrust into customary situations for which there is little precedent. Custom itself is ambivalent: it is both a background for change and part of the new design for which history seems to be searching.

Attitudes towards Change

Although highly individualistic in style and content, Rodulf Glaber sits midway between a world that is oral, gestural, and symbolic, and one that is textual, interpretive, and factually oriented. As such, he offers a convenient point of departure for exploring broader attitudes towards change between two peaks of sensibility, namely, the later Carolingian empire and the consolidation of the duchy of Normandy and its dependent regions in the generation after the death of William the Conqueror.

Then, as now, a distinction must be made between the objective and the subjective. Those living through the times were often confronted with changes whose violence was all too vivid and real, such as invasion, famine, or natural catastrophe. But, what one invariably finds in their letters, histories, and works of literature is an unjudicious mixture of what actually took place and their personal thoughts about the events.

Like people at any time and place, they did not fully comprehend the changes in settled patterns of thought and action going on all around them. But, they did not on that account view them as a series of totally unconnected actions. Mutations were "causally" interrelated; the past, the present, and the future indissolubly linked. Attachments were not limited to the empirical: ancestors, biblical figures, and pagan spirits were as influential on conduct as the exigencies of survival. Forces which for us can only be brought to the surface through psychoanalysis were felt as tangible realities. The visible and the invisible coexisted like body and soul in mutual interdependence. Symbols and rituals, as noted, were not objects of study; they informed and gave immediately apprehensible meaning to life. Experience, if somewhat disordered by contemporary standards, was immeasurably richer in range and depth. For better or worse, men lacked as yet the instruments for turning what they felt and sensed into a set of logical concepts.[44] What Husserl said of the period preceding Descartes can

---

[44] M. Bloch, *Feudal Society*, vol. 1, p. 108.

be said of the early Middle Ages in general: men had not yet discovered "science," but they had not yet lost touch with "the world."[45]

From time to time the subjective and the objective coincided in time. Anticipations were confirmed, expectations fulfilled. Earlier models for conduct seemed to live again. But such occasions were rare. More commonly, change in the external world and one's appreciation of it were separated by an unbridgeable gulf. The result was anxiety, lack of comprehension, and a whole range of compensatory techniques. For, if the hard facts of life could not be altered, at least they could be fitted into a system of belief that made them understandable and acceptable.

There were many methods of explanation, most of which worked along internalist lines. Like all abstract systems detached from actual change, they had their own principles of development and their often arbitrary ways of accounting for why things happened. Instead of dealing with the phenomenal content of reality, they described its modes of appearance, its organic patterns, and its hidden, inner meanings. The contemporary student normally looks upon these analytical tools in a somewhat disparaging manner: they would seem to represent the symbolic universe of those who had not yet learned to limit investigations of reality to the empirical. But, to those employing them, they comprised a system of signs for communicating between form and content, sound and sense, design and function. Attempts were sometimes made at codification, but they were only partially successful. Men could never fully agree. Even religion, the largest repository of significant objects and events, harboured not easily reconcilable notions side by side. What crossed educational levels and the boundaries of estates was not hard-and-fast philosophy: it was the widely shared if often naive faith in the value of interpretation.[46]

Change, not surprisingly, was frequently viewed with suspicion, as it led to uncertainty. *Mutatio* carried pejorative connotations.[47] Novelty did not generate enthusiasm but fear, not adaptation but resistance.

Indeed, throughout the tenth and eleventh centuries, as the tempo of social change increased in northwest Europe, so, to some degree,

[45] For a theoretical review of the issues, see A. Schutz, *The Phenomenology of the Social World*, trans. G. Walsh and F. Lehnert (Evanston, Ill., 1967), 45-96.

[46] Cf. G. Duby, *L'an mille* (Paris, 1967), 59-60; 65.

[47] E.g., Ordericus Vitalis, *Historia Ecclesiastica* 5.19, ed. Chibnall (1972), 172; 8.1 (1973), 112f.

did the incapacity of individuals to understand and to interpret what was taking place.

The reason is not hard to find. All the transformations seemed to be leading an already troubled society into worse times. In Charles the Bald, who died in 877, the cultural if not political unity of the Carolingian empire still appeared to be intact. But, just thirty-four years later, the "coastal counties," as Flodoard put it,[48] along the Seine were ceded in fief by the French to Rollo, who was named the first "duke of Normandy." The "invasions" perhaps brought about less physical than psychological damage. Whether or not they marked the decisive end of the old order, they compelled men and women of all social strata to reflect upon the direction in which civilization was heading.[49]

Speculation, of course, varied inversely with the quantity of objective documentation. To take Normandy, around which, our following discussion is chiefly oriented:[50] from the first two dukes, Rollo (d. 931) and William Longsword (d. 942), we possess no official acts at all. Richard I, the third duke, reigned for over fifty years from 942 to 996 but left only three diplomas. Acts become a little more plentiful from the time of Richard II (d. 1026) and Robert the Magnificent (d. 1035), but they do not come to light in any real abundance until the time of William the Conqueror. A certain amount of information can be gleaned from saints' lives. But the early chronicles are disappointing. Dudo of St. Quentin, the official spokesman of the first three dukes, is virtually silent on institutions beyond obvious feudal loyalties. William of Jumièges, who continued his history into succeeding reigns, is hardly more instructive. The earliest genuine inventory of ducal rights and powers is found in an inquest made by his sons after the Conqueror's death in 1091.[51] But its function was merely "to record" what had always been said and done; only with caution could its principles be applied to earlier duchies, or for that matter to William's own ascendancy.

The legislation of the later Carolingians provides a similar picture of evaporating documentation. The last capitulary of the kings of *Francia Occidentalis* is from 884.[52] During the tenth century the num-

---

[48] *Hist. Eccles. Remensis* 4.14, MGH SS 13, p. 577.

[49] E.g., Rodulf Glaber, *Historiae* 1.5.17-20, ed. Prou, pp. 17-20.

[50] Summarized from J. Yver, "Les premières institutions du duché de Normandie," *I Normanni e la loro espansione in Europa nell'alto medioevo* (Spoleto, 1969), 299-366.

[51] C. H. Haskins, *Norman Institutions* (Cambridge, Mass., 1925), Appendix D, p. 281.

[52] MGH Leges, Sectio II: *Capitularia Regum Francorum*, vol. 2, pt. 2, No. 287, pp. 371-75.

ber of dispositive acts decreases with each successive monarch: 120 acts for Charles the Simple in 30 years (i.e., about four per year), 53 for Louis IV in 18 (less than three per year), 56 for Lothair in 32 (less than two per year). Gradually control over the classical prerogatives of minting, tonlieu, forests, and the construction of châteaux was lost. More and more frequently, concessions were made to local "counts" whose lineage may have been suspect but whose military authority was undeniable.

Early historians, as a rule, attributed the psychological breakup of the old order to abrupt, irreversible changes of one sort or another. In doing so, they followed in the footsteps of medieval commentators, who tended to speak of the transformations in highly dramatic terms. Even Haskins, who was sensitive to the sources' literary qualities, overemphasized the degree to which the founding of the Norman state was a discontinuous break with the past.[53]

Certainly, the fear of the millennium and the Antichrist played on men's minds, as Adso of Montierender bears witness. Nor should the destructive and creative energies of invasion, immigration, and settlement be underestimated. Who, for instance, among contemporary chroniclers, could see a larger, divine purpose in the random looting of the Magyars; in Hasting's raids on the coasts of France, Spain, and Italy; or in the long-remembered Moslem attacks which desecrated St. Peter's in 846 and Montecassino in 881?

On the other hand, the commentators' bias should not be forgotten. A well-known example is the complaint of Hervé, archbishop of Reims, to the council of Troli on 26th June 909, that the province's bishops have been unable to meet for several years owing to "the influx of pagans and the grave disturbance of the realm."[54] In his opinion, God's wrath was evident: towns were depopulated, monasteries laid waste, and farms deserted. Adultery, fornication, and mindless slaughter were common occurrences. Bishops neglected their flocks; laymen

---

[53] D. C. Douglas, *William the Conqueror* (London and Berkeley, 1964), 98. For an *aperçu* of scholarship since W. Vogel's 1906 thesis, see A. d'Haenens,"Les invasions normandes dans l'empire franc au IXe siècle," *I Normanni*, 233-98. The same question is reviewed more briefly by P. H. Sawyer, *The Age of the Vikings*, 2nd ed. (London, 1971), ch. 6 (pp. 120-47). On the continuity of Carolingian and Norman estates, see above all L. Musset, "Les domaines de l'époque franque et les destinées du régime domanial," *Bulletin de la Société des antiquaires de Normandie* 49 (1942-45), 7-97; on the continuity of the first Capetians, see J. F. Lemarignier, "Structures monastiques et structures politiques dans la France de la fin du Xe et des débuts du XIe siècle," *Il monachesimo nell'alto medioevo e la formazione della civiltà occidentale* (Spoleto, 1957), esp. 360-61, 398-400.

[54] *Concilium Troslejanum*, Mansi 18, 264-65.

usurped ecclesiastical offices; canons and nuns pledged allegiance to foreigners. It was, he concluded, nothing less than a return to primitive chaos.

Michelet, among others, regarded the council as an accurate reflection of events. But how much can we really believe? The "terrors of the year 1000" were copied in part from the *Dialogues* of Gregory the Great.[55] Their sombre evocations are echoed by few other chroniclers. In truth, the "invasions" may not have been as uniformly disruptive as was once thought. Even Normandy, whose boundaries were "an expression of history rather than the product of geographical conditions," illustrated a large amount of "tenurial continuity" with its own agrarian past.[56] Norman society was not a new society: it was a hybrid, a mixture of old and new.[57] The forces which helped to fragment the enfeebled empire and to pave the way for the Scandinavian colonization also laid the foundations for what later became known as "the feudal system." But it took juridic structures nearly a century to catch up with social realities. In the meanwhile, what men noticed most was not the appearance of the new order but the gradual disappearance of the old one.

It was at once a society which was old, and therefore confronted with its apparent youthfulness, and, at the same time, rather immature, and for that reason preoccupied with creating for itself a sufficiently credible past.

Old age and youth—witnesses, so to speak, to the sense of discontinuity—are recurrent themes in the period's literature, hagiography, and historical writing. Perhaps better than mute statistics they provide an index of reactions to change: not only to the subjective experience, but, more importantly, to the models of interpretation which individuals used to characterize their hopes, desires, and inevitable disappointments.

Wandering and Youth

Let us look first at two of society's basic metaphors for change, namely physical displacement and the stages of the life-cycle.

During the period under consideration, it appeared normal to most thinkers that life-styles should remain unfixed for a certain length of

[55] *Dialogi* 3.38, PL 77.316C.

[56] Douglas, *William the Conqueror*, 17 and 22.

[57] C. W. Hollister and J. W. Baldwin, "The Rise of Administrative Kingship: Henry I and Philip Augustus," 889-90.

time. *Peregrinus* had not acquired the specialized sense of "pilgrim," still less of "crusader";[58] it simply meant "exile" or "wanderer."[59]

However, from the tenth century, the notion gradually began to be looked upon in another light.[60] While retaining its older meanings, "wandering" also started to function as a symbol of psychological indecision. Physical movement, so to speak, gave individuals a period of reflection, not only between the poles of birth and death, but, as became increasingly clear, between the apparently immobile models for behaviour inherited from their ancestors and the new forms towards which they were not always successfully groping. It was a time of testing, of *aventure*. And, for both sexes, the period of instability was youth.

Here, as we have elsewhere emphasized, the early feudal age marks a dividing line between two contrasting *mentalités*.

In the world of Germanic folklore, movement was an intimate part of the social ethic itself. The essential features of this belief were beautifully summed up in the Anglo-Saxon poems *The Wanderer* and *The Seafarer*. The warriors regret the loss of their kinsmen, the warm hearth, and the mead-hall of their "protectors," but they are compelled to lead a life of restless exile over "the dark waves," where "frost and snow are falling, mingled with hail." A similar atmosphere surrounds the judicial exile of the early medieval pilgrimage. The *Penitential of St. Columbanus* states that a cleric who commits murder without making sufficient retribution "may never again be restored to his native land, but, like Cain, must roam the earth a wanderer and fugitive (*uagus et profugus*)."[61] Other examples of socially inspired movement come easily to mind: at the top of the social scale, for

[58] For a brief review, see J. A. Brundage, *Medieval Canon Law and the Crusader* (Madison, 1969), 10-11.

[59] See B. de Gaiffier, "Pèlerinage et culte des saints: thème d'un congrès," *Etudes critiques d'hagiographie et d'iconologie* (Brussels, 1967), 31-34. Useful introductions to the pilgrimage ideal include H. von Campenhausen, "Die asketische Heimatlosigkeit im altkirchlichen und frühmittelalterlichen Mönchtum," repr. in *Tradition und Leben. Kräfte der Kirchengeschichte. Aufsätze und Vorträge* (Heidelberg, 1960), 302-17; J. Leclercq, "Monachisme et pérégrination," *Aux sources de la spiritualité occidentale. Etapes et constantes* (Paris, 1964), 35-90; and G. Constable, "Monachisme et pèlerinage au Moyen Age," *Revue historique* 258 (1977), 3-27. On abuse of the idea, see G. Constable, "Opposition to Pilgrimage in the Middle Ages," *Studia Gratiana* 19 (1976), 125-46.

[60] For an unsophisticated survey of the literature, see M. Bechthum, *Beweggründe und Bedeutung des Vagantentums in der lateinischen Kirche des Mittelalters* (Jena, 1941), 44-71.

[61] *Paenitentiale S. Columbani*, B.1, ed. L. Bieler, *The Irish Penitentials* (Dublin, 1963), 98. The distinction between *monachi* and *gyrovagi* had become common by the eleventh century; e.g., Peter Damian, *De Communi Vita Canonicorum* . . . , c. 3, PL 145.507C-D.

instance, the Carolingian emperors, who, being somewhat nomadic, travelled from estate to estate, liberally dispensing gifts to their "families." The early English king, wrote A. L. Poole, "moves ceaselessly from place to place . . . and with him moves also all the paraphernalia of government. . . ."[62]

What was true of William Rufus and Henry I on one side of The Channel, of course, was still applicable on the other to Philip Augustus, who died in 1223.[63] But, by this date, "wayfaring," was well on the way to becoming a disreputable sort of activity. Did the aristocratic Otto of Freising not derive the name of the Norman soldier of fortune, "Guiscard," from wanderer or vagabond (*oberrator vel girator*),[64] pointedly recalling an ancient monastic opprobrium? It is not clear just when the turning-point came. A last gasp of the older idealism with respect to physical movement can still be felt in the Children's Crusade of 1212: it began in an atmosphere of pure piety; it ended in brigandage, kidnapping, slavery, and murder. By this date many types of travellers had acquired a special status: pilgrims and crusaders above all, both furnished with letters and recognizable garments; but also, by the mid-century, mendicant friars, merchants, and troubadours, along with pedlars, jongleurs, and, perhaps more frequently than the sources admit, preachers of popular but unauthorized doctrines. On the fringes of this substantial group was an even larger number of vagabonds, whose ranks included the poor and homeless, together with those for whom displacement· was a convenient means of remaining outside the largely localized network of law and order.

Yet, if the thirteenth century witnessed the final stages of this evolution, the eleventh saw the early and later medieval conceptions of human movement come face to face. Wandering had not lost its ritual associations, and still exerted a strong, primitive force on men's minds. But it had also begun to take on specific social and religious connotations. What is more, it was suddenly taken up by the lower echelons of society. By 1100, all but the greatest lords were leading sedentary lives. But the masses were now on the move.[65] They crowded after the wandering preachers. They huddled together on the dusty pilgrimage roads. They filled Italian town squares in search of civil

[62] *From Domesday Book to Magna Carta* (Oxford, 1951), 7.

[63] Hollister and Baldwin, "The Rise of Administrative Kingship," 895-905.

[64] *Gesta Friderici Imperatoris* 1.3, MGH SS 20, 353.

[65] Cf. R. I. Moore, "Family, Community and Cult on the Eve of the Gregorian Reform," *Transactions of the Royal Historical Society*, 5th Series, vol. 30 (London, 1980), 49-56.

rights. In the north, they infiltrated the councils devoted to the peace and truce of God.[66] Making their first effective appearance in medieval history, they breathed new life into the conventional connection between displacement through space or time and spiritual improvement.

"Wandering," in this context, illustrates a typically medieval and early modern cultural process, the manner in which one model of behaviour works its way down the social scale while another begins to move upwards, both dependent on putative exemplars, which, for the sake of simplicity, may be called "texts."

A related process is the formation of new bonds of solidarity within well-defined social categories, the most remarkable example of which in the later eleventh century is the crisis of "youth."

In every society, of course, the passage from youth to maturity is an important rite. Crossing the frontier from one stage of life to another inevitably brings with it a time of instability.[67] The contrast between old age and youth—that is, between the ancients and the moderns—is already a familiar theme in the Carolingians, as it is in later commentators such as Rodulf Glaber. But the metaphor and its associations entered a new phase in the last half of the eleventh century. More precisely, in the north of France from about 1060 on— that is, from the moment when William, after some fourteen years of uninterrupted combat, managed to consolidate his hold over the duchy of Normandy—growing up and taking a position in society seems to have been an especially difficult change for many well-born young men and women.

It was different in the south, where wealth, courtly ideals, and orderly relations between church and state helped to ease the tensions of socialization. There, despite the presence of a knightly class, youthful energies found outlets in lay piety, vernacular literature, and even heresy.[68] William IX sublimated battle into poetry: the conflicts of the real world were transformed into a vehicle for resolving the opposites of love.[69] In the north, the real battlefield was never far away. Society was more directly shaped by the survival of the fittest. Wil-

---

[66] L. C. MacKinney, "The People and Public Opinion in the Eleventh-Century Peace Movement," *Speculum* 5 (1930), 186-99; G. Duby, "Les laïcs et la paix de Dieu," in *Hommes et structures du moyen âge*, 227-40.

[67] A. van Gennep, *The Rites of Passage*, trans. M. B. Vizedom and G. L. Caffee (Chicago, 1960), 2-3; 76. For a recent review of the issues, see S. F. Moore and B. G. Myerhoff, "Secular Ritual: Forms and Meanings," in *Secular Ritual*, 3-24, and the extensive bibliography, 283-93.

[68] G. Volpe, *Movimenti religiosi e sette ereticali nella società medievale italiana*, 38.

[69] Cf. L. T. Topsfield, "The Burlesque Poetry of Guillhem IX of Aquitaine," *Neuphilologische Mitteilungen* 69 (1968), 280-302; on *joven*, pp. 285-87.

liam the Conqueror was a strong leader and administrator. Those of his generation who prospered were like him. A kindly, sensitive, and humane individual like Arnold of Echauffour, whose only sin was his lack of fortune, might have led a reasonably untroubled life in the south. Friendless in his own country, he was first tricked by William's false promises and later murdered by Mabel Talvas.[70] The power, ruthlessness, and fragility of the Norman aristocracy under William was a virtual guarantee that a "generational gap" would exist between the elders and their offspring. Few of the children could fill their parents' boots: fewer still wanted to.

Care must be exercised in defining what was meant by "youth." But here, classical and sociological canons are in reasonable agreement. Isidore of Seville placed *iuuentus* between the ages of fifteen and fifty.[71] Later authorities imitated his classification of the *aetates hominum* with only minor changes.[72] For instance, Guibert of Nogent, although over forty at the time of writing, speaks of himself as "timid in his youthfulness."[73] *Iuuentus*, moreover, not only referred to a span of time but "to a specific position in military society and family structure."[74] In other words, youth was defined by a social role and by a strong horizontal bond within a peer group. A brotherhood or *maisnie* was often formed on the day following the ceremony of knighthood.[75] Membership was shared by all those who had undergone the "rites of passage" together and who, in the service of a wealthy retainer, constituted a new cohesive *familia* devoted to battles, tournaments, wenching, and conquest.

Georges Duby has indicated why the new "family" was needed as a substitute for the old.[76] Problems arose within the system of primogeniture. Often a young nobleman received arms when he was between sixteen and twenty-two, that is, at a time when his father,

[70] Orderic Vitalis, *Eccles. Hist.*, 3.9, vol. 2, 122, 124.

[71] *Etymologiae* 11.2, ed. W. M. Lindsay.

[72] E.g., Rabanus Maurus, *De Universo* 7.1, PL 111.179. In general see A. Hofmeister, "Puer, Iuvenis, Senex: Zum Verständnis der mittelalterlichen Altersbezeichnungen," in A. Brackmann, ed., *Papsttum und Kaisertum . . . Paul Kehr zum 65. Geburtstag* (Munich, 1926), 287-316; J. de Ghellinck, "Iuventus, gravitas, senectus," *Studia Mediaevalia R. J. Martin*, 55, and, on the terms for youth in medieval canon law, R. Metz, "L'enfant dans le droit canonique médiéval," *L'enfant 2e partie, Europe médiévale et moderne* (Brussels, 1976), 12-14.

[73] *De Vita Sua* 3.4, ed. G. Bourgin (Paris, 1907), 141.

[74] G. Duby, "Les jeunes dans la société aristocratique dans la France du Nord-Ouest au XIIe siècle," *Hommes et structures du moyen âge*, 214.

[75] M. Bloch, *Feudal Society*, I, 238.

[76] "Les jeunes," 214-17.

who was frequently in his fifties, had no intention of relinquishing his estate or its prerogatives. Disputes over the distribution of family resources inevitably resulted in confrontations, mounting tensions, and physical assaults. No wonder it was fashionable in reality as well as in romance for a young knight to spend a good deal of time away from home.

Property within the family was not the only source of conflict. The other medieval method of transferring the means of production among lineages was through marriage. In principle, youth ended with marriage: the *iuuenis* became a *uir*, that is, a man with a family and stable ethical values. But marriages were often negotiated with a mind to protecting the integrity of estates, and younger sons were both a nuisance and a threat. Frustrated, many young men chose to become permanent exiles.

Young Normans are found as mercenaries in southern Italy from 1016. By 1038 the infamous sons of Tancred d'Hauteville were present. The subsequent story of displaced aggressivity is well known. Robert Guiscard, aided by his youngest brother, Roger, proceeded to subdue all of Apulia after 1058. In 1071 he captured Bari, the last Byzantine stronghold. Roger took Messina in 1061 and Palermo in 1072. Of course, not all the dissatisfied young men of Normandy left for the Mediterranean frontier, and chroniclers differ on the real as opposed to mythical vitality of the Italian connections.[77] Of those who did leave, many managed to return. Still others remained, and attempted to work out their fates on local soil.

Two portraits from the last decades of the eleventh century paint a vivid picture of the inner conflicts and uncertainties of the aristocratic Norman youth.

The best known is Orderic Vitalis's description of the court of William Rufus in the 1090s,[78] which provided him with an occasion for a general lament on the decline of "our ancestors' honorable customs" since the death of the Conqueror and of Gregory VII.

In rhetorical phrases, Orderic depicted the younger generation as turning away from the firm piety and virulent manhood of their eld-

---

[77] This is particularly true of Orderic's account; M. Chibnall, *The Ecclesiastical History*, vol. 2 (1969), xxx-xxxii; R.H.C. Davis, *The Normans and their Myth* (London, 1976), 14-16, 63-65.

[78] *Hist. Eccles.*, 8.10, vol. 4 (1973), 187-90. Cf. Eadmer, *Historia Novorum in Anglia*, bk. 1, ed. M. Rule (London, 1884), 48, who speaks similarly of the *curialis juventus*. Of course, not only the Norman youth were criticized for long hair. Gerard of Cambrai levelled the same charge at the heretics judged in 1025; *Acta Synodi Atrebatensis*, c. 3, PL 142.1286D. See above, ch. 2, pp. 120ff.

ers. They appeared to him to act, to look, and to dress more like women than men. They were *effeminati*; and, as stable boundaries of gender were trespassed, so were traditional norms of conduct. He was particularly incensed at the fashions in footwear, clothing, and hair styles. Long pointed shoes, he related, were invented for Fulk-le-Rechin, who suffered from bunions; they were introduced to court by a certain Robert (soon after nicknamed *cornardus*). Shirts and tunics, he continued, were too ornate. Rufus's forbears were content with modest dress, equally suited to walking or riding. There were no tight shirts, oversized gloves, or capes that swept the ground. The new hair styles were similarly non-functional. The short-cropped, militaristic cut of earlier times had been abandoned in favour of long hair, which, he noted, was frequently parted at the middle and hung down in ringlets.

In effect, Orderic observed, Rufus's friends shaved the front part of their heads like thieves, while they let their hair grow long at the back like harlots. In this way, he added, they parodied a style reserved for penitents, prisoners, and pilgrims. His image was apt, for, consciously or unconsciously, these young men had broken with the ways of their fathers. They had become "wanderers" of a new type. Orderic felt that in his own day "the older life-style had almost entirely been given up for novel diversions." In his view, the outward appearance of Rufus's companions mirrored the shallowness of their inner lives.

Yet, leaving aside the allegations of degeneracy, how characteristic is Orderic's picture of the moral predicament? It is instructive to compare his observations with a different sort of personality crisis related in Guibert of Nogent's *Memoirs* in which the social milieu is somewhat similar.[79]

Guibert told the story as part of a larger discussion of "the conditions of religious life and the conversions" he saw in his day. The hero was Evrard of Breteuil, who died in 1095. Evrard was "in the flower of youth" and known throughout Normandy for his wealth and refinement. However, at length, Guibert tells us, he began to reflect on the purposelessness of his existence, which, in the narrator's terms, consisted of nothing "but consuming and being consumed."

He talked over the problem with some of his friends, and they decided to pursue the religious life together as members of a lay confraternity. Leaving the comforts of their great houses, they went into "exile" in a region unknown to them, where they earned their liveli-

---

[79] *De Vita Sua* 1.9, pp. 24-27.

hood by selling charcoal. Evrard, Guibert says, remained in apostolic poverty until one day when he found himself in a village, where before him stood a young man ridiculously dressed in a scarlet cloak, fancy silk trousers, and obscenely short leggings. His hair, parted in front, swept down girlishly over his shoulders: he looked, Guibert notes, "more like a lover than a traveller." Evrard, who had kept his own identity a secret, was eager to learn who this person was. When asked, the young man replied: "You must not tell anyone, but I am actually Evrard of Breteuil! I was once a count, but I have voluntarily gone into exile to do penance for my sins." Evrard was shocked, but interpreted the meeting as a divinely inspired sign that his period of "wandering" was finished. Accordingly, he and his companions immediately left for Marmoutier, where they became monks.

Even if we put aside the moralities of the two authors, there is a fundamental similarity and an important difference in the two stories. In both, the life-style of the previous generation is rejected, even though inheritance poses no problem. But the two groups are at separate stages of their dissociation from traditional norms of behaviour. William Rufus's court has merely left them behind, while Evrard and his friends, at least in Guibert's view, have found their chosen goal. Perhaps he was overly optimistic: even so, their youthful "rites of passage" involved the isolation from one set of relations, a transitional or liminal stage, and incorporation into a new "family." Territorial displacement thereby symbolized spiritual growth.

These stories also illustrate two different uses of textual models. In Orderic, the customs of the past have become an inviolable standard for the present. In Guibert, we witness the progress through two stages of a "textual community," first appearing as a confraternity and later adopting the *Rule*.

There were, of course, more idealistic renderings of Christian knighthood.[80] For, in a society, as Glaber noted, which seemed to be growing old without growing wise, the *puer senex*[81] or wise young man

[80] The considerable literature on the Merovingian prehistory of the idea is reviewed by B. de Gaiffier, "Hagiographie et historiographie," *La storiografia altomedievale*, 141-45 and by F. Graus, "Sozialgeschichtliche Aspekte der Hagiographie der Merowinger-und Karolingerzeit. Die Viten der Heiligen des südalemannischen Raumes und die sogenannten Adelsheiligen," in A. Borst, ed., *Mönchtum, Episkopat und Adel zur Gründungszeit des Klosters Reichenau* (Sigmaringen, 1974), 131-76. Of capital importance is the same author's *Volk, Herrscher und Heiliger im Reich der Merowingerzeit* (Prague, 1965). D. Illmer points out that, in contrast to ancient practice, the Merovingian knight came to court as a "youth"; "Zum Problem der Emanzipationsgewohnheiten im merowingischen Frankenreich," *L'enfant: 2e partie, Europe médiévale et moderne*, 146.

[81] On the topos, see E. R. Curtius, *European Literature and the Latin Middle Ages*, 98-101.

was an especially important link between the past and the present. For an outstanding example we need only step back a few years to the reign of Robert the Pious, who died in 1031. He was the subject of a famous poem by Adalbero of Laon, perhaps composed between 1010 and 1020,[82] and a lengthier life by Helgaud of Fleury, completed by 1033.[83] Although drawn in his later years, both portraits present Robert as a young man. Helgaud's *vita* is really an example of secular hagiography. He saw the king as a new church father, capable as were the ancients of transmitting to earth the *celestis imperii dignitas*.[84] Robert in his view lived at a time when God was looking over "the sons of men" in an effort to find someone who truly understood and desired him.[85]

Adalbero had a larger view. On the one hand, he saw Robert as a transitional figure between the Carolingian and Capetian dynasties. As such, he represented both *sapientia* and *iuuentus*.[86] Although aging himself, Adalbero greets the king on behalf of the younger and older brethren in Laon (*flos juvenum fructusque senum*).[87] Also, he idolizes the early years of the prince who helped Hugh Capet to govern the country from 987 to 996, and who became sole ruler at twenty-seven: "Your image," he stated, "is now resplendent with the flower of youth. . . . The common people are happy, even the wise rejoice."[88]

But, in his later years, Adalbero feared that many long-established traditions were under attack. In particular, he saw the Cluniacs under Odilo as a threat to the inherited link between the nobility and the bishops which was a bulwark of Carolingian polity, and, in broader terms, as a desacralization of the threefold division of society—those who laboured, prayed, and fought—in which he perceived a reflection of divine law on earth.[89] The Cluniacs were viciously satirized: their so-called ancient law had no authority; their superior usurped the

[82] R. T. Coolidge, "Adalbero, Bishop of Laon," *Studies in Medieval and Renaissance History* 2 (1965), 71-72.

[83] R.-H. Bautier and G. Labory, eds., *Helgaud de Fleury, Vie de Robert le Pieux* (Paris, 1965), 37.

[84] *Epitoma Vitae Regis Rotberti Pii* 1, *ibid.*, 56.

[85] *Ibid.*, 2, p. 58.

[86] Cf. Cl. Carozzi, "Les fondements de la tripartition sociale chez Adalbéron de Laon," *Annales, E.S.C.*, 33 (1978), 683-84, 691, and G. Duby, *Les trois ordres ou l'imaginaire du féodalisme*, 63-66.

[87] *Adalberonis Episcopi Laudunensis Carmen ad Rotbertum Regem Francorum*, RHF, vol. 10, vv. 2-3.

[88] *Ibid.*, vv. 13-14.

[89] Coolidge, "Adalbero, Bishop of Laon," 72-74.

secular functions of royalty; and learned bishops were replaced by illiterates. In the abortive attempt to halt the Moslem advance, the roles of old age and youth were predictably reversed, the young knights ascending "slow chariots" and the horses stooping "to a crowd of old men."[90] Adalbero even regretted spending his own youth acquiring learning, since, as he put it, warfare and agriculture were now so much more fashionable.[91]

Adalbero did not approve of the *miles-monachus*,[92] but in general the eleventh century did.[93] Although less remarkable as a literary work, Helgaud's *Vita* is more characteristic of a period that increasingly sought to combine secular and ecclesiastical heroic types into a single image.

An early classic of the genre was Odo of Cluny's *Life of Gerald of Aurillac*.[94] Gerald, who died in 909, never actually became a monk, but, Mabillon observed, "the Benedictines owe so much to him . . . that he justly has a place among the Order's holy men."[95] The social and religious pressures of the decades following the death of Robert the Pious reopened the issues. Yet, for the most effective portraits, we must look forward to the historians of the First Crusade. An example is Tancred, whose *Gesta* were narrated by Ralph of Caen around 1113. Ralph's problem was how to make his hero attractive to a society which had all but had its fill of aggressive young men. He did so by fitting the real person into two irreproachable models from the past, Christian virtue and wise youth. Despite a rich family, Tancred is said to be unconsumed by pride. He is vigorous and yet reflective: "An acute observer of God's precepts, he strove with great effort to give meaning to what he heard and, to the degree that his peers allowed, to transform thought into action."[96] Accepting no praise for himself, he led an ascetic life, putting off sleep for vigil, rest for work,

---

[90] *Carmen*, respectively vv. 34-35, 115, 37-49 and 141-42.

[91] *Ibid.*, vv. 174-75.

[92] *Ibid.*, vv. 110-15.

[93] On the social history, see A. Schulte, *Der Adel und die deutsche Kirche im Mittelalter* (Stuttgart, 1922), G. Duby, *La société aux XIe et XIIe siècles dans la région mâconnaise*, 109-33, 215-33, J. Fechter, *Cluny, Adel und Volk. Studien über der Verhältnis des Klosters zu den Ständen* (910-1156) (Stuttgart, 1966), G. Tellenbach, ed., *Studien und Vorarbeiten zur Geschichte des grossfränkischen und frühdeutschen Adels* (Freiburg-im-Breisgau, 1957), and, from the monastic perspective, H. Grundmann, "Adelsbekehrungen im Hochmittelalter. *Conversi* und *nutriti* im Kloster," *Ausgewählte Aufsätze* I (Stuttgart, 1976), 124-49.

[94] *De Vita S. Geraldi . . .* , PL 133.639A-704A.

[95] *Vitae S. Geraldi Compendium, ibid.*, 703B.

[96] *Gesta Tancredi*, c.1, *Recueil des historiens des croisades* (Paris 1841-1906), 3, 605.

satiety for hunger, and leisure for effort.[97] Robert the Monk, writing of Godefrey of Bouillon, was a little less explicit. As a knight from Lorraine taking up the crusade, Godefrey fell heir to the legendary obligation of Charlemagne, who was reputed to have carried the cross of northern Christianity as far as Constantinople.[98] Yet, in spirit, he was "more monk than soldier."[99]

These of course are literary portraits.[100] We come closer to reality in the Norman nobility who fill the pages of Orderic's *Ecclesiastical History*, a work which, Marjorie Chibnall observes, has perhaps no equal as a living portrait of eleventh-century society.[101] Here, too, the contrast between lay and religious ideals provides refreshing insights into the growth of literate concerns.

Let us look at a few of these youths, then attempt some general remarks on the manner in which Orderic conceives the rituals of entering mature life.

We may begin with Ansold, the eldest son of Peter of Maule, who died on 12 January 1100 or 1101.[102] According to Orderic, Ansold's career after his father's death was a textbook version of Christian knighthood. He had all the expected virtues: he was tall and strong, an excellent leader, an impartial judge, and a generous, intelligent person.[103] But his life was "ideal-typical" in other respects. As a young knight or *tiro*, he displayed outstanding capacity for combat. Then, forced into exile during his father's lifetime, he campaigned successfully with Robert Guiscard at Constantinople. He returned to Normandy on finding a suitable bride, Odeline, the daughter of Ralph, the castellan of Mantes. He married her as a young girl, apparently educated her, and had by her seven sons and two daughters. In Orderic's view, Ansold evolved from a knighthood graced with monastic spirituality to a disciplined fatherhood in which youthful exuberance was barely a memory. So notable was his religious commitment, his

[97] *Loc.cit.*

[98] R. Folz, *Le Souvenir et la Légende de Charlemagne dans l'Empire germanique médiéval* (Paris, 1950), 134-42, and, on the archaeology, see A. Kleinclausz, "La légende du protectorat de Charlemagne sur la terre sainte," *Syria* 7 (1926), 211-33.

[99] *Historia Iherosolimitana* 1.5, *Recueil*, vol. 3, 731-32. On Godefrey's youth, see H. Glaesener, "Godefroid de Bouillon. Etait-il 'un médiocre?' " RHE 39 (1943), 310-20.

[100] Trustworthy accounts of the First Crusade record a number of lay internalizations of monastic discipline. On the background, see above all C. Erdmann, *The Origin of the Idea of Crusade*, chs. 2 and 7.

[101] *Eccles. Hist.*, vol. 2, p. xxix.   [102] *Ibid.*, vol. 3, 178n2.

[103] *Ibid.*, 5.19, vol. 3, 178-80.

biographer observes, that "he even provided a model for persons living under the *Rule*."[104]

In families with two sons, one often became a knight, the other a monk. Such was the fate of a pair of the impoverished progeny of Arnold of Giroie. After their father's death, the eldest, William of Echauffour, went to the French court "as soon as he reached adolescence."[105] He served the king until he was old enough to bear arms; then he journeyed to Apulia, where he was well received by his Norman relatives already established in Italy. He married a Lombard woman, and, while in the service of Guiscard's nephew, Robert of Loritello, got possession of some thirty *castelli*. His wife, Orderic notes, bore him many children, and he lived for some forty years among her people, "forgetting Normandy."[106]

His younger brother Reginald was a more interesting case. He was given with one ploughland to Orderic's house, St. Evroul, at the age of five. Disciplined and clever, he stood out among the novitiates of his generation. He was, the chronicler recalls, gifted with an exceptional memory, and was especially skilled in *divina lectio*.[107] But his scholastic achievement appears to have camouflaged inner conflicts. He was a fanatically strict interpreter of the *Rule*, and, it was reported, highly critical of those who bore life's burdens less easily than he. According to Orderic, this behavioural pattern first became apparent when he was quite young. Even as a boy Reginald overdid things: once, for instance, when transporting a load of earth, he incurred a hernia. Repeated overexertions eventually rendered his condition incurable.[108] The examples of William and Reginald are not unusual.[109] A similar destiny awaited Bernard and Drogo, the sons of Geoffrey of Neufmarché.[110]

In such lives, the period of "wandering" was necessary but impermanent. Whichever direction the human spirit took, in Orderic's view, secular and religious values reinforced each other. Successful decisions were often taken before youth's end. But a high emotional price was paid during adolescence, the interest, so to speak, accumulating in small amounts until later in life, when it could bring about psychological bankruptcy. Overindulgence in ascetic exercises was one answer to uncertainty, but it brought new problems in its wake.

An even more decisive change of character sometimes occurred in a

---

[104] *Ibid.*, 180.   [105] *Ibid.*, bk. 3, vol. 2, p. 126.
[106] *Loc.cit.*   [107] *Loc.cit.*   [108] *Ibid.*, 128.
[109] Cf. Erlembald, Landulf Senior, *Historia Mediolanensis* 3.14, MGH SS 8, p. 83.
[110] *Hist. Eccles.*, 6.8, vol. 3, p. 254.

single person, dramatically uniting the notions of wandering and reform. Throughout the eleventh century, monastic confraternity offered a viable substitute for declining joint families and networks of
kin.[111] Also, the change from a secular to a religious style of life was
still relatively easy.[112] The *fraternitas* of the monastic community could
even act as a vehicle for social mobility. A certain Geoffrey, an unti-
tled Breton, was said to have committed a number of thefts *in iuuen-
tute*; but, later in life, either, as Orderic would have it, *inspirante Deo*,
or, as was more likely, on finding a rich wife, he mended his ways,
stopped consorting with rowdies, and, adopting monastic habits, attempted "to procure by his own hands' labour all that was necessary
for his existence."[113] His newly acquired goods were used for charitable purposes: he gave alms, supported hermits, and kept only the
bare necessities for himself. Later, he asked for and was granted confraternity with St. Evroul.[114]

Literary texts like these are notoriously unreliable indicators of real
social changes. Yet, at least one interesting pattern is reiterated.

Its most remarkable feature is the manner in which social and cultural values became interlocked. The behavioural sequence normally
began with a *familia* that had temporarily or permanently broken
down. It was replaced by an equally impermanent peer group, a loose
organization which delimited the passage from adolescence to youth
or from youth to manhood. Eventually a new *familia* or *fraternitas* was
formed. Only in the last phase were kin and ethical bonds reunited:
that accounts, perhaps, for its appeal.

Yet the wandering between two periods of relative stability was
also essential. It was, so to speak, every young man's personal *Bil-
dungsroman*, through which he recreated, interpreted, and re-expressed
his individual development for himself. It was a hermeneutic exercise
whose text was life itself. Usually it involved physical displacement
or a change in station, as in the case of Evrard of Breteuil. But the
period of uncertainty provided an opportunity for introspection. It
forced men onto their own resources and tested them out. As a consequence, they were compelled to adapt older values to new circumstances. Manual labour, self-denial, and voluntary poverty were fa-

[111] H.E.J. Cowdrey, "Unions and Confraternity with Cluny," *Journal of Ecclesiastical History*
16 (1965), 153-54, 162.
[112] See in general E. Amman and A. Dumas, *L'Eglise au pouvoir des laïques (888-1057)* (Paris,
1942), 296-315, 341-64.
[113] *Hist. Eccles.*, 6.10, vol. 3, p. 342.
[114] *Loc.cit.*

miliar themes, as was the tension between family, whose bonds operated vertically, and fraternity, in which they functioned horizontally. In all three stages of the "rites of passage," as instability increased, there arose a corresponding desire to internalize inherited religious values.

No wonder the resulting structures were somewhat unstable. Youth, as even unwise young men knew, was a two-sided coin: it could bring radical good fortune or bad. Men like Geoffrey were lucky. Many others were slain before their values had a chance to mature. Still others drank away their lives or spent them in wanton destruction. A number of young noblemen revolted against their parents and were crushed. A few, like Ranulf Flambard, were drawn from obscurity into a limelight that threw their worst and best qualities into stark relief.[115] Above all, most wasted all or a part of their youth in senseless movement. They were simply drifters, *peregrini* who set forth on a quest but who never reached their goal.

Odyssey and Vision

Rhetorical sketches like those of Evrard of Breteuil or the court of William Rufus were designed by their authors as points of reference in an age of transition. Yet they bore witness to a genuine paradox. During the eleventh century life expectancy was still short. "Old age," remarked Marc Bloch, "seemed to begin very early, as early as mature adult life with us. This world, which . . . considered itself very old, was in fact governed by young men."[116]

Youth, as a consequence, was not only a time of instability in the real world. It also made a deep impression on the poetic and unconscious life of the period. It is a common theme in the literature of the south and the north of France. The earliest work in Provençal, the eleventh-century *Poëme sur Boece*, opens with a reflection on the *follia* of *nos jove omne*, who have apparently deserted the ethical models of the past and think it nothing to betray one's parents.[117] A similar disregard for inherited values by *aquest foll jovent* is echoed in the contemporary *Chanson de Ste. Foi*.[118] The manysided problems of youth were profoundly explored by the early troubadours, as witness the

[115] For a balanced assessment, see R. W. Southern, "Ranulf Flambard," *Medieval Humanism and Other Studies* (Oxford, 1970), 183-205.

[116] *Feudal Society*, vol. 1, 72-73.

[117] Ll. 1-8, ed. C. Appel, *Provenzalische Crestomathie* (Marburg, 1904), 1.

[118] Ll. 248-55, ed. E. Hoepffner (Paris, 1926), 293-94.

difficulty of finding a straightforward translation for *jovens*.[119] The term can either refer to a group of virtues which, ideally, the young should possess, or, on occasion, to "a body of youths," "an association of youthful people,"[120] perhaps as a parallel to the fraternity (*la gen frairina*) of the poets themselves. Marcabru caught the range and subtlety of troubadour sentiments in a generalized invective against false love:

> Tant cant bos Jovens fon paire
> Del segle e fin'Amors maire,
> Fon Proeza mantenguda
> A celat et a saubuda,
> Mas et l'ant avilanada
> Duc e rei et emperaire.
>
> Qu'ieu sui assatz esprovaire,
> Deffendens et enquistaire,
> E vei cum Jovens se tuda,
> Per que Amors es perduda
> E de Joi deseretada
> E cum Amors es cujaire.[121]
>
> As long as true youth was father
> To the world and pure love mother,
> Prowess was maintained
> Secretly and publicly,
> But now it is debased
> By duke, king, and emperor.
>
> Because I am a good judge,
> As defender and inquisitor,
> I see how youth stifles itself,
> How affection is lost,
> Joy deserted,
> and love troubled.

[119] A. J. Denomy, "Jovens: the Notion of Youth among the Troubadours, its Meaning and Source," *Mediaeval Studies* 11 (1949), 1-22. For speculations on the possible social origins, see E. Köhler, "Sens et fonction du terme 'jeunesse' dans la poésie des troubadours," *Mélanges R. Crozet* (Poitiers, 1966), vol. 1, 569-83; and, more generally, the articles edited by W. Haubrichs, *Höfische Dichtung oder Literatur im Feudalismus?* in the *Zeitschrift für Literaturwissenschaft und Linguistik* 7 (1977).

[120] Denomy, "Jovens," 3-13, discusses the range.

[121] Ed. J.M.L. Dejeanne, *Poésies complètes du Troubadour Marcabru* (Toulouse, 1909), 5, vv. 37-48.

In the north, the theme of youth found quite a different form of expression in the *Vie de St. Alexis*, which was possibly written by Tedbalt de Vernon, a canon of Rouen, around 1040. The poem was an immediate success: the original strophic version is known in some seven manuscripts; translations later appeared in Old French, Provençal, Spanish, German, Old Norse, and Russian.[122] Among the oldest Italian minstrel poems is the *Ritmo di Sant'Alessio* from the late twelfth or thirteenth century. In Italy the story also influenced a Hebrew elegy on the captivity and martyrdom of two noble Christian children.[123] Although Syriac and Byzantine *vitae* existed, the Latin life and cult can be traced no further back than the tenth century.[124] The life, therefore, although based on an ancient story, achieved its popularity during the Middle Ages.

Its attractiveness in the eleventh century was partly due to the central theme of apostolic poverty.[125] But it also struck close to the problems affecting family and youth. The Anglo-Norman version has little action and is built instead around a single moral decision, which is aptly summed up in the statement that Alexis *plus aimet Deu que trestot son lignage* (Alexis loved God more than he treasured his lineage).[126] The plot involves none of the typically medieval machinery of demons, miracles, or divine intercessions. The well-known story is really one of conversion away from the world, and spiritual development is framed within Alexis's wandering from Rome to Edessa and back to Rome again. Living under his parents' doorstep for some seventeen years, he is nonetheless unmoved by their anguish and laments. Only after their death is his identity revealed.

The story, then, was a victory of spirit over flesh, and of youth over old age, as was obvious to Christina of Markyate, who had a version of the Old French life transcribed into the *St. Alban's Psalter*

[122] For a brief review, see *La vie de saint Alexis*, ed. C. Storey (Oxford, 1946), ix-xii; on vernacular versions of other eleventh-century saints' lives, see B. de Gaiffier, "L'hagiographe et son public au XIe siècle," *Miscellanea Historica . . . L. van der Essen* (Paris and Brussels, 1947), I, 156-57.

[123] See B. Migliorini, *The Italian Language*, ed. and trans. T. G. Griffith (London, 1966), 71-73.

[124] The Latin lives are classified by M. Rösler, *Die Fassungen der Alexius-Legende* (Vienna, 1905) pp. 35-76; on the cult, see L. Duchesne, "Notes sur la topographie de Rome au moyen-âge VII: les légendes chrétiennes de l'Aventin," *Mélanges de l'Ecole française de Rome* 10 (1890), 234-50.

[125] Interpretations are reviewed briefly by B. de Gaiffier, "Intactam sponsam relinquens. A propos de la vie de S. Alexis," *Analecta Bollandiana* 65 (1947), 157-62.

[126] L. 250, ed. G. Paris (Paris, 1911), 9.

made for her sometime before 1123. Like Alexis, her early marriage
had been arranged without her consent; she escaped only by requesting her husband to respect her prior vow of chastity.[127] The numerous
overlappings between Alexis's *vita* and her life led Otto Pächt to remark: ". . . Either . . . in Christina's case reality was moulded strictly
according to a literary pattern, so to speak as an 'Imitatio Alexii,' or
. . . the story of Alexis was introduced 'after the event' as a meaningful allusion and suitable parallel to Christina's own experiences. . . ."
Consciously or unconsciously, Christina lived a text in such a way
that her life became a paradigm of Christian sainthood.[128]

Of course, precocious saints were not original in the post-Carolin-
gian age, but changes in religious sensibilities found a number of
occasions for breathing new life into the topoi. An example is the *vita*
of Bernwald, bishop of Hildesheim, by Thangmar the Saxon. Bernwald was elected on 15 January 993. The "venerable Gerdagus" having died, relates Thangmar, "the consensus of all settled on the young
man (*iuvenis*),"[129] who, although tender in years, amazed the elders
(*senes*) with the gravity of his ways (*morum . . . gravitate*).[130] Odilo,
who died in 1049, met Maieul of Cluny as a young lad and was taken
under his wing "like a son."[131] Such examples reinforced the continuity with the past. But, in the next generation, the same hagiographic conventions could symbolize a break with custom. For instance, Vitalis of Savigny was so zealous as a boy that he earned the
somewhat condescending epithet of *parvus abbas*.[132] Bernard of Tiron
"was so inflamed with religious affection that he covered himself with
the gown of a regular canon. . . . His school chums laughed, calling
him a 'monk.'. . ."[133]

A literary work which came at the question of youth, movement,
and spiritual growth from a different angle, but which nonetheless

---

[127] The theme is fully explored by C. J. Holdsworth, "Christina of Markyate," in D. Baker, ed., *Medieval Women* (Oxford, 1978), 190-94 and more generally in R. W. Hanning, *The Individual in Twelfth-Century Romance*, 34-50.

[128] *The St. Albans Psalter (Albani Psalter)* (London, 1960), 136-37. Cf. H. Sckommodau, "Alexius in Liturgie, Malerei und Dichtung," *Zeitschrift für romanische Philologie* 72 (1956), 165-94.

[129] *Vita Bernwardi*, c. 4, MGH SS IV, 759.

[130] *Ibid.*, c. 5.

[131] *Vita S. Odilonis*, c. 1, PL 142.899C: Fit inter eos familiare colloquium, junior seniori suum prodit desiderium; senex ut praemeditata perficiat, modis quibus potuit junioris instruit animum.

[132] *Vita S. Vitalis*, c. 2, ed. *anon.*, *Analecta Bollandiana* 1 (1882), 360.

[133] *Vita S. Bernardi*, 1.7, PL 172.1374B-C.

belongs to the sensibilities of the same period, is the *Navigatio Sancti Brendani*, manuscripts of which date from tenth-century Lotharingia.[134] The text reached French readers by 1047[135] and was beautifully translated into Anglo-Norman from a new Latin version as early as 1106.[136]

The real Brendan was born around 489 and died between 570 and 583, after reportedly visiting the Shetlands, Brittany, and England. His life and adventures inspired an Irish *immram* (a sea voyage interspersed with remarkable events), which involved two visits to the threshold of "the land of promise." One was made by Brendan's fellow monk, Barinthus, who told him about it on his return. Barinthus said that he had travelled over sea to the Isle of Delights to visit his hermit son Mernoc. There he found a large number of monks living in complete spiritual harmony. To the west, he was told, lay another island, the *terra repromissionis*, a marvellous place of precious stones, eternal blooms, and ever-ripening fruit, where physical needs were unknown. Barinthus and Mernoc visited the island and wandered about for some fifteen days, coming finally to a river which flowed from east to west. A man bathed in light then appeared and told them to turn back, intimating that they had reached the gates of paradise.

On hearing Barinthus's account, Brendan resolved to visit the islands himself. After fasting for forty days, he set out with some fourteen chosen brethren. A lengthy odyssey ensued, in which Brendan's boat passed from isle to isle, alternately experiencing marvels, threats, and temptations through the course of the liturgical year. One island turned out to be a large fish, which simply swam away. Another seemed to be a paradise filled with exotic birds, but was in reality the abode of fallen angels. The voyagers were even greeted on one occasion by Judas Iscariot. At length they arrived in the promised land and found themselves at the same river which flowed from east to west. The same young man appeared before them, embraced them, and said: "Before you lies the land you seek, which to this point God has deliberately concealed from you. Return whence you came, taking as

---

[134] C. Selmer, ed., *Navigatio Sancti Brendani Abbatis* (Notre Dame, 1959), xxviii-ix. J. Carney, *Medium Aevum* 32 (1963), 40, criticizes Selmer and places the original around 800. On the early Irish parallels, see H.P.A. Oskamp, *The Voyage of Máel Dúin*, 16-35, and, on the motivation, K. Hughes, "The Changing Theory and Practice of Irish Pilgrimage," *Journal of Ecclesiastical History* 11 (1960), 148-50.

[135] J. F. Kenney, *The Sources for the Early History of Ireland*, vol. 1 (New York, 1929), 415.

[136] I. Short and B. Merrilees, eds., *The Anglo-Norman Voyage of St. Brendan* (Manchester, 1979), 2.

many fruits and precious stones as you can carry. For the final day of your earthly pilgrimage draws near." Thus enlightened, Brendan and his companions sailed for home, where the saint died shortly afterwards.

The *Navigatio* has been chiefly studied for what it tells us about earlier Irish literature. But attention should also be paid to the sources of its popularity as a Latin work down to the fifteenth century.[137] Its hero was admittedly an attractive saint and its charming exotica enticed many readers. Yet, the eleventh-century themes which we have been discussing make an appearance as well. The rite of passage achieved its goal, and the visionary qualities were sure to be of interest to men already drawn to those other ancient forms of prognostication, dreams, and prophecies. The quest for the *terra repromissionis* was itself on men's minds. In effect, the *Navigatio* presented a fabulous version of the search for the earthly and spiritual Jerusalem which was the meeting point of the pilgrimage and the crusade.[138] The story was also rich in symbolism that struck at the core of contemporary spirituality. The ocean represented the desert of the wandering preachers; the crossing was a time of testing, self-analysis, and discovery. The images and anecdotes combined mortification, purification, and the desire for inner perfection—concerns which Irish missionary activity had brought to the Continent and which, in the eyes of many, were just then beginning to mature. In a sense, as he set out on his penitential journey, Brendan stood for all "exiles" seeking to be reunited with their permanent homes, whether they were monks desiring paradise or knights yearning for their *patria*. Typology, too, played a role in uniting the past and the present. There were really two paradises, the one narrated by Barinthus anticipating the other seen by Brendan, just as the Old Testament foretold the New. But above all the story echoed the theme of old age and youth, aptly represented by the eternally young and yet ageless paradise itself. Barinthus was guided there by his more intensely spiritual son, Mernoc. Brendan was told he was near his journey's end by a *iuuenis*.[139] In his Anglo-Norman version, Benedeit elaborated the point: Brendan was given two guides, "a white-haired man, his eyes youthful," who followed the boat and provided food, and *un juvencel*, an angelic personage at paradise's door-

---

[137] Selmer, *Navigatio*, xvii.

[138] P. Alphandéry, *La Chrétienté et l'idée de croisade*, ed. A. Dupront, 2 vols. (Paris, 1954, 1959), I, 22.

[139] *Navigatio S. Brendani*, c. 28, p. 79, 20.

step,[140] the latter possibly drawn from Claudian and anticipating Alan of Lille.[141]

An eleventh-century vision which more closely interrelated the imaginary and the real was the story of Walchelin, a young priest of St. Aubin's, near Angers. According to Orderic, who reported it from a verbal account, the episode took place on 1 January 1091.[142] Like the testings and conversions of the wandering preachers, it occurred in a deserted region of the northwest, "far from the dwellings of men."[143]

The most notable feature of Walchelin's character, twice repeated in the vision, is his combination of religious piety and youthful uncertainty. The story's inevitable moral lesson is also presented through images uniting the problems of youth and family.

The events are as follows. One night Walchelin was returning home along a deserted road after visiting a sick parishioner when he heard the hoofbeats of a large cavalry force in the distance. At first he thought it was the infamous marauders of Robert Bellême, rushing to the siege of Courcy. The young priest was frightened, and turned over several courses of action in his mind. As the band approached, he tried to reach the cover of four medlar trees which he saw in the distance through the moonlight. But a giant wielding a mace barred his way and shouted from his horse that he was to proceed no further.

Then Walchelin bore witness to a lengthy purgatorial procession. First, a great crowd passed on foot, carrying domestic animals, clothing, and household utensils like so much booty, nagging one another as they hurried along. Among their number Walchelin recognized individuals from his own diocese who had recently died. Now, he reasoned, they were paying for their sins.

The spirits who followed were more bizarre. Walchelin stood in amazement as some thousand men walked by, each pair supporting a litter on which sat a dwarf with a large, barrel-like head. Behind this troop came two huge blacks carrying a man bound to a tree-trunk; on top of him rode a fierce demon who periodically thrust a hot poker into his genitals. Walchelin recognized him as well: it was a certain

---

[140] Ed. Short and Merrilees, respectively ll. 356ff. (announced at l. 140) and ll. 1715ff. For another from among the numerous examples of the topos in Anglo-Norman literature, see the dialogue between *le veillard* and *l'enfant* in *Le Petit Plet*, ed. B. S. Merrilees (Oxford, 1970).

[141] M. D. Legge, *Anglo-Norman Literature and its Background*, 11.

[142] *Eccles. Hist.*, 8.17, vol. 4, pp. 236-50.

[143] *Ibid.*, 238.

Stephen, a priest, who, he recalled, had committed a murder but had not completed his penance.

Next came a stream of women which seemed to him to be almost limitless. As punishment for their "seductions and obscene pleasures," they were mounted side-saddle on steeds whose backs were covered with hot nails. Some were noble, Walchelin noted, and quite a few horses still awaited their riders. After them came bishops, abbots, and monks, all holding the pastoral staffs they had wilfully neglected in this life. Finally Walchelin saw a large number of knights, among whose ranks he picked out Landry of Orbec, who rose above his lowly origins only to be corrupted by bribery and greed.

After the immense army of the dead had passed, Walchelin realized that he had been observing the *familia* or *mesnie* of Hellequin. According to legend, such spirits roamed the dark wastes of Normandy and Brittany by night, leading those in purgatory on ghastly hunts. He feared that no one would believe his tale, and so he decided to catch hold of a riderless horse and to take it back with him as proof. He reached for one of the coal-black steeds, but it eluded him and galloped swiftly away. In order not to miss another, he placed himself squarely in the middle of the road. When a second horse stopped, he attempted to mount. However, no sooner had he put his foot in the stirrup than he felt a burning pain shoot up his leg. His hands, which had lightly taken the reigns, turned to ice.

Meanwhile, four great knights rode up and scolded him for interfering with the horses. Three of them were on the point of taking hold of him, but the forth asked them to leave off, as he wanted the priest to take a message to his wife. He was, he said, William of Glos, and his sin was usury. He had once loaned a poor man some money and had taken his mill as a pledge. When the debt was not repaid, he annexed the mill and eventually willed it to his heirs. As punishment for his sin he was forced to carry a burning mill-shaft perpetually in his mouth. He asked Walchelin to tell his wife and son to return the illegally acquired property to its rightful owners.

Walchelin was undecided as to what he should do. Whether William merited consideration or not, he concluded, delivering such a message was a risky business. William continued to repeat his request, and finally the priest pretended to assent in order to be rid of him. But William, being a spirit, immediately saw through the duplicity and threatened Walchelin with attack. The priest rapidly recited a prayer to the Virgin and was rescued by a mysterious horseman who appeared out of nowhere bearing a large sword.

When all the other knights had passed, Walchelin noticed a solitary figure lingering on the road. The rider approached and asked pointedly whether he recognized him. When the priest said he did not, the stranger revealed his identity: he was his own brother, Robert, the son of Ralph the Fair. As proof, he related intimate details of their childhood together. Once again, Walchelin was unsure just what to do. He was even reluctant to acknowledge his own flesh and blood! Somewhat taken aback, Robert reminded him that, after their father's untimely death, it was he who virtually raised, clothed, and educated him. Without his aid, he informed his brother, he would never have succeeded in pursuing a religious vocation. Confronted with these facts, Walchelin broke down in tears. Robert then told him that he had narrowly escaped being slain for trying to steal one of Hellequin's horses. Only prayer had saved him. Finally, he added a word of advice. Their father, he stated, had only escaped in part from purgatory when Walchelin sang his first mass. Therefore, he must continue to be a good priest and to pray for them both.

This vision is rich in associations, and effectively blends a number of themes from popular religion in the eleventh century. In the background stand the absolutes of good and evil: the four medlars, possibly representing the apostles, are balanced by the four condemned riders of the miniature apocalypse. Prayer is a primitive "science" whose efficacy in the external world is immediate. Although, as in any dream, details from fact and fiction are interwoven, Walchelin, or, as is more likely, Orderic himself, arranged them from oral record so that they fitted the literary genres of the vision and the estates satire. The actors, all persons lately deceased, are placed in a landscape made up of Christian symbolism and the folklore of Hellequin, a figure who also makes a shadowy appearance in Walter Map, William of Malmesbury, and Peter of Blois.[144] Among the commoners in the procession Walchelin recognizes some neighbours; among the clergy, Hugh of Lisieux, Mainer of St. Evroul, and Gerbert of Wandrille; and among the nobility, as noted, Landry of Orbec and William of Glos. Moreover, the various classes and their typical sins are listed in order: the peasantry, who simply disregard law and order; the women, who are given over to sensual pleasures; the clergy, who desert their flocks; and the nobility, who are guilty of abuses of power. The fat-

---

[144] *Ibid.*, Intro., xxxix. Cf. C. Ginzburg, "Charivari, associations juvéniles, chasse sauvage," in J. Le Goff and J.-C. Schmitt, eds., *Le charivari* (Paris, 1981), 134-36.

headed dwarfs and their giant bearers may even recall a more famous metaphor of Bernard of Chartres.[145]

But the story's major subject is one man's indecision. Walchelin, in effect, is put to the test three times, once at the outset, a second time before William of Glos, and finally in the presence of his brother. On the first two occasions he fails; on the last he succeeds, but, it is arguable, in spite of himself. His brother draws into the open the real source of his uncertainty, that is, the tension produced by his having to forsake ties of kin for an extrapersonal relationship of presumably greater value. The vision not only underlines the need for prayer and vigilance—that is its justification; it also reinforces Walchelin's personal resolve during a period of psychological instability, when he passes from one style of life to another.

The timing, too, is important. Walchelin was only recently ordained; he is still called a *iuuenis*.[146] His unquelled audacity almost costs him his life when he tries to make off with one of Hellequin's ghostly steeds. The purgatorial procession, of course, is no surprise in a medieval vision. But, here too contemporary concerns directly affecting his life make themselves felt. Religious reform is just beneath the surface: the condemned clerics are in fact all black monks. Further, the events take place in the unsettled wilderness of Maine, which often doubles for the Mediterranean retreats of the desert fathers in the lives of eleventh-century wandering preachers.[147] Economic change is another source of anxiety. Landry of Orbec is accused of profiting from office and William of Glos of usury. Reference is made to the two devices which played an important role in transforming northerly agriculture, namely the water-mill and the stirrup.[148] Even the Moslem menace, which was still on men's minds, makes a dim appearance in the black bearers.[149]

In this sense, the vision is a catalogue of the concerns which might have affected a young priest of noble origins but of little financial security in a rapidly changing world. This view is reinforced by the conversation with his brother, which is more than an exercise in nos-

[145] See B. Stock, "*Antiqui* and *Moderni* as 'Giants' and 'Dwarfs': A Reflection of Popular Culture?" *Journal of Modern Philology* 76 (1979), 370-74; on Bernard, see below, p. 517.

[146] *Hist. Eccles.*, p. 238.

[147] E.g., Robert of Arbrissel, *Vita*, c. 2, AASS 25 February, vol. 6, 610E-F; *Vita B. Bernardi Tironiensis*, c. 3.20, PL 172.1380D.

[148] *Hist. Eccles.*, p. 244: *molendinum, teripedes*, the latter an early use; cf. R. E. Latham, *Revised Medieval Latin Word-List* (Oxford, 1965), 480. On the stirrup, see L. White, Jr., *Medieval Technology and Social Change*, 1-38.

[149] Cf. N. Daniel, *Islam and the West* (Edinburgh, 1960), 6-7.

talgia. The interview attempts in effect through the most powerful of evocations—the deceased—to transcend living human bonds and to re-express them in spiritual terms. There are really two "families" active in the vision, the band of Hellequin and Walchelin's own present and future religious brotherhood. The one is a folkloric "text" brought to life through being recorded. The other is an internalized "text," in which the image of Walchelin's personal family for two previous generations is used to strengthen his membership in a new association.

Guibert's Mother

Uncertainty, of course, affected women as deeply as men, although the chroniclers, being males, have left us nothing like as complete a record of their trials.

Yet, the historical forces against which women were reacting were not the same. From the eleventh century, women appear to have begun to live longer than men, reversing an early medieval trend.[150] Population growth overcrowded the marriage market with young ladies who had no dowries and hence little possibility of attracting a suitable mate. Consensual marriage was not yet the rule,[151] and decision-making was generally a family rather than an individual responsibility. Among the lower strata, strict monogamy was not always practiced,[152] and many peasant women were concubines of the regular clergy. The imposition of the feudal system gradually impoverished such women's families, while the promulgation of the Gregorian reforms demanding strict clerical celibacy deprived many of their sole means of support.

On the positive side, older boundaries began, if not to be obliterated, at least to be challenged. A number of tenth-century women took to arms to secure what was theirs. Alpert of Metz mentions Liutgarda, who, on her sister's death, took over her estates by force, then captured Elten on the Rhine.[153] Thietmar of Merseburg writes

---

[150] D. Herlihy, "Life Expectancies for Women in Medieval Society," in R. T. Morewedge, ed., *The Role of Women in the Middle Ages* (Albany, 1975), 9-11.

[151] See M. M. Sheehan, "Choice of Marriage Partner in the Middle Ages: Development and Mode of Application of a Theory of Marriage," *Studies in Medieval and Renaissance History*, n.s. 1 (1978), 7-8.

[152] For a general review of the issues before 1100, see *Il matrimonio nella società altomedievale*, 2 vols. (Spoleto, 1977); for a later parallel, see J. Scammell, "Freedom and Marriage in Medieval England," *Economic History Review* 27 (1974), 531-32.

[153] *De Diversitate Temporum* 1.2-3, MGH SS 4, 702-03.

of a certain Christianized Hungarian called Deviux around 1018. His beautiful wife "drank quite a bit, rode to battle like a knight, and even once killed a man in anger."[154] Closer to the society we have been discussing, Orderic speaks of a number of women who openly played male roles, like Isabel of Conches, who fought "as fiercely as Camilla."[155] Other Norman women refused to accept the permanent desertion of their husbands for the battlefield. When the Conqueror called upon his vassals to quell the revolt at York in 1068, a number of spouses gave their husbands the choice of returning immediately or of finding them remarried when they did.[156] Contemporary portraits of women also show them emerging from two-dimensionality. An example is Mabel, the notorious niece of the bishop of Séez, who was, Orderic notes, "very forceful and worldly, clever, quick with her tongue, and above all cruel."[157]

The most popular woman in transition in the entire age is undoubtedly Héloïse, while the most fervent reformer is Hildegard of Bingen. But the most typical of the tensions of the later eleventh century is perhaps the mother of Guibert of Nogent.[158]

Guibert's portrait forms an important part of his *Memoirs*, which were written in 1115.[159] His mother's conversion is interwoven with his own spiritual development, about which he gives the reader some insights in the opening chapters. The first image is that of perpetual movement between two extremes, that is, *decursus* and *recursus*, a continual falling into sin and attempted recovery.[160] *Decursus* is also a sort of waywardness, a wandering from the straight path and the chosen goal.[161] Guibert's God is at once inflexible and compassionate; he is both a deity outside man, influencing him objectively, and a deity within, who is perceived subjectively. Above all, he appears to understand the many dark corners of Guibert's mind: He knows that he has sinned; and He knows that he will sin again. And a large part of

[154] *Chronicon* 9.4, ed. F. Kurze (Hanover, 1889), 241.

[155] *Hist. Eccles.*, 8.14, vol. 4, pp. 212, 214.

[156] *Ibid.*, bk. 4, vol. 2, 218, 220.

[157] *Ibid.*, bk. 3, vol. 2, 48. Cf. E. Auerbach, *Mimesis*, trans. W. Trask (Princeton, 1968), 147.

[158] For useful contrasts between Abelard and Guibert, see M. McLaughlin, "Abelard as Autobiographer: The Motives and Meaning of the Story of the Calamities," *Speculum* 42 (1967), 486-87.

[159] J. F. Benton, *Self and Society in Medieval France*, 237.

[160] *De Vita Sua* 1.1, ed. Bourgin, p. 1. Cf. F. Amory, "The Confessional Superstructure of Guibert of Nogent's *Vita*," *Classica et Mediaevalia* 25 (1964), 233-34.

[161] Guibert, *De Vita Sua*, Cf. *ibid.*, 1.3, p. 10: Nihil in te solidus, nihil constans habui.

Guibert's anguish arises from the simple fact that he too knows that God understands. His crisis, as John Benton emphasizes, is one of self-knowledge.

His troubles, as he sees them, started in early youth, indeed, almost from the moment of birth. He was a sickly baby, and, as a boy, a slow learner, who never lived up to his tutor's expectations.[162] He saw himself, in fact, as a latter-day Augustine, that is, as a person in whom original sin had taken the form of youthful irrationality, which he had to strive to overcome. "I confess," he wrote, "the evil deeds of my childhood and adolescence, which still smoulder in this, my mature stage of life, the deep-rooted longings after forbidden pleasures, which, despite the weariness of my frame, have never ceased."[163] Guibert was over fifty when he wrote these words.[164] He was looking back on his "youth" as well as on broader problems which were indirectly connected to his own spiritual development, namely, religious revivals, civil disobedience, and the breakdown of formerly irreproachable codes of conduct. Even his style brings together the personal and the general. The *Memoirs* have no linear design; each episode is linked emotionally to the next. Each, as well, involves many feelings at once: dignity and shame, charity and regret, attraction and revulsion. His story, in short, is an effort to bring order to the chaos of his own experience through literature.[165] It does not always succeed. Similarly, in real life, he was continually struggling to be free: but he never was.

Nor was his mother. But her anxieties were not the same as his. Guibert's turmoil was almost entirely internal; hers arose in large part from her treatment in a male-dominated world. Insight, when it came to her, came as one by one society's supports were denied her.

The details of her predicament are not clarified until the twelfth chapter of book one. By then, Guibert has acquainted the reader with his own tensions, as well as the new fashion for religious conversion in men like St. Bruno and Evrard of Breteuil. Ironically, he adds, his mother "did not yet understand what hope, what certainties, she ought to have derived" from faith.[166]

As he depicts his mother, the intense desire for solid relations, which was undercut by her inability to control her fate, engendered

---

[162] *Ibid.*, 1.3, p. 9; 1.5-6, pp. 14-19.

[163] *Ibid.*, 1.1, p. 1; cf. Amory, "The Confessional Superstructure," 224-40.

[164] Benton, *Self and Society*, 233.   [165] *De Vita Sua* 1.12, p. 41.

[166] *Ibid.*, 1.7, p. 22.

in her a blind fear of God.[167] She often imagined, he said, that He would actually strike her.[168] Worse, she was forced into a bad marriage. When scarcely past puberty, she was given to Guibert's father, who was himself still in adolescence.[169] The match had been arranged by her grandfather. But her stepmother, hoping to promote one of her own nieces, bewitched her, and for three years the marriage remained unconsummated.

Her husband, questioned repeatedly by his relatives, at length revealed the state of affairs. His family tried to obtain an annulment and to persuade him to enter a monastery. Failing in this, they began to harass the young bride, whom they were eager to disinherit. Wealthy bachelors in the region assumed that she was still a virgin and began to pay her suit. But, after some seven years of barrenness, the spell was broken and several children were born. Guibert's father died when he was only eight months old; he was raised entirely by his mother and his tutor. His mother, who was increasingly preoccupied with both material and spiritual questions, retired when he was twelve to a house near the monastery of Clermont-en-Beauvaisis. His tutor became a monk in the same abbey and later its prior.[170] For a brief period Guibert pretended to take part in the youthful diversions fashionable in his day. Then, to his mother's disappointment, he entered the nearby monastery of St. Germer.[171]

Guibert's story is rich, perhaps too rich, in suggestions for psychohistory.[172] A virtually fatherless child, he looked for strong support in his tutor and his mother. His tutor, he claimed, appeared to him before they met in a dream as an archetypal father-figure, towards whose kindly features and white flowing hair Guibert immediately adopted an attitude of blind devotion.[173] He found his mother irresistibly beautiful. His attempts to transform his physical attraction into Platonic images were not altogether convincing.[174]

Yet, at critical moments in his youth, both parents treated him cruelly and left his needs unattended. Guibert lived at home and, so far as we know, had no outside friends. He therefore developed an

[167] Ibid., 1.12, pp. 36-37.   [168] Loc.cit.   [169] Loc.cit.

[170] Ibid., 1.14-15, pp. 48-52.   [171] Ibid., 1.15, p. 53.

[172] On the merits of psychological interpretation, see Benton, Self and Society, 21-23.

[173] De Vita Sua 1.4, p. 13; 1.17, p. 64. Guibert modelled the story of his education (c. 5, p. 15) on Quintilian, Institutiones Oratoriae 1.3, ed. Meister, (Leipzig, 1886), 17; A. Mollard, "L'imitation de Quintilien dans Guibert de Nogent," Le Moyen Age, 3rd series, 5 (1934), 81-87. On the historical context, see L. Halphen, "Un pédagogue," A travers l'histoire du moyen âge (Paris, 1950), 277-85.

[174] De Vita Sua 1.12, pp. 5-6.

acute awareness of the differences between his own system of values and those which prevailed in the male-dominated society at large.[175] He both cherished and dreaded the two chief influences in his life:[176] his attitude foreshadowed his later ambivalence towards physical violence and sexuality. Neglect, perhaps, also provided the springs for his unceasing search for someone or something to cling to during periods of anxiety and indecision.

These contradictory forces produced a deeply troubled personality. He had a tendency towards authoritarianism which occasionally masqueraded as patriotism. He loathed heretics[177] and Jews,[178] upon whose comparatively innocent heads he often brought down his pent-up aggression. Like Augustine, he transformed the distinction between body and soul into a series of poetic images describing the most unpleasant aspects of physiology. But, just beneath the surface of his rage, one senses a secret desire, a mixture of terror and anticipation, which surfaced in his uncontrollable nightmares.[179] In a curious way, the same qualities which make Guibert unlikable as a human being compel the historian to take his insights seriously. Indeed, his inward turning away from a potentially hostile yet sensually fascinating world is perhaps more typical of the period's real problems than the arid triumphs of pure thinkers.

We witness his mother's conversion through his eyes; we never see her face to face. We do not even learn her first name. The story begins in book one, chapter nine, in a series of deliberate foreshadowings; it concludes with the visions and apparitions which precede her death in chapter twenty-four.

Of course, Guibert is not merely attempting to explain his mother's case. He is placing a number of contemporary conversions under a single panoply. These experiences have to his mind essentially three features in common. First, conversion is not chiefly an intellectual change; it is behavioural. Consequently, what happens in the outside world has a direct bearing on the convert's inner comprehension of things. Conversion is not on that account socially determined; but, in Guibert's view, the external world—its forms, rituals, and realities—is a foe with which the inner self continuously engages in battle,

---

[175] Cf. Benton, *Self and Society*, 23.

[176] On his tutor, *De Vita Sua* 1.4, p. 13: " 'Vade,' inquit, 'ad eum, quia iste te plurimum amaturus est.' " On his mother, 1.16, p. 59: "Cui (matri) cum sic more gererem, ut ei nullatenus negarem. . . ."

[177] *Ibid.*, 3.17, pp. 212-15.   [178] *Ibid.*, 2.5, pp. 118-24; 3.16, 208-11.   [179] E.g., 1.15, p. 56.

just as, centuries before, the desert fathers struggled against hoards of demons. Thirdly, conversion is not only directed towards the other-world; it emerges from active engagement with the world, and, at least in part, remains innerworldly in orientation. These features of the experience are united in the converts' minds by the invoking of models from the distant past, that is, by looking upon unprecedented activity as something structured long ago.

Conversion then, in the cases of Simon of Valois, St. Bruno, or Evrard of Breteuil, illustrates the sense of cultural discontinuity which we see emerging elsewhere. "What was achieved," Guibert noted, "was the same as in ancient martyrdoms."[180] The "modern" age and its corrupting influences were superseded.[181]

For Guibert's mother, at least in his view, the essential problem was how to maintain a proper, that is, inherited, form of behaviour in a changing world. Her inability to adjust began very early. She was born, or so he thought, into a world of unquestioned loyalties, which he identified with moral absolutes. Her troubles began when she was given as a girl to his father. One by one her former standards of conduct and guides for decision-making were invalidated. As the real norms vanished, psychological sanctions and boundaries took their place: they appeared as successive sets of tests which she had to pass in order to proceed from one level of self-assurance to the next. Her chastity was enforced by witchcraft;[182] the sexual barrier was put in place again after her husband's capture and death.[183] In both instances, personal relations provided a point of departure for the eventual appearance of extrapersonal values.

Guibert himself played a role in the implanting of the psychological fenceposts. In many respects the child was father to the parent. As he saw it, his spiritual enlightenment preceded hers.[184] His wayward adolescence and introspection served to remind her of her penitential obligation.[185] His fears were also reflected in her character. Throughout the story, her own anxieties took the form of direct physical peril, as, for example, when the devil finally appeared before her and almost crushed her to death.[186] Fear of rape, also diabolically inspired, was another recurrent source of concern. In fact, just before her final conversion, the rumour was spread about that her loins were bewitched.[187] Was the juxtaposition not significant? The world of sexual liberty seems to have become a sort of underground governed by de-

[180] Ibid., 1.11, p. 35.   [181] Ibid., 1.12, p. 38.   [182] Ibid., 1.12, p. 37.
[183] Ibid., 1.13, pp. 45-46.   [184] Ibid., 1.19, p. 74.   [185] Ibid., 1.15, pp. 51-52.
[186] Ibid., 1.13, pp. 43-44.   [187] Ibid., 1.14, p. 47.

monic powers. Guibert's mother could not find the stability she desired in the old family relations, which, in her mind, were linked to the devil's realm. She did not regain tranquillity until she found a suitably strong institutional structure to replace it. The walls had to be high enough to keep the evil spirits out:[188] one wonders if they really were.

How are we to assess the accuracy of Guibert's portrait of his mother's spiritual development? Like Orderic, Guibert uses the alleged decadence of the present as a foil in order to establish the superiority of earlier patterns of conduct. "In those days," he tells us, "a marriage was hardly ever slandered by hearsay."[189] Motherly guidance, in his view, had gone astray. The women of his time were devoted only to gossip, flirtation, and amorous pranks. They swaggered like tarts; their oversized sleeves, sexy slips, and pointed Cordovan shoes were "the antithesis of the old modesty." Their only misery was a lack of "mad lovers" to chase them; their only nobility derived from the odious court in which they placed them. In former times, Guibert concludes, men would have blushed to keep the company of these so-called virgins, who, "by their sly business operations, turned true lovers into windbags in the public market."[190]

The flaw, of course, in Guibert's thinking is his association of virtue in the past with sexual puritanism, a familiar theme of many ascetic utopias. How far back did his information go? Only far enough, the evidence suggests, to rationalize the gradual slide down the social scale of his mother's family. In his opinion, the decline had set in just one generation before. The "present age," he thought, made the older, inviolable marriages difficult, if not impossible. The new attitudes among females signified personal pleasure over the common good, the individual over the general.

In reality, his mother had not gone from a position of security in her family to one of insecurity in his. Guibert had merely projected his anxieties into the past, where they could be more easily typified and dealt with. Morality in these terms was synonymous with immobility. Similarly, he read his own need for certainty into his mother's conversion. In his mind, as, very possibly, in hers, proper behaviour was a "text" set down in the past: it could not now be altered.

Not the least of Guibert's positive achievements is the stylistic interplay of his mother's point of view and his own. Her spiritual development is not only seen through his eyes; it is a tangible reality

[188] *Ibid.*, 1.18, pp. 73-74.   [189] *Ibid.*, 1.12, p. 38.   [190] *Ibid.*, 39.

which he lives and feels as he writes about it. His shifting, staccato periods, overrich in poetic turns of phrase, mirror the tensions of his own mind. As noted, he tells the story of his mother's conversion by the piling up of different events which seem to him to have the same emotional weight. Chapters twelve, thirteen, and fourteen, to which we have alluded, have the effect on the reader of figures in a cubist painting, in which the artist's intention is to present two perspectives at once.

The interlacing of the two personalities reaches its highest point in chapter fourteen, in which he fully reveals his ambivalence towards his mother's leaving the world. For, in order to obey her religious calling, she was obliged to abandon her son at the age of twelve. Although, at a cognitive level, Guibert understood the reasons for his mother's decision, he was unable to overcome his dependence on her.

The separation was therefore a critical moment in his life, and he narrates it in two stages. First, his mother went to the manor of Catenoy,[191] situated about two miles from town. While staying there, she apparently made up her mind to withdraw permanently to the monastery of Fly. At the intervention of Guibert's tutor, a modest dwelling was found and at length she set out for her new home. In Guibert's description, she passes from one stage of life to the next, while, as the tension builds, he informs her mind with his own emotions: "She knew," he says, "that I would become an orphan. There was no one on whom I could depend. For, despite many relatives, no one else could provide for a young lad in this tender stage of life. . . . Yet, through fear and love of you, dear God, she hardened her heart. En route to Fly she passed beneath the town where I was staying. Her heart was torn by such pangs that she could not bear to look back. Bitter remorse consumed her when she turned over in her mind what she had left behind."[192]

In these few sentences, Guibert inserts into his mother's moment of decision a number of themes which one finds expressed elsewhere in the *Memoirs* and in the other lives we have discussed. Conversion involves internal reflection (*delibero*). An impermanent journey (*demigro*) is a prelude to a permanent change in life-style, implying the abandonment of ties of kinship and their replacement with spiritual values. But it is also a consciousness filled with reminiscences of things

[191] *Ibid.*, 1.14, p. 48.
[192] *Ibid.*, 49.

past. In Guibert's case, it is a youth that has all the regret, sadness, and frailty of old age.

Interpreting Social Conflict

Guibert did not completely understand his mother's motives for conversion, but he nonetheless provided an interpretive model into which the stages of her spiritual development could conveniently be fitted. However, not all interpretations of real or imaginary "events" in the period reveal so thorough a grasp of the situation. Just the opposite is often the case: older traditions are superseded by radical forces, but, apart from God's ineffable ways, no obvious explanation can be found.

Either reality and hermeneutics remain rather far apart; or, what is perhaps worse, the interpretive process gives the impression of coherence and continuity where there is none. Also, as the inability to analyse increases, the modes of explanation themselves inevitably become more and more archaic. And, as attempts to interpret and to explain events grow, so does the complexity of interplay between society and ideas. Incomprehensibility, in this sense, reaches beyond the lack of understanding among individuals and attains the status of a literary topos.

Nowhere in the period's writings is the inability to account for historical changes better demonstrated than in Guibert's account of the murder of Gerard of Quierzy and the subsequent social disorder in Laon in 1112, which comprise chapters one to six of his *Memoir*'s third book.[193]

Guibert's initial explanation of the causes of the civil strife once again takes us into the symbolic realm of youth and old age. In his view, the entire problem went back to the time of Adalbero, bishop from 977 to 1030, who betrayed the interests of Charles of Lorraine in favour of Hugh Capet. He thereby increased the bishopric's wealth but reduced its spiritual credibility. For, while he won the local nobility's patronage, he effectively betrayed his king while he was still a boy. Sooner or later, Guibert reasoned, God would punish such infidelity.[194]

[193] Cf. J. Chaurand, "La conception de l'histoire de Guibert de Nogent (1053-1124)," 390-91, and, on the link in Guibert's imagination between the sexual excesses of his mother's day and the conjugal problems in Laon, see G. Duby, *Le chevalier, la femme et le prêtre* (Paris, 1981), 151-72.

[194] *De Vita Sua* 3.1, p. 130.

Adalbero was followed by Hélinand, a man of poor family and little education. Then came Enguerrand of Coucy, who became bishop in 1098 or 1099 and died in 1104, during whose administration, Guibert noted, the bishopric's moral force was further weakened. Hélinand had persuaded Philip to give back certain revenues that had been taken by force, but Enguerrand eventually returned everything to the king. Not only was the see materially impoverished; the door was also opened to simony, for no bishop could thenceforth demand the surrender of revenues by those who guaranteed his election. To make matters worse, Enguerrand was a worldly man, bereft, in Guibert's opinion, of true piety, who spent a good deal of his time spreading idle gossip. The gradual accumulation of abuses provided what the narrator called "opportunities for the destruction of the town and its churches, opportunities for which, as it turned out, there were not happy endings."[195]

About this time there appeared on the scene Enguerrand of Boves, the bishop's first cousin, who was generous to the churches but also an inveterate philanderer. An elderly man, unfortunate in marriage, he finally set his sights on Sybille, the wife of Godefrey, the youthful, handsome count of Namur. Guibert argues that Godefrey might have incurred his wife's enmity through the tardiness with which he paid off an inherited marriage debt. Enguerrand seduced her, and proceeded to disavow his own spouse by accusing her falsely of adultery. Then, to everyone's consternation, he married Sybille.

Despite a public scandal, the combination of Enguerrand's influence and Sybille's flattery lulled the bishop into inaction. Deprived through treachery of his wife, Godefrey took his revenge on the county of Porcien to the west of Laon, which belonged to Enguerrand. Many men were killed or mutilated: "and thus Venus," Guibert reflected, "not having conceived Vulcan, proceeded to Mars."[196] Throughout these events the bishop did nothing; and, on his deathbed, he received his cousin over the protests of local monks, and absolved him, or so it appeared, of any guilt.

The episcopal see was vacant for the following two years, that is, from 1104 to 1106. Then, as was the custom, the local nobility and higher clergy met to elect a new bishop. Enguerrand of Boves, together with the churchmen, favoured a candidate on the king's side, Gaudry, chancellor to Henry I. But, as Anselm of Laon raised legitimate objections, the matter was brought before Paschal II, who was

<hr/>

[195] *Ibid.*, 3.3, p. 133.   [196] *Ibid.*, 3.3, p. 136.

then travelling through France. The case was heard at Langres on 24th February 1107. After a number of speeches, including Guibert's on Gaudry's behalf, the election was confirmed. The consecration took place shortly afterwards in St. Ruf of Avignon, as Guibert puts it, to the subsequent "destruction of the town, indeed, of the entire region."[197]

Gaudry's bishopric passed three years peacefully enough, but the seeds of so many evil actions were bound sooner or later to bear fruit. The dissolution of order was eventually occasioned by the malicious gossip of one of the town's procurers, Gerard of Quierzy. A man of great physical strength and a hero of the First Crusade, he became, through Enguerrand's preferment, the protector of a girl's monastery in Laon. His Achilles heel, Guibert observes, was speaking ill of others, although never, he adds, without cause. His first object of disparagement was Sybille. Before her marriage to Enguerrand, she had been his lover. On marrying, he had stopped seeing her, but she, he maintained, still desired him. Gerard's insults were echoed by his wife, who began to exchange abuse with Sybille.

Having thus attacked Enguerrand, Gerard next turned on Gaudry, who, Guibert remarks, bore his jibes "silently but not patiently."[198] A calculating man, Gaudry waited for his moment. An official visit to Rome provided him with the opportunity of arranging Gerard's murder at a convenient distance. The deed was to be carried out by a group of local laymen and their wives, supported on the inside by two archdeacons. The actual scene is one of the most vivid in the *Memoirs*. Gerard, Guibert tells us, came to the cathedral to pray clad in "Tyrian purple." Fearing his strength, the conspirators came at him from behind. His cape was held around him so that he could not move: then he was cut down. The poor people who happened to be in the church cried out, but they were too frightened to come to Gerard's aid. When Ivo, the royal delegate, heard the news, he rounded up and killed many of those who had taken part. The fuse was lit; the town exploded.

The remaining chapters of book three confirm the picture of inevitable civil strife as a hangover from the past. But, even if we follow Guibert's account carefully, we are never sure what precisely caused the communal riots in Laon in 1112. Not only is he unable to perceive economic and social rivalries as such. Even within his own explanation—ecclesiastical abuse of long standing—there is much unclear

[197] *Ibid.*, 3.4, p. 137.   [198] *Ibid.*, 3.5, p. 146.

thinking. One must distinguish between his position and his interpretation. He defended Gaudry, as noted, before Paschal II,[199] and,
like most contemporary churchmen, took an unremitting stand against
the commune.[200] Yet, as the story proceeds, the intermingling of
images and motives leaves one with the impression that he is unconvinced by his own analysis. He never really steps back from the grip-
ping narrative. Instead, he engages in periodic, half-hearted attempts
to persuade the reader and himself of a few large truths.

However, as early as his initial prognosis of doom, a more personal
interpretation makes its appearance, one which, not surprisingly, involves his own life history as well as the *Memoirs*' wider concerns. The
seeds which bring forth disorder are the betrayals and indiscretions of
youth. As in his own life, the wrongs are those of adults against
children. Adalbero, as noted, from whose bishopric, in Guibert's view,
the original sins descended, betrayed the boy Charles of Lorraine.
Godefrey of Namur, a *iuuenis*, was deprived of his legitimate wife by
an older man, Enguerrand of Boves. Moreover, the failures of youth
bring down all the central characters. Godefrey is said to have neglected his wife's debts and his wife to have taken early lovers, including Gerard. He, although free of youth's wantonness, is propelled
back into the affair through his own immaturity, which results in
taunts to his former mistress. As in his own childhood, Guibert also
links the betrayal of adults to sexual repression. Just as he fought all
his life to control his unruly passions, so Enguerrand and Gerard,
each in his way, carries with him the flaw of overindulgence. With
biblical precedents in mind, Guibert attempts to trace all the wrong-
doings to a single point in time. But, in doing so, he confuses rather
than clarifies an already obscure picture. What results is a series of
images which contrast the past and the present, the familial and the
extrafamilial. The only indisputable conclusion the reader can reach
is that, in Guibert's mind, older models of explanation are breaking
down. Lust, irreverent youth, and divided loyalties are replacing moral
absolutes. He does not know quite what has gone wrong: but something definitely has.

Symbols Unearthed

The theme of old age and youth not only made a frequent appearance in real lives and in their literary representations. It also found
its way into symbolic statements of cultural discontinuity.

[199] *Ibid.*, 3.4, pp. 139-40.   [200] *Ibid.*, 3.7, p. 156.

Those who could neither read nor write, or who were only slightly acquainted with the written word, needed concrete vestiges of the past. Somewhat paradoxically, in this period of increasing complexity in modes of interpretation, ever greater interest was also shown in physical symbols interrelating the past and the present, that is, in relics, cults of local saints, the veneration of the cross, and so forth. Rodulf Glaber is an eloquent witness to the reawakened archaeological instincts. As noted earlier, he maintained that, within a few years of the millennium, there was widespread evidence of religious revival. Reform was in the air;[201] and, in 1008, a number of relics that had been lost for centuries were suddenly rediscovered.[202]

Moving outside the confines of Norman society, let us look briefly at two examples of the rehabilitation of physical objects, occurring respectively in the early and later years of the eleventh century.

One of the copies of Ademar of Chabannes' *Chronicon* records that, shortly before his death in 1002, Otto III was told in a dream that he must exhume the body of Charlemagne at Aachen.[203] But no one was any longer sure where the emperor lay. His burial place was discovered after a three-day fast. He was found seated on a golden chair in a vaulted crypt beneath the basilica of St. Mary. He held his sword and his sceptre and wore a gem-studded crown; and, despite the passage of time, his body was perfectly preserved.

His remains, Ademar records, were taken out of their resting place and put on public display. Among those who admired the marvel was a canon called Adalbert. He was a man of immense size, and, being perhaps bolder than the others, he tried on the imperial crown and measured his legs against those of Charlemagne. The crown did not fit; and, as if by miracle, one of his own legs suddenly broke, leaving him crippled for some forty years afterwards. Charlemagne's body, Ademar continues, was then placed on the right side of the church behind the altar of John the Baptist. Over it was built a magnificent crypt lined with gold. Before long, the shrine became well known for revealing divinely inspired signs. Nonetheless, Ademar adds, the emperor's anniversary was not celebrated there by a special liturgy.

Otto's dream is an interesting specimen of interplay between popular and learned culture which also touches upon the symbolism of old age and youth.

[201] *Historiae* 3.4.13, p. 62.
[202] *Ibid.*, 3.6.19, p. 68.
[203] *Chronicon* 3.31, ed. J. Chavanon, 153-54, from MS Paris, B.N., lat. 5296. For other versions in their historical setting, see R. Folz, *Le Souvenir et la Légende de Charlemagne*, 87-93.

Otto, who was himself near death, was sensitized in his dream to the fact that Charlemagne belonged to a distinctive cultural period in the past. He himself therefore represented modernity. The hiatus was symbolized by the need to dig up the body and to verify its physical existence. Yet, in distancing himself from his illustrious predecessor, Otto nonetheless interrelated the past and the present in a new way. For the revelation only took place after an interlude of purification and psychological transformation. The entire search, therefore, may be viewed as a rite, the first stages consisting of the dream and the fast, the second of the unearthing and the subsequent observances.

The story in fact is told on two levels at once. For higher culture, Charlemagne remains a symbol; for popular culture, at least as Ademar conceives it, he is simply a sign. Although aging and possibly forewarned of his own death, Otto found the emperor's body *incorruptum*. This, as noted, was a reaffirmation of the continuity between the two dynasties which superseded the temporal gap between them. But, even to those who knew nothing of the dream or could not interpret it, the discovery had deep significance. In their case, the relation between the past and the present was made clear through eternally sanctioned differences in social levels. On the one hand, popular participation was encouraged. Adalbert, a mere canon, tried on the imperial crown and compared leg sizes. By implication, any ordinary person looking on or hearing later of the event could imagine doing the same. On the other hand, higher culture was definitely reasserted. Adalbert's boldness was a minor sacrilege; *divina virtus*, Ademar notes, punished him with lameness. Further, once exhumed, Charlemagne was placed in a gilded crypt just behind John the Baptist, who, of course, announced Christ's coming just as the Carolingian preceded the Ottonian emperors. The popular element was retained: the crypt's richness made it a natural shrine, where, it was said, many illnesses were eventually cured. As a final unifying touch, one is told that Charlemagne's anniversary is celebrated *communi more*. Although divine, the emperor is thus made personable, approachable, and understandable.

Rarely, however, were imperial remains the symbols that united the past and the present. As Glaber suggests, more often they were physical objects which had acquired important associations in the past. Reappearing in the present, they offered men still strongly influenced by ritual some tangible guides through the vicissitudes of a changing universe of interpretation.

One of the most renowned objects of this kind in the Middle Ages was the holy lance, which, although not normally examined in this context, reasserts a number of basic patterns involving old age and youth.

The lance was said to have been discovered by a poor peasant, Peter Barthelemy, in Antioch, on 14th June 1098. The mystical details of the story are most successfully related by Raymond d'Aguilers in a series of visions which preceded the final fall of the city to the combined forces of Bohemund and Raymond of St. Gilles some two weeks later. Raymond's account is not echoed by contemporary historians of the First Crusade,[204] and may in fact reflect a purely personal interpretation of events.[205] But the internal structure of the narrative is significant in its own right.

As Raymond tells it, the story runs as follows.[206] On 10th June, Peter Barthelemy told Raymond, the count of Toulouse, and Ademar, the bishop of Le Puy, that St. Andrew had appeared before him some four times, stating on each occasion that, as soon as Antioch fell, the holy lance, which had been lost since the time of Christ, would be recovered. The first vision had occurred on the preceding 30th of December during an earthquake and coincided with the beginning of the siege. Alone and afraid, Peter lay trembling in his hut when two men suddenly appeared before him. One was elderly; he was moderate in stature and had white hair, a flowing white beard, and piercing black eyes. The other was a younger, taller, and better-looking man, who remained silent. The elder of the pair revealed himself to be St. Andrew. He told Peter to summon the count, the bishop, and Ray-

---

[204] The episode receives only brief notices in other historians. See Peter Tudebode, c. 10, *Recueil des historiens des croisades*, vol. 3, 70-71; Fulcher of Chartres, c. 18, *ibid.*, 344-45; Albert of Aix 4.43, vol. 4, 419-20; Baudri of Bourgueil 3.9, *ibid.*, 67-68; and Robert the Monk 7.3, vol. 3, 823. P. Alphandéry, *La Chrétienté et l'idée de croisade*, vol. 1, p. 102, draws attention to the popular elements in the anonymous *Gesta Dei per Francos*; but here too the account is very brief (*Tudebodus Abbreviatus*, c. 3, *Recueil* . . . , vol. 3, 147). For a critical account of the sources, see S. Runciman, "The Holy Lance Found at Antioch," *Analecta Bollandiana* 68 (1950), 197-209; cf. H. Fichtenau, "Zum Reliquienwesen im früheren Mittelalter," MIöG 60 (1952), /1, 78-79; and, on the relations of the episode to other visions of the First Crusade, see H. Hagenmeyer, *Le vrai et le faux sur Pierre l'hermite*, trans. F. Raynaud (Paris, 1883), 74-101.

[205] See P. Alphandéry, *La Chrétienté*, I, 101-02, and, for a different view, E. O. Blake, "The Formation of the 'Crusade Idea,' " *Journal of Ecclesiastical History* 21 (1970), 20. For an interpretation which places the episode in the wider context of the piety of the First Crusade, see the thoughtful remarks of B. McGinn, "*Iter Sancti Sepulchri*: The Piety of the First Crusaders," in B. K. Lackner and K. R. Philip, eds., *The Walter Prescott Webb Memorial Lectures* (Austin and London, 1978), 51-53.

[206] Summarizing Raymond d'Aguilers, *Historia Francorum qui Ceperunt Iherusalem*, cc. 10-11, *Recueil* . . . , vol. 3, 253-57.

mond d'Hautepoul, and to ask why the bishop had neither preached before Antioch nor carried the cross as a symbol for the common people. He then led Peter through the streets of Antioch to the church of St. Peter, where he displayed the holy lance. Peter offered to take the relic back to the Christian side, but Andrew told him that the city had first to be taken. The two spirits then led Peter back to his hut, where they left him.

In relating his tale to count Raymond and bishop Ademar, Peter claimed that he had not immediately come forward because of his poverty and low station. But Andrew reappeared before him at the beginning of Lent and told him that he had been chosen as God's messenger precisely because of his humble origins. Peter still hesitated: surely, he reasoned, in such harsh times, the count would accuse him of simply trying to secure a little extra nourishment for himself. Andrew, however, appeared again, on this occasion while Peter was in the company of his own lord, William Peter. William heard the saint explain that, when the count reached the Jordan, he was not to immerse himself in it but to take a boat to the other side, where, dressed in fresh attire, he was to sprinkle a little water over himself. Peter once again tried to avoid his duty by sailing to Cyprus in search of food. But, after a series of misadventures, he found himself back at the port of St. Simeon. Meanwhile, on 11th June, a priest named Stephen had a vision while praying for his lost brethren. An angry Christ appeared before him, and, despite the good offices of Mary, chastised the crusaders for their failure of will on the threshold of victory. The following day the assembled knights pledged to take Antioch. Signs appeared in the sky; and, on the 14th, Peter, accompanied by twelve crusaders, invaded the church of St. Peter. Barthelemy dug up the lance, and St. Andrew reappeared to confirm the discovery's significance. Thus emboldened, Raymond d'Aguilers concludes, the Christians eventually took the city.

The historical context of the story is different from the others in this chapter, and a full reconstruction would have to include an account of popular piety in other episodes of the First Crusade. Our concern is limited to the narrative's internal features, and, more particularly, to the function of symbol and ritual within the text.

So restricted, the central events clearly relate thematically to issues already dealt with. The story of Peter Barthelemy is essentially one of prediction and fulfilment. It links old age and youth, not only through the physical symbol of the lance but also through the figures of St. Andrew and Christ. The simplest typological connection is between the youthful Christ and Peter himself. But the contrast between old age and youth also reflects a concern with learned and popular culture. Old age, through Andrew, leads youth; similarly, through Peter, the high culture vision of Stephen, which is largely an explanation for suffering and a plea for penance, reinforces the simpler visions of the Provençal peasant, whose message is popular election and the confirmation of the crusade's inner spiritual life.

These features become evident if we look at the episode in greater detail.

The story covers chapter ten and the first part of eleven in Raymond d'Aguilers' *Historia Francorum qui Ceperunt Iherusalem*. Peter relates his experiences in the first person, the style, so to speak, deliberately mirroring his fear, hesitation, and insecurity. He is really confessing his failure to act, despite divine command. His tale thereby provides a popular counterweight to the crusaders' inability to take Antioch, and, through it, to the more general frustration of the crusade's higher mission.

The parallels of which we have been speaking—old age and youth, prediction and fulfilment, and the learned and the popular—are maintained throughout.

To review them in the order in which they appear: the first vision, as noted, coincided with the beginning of the siege; it thus marked a turning-point in the real crusade. Also, it came about during an earth tremor, a sign of God's wrath easily understood by the non-lettered. From the outset there were two age levels, *senior* and *junior*.[207] Only the elder St. Andrew actually spoke, signifying the old predicting the new. Christ, representing fulfilment, remained silent, if expectant. Physical symbolism plays a role as well within St. Andrew's complaint. Ademar, he alleges, both failed to preach and to bless the common people with the cross (*cum cruce . . . signare populum*).[208] Thus, Ademar's refusal to venerate one concrete object provides a reason for the eventual revelation of another.

Peter sees himself being led through the streets of Antioch wearing only a shirt. In this state of spiritual innocence—that is, while there is little covering for his body, and, by implication, for his soul—he is a suitable recipient of the lance. He sees the relic and holds it in his hands; and the contact is accompanied by St. Andrew's explanation: this is the lance, he relates, which pierced Christ's side and

[207] *Historia*, c. 10, p. 254.
[208] *Loc.cit.*

which, for that reason, is a token of future salvation. Andrew adds that Peter must return to the church of his patron apostle in the company of only twelve other men, another clear parallel with the gospels. Peter's subsequent vacillation only serves to add credibility to the story. Were it false, the narrator implies, he would surely have tried his ruse immediately. Andrew visited him a second time at the beginning of Lent. Again, the symbolism is transparent: while the "first cock" crowed, the saint asked him whether he was still "asleep." Peter's excuses confirm the story's inner message. He claimed he was too uneducated, but Andrew refused to choose another. His spirit, he said, was weak, his flesh even weaker. Yet, against Andrew's spiritual designs he could only set up physical impediments to action such as poverty, hunger, and the "illness" which underlined his soul's inactivity.

On Palm Sunday Andrew paid him another visit. Once again Peter asked that someone more suitably educated (*sapientior*) be selected. Andrew again refused, and offered a parallel for the Easter procession which ought to have been held that year in Jerusalem.

Before William Peter, a presumably reliable witness, he told Barthelemy that Raymond of St. Gilles was to re-baptize himself in the Jordan in a manner which inverted the normal symbolic relationships. He was in effect to cross the river by boat, to put on new clothes, and, once he reached the other side, to sprinkle water on the garments. Once again, the old was to be put aside, the new reborn. Raymond's clothes even attained the status of relics, since they were to be preserved along with the holy lance. It is also significant that William Peter heard St. Andrew, but did not see him. The direct experience of divinity was thereby reserved for the common man, who, the narrator would seem to suggest, believes through physical representations, not through words, texts, and meanings alone. Stephen's vision, which is interjected after Peter's abortive attempt to escape to Cyprus, provides a necessary confirmation of divine intentions, since, within the story, while Raymond of Toulouse believed Peter, Ademar of Le Puy did not. And Stephen's vision itself returns the story to a higher cultural level. Christ asks the priest to define what a Christian is, and Stephen replies by quoting the creed. Christ then exhorts the flagging troops with quotations from the Psalms.

On the following day, the knights swear a new oath not to flee before the Turks. The common people, through whose eyes the reader witnesses the final scene, are reassured. The church of St. Peter is stormed and the twelve chosen search for the lance from morning to nightfall, without success. They need the help of Peter, the *iuuenis*. When the lance is finally recovered, Andrew reappears: God, he says, gave to count Raymond what had been given to no other man, a sacred standard as a demonstration of his love.

Ancients and Moderns

From the complex use of the topos of old age and youth in Raymond d'Aguilers it is a short step to cultural assessments of the period itself, to which, in conclusion, we briefly direct our attention.

Once the pastness of the past was widely recognized, archaic modes of thought were no longer able to envelop the present and to dissolve it as an independent realm of experience. The present became a vantage point from which the past could be discussed and debated. The inevitable contrast between the old and the new resulted in the first tentative stages of the *"querelle des Anciens et Modernes."*[209]

The differing positions were most clearly reflected in higher culture. The best-known summation is that of Bernard of Chartres as reported by John of Salisbury. Bernard, as frequently noted, said that students of classical tradition in his own time were like dwarfs standing on the shoulders of the giants. They were able to see farther than the ancients not because of better vision but owing to the height to which they had been inadvertently raised.[210]

His famous comparison dates from the 1120s,[211] but behind it lay a century's quiet growth in historical consciousness. The key term was *modernus*, which, in general usage, referred to "the present period" or "the present generation," and, hence, as time went on, to modernity itself. The sense was first established by Cassiodorus,[212] who was followed by a wide variety of medieval authors for whom the *moderni* had little in common besides distinctiveness from the patristic era.[213] Thus,

---

[209] See E. R. Curtius, *European Literature and the Latin Middle Ages*, 251-55 and E. Gössmann, *Antiqui und Moderni im Mittelalter* (Paderborn, 1974), 9-19.

[210] *Metalogicon* 3.4, ed. C.C.J. Webb (Oxford, 1929), 136, 23-27.

[211] E. Jeauneau, " 'Nani gigantum humeris insidentes.' Essai d'interprétation de Bernard de Chartres," *Vivarium* 5 (1967), 56-60. Cf. H. Silvestre, " 'Quanto iuniores, tanto perspicaciores'. Antécédents à la Querelle des Anciens et des Modernes," in *Recueil commémoratif . . . de l'Université Lovanium de Kinshasa* (Louvain and Paris, 1968), 236-37, 251-55. An important, unnoticed use of Priscian's comparison is found in John of Fécamp, *Confessio Fidei* 3.40, PL 101.1084A.

[212] E.g., *Variae* 3.5.3, MGH Auctores Antiquissimi 12, 81; 4.51.12, *ibid.*, 139.

[213] W. Hartmann, " 'Modernus' und 'Antiquus': Zur Verbreitung und Bedeutung dieser Bezeichnungen in der wissenschaftlichen Literatur vom 9. bis zum 12. Jahrhundert," in A. Zimmermann, ed., *Antiqui et Moderni: Traditionsbewusstsein und Fortschrittsbewusstsein im späten Mittelalter* (Berlin, 1974), 23.

Paschasius Radbertus, whose eucharistic theories reinterpreted the traditional teaching, spoke of the ninth century as "a modern period, after the first fathers' authority."[214] The same notion was carried over with little change to the eleventh century, when the disciplines attributed to *moderni* were expanded to include dialectics and musical theory.[215] Perspective on the past gradually matured: by the twelfth century, *antiqui* and *moderni* came to represent cultural positions in law, history, theology, natural philosophy, and the plastic arts.[216] The "renaissance" was in part an awareness of progress through difference.

Wherever ancient models were recognized as such, their relevance to contemporary interpretation therefore became a subject of inquiry. In general, *modernus* retained negative connotations; innovation was often equated with unwelcome novelty.[217] However, some writers had a more nuanced view. Adalbold of Utrecht, for instance, took up the question briefly in the preface to his life of Henry II, which was begun around 1004. Everywhere, he remarked, we are taught to venerate *antiquitas* and to disparage *novitas*. But all that we call ancient was once new. "*Novitas* merely preceded in order that what we call *antiquitas* might follow." Spurning innovation, therefore, was largely a matter of prejudice: "For rarely is a river sought by a thirsty man when he possesses its source." The ancients and the moderns, he concluded, have a roughly similar value.[218]

His views were echoed by later authors. Writing in the spring of 1046, Wipo reminded his readers in the preface to his *Gesta Chuonradi Imperatoris* that the Old Testament "prefigured and taught that the fruit of recent events ought to be gathered up and stored away in the memory"[219] with the aid of scribal methods perfected by the *moderni*.[220] An even more forthright statement was made by Guitmund of Aversa, who, in arguing against Berengar, said that he had superseded the arguments of both the ancients and of authors of his own time.[221]

---

[214] *Expositio in Evangelium Mattaei, prologue*, PL 120.32D-33A. On the context, see G. Mathon, "Pascase Radbert et l'évolution de l'humanisme carolingien," *Corbie, abbaye royale*, 140-42.

[215] W. Hartmann, " 'Modernus' und 'Antiquus,' " 28.

[216] See in general, J. Spörl, "Das Alte und das Neue im Mittelalter I-II," *Historisches Jahrbuch* 50 (1930), 297-341, 498-524, and M.-D. Chenu, "Conscience de l'histoire et théologie," in *La théologie au douzième siècle*, 62-97. On philosophy, see Chenu, "Antiqui, Moderni," RSPT 17 (1928), 82-94; and more generally, Gössmann, *Antiqui und Moderni*, chs. 2-5.

[217] E.g., Andrew of Strumi, *Vita S. Arialdi*, c. 1, MGH SS 30.2, p. 1050.

[218] *Vita Heinrici II*, MGH SS 4, p. 683, 35-42.

[219] *Gesta Chuonradi Imperatoris, prol.*, ed. H. Bresslau, 3rd ed. (Hanover, 1919), 5.

[220] *Ibid.*, 5-6.

[221] *De Corporis et Sanguinis Veritate in Eucharistia, lib.* 3, PL 149.1480A.

William of Malmesbury, who died in 1143, wondered why so little attention had been paid to his period's intellectual achievements. Everywhere, he complained, inveterate usage is accepted without question. New facts, even when verified, are placed in a doubtful light. Everyone repaired to the wisdom of the ancients. Nothing of recent origin was given sufficient credit.[222]

Such contrasts blended easily with the biological metaphor of old age and youth. Anselm of Havelberg saw youth as the most appropriate symbol of successive church renewals.[223] At the climax of the *De Planctu Naturae*, Alan of Lille brilliantly caught the flavour of Bernard of Chartres's image in portraying Hymen, the god of marriage. His appearance fluctuated between adolescence and senility: his stature correspondingly rose from the insignificant to rival "the giants."[224]

There were of course more systematic reflections upon change involving growth, education, and the uses of literacy. In the third book of *De Concordia*,[225] for example, Anselm used the analogy of the agrarian cycle to depict the relationship between free will, language, and Scripture. Divine words, he said, ought to be understood in such a way that neither grace nor free will alone insures man's salvation. Yet, he added, in biblical passages dealing with free choice, the following comparison holds. The earth produces many plants without man's help; but those which nourish man require a seed, a farmer, and hard work. Similarly, without doctrine, the human spirit produces many thoughts and volitions not useful for salvation. Human beings, too, need "their own kind of seed and laborious cultivation." This, he states, is the *agricultura Dei*: the word of God—or rather, the meaning which lies behind it—is the seed of "every understanding of righteousness," whether originating in the mind, in words, in texts, or in reasoning based upon them. What is more, he argued, as the Word reaches us largely through preaching, "what the mind conceives from hearing the Word may be considered the preacher's seed." Righteousness of will is by implication the increase given by God. Therefore, in the beginning, just as God miraculously created plants without cultivation, so he made the gospels without human learning, placing

[222] *Gesta Regum Anglorum* 3.292, ed. W. Stubbs (London, 1889), vol. 2, p. 345.
[223] *Dialogi* 1.6, PL 188.1149A.
[224] *De Planctu Naturae, prosa* 8, ed. N. Häring, p. 865, 1-9.
[225] *De Concordia Praescientiae et Praedestinationis et Gratiae Dei cum Libero Arbitrio* 3.5, ed. F. S. Schmitt, *Opera Omnia*, vol. 2 (Rome, 1940), 269, 2-8.

the seeds of future salvation in the hearts of the prophets and of the apostles.

In a letter written a generation later, Peter the Venerable used a similar metaphor to exhort an otherwise unknown hermit named Gilbert to combine solitude and manual labour with divine reading: "Let your hand be turned from the plough to the pen, let pages be tilled with divine letters rather than fields, and let the plot be sown in the text of God's word." Thereby, Peter continued, Gilbert would become the "silent preacher of God's word"; and, although remaining mute, his message would reach "many peoples."[226]

These statements from within the monastery contrasted with the broader perspectives of those living in the world.

Otto of Freising, for instance, united the notion of the life-cycle with the idea of cumulative understanding. Children, he observed, are always told that, the younger they are, the more they are able to apprehend. So it is in history. On the one hand, we are taught by the writings and institutions of our ancestors, together with experience and the passage of time. Therefore, the later we live within the span of history, the more rapidly we are able to learn. And, after mastering the knowledge that has come before, we are able to invent new ideas with the same innovativeness as our ancestors.[227]

The role of rationality, and, by implication, of textual studies in the transition from a youthful to a mature state of mind was perhaps best summed up by Abelard in the opening paragraphs of the *Dialogue of a Philosopher with a Jew and a Christian*. The dialogue is begun by the rationalist Philosopher, who claims to be content with an ethical position established only by "natural law," that is, in his terms, by the first law of reason, composed only of *scientia morum*, in which there are no superadded texts (*superaddita scripta*) or superfluous external signs (*exteriora signa*).[228] He begins his defence of pure reason in religion by attempting to relativize the social origins of belief. He asks the Jew and the Christian: were you, who rely chiefly on scriptures, actually led to your respective beliefs by reason or merely by men's opinion and by loving respect for your own peoples?[229] The latter, he

[226] *Ep.* 20, *Ad Gislebertum*, ed. G. Constable, *The Letters of Peter the Venerable*, vol. 1, p. 38 (= PL 189.97C-98A).

[227] *Ottonis Episcopi Frisingensis Chronica* . . . , ed. A. Hofmeister (Hanover and Leipzig, 1912), 226, 14-25.

[228] *Dialogus inter Philosophum, Iudaeum et Christianum*, ed. R. Thomas (Stuttgart-Bad Cannstatt, 1970), p. 44, ll. 80-89.

[229] *Ibid.*, ll. 92-95.

argues, is the common heritage of all traditional belief, which, as Sallust notes, effectively turns custom into nature: for, whatever one has learned as a child, one obstinately adheres to as an adult, and, before one truly understands what is said, one claims to believe it.[230] It is astonishing, he adds, that, although human understanding grows cumulatively through the ages, in matters of faith, where the danger of error is greatest, there appears to be little real progress. "For youths as well as grownups, *rustici* as well as *literati*, are said to feel the same way; and he who is said to be the most firm in faith is the one who does not go beyond the common thoughts of the people."[231]

These statements on the nature of modernity do not add up to a distinctive view of the world, but they take us far from the monolithic eschatology of Rodulf Glaber, with which our reflections began. For each in its way acknowledges the possibility of cultural progress, even if incorporating it into a recognizable metaphorical framework. The stress on continuity with the past is of course in part a plea for reassurance. By admitting the reality of change, a Bernard of Chartres or an Otto of Freising also suggests that the world can never be quite the same again. The situation of Abelard's Philosopher is particularly telling. The text on natural law which he invents through reason is answered by the already established texts of the Jew and the Christian. The debate between the three is mainly over the foundations of ethics, but the questions often spill over into areas treated elsewhere in this volume, such as custom versus law, external versus internal forms of worship, and of course ageless tradition versus youthful innovation. As the *Dialogue* ends before a final judgment is rendered, we are not sure just where Abelard stood on many of these problems, which were central to a period that was even less sure of inherited certainties than himself.

[230] *Ibid.*, p. 45, ll. 107-13.

[231] *Ibid.*, p. 45, ll. 117-23: "Quod enim mirabile est, cum per etatum seriem et temporum successionem humana in cunctis rebus ceteris intelligentia crescat, in fide, cuius erroris summum periculum imminet, nullus est profectus. Sed eque minores ut maiores, eque rustici ut literati de hac sentire asserentur, et ille firmissimus in fide dicitur, qui communem populi non excedit sensum."

CONCLUSION

This book has dealt with the realignment of oral discourse within a cultural reference system based on the logical priorities of texts in a number of different aspects of medieval life and thought. By way of conclusion, it may be useful to reiterate the central features of the argument, and, in particular, to indicate how the major themes of Chapters Two to Five impinge upon each other.

As noted, there are four general topics, of which the first and most basic is literacy and social organization. The issues may be framed as follows. Where there are texts, there are also presumably groups to study them. The process of learning and reflection inevitably influences the members: how individuals behave towards each other and how the group, if it is not transitory, behaves towards the outside world, will bear some relation to attitudes formed during the educational experience.

From reading, dialogue, and the absorption of texts, therefore, it is a short step to "textual communities," that is, to groups of people whose social activities are centred around texts, or, more precisely, around a literate interpreter of them. The text in question need not be written down nor the majority of auditors actually literate. The *interpres* may relate it verbally, as did the medieval preacher. It may be lengthy, as were, for instance, genealogies or monastic rules; but normally it is short enough that its essentials can be easily understood and remembered—a few proverbial maxims, let us say, of St. Paul, rather than an entire epistle. Moreover, the group's members must associate voluntarily; their interaction must take place around an agreed meaning for the text. Above all, they must make the hermeneutic leap from what the text says to what they think it means; the common understanding provides the foundation for changing thought and behaviour.

The examples taken of this activity are a series of relatively isolated outbursts of heresy between roughly A.D. 1000 and 1050, and three accounts of the Patarene reform movement in Milan between 1057 and 1075. Yet the principles involved take us to the heart of broader issues linking literacy, heresy, reform, and group organization. The central motor of change was the literate interpreter of a text working within a less lettered community. Within smaller groups contact was informal and personal; in larger ones, or when the audience was dispersed, a more formal means of communication was adopted, normally preaching, through which a heretical or reformist text was transmitted and commented upon orally. However, in both cases, the group adopted as a norm for behaviour within a given context a type of rationality inseparable from the text. The sense of logical interconnection thereby established could then be applied critically to other issues, as was the case of the Orléans heretics, who, under questioning by bishop Guarin of Beauvais, confronted the church with the notion of autonomous natural law. As a consequence of this manner of thinking, heretics, and, to a lesser degree, reformers as well, tended to dismiss as "popular" all that could not be legitimized by textual means. The search for precedent with its scholastic overtones supplanted the experiential relationship between theory and practice, for which no better defence could often be found than that things had always been done that way. Laymen, as it turns out, played a larger role in such groups than has frequently been supposed. They were rarely among the literate or clerical organizers, but, as in the case of the Pataria, they comprised the mass of less-lettered followers, whose unsystematic thoughts were transformed into a platform for change by means of a verbally transmitted text. The principles embodied in such programmes, rather than the allegedly underlying social, economic, or even religious discontents, provided perhaps the most radical challenge to authority.

From the formation of communities to implement ideas and to draw up lines of debate, it was a short step to focusing on inherited attitudes towards ritual and symbol and to the evolution of a critique of the nature of observable reality.

An obvious consequence of the rise in general levels of literacy was the new appeal of a systematic, reflective theology, which gradually emerged as the most cohesive intellectual force of the eleventh century. The ideal of a higher religious culture was thereby extended beyond a small group of professionals, effectively expressing confidence in indigenous achievement but militating against the preservation of the local, the particular, and the unwritten. If the "great" did not actually predominate over "the little traditions" in Redfield's terms,[1] it offered what the unlettered often considered an acceptable

---

[1] "The Social Organization of Tradition," in *Peasant Society and Culture. An Anthropological Approach to Civilization* (Chicago, 1956), 70-74.

alternative, and contributed by its universalism another discouragement to "popular" culture. More specifically, the recognition of different levels of understanding between *litterati* and *illitterati* implied a turning away from ritual and symbol and towards an intellectualism inseparable from the study of texts: that is, a movement away from the performance of rites and from devotion to representational objects and towards the consideration of both primarily in terms of an inner lesson, meaning, or kernel of truth.

The natural field for this debate was the sacraments, which not only harboured the most respected repositories of rites and symbols but also provided the raw material for medieval Europe's first sustained inquiry into allegory. Was it entirely by accident that followers of Radbert and later Lanfranc insisted on an interpretation of the eucharist stressing the spoken, the concrete, and the performative, while Ratramn and Berengar emphasized the allegorical and the search for a sense beneath the formalistic surface? The resolution of the eucharistic controversy, which is the major theme of Chapter Three, not only brought about a permanent intellectualization of the sacraments. As a byproduct, it also created an interest in physical change. For whether, as the traditionalists urged, the body and blood of Christ were "really" on the altar, or whether, as their opponents argued, they were only configured by the objects present, an explanation had to be found for an important phenomenon of observable nature. The tentative inquiries into relations between nature and texts—how, for example, changes in reality paralleled those of logic—set the stage for a broader investigation of nature in scholastic science.

A full account of the development of naturalism lay outside the central interest of the study. Yet, it is important to recognize certain parallels between the isolation of learned and popular elements in the eucharistic debate and in the growing discussion of nature and change. The positions may conveniently be viewed from the vantage point of the early twelfth century, that is, the period in which a genuinely scientific appreciation of nature first emerged. As in the broader development of literacy, we may speak of two points of view from within medieval tradition. From the perspective of literate culture, the consequence was a "discovery of nature," a penetration of "the idea of nature" into Latin and vernacular literature, political philosophy, and theology, in short, the much studied "desacralization" of the natural universe.[2] However, from within oral culture the issues were seen

[2] M.-D. Chenu, "La nature et l'homme. La Renaissance du XIIe siècle," in *La théologie au douzième siècle*, 21-30.

differently. Oral tradition accepted without question nature's physicality, tangibility, and concreteness.[3] To use the analogy of law, the dominant conception was similar to early medieval *traditio*, which required the tactile, the seen, the heard, and the performed. In this sense, nature did not have to be discovered; it already existed. But it had to be explained, interpreted, and above all authenticated by texts. A naive, pre-existing notion of the phenomenal had to be adapted to the principles by which the human mind was thought to function. In sum, from within literate tradition the interpretive model was that of the renaissance or classical revival. For oral culture the problem was posed at a more basic level. How could the given physicality of things be reconciled with forms of thought which suggested a more real existence at their core? Worse, following the diluted Platonism of the early medieval schools, how could one maintain that what was before one's eyes had little or no reality at all?

The rise of organized groups for studying texts and the appearance of a more systematic theology of the sacraments were accompanied by Europe's first sustained inquiry into the relationship between language and reality. There were, of course, ancient precedents for the central lines of debate and a wide variety of methods developed in cathedral schools and in the nascent university of Paris. Yet, as contributors to the overall discussion of literacy's uses, three authors stand out in importance, Anselm of Canterbury, Peter Abelard, and Bernard of Clairvaux.

Their ideas and approaches overlapped in ways that are not fully revealed by the period's intense polemics or by the modern, overly rigid categories of "monastic" as opposed to "scholastic" thought. Anselm, the "father of scholasticism" in Grabmann's words, wrote chiefly for the benefit of other monks. Abelard, whose *Sic et Non* confirmed the use of the scholastic method, was more than occasionally monastic in spirit, as revealed by his biblical commentaries, his founding of the reformist Paraclete, and his fervently ascetic rule for religious women. And Bernard, while misunderstanding Abelard's intentions, nonetheless resorted from time to time to a scholastic type of allegorism, as did, in a more systematic way, his fellow Cistercian critic of the master from Le Pallet, William of St. Thierry.

Beneath the surface of the controversies, the councils, and the accusations of heresy lay a growing awareness of the subjective and objective dimensions of philosophical or theological issues which arose from the different uses of texts. Anselm occupies a middle position.

---

[3] C. Lévi-Strauss, *La pensée sauvage* (Paris, 1962), esp. ch. 1.

His meditations are both personal reflections on the Bible and examples of the mental process by which, proceeding from word to text, the individual in search of God achieves theological certainty. For Anselm, texts are largely memoranda. Like early medieval legal documents, they set down an oral discourse in writing without significantly altering the mentality which lies behind it. For Abelard, to use the same analogy, texts are dispositive, or, at the very least, have in themselves the potential to reveal aspects of objective reality. Abelard's central problem is at once linguistic and semantic, thereby interrelating words, facts, things, and meanings. For him, universality is imputable "to words alone." Yet this celebrated phrase should not be taken out of context and made to defend the sort of verbalism he opposed. Words, in Abelard's view, are subject to grammar and logic; they are in effect spoken elements of discourse in relation to real or imagined texts. Taking priority over texts, they do not on that account negate the relevance of texts. In Bernard of Clairvaux we find a quite different approach to these questions, but one which presupposes the existence of scholastic tendencies and derives its strength from an implied contrast to them. Bernard's sermons on the Song of Songs, the twelfth century's most remarkable example of mystical theology, are largely a subjective expression of faith. But textuality played a major role in their production, audience relations, and subsequent transmission. For, although he was himself a charismatic preacher who extolled the power of God's unadorned Word, Bernard in fact reproduced the ritualistic and symbolic world of oral discourse in the form of a text. As such, his dicta became a set of quasi-sacramental bonds for the period's most exemplary textual community, the Cistercian Order. And, within his sermons, the experience of the text and the experience of the religious life were intermingled, offering a structure to both at once.

The final chapter of the book turns to the question of ideas and society. How, we may ask, did the gradual increase in the use of texts act as an intermediary between group interests and their ideological expression?

The later eleventh and twelfth centuries were times of intensive economic, social, and cultural upheaval—that was recognized by many contemporary observers of events. But how was one to explain or to understand the transformations? In general, witnesses found that their inherited tools of interpretation were inadequate. A programme was therefore undertaken, not primarily to study the roots of change, but to develop techniques of the intellect. Those categories of thought rather than an objective evaluation of the forces involved represent one of the period's most distinctive cultural products. From the diverse contributions, commentators gradually built up an inventory of inter-preted experience and evolved both personal and general styles of her-meneutics. The effects were not only felt in the intellectual domain, where one saw a proliferation of exegesis, historical writing, philoso-phy, and theology. As noted, the new structures also fed into and were in turn nourished by the world of lived experience.[4] It was not only the educated, who were in direct contact with classical or Chris-tian tradition, who began to adopt textual models for behaviour. Through preaching and other verbal communication, the unlettered were also affected. Texts gradually acquired the capacity to shape ex-perience itself and to operate as intermediaries between orally trans-mitted ideas and social change.

Eleventh-century *mentalité* therefore reveals orientations similar to heresy, reform, and intellectual debate. The starting point of Chapter Five is the *Historiae* of Rodulf Glaber, in which action is largely sym-bolic and interpretation an afterthought. However, as the century progressed, and, in particular, during the literary revival which fol-lowed the consolidation of the Norman duchy by William the Con-queror, traditional and modernistic patterns of conduct were con-trasted more directly. Perhaps the most popular metaphor for portraying change was the notion of "old age and youth," a well-known rhetor-ical topos which was reworked in a variety of circumstances. Fre-quently, in fact, changes were viewed as unprecedented events, and the perceived novelty was difficult for those used to a static universe to accept. As a result, there arose a series of imaginative attempts to fit contemporary experience into models from the distant past—to see youth, so to speak, as old age—in which the *moderni*, that is, the more recent thinkers, gradually distinguished their attitudes and hab-its of mind from the *antiqui*. The awareness of similarities and differ-ences between the present and the past offered for the first time in some two centuries the alternatives normally open to a voluntarist society: either to recognize the newness of the "modern" age, or, as many preferred, to reshape what it actually was in the image of what it was once thought to be.

The subjects chosen for this study are not of course the only pos-sible illustrations of literacy's ramifications during the eleventh and

---

[4] Cf. A. Schutz and T. Luckmann, *The Structures of the Life-World* (Evanston, Ill., 1973), 3-8 *et passim*.

twelfth centuries. For reasons of space, such important topics as music, iconography, architecture, and Latin poetry were omitted: it was better, I felt, to say nothing than to offer a superficial treatment. Even within the disciplines discussed a selection of the available material had to be made. As a consequence, little is said about the development of grammar and logic during the eleventh century, which undoubtedly influenced the pattern of mature philosophical concerns in the twelfth, or, to take another example, the twelfth-century interconnections between theories of language and theology, as witnessed by such writers as Hugh of St. Victor, Gilbert of Poitiers, and Alan of Lille.

On the other hand, the questions taken up have the advantage of being naturally interrelated, both through historic and thematic development. As noted, the problems treated in Chapters Two to Five, heresy, reform, linguistic philosophy, mystical theology, and the social uses of ideas, have long been known to have interpenetrated each other. In this sense, the book follows the lines of inquiry laid down by such notable previous students of the subject as M.-D. Chenu. The thematic continuities are equally evident. The criticism of ritual and symbol by heretics and reformers was inseparable from the eucharistic debate, which reassessed the meaning of the sacraments as a whole. The issues raised by Lanfranc and Berengar led naturally to a consideration of language, texts, and reality at a more abstract level, as well, indirectly, to the polarization of attitudes towards textual methodologies in such writers as Abelard and Bernard. Their discussions, which represent high peaks of development in their respective fields, contributed to the more general interest in interpretive systems, which, in turn, inevitably fed back into conceptions of the individual and of society.

Running through the essays is also a larger set of theoretical concerns involving speakers, writers, readers, and audiences in a period reawakening to the potential of literate communication. In Saussurian terms, one could say that we are witnessing the historical emergence of the distinction between *langue* and *parole*, that is, in medieval terms, the distinction between an inner linguistic model, based upon Latin's explicit grammar, and common, at least in theory, to many members of a group, and an outer, speaking-capacity, chiefly associated with the vernaculars, which demanded individual performance and flexible social allegiances. On the one hand, contact with texts caused "deeply rooted" layers of oral tradition to be articulated both in spoken and in written form.[5] On the other, the appearance of texts often preserved the record of oral traditions in a scribal museum in which, like the physical symbols in the eucharist, they seemed to say one thing and to mean another. Everywhere, the presence of texts forced the elements of culture embedded in oral discourse to redefine their boundaries with respect to a different type of human exchange. This invariably resulted in contrasts between the "popular" and the "learned" which were themselves the byproducts of literate sensibilities. Other opposites also became polarized: custom versus law, things versus linguistic ideas, synchrony versus diachrony, and sense versus interpreted experience. In many cases, the persistence, if somewhat transformed, of orality was merely disguised by medieval textuality and its later mechanization in the age of print.[6]

The story can be told *in nuce* in the gradual expansion of the notion of ritual. Europe after the eleventh century created a cultural distance from a certain type of ritualism, which was classified as primitive by such critics of popular religion as Bernard of Angers and Guibert of Nogent. Similarly, by the mid-twelfth century, monarchy centred upon written law took the place of the legitimation of royal authority through sacral rites. Customary ritual, in sum, was on the wane, often demoted to mere ceremonial. However, the same period saw the growth of new ritual activities, which had nothing in common except a loose adherence to a textual base. As texts gradually invaded the institutional sphere of life, experience in all domains was restructured to conform to external norms of behaviour, and these were almost invariably independent of the individual. The influence of textually oriented rituals on group conduct was particularly dramatic. Among heretical and reformist communities, ritual was chiefly expressed as a form of interaction among the members; that is, the rules or dicta were written, but the consequences were acted out orally. The verbal yet structured level of hermeneutic activity was a means of separating the old from the new, of defining world-renouncing as opposed to world-embracing views of the religious life. At another level, rituals also began to work within society as a whole by means of texts that were transmitted by word of mouth. Obvious examples of this phenomenon are the widespread notions of pilgrimage and crusade, through

[5] Cf. C. Ginzburg, *Il formaggio e i vermi. Il cosmo di un mugnaio del '500*, 135.
[6] Cf. N. Z. Davis, "Printing and the People," in *Society and Culture in Early Modern France*, 189-226.

which texts united in symbolic action peoples who had little in common besides occupying the same temporal and geographical space.[7]

In higher medieval culture, textuality lay at the basis of a growing intellectualism. The fundamental divisions of communications in the eleventh and twelfth centuries were all derived from analogies like word and text, spirit and letter, inner and outer meaning, etc. The ordering of the phenomenal universe, on which most natural-scientific achievement rested, took its direction from the opposition of the visible and the invisible. The intellectual roots lay in Christian Platonism, but the redeployment, as in William of Conches, was often tied to a contrast between popular and learned traditions. For, what met the eye was, like the letter, both a source of deeper insight into the spirit and an impediment to realizing it. Again, the most frequently reiterated dichotomy among both heretics and reformers was between the material and the immaterial, in which the rise of a legally oriented, institutionally centralized papacy held an ambivalent position. The terms of such discussions were clearly drawn from St. Paul and Augustine, but the critical instincts with which they were reapplied presupposed an agreement on matters like precedent, scholastic arrangement, and the equivalence of law and truth. Practice, too, in such areas as education and politics, was informed by a new access to theory. The distinction was increasingly thought to lie between what was considered to be oral, customary, and transient, as opposed to what was written, canonical, and permanent. The use and reuse of such familiar polarities as time and eternity, image and reality, and *figura* and *veritas*, whatever their particular sources, were justified by the belief that within the ontology of the written word lay an intimate reflection of reality, which the study of grammar, syntax, and hermeneutics could reveal.

In the content, then, and even the forms of thought, the medievals appear to have consciously imitated their ancient predecessors. Yet, as their imprecisions, misinterpretations, and sources of anxiety demonstrate, they were unlike their forbears in fundamental ways. The roots of these differences are traceable to the conceptual vocabulary, if not to the process of conceptualization itself, which derived from a few linguistic models, all directly or indirectly based on the relation of oral to written exchange. These complexes of ideas provided the period after the millennium with a rationale for both cultural progress and decline.

[7] Cf. V. Turner, "Pilgrimages as Social Processes," in *Dramas, Fields, and Metaphors*, 166-230.

CONCLUSION

The presence of a number of different theoretical concerns relevant to history, literature, and the social sciences naturally raises the question of theory's role in the volume as a whole.

In general it appears on two levels. The study assumes that the transition to new working relations between oral and written modes of communication was an important shaping instrument both for the forces of change themselves and for the processes of thought by which they were simultaneously interpreted. In a broader context, the volume also takes a more positive view of the contribution of historical research to an interpretive social science than is nowadays fashionable, and that of course amounts to a theoretical standpoint in itself.

The argument for the second role of theory derives in part from the working hypotheses of the book as a whole, and may be summed up as follows. Texts, as noted, when introduced into a largely oral society, not only created a contrast between two different ways of looking at the world. They also raised the possibility that reality could be understood as a series of relationships, such as outer versus inner, independent object as opposed to reflecting subject, or abstract sets of rules in contrast to a coherent texture of facts and meanings. Experience in other words became separable, if not always separated, from ratiocination about it; and the main field of investigation turned out to be, not the raw data of sense or the platonized ideal of pure knowledge, but rather the forms of mediation between them. This set of changes resulted in a rebirth of hermeneutics as a critical philosophy of meaning, in a renewed search for epistemological order, and in a widespread interest in diachrony, development, and processual evolution. Understanding as a consequence began to emerge from the accumulation of reiterated and reinterpreted experience, even though, as was recognized, the tools of methodological analysis were not given in each concrete set of events; and an understanding formed of similar elements links the contemporary reader to the past through the preservation of those very written artefacts which originated new patterns of thought and action themselves. A theory which attempts to account for such transformations cannot operate aprioristically; it cannot divorce itself artificially from the general flow of events, which includes the present. Indeed, if the issue of causality is to be raised at all, it cannot be limited to the technical, the economic, the societal, or the intellectual. As crucial aspects of reiterated experience, historical factors have priority.

SELECTED BIBLIOGRAPHY

Abbreviations

AASS	*Acta Sanctorum*
AHDLMA	*Archives d'histoire doctrinale et littéraire du moyen âge*
BIS	*Bullettino dell'Istituto storico italiano e archivio muratoriano*
CCCM	*Corpus Christianorum, Continuatio Mediaevalis*
CCSL	*Corpus Christianorum, Series Latina*
CCM	*Cahiers de civilisation médiévale, Xe-XIIe siècles*
CSEL	*Corpus Scriptorum Ecclesiasticorum Latinorum*
DACL	*Dictionnaire d'archéologie chrétienne et de liturgie*
DTC	*Dictionnaire de théologie catholique*
Mansi	*Sacrorum Conciliorum Nova et Amplissima Collectio*, ed. G. D. Mansi (Florence, 1759-98)
MGH SS	*Monumenta Germaniae Historica, Scriptores* (in folio)
MIöG	*Mitteilungen des Instituts für Österreichische Geschichtsforschung*
NRHD	*Nouvelle revue historique du droit français et étranger*
PL	*Patrologia Latina*
Rben	*Revue bénédictine*
RHE	*Revue d'histoire ecclésiastique*
RHF	*Recueil des historiens des Gaules et de la France*, 2nd ed. (Paris, 1868-80)
RSPT	*Revue des sciences philosophiques et théologiques*
ZRG GA	*Zeitschrift der Savigny-Stiftung für Rechtsgeschichte, Germanistische Abteilung*
ZRG KA	*Idem, Kanonistische Abteilung*

Abelard, Peter, *Peter Abaelards philosophische Schriften*, ed. B. Geyer:
 I. *Die "Logica Ingredientibus"*:
  1. *Die Glossen zu Porphyrius* (Beiträge zur Geschichte der Philosophie des Mittelalters, Bd. 21, Heft 1, Münster, 1919);
  2. *Die Glossen zu den Kategorien* (*ibid.*, 21, 2, 1921);
  3. *Die Glossen zu* ΠΕΡΙ ΕΡΜΗΝΕΙΑΣ (*ibid.*, 21, 3, 1921).
 II. *Die Logica "Nostrorum Petitioni Sociorum." Die Glossen zu Porphyrius* (*ibid.*, 21, 4, 1933).
————, *Peter Abaelards Theologia "Summi boni" zum ersten Male vollständig herausgegeben*, ed. T. H. Ostendler (Beiträge zur Geschichte der Philosophie und Theologie des Mittelalters, Bd. 35, Heft 2/3, Münster, 1939).
————, *Peter Abailard, "Sic et Non." A Critical Edition*, ed. B. B. Boyer and R. McKeon (Chicago and London, 1976-1977).
————, *Peter Abelard's "Ethics." An Edition with Introduction, English Translation and Notes*, ed. D. E. Luscombe (Oxford Medieval Texts, Oxford, 1971).
————, *Petri Abaelardi Opera Theologica*, ed. E. M. Buytaert, 2 vols. (CCCM 11-12, Turnhout, 1969).
————, *Petrus Abaelardus Dialectica: First Complete Edition of the Parisian Manuscript with an Introduction*, ed. L. M. de Rijk (Wijsgerige Teksten en Studies. Philosophical Texts and Studies, vol. 1, 2nd ed., Assen, 1970).
————, *Petrus Abaelardus. Dialogus inter Philosophum Iudaeum et Christianum. Textkritische Edition*, ed. R. Thomas (Stuttgart-Bad Cannstatt, 1970).
————, *Pietro Abelardo, Scritti filosofici. Editio super Porphyrium. Glossae in Categorias. Super Aristotelem De Interpretatione. De divisionibus. Super Topica glossae*, ed. M. del Pra (Nuova Biblioteca Filosofica, Serie 2, vol. 3, Milan, 1954).
Acta Synodi Atrebatensis in Manichaeos, PL 142.1269-1312.
Adalbero of Laon, *Adalberonis Episcopi Laudunensis Carmen ad Rotbertum Regem Francorum*, RHF, vol. 10, pp. 65-72.
Adam, K., *Die Eucharistielehre des hl. Augustin* (Forschungen zur christlichen Literatur-und Dogmengeschichte, Bd. 8, Heft 1, Paderborn, 1908).
Adamson, J. W., " 'The Illiterate Anglo-Saxon,' " in *"The Illiterate Anglo-Saxon" and Other Essays on Education Medieval and Modern* (Cambridge, 1946), 1-20.
Adémar de Chabannes, *Chronique. Publiée d'après les manuscrits*, ed. J. Chavanon

(Collection de textes pour servir à l'étude et à l'enseignement de l'histoire, fasc. 20, Paris, 1897).

Adlhoch, B., "Roscelin und Sanct Anselm," *Philosophisches Jahrbuch der Görresgesellschaft* 20 (1907), 442-56.

Agricoltura e mondo rurale in occidente nell'alto medioevo italiano (Settimane di studio del Centro italiano di studi sull'alto medioevo, vol. 13, Spoleto, 1966).

Alan of Lille: see Häring, N.

Alphandéry, P., "De quelques faits de prophétisme dans les sectes latines antérieures au Joachisme," *Revue de l'histoire des religions* 52 (1905), 177-218.

————, *La Chrétienté et l'idée de croisade*, ed. A. Dupront, 2 vols. (L'évolution de l'humanité. Synthèse collective, vols. 38-38bis, Paris, 1954, 1959).

Ambrosioni, A., "Il più antico elenco di chierici della diocesi ambrosiana ed altre aggiunte al *Decretum* di Burcardo in un codice della Biblioteca Ambrosiana (E 144 sup.) Una voce della polemica antipatarinica?" *Aevum* 50 (1976), 274-320.

Amira, K. von, "Der Stab in der germanischen Rechtssymbolik," *Abhandlungen der königlich Bayerischen Akademie der Wissenschaften, philos.-philolog., und historische Kl.*, 25. Bd., 1. Abh. (Munich, 1911), 1-180.

Amelotti, M., and G. Costamagna, *Alle origini del notariato italiano* (Studi storici sul notariato italiano, vol. 2, Rome, 1975).

Amory, F., "The Confessional Superstructure of Guibert of Nogent's *Vita*," *Classica et Mediaevalia* 25 (1964), 224-40.

Anciaux, P., *La Théologie du Sacrement de Pénitence au XIIe siècle* (Universitas Catholica Lovaniensis. Dissertationes ad gradum magistri in Facultate Theologica vel in Facultate Iuris Canonica consequendum conscriptae, Series 2, tomus 41, Louvain and Gembloux, 1949).

Andrea da Strumi, *Vita Sancti Arialdi auctore Andrea Abbate Strumensi*, ed. F. Baethgen, MGH SS 30.2, pp. 1047-75.

Andrew of Fleury, *Vita Gauzlini Abbatis Floriacensis Monasterii*, ed. R.-H. Bautier and G. Labory (Sources d'histoire médiévale publiées par l'Institut de Recherche et d'Histoire des Textes, vol. 2, Paris, 1969).

Anselm of Canterbury, *Anselme de Cantorbéry. Pourquoi Dieu s'est fait homme*, ed., intro., and trans., R. Roques (Sources chrétiennes, no. 91, Paris, 1963).

————, *S. Anselmi Cantuariensis Archiepiscopi Opera Omnia*, ed. F. S. Schmitt, 6 vols.: vol. 1 (Seckau, 1938, repr. Edinburgh, 1946); vol. 2 (Rome, 1940); vol. 3 (Edinburgh, 1946); vol. 4 (Edinburgh, 1949); vol. 5 (Edinburgh, 1951); vol. 6 (Edinburgh, 1961); repr. with a new introduction by F. S. Schmitt (Stuttgart-Bad Cannstatt, 1968).

Arnulf of Milan, *Arnulfi Gesta Archiepiscoporum Mediolanensium*, ed. L. C. Bethmann and W. Wattenbach, MGH SS 8, pp. 1-31.

Aston, M., "Lollardy and Literacy," *History* 62 (1977), 347-71.

Audet, Th. A., "Une source augustinienne de l'argument de saint Anselme," in J. Maritain. *et al.*, eds., *Etienne Gilson, philosophe de la chrétienté* (Rencontres, 30, Paris, 1949), 105-42.

Auerbach, E., *Literary Language and its Public in Late Latin Antiquity and in the Middle Ages*, trans. R. Manheim (Bollingen Series, vol. 74, London and New York, 1965).

————, *Mimesis. The Representation of Reality in Western Literature*, trans. W. Trask (Princeton, 1953).

Avalle, D'A. S., *Alle origini della letteratura francese. I giuramento di Strasburgo e la sequenza di santa Eulalia*, ed. L. Borghi (Turin, 1966).

Ayer, A. J., *The Foundations of Empirical Knowledge* (London, 1940).

Bäuml, F. H., "The Unmaking of the Hero: Some Critical Implications of the Transition from Oral to Written Epic," in H. Scholler, ed., *The Epic in Medieval Society, Aesthetic and Moral Values* (Tübingen, 1977), 86-99.

————, "Varieties and Consequences of Medieval Literacy and Illiteracy," *Speculum* 55 (1980), 237-65.

Balogh, J., "*Voces paginarum*: Beiträge zur Geschichte des lauten Lesens und Schreibens," *Philologus* 82 (1927), 84-109, 202-40.

Barth, K., *Anselm: Fides Quaerens Intellectum. Anselm's Proof of the Existence of God in the Context of his Theological Scheme*, Eng. trans. from the 2nd ed., Zürich, 1958 (The Library of Philosophy and Theology, London, 1960).

Bartlett, F. C., *Remembering. A Study in Experimental and Social Psychology* (The Cambridge Psychological Library, Cambridge, 1932).

Bautier, R.-H., "L'hérésie d'Orléans et le mouvement intellectuel au début du XIe siècle. Documents et hypothèses," in *Enseignement et vie intellectuelle (IXe-XVIe Siècle)* (Actes du 95e Congrès national des sociétés savantes, Reims, 1970, Section de philologie et d'histoire jusqu'à 1610, tome 1, Paris, 1975), 63-88.

Bechthum, M., *Beweggründe und Bedeutung des Vagantentums in der lateinischen Kirche des Mittelalters* (Beiträge zur mittelalterlichen, neueren und allgemeinen Geschichte, Bd. 14, Jena, 1941).

Becquet, J., "L'érémitisme clérical et laïc dans l'ouest de la France," in *L'eremitismo in occidente nei secoli XI e XII* (Pubblicazioni dell'Università Cattolica del Sacro Cuore, contributi, serie terza, varia 4: Miscellanea del Centro di studi medioevali 4, Milan, 1965), 182-203.

Benedeit, *The Anglo-Norman Voyage of St. Brendan*, ed. I. Short and B. Merrilees (Manchester, 1979).

Benson, R. L., *The Bishop-Elect. A Study in Medieval Ecclesiastical Office* (Princeton, 1968).

————, and G. Constable, eds., with C. D. Lanham, *Renaissance and Renewal in the Twelfth Century. From a conference held under the auspices of UCLA Center for Medieval and Renaissance Studies Harvard University Committee on Medieval Studies 26-29 November 1977. Cambridge, Massachusetts* (Cambridge, Mass., 1982).

Benton, J. F., *Self and Society in Medieval France. The Memoirs of Abbot Guibert of Nogent (1064?-c. 1125). The Translation of C. C. Swinton Bland revised by the Editor* (New York, 1970).

Béraudy, R., "Les catégories de pensée de Ratramne dans son enseignement eucharistique," in *Corbie, abbaye royale*, 157-80.

Berengar of Tours, *Berengarius in purgatoria epistola contra Almannum*, ed. J. de Montclos, in *Lanfranc et Bérenger*, pp. 531-38.

————, *Berengarius Turonensis de Sacra Coena adversus Lanfrancum* ed. W. H. Beekenkamp, (Kerkhistorische Studien behoorende bijhet Nederlandscharchief voor Kerkgeschiednis, Deel 2, The Hague, 1941).

————, *Epistola ad Ascetinum*, PL 150.66; also ed. R.B.C. Huygens, "Les lettres de Bérenger de Tours et d'Ascelin de Chartres," in *Texts and Manuscripts. Essays presented to G. I. Lieftinck*, vol. 2 (Litterae Textuales, Amsterdam, 1972), 18-19.

Berkout, C. T., and J. B. Russell, *Medieval Heresies. A Bibliography 1960-1979* (Pontifical Institute of Mediaeval Studies. Subsidia Mediaevalia 11, Toronto, 1981).

Berschin, W., *Bonizo von Sutri, Leben und Werk* (Beiträge zur Geschichte und Quellenkunde des Mittelalters, Bd. 2, Berlin and New York, 1972).

Bernard of Angers, *Liber Miraculorum Sancte Fidis*, ed. A. Bouillet (Collection de textes pour servir à l'étude et à l'enseignement de i'histoire, fasc. 21, Paris, 1897).

Bernard of Clairvaux, *S. Bernardi Opera*, ed. J. Leclercq and H. M. Rochais, 8 vols. (Rome, 1957-1977); vols. 1-2 also ed. C. H. Talbot.

Bernard of Clairvaux. Studies Presented to Dom Jean Leclercq (Cistercian Studies No. 23, Washington, D.C., 1973).

Bernhard von Clairvaux, Mönch und Mystiker. Internationaler Bernhardkongress, Mainz, 1953 (Veröffentlichen des Instituts für europäische Geschichte Mainz, Bd. 6, Wiesbaden, 1955).

Bertola, E., "I precedenti storici del 'Sic et Non' di Abelardo," *Rivista di filosofia neo-scolastica* 53 (1961), 255-80.

————, "Le critiche di Abelardo ad Anselmo di Laon ed a Guglielmo di Champeaux," *Rivista di filosofia neo-scolastica* 52 (1960), 495-522.

Besnier, R., " 'Inquisitiones' et 'Recognitiones.' Le nouveau système des preuves à l'époque des Coutumiers normands," NRHD, 4th Series, 28 (1950), 183-212.

————, *La coutume de Normandie, histoire externe* (Paris, 1935).

————, " 'Vadiatio legis et leges.' Les preuves de droit commun à l'époque des coutumiers normands," NRHD, 4th Series, 19-20 (1940-41), 88-135.

Bieler, L., ed., *The Irish Penitentials, with an appendix by D. A. Binchy* (Scriptores Latini Hiberniae, vol. 5, Dublin, 1963).

Bischoff, B., "The Study of Foreign Languages in the Middle Ages," *Speculum* 36 (1961), 209-24; repr. *Mittelalterliche Studien*, vol. 2 (Stuttgart, 1967), 227-45.

Bishop, T.A.M., *Scriptores Regis. Facsimiles to identify and illustrate the hands of royal scribes in original charters of Henry I, Stephen, and Henry II* (Oxford, 1961).

Blake, E. O., "The Formation of the 'Crusade Idea,' " *Journal of Ecclesiastical History* 21 (1970), 11-31.

Bloch, M., *La société féodale*, 2 vols. (L'évolution de l'humanité. Synthèse collective, vols. 34-34bis, Paris, 1939-40); English trans., *Feudal Society*, trans. L. A. Manyon, 2 vols. (London, 1961).

———, "Les formes de la rupture de l'hommage dans l'ancien droit féodal," NRHD 36 (1912), 141-77; repr. *Mélanges historiques*, vol. 1 (Paris, 1963), 189-206.

Blok, D. P., "Les formules de droit romain dans les actes privés du haut Moyen Age," *Miscellanea Mediaevalia in memoriam Jan Frederik Niermeyer* (Groningen, 1967), 17-28.

Bodard, C., "La Bible, expression d'une expérience religieuse chez S. Bernard," *Saint Bernard théologien*, pp. 24-45.

Boesch, S., "Giovanni Gualberto e la vita comune del clero nelle biografie di Andrea da Strumi e di Atto da Vallombrosa," *La vita comune del clero nei secoli XI e XII*, vol. 2, 228-35.

Boesch Gajano, S., "Storia e tradizione vallombrosane," BIS 76 (1964), 99-215.

Boethius, *Anicii Manlii Severini Boetii Commentarii in Librum Aristotelis ΠΕΡΙ ΕΡΜΗΝΕΙΑΣ*, ed. C. Meiser, 3 vols. (Leipzig, 1887-1880).

———, *Commentaria in Porphyrium a se translatum*, PL 64.71-158.

Boissard, E., "La doctrine des anges chez S. Bernard," *Saint Bernard théologien*, 114-35.

Boler, J. F., "Abailard and the Problem of Universals," *Journal of the History of Philosophy* 1 (1963), 37-51.

Bongert, Y., *Recherches sur les cours laïques du Xe au XIIIe siècle* (Paris, 1949).

Bonizo of Sutri, *Bonizonis Episcopi Sutrini Liber ad Amicum post Editionem Iaffeanam*, ed. E. Dümmler (MGH Libelli de Lite Imperatorem et Pontificum Saeculis XI. et XII. conscripti, vol. 1, Hanover, 1891), 568-620.

Borino, G. B. Salesiano, "L'arcidiaconato di Ildebrando," *Studi gregoriani* 3 (1948), 463-516.

Borst, A., "Abälard und Bernhard," *Historische Zeitschrift* 186 (1958), 497-526.

———, *Die Katharer* (Schriften der MGH 12, Stuttgart, 1953).

Bossi, G., *I Crescenzi. Contributo alla storia del 900 al 1012* (Vatican City, 1915).

Boüard, A. de, *Manuel de diplomatique française et pontificale*: vol. 1, *Diplomatique générale. Avec un album de 54 planches en phototypie* (Paris, 1929); vol. 2: *L'acte privé* (Paris, 1948).

Bouhot, J.-P., *Ratramne de Corbie. Histoire littéraire et controverses doctrinales* (Paris, 1976).

Bouillet, A., and L. Servières, *Sainte Foy, vièrge et martyr* (Rodez, 1900).

Bouton, J. de la Croix, *Bibliographie bernardine 1891-1957* (Commission d'histoire de l'Ordre de Cîteaux, No. 5, Paris, 1958).

Boutruche, R., *Seigneurie et féodalité* (Collection historique): vol. 1: *Le premier âge des liens d'homme à homme*, 2nd ed. (Paris, 1968); vol. 2: *L'apogée (XIe-XIIIe siècles)* (Paris, 1970).

Boyle, L. E., *A Survey of the Vatican Archives and of its Medieval Holdings* (Pontifical Institute of Mediaeval Studies. Subsidia Mediaevalia 1, Toronto, 1972).

———, "Montaillou Revisited: *Mentalité* and Methodology," in J. A. Raftis, ed., *Pathways to Medieval Peasants* (Pontifical Institute of Mediaeval Studies. Papers in Mediaeval Studies, no. 2, Toronto, 1981) 119-40.

Braudel, F., "Histoire et sciences sociales: la longue durée," *Annales, E.S.C.*, 13 (1958), 725-53; repr. in *Ecrits sur l'histoire* (Paris, 1969), 41-83.

Brenner, R., "Agrarian Class Structure and Economic Development in Pre-Industrial Europe," *Past and Present* 70 (1976), 30-75.

Bresslau, H., *Handbuch der Urkundenlehre für Deutschland und Italien*, vol. 1 (Leipzig, 1912), vol. 2, also ed. H.-W. Klewitz (Berlin, 1931).

Brissaud, J., *A History of French Private Law*, trans. R. Howell (The Continental Legal History Series Published under the auspices of the Association of American Law Schools, vol. 3, Boston, 1912).

Browe, P., *Die eucharistischen Wunder des Mittelalters* (Breslauer Studien zur historischen Theologie, neue Folge, Bd. 4, Breslau, 1938).

Brown, E.E.R., "The Tyranny of a Concept: Feudalism and Historians of Medieval Europe," *American Historical Review* 79 (1974), 1063-88.

Brundage, J. A., *Medieval Canon Law and the Crusader* (Madison, Wisconsin, 1969).

Brunner, H., *Die Entstehung der Schwurgerichte* (Berlin, 1972).

———, *Zur Rechtsgeschichte der römischen und germanischen Urkunde*, Bd. 1 (Berlin, 1880).

Brunton, J. A., "The Logic of God's Necessary Existence," *International Philosophical Quarterly* 10 (1970), 276-90.

Bynum, C. W., "Jesus as Mother and Abbot as Mother: Some Themes in Twelfth-Century Cistercian Writing," *Harvard Theological Review* 70 (1977), 257-84; repr. *Jesus as Mother. Studies in the Spirituality of the High Middle Ages* (Berkeley, Los Angeles, and London, 1982), 110-69.

———, "The Cistercian Conception of Community," *Harvard Theological Review* 68 (1975), 273-86; repr., *Jesus as Mother . . .*, pp. 59-81.

Caenegem, R. C. van, *Royal Writs in England from the Conquest to Glanvill. Studies in the Early History of the Common Law* (Publications of the Seldon Society, vol. 77, London, 1959).

———, *The Birth of the English Common Law* (Cambridge, 1973).

———, "The Law of Evidence in the Twelfth Century: European Perspectives and Intellectual Background," *Proceedings of the Second International*

Congress of Medieval Canon Law, ed. S. Kuttner and J. J. Ryan (Monumenta Iuris Canonici, Series C, Subsidia, vol. 1, Vatican City, 1965), 297-319.

Calasso, F., *La "convenientia." Contributo alla storia del contratto in Italia durante l'alto medio evo* (Biblioteca della Rivista di storia del diritto italiano, no. 9, Bologna, 1932).

Caliaro, M., "Lo spirito santo nella vita spirituale secondo S. Bernardo," *Divus Thomas. Commentarium de Philosophia et Theologia* 51 (1947), 304-18.

Camelot. P.-Th., "Réalisme et symbolisme dans la doctrine eucharistique de saint Augustin," RSPT 31 (1947), 394-410.

————, " 'Sacramentum.' Notes de théologie sacrementaire augustinienne," *Revue thomiste* 57 (1957), 429-49.

Campenhausen, H. Freiherr von, "Die asketische Heimatlosigkeit im alt-kirchlichen und frühmittelalterlichen Mönchtum," in *Tradition und Leben. Kräfte der Kirchengeschichte. Aufsätze und Vorträge* (Heidelberg, 1960), 302-17.

Capelle, C., *Le voeu d'obéissance des origines au XIIIe siècle. Etude juridique* (Bibliothèque d'histoire du droit et droit romain, tome 2, Paris, 1959).

Capitani, O., "Esiste un 'età gregoriana'? Considerazioni sulle tendenze di una storiografia medievistica," *Rivista di storia et letteratura religiosa* 1 (1965), 454-81.

————, *Immunità vescovile ed ecclesiologia in età "pregregoriana" e "gregoriana."* *L'avvio alla "restaurazione"* (Biblioteca degli "Studi medievali," vol. 3, Spoleto, 1966).

————, "La lettera di Goffredo II Martello conte d'Angiò a Ildebrando (1059)," *Studi gregoriani* 5 (1956), 19-31.

————, "Per la storia dei rapporti tra Gregorio VII e Berengario di Tours," *Studi gregoriani* 6 (1959-61), 99-145.

————, "Storiografia e riforma della chiesa in Italia (Arnolfo e Landolfo seniore di Milano)," in *La storiografia altomedievale*, 557-629.

————, "Studi per Berengario di Tours," BIS 69 (1957), 67-173; repr. *Studi su Berengario di Tours* (Collezione di studi e testi, vol. 2, Lecce, 1966), 9-191.

Carozzi, Cl., "Les fondements de la tripartition sociale chez Adalbéron de Laon," *Annales, E.S.C.*, 33 (1978), 683-701.

Cartulaire de l'abbaye de Saint-Père de Chartres, ed. B. Guérard (Collection des documents inédits sur l'histoire de France publiés par l'ordre du roi et par les soins du ministre de l'instruction publique. Première série: histoire politique. Collection des cartulaires de France, tome 1-2, Paris, 1840).

Casel, O., "Das Mysteriengedächtnis der Messliturgie im Lichte der Tradition," *Jahrbuch für Liturgiewissenschaft* 6 (1926), 113-204.

Cattaneo, E., "La participazione dei laici alla liturgia," in *I laici nella "societas christiana,"* 396-423.

Cecchelli, C., *I Crescenzi, i Savelli, i Cenci* (Le grande famiglie romane, vol. 2, Rome, 1942).

Cencetti, G., "Il notaio medievale italiano," *Atti della Società ligure di storia patria*, n.s. 4 (1964), vii-xxiii.

Certeau, M. de, *L'écriture de l'histoire* (Bibliothèque des histoires, Paris, 1975).

Chaurand, J., "La conception de l'histoire de Guibert de Nogent," CCM 8 (1965), 381-95.

Cheney, C. R., *English Bishops' Chanceries 1100-1250* (Publications of the Faculty of Arts of the University of Manchester, No. 3, Manchester, 1950).

Chénon, E., *Histoire générale du droit français public et privé des origines à 1815*, 2 vols. (Paris, 1926).

———, "Recherches historiques sur quelques rites nuptiaux," NRHD 36 (1912), 573-660.

Chenu, M.-D., *La théologie au douzième siècle* (Etudes de philosophie médiévale, vol. 14, Paris, 1957).

———, *L'éveil de la conscience dans la civilisation médiévale* (Conférence Albert-le-Grand 1968, Montréal and Paris, 1969).

Christian, W. A., Jr., *Person and God in a Spanish Valley* (Studies in Social Discontinuity, vol. 1, New York and London, 1972).

Cipolla, C., *Literacy and Development in the West* (Harmondsworth, 1969).

Cristiani, M., "La controversia eucaristica nella cultura del secolo IX," *Studi medievali*, 3rd Series, 9 (1968), 167-233.

Clanchy, M. T., *From Memory to Written Record. England, 1066-1307* (London, 1979).

———, "Remembering the Past and the Good Old Law," *History* 55 (1970), 166-72.

Classen, P., "Eschatologische Ideen und Armutsbewegungen im 11. und 12. Jahrhundert," in *Povertà e ricchezza nella spiritualità dei secoli XI e XII* (Convegni del Centro di studi sulla spiritualità medievale, vol. 8, Todi, 1969), 126-62.

———, "Fortleben und Wandel spätrömischen Urkundenwesens im frühen Mittelalter," in *Recht und Schrift im Mittelalter*, pp. 13-54.

———, "Kaiserreskript und Königsurkunde. Diplomatische Studien zum römisch-germanischen Kontinuitätsproblem I-II," *Archiv für Diplomatik, Schriftgeschichte, Siegel-und Wappenkunde* 1 (1955), 1-87; 2 (1956), 1-115.

Clerval, A., *Les écoles de Chartres au moyen âge du Ve au XVIe siècle* (Mémoires de la Société archéologique d'Eure-et-Loire, tome 11, Chartres, 1895).

Coing, H., ed., *Handbuch der Quellen und Literatur der neueren europäischen Privatrechtsgeschichte. Erster Bd.: Mittelalter (1100-1500). Die Gelehrten Rechte und die Gesetzgebung* (Veröffentlichung des Max-Planck-Instituts für europäische Rechtsgeschichte, Munich, 1973).

Colish, M., *The Mirror of Language. A Study in the Medieval Theory of Language* (Yale Historical Publications, Miscellany 88, New Haven, 1968).

Colman, R. V., "Reason and Unreason in Early Medieval Law," *Journal of Interdisciplinary History* 4 (1974), 571-91.

Columbo, A., "Il testamento di Landolfo Seniore?" *Archivio storico lombardo* 57 (1930), 128-40.

Congar, Y., " 'Arriana haeresis' comme désignation du néo-manichéisme au XIIe siècle. Contribution à l'histoire d'une typification de l'hérésie au moyen âge," RSPT 43 (1959), 449-61.

————, "L'ecclésiologie de S. Bernard," in *Saint Bernard théologien*, pp. 136-90.

————, "Les laïcs et l'ecclésiologie des 'ordines' chez les théologiens des XIe et XIIe siècles," in *I laici nella "societas christiana" dei secoli XI e XII*, pp. 83-117.

Conrat (Cohn), M., *Geschichte der Quellen und Literatur des römischen Rechts in früheren Mittelalter*, Bd. 1 (Leipzig, 1891).

Constable, G., *Letters and Letter-Collections* (Typologie des sources du moyen âge occidental, fasc. 17, Turnhout, 1976).

————, "Monachisme et pèlerinage au Moyen Age," *Revue historique* 258 (1977), 3-27.

————, "Opposition to Pilgrimage in the Middle Ages," *Studia Gratiana* 19 (1976), 125-46.

————, *The Letters of Peter the Venerable*, 2 vols. (Harvard Historical Studies 78, Cambridge, Mass., 1967).

✗ ————, "Twelfth-Century Spirituality and the Late Middle Ages," in O. B. Hardison, Jr., ed., *Medieval and Renaissance Studies*, no. 5 (Chapel Hill, 1971), 27-60.

Coolidge, R. T., "Adalbero, Bishop of Laon," *Studies in Medieval and Renaissance History* 2 (1965), 3-114.

Corbie, abbaye royale. Volume du XIIIe centenaire (Lille, 1963).

Cottiaux, J., "La conception de la théologie chez Abélard," RHE 28 (1932), 247-95, 533-51, and 788-828.

? Courtenay, W. J., "Sacrament, Symbol, and Causality in Bernard of Clairvaux," in *Bernard of Clairvaux*, pp. 111-22.

————, "The King and the Leaden Coin: The Economic Background of 'Sine qua non' Causality," *Traditio* 28 (1972), 185-209.

Cousin, P., *Abbon de Fleury-sur-Loire. Un savant, un pasteur, un martyr à la fin du Xe siècle* (Paris, 1954).

Couturier, C., " 'Sacramentum' et 'mysterium' dans l'oeuvre de saint Augustin," in H. Rondet, M. le Landais, A. Lauras, and C. Couturier, eds., *Etudes augustiniennes* (Théologie, vol. 28, Paris, 1953), 161-332.

Cowdrey, H.E.J., "Anselm of Besate and Some North-Italian Scholars of the Eleventh Century," *Journal of Ecclesiastical History* 23 (1972), 115-24.

————, "Archbishop Aribert II of Milan," *History* 51 (1966), 1-15.

————, *The Cluniacs and the Gregorian Reform* (Oxford, 1970).

————, "The Papacy, the Patarenes and the Church of Milan," *Transactions of the Royal Historical Society*, 5th Series, 18 (London, 1968), 25-48.

Cowdrey, H.E.J., "Unions and Confraternity with Cluny," *Journal of Ecclesiastical History* 16 (1965), 152-62.

Cracco, G., "Pataria: *opus* e *nomen* (tra verità e autorità)," *Rivista della storia della chiesa in Italia* 28 (1974), 357-87.

————, "Riforma ed eresia in momenti della cultura europea tra X e XI secolo," *Rivista di storia e letteratura religiosa* 7 (1971), 411-77.

Curtius, E. R., *European Literature and the Latin Middle Ages*, trans. W. R. Trask (Bollingen Series, vol. 36, Princeton, 1953).

————, "Rhetorische Naturschilderung im Mittelalter," *Romanische Forschungen* 56 (1942), 219-56.

Daly, L. W., *Contributions to a History of Alphabetization in Antiquity and the Middle Ages* (Collection Latomus, vol. 90, Brussels, 1967).

Daly, L. W., and B. A. Daly, "Some Techniques in Mediaeval Latin Lexicography," *Speculum* 39 (1964), 231-39.

David, M., "Le serment du sacre du IXe au XVe siècle. Contribution à l'étude des limites juridiques de la souveraineté," *Revue du moyen âge latin* 6 (1950), 5-272.

Davis, N. Z., "Les conteurs de Montaillou," *Annales, E.S.C.*, 34 (1979), 61-73.

————, *Society and Culture in Early Modern France. Eight Essays* (Stanford, 1975).

————, "Some Themes in the Study of Popular Religion," in C. Trinkaus and H. Oberman, eds., *The Pursuit of Holiness in Late Medieval and Renaissance Religion. Papers from the University of Michigan Conference* (Studies in Medieval and Reformation Thought, vol. 10, Leiden, 1974), 307-36.

Davis, R.H.C., *The Normans and their Myth* (London, 1976).

d'Ales, A., "Le mysticisme de saint Bernard," *Recherches des sciences religieuses* 25 (1935), 364-84.

d'Alverny, M.-T., "Le cosmos symbolique du XIIe siècle," AHDLMA 20 (1954), 31-81.

Déchanet, J.-M., "La christologie de saint Bernard," *Bernhard von Clairvaux*, pp. 63-75.

————, "La christologie de S. Bernard," *Saint Bernard théologien*, pp. 78-91.

Delhaye, Ph., *Le problème de la conscience morale chez S. Bernard étudié dans ses oeuvres et dans ses sources* (Analecta Mediaevalia Namurcensia 9, Namur, Louvain, and Lille, 1957).

————, "L'organisation scolaire au XIIe siècle," *Traditio* 5 (1947), 211-68.

Delaruelle, E., *La piété populaire au moyen âge*, pref. Ph. Wolff, intro. R. Manselli and A. Vauchez (Turin, 1975).

Denomy, A. J., "Jovens: the Notion of Youth among the Troubadours, its Meaning and Source," *Mediaeval Studies* 11 (1949), 1-22.

d'Haenens, A., "Les invasions normandes dans l'empire franc au IXe siècle. Pour une rénovation de la problématique," in *I Normanni*, pp. 233-98.

Diringer, D., *Writing* (Ancient People and Places, vol. 25, London, 1962).

Dondaine, A., "L'origine de l'hérésie médiévale. A propos d'un livre récent," *Rivista di storia della chiesa in Italia* 6 (1952), 47-78.

Douglas, D. C., *William the Conqueror. The Norman Impact upon England* (London and Berkeley, 1964).

Dronke, P., *Fabula. Explorations into the Uses of Myth in Medieval Platonism* (Mittellateinische Studien und Texte, Bd. 9, Leiden and Cologne, 1974).

Duby, G., *Hommes et structures du moyen âge. Recueil d'articles* (Le savoir historique, vol. 1, Paris and The Hague, 1973).

————, *Guerriers et paysans VIIe-XIIe siècle. Premier essor de l'économie européenne* (Bibliothèque des histoires, Paris, 1973).

————, "La féodalité? Une mentalité médiévale," *Annales, E.S.C.*, 13 (1958), 765-71; repr. *Hommes et structures*, pp. 103-10.

————, *L'an mille* (Collection Archives, no. 30, Paris, 1967).

————, *La société aux XIe et XIIe siècles dans la région mâconnaise*, 2nd ed. (Bibliothèque générale de l'Ecole pratique des hautes études, VIe section, Paris, 1971).

————, *Le chevalier, la femme et le prêtre. Le mariage dans la France féodale* (La force des idées, Paris, 1981).

————, "Les jeunes dans la société aristocratique dans la France du Nord-Ouest au XIIe siècle," *Annales, E.S.C.*, 19 (1964), 835-46; repr. *Hommes et structures*, pp. 214-25.

————, "Les laïcs et la paix de Dieu," in *I laici nella "societas christiana" dei secoli XI e XII*, pp. 448-61; repr. *Hommes et structures*, pp. 228-40.

————, *Rural Economy and Country Life in the Medieval West*, trans. C. Postan (Columbia, S.C., 1968).

Duchesne, L., "Notes sur la topographie de Rome au moyen âge VII: les légendes chrétiennes de l'Aventin," *Mélanges de l'Ecole française de Rome* 10 (1890), 225-50.

Dumas, A., "La parole et l'écriture dans les capitulaires carolingiens," *Mélanges Louis Halphen*, pp. 208-16.

Dumézil, G., *Mythe et épopée*, 3 vols. (Bibliothèque des sciences humaines, Paris, 1968-73).

Dumontier, M., *Saint Bernard et la Bible*, intro. J.-M. Déchanet (Bibliothèque de spiritualité médiévale, Paris, 1953).

Dupront, A., "De l'Acculturation," *XIIe Congrès International des Sciences Historiques, Vienne, 29 Août-5 Septembre 1965. Rapports I: Grands thèmes* (Vienna, 1965), 7-36.

————, "La spiritualité des croisés et des pèlerins d'après les sources de la première croisade," in *Pellegrinaggi e culto dei santi*, pp. 451-83.

Durand of Troarn, *Domni Durandi Abbatis Troarnensis Liber de Corpore et Sanguine Christi contra Berengarium et ejus Sectatores*, PL 149.1375-1424.

Dutton, P., "Raoul Glaber's *De Divisione Quaternitate*: An Unnoticed Reading of Eriugena's Translation of the *Ambigua* of Maximus the Confessor," *Mediaeval Studies* 42 (1980), 431-53.

Eadmer, *Eadmeri Historia Novorum in Anglia et Opusculo duo de Vita Sancti Anselmi et quibusdam Miraculis ejus*, ed. M. Rule (Rerum Britannicarum Medii Aevi Scriptores, vol. 81, London, 1884).

———, *The Life of St. Anselm Archbishop of Canterbury*, ed., intro., and trans. R. W. Southern, repr. (Oxford Medieval Texts, 1972).

Ebel, W., "Über den Leihegedanken in der deutschen Rechtsgeschichte," in T. Mayer, ed., *Studien zum mittelalterlichen Lehenswesen* (Vorträge und Forschungen, Bd. 5, Constance, 1960), 11-36.

✶Eisenstein, E., *The Printing Press as an Agent of Change. Communications and Cultural Transformations in Early Modern Europe*, 2 vols. (Cambridge, 1979).

Elcock, W. D., *The Romance Languages* (The Great Languages, London, 1960).

Endres, J. A., *Forschungen zur Geschichte der frühmittelalterlichen Philosophie* (Beiträge zur Geschichte der Philosophie des Mittelalters, Bd. 17, Heft 2-3, Münster, 1915).

Epistola A. Civis Spirensis ad Heribertum Coloniensem archiepiscopum adversus praeproperas peccatorum absolutiones, in Martène and Durand, *Veterum Scriptorum Monumentorum . . . Amplissima Collectio*, vol. 1 (Paris, 1724), cols. 357-59.

Epistola Trajectensis Ecclesiae ad Fridericum Episcopum Coloniensem de Tanchelmo seductore, AASS June, I, 832-33.

Erdmann, C., "Gregor VII. und Berengar von Tours," *Quellen und Forschungen aus italienischen Archiven und Bibliotheken* 28 (1937-38), 48-74.

———, *The Origin of the Idea of Crusade*, trans. M. W. Baldwin and W. Goffart (Princeton, 1977).

Esmein, A., *Cours élémentaire du droit français à l'usage des étudiants de première année*, 13th ed. (Paris, 1920).

Evans, A. P., "Social Aspects of Medieval Heresy," in *Persecution and Liberty. Essays in Honor of George Lincoln Burr* (New York, 1931), 93-116.

Evans, G. R., *Anselm and a New Generation* (Oxford, 1980).

———, *Anselm and Talking about God* (Oxford, 1978).

Eynde, D. van den, *Les Définitions des Sacrements pendant la première période de la théologie scolastique (1050-1240)* (Rome and Louvain, 1950).

Farkasfalvy, D., *L'inspiration de l'Ecriture sainte dans la théologie de saint Bernard* (Studia Anselmiana, fasc. 53, Rome, 1964).

Fasoli, G., "Gouvernants et gouvernées dans les communes italiennes du XIe au XIIIe siècle," in *Gouvernés et gouvernants*, 4e partie, pp. 47-86.

Fechter, J., *Cluny, Adel und Volk. Studien über der Verhältnis des Klosters zu den Ständen (910-1156)* (Stuttgart, 1966).

Fedele, P., "Richerche per la storia di Roma e del papato nel secolo X," *Archivio della Reale Società Romana di Storia Patria* 33 (1910), 177-247; 34 (1911), 75-115, 393-423.

Ferguson, W. K., *The Renaissance in Historical Thought* (Cambridge, Mass., 1948).

Ferrai, L. A., "Gli Annali di Dazio e i Patarini," *Archivio storico lombardo* 19 (1892), 509-48.

——, "I fonte di Landolfo Seniore," BIS 14 (1895), 7-70.

Festgabe zum 60. Geburstag Clemens Baeumker gewidmet von seinen Schülern und Freunden, 2 vols. (Beiträge zur Geschichte der Philosophie des Mittelalters, Supplementbd. I, Münster, 1913).

Festschrift zum 800-Jahresgedächtnis des Todes Bernhards von Clairvaux (Oesterreichische Beiträge zur Geschichte des Cistercienserordens, Vienna and Munich, 1953).

Fichtenau, H., " 'Carta' et 'Notitia' en Bavière du VIIIe au Xe siècle," *Le Moyen Age* 69 (1963), 105-20.

——, "Zum Reliquienwesen im früheren Mittelalter," MIöG 60 (1952), 60-89.

*Finucane, R. C., *Miracles and Pilgrims. Popular Beliefs in Medieval England* (London, 1977).

——, "The Use and Abuse of Medieval Miracles," *History* 60 (1975), 1-10.

Finnegan, R., *Oral Literature in Africa* (Oxford Library of African Literature, Oxford, 1970).

Fischer, J., *Die Erkenntnislehre Anselms von Canterbury nach den Quellen dargestellt* (Beiträge zur Geschichte der Philosophie des Mittelalters, Bd. 10, Heft 3, Münster, 1911).

Flach, J., "Le droit romain dans les chartes du IXe au XIe siècle," *Mélanges Fitting. LXXVe anniversaire M. le Professeur Hermann Fitting*, vol. 1 (Montpellier, 1902), 383-421.

Flasch, K., "Der philosophische Ansatz des Anselm von Canterbury im Monologion und sein Verhältnis zum Augustinischen Neuplatonismus," *Analecta Anselmiana* 2 (1970), 1-43.

——, "Zum Begriff der Wahrheit bei Anselm von Canterbury," *Philosophisches Jahrbuch* 72 (1965), 322-52.

Fliche, A., *La réforme grégorienne*, 3 vols. (Spicilegium Sacrum Lovaniense. Etudes et documents, fasc. 6, 9, and 16, Paris, 1924, 1925, and 1937).

Folghera, J.-D., "La verité définie par saint Anselme," *Revue thomiste* 8 (1900), 413-26.

Folkerts, M., *"Boethius" Geometrie II. Ein mathematisches Lehrbuch des Mittelalters* (Boethius. Texte und Abhandlungen zur Geschichte der exakten Wissenschaften, Bd. 9 Wiesbaden, 1970).

Folz, R., *Le Souvenir et la Légende de Charlemagne dans l'Empire germanique médiéval* (Publications de l'Université de Dijon, vol. 7, Paris, 1950).

Fournier, P., "Etude sur les fausses décrétales," RHE 7 (1906), 33-51, 310-16, 543-64, 761-84; 8 (1907), 19-56.

——, *Les officialités au moyen âge. Etude sur l'organisation, la compétence et la procédure des tribunaux ecclésiastiques ordinaires en France de 1180 à 1328* (Paris, 1880).

Fournier, P., and G. le Bras, *Histoire des collections canoniques en Occident depuis les fausses décrétales jusqu'au Décret de Gratien*, 2 vols. (Bibliothèque d'histoire du droit publiée sous les auspices de la Société d'histoire du droit, Paris, 1931-1932).

Fossier, R., "Les mouvements populaires en occident au XIe siècle," *Comptes rendus de l'Académie des Inscriptions et Belles-Lettres*, Année 1971, pp. 257-69.

France, J., "The Divine Quaternity of Rodulfus Glaber," *Studia Monastica* 17 (1975), 283-94.

Frank, R., *Old Norse Court Poetry. The Dróttkvaett Stanza* (Islandica, vol. 42, Ithaca and London, 1978).

Fredericq, P., *Corpus Documentorum Inquisitionis Haereticae Pravitatis Neerlandicae. Verzameling van stukken betreffende de pauselijkeen bisschoppelijke inquisitie in de Nederlanden*, vol. 1 (Hoogeschool van Gent. Werken van den practischen leergang van vaderlandsche geschiednis, 9, Ghent, 1889).

Frischmut, G., *Die paulinische Konzeption in der Frömmigkeit Bernhards von Clairvaux* (Beiträge zur Forderung Christlichen Theologie, vol. 37, fasc. 4, Gütersloh, 1933).

Frugoni, A., "Due schede: 'Pannosus' e 'Patarinus,' " BIS 65 (1953), 129-35.

Fuhrmann, H., "Das frühmittelalterliche Papsttum und die konstantinische Schenkung. Meditationen über ein unausgeführtes Thema," *I problemi dell'occidente nel secolo VIII*, pp. 257-92.

———, "Das Reformpapsttum und die Rechtswissenschaft," in J. Fleckenstein, ed., *Investiturstreit und Reichsverfassung*, pp. 175-203.

———, "Die Fälschungen im Mittelalter. Überlegungen zum mittelalterlichen Wahrheitsbegriff," *Historische Zeitschrift* 197 (1963), 529-54.

———, *Einfluss und Verbreitung der pseudoisidorischen Fälschungen. Von ihrem Auftauchen bis in die neuere Zeit* (Schriften der MGH, Bd. 24, 1-3, Stuttgart, 1972, 1973, and 1974).

Funke, B., *Grundlagen und Voraussetzungen der Satisfaktionstheorie des hl. Anselm von Canterbury, I. Teil*, diss. (Münster, 1903).

Gaiffier, B. de, "Hagiographie et historiographie," in *La storiografia altomedievale*, pp. 139-66.

———, "Intactam sponsam relinquens. A propos de la vie de S. Alexis," *Analecta Bollandiana* 65 (1947), 157-95.

———, "L'hagiographe et son public au XIe siècle," in *Miscellanea Historica in honorem Leonis van der Essen Universitatis Catholicae in Oppido Lovaniensi iam annos XXXV Professoris* (Brussels and Paris, 1947), vol. 1, pp. 135-66.

———, "Mentalité de l'hagiographe médiéval d'après quelques travaux récents," *Analecta Bollandiana* 86 (1968), 391-99.

———, "Pèlerinage et culte des saints: thème d'un congrès," in *Pellegrinaggi e culto dei santi*, pp. 11-35; repr. *Etudes critiques d'hagiographie et d'iconologie* (Brussels, 1967), 31-49.

Galbraith, V. H., "Raleigh Lecture on History. The Literacy of the Medieval English Kings," *Proceedings of the British Academy*, 5th Series, 21 (1935), 201-38.

Ganshof, F. L., "Charlemagne et l'usage de l'écrit en matière administrative," *Le Moyen Age* 57 (1951), 1-25.

————, *Feudalism*, trans. P. Grierson, with a foreword by Sir F. M. Stenton (London, 1952) (= *Qu'est-ce que la féodalité*, 2nd ed., Brussels and Neuchâtel, 1947, with corrections and additions).

————, *Frankish Institutions under Charlemagne*, trans. B. and M. Lyon (New York, 1970).

————, "La preuve dans le droit franc," in *La preuve, 2e partie*, pp. 71-98.

————, "Les relations féodo-vassaliques aux temps post-Carolingiens," *I problemi comuni dell'Europa post-carolingia* (Settimane di studio del Centro italiano di studi sull'alto medioevo, vol. 2, Spoleto, 1955), 67-114.

————, "L'origine des rapports féodo-vassaliques," *I problemi della civiltà carolingia* (Settimane di studio del Centro italiano di studi sull'alto medioevo, vol. 1, Spoleto, 1954), 27-69.

Gaudemet, J., "Les ordalies au moyen âge: doctrine, législation et pratique canoniques," *La preuve, 2e partie*, pp. 99-135.

Geiselmann, J., "Der Einfluss des Remigius von Auxerre auf die Eucharistielehre des Heriger von Lobbes," *Theologische Quartalschrift* 114 (1933), 222-44.

————, *Die Abendmahlslehre an der Wende der christlichen Spätantike zum Frühmittelalter. Isidor von Sevilla und das Sakrament der Eucharistie* (Munich, 1933).

————, *Die Eucharistielehre der Vorscholastik* (Forschungen zur christlichen Literatur-und Dogmengeschichte, Bd. 15, Paderborn, 1926).

————, "Die Stellung des Guibert von Nogent (†1124) in der Eucharistielehre der Frühscholastik," *Theologische Quartalschrift* 110 (1929), 67-84, 279-305.

————, "Ein neuentdecktes Werk von Tours über das Abendmahl?" *Theologische Quartalschrift* 118 (1937), 1-31, 133-72.

Gennep, A. van, *The Rites of Passage*, trans. M. B. Vizedom and G. L. Caffee (Chicago, 1960).

Gerstenberg, O., "Studien zur Geschichte des römischen Adels im Ausgange des 10. Jahrhunderts," *Historische Vierteljahrschrift* 31 (1937), 1-26.

Geyer, B., "Die alten lateinischen Übersetzungen der aristotelischen Analytik, Topik und Elenchik," *Philosophisches Jahrbuch* 30 (1917), 25-43.

————, "Die Stellung Abaelards in der Geschichte der Logik," in *Peter Abaelards philosophische Schriften II* (Beiträge . . . , 21, 4, 1933), 622-33.

Geyer, B., "Die Stellung Abaelards in der Universalienfrage nach neuen handschriftlichen Texten," *Festgabe Clemens Baeumker*, vol. 1, pp. 102-27.

Ghellinck, J. de, "Dialectique et dogme aux Xe-XIIe siècles. Quelques notes," *Festgabe Clemens Baeumker*, vol. 1, pp. 79-99.

————, "Iuventus, gravitas, senectus," *Studia Mediaevalia R. J. Martin*, pp. 39-59.

————, "Latin chrétien ou langue latine des chrétiens," *Les études classiques* 8 (1939), 449-78.

————, ed., *Pour l'histoire du mot "Sacramentum" I. Les anténicéens* (Spicilegium Sacrum Lovaniense. Etudes et documents, fasc. 3, Louvain and Paris, 1924).

Gibson, M., *Lanfranc of Bec* (Oxford, 1978).

Gilchrist, J. T., ed., *Diuersorum patrum sententie siue Collectio in LXXIV titulos digesta* (Monumenta Iuris Canonici, Series B: Corpus Collectionum, vol. 1, Vatican City, 1973).

————, "Gregory VII and the Juristic Sources of his Ideology," *Studia Gratiana* 12 (1967), 1-38.

————, "The Reception of Pope Gregory VII into the Canon Law (1073-1141)," ZRG KA 59 (1973), 35-82.

Gilson, E., *La théologie mystique de saint Bernard* (Etudes de philosophie médiévale, vol. 20, Paris, 1934).

————, " 'Regio dissimilitudinis' de Platon à Saint Bernard," *Mediaeval Studies* 9 (1947), 108-30.

————, "Sens et nature de l'argument de Saint Anselme," AHDLMA 9 (1934), 5-51.

Ginzburg, C., *Il formaggio e i vermi. Il cosmo di un mugnaio del '500*, 3rd ed. (Turin, 1976).

Giry, A., *Manuel de diplomatique. Diplômes et chartes, Chronologie technique, Eléments critiques et parties constitutives de la teneur des chartes, les chancelleries, les actes privés*, 2nd ed. (Paris, 1925).

Glaesener, H., "Godefroid de Bouillon. Etait-il 'un médiocre'?" RHE 39 (1943), 310-41.

Gliozzo, G., *La dottrina della conversione eucaristica in Pascasio Radberto e Ratramno, monaci di Corbia* (Pubblicazioni dell'Ignatianum, Messina, Serie teologica 1, Palermo, 1945).

Gössmann, E., *Antiqui und Moderni im Mittelalter. Eine geschichtliche Standortsbestimmung* (Veröffentlichen des Grabmann-Institutes zur Erforschung der mittelalterlichen Theologie und Philosophie, Neue Folge, vol. 23, Munich, Paderborn, and Vienna, 1974).

Goffart, W., *The Le Mans Forgeries. A Chapter from the History of Church Property in the Ninth Century* (Harvard Historical Studies, vol. 76, Cambridge, Mass., 1966).

Goldman, E., "Cartam levare," MIöG 35 (1914), 1-59.

Gombocz, W. L., "Abaelards Bedeutungslehre als Schlüssel zum Universalienproblem," in *Petrus Abaelardus*, pp. 153-64.

Goody, J., "Literacy and the Non-Literate," *Times Literary Supplement* (12 May 1972), 539-40.

——, ed., *Literacy in Traditional Societies* (Cambridge, 1968).

——, *The Domestication of the Savage Mind* (Cambridge, 1977).

Goody, J., and I. Watt, "The Consequences of Literacy," *Comparative Studies in Society and History* 5 (1962-1963), 304-45; repr. *Literacy in Traditional Societies*, pp. 27-68.

Gossen, C.-Th., "Graphème et phonème: le problème central de l'étude des langues écrites du moyen âge," *Revue de linguistique romane* 32 (1968), 1-16.

——, *Französische Skriptastudien. Untersuchungen zu den nordfranzösischen Urkundensprachen des Mittelalters* (Oesterreichische Akademie der Wissenschaften, phil.-hist. Kl., Sitzungsberichte, 253. Bd., Vienna, 1967).

Gougaud, L., "Muta Praedicatio," Rben 42 (1930), 168-71.

Gouvernés et gouvernants, deuxième partie: Antiquité et haut moyen âge; quatrième partie: Bas moyen âge et temps modernes (II) (Recueils de la Société Jean Bodin pour l'histoire comparative des institutions, vols. 23 and 25, Brussels, 1968, 1965).

Grabmann, M., "Die Entwicklung der mittelalterlichen Sprachlogik," in *Mittelalterliches Geistesleben. Abhandlungen zur Geschichte der Scholastik und Mystik*, vol. 1 (Munich, 1926), 104-46.

——, *Die Geschichte der scholastischen Methode. Nach den Gedructen und Ungedructen Quellen dargestellt*, 2 vols. (Freiburg-im-Breisgau, 1909-1911).

Graus, F., "Sozialgeschichtliche Aspekte der Hagiographie der Merowinger- und Karolingerzeit. Die Viten der Heiligen des südalemannischen Raumes und die sogennanten Adelsheiligen," in A. Borst, ed., *Mönchtum, Episkopat und Adel zur Gründungszeit des Klosters Reichenau* (Vorträge und Forschungen, Bd. 20, Sigmaringen, 1974), 131-76.

——, *Volk, Herrscher und Heiliger im Reich der Merowingerzeit. Studien zur Hagiographie der Merowingerzeit* (Prague, 1965).

Greenberg, J. H., *Language, Culture and Communication. Essays by Joseph H. Greenberg*. Selected and intro., A. S. Dil (Language, Science and National Development, Stanford, 1971).

Gregory, T., "Considérations sur Ratio et Natura chez Abélard," in *Pierre Abélard, Pierre le Vénérable*, pp. 569-81.

——, "L'idea di natura nella filosofia medievale prima dell'ingresso della fisica di Aristotle: il secolo XII," in *La filosofia della natura nel medioevo* (Atti del terzo Congresso internazionale di filosofia medioevale, Milan, 1966), 27-65.

——, *Anima Mundi. La filosofia di Guglielmo di Conches e la scuola di Chartres* (Florence, 1955).

Grossi, P., "Problematica strutturale dei contratti agrari nella esperienza giuridica dell'alto medioevo italiano," in *Agricoltura e mondo rurale*, pp. 487-529.

Grossus, G., *Vita Beati Bernardi Fundatoris Congregationis de Tironio in Gallia*, PL 172.1363-1446.

Grund, K., *Die Anschauungen des Radulfus Glaber in seinen Historien*, diss. (Greifswald, 1910).

Grundmann, H., "Adelsbekehrungen im Hochmittelalter. *Conversi* und *nutriti* im Kloster," in *Adel und Kirch. Gerd Tellenbach zum 65. Geburstag dargebracht von Freunden und Schülern*, ed. J. Fleckenstein and K. Schmid (Freiburg, Basle, and Vienna, 1968), 325-45; repr. *Ausgewählte Aufsätze*, vol. 1, 124-49.

————, *Ausgewählte Aufsätze*, 3 vols. (Schriften der MGH, Bd. 25, 1-3, Stuttgart, 1976, 1977, 1978).

————, *Bibliographie zur Ketzergeschichte des Mittelalters (1900-1966)* (Edizioni di storia e letteratura. Sussidi eruditi, vol. 20, Rome, 1967); repr. in *Hérésies et sociétés*, pp. 407-67.

————, "Hérésies savantes et hérésies populaires au moyen âge," in *Hérésies et sociétés*, pp. 209-14.

————, "Litteratus-illitteratus. Der Wandel einer Bildungsnorm vom Altertum zum Mittelalter," *Archiv für Kulturgeschichte* 40 (1958), 1-65; repr. in *Ausgewählte Aufsätze*, vol. 3, pp. 1-66.

————, "Neue Beiträge zur Geschichte der religiösen Bewegungen im Mittelalter," *Archiv für Kulturgeschichte* 37 (1955), 129-82; repr. in *Ausgewählte Aufsätze*, vol. 1, pp. 38-92.

————, *Religiöse Bewegungen im Mittelalter. Untersuchungen über die geschichtlichen Zusammenhänge zwischen der Ketzerei, den Bettleorden und der religiösen Frauenbewegung im 12. und 13. Jahrhundert and über die geschichtlichen Grundlagen der Deutschen Mystik* (Historische Studien, Heft 267, Berlin 1935; 2nd ed., Darmstadt, 1970).

Guenée, B., "Histoire, annales, chroniques. Essai sur les genres historiques au Moyen Age," *Annales, E.S.C.*, 28 (1973), 997-1016.

————, *Histoire et culture historique dans l'Occident médiéval* (Paris, 1981).

Guibert of Nogent, Ven. *Guiberti Abbatis in libros quatuor De Pignoribus Sanctorum*, PL 156.607-80.

————, *Histoire de sa vie (1053-1124)*, ed. G. Bourgin (Collection de textes pour servir à l'étude et à l'enseignement de l'histoire, fasc. 40, Paris, 1907).

Guitmund of Aversa, *Guitmundi Archiepiscopi Aversani De Corporis et Sanguinis Christi Veritate in Eucharistia libri tres*, PL 149.1427-94.

Gurevič, A., "Représentations et attitudes à l'égard de la propriété pendant le haut moyen âge," *Annales, E.S.C.*, 27 (1972), 523-47.

Guth, K., *Guibert von Nogent und die hochmittelalterliche Kritik an der Reliquienverehrung* (Studien und Mitteilungen zur Geschichte des Benediktiner-Ordens und seiner Zweige, 21. Ergänzungsbd., Ottobeuren, 1970).

Häring, N., "Abelard Yesterday and Today," in *Pierre Abélard, Pierre le Vénérable*, pp. 341-403.

————, "Alan of Lille, 'De Planctu Naturae,' " *Studi medievali*, 3rd Series, 19 (1978), 797-879.

————, "*Character, Signum* und *Signaculum.* Die Entwicklung bis nach der karolingischen Renaissance," *Scholastik* 30 (1955), 481-512.

————, "Die Vierzehn Capitula Heresum Petri Abaelardi," *Cîteaux. Commentarii Cistercienses* 31 (1980), 35-52.

————, "A Study in the Sacramentology of Alger of Liège," *Mediaeval Studies* 20 (1958), 41-78.

————, "The Creation and Creator of the World according to Thierry of Chartres and Clarenbaldus of Arras," AHDLMA 22 (1956), 138-216.

Häussling, A. A., *Mönchskonvent und Eucharistiefeier. Eine Studie über die Messe in der abendländischen Klosterliturgie des frühen Mittelalters und zur Geschichte der Messhäufigkeit* (Liturgiewissenschaftliche Quellen und Forschungen, Heft 58, Münster, 1973).

Hafstöm, G., "Die politischen Institutionen des skandinavischen Wikinger und deren Probleme," in *Agricoltura e mondo rurale*, pp. 57-69.

Hagenmeyer, H., *Le vrai et le faux sur Pierre l'Ermite. Analyse critique des témoignages historiques relatifs à ce personnage et des légendes auxquelles il a donné lieu*, trans. F. Raynaud (Paris, 1883).

Halbwachs, M., *Les cadres sociaux de la mémoire* (Bibliothèque de philosophie contemporaine. Travaux de l'Année sociologique, Paris, 1925).

Hall, R. A., "The Reconstruction of Proto-Romance," *Language* 26 (1950), 6-27.

Halphen, L., "Un pédagogue," *A travers l'histoire du moyen âge* (Paris, 1950), 277-85.

Hanning, R. W., *The Individual in Twelfth-Century Romance* (New Haven, 1977).

Hartmann, W., " 'Modernus' und 'Antiquus': Zur Verbreitung und Bedeutung dieser Bezeichnungen in der wissenschaftlichen Literatur vom 9. bis zum 12. Jahrhundert," in A. Zimmermann, ed., *Antiqui et Moderni: Traditionsbewusstsein und Fortschrittsbewusstsein im späten Mittelalter* (Miscellanea Mediaevalia. Veröffentlichen des Thomas-Instituts der Universität zu Köln, Bd. 9, Berlin, 1974), 21-39.

Haskins, C. H., *Norman Institutions* (Harvard Historical Studies, vol. 24, Cambridge, Mass., 1925).

————, *The Renaissance of the Twelfth Century* (Cambridge, Mass., 1927).

Hauck, A., *Kirchengeschichte Deutschlands*, (vol. 5.2 ed. H. Böhmer), 5 vols. (Leipzig, 1887-1920).

Havelock, E., *Preface to Plato* (Cambridge, Mass., 1963).

Hazeltine, H. D., "Comments on the Writings Known as Anglo-Saxon Wills," in D. Whitelock, ed., *Anglo-Saxon Wills* (Cambridge, 1930), vii-xl.

Helgaud de Fleury, *Vie de Robert le Pieux. Epitoma Vitae Regis Rotherti Pii*, ed. R.-H. Bautier and G. Labory (Sources d'histoire médiévale publiée par l'Institut de Recherche et d'Histoire des Textes, Paris, 1965).

Hendrickson, G. L., "Ancient Reading," *The Classical Journal* 25 (1929), 182-96.

Henry, D. P., *The 'De Grammatico' of St. Anselm. The Theory of Paronymy* (Publications in Mediaeval Studies. The University of Notre Dame, vol. 17, Notre Dame, 1964).

———, *The Logic of St. Anselm* (Oxford, 1967).

———, "Why 'Grammaticus'?" *Archivum Latinitatis Medii Aevi* 28 (1958), 165-80.

Hérésies et sociétés dans l'Europe pré-industrielle 11e-18e siècles. Communications et débats du Colloque de Royaumont présenté par J. Le Goff (Ecole pratique des hautes études, Sorbonne, VIe Section: sciences économiques et sociales. Centre de recherches historiques. Civilisations et sociétés, vol. 10, Paris and The Hague, 1968).

Heriger of Lobbes, *Gerberti postmodum Silvestri II papae Libellus de Corpore et Sanguine Domini* (wrongly attributed), PL 139.177-88.

Herlihy, D., "Life Expectancies for Women in Medieval Society," in R. T.
✦ Morewedge, ed., *The Role of Women in the Middle Ages. Papers of the Sixth Annual Conference of the Centre for Medieval and Early Renaissance Studies, State University of New York at Binghamton, 6-7 May 1972* (Albany, 1975), 1-22.

Hesbert, R.-J., "Saint Bernard et l'eucharistie," *Mélanges saint Bernard*, pp. 156-86.

Heurtevent, R., *Durand de Troarn et les origines de l'hérésie bérengarienne* (Etudes de théologie historique, vol. 5, Paris, 1912).

Heusler, A., *Institutionen des Deutschen Privatrechts*, 2 vols. (Systematisches Handbuch der Deutschen Rechtswissenschaft, Zweite Abtheilung, zweiter Theil, 1-2. Bd., Leipzig, 1885-1886).

Hiss, W., *Die Anthropologie Bernhards von Clairvaux* (Quellen und Studien zur Geschichte der Philosophie, Bd. 7, Berlin, 1964).

Hödl, L., "Die confessio Berengarii von 1059. Eine Arbeit zum frühscholastischen Eucharistietraktat," *Scholastik* 37 (1962), 370-94.

Höfische Dichtung oder Literatur im Feudalismus?, special number of the *Zeitschrift für Literaturwissenschaft und Linguistik*, Jahrgang 7, Heft 26 (1977).

Hoepffner, E., *La chanson de sainte Foy, tome 1er. Fac-similé du manuscrit et texte critique. Introduction et commentaire philologiques* (Publications de la Faculté des lettres de l'Université de Strasbourg, fasc. 32, Paris, 1926).

Hoffmann, H., *Gottesfriede und Treuga Dei* (Schriften der MGH, vol. 20, Stuttgart, 1964).

———, "Von Cluny zum Investiturstreit," *Archiv für Kulturgeschichte* 45 (1963), 165-203; revised in H. Richter, ed., *Cluny. Beiträge zur Gestalt und Wirking der cluniazensischen Reform* (Wege der Forschung, vol. 241, Darmstadt, 1975), 319-70.

Hofmeister, A., "Puer, Iuvenis, Senex: Zum Verständnis der mittelalterlichen Altersbezeichnungen," in A. Brackmann, ed., *Papsttum und Kai-*

sertum. Forschungen zur politischen Geschichte und Geisteskultur des Mittelalters. Paul Kehr zum 65. Geburstag (Munich, 1926), 287-316.

Holböck, F., *Der eucharistische und der mystische Leib Christi in ihren Beziehungen zueinander nach der Lehre der Frühscholastik* (Rome, 1941).

Holdsworth, C. J., "Christina of Markyate," in D. Baker, ed., *Medieval Women* (Studies in Church History, Subsidia 1, Oxford, 1978), 185-204.

Hollister, C. W., and J. W. Baldwin, "The Rise of Administrative Kingship: Henry I and Philip Augustus," *American Historical Review* 83 (1978), 867-905.

Hopkins, J., *A Companion to the Study of St. Anselm* (Minneapolis, 1972).

——, "Anselm's Debate with Gaunilo," *Analecta Anselmiana* 5 (1976), 25-53.

Hubert, J., "La vie commune de clercs et l'archéologie," in *La vita comune del clero*, vol. 1, pp. 90-111.

Huebner, R., *A History of Germanic Private Law*, trans. F. S. Philbrick (The Continental Legal Series Published under the auspices of the Association of American Law Schools, vol. 4, Boston, 1918).

Hugh of Langres, *Hugonis Tractatus de Corpore et Sanguine Christi contra Berengarium*, PL 142.1325-34.

Hugh of St. Victor, *Hugonis de Sancto Victore Didascalicon de Studio Legendi. A Critical Text*, ed. C. H. Buttimer (Catholic University of America. Studies in Medieval and Renaissance Latin, vol. 10, Washington, 1939).

Hughes, K., "The Changing Theory and Practice of Irish Pilgrimage," *Journal of Ecclesiastical History* 11 (1960), 143-51.

Huygens, R.B.C., "A propos de Bérenger et son traité de l'eucharistie," Rben 76 (1966), 133-39.

——, "Textes latins du XIe au XIIIe siècle," *Studi medievali*, 3rd Series, 8 (1967), 451-503.

I laici nella 'Societas Christiana' dei secoli XI e XII (Pubblicazioni dell'Università Cattolica del Sacro Cuore, Contributi, serie terza, varia 5: Miscellanea del Centro di studi medioevali, Milan, 1968).

Ilarino da Milano, "Le eresie populari del secolo XI nell'Europa occidentale," *Studi gregoriani* 2 (1947), 43-89.

Il matrimonio nella società altomedievale, 2 vols. (Settimane di studio del Centro italiano di studi sull'alto medioevo, vol. 24, Spoleto, 1977).

Illmer, D., *Formen der Erziehung und Wissensvermittlung im frühen Mittelalter. Quellenstudien zur Frage der Kontinuität des abendländischen Erziehungswesen* (Münchener Beiträge zur Mediävistik und Renaissance-Forschung, vol. 7, Munich, 1971).

——, "Zum Problem der Emazipationsgewohnheiten im merowingischen Frankenreich," in *L'enfant, 2e partie*, pp. 127-68.

Innis, H. A., *Empire and Communications*, revised by M. Q. Innis, foreword by M. McLuhan (Toronto, 1972).

——, *The Bias of Communication* (Toronto, 1951; repr. 1964).

I Normanni e la loro espansione in Europa nell'alto medioevo (Settimane di studio del Centro italiano di studi sull'alto medioevo, vol. 16, Spoleto, 1969).

Investiturstreit und Reichsverfassung, ed. J. Fleckenstein (Vorträge und Forschungen, Bd. 17, Sigmaringen, 1973).

I problemi dell'occidente nel secolo VIII (Settimane di studio del Centro italiano di studi sull'alto medioevo, vol. 20, Spoleto, 1973).

Ivánka, E. von, "La structure de l'âme selon S. Bernard," in *Saint Bernard théologien*, pp. 202-08.

Jacobi, E., "Der Prozess im Decretum Gratiani und bei den ältesten Dekretisten," ZRG KA 3 (1913), 223-343.

Jacobi, K., "Discussionen über Prädikationstheorie in den logischen Schriften des Petrus Abailardus," in *Petrus Abaelardus*, pp. 165-79.

Jacquin, A. M., "Le *De Corpore et Sanguine Domini* de Pascase Radbert," RSPT 8 (1914), 81-103.

———, "Les 'rationes necessariae' de saint Anselme," *Mélanges Mandonnet*, vol. 2, pp. 67-78.

Janauschek, L., *Bibliographia Bernardina qua Sancti Bernardi primi Abbatis Claravallensis Operum cum omnium tum singulorum Editiones ac Versiones Vitas et Tractatus de eo Scriptus quotquot usque ad Finem anni MDCCCXC reperire potuit* (Xenia Bernardina, pars quarta, Vienna, 1891).

Jason, H., "A Multidimensional Approach to Oral Literature," *Current Anthropology* 10 (1969), 413-26.

Jeauneau, E., " 'Nani gigantum humeris insidentes.' Essai d'interprétation de Bernard de Chartres," *Vivarium* 5 (1967), 79-99; repr. *Lectio Philosophorum. Recherches sur l'Ecole de Chartres* (Amsterdam, 1973), 55-73.

Jenkinson, H., *Palaeography and the Practical Study of Court Hand* (Cambridge, 1915).

John of Fécamp, *Albini Confessio Fidei* (wrongly attributed), PL 101.1027-98.

John of Salisbury, *Historia Pontificalis*, trans. M. Chibnall (Nelson's Medieval Texts, London, 1956).

———, *Ioannis Saresberiensis episcopi carnotensis Metalogicon libri IIII*, ed. C.C.J. Webb (Oxford, 1929).

Jolivet, J., *Arts du langage et théologie chez Abélard* (Etudes de philosophie médiévale, vol. 57, Paris, 1969).

Jorissen, H., *Die Entfaltung der Transsubstantiationslehre bis zum Beginn der Hochscholastik* (Münsterische Beiträge zur Theologie, Heft 28, 1, Münster, 1965).

Jousse, M., *Etudes de psychologie linguistique. Le style oral rhythmique et mnémotechnique chez les Verbo-moteurs* (Archives de philosophie, vol. 2, Paris, 1924).

Jungmann, J. A., *The Mass of the Roman Rite: its Origin and Development (Missarum Sollemnia)*, trans. F. A. Brunner, 2 vols. (New York, 1951, 1955).

Kantorowicz, H., ed., with the collaboration of W. W. Buckland, *Studies in the Glossators of the Roman Law. Newly discovered Writings of the Twelfth Century* (Cambridge, 1938); repr. ed., P. Weimar (Aalen, 1969).

Kaser, M., *Das römische Privatrecht, zweiter Abschnitt: Die nachklassischen Entwicklungen*, 2nd ed. (Rechtsgeschichte des Altertums im Rahmen des Handbuchs der Altertumswissenschaft, dritter Teil, dritter Bd., zweiter Abschnitt, Munich, 1975).

————, *Das römische Zivilprozessrecht* (Rechtsgeschichte des Altertums im Rahmen des Handbuchs der Altertumswissenschaft, dritter Teil, vierter Bd., Munich, 1976).

Kehr, P., "Scrinium und Palatium. Zur Geschichte des päpstlichen Kanzleiwesens im XI. Jahrhundert," MIöG VI. Ergänzungsbd. (1901), 70-112.

Keller, H., "Pataria und Stadtverfassung, Stadtgemeinde und Reform: Mailand im 'Investiturstreit,' " in *Investiturstreit und Reichsverfassung*, pp. 321-50.

Kenny, J. F., *The Sources for the Early History of Ireland. An Introduction and Guide* (Records of Civilization, Sources and Studies, no. 11, New York, 1929).

Kitzinger, E., *Early Medieval Art in the British Museum* (London, 1940).

Kleinclausz, A., "La légende du protectorat de Charlemagne sur la terre sainte," *Syria* 7 (1926), 211-33.

Kleineidam, E., "Wissen, Wissenschaft, Theologie bei Bernhard von Clairvaux," in *Bernhard von Clairvaux*, pp. 128-67.

Klewitz, H.-W., "Cancelleria. Ein Beitrag zur Geschichte des geistlichen Hofdienstes," *Deutsches Archiv für Geschichte des Mittelalters* 1 (1937), 44-79.

Knox, R., "Finding the Law. Developments in Canon Law during the Gregorian Reform," *Studi gregoriani* 9 (1972), 421-66.

Koch, G., *Frauenfrage und Ketzertum im Mittelalter. Die Frauenbewegung im Rahmen des Katharismus und des Waldensertums und ihre sozialen Wurzeln (12.-14. Jahrhundert)* (Forschungen zur mittelalterlichen Geschichte, Berlin, 1962).

Köhler, E., "Sens et fonction du terme 'jeunesse' dans la poésie des troubadours," *Mélanges R. Crozet*, vol. 1, pp. 569-83.

Kohlenberger, H. K., *Similitudo und Ratio. Überlegungen zur Methode bei Anselm von Canterbury* (Bonn, 1972).

————, "Zur Metaphysik des Visuellen bei Anselm von Canterbury," *Analecta Anselmiana* 1 (1969), 11-37.

Konrad, R., "Das himmlische und das irdische Jerusalem im mittelalterlichen Denken. Mystische Vorstellung und geschichtliche Wirkung," in C. Bauer, L. Boehm, and M. Müller, eds., *Speculum Historiale. Geschichte im Spiegel von Geschichtsschreibung und Geschichtsdeutung* (Freiburg and Munich, 1965), 523-40.

Kos, M., "Carta sine litteris," MIöG 62 (1954), 97-100.

Kunkel, W., *An Introduction to Roman Legal and Constitutional History*, trans. J. M. Kelly (Oxford, 1966).

Kuttner, S., "The Revival of Jurisprudence," in R. L. Benson *et al.*, eds., *Renaissance and Renewal in the Twelfth Century*, pp. 299-323.

Laarhoven, J. van, " 'Christianitas' et réforme grégorienne," *Studi gregoriani* 6 (1959-61), 1-98.

Labande, E.-R., " 'Ad limina.' Le pèlerin médiéval au terme de sa démarche," in *Mélanges R. Crozet*, vol. 1, pp. 283-91.

————, "Recherches sur les pèlerins dans l'Europe des XIe et XIIe siècles," CCM 1 (1958), 159-69, 339-47.

Lacroix, B., *L'historien au moyen âge* (Conférence Albert-le-Grand, Montréal and Paris, 1971).

Ladner, G., *Theologie und Politik vor dem Investiturstreit. Abendmahlstreit, Kirchenreform, Cluni und Heinrich III* (Veröffentlichen des Österreichischen Instituts für Geschichtsforschung, Bd. 2, Baden near Vienna, Leipzig, and Prague, 1936).

————, "Two Gregorian Letters on the Sources and Nature of Gregory VII's Reform Ideology," *Studi gregoriani* 5 (1956), 221-42.

Laistner, M.L.W., *Thought and Letters in Western Europe A.D. 500 to 900* (London, 1957).

✦Lambert, M., *Medieval Heresy. Popular Movements from Bogomil to Hus* (London and New York, 1977).

Landgraf, A., "Das Sacramentum in Voto in der Frühscholastik," *Mélanges Mandonnet*, vol. 2, pp. 97-143.

————, "Zur Methode der biblischen Textkritik im 12. Jahrhundert," *Biblica* 10 (1929), 445-74.

Landulf Senior, *Landulfi Historia Mediolanensis*, ed. L. C. Bethmann and W. Wattenbach, MGH SS 8, 32-100.

————, *Mediolanensis Historiae libri quattuor*, ed. A. Cutolo (Rerum Italicarum Scriptores . . . ordinata da L. A. Muratori . . . , nuova edizione ridevuta, ampliata e corretta, eds., G. Carducci, V. Fiorini, and P. Fedele, tomo 4, parte 2, Bologna, 1942).

Lanfranc of Bec, *Beati Lanfranci Cantuariensis Archiepiscopi De Corpore et Sanguine Domini adversus Berengarium Turonensem*, PL 150.407-442.

La Normandie bénédictine au temps de Guillaume le conquérant (XIe siècle) (Lille, 1967).

La piété populaire au moyen âge (Actes du 99e Congrès national des sociétés savantes, Besançon, 1974, section de philologie et d'histoire jusqu'à 1610, Paris, 1977).

La preuve, deuxième partie: Moyen âge et temps modernes (Recueils de la Société

Jean Bodin pour l'histoire comparative des institutions, vol. 17, Brussels, 1965).

La storiografia altomedievale, 2 vols. (Settimane di studio del Centro italiano di studi sull'alto medioevo, vol. 17, Spoleto, 1970).

La vie de saint Alexis, ed. C. Storey (Blackwell's French Texts, Oxford, 1946).

La vie de saint Alexis. Poème du XIe siècle, ed. G. Paris (Les classiques français du moyen âge, Paris, 1885; repr. up to 1925).

La vita comune del clero nei secoli XI e XII, 2 vols. (Pubblicazioni dell'Università Cattolica del Sacro Cuore, serie terza, scienze storiche 3: Miscellanea del Centro di studi medioevali 3, Milan, 1962).

Lavorel, L., "Oblats et corps du Christ sur l'autel d'après saint Ambrose," *Recherches de théologie ancienne et médiévale* 24 (1957), 205-24.

Leach, E. R., "Two Essays concerning the Symbolic Representation of Time," in E. R. Leach, *Rethinking Anthropology* (London, 1966), 124-36.

Lebon, J., "Sur la doctrine eucharistique d'Hériger de Lobbes," *Studia mediaevalia R. J. Martin*, pp. 61-84.

Leclercq, J., "Christusnachfolge und Sakrament in der Theologie des heiligen Bernhard," *Archiv für Liturgiewissenschaft* 8 (1963), 58-72.

———, "La date du 1er sermon sur le Cantique des cantiques," *Saint Bernard mystique* (Les grands mystiques, Paris, 1948), 480-83.

———, "Les formes successives de la lettre-traité de S. Bernard contre Abélard," Rben 78 (1968), 89-105.

———, "Les sermons sur les Cantiques ont-ils été prononcés?" Rben 65 (1955), 71-89; repr. *Recueil*, vol. 1, 193-212.

———, "Lettres de S. Bernard: histoire ou littérature," *Studi medievali*, 3rd Series, 12 (1971), 1-74.

———, "Monachisme et pérégrination," in *Aux sources de la spiritualité occidentale. Etapes et constantes* (Tradition et spiritualité, vol. 4, Paris, 1964), 35-90.

———, "Passage authentique inédit de Guitmond d'Aversa," Rben 57 (1947), 213-14.

———, *Recueil d'études sur S. Bernard et ses écrits*, 3 vols. (Storia e letteratura. Raccolta di studi et testi, vols. 92, 104 and 114, Rome, 1962, 1966 and 1969).

———, "Saint Bernard écrivain," Rben 70 (1960), 562-90; repr. in *Recueil*, vol. 1, pp. 321-51.

———, "S. Bernard et la tradition biblique d'après les Sermons sur les Cantiques," *Sacris Erudiri* 11 (1960), 225-48.

———, "Spiritualitas," *Studi medievali*, 3rd Series, 3 (1962), 279-96.

———, *The Love of Learning and the Desire for God. A Study of Monastic Culture*, trans. C. Misrahi (New York, 1961).

———, "The Renewal of Theology," in R. L. Benson *et al.* eds., *Renaissance and Renewal in the Twelfth Century*, pp. 68-87.

Leclercq, J., and J.-P. Bonnes, *Un maître de la vie spirituelle au XIe siècle: Jean de Fécamp* (Etudes de théologie et d'histoire de la spiritualité, vol. 9, Paris, 1946).

Lefranc, A., "Le traité des reliques de Guibert de Nogent et les commencements de la critique historique au moyen âge," *Etudes d'histoire du moyen âge dédiées à Gabriel Monod* (Paris, 1896), 285-306.

Legge, M. D., *Anglo-Norman Literature and its Background* (Oxford, 1963).

Le Goff, J., "Le rituel symbolique de la vassalité," in *Simboli e simbologia nell'alto medioevo* (Settimane di studio del Centro italiano di studi sull'alto medioevo, vol. 23, Spoleto, 1976), 679-788; repr. *Pour un autre Moyen Age*, pp. 349-420.

———, *Les intellectuels au moyen âge* (Paris, 1962).

———, *Pour un autre Moyen Age. Temps, travail et culture en Occident: 18 essais* (Bibliothèque des histoires, Paris, 1977).

Lemarignier, J.-F., "Structures monastiques et structures politiques dans la France de la fin du Xe et des débuts du XIe siècle," in *Il monachesimo nell'alto medioevo e la formazione della civiltà occidentale* (Settimane di studio del Centro di studi sull'alto medioevo, vol. 4, Spoleto, 1957), 357-400.

L'enfant, deuxième partie: Europe médiévale et moderne (Recueils de la Société Jean Bodin pour l'histoire comparative des institutions, vol. 36, Brussels, 1976).

L'eremitismo in occidente nei secoli XI e XII (Pubblicazioni dell'Università Cattolica del Sacro Cuore, contributi, seria terza, varia 4: Miscellanea del Centro di studi medioevali, vol. 4, Milan, 1965).

Le Roy Ladurie, E., *Montaillou, village occitan de 1294 à 1324* (Bibliothèque des histoires, Paris, 1975).

Lessing, G. E., *Berengarius Turonensis oder eine Ankündigung eines wichtigen Werkes desselben, wovon in der herzoglichen Bibliothek zu Wolfenbüttel ein manuscript befindlich, welches bisher völlig unerkannt geblieben* (Brunswick, 1770).

Lévi-Provençal, E., *España musulmana hasta la caída del califato de Córdoba (711-1031 de J.C.)*, 3rd ed. (Madrid, 1957).

Lévi-Strauss, C., *La pensée sauvage* (Paris, 1962).

Levy, E., *Gesammelte Schriften. Zu seinem achtigsten Geburtstag mit Unterstützung der Akademien der Wissenschaften zu Göttingen, Heidelberg und München sowie von Basler Freunden ihm dargebracht*, ed. W. Kunkel and M. Kaser, 2 vols. (Cologne and Graz, 1963).

———, *West Roman Vulgar Law. The Law of Property* (Memoirs of the American Philosophical Society Held at Philadelphia for Promoting Useful Knowledge, vol. 29, Philadelphia, 1951).

———, *Weströmisches Vulgarrecht. Das Obligationenrecht* (Forschungen zum römischen Recht, 7. Abhandlung, Weimar, 1956).

Lévy, J.-P., "L'évolution de la preuve des origines à nos jours," *La preuve, 2e partie*, pp. 9-70.

Leyerle, J., "The Interlace Structure of *Beowulf*," *University of Toronto Quarterly* 37 (1967), 1-17.

Liebeschütz, H., "Kosmologische Motive in der Bildungswelt der Frühscholastik," *Vorträge der Bibliothek Warburg 1923-1924* (Leipzig and Berlin, 1926), 83-148.

Lindberg, D. C., "Alhazen's Theory of Vision and its Reception in the West," *Isis* 58 (1967), 321-41.

Linhardt, R., *Die Mystik des hl. Bernhard von Clairvaux* (Munich, 1923).

Little, E., "Bernard and Abelard at the Council of Sens, 1140," in *Bernard of Clairvaux*, pp. 55-71.

Löfstedt, E., *Late Latin* (Instituttet for sammenlignende Kulturforskning, Serie A: forelesinger 25, Oslo, 1959).

ᐧ.Lopez, R. S., "An Aristocracy of Money in the Early Middle Ages," *Speculum* 28 (1953), 1-43.

ᐧ.————, "The Culture of the Medieval Merchant," in D.B.J. Randall, ed., *Medieval and Renaissance Studies. Proceedings of the Southeastern Institute of Medieval and Renaissance Studies, 1976* (Medieval and Renaissance Series, No. 8, Durham, 1979), 52-73.

Lord, A. B., "Perspectives on Recent Work on Oral Literature," in J. J. Duggan, ed., *Oral Literature. Seven Essays* (Edinburgh and London, 1975).

Lot, F., "Le mythe des terreurs de l'an mille," *Mercure de France* 300 (1947), 639-55; repr. in *Recueil des travaux de F. Lot*, vol. 1 (Centre de recherches d'histoire et de philosophie de la IVe Section de l'Ecole pratique des hautes études, 5: Hautes études médiévales et modernes, vol. 4, Geneva and Paris, 1968), 398-414.

Lubac, H. de, *Corpus Mysticum. L'eucharistie et l'Eglise au moyen âge. Etude historique* (Théologie, vol. 3, Paris, 1954).

————, *Exégèse médiévale. Les quatre sens de l'Ecriture*, 4 vols. (Théologie, vols. 41, 42, and 59, Paris, 1959-1964).

Lüdke, H., "Die Entstehung romanischer Schriftsprachen," *Vox Romanica* 23 (1964), 4-21.

————, *Geschichte des romanischen Wortschatzes*, 2 vols. (Freiburg-im-Breisgau, 1968).

Luscombe, D. E., *The School of Peter Abelard. The Influence of Abelard's Thought in the Early Scholastic Period* (Cambridge Studies in Medieval Life and Thought, New Series, vol. 14, Cambridge, 1969).

Macdonald, A. J., *Berengar and the Reform of Sacramental Doctrine* (London, 1930).

MacKinney, L. C., "The People and Public Opinion in the Eleventh-Century Peace Movement," *Speculum* 5 (1930), 181-206.

Mallon, J., *Paléographie romaine* (Scripturae Monumenta et Studia, vol. 3, Madrid, 1952).

Manitius, M., *Geschichte der lateinischen Literatur des Mittelalters*, 3 vols. (Handbuch der klassischen Altertumswissenschaft, 9, 2, 1-3, Munich, 1911-1931).

Manselli, R., *L'eresia del male* (Collana di storia, vol. 1, Naples, 1963).

Manselli, R., "Una designazione dell'eresia catara: 'Arriana Heresis,' " BIS 68 (1956), 233-46.

Markus, R. A., ed., *Augustine. A Collection of Critical Essays* (Modern Studies in Philosophy AP 13, New York, 1972).

Marrou, H. I., *A History of Education in Antiquity*, trans. G. Lamb (London, 1956).

Mastrelli, C. A., "Romania-Germania: Mündliche und schriftliche Überlieferung," in *Oral Tradition, Literary Tradition*, pp. 83-92.

———, "Vicende linguistiche del secolo VIII," in *I problemi dell'occidente nel secolo VIII*, vol. 2, 803-31.

Mathon, G., "Jean de Fécamp, théologien monastique? (Notes de lecture de *Confessio fidei* III, 36-40)," in *La Normandie bénédictine*, pp. 485-500.

———, "Pascase Radbert et l'évolution de l'humanisme carolingien. Recherches sur la signification des Préfaces des livres I et III de l'*Expositio in Matthaeum*," in *Corbie, abbaye royale*, pp. 135-55.

Mattoso, J., "A 'lectio divina' nos autores monásticos da alta Idade Média," *Studia Monastica* 9 (1967), 167-87.

Matronola, M., *Un testo inedito di Berengario di Tours e il concilio romano del 1079* (Milan, 1936).

Mauss, M., "Essai sur le don. Forme et raison de l'échange dans les sociétés archaïques," in M. Mauss, *Sociologie et anthropologie*, intro. C. Lévi-Strauss, 4th ed. (Paris, 1968), 145-71.

McGinn, B., "*Iter Sancti Sepulchri*: The Piety of the First Crusaders," in B. K. Lackner and K. R. Philip, eds., *The Walter Prescott Webb Memorial Lectures. Essays on Medieval Civilization by Richard E. Sullivan, Bernard McGinn, Bede Karl Lackner, David Herlihy, Frederic L. Cheyette* (Austin and London, 1978), 33-71.

———, "Saint Bernard and Eschatology," in *Bernard of Clairvaux*, pp. 161-85.

McIntyre, J., "Premises and Conclusions in the System of Anselm's Theology," *Spicilegium Beccense I*, pp. 95-101.

———, *St. Anselm and his Critics. A Re-Interpretation of the 'Cur Deus Homo'* (London, 1954).

McLuhan, M., *The Gutenberg Galaxy. The Making of Typographic Man* (Toronto, 1962).

⬩McLaughlin, M., "Abelard as Autobiographer: The Motives and Meaning of the 'Story of the Calamities,' " *Speculum* 42 (1967), 463-88.

Meersseman, G. G., "Eremitismo e predicazione itinerante dei secoli XI e XII," in *L'eremitismo in occidente nei secoli XI e XII*, pp. 164-79.

Mélanges d'histoire du moyen âge dédiés à la mémoire de Louis Halphen, intro. C.-E. Perrin (Paris, 1951).

Mélanges Mandonnet. Etudes d'histoire littéraire et doctrinale du moyen âge, 2 vols. (Bibliothèque thomiste, vols. 13-14, Paris, 1930).

Mélanges offerts à René Crozet à l'occasion de son soixante-dixième anniversaire par ses amis, ses collègues, ses élèves et les membres du C.E.S.C.M., ed. P. Gallais and Y.-J. Riou, 2 vols. (Poitiers, 1966).

Mélanges saint Bernard. XXVe Congrès de l'Association bourguignonne des sociétés savantes (Dijon, 1953).

Menéndez Pidal, R., *Orígenes del español, estado lingüístico de la península iberíca hasta el siglo XI*, 3rd ed. (Madrid, 1950).

Metz, R., "L'enfant dans le droit canonique médiéval. Orientations de recherche," in *L'enfant, 2e partie*, pp. 9-96.

Mews, C., "The Development of the Theologia of Peter Abelard," in *Petrus Abaelardus*, pp. 183-98.

Meynial, E., "Remarques sur la réaction populaire contre l'invasion du droit romain en France aux XIIe et XIIIe siècles," *Mélanges Chabaneau. Volume offert à Camille Chabaneau à l'occasion du 75e anniversaire de sa naissance (4 mars 1906) par ses élèves, ses amis et ses admirateurs* (Erlangen, 1907), 557-84.

Miccoli, G., *Chiesa gregoriana. Ricerche sulla Riforma del secolo XI* (Storici antichi e moderni, nuova serie, vol. 17, Florence, 1966).

Michaud-Quantin, P., "Notes sur le vocabulaire psychologique de saint Anselme," *Spicilegium Beccense I*, pp. 23-43.

Migliorini, B., *The Italian Language*, ed. and trans. T. G. Griffith (The Great Languages, London, 1966).

Millàs Vallicrosa, J., "La introducción del cuadrante con cursor en Europa," *Isis* 17 (1932), 218-58.

Mingroot, E. van, "Acta Synodi Atrebatensis (1025): problèmes de critique de provenance," *Studia Gratiana* 20 (1976), 201-29.

Mireux, M.-D., "Guibert de Nogent et la critique du culte des reliques," in *La piété populaire au moyen âge*, pp. 293-301.

Mitteis, H., *Die Rechtsgeschichte und das Problem der historischen Kontinuität* (Abhandlungen der Deutschen Akademie der Wissenschaften zu Berlin, Jahrgang 1947, phil.-hist. Kl., Berlin, 1947).

Mohr, W., "Tanchelm von Antwerpen. Eine nochmalige Überprüfung der Quellenlage," *Annales Universitatis Saraviensis, philosophie-lettres*, 3 (1954), 234-47.

Mohrmann, C., *Etudes sur le latin des chrétiens*, 4 vols. (Storia e letteratura. Raccolta di studi e testi, vols. 65, 87, 103, and 143, Rome, 1958 [2nd ed., 1961], 1961, 1965, and 1977).

———, *Latin vulgaire, latin des chrétiens, latin médiéval* (Paris, 1955).

———, "Observations sur la langue et le style de saint Bernard," in *S. Bernardi Opera*, vol. 2 (1958), ix-xxxiii.

Mollard, A., "L'imitation de Quintilien dans Guibert de Nogent," *Le Moyen Age*, 3rd Series, 5 (1934), 81-87.

Moneta e scambi nell'alto medioevo (Settimane di studio del Centro italiano di studi sull'alto medioevo, Spoleto, 1961).

Monod, B., *Le moine Guibert et son temps*, intro. E. Gebhart (Paris, 1905).

Montclos, J. de, *Lanfranc et Bérenger. La controverse eucharistique du XIe siècle* (Spicilegium Sacrum Lovaniense. Etudes et documents, fasc. 37, Louvain, 1971).

Moore, R. I., "Family, Community and Cult on the Eve of the Gregorian Reform," *Transactions of the Royal Historical Society*, 5th Series, vol. 30 (London, 1980), 49-69.

————, "Heresy as Disease," in *The Concept of Heresy*, pp. 1-11.

————, *The Origins of European Dissent* (London, 1977).

————, "The Origins of Medieval Heresy," *History* 55 (1970), 21-36.

Moore, S. G., and B. G. Myerhoff, "Secular Ritual: Forms and Meanings," in *Secular Ritual*, ed. S. G. Moore and B. G. Myerhoff (Assen, 1977), 3-24.

Mor, G. C., "Gouvernés et gouvernants en Italie du VIe au XIIe siècle," *Gouvernés et gouvernants, 2e partie*, pp. 395-420.

Mordek, H., *Kirchenrecht und Reform im Frankenreich. Die Collectio Vetus Gallica, die älteste systematische Kanonessammlung des fränkischen Gallien. Studien und Edition* (Beiträge zur Geschichte und Quellenkunde des Mittelalters, Bd. 1, Berlin and New York, 1975).

Moreau, E. de, *Histoire de l'Eglise en Belgique*, vol. 2: *La formation de l'Eglise médiévale* (Museum Lessianum, Section historique, No. 2, Brussels, 1945).

Morghen, R., "Il cosidetto neo-manicheismo occidentale del secolo XI," in *Oriente ed Occidente nel Medio Evo*, pp. 84-104.

————, "Problèmes sur l'origine de l'hérésie au Moyen Age," *Revue historique* 336 (1966), 1-16; repr. and revised in *Hérésies et sociétés*, pp. 121-38.

Morin, G., "Un critique en liturgie au XII siècle. Le traité inédit d'Hervé de Bourgdieu *De correctione quarundam lectionum*," Rben 24 (1907), 36-61.

Mouroux, J., "Sur les critères de l'expérience spirituelle d'après les sermons sur le Cantique des cantiques," in *Saint Bernard théologien*, pp. 253-67.

Mumford, L., *Technics and Civilization* (New York, 1934).

✱ Murray, A., *Reason and Society in the Middle Ages* (Oxford, 1978).

Musset, L., "Les domaines de l'époque franque et les destinées du régime domanial," *Bulletin de la Société des antiquaires de Normandie* 49 (1942-45), 7-97.

Musy, J., "Mouvements populaires et hérésies au XIe siècle en France," *Revue historique* 253 (1975), 33-76.

Nash, M., *Primitive and Peasant Economic Systems* (Scranton, Penn., 1966).

Navigatio Sancti Brendani Abbatis from Early Latin Manuscripts, ed. C. Selmer (Publications in Mediaeval Studies. The University of Notre Dame, vol. 16, Notre Dame, 1959).

Nichols, S. G., Jr., *Formulaic Diction and Thematic Composition in the Chanson de Roland* (North Carolina University. Studies in the Romance Languages and Literatures, vol. 36, Chapel Hill, 1961).

Nock, A. D., "Hellenistic Mysteries and Christian Sacraments," *Mnemosyne*, 4th Series, 5 (1952), 177-213.

Noiroux, J.-M., "Les deux premiers documents concernant l'hérésie au Pays-Bas," RHE 49 (1954), 842-55.

Notopoulos, J. A., "Mnemosyne in Oral Literature," *Transactions and Proceedings of the American Philological Association* 69 (1938), 465-93.

Ogden, C. K., and I. A. Richards, *The Meaning of Meaning. A Study of the Influence of Language upon Thought and of the Science of Symbolism, with supplementary essays by B. Malinowski and F. G. Crookshank* (London, 1923).

✗ Ong, W., *The Presence of the Word. Some Prolegomena for Cultural and Religious History* (The Terry Lectures, New Haven, 1967).

Oral Tradition, Literary Tradition. A Symposium. Proceedings of the First International Symposium organized by the Centre for the Study of Vernacular Literature in the Middle Ages, Odense University, 22-23 November, 1976 (Odense, 1977).

Orderic Vitalis, *Orderici Vitalis Historia Aecclesiastica. The Ecclesiastical History of Orderic Vitalis*, ed. and trans. M. Chibnall, 6 vols. (Oxford Medieval Texts, Oxford, 1969-1980).

Oriente e Occidente nel Medio Evo (Convegno "Volta" di scienze morale, storiche e filologiche, 27 maggio-1 guigno 1956. Accademia nazionale dei Lincei, Atti, 8th Series, vol. 12, Rome, 1957).

Orsi, P., "L'anno Mille (saggio di critica storia)," *Rivista storica italiana* 4 (1887), 1-56.

Otto of Freising, *Ottonis Episcopi Frisingensis Chronica sive Historia de Duabus Civitatibus*, ed. A. Hofmeister (Scriptores Rerum Germanicarum in Usum Scholarum ex Monumentis Germaniae Historicis separatim editi, vol. 45, Hanover and Leipzig, 1912).

Ourliac, P., and J. de Malafosse, *Histoire du droit privé*, 3 vols. (Thémis. Manuels juridiques, économiques et politiques, Paris, 1957, 1961, and 1968).

Oury, G., "L'idéal monastique dans la vie canoniale. Le Bienheureux Hervé de Tours (†1022)," *Revue Mabillon* 52 (1962), 1-31.

Oskamp, H.P.A., *The Voyage of Máel Dúin. A Study in Early Irish Voyage Literature, followed by an Edition of Immram curaig Máele Dúin from the Yellow Book of Lecan in Trinity College, Dublin* (Groningen, 1970).

Pächt, O., C. R. Dodwell, and F. Wormald, *The St. Albans Psalter (Albani Psalter)* (Studies of the Warburg Institute, vol. 25, London, 1960).

Palmer, R. E., *Hermeneutics. Interpretation Theory in Schleiermacher, Dilthey, Heidegger, and Gadamer* (Northwestern University Studies in Phenomenology and Existential Philosophy, Evanston, Ill., 1969).

? Panofsky, E., *Gothic Architecture and Scholasticism. An Inquiry into the Analogy of the Arts, Philosophy and Religion in the Middle Ages* (Wimmer Lecture, 1948, Latrobe, Penn., 1951).

———, *Renaissance and Renascences in Western Art. Text* (Stockholm, 1960).

Paratore, E., "San Bernardo scrittore," in *Studi su San Bernardo*, pp. 261-79.

Parent, J.-M., *La doctrine de la création dans l'école de Chartres. Etude et textes*

(Publications de l'Institut d'Etudes Médiévales d'Ottawa, vol. 8, Paris and Ottawa, 1938).

✱Parkes, M., "The Influence of Concepts of *Ordinatio* and *Compilatio* on the Development of the Book," in J.J.G. Alexander and M. T. Gibson, eds., *Medieval Learning and Literature. Essays presented to Richard William Hunt* (Oxford, 1976), 115-41.

————, "The Literacy of the Laity," in D. Daiches and A. Thorlby, eds., ✱ *The Mediaeval World* (Literature and Western Civilization, vol. 2, London, 1973), 555-77.

◀ Partner, N. F., *Serious Entertainments. The Writing of History in Twelfth-Century England* (Chicago, 1977).

Paschasius Radbertus, *De Corpore et Sanguine Domini*, ed. B. Paulus (CCCM 16, Turnhout, 1969).

————, *S. Paschasii Radberti Abbatis Corbeiensis Expositio in Evangelium Matthaei*, PL 120.31-994.

Pellegrinaggi e culto dei santi in Europa fino alla IA Crociata (Convegni del Centro di studi sulla spiritualità medievale, vol. 4, Todi, 1963).

Pellegrini, C., "Fonti e memorie storiche di S. Arialdo," *Archivio storico lombardo*, anno 27, vol. 14 (1900), 209-36.

Peter Abelard. Proceedings of the International Conference Louvain May 10-12, 1971, ed. E. M. Buytaert (Mediaevalia Lovaniensia, Series 1, Studia 2, Louvain, 1974).

Petrucci, A., ed., *Notarii. Documenti per la storia del notariato italiano* (Milan, 1958).

Petrus Abaelardus (1079-1142). Person, Werk und Wirkung, ed. R. Thomas, with the collaboration of J. Jolivet, D. E. Luscombe, and L. M. de Rijk (Trier theologische Studien, Bd. 38, Trier, 1980).

Phillips, H., *John Wyclif's "De Eucharistia" in its Medieval Setting*, diss. (Toronto, 1980).

Picavet, F., *Roscelin philosophe et théologien d'après la légende et d'après l'histoire. Sa place dans l'histoire générale et comparée des philosophes médiévales* (Paris, 1911).

Pierre Abelard, Pierre le Vénérable. Les courants philosophiques, littéraires et artistiques en occident au milieu du XIIe siècle, ed. R. Louis, J. Jolivet, and J. Châtillon (Colloques internationaux du Centre national de la recherche scientifique, no. 546, Paris, 1975).

Pirenne, H., "L'instruction des marchands au moyen âge," *Annales d'histoire économique et sociale* 1 (1929), 13-28.

————, "Tanchelm et le projet de démembrement du diocèse d'Utrecht vers 1100," *Académie royale de Belgique. Bulletins de la Classe des lettres et des sciences morales et politiques*, série 5, vol. 13 (1927), 112-19.

Plaine, F., "Les prétendues terreurs de l'an mille," *Revue des questions historiques* 13 (1873), 145-64.

Polanyi, K., "The Economy as an Instituted Process," in K. Polanyi, C. M.

Arensberg, and H. W. Pearson, eds., *Trade and Market in Early Empires. Economics in History and Theory* (New York, 1957), 243-70.

Pollock, Sir F., and F. W. Maitland, *The History of English Law before the time of Edward I*, 2nd ed., intro. S.F.C. Milsom, 2 vols. (Cambridge, 1968).

Poole, R. L., *Lectures on the History of the Papal Chancery down to the Time of Innocent III* (Cambridge, 1915).

Pope, M. K., *From Latin to Modern French with Especial Consideration of Anglo-Norman. Phonology and Morphology*, 2nd ed. (Publications of the University of Manchester, 229, French Series, No. 6, London, 1952).

Poschmann, B., *Die abendländische Kirchenbusse im frühen Mittelalter* (Breslauer Studien zur historischen Theologie, Bd. 16, Breslau, 1930).

——, *Penance and the Anointing of the Sick* (Herder History of Dogma, vol. 4, part 3, Freiburg, 1964).

Postan, M. M., *Essays on Medieval Agriculture and General Problems of the Medieval Economy* (Cambridge, 1973).

Pouchet, R., *La rectitudo chez saint Anselme. Un itinéraire Augustinien de l'Ame à Dieu* (Paris, 1964).

Pra, M. del, *Logica e realtà. Momenti di pensiero medievale* (Biblioteca di Cultura Moderna 765, Bari, 1974).

Prevenier, W., "La chancellerie des comtes de Flandre dans le cadre européen à la fin du XIIe siècle," *Bibliothèque de l'Ecole des Chartes* 125 (1967), 34-93.

Prou, M., *Manuel de paléographie latine et française du Ve au XVIIe siècle suivi d'un dictionnaire des abbréviations avec 23 fac-similés en phototypie*, 2nd ed. (Paris, 1892).

Puech, H.-C., "Catharisme médiéval et Bogomilisme," in *Oriente e Occidente nel Medio Evo*, pp. 56-84.

Pulgram, E., "Graphic and Phonic Systems: Figurae and Signs," *Word* 21 (1965), 208-24.

——, "Phoneme and Grapheme: a Parallel," *Word* 7 (1951), 15-20.

Rassow, P., "Die Kanzlei St. Bernhards von Clairvaux," *Studien und Mitteilungen zur Geschichte des Benedikten-Ordens und seiner Zweige* 34 (1913), 63-103, 243-93.

Ratramnus of Corbie, *Ratramnus de Corpore et Sanguine Domini. Texte établi d'après les manuscrits et notice bibliographique*, ed. J. N. Bakhuizen van den Brink (Verhandelingen der Koninklijke Nederlandse Akademie van Wetenschappen, Afd. Letterkunde, Nieuwe Reeks, Deel 61, No. 1, Amsterdam, 1954).

Ray, R. D., "Orderic Vitalis and his Readers," *Studia Monastica* 14 (1972), 18-33.

Raymond d'Aguilers, *Raimundi de Aguilers Canonici Podiensis Historia Francorum qui Ceperunt Iherusalem* (Recueil des historiens des croisades. Historiens occidentaux, vol. 3, Paris, 1866), part 4, pp. 230-309.

Raynaud de Lage, G., *Alain de Lille, poète du XIIe siècle* (Université de Montréal. Publications de l'Institut d'études médiévales, vol. 12, Montréal and Paris, 1951).

Recht und Schrift im Mittelalter, ed. P. Classen (Vorträge und Forschungen, Bd. 23, Sigmaringen, 1977).

Redfield, R., *Peasant Society and Culture. An Anthropological Approach to Civilization* (Chicago, 1956).

————, *The Primitive World and its Transformations* (Ithaca, 1953).

Relazioni del X Congresso Internazionale di Scienze Storiche, Roma, 4-11 settembre, 1955, vol. 3: *Storia del medioevo* (Biblioteca Storica Sansoni, nuova serie, vol. 24, Florence, 1955).

Renouard, Y., *Les villes d'Italie de la fin du Xe siècle au début du XIVe siècle*, ed. Ph. Braunstein, 2 vols. (Regards sur l'histoire, vols. 8-9, Paris, 1969).

Reynolds, R. E., "Liturgical Scholarship at the Time of the Investiture Controversy," *Harvard Theological Review* 71 (1978), 112-18.

Riché, P., *Education and Culture in the Barbarian West From the Sixth through the Eighth Century*, trans. J. J. Contreni, intro. R. E. Sullivan (Columbia, S.C., 1976).

————, "L'instruction des laïcs au XIIe siècle," *Mélanges Saint Bernard*, pp. 214-17.

————, "Recherches sur l'instruction des laïcs du IXe au XIIe siècle," CCM 5 (1962), 175-82.

Richter, D., "Die Allegorie der Pergamentbearbeitung. Beziehungen zwischen handwerklichen Vorgängen und der geistlichen Bildersprache des Mittelalters," in G. Keil, R. Rudolf, W. Schmitt, and H. J. Nermeer, eds., *Fachliteratur des Mittelalters. Festschrift für Gerhard Eis* (Stuttgart, 1968), 83-92.

Richter, M., "Kommunikationsprobleme im lateinischen Mittelalter," *Historische Zeitschrift* 222 (1976), 43-80.

Ries, J., *Das geistliche Leben in seinen Entwicklungsstufen nach der Lehre des hl. Bernhard, Quellenmässig dargestellt* (Freiburg-im-Breisgau, 1906).

————, "Die Kontemplationsarten nach der Lehre des hl. Bernhard," *Jahrbuch für Philosophie und Spekulative Theologie* 23 (1909), 150-78.

Rijk, L. M. de, *Garlandus compostista, Dialectica. First Edition of the Manuscripts with an Introduction on the Life and Works of the Author and on the Contents of the Present Work* (Wijsgerige Teksten en Studies, vol. 3, Assen, 1959).

Rivière, J., *Le dogme de la rédemption au début du moyen âge* (Bibliothèque thomiste, vol. 19, Paris, 1934).

Robson, C. A., "Literary Language, Spoken Dialect and the Phonological Problem in Old French," *Transactions of the Philological Society, 1955* (Oxford, 1956), 117-80.

Rochais, H., and J. Leclercq, "La tradition des sermons liturgiques de S. Bernard," *Scriptorium* 15 (1961), 240-84.

Rodulfus Glaber, *Raoul Glaber. Les cinq livres de ses histoires (900-1044)*, ed.

M. Prou (Collection de textes pour servir à l'étude et à l'enseignement de l'histoire, fasc. 1, Paris, 1886).

Roques, R., "Derisio, Simplicitas, Insipientia. Remarques mineurs sur la terminologie de saint Anselme," in L'homme devant Dieu. Mélanges offerts au Père Henri de Lubac (Théologie, vol. 57, Paris, 1963), vol. 2, pp. 47-61.

————, "Structure et caractères de la prière Anselmienne," in Sola ratione, pp. 119-87.

Rouse, R., "Biblical Distinctiones in the Thirteenth Century," AHDLMA 41 (1974), 27-37.

Rouse, R., and M. A. Rouse, Preachers, Florilegia and Sermons: Studies in the 'Manipulus florum' of Thomas of Ireland (Pontifical Institute of Mediaeval Studies. Studies and Texts, vol. 47, Toronto, 1979).

————, "Statim invenire: Schools, Preachers, and New Attitudes to the Page," in R. L. Benson et al eds., Renaissance and Renewal in the Twelfth Century, pp. 201-25.

Runciman, S., "The Holy Lance Found at Antioch," Analecta Bollandiana 68 (1950), 197-209.

Russell, J. B., "A propos du synode d'Arras en 1025," RHE 57 (1962), 66-87.

————, Dissent and Reform in the Early Middle Ages (Publications of the Center for Medieval and Renaissance Studies, vol. 1, Berkeley and Los Angeles, 1965).

————, "Interpretations of the Origins of Medieval Heresy," Mediaeval Studies 25 (1963), 26-53.

Rychner, J., La Chanson de geste. Essai sur l'art épique des jongleurs (Société de publications romanes et françaises, vol. 53, Geneva and Lille, 1955).

Sabatini, F., "Dalla 'scripta latina rustica' alle 'scriptae' romanze," Studi medievali, 3rd Series, 9 (1968), 320-58.

Sackur, E., Die Cluniacenser in ihrer kirchlichen und allgemeingeschichtlichen Wirksamkeit bis zur Mitte des elften Jahrhunderts, 2 vols. (Halle, 1892-1894).

Saint Bernard théologien. Actes du Congrès de Dijon 15-19 septembre 1953 (Analecta Sacri Ordinis Cisterciensis, vol. 9, 1953).

Sahlins, M., Stone Age Economics (Chicago, 1972).

Santifaller, L., "Beiträge zur Geschichte der Beschreibstoffe im Mittelalter. Mit besonderer Berücksichtigung der päpstlichen Kanzlei. Erster Teil: Untersuchungen," MIöG, 16, Ergänzungsbd., Heft 1 (1953).

————, "Saggio di un elenco dei funzionari, impiegati e scrittore della Cancelleria Pontificia dall'inizio all'anno 1099," BIS 56, 1-2 (1940).

Sawyer, P. H., The Age of the Vikings, 2nd ed. (London, 1971).

Schiaparelli, L., "Note diplomatiche sulle Carte longobarde: 1. I notai nell'età longobarda," ASI, 7th Series, 17 (1932), 1-34; repr. Note di diplomatica (1896-1934), ed. A. Pratesi (Turin, 1972), 183-214.

Schreiner, K., " 'Discrimen veri ac falsi.' Ansätze und Formen der Kritik in der Heiligen-und Reliquienverehrung des Mittelalters," *Archiv für Kultur-geschichte* 48 (1966), 1-53.

Schmidt, T., *Alexander II. (1061-1073) und die römische Reformgruppe seiner Zeit* (Päpste und Papsttum, Bd. 11, Stuttgart, 1977).

Schmitt, F. S., "Anselm und der (Neu-)Platonismus," *Analecta Anselmiana* 1 (1969), 39-71.

————, "Cinq recensions de l'Epistola de Incarnatione Verbi de S. Anselme de Cantorbéry," Rben 51 (1939), 275-87.

————, "Die wissenschaftliche Methode Anselms 'Cur Deus Homo,' " *Spicilegium Beccense I*, pp. 349-70.

————, "Les corrections de S. Anselme à son Monologion," Rben 50 (1936), 194-205.

————, "Zur Chronologie der Werke des hl. Anselm von Canterbury," Rben 44 (1932), 322-50.

Schmitt, J.-C., " 'Religion populaire' et culture folklorique," *Annales, E.S.C.*, 31 (1976), 941-53.

Schuck, J., *Das religiöse Erlebnis beim hl. Bernhard von Clairvaux. Ein Beitrag zur Geschichte der christlichen Gotteserfahrung* (Abhandlungen zur Philosophie und Psychologie der Religion, Heft 1, Würzburg, 1922).

Schulte, A., *Der Adel und die deutsche Kirche im Mittelalter. Studien zur Social-, Rechts-und Kirchengeschichte* (Kirchenrechtliche Abhandlungen, Heft 63 and 64, Stuttgart 1910; 2nd ed., 1922).

Schurr, A., *Die Begründung der Philosophie durch Anselm von Canterbury. Eine Erörterung des ontologischen Gottesbeweises* (Stuttgart, 1966).

Schutz, A., *The Phenomenology of the Social World*, trans. G. Walsh and F. Lehnert (Northwestern University. Studies in Phenomenology and Existential Philosophy, Evanston, Ill., 1967).

Schutz, A., and T. Luckmann, *The Structures of the Life-World*, trans. R. M. Zaner and H. T. Engelhardt, Jr. (Northwestern University. Studies in Phenomenology and Existential Philosophy, Evanston, Ill., 1973).

Sckommodau, H., "Alexius in Liturgie, Malerei und Dichtung," *Zeitschrift für romanische Philologie* 72 (1956), 165-94.

Sheehan, M. M., "Choice of Marriage Partner in the Middle Ages: Development and Mode of Application of a Theory of Marriage," *Studies in Medieval and Renaissance History*, n.s., 1 (1978), 3-33.

————, *The Will in Medieval England From the Conversion of the Anglo-Saxons to the End of the Thirteenth Century* (Pontifical Institute of Mediaeval Studies. Studies and Texts, vol. 6, Toronto, 1963).

Sikes, J. G., *Peter Abailard*, intro. A. Nairne (Cambridge, 1932).

Silagi, G., *Untersuchungen zur "Deliberatio supra Hymnum Trium Puerorum" des Gerhard von Csanád* (Münchener Beiträge zur Mediävistik und Renaissance-Forschung, Munich, 1967).

Silverstein, T., "Elementatum: Its Appearance Among the Twelfth-Century Cosmogonists," *Mediaeval Studies* 16 (1954), 156-62.

Silvestre, H., "Le problème des faux au Moyen Age," *Le Moyen Age* 66 (1960), 351-70.

——, "Notice sur Adelman de Liège, évêque de Brescia (†1061)," RHE 56 (1961), 855-71.

——, " 'Quanto iuniores, tanto perspicaciores'. Antécédents à la Querelle des Anciens et des Modernes," in *Recueil commémoratif du Xe anniversaire de la Faculté de philosophie et lettres* (Publications de l'Université Lovanium de Kinshasa, vol. 22, Louvain and Paris, 1968), 231-55.

Simson, O. von, *The Gothic Cathedral. Origins of Gothic Architecture and the Medieval Concept of Order* (Bollingen Series, vol. 48, New York, 1962).

✳Skorupski, J., *Symbol and Theory. A Philosophical Study of Theories of Religion in Social Anthropology* (Cambridge, 1976).

Smalley, B., "La Glossa Ordinaria. Quelques prédécesseurs d'Anselme de Laon," *Recherches de théologie ancienne et médiévale* 9 (1937), 365-400.

Sola ratione: Anselm-Studien für Pater Dr. h.c. Franciscus Salesius Schmitt OSB zum 75. Geburtstag am 20. Dezember 1969, ed. H. Kohlenberger (Stuttgart, 1970).

Soden, H. von, "MYSTHPION und sacramentum in den ersten drei Jahrhunderten der Kirche," *Zeitschrift für die neutestamentliche Wissenschaft und die Kunde des Urchristentums* 12 (1911), 188-227.

Somerville, R., "The Case Against Berengar of Tours: A New Text," *Studi gregoriani* 9 (1972), 53-75.

Somigli, C., "San Pietro Damiano e la Pataria (Relazioni e amicizie)," *San Pier Damiano nel IX centenario della morte (1072-1972),* vol. 3 (Cesena, 1973), 193-206.

Sommerfeldt, J., "Charismatic and Gregorian Leadership in the Thought of Bernard of Clairvaux," in *Bernard of Clairvaux,* pp. 73-90.

——, "Epistemology, Education and Social Theory in the Thought of Bernard of Clairvaux," in *Saint Bernard of Clairvaux,* pp. 169-79.

——, "The Epistemological Value of Mysticism in the Thought of Bernard of Clairvaux," *Studies in Medieval Culture* 1 (1964), 48-58.

Southern, R. W., *Medieval Humanism and Other Studies* (Oxford, 1970).

——, *St. Anselm and his Biographer. A Study of Monastic Life and Thought 1059-c. 1130* (Cambridge, 1963).

——, "The Canterbury Forgeries," *English Historical Review* 73 (1958), 193-226.

Spicilegium Beccense I. Congrès international du IXe centenaire de l'arrivée d'Anselme au Bec (Le Bec-Hellouin and Paris, 1959).

Spinelli, G., "Il sacerdozio ministeriale nella predicazione della Pataria milanese," *Benedictina* 22 (1975), 91-118.

Spörl, J., "Das Alte und das Neue im Mittelalter. Studien zum Problem des mittelalterlichen Fortschrittsbewusstseins I-II," *Historisches Jahrbuch* 50 (1930), 297-341, 498-524.

Sprandel, R., "Über das Problem neuen Rechts im früheren Mittelalter," ZRG KA 48 (1962), 117-37.

Standaert, P. M., "La doctrine de l'image chez saint Bernard," *Ephemerides Theologicae Lovanienses* 23 (1947), 70-129.

Steiger, L., "Contexe syllogismos: Über die Kunst und Bedeutung der Topik bei Anselm," *Analecta Anselmiana* I (1969), 107-43.

Steinacker, H., *Die antiken Grundlagen der frühmittelalterlichen Privaturkunde* (Grundriss der Geschichtswissenschaft zur Einführung in das Studium der deutschen Geschichte des Mittelalters und der Neuzeit, Erganzungsbd. 1, Leipzig and Berlin, 1927).

————, " 'Traditio cartae' und 'traditio per cartam,' ein Kontinuitätsproblem," *Archiv für Diplomatik, Schriftgeschichte, Siegel-und Wappenkunde* 5-6 (1959-60), 1-72.

Stock, B., "*Antiqui* and *Moderni* as 'Giants' and 'Dwarfs': A Reflection of Popular Culture?" *Journal of Modern Philology* 76 (1979), 370-74.

————, *Myth and Science in the Twelfth Century. A Study of Bernard Silvester* (Princeton, 1972).

Stolz, A., "Das Problem des hl. Anselm," Rben 47 (1955), 331-47.

Storia di Milano, 16 vols. (Milan, 1953-1962).

Stouff, L., "Etude sur la formation des contrats par l'écriture dans le droit des formules du Ve au XIIe siècle," NRHD 11 (1887), 249-87.

Studi su S. Bernardo di Chiaravalle nell'ottavo centenario della canonizzazione. Convegno internazionale, Certosa di Firenze, 6-9 novembre 1974 (Bibliotheca Cisterciensis, vol. 6, Rome 1975).

Studia Mediaevalia in honorem admodum Reverendi Patris Raymundi Josephi Martin Ordinis Praedicatorum, S. Theologiae Magistri, LXXum Natalem Diem Agentis (Bruges, 1948).

Synan, E., "Prayer, Proof, and Anselm's *Proslogion*," in *Standing Before God. Studies on Prayer in Scriptures and in Tradition with Essays in Honor of John M. Oesterreicher*, ed. A. Finkel and L. Frizzell (New York, 1981), 267-88.

Tannery, P., "La géometrie au XIe siècle," in *Mémoires scientifiques*, ed. J.-L. Heiberg and H.-G. Zeuthen, vol. 5: *Sciences exactes au moyen âge, 1877-1921* (Toulouse, 1922), 79-102.

Taviani, H., "Naissance d'une hérésie en Italie du Nord au XIe siècle," *Annales, E.S.C.*, 29 (1974), 1224-52.

Tellenbach, G., *Church, State and Christian Society at the Time of the Investiture Contest*, trans. R. F. Bennett (Studies in Mediaeval History, vol. 3, Oxford, 1940).

————, *Studien und Vorarbeiten zur Geschichte des grossfränkischen und frühdeutschen Adels* (Forschungen zur oberrheinischen Landesgeschichte, Bd. 4, Freiburg-im-Breisgau, 1957).

Tessier, G., *Diplomatique royale française* (Paris, 1962).

Theoduin of Liège, *Deoduini Leodiensis ad Henricum Regem Contra Brunonem et Berengarium Epistola*, PL 146.1439-42.

Thévenin, M., "Contributions à l'histoire du droit germanique," NRHD 3 (1879), 323-50; 4 (1880), 69-99.

————, *Textes relatifs aux institutions privées et publiques aux époques mérovingiennes et carolingiennes* (Collection de textes pour servir à l'étude et à l'enseignement de l'histoire, fasc. 3, Paris, 1887).

Thomas, R., *Der philosophisch-theologische Erkenntnisweg Peter Abaelards im Dialogus inter Philosophum, Judaeum et Christianum* (Untersuchungen zur allgemeinen Religionsgeschichte, Neue Folge, Heft 6, Bonn, 1966).

Thompson, J. W., *The Literacy of the Laity in the Middle Ages* (University of California Publications in Education, vol. 9, Berkeley, 1939).

Thompson, P., *The Voice of the Past. Oral History* (New York and Oxford, 1978).

Thorndike, L., "Invention of the Mechanical Clock about 1271 A.D.," *Speculum* 16 (1941), 242-45.

Tierney, B., "Natura Id Est Deus: A Case of Juristic Pantheism?" *Journal of the History of Ideas* 24 (1963), 307-22.

Tonini, S., "La scrittura nelle opere sistematiche di S. Anselmo: concetto, posizione, significato," *Analecta Anselmiana* 2 (1970), 57-116.

Topsfield, L. T., "The Burlesque Poetry of Guilhem IX of Aquitaine," *Neuphilologische Mitteilungen* 69 (1968), 280-302.

Toubert, P., *Les structures du Latium médiévale. Le Latium méridional et la Sabine du IXe à la fin du XIIe siècle*, 2 vols. (Bibliothèque des Ecoles françaises d'Athènes et de Rome, fasc. 201, Rome, 1973).

Tout, T. F., "Medieval Forgers and Forgeries," *The Bulletin of the John Rylands Library* 5 (1918-20), 208-34.

Troeltsch, E., *Die Soziallehren der christlichen Kirchen und Gruppen* (Gesammelte Schriften von Ernst Troeltsch, vol. 1, 3rd reprinting, Tübingen, 1923); English trans.: *The Social Teachings of the Christian Churches*, trans. O. Wyon, intro. C. Gore (Halley Stewart Publications, vol. 1, London and New York, 1931).

The Concept of Heresy in the Middle Ages (11th to 13th C.) (Mediaevalia Lovaniensia, Series 1, Studia 4, Louvain and The Hague, 1976).

Turner, V., *Dramas, Fields, and Metaphors. Symbolic Action in Human Society* (Symbol, Myth, and Ritual Series, Ithaca, 1974).

Tweedale, M. M., *Abailard on Universals* (Amsterdam, 1976).

Ullmann, W., *The Growth of Papal Government in the Middle Ages*, 2nd ed. (London, 1962).

Vacandard, E., *Etudes de critique et d'histoire religieuse*, 2 vols., 2nd ed. (Paris, 1906, 1910).

————, *Vie de Saint Bernard, Abbé de Clairvaux*, 2 vols., 2nd ed. (Paris, 1897).

Vachek, J., *Written Language. General Problems and Problems of English* (Janua linguarum. Series critica, vol. 14, The Hague, 1973).

Vagaggini, C., "La hantise des rationes necessariae de saint Anselme dans la théologie des processions trinitaires de saint Thomas," *Spicilegium Beccense I*, pp. 105-39.

Vandenbrouke, Fr., "La lectio divina du 11e au 14e siècle," *Studia Monastica* 8 (1966), 267-93.

Vanni Rovighi, S., "L'etica de S. Anselmo," *Analecta Anselmiana* 1 (1969), 73-99.

————, "Notes sur l'influence de saint Anselme au XIIe siècle," CCM 7 (1964), 423-37; 8 (1965), 43-58.

————, "*Ratio* in S. Anselmo d'Aosta," in *Sapientiae procerum amore. Mélanges médiévistes offerts à Dom Jean-Pierre Müller, o.s.b.* (Studia Anselmiana, vol. 63, Rome, 1974), 65-79; repr. *Studi di filosofia medioevale I. Da sant'Agostino al XII secolo* (Vita e Pensiero. Pubblicazioni della Università Cattolica del Sacro Cuore, scienze filosofiche, vol. 19, Milan, 1978), 22-36.

————, "San Bernardo e la filosofia," in *S. Bernardo. Pubblicazioni commemorativa nell'VIII centenario della sua morte* (Vita e Pensiero. Pubblicazioni dell'Università Cattolica del Sacro Cuore, Milan, 1954), 132-50; repr. *Studi di filosofia I*, pp. 142-62.

Vansina, J., *Oral Tradition. A Study in Historical Methodology*, trans. H. M. Wright (London, 1965).

————, "The Power of Systematic Doubt in Historical Enquiry," *History in Africa. A Journal of Method*, 1 (1974), 109-27.

Vauchez, A., "La piété populaire au moyen âge. Etat des travaux et position des problèmes," in *La piété populaire au moyen âge*, pp. 27-42.

————, *La sainteté en Occident aux derniers siècles du Moyen Age d'après les procès de canonisation et les documents hagiographiques* (Bibliothèque des Ecoles françaises d'Athènes et de Rome, fasc. 241, Rome, 1981).

————, *La spiritualité du Moyen Age occidental, VIIe-XIIe siècles* (Collection SUP, L'historien, No. 19, Paris, 1975).

Vernant, J.-P., "Du mythe à la raison: la formation de la pensée positive dans la Grèce archaïque," *Annales, E.S.C.*, 12 (1957), 183-206.

Vinaver, E., *The Rise of Romance* (Oxford, 1971).

Vignaux, P., "La méthode de saint Anselme dans le *Monologion* et le *Proslogion*," *Aquinas* 8 (1965), 110-29.

————, "Structure et sens du *Monologion*," RSPT 31 (1947), 193-212.

Vogel, C., "La réforme culturelle sous Pépin le Bref et sous Charlemagne (deuxième moitié du VIIIe siècle et premier quart du IXe siècle)," in E. Patzelt, *Die karolingische Renaissance*, C. Vogel, *La réforme culturelle* . . . 2 vols. in one (Graz, 1965), 171-242.

————, *Les 'libri paenitentiales'* (Typologie des sources du moyen âge occidental, fasc. 27, Turnhout, 1978).

Volpe, G., *Movimenti religiosi e sette ereticali nella società medievale italiana (secoli XI-XIV)* (Collana storica, vol. 6, Florence, 1922); new ed. (Biblioteca storica Sansoni, N.S., 37, Florence, 1961).

Voltelini, H., "Die Imbreviatur des Johannes Scriba im Staatsarchiv zu Genua," MIöG 41 (1926), 70-79.

Violante, C., *La pataria milanese e la riforma ecclesiastica. Le premesse (1045-1057)* (Istituto storico italiano per il Medio Evo, Studi storici, vol. 11, Rome, 1955).

————, *La società milanese nell'età precomunale* (Istituto italiano per gli studi storici, Pubblicazioni, vol. 4, Bari, 1953).

————, *Studi sulla cristianità medioevale. Società, istitutioni, spiritualità*, ed. P. Zerbi (Cultura e Storia, vol. 8, Milan, 1972).

Wadstein, E., *Die eschatologische Ideengruppe: Antichrist—Weltsabbat—Weltende und Weltgericht in den Hauptmomenten ihrer christlich-mittelalterlichen Gesamtentwickelung* (Leipzig, 1896).

Wakefield, W. L., and A. P. Evans, trans., *Heresies of the High Middle Ages. Selected Sources Translated and Annotated* (Records of Civilization. Sources and Studies, vol. 81, New York, 1969).

Walter, J. von, *Die ersten Wanderprediger Frankreichs. Studien zur Geschichte des Mönchtums, 2 Teile: 1. Robert von Arbrissel; 2. Bernhard von Thiron, Vitalis von Savigny, Girald von Salles, Bemerkung zu Norbert von Xanten und Heinrich von Lausanne* (Studien zur Geschichte der Theologie und der Kirche, Bd. 9, Heft 3, Leipzig, 1903-06; repr. Aalen, 1972, 2 vols. in one).

Warnach, V., "Wort und Wirklichkeit bei Anselm von Canterbury," *Salzburger Jahrbuch für Philosophie* 5-6 (1961-62), 157-76.

Wartburg, W. von, *Die Entstehung der romanischen Völker*, 2nd ed. (Tübingen, 1951).

————, *Einführung in Problematik und Methodik der Sprachwissenschaft* (Halle, 1943).

Watts, A. C., *The Lyre and the Harp. A Comparative Reconsideration of Oral Tradition in Homer and Old English Epic Poetry* (Yale Studies in English, vol. 169, New Haven, 1969).

Weber, M., *Die protestantische Ethik und der Geist des Kapitalismus*, in J. Winckelmann, ed., *Max Weber. Die protestantische Ethik I. Eine Aufsatzsammlung*, 3rd ed. (Hamburg, 1973), 27-374.

————, *Wirtschaft und Gesellschaft*, 5th ed., ed. J. Winckelmann (Tübingen, 1972).

Werner, E., *Häresie und Gesellschaft im 11. Jahrhundert* (Sitzungsberichte der sächsischen Akademie der Wissenschaften zu Leipzig, Philol.-hist. Kl., Bd. 117, Heft 5, Leipzig, 1975).

————, *Pauperes Christi. Studien zu Sozial-religiösen Bewegungen im Zeitalter des Reformpapsttums* (Leipzig, 1956).

Werner, E., and M. Erbstösser, "Sozial-religiöse Bewegungen im Mittelalter," *Wissenschaftliche Zeitschrift der Karl-Marx Universität* 7 (1957-58), 257-82.

Wetherbee, W., *Platonism and Poetry in the Twelfth Century. The Literary Influence of the School of Chartres* (Princeton, 1972).

⌐. White, L., Jr., *Medieval Technology and Social Change* (Oxford, 1962).

———, "Natural Science and Naturalistic Art in the Middle Ages," *American Historical Review* 52 (1947), 421-35.

Wieacker, F., *Allgemeine Zustände und Rechtszustände gegen Ende des Weströmischen Reiches* (Ius Romanum Medii Aevi, vol. 1, 2a, Milan, 1963).

———, *Vulgarizmus und Klassicizmus im Recht der Spätantike* (Sitzungsberichte der Heidelberger Akademie der Wissenschaften, Phil.-hist. Kl., Abh. 3, 1955, Heidelberg, 1955).

William of Conches, *Glosae super Platonem*, ed. E. Jeauneau (Textes philosophiques du moyen âge, vol. 13, Paris, 1965).

———, *Wilhelm von Conches, Philosophia*, ed. and trans. G. Maurach, with the aid of H. Telle (Pretoria, 1980).

Williams, G. H., *Anselm: Communion and Atonement* (St. Louis, 1960).

Williams, S., "The Oldest Text of the 'Constitutum Constantini,'" *Traditio* 20 (1964), 448-61.

Wilson, B. R., *Religious Sects. A Sociological Study* (World University Library, London and New York, 1970).

Wipo, *Die Werke Wipos*, ed. H. Bresslau (Scriptores Rerum Germanicarum in Usum Scholarum ex Monumentis Germaniae Historicis separatim editi, 3rd ed., Hanover and Leipzig, 1915).

Wright, R., "Speaking, Reading and Writing Late Latin and Early Romance," *Neophilologus* 60 (1976), 178-89.

Yates, F., *The Art of Memory* (London, 1966).

Yver, J., "Les premières institutions du duché de Normandie," in *I Normanni*, pp. 299-366.

Zerbi, P., "Alcuni risultati e prospettive di ricerca sulla storia religiosa di Milano dalla fine del secolo XI al 1144," in *Problemi di Storia religiosa Lombarda. Ente Villa Monastero di Varenna. Tavola Rotonda sulla storia religiosa lombarda, 2-4 settembre, 1969* (Como, 1972), 17-26.

———, "Il termine 'fidelitas' nelle lettere di Gregorio VII," *Studi gregoriani* 3 (1948), 129-48.

———, "Monasteri e riforma a Milano dalla fine del secolo X agli inizi del XII," *Aevum* 24 (1950), 44-60, 166-78.

———, "San Bernardo di Chiaravalle e il Concilio di Sens," in *Studi su S. Bernardo*, pp. 49-73.

Zeumer, K., "'Cartam levare' in Sanct Galler Urkunden," ZRG GA 4 (1883), 113-17.

———, "Zum westgothischen Urkundenwesen, 1. Subscriptio und Signum," *Neues Archiv* 24 (1899), 15-29.

Zink, M., *La prédication en langue romane avant 1300* (Nouvelle Bibliothèque du Moyen Age, vol. 4, Paris, 1966).

———, "Les destinaires des recueils de sermons en langue vulgaire au XIIe et au XIIIe siècle. Prédication effective et prédication dans un fauteuil," in *La piété populaire au moyen âge*, pp. 59-74.

Zumthor, P., *Essai de poétique médiévale* (Paris, 1972).

INDEX

INDEX

dualism: 99, 102, 141, 146, 152; *see also*
Catharism, Manichaeism
Duby, G.: 17n, 49n, 51n, 55n, 86n, 122n,
458n, 466n, 470n, 473n, 479n, 484n,
480f, 485n, 507
Du Cange: 204n
Duchesne, L.: 491n
Dudo of St. Quentin: 76n, 474
Duggan, J.: 80n
Dulcidius, St.: 64
Dumas, A.: 16n, 488n
Dumézil, G.: 15n
Dumontier, M.: 417n, 452n
Dupront, A.: 9n
Durand of Troarn: 272, 282, 287, 290-95
Durkheim, E.: 14
Dutton, P.: 457n
Dvornik, F.: 460n
dwarfs and giants, as metaphor: 495, 498,
517, 519; *see also* ancients and moderns

Eadmer: 62, 331n, 481n
Ebel, W.: 49n
ecclesia primitiva: 199, 207, 213
Ecclesiastes: 411, 413, 414
Eden: 87; *see also* Adam
Edict of Milan: 35
Easter, liturgy of: 305, 516
Eisenstein, E. L.: 13n
Elcock, W.: 23n
elect, the: 187, 220f
elementum: as letter, 319; as matter, 374; as
sound, 372, 373, 374; *elementatum*, 319f
Elias: 292
Elijah: 430f
Elisha: 430f
empiricism: 11, 253n, 316, 456, 473; uned-
ucated, 243; *see also* nature
enactment: 290, 306, 457; and re-enact-
ment, 291; of sacraments, 258
Endres, J.: 146n, 299n
encyclopedism, in oral tradition: 13, 80
Engels, F.: 93
Enguerrand of Boves: 508, 510
Enguerrand of Coucy, bishop of Laon: 508
Eon de l'Etoile: 151, 235
Erbstösser, M.: 93n
Erdmann, C.: 203n, 272n, 486n
Eriugena, Johannes Scottus: 118, 221, 292;
Ratramn mistaken as, 274, 279
eschatology: 457, 458n, 521
Esmein, A.: 51n, 52n, 53n, 55n, 56, 57n
esse: ens, 338; *esse*, 338, 388; essence, defini-
tion of, 354; *essentia*, 338, 343; *essentia di-*

vinitatis, 333; *essentia, esse*, and *ens*, 343;
essentia, summa, 340; *essentialiter*, 311; *exis-
tens*, 338
Etcheverry, F.: 244n
ethics: 462, 520f; in Anselm, 361
Etienne de Garlande: 38
eucharist: 100, 111, 123, 128, 133f, 136,
138, 139, 143, 144n, 241-325, 360,
402, 406, 419, 420, 524, 528, 529
Eudes of Chartres: 467
Eudes of St. Symphorien: 244, 249
Eugenius, archbishop of Milan: 178
Eusebius: 135, 272, 290
euthanasia, among heretics: 143
Evans, A. P.: 93n, 96n, 107n, 121n, 126n,
144n
Evans, G. R.: 330n, 339n, 352n, 361n
Evdokimov, P.: 361n
Eve: 207, 314
Evrard of Breteuil: 482f, 488, 489, 501,
504
Evrard, sacristan at Chartres: 107, 110
Evroul, St.: 76; monastery of, 488; *see also*
Orderic Vitalis
exchange: and communication, 85-87, 370f;
gift, 453; symbolic, 50f
exemplum: 108f, 111, 113, 194, 196, 245,
336, 338, 466; *meditationis*, 331, 344,
354; *modernum*, 248; *primitivae ecclesiae*,
152; *sanctae vitae*, 290; *exemplares formae*,
379; *exemplo docet*, 413
exile: 133, 445, 463, 477, 481, 482, 494
existence: in Anselm, 336f; in reality and in
thought, 388-91 *see also esse*
experience: 455, 472; and reform, 432f; and
understanding, 531; everyday or lived,
313, 317, 465, 527; mystical, 412, 415;
of the text, 4, 413f, 417, 439, 452, 517;
experientia, 245, 419; *experimentum*, 317
experimentation, scientific: 243
expertus: 417, 420, 442n; *see also* interpretation
explanatio: as interpretation, 79
explanation, methods of: 473
expression: as *locutio*, 339f; of highest substance, 340-43
exteriority: 399, 453, 458; *see also* interiority
Exuperus, St.: 250
Eynde, van den, D.: 254n

Fairweather, E.: 353n
faith: 245, 269, 286, 306, 407; and certainty, 501; and intellectual progress,
521; and reason, 247, 264, 297, 303,

Heriger of Lobbes: 271f

Herlihy, D.: 499n

hermeneutics: 10n, 101, 108, 115, 139, 142f, 152f, 217, 219-21, 234, 249, 252, 260, 265f, 271f, 273, 278, 279f, 282, 284f, 293f, 301, 309, 317, 320, 363, 403-06, 415, 429f, 452, 488, 507, 522, 527, 530, 531; *see also* allegory, interpretation

hermit: life of, 103; right to preach, 233f

Herodias; 216

Herold, M.: 403n

Hervé, archbishop of Reims: 475

Hervé de Bourgdieu: 63

Hesbert, R.-J.: 453n

Heubner, R.: 50n, 55n

Heurtevent, R.: 274n, 290n, 294n

Heusler, A.: 47n, 50n

Hilary of Poitiers: 290, 292, 316

Hildebrand: 36f, 160, 174, 197, 200, 201, 202, 206, 210, 228, 276; *see also* Gregory VII

Hildegard of Bingen: 500

Hilduin, count of Milan: 178-80

Hincmar of Reims: 290

Hispana Gallica Augustodunensis: 61

Hiss, W.: 427n, 444n

Hödl, L.: 277n

Hoffmann, H.: 36n, 55n

Hofmeister, A.: 480n

Hölbock, F.: 268n

Holdsworth, C. J.: 492n

Holdsworth, W. S.: 57n

Hollister, C. W.: 38n, 476n, 478n

homage: 50f

Homer: 32, 33

Honoratus, archbishop of Milan: 178-80

Honorius II: 161

Hopkins, J.: 330n, 346n

Horace: 20, 28

Hourlier, J.: 417n

Hubert, J.: 230n

Hubert, St., abbey of: 60

Hugh, archbishop of Lyons: 345

Hugh Capet: 38, 484, 507

Hugh of Burgundy: 164

Hugh of Langres: 272, 282, 287-89, 291

Hugh of Lisieux: 497

Hugh of St. Victor: 87, 253, 316, 322-25, 327, 528

Hughes, K.: 493n

Huguccio of Pisa: 27n, 63

Humbert of Silva Candida: 276, 278, 280, 281, 295, 297, 299, 306

Hungary: 23, 180, 457, 475, 500; heresy in, 146

Husserl, E.: 472f

Huygens, R.B.C.: 277n, 284n

Ibn Abī ʾĀmir Mohammed: 462n

Ibn al-Haitham: 82f

iconoclasm: 105; and heresy, 102

ideas, collective: 457, 458, 471; *see also* interpretation

idiota: 28-30, 70, 199, 224n, 240, 298, 403; as heretic, 88; as illiterate, 27, 68, 166, 235; as uneducated, 117, 149; as unskilled in interpretation, 308; *see also* literacy, illiteracy, *rusticus*

idolatry: 424

idols, worship of: 140; *see also* heresy

ignorance: allegorized, 431; and self-knowledge, 444-47; before Christ, 423f; *see also* knowledge

Ilarino da Milano: 93n, 97n, 107n, 118n, 119n, 127n, 139n, 144n, 145n

illiteracy: 7, 19, 61n, 100, 105, 132, 225, 227f, 286, 294, 296, 485, 511, 515; and fables, 136; and foolishness, 346; and language use, 369; as byproduct of literacy, 242; as childhood, 126; as *imperita multitudo*, 79; defined by literates, 6-8; legal, 43-45; *see also* literacy

illitterati: 27, 68, 73n, 136, 149, 215, 263, 265; *Angli*, 75n; *conversi*, 406; *et idiotae*, 235; *et vulgares*, 250; *Patarini*, 171n, 200; *see also idiota, litterati, rusticus*

Illmer, D.: 44n, 100n, 483n

illumination: 99, 103, 105, 110, 111, 114, 119, 125, 145, 217, 220, 221, 227, 323, 411, 419, 424, 428, 429

image: 136; images, divine, 128; image and likeness, 303, 323, 341, 432, 438-51, 530; images as language for unlettered, 136f; image formation, 15, 370, 378, 380, 383f, 408f, 442, 448; images, mental, 397, 401; of corporeal things, 339; *imago*, 342, 379, 383; *Dei*, as *pignus*, 248; as wall-painting, 70; *imaginatio*, 388; as *confusa animi conceptio*, 380; *et sensus*, 380; *significandi*, 367; *imaginaliter*, 69

imitation of Christ: 222, 227, 228, 233n; *imitatio*, 305, 492

immram: 493; *see also* wandering

imperitus: 301, 308; *see also* interpretation, *peritus*

imposition of hands: 135, 147

incantation: 134, 213; *see also* heresy

INDEX

incest: 147, 470
indecision, behavioural: 477, 503; *see also* decision-making
indexing, beginnings of: 63
individualism: 15, 225, 232f, 239f, 252, 274, 297f, 309, 310, 317, 459; and man-oriented theology, 360; and moral integrity, 234; resisted, 415; versus collectivism, 456
Indovinello Veronese: 25
inexpertus: as inexperienced with text, 417; as illiterate, 68, 74; *see also expertus*, hermeneutics
initiation: 426-28, 437, 450, 452
Innis, H. A.: 16n
Innocent III: 35, 62
inquisition: 55, 104, 113, 118, 120, 124, 126f, 143; *inquisitio*, in law, 59
insanity: 199; and heresy, 104, 106, 123; and physicalism, 276
integumentum: 248; *see also* covering, allegorical
intellectualism: 129, 145, 152, 191, 204, 212, 241, 242, 244, 260, 282, 303, 402, 405, 524, 530
intellectus: 324, 325, 354, 366, 386, 396f, 450; *et imaginatio*, 378-80; *et res*, 350f, 364, 377, 381f; *et sensus*, 380; *divinarum scientiarum*, 144; *in anima*, 368; *intellectu concipere*, 388; *orationis*, 375; *significatio intellectus*, 378; *spiritualis*, 258
intelligentia: 341, 399; *verborum*, 308; *intelligo*, 349, 350; *et cogito*, 341n, 361
intentions: 251, 331n, 447; moral, 128, 454; of author, 364; of speaker, 377
interiority: 78f, 84, 115, 128, 130, 137, 221, 275, 283, 332, 334, 389, 409, 430-38, 452, 454, 494, 501; and exteriority, 77, 79, 84, 90, 91, 101, 116, 222, 224, 248, 249, 250f, 253f, 259, 262f, 266, 269, 286, 291, 313, 320, 323f, 325, 327, 331, 405, 406f, 415, 417, 432, 438, 439, 446f, 503, 521, 530, 531; interior versus exterior history, 11
interpretation: 5, 11, 44, 82, 90, 91, 101, 104, 105, 106, 108, 114, 119, 127, 128, 130, 136, 137, 141, 148, 150, 151, 152, 163, 167, 168, 169, 174, 176, 183, 196, 198, 220, 227, 246, 249, 251, 252, 258, 259-61, 264-66, 269f, 274f, 276, 279, 280f, 282, 283, 288, 291, 293f, 313f, 316, 320-22, 328, 344, 363, 384f, 404, 414, 415, 453f, 455f, 457, 459, 473, 476, 507, 510, 511, 512, 513, 517-21, 525,

526f, 528, 531; and classification, 14; and logic, 273f; as digestion of text, 234; as *explanatio*, 79; in Paul, 29f; opposition to, 291, 306f, 407, 425, 473; Patarene, 207, 208; rational, 139; *interpres*, 105, 167, 247, 522; *interpretatio*: 310, 367-69, 378; *see also* hermeneutics
inventories, Carolingian: 84
investiture: 49, 162, 195, 232, 234, 252, 254, 453
Irenaeus: 257
Irminon, polyptique of: 16
Irnerius of Bologna: 56
irrationality: 421, 501; *see also* literacy, rationality
Isaac: 441
Isabel of Conches: 500
Isaiah: 312, 315, 417, 418
Isidore of Seville: 135, 267, 276, 480
Islam: 23, 459, 461, 468f; as menace, 463, 475, 498
Italy: 185; and Normandy, 481; as source of heresy, 117, 123, 125, 145n; as source of reform, 466; as bearer of blight, 470
Ivánka, E. von: 414n, 441n
Ivo of Chartres: 37, 61
involucrum: 287f; *see also integumentum*

Jackson, B. D.: 259n
Jacobi, E.: 55n
Jacobi, K.: 386n
Jacquin, A. M.: 263n, 332n
James, St.: 130
Janauschek, L.: 403n
Jason, H.: 80n
Jeauneau, E.: 320, 517n
Jenkinson, H.: 18
Jeremiah: 226, 418
Jerome St.: 29n, 79, 135, 177n, 272, 278, 285
Jerusalem: 203, 216, 463, 466, 468, 469, 470; earthly and spiritual, 494
Jews: 67, 97, 135, 140, 141, 407, 468f, 471, 491, 521; and heresy, 104; in Sens, 467f; legalism of, 257; stereotype of, 520f
Jolivet, J.: 362n, 363n, 364n, 378n, 385n, 386n
John, St.: 29, 131, 269, 279, 280, 291, 294, 420
John Chrysostom: 290
John Gualbert: 215
John of Fécamp: 282f, 517n
John of Gorze: 103n
John of Reims: 75

589

of Ariald, 223-28; in Milan, 168; wandering preachers, 478, 494
predestination: 131
prefiguration: 292; *see also* typology
preliteracy: 6, 19; *see also* literacy
Premonstratensian Order: 152
Prevenier, W.: 39n
pride, sin of: 467
priests: in Pataria, 236; rejection of, 142, 143, 145, 233
print, age of: 26, 529
Priscian: 373, 374, 377, 379, 394, 396, 398, 399, 401, 402, 517n
prodigies: 68, 246
progress: cultural, 8, 530; spiritual, 419, 420, 426, 427, 434, 435, 448, 458, 483, 504, 505; via knowledge, 323
proof: 247, 248, 332, 336; Anselmic, 344, 361; Germanic, 58, 66
prophecy: 29, 74, 103, 118, 151, 168f, 177, 196, 219, 246, 257, 442, 448, 463, 494
prostitution: 209, 321, 482
Protaxius, St., church of, Milan: 185
Prou, M.: 17n, 456
Proverbs: 411, 413, 414
Prudentius: 69
Psalms: 63, 230f, 245, 292, 345, 412, 414, 427, 516
pseudo-Denis: 82, 135
pseudo-Isidore: 61n, 290
public, the: versus the private, 116, 199, 212, 218 226f, 234, 239; *publica fides*, 39, 40
Puech, H. C.: 99, 121n
puer senex, topos of: 483; *see also* youth
Pulgram, E.: 19n
purification: 95, 132, 133, 141, 212, 213, 223, 228, 232, 305, 426-28, 494, 512
purgatory, theme of: 495-99
Pye, M.: 94n
Pyron, St.: 246

Quintilian: 28, 502n

Rabikauskas, P.: 36n
Rabanus Maurus: 480n
Raftis, J. A.: 95n
Rainard, count of Sens: 467, 468
Ralph, castellan of Mantes: 486
Ralph of Caen: 485
Ralph the Fair: 497
Ramihrd: 232
Ramiro III of León: 462n

Randall, D.J.B.: 17n
Ranulf Flambard: 489
Raoul the Monk: 235
Rassow, P.: 410n
ratio: 133, 196, 208, 246, 251, 264, 265, 274, 276, 282, 293, 296, 307, 309, 310, 320, 323, 324, 325, 332n, 338, 339n, 342, 343, 353, 360, 361, 388, 390, 414, 422, 425, 436; and *auctoritas*, 295, 308f, 334; and *veritas*, 63; and wisdom, 323; *divina*, 324; *fidei*, 344; *logos*, and *verbum*, 405; *rationis necessitas*, 67, 332, 334, 343; *sola*, 245, 247, 331; *scripta*, 57, 318, 362, 390; *rationalis anima*, 422; *ratiocinatio*, 251; *see also* rationality, textuality
rationality: 119, 145, 149, 150, 208, 252, 261, 273f, 278, 279, 280, 301, 320, 342, 346, 354, 361, 378, 384, 406f, 433-35; and mysticism, 422f; and the study of texts, 10, 111f, 252, 335, 363, 391, 520f, 523; *see also* textuality
Rathe, E.: 403n
Rather of Verona: 102n
Ratramnus of Corbie: 241, 253, 259-72, 288, 402, 524; mistaken for Eriugena, 274
Ravenna: 156, 159, 164; heresy at, 97, 98, 146
Ray, R. D.: 76n
Raymond d'Aguilers: 513-17
Raymond d'Hautepoul: 513n
Raymond of St.-Gilles, count of Toulouse: 513, 514, 516, 517
Raynaud de Lage, G.: 321n
real presence, the: 122, 265, 269, 270, 283, 307, 308; *see also* eucharist, transubstantiation
realism: 290, 321f, 351, 524; and literalism, 278; crude, in law, 44f; limits of, 391-93; opposition to, 385, 406; sacramental, 132, 136, 137, 139, 141, 260, 287, 290f, 299, 361
reality: 243, 270; and abstraction, 336; and figure, 300; and hermeneutic method, 320; and image, 397; and intellect, 388; and language, 278, 350, 364, 380-85; and symbol, 280, 305; intelligible, 421; observable, 242, 271, 523-25; objective, 386; textually defined, 241, 278f, 321f, 447
reason: 82, 136, 145, 306, 349, 461; and authority, 278, 307; and nature, 114; and sense, 251; and texts, 335; as law, 320; authenticated, 245; divine, 133; in An-

reason (*cont.*)
  selm, 343; limits of, 283, 285-88, 306, 425; necessary, 332, 364; will, and memory, 427; *see also ratio*, rationality
reason and faith: see faith
recognitio: in law, 59
Redfield, R.: 16n, 523
reform, religious: 4, 88-92, 113, 115, 117, 129, 132, 133, 147, 149, 151-53, 157, 159, 164, 167-70, 173, 175, 177, 183f, 186, 191, 192, 195, 198, 200, 202-204, 206-10, 214, 215-31, 226, 233, 236, 253, 263, 265, 272f, 364, 414, 432f, 430-38, 458, 465f, 470, 471, 488, 498, 511, 522f, 525, 527-30; *reformare*, 434, 435
Reformation, the: 92, 252, 254n
Reginald of Echauffour: 487
registers: episcopal, 39; notarial, 41f; papal, 36f; papal, of Gregory VII, 35
relics: 70, 72, 90, 231, 244-52, 315, 466f, 468, 470, 511, 513-17
religion, popular: 496f, 529; *see also* culture
Rémi of Auxerre: 271
renaissance: 5; Carolingian, 25; Justinian, 45; literacy, and rationality, 31f; of higher disciplines, 455; of law, 55f; of the fifteenth century, 21; of the twelfth century, 32, 326, 327; *see also* reform
renewal, millenarian: see millenarianism
Renouard, Y.: 155n, 165n, 214n
res: 269, 325, 437; and *forma loquendi*, 359; and *intellectus*, 350f, 364, 377, 381f, 384; and intentions, 447; and *nomen*, 300, 356, 402; *sacramenti*, 91, 286, 302f, 304; and *signum*, 258f, 275, 288, 302; and *similitudo*, 366; and *verba*, 345-51, 358; and *voces*, 339, 402; *divina*, 283; *enuntiata*, 352; *status rei*, 383, 395; *significans*, 305; *subjecta*, 395
resemblance: see image
resurrection, the: 132, 248, 261, 269, 293, 305, 306, 312, 316
revival, religious: 458, 501, 511; *see also* reform
Reynold of Tours: 67
Reynolds, R. E.: 63n
rhetoric: 16, 22f, 28, 36, 43, 65, 74, 144, 165n, 208, 243, 249, 264, 284, 293, 300, 304, 310, 322, 329, 332n, 445, 527
Richard I, duke of Normandy: 474
Richard II, duke of Normandy: 107, 108, 118, 474
Richard of St. Vannes: 103

Richards, I. A.: 16n
Riché, P.: 17n, 44n, 143n
Richer of Reims: 83
Richter, D.: 145n
Richter, M.: 26n
Ries, J.: 414n
Rijk, L. M. de: 84n, 362n, 363, 384n
Risorgimento, the: 175
rites of passage: 494, 506; *see also* youth
ritual: 11, 15, 33, 47f, 49, 50, 57, 58, 64, 69, 71, 90f, 100, 106, 110, 111, 114, 116, 118, 119, 129, 130f, 134, 137, 139, 140, 141, 212f, 230f, 233, 241, 242, 265, 267, 273, 281, 292, 295, 298, 303, 304, 307, 405, 408, 416, 417, 426-28, 452, 455f, 460, 478, 512, 523-26, 428-30; and the eucharist, 263, 266, 289, 291; and *sacramentum*, 255-58
Rivière, J.: 360n
Robert Bellême: 495
Robert of Arbrissel: 103n, 234, 498n
Robert of Loritello: 487
Robert II, count of Flanders: 233
Robert, son of Ralph the Fair: 497
Robert the Magnificent: 474
Robert the Monk: 486, 513n
Robert the Pious: 17, 38, 107, 110, 113, 118, 467, 484, 485
Robson, C. A.: 26n
Roch, F.: 403n
Rochais, H. M.: 55n, 453n
Rodulf Glaber: 64, 77n, 97n, 98, 101f, 103, 104, 105, 106, 107, 115, 117, 139, 140f, 143, 150, 248, 456-72, 474n, 479, 483, 511, 512, 521, 527
Rösler, M.: 491n
Roger Bacon: 83
Roger I, bishop of Châlons-sur-Marne: 121
Roger II, bishop of Châlons-sur-Marne: 147-50
Roger of Sicily: 481
role, social: 14, 91, 328
Rollo, duke of Normandy: 474
Romanesque, the: 82
Rome: 160, 161, 228, 491, 509; *see also* papacy
Romanus III, emperor: 140, 469n
Romussi, C.: 175
Roques, R.: 332n, 346n, 360n
Roscelin, Johannes: 359f
Rouen: 108n, 117, 491
Rouse, R. and M.: 62n, 63
Rousse, J.: 408n
Rousselet, P.: 414n
Rozone, S. Trinità di, Milan: 227n, 236n

senses, the (*cont.*)
370, 444; versus reason, 276, 378, 405, 424
sensualitas: exterior, 399; and *intellectualitas*, 250; *sensualiter*, of material birth of Christ, 142, 144
sensus: 435; *carnalis*, 313; *imaginatio*, and *ratio*, 386; *see also* senses
sermo: 332, 419, 429; and *vox*, in Abelard, 378; as discourse, 324; as sound, 384; *divinus*, 265; *sacer theoricusque*, 414
Severus, St.: 179
Servières, L.: 64n
Sheehan, M. M.: 48n, 49n, 499n
Shippey, T. A.: 80n
signaculum: 256; *et imago Dei*, 319; *sanctae crucis*, 110; *veritatis*, 448; *see also sacramentum*
significatio: 259, 269, 353, 367, 375, 381; in Abelard, 376-85; *nominum*, 400; *vocis*, 347; *significare*, 304, 305, 367, 378, 391; *significativa (vox) ad placitum*, 373; *significativum* and *appellativum*, 357; *see also* signification
signification: 339, 346-51, 358, 368, 371, 372, 381, 385, 388; and the hearer's mind, 376, 377; and universals, 395; genus, and species, 387-91; through things, 324; via sound, 367
sign, in language: 122, 125, 136, 249, 250, 275, 321, 353, 359, 366, 371, 427, 512; divine signs, 118, 140, 303, 483, 511; mental consideration of, 339; physical, 246f, 315, 319, 324, 339, 431, 447f, 452, 466f, 514; types of, 246; textual, 13, 279, 371, 378; sign language, 353; *see also significatio*, signification
signum: 68, 256, 308, 316, 339, 353, 366, 384, 427; and *figura*, 315; and *res*, 258f, 288, 302; *exteriora*, 520; *sacrum*, 275, 315, 453; *intersigna rerum*, 379; *see also* sign
Sikes, J. G.: 386n, 392n
Silagi, G.: 146n
Silverstein, T.: 319n
Silvestre, H.: 61n, 284n, 517n
similitudo: 221, 257n, 275, 279, 280, 291, 293, 294, 300, 304, 308, 312, 338, 340, 341, 342, 343, 366, 371, 379, 390, 395, 397, 439, 448; *see also* image
Simon of Valois: 504
Simon Magus: 224f, 228
simony: 105n, 138, 146, 153, 156, 160, 161, 162, 164, 166, 168, 170, 172, 195, 204, 205, 206, 217, 218, 224, 226, 227,

228, 229, 232, 235, 236, 241, 252, 436, 475f, 508
simplices: as uneducated, 117, 124, 136f, 199, 240, 251, 265, 440; *see also idiota*
simplicity: and physicalism, 272; of faithful, 264; of ignorance, 264
Simson, O. von: 82n
simulacrum: 71, 324f, 379
Sirus, Patarene priest: 215, 227f, 231n, 235
Sismondi, Jean: 458n
Skorupski, J.: 242n
Smalley, B.: 275n
S. Maria Yemale, church of, Milan: 193, 210
Smith, D. E.: 84n
Socrates: 34; *see also* Plato
Solomon: 313, 411, 412, 416, 432, 441; *see also* Song of Songs
Sommerfeldt, J.: 414n, 445n
Somerville, R.: 272n
Somigli, C.: 161n
Song of Songs: 410-51, 452, 453, 526
sorcery: 104f; *see also* magic
sound: and sense, 313, 372; articulated versus signified, 377; diachronic nature of, 325; qualitative aspects of, 374; quantitative aspects of, 373; *see also* sign
Southern, R. W.: 62n, 304n, 329n 330n, 331n, 360, 489n
Speier, anonymous citizen of: 77-79
Spicq, C.: 29n
Spinelli, G.: 215n, 222n
spirit: as highest substance, 340f; as human intelligence, 142, 148, 227; holy, 142, 407; holy, and communication, 144f; and literacy, 176; as human intelligence, 144f; as Mani, 147; as the understanding of divine matters, 142; spirit versus letter, 130, 134f, 145, 293, 307, 435, 453, 468, 530 (see also letter); spiritual, the, and the physical: 260, 266f, 279, 424, 438; and the secular, 413; in Berengar, 277; in the eucharist, 263; *see also spiritus*
spiritualitas: 277n; *spiritualiter*, as *invisibiliter*, 308
spirituality: 90, 406
spiritus: creans, 341; *duplex*, 431; in sound, 374; *sapientiae et intellectus*, 425
Spörl, J.: 518n
Sprandel, R.: 46n
Standaert, P. M.: 417n, 444n
statuary: 68
status, inherited: 14, 16, 18, 95
status: in Abelard, 395, 396, 399
Steiger, L.: 354n, 355n

INDEX

William of Gascony: 462
William of Glos: 496, 497, 498
William of Jumièges: 474
William of Malmesbury: 75, 497, 519
William of Newburgh: 235
William of St.-Bénigne: 466, 469-71
William of St. Thierry: 363, 406, 417n,
  525
William of Volpiano: 282
William, St.: 75
William the Conqueror: 76n, 472, 474,
  479, 480, 481, 500, 527
Williams, G. H.: 360n
Williams, S.: 60n
Wilson, B. R.: 95
Winckelmann, J.: 10n
Wipo: 74n, 151, 518
wisdom: 319, 323, 411, 426, 429, 437,
  445, 446f, 451
witchcraft: 502, 504; see also magic, sorcery
Witelo: 83
Wolff, A.: 42n
woman: and man, in imagery, 425f; as Cathar heretic, 469; creation of, 294; Guibert's mother, 499-507; women: 189,
  210, 213, 232, 482; abuse of, 310; and
  sensuality, 496f; as bearers of rumour,
  247; in the church, 214; in the Milanese
  church, 190; in the Pataria, 171, 207; life
  expectancy of, 499; rule for, 525
word, the: 79, 105, 106, 127, 136, 150,
  167, 179, 212, 217, 219, 233, 262, 264,
  269, 285, 291, 295, 302, 342f; and the
  text, 270, 292f, 301, 304, 308f, 324,
  336, 344, 351, 415, 416, 417-30, 434,
  442-44, 451, 452f, 519n, 520, 526; descent of, in allegory, 219; interiority, and
  reform, 430-38; of the creator and the
  word in things, 341, 420-22; see also orality, texts

words: and images, 398; and intellections,
  324; and sense, 354f; and things, 279,
  324f, 339, 341, 342, 343, 345, 346,
  353, 356, 360, 368, 391-93, 402, 526,
  529; and thoughts, 243, 312f; as mental
  concepts, 342f; as universals, 396-402
work: and knowledge, 322; and salvation,
  126; as manual labour, 520; as metaphor,
  519f; works, good, 131, 245, 451
worldliness, in the clergy: 153, 175f, 217f,
  235f, 429, 440, 508; rejection of, 208
Wright, R.: 24n
writ, the sealed: 57f
writing: and the study of language, 19, 368-
  71, 384, 416; as preserved oral record,
  336, 455, 474; dispositive functions of,
  42, 48f, 270, 453, 475, 526; evidential
  functions of, 42, 64, 70, 119, 247, 282,
  301, 348, 361, 452; dispositive versus evidential functions of, 42f, 270f, 361, 407,
  452f; general functions of, 3-10, 13-18;
  see also text
Wunderle, P.: 19n

Yates, F. A.: 15n
youth: 476-89, 493f, 501; and family, 491,
  495-99; and old age, in reality and metaphor, 53, 132, 169, 179, 180, 216, 468,
  476-89, 492, 494f, 507, 510-21, 527; as
  social role, 480; betrayals of, 510; defined,
  480; errors of, 265; rites of, 479f, 483,
  489; see also iuuentus
Yver, J.: 56n, 474n

Zerbi, P.: 153n, 159n, 226n, 404n
Zeumer, K.: 46n, 47n, 48n
Zink, M.: 72n
Zumthor, P.: 25n, 80n

604

Library of Congress Cataloging in Publication Data

Stock, Brian.
The implications of literacy.
Bibliography: p.
Includes index.
1. Written communication—Europe—History.
2. Civilization, Medieval.   I.   Title.
P211.S69 1982   001.54'3'094   82-47616
ISBN 0-691-05368-5